AMERICAN CORRECTIONS

THEORY, RESEARCH, POLICY, AND PRACTICE

Matt DeLisi, PhD
Iowa State University

Peter J. Conis, PhD
Iowa State University

JONES AND BARTLETT PUBLISHERS
Sudbury, Massachusetts
BOSTON TORONTO LONDON SINGAPORE

World Headquarters
Jones and Bartlett Publishers
40 Tall Pine Drive
Sudbury, MA 01776
978-443-5000
info@jbpub.com
www.jbpub.com

Jones and Bartlett Publishers Canada
6339 Ormindale Way
Mississauga, Ontario L5V 1J2
Canada

Jones and Bartlett Publishers International
Barb House, Barb Mews
London W6 7PA
United Kingdom

Jones and Bartlett's books and products are available through most bookstores and online booksellers. To contact Jones and Bartlett Publishers directly, call 800-832-0034, fax 978-443-8000, or visit our website, www.jbpub.com.

Substantial discounts on bulk quantities of Jones and Bartlett's publications are available to corporations, professional associations, and other qualified organizations. For details and specific discount information, contact the special sales department at Jones and Bartlett via the above contact information or send an email to specialsales@jbpub.com.

Production Credits
Publisher: Cathleen Sether
Acquisitions Editor: Jeremy Spiegel
Editorial Assistant: Kyle Hoover
Production Director: Amy Rose
Senior Production Editor: Renée Sekerak
Production Assistant: Jill Morton
Marketing Manager: Jessica Faucher
Manufacturing and Inventory Control Supervisor: Amy Bacus
Composition: Shepherd, Inc.
Cover Design: Anne Spencer
Cover and Title Page Image: © Paul Doyle/Alamy Images
Cover and Title Page Design Image: © wheatley/ShutterStock, Inc.
Assistant Photo Researcher: Bridget Kane
Text Printing and Binding: Courier Kendallville
Cover Printing: Courier Kendallville

Library of Congress Cataloging-in-Publication Data
DeLisi, Matt.
American corrections : theory, research, policy, and practice / by Matt DeLisi and Peter J. Conis.
p. cm.
Includes bibliographical references and index.
ISBN-13: 978-0-7637-5487-7
ISBN-10: 0-7637-5487-0
1. Corrections--United States--Textbooks. I. Conis, Peter John. II. Title.
HV9304.D45 2009
364.60973--dc22
2008037054

6048

Printed in the United States of America
13 12 11 10 09 10 9 8 7 6 5 4 3 2 1

DEDICATION

To Missa, our three little bears, and the quiet genius.
—Matt

To Barb.
—Peter

BRIEF CONTENTS

Part I The Foundation of Corrections

Part II Corrections: The Management of Offender Risk

Part III Prison and Offender Reentry

Part IV Special Topics in Corrections

CONTENTS

Part III Prison and Offender Reentry

Part IV Special Topics in Corrections

PREFACE

THE CORRECTIONAL SYSTEM HAS A DIFFICULT JOB TO DO. It must provide monitoring, supervision, punishment, and treatment for the range of offenders who are convicted of violations of the law. This range of offenders is tremendous. It spans those whose only violations of the law include relatively minor traffic crimes such as speeding, driving with an expired license, or driving with expired registration to those convicted of predatory crimes such as murder, kidnapping, and rape. The correctional system imposes punishments including diversion and deferred sentences where there is effectively no sentence to situations where the state lawfully kills the offender. Correctional clients range from upstanding citizens with strong ties to the community to the most disadvantaged and pathological of our fellow citizens. Across these variations, the correctional system must perform its functions with the ideal of balanced justice in mind.

While there are problems and negative aspects of the correctional system, the American correctional system does an admirable job of providing appropriate justice to the correctional clients that it serves. The logic of *American Corrections: Theory, Research, Policy, and Practice* is consistent with the triage system used in the medical community: the most serious cases demand the most immediate and serious treatment and the less serious cases must wait.

American Corrections: Theory, Research, Policy, and Practice is divided into four parts. Part I, The Foundation of Corrections, provides a general overview of the correctional system and its place in the criminal justice system, the philosophy and history of the correctional system in the United States, and the laws that govern the ability of the state to correct criminal offenders. As you will see, there are many philosophies about the best way to supervise criminal offenders and some of these are conflicting and even difficult to reconcile.

Part II, Corrections: The Management of Offender Risk, delves into the triage approach beginning with the various sentences that the criminal courts impose on offenders and the ways that the correctional system classifies offenders according to the various risks they exemplify. From there, a continuum of sentences is used to meet the diverse risks and needs of the offenders. In severity, the continuum of sentences is generally representative of the continuum of offenders.

Part III, Prison and Offender Reentry, explores one of the most serious parts of the correctional system: prison. In this section, the journey of prisoners as they navigate prison, parole, and ultimate reentry into society is examined.

Part IV, Special Topics in Corrections, examines three somewhat special populations of offenders: juveniles, women, and the small portion of offenders who receive the most severe treatment by the system—namely capital punishment and civil commitment.

American Corrections: Theory, Research, Policy, and Practice offers 15 chapters of useful information based on scholarship from the social and behavioral sciences. It is a comprehensive, student-friendly text for introductory corrections courses at the community college and university levels. It does not stray into material that is more suitable for other courses (e.g., criminal justice, corrections management, etc.) and it does not present a point of view. *American Corrections: Theory, Research, Policy, and Practice* does not lionize the criminal offender and malign the system and it does not pretend that the correctional system is beyond reproach. Instead, in a fun, scholarly, and student-friendly way, *American Corrections: Theory, Research, Policy, and Practice* explores the correctional system in the United States. We hope you enjoy it.

ACKNOWLEDGMENTS

Although we did all the typing, *American Corrections: Theory, Research, Policy, and Practice* was enhanced or influenced by the friendship, input, and/or scholarship of a number of colleagues. We would like to acknowledge Craig Anderson, Simon Baron-Cohen, Kevin Beaver, Mark Berg, James Byrne, Avshalom Caspi, Frank Cullen, Mark Cunningham, Brendan Dooley, Alan Drury, Robert Hare, John Hewitt, George Higgins, Don Hummer, Anna Kosloski, Paul Lasley, Edward Latessa, Christopher Lowenkamp, Doris Layton MacKenzie, Dan Mears, Terrie Moffitt, Joan Petersilia, Travis Pratt, Robert Regoli, Gene Simmons, Jon Sorensen, Chad Trulson, Michael Vaughn, Glenn Walters, James Q. Wilson, Nancy Wolff, John Paul Wright, Kevin Wright, the Bureau of Justice Statistics, and the National Institute of Corrections.

The authors would like to thank the following reviewers for their comments.

Larry Chandler, MS
Warden, Kentucky State Reformatory

Harry Dammer, PhD
Professor and Chair, Department of Sociology/Criminal Justice
University of Scranton

Noelle E. Fearn, PhD
Assistant Professor, Department of Sociology and Criminal Justice
Saint Louis University

Laura L. Hansen, PhD
Assistant Professor, Department of Sociology
University of Massachusetts, Boston

Jessie L. Krienert, PhD
Associate Professor, Department of Criminal Justice
Illinois State University

Iryna Malendevych, MS
Instructor, Department of Criminal Justice and Legal Studies
University of Central Florida

Sheree Morgan, MS
Coordinator of Off Campus Programs
St. Cloud State University

John Neiswender, PhD

Michael Seredycz, PhD
Assistant Professor, Department of Criminal Justice
University of Wisconsin, Parkside

Isis N. Walton, PhD
Associate Professor, Department of Criminal Justice
Virginia State University

Cortney A. Franklin, PhD
Assistant Professor, College of Criminal Justice
Sam Houston State University

Travis Franklin, PhD
Assistant Professor, College of Criminal Justice
Sam Houston State University

LAW
LAW

PART

I

The Foundation of Corrections

CHAPTER

1

Corrections and Its Place in the Criminal Justice System

"The nation has invested billions of dollars into locking up offenders. The policies around reentry have become increasingly an avoidance of risk. As a result, we have created a revolving door of offenders who will be committed to prison time and again as they fail in the community."[1, p. 381]

OBJECTIVES

- Understand the role of corrections in the criminal justice system and its relationship to police and courts.
- Recognize the different sentences and sanctions that comprise the correctional system.
- Identify the offender-based characteristics that are used to determine placement in the correctional system.
- Compare community corrections and institutional corrections and understand examples of each.
- Learn the statistical profile of the correctional system, correctional populations, and collateral issues raised by corrections.
- Explore the federal criminal justice system and its role in American corrections.

CASE STUDY

Three Meals and a Deal

Paris Hilton was sentenced to serve 45 days in a Los Angeles County Jail for having violated her probation—a probation that stemmed from an alcohol-related reckless driving incident.

On February 27, 2007, at approximately 11:00 p.m., Hilton was stopped by a Los Angeles County sheriff's deputy who had observed her operating a motor vehicle with its headlights off. She had also exceeded the speed limit, according to court records. A check of her driver's license revealed her driving privileges had been under suspension—another traffic violation. It had also been determined by the courts that Paris had failed to meet another condition of her probation when the court learned she had not enrolled in an alcohol education program.

1. What's life like in a county jail?
2. How much time did she actually serve?
3. Was she guilty of violating her probation?

Paris Hilton's criminal justice experience contributes to popular beliefs that fame and fortune influence the type of justice one receives.

"Under current conditions, probation and parole are probably best thought of as legal statuses allowing swifter incarceration or re-incarceration when fresh offenses are detected rather than as programs with independent incapacitative or rehabilitative effects."[2, p. 1917]

Overview of the Correctional System

The criminal justice system is comprised of three broad areas. First, the **police**, also known as law enforcement, respond to citizen complaints, provide basic services, such as traffic control, enforce the criminal law, and in doing so, initiate criminal cases. To be blunt, the police catch the bad guys. The police are the first line in the investigative process that creates a criminal complaint against a suspect or **defendant**—the person accused of a criminal violation. As shown in FIGURE 1-1 and FIGURE 1-2, the police are aware of only a fraction of actual crimes because offenders, victims, or witnesses never notify them, and even fewer cases result in arrest. In this way, every time the police choose not to make an arrest, they filter or divert cases from the criminal justice system. Overall, less than half of crimes are reported to police.

The second component of the criminal justice system is the judicial system or **courts**. The courts, which are comprised of prosecutors, defense counsel, and judges, serve a variety of functions, foremost of which is to serve as a check and balance on the police. The primary judicial officer or member of the courts is the prosecutor. Variously known as the district attorney, county attorney, or state's attorney, the prosecutor examines arrests to ensure that the arrests were lawful and compliant with the United States Constitution. Also, the prosecutor uses his or her **discretion**, the latitude to choose one course of action or another, to decide whether prosecuting a case would serve the interests of justice. Here there are many considerations, including the seriousness of the accused crime, the evidence, the witnesses and alleged victims, the criminal background of the defendant, possible political considerations, and others. Resource availability is another important consideration: Does the state have the time, money, and staff to prosecute a case originally brought by the police?

"*Probation and parole, systems developed in the United States more by accident than by design, now threaten to become the tail that wagged the corrections' dog.*"[3, p. 493]

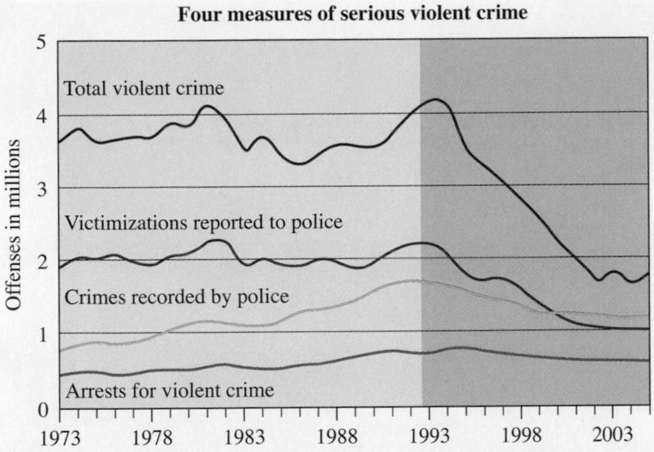

FIGURE 1–1 Estimates of Serious Violent Crime, 1973–2003. *Source*: Bureau of Justice Statistics. (n.d.). *Serious violent crime levels decrease since 1993*. Retrieved May 13, 2007, from http://www.ojp.usdoj.gov/bjs/glance/cv2.htm.

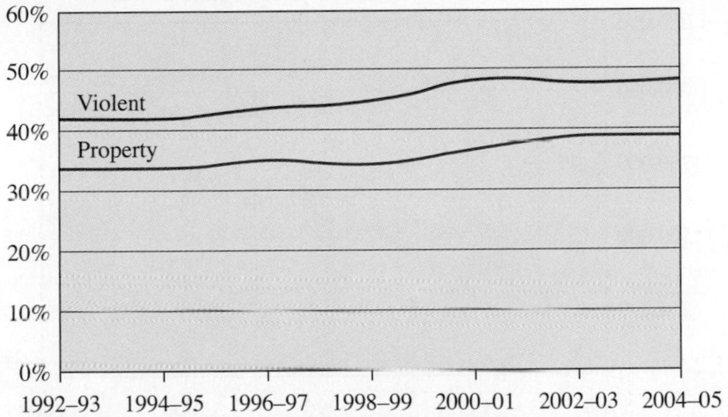

FIGURE 1–2 Percent of Crime Reported to Police, 1992–2005. *Source*: Bureau of Justice Statistics. (n.d.). *The percentage of crimes reported to the police has been increasing*. Retrieved May 13, 2007, from http://www.ojp.usdoj.gov/bjs/glance/reportingtype.htm.

According to the most recent data, more than 1.14 million felons are convicted in courts (see **FIGURE 1–3**). About 94 percent of these cases are decided at the state level with 6 percent at the federal level. Even among convicted felons, there is a great screening out of offenders from the criminal justice system. For instance, 31 percent of felons convicted in state courts are sentenced to probation and receive no jail or prison time whatsoever. As shown in **FIGURE 1–4**, convicted felons are sentenced to a variety of punishments, some in the community and some in institutions.[6]

Terry Baumer reports how some jurisdictions attempt to control its lockup population through creation of a separate processing center designed to expedite initial processing of individuals charged with misdemeanors and minor felonies. In the new center, cases were screened and initial hearings held around the clock, 7 days per week. Before and after samples of arrestees were compared on prosecutorial screening time, time to court, and time in custody, and Baumer found significant reductions in case screening and length of time to initial court hearing. Individuals released on recognizance and those with no charges filed spent significantly less time in custody and saved considerable bed space for the jurisdiction. Individuals with bond set experienced no reductions in length of custody.[7]

"Imprisonment now rivals or overshadows the frequency of military service and college graduation for recent cohorts of African American men."[4, p. 164]

Due to the sheer volume of crime, correctional systems use discretion to detain only the most serious and chronic offenders.

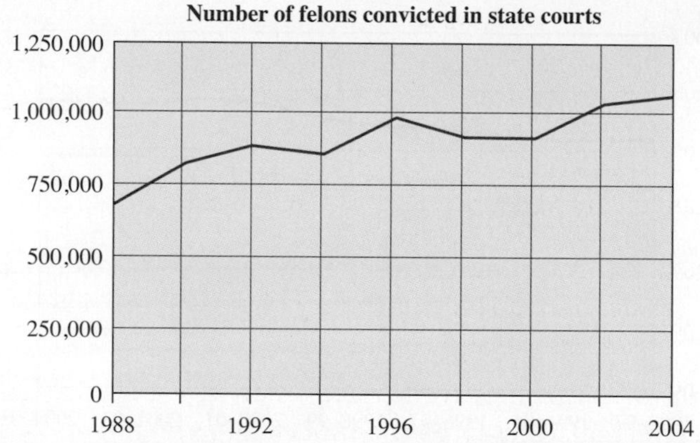

FIGURE 1–3 Felons Convicted in State Courts, 1988–2004. *Source*: Durose, M. R., & Langan, P. A. (2007). *Felony sentences in state courts, 2004*. Washington, DC: U.S. Department of Justice, Office of Justice Programs, Bureau of Justice Statistics.

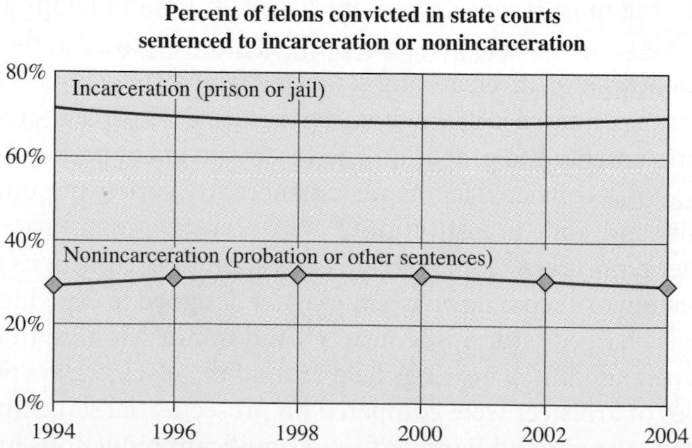

FIGURE 1–4 Sentence Outcomes, 1988–2002. *Source*: Durose, M. R., & Langan, P. A. (2007). *Felony sentences in state courts, 2004*. Washington, DC: U.S. Department of Justice, Office of Justice Programs, Bureau of Justice Statistics.

The third component of the criminal justice system is corrections. **Corrections** or the correctional system is the collection of local, state, and federal agencies that supervise and treat criminal defendants. Although the correctional system is considered the final stage of the criminal justice process, there are important points to understand about the role of corrections in the criminal justice system. A schematic of the criminal justice system appears in FIGURE 1-5. The following points provide a guide to understand the role and purpose of corrections within the criminal justice system.

"In late twentieth-century America, prisons and jails have become the imposing physical embodiment of the nation's crime control policy."[5, p. ix]

- The constitutionality of corrections is found in the **Eighth Amendment**, which states that "excessive bail shall not be required, nor excessive fines imposed, nor cruel and unusual punishments inflicted." Implicit in this language is the application of corrections to the pretrial and posttrial or postadjudication phases of the judicial process. In other words, *defendants are subject to correctional supervision both before and after they actually have been convicted.*
- The correctional system begins with the pretrial supervision of defendants on bond. **Pretrial supervision** is the correctional supervision of a defendant who has been arrested, booked, and bonded out of jail. Often, there are conditions of **bond**, the release from jail custody in exchange for collateral or recognizance whereby the defendant promises to appear for future court dates. Bond conditions can include no contact with alleged victims in the case, no possession of weapons, no driving, substance abuse monitoring, mental health treatment, and others. Bond conditions are monitored by pretrial service personnel who are a component of probation departments in many jurisdictions.
- The correctional system also pertains to defendants after they have pleaded guilty or been found guilty, a stage known as **posttrial or postadjudication**. Often, the conditions of bond are continued until the defendant is formally sentenced or receives a penalty of punishment from a judge upon conviction.
- Unlike law enforcement, which is basically limited to police, corrections is staffed by multiple and sometimes overlapping agencies. Criminal defendants can serve multiple correctional sentences or be under correctional supervision in different agencies at the same time. For instance, one could be on bond in one county, on probation in another, be awaiting sentencing in still another, and have new criminal charges.
- Correctional supervision occurs in both community and institutional settings. **Community corrections** refers to sanctions that allow criminal offenders to remain in the community as long as they abide by certain conditions, such as maintaining employment, participating in drug treatment, or undergoing psychological treatment. Community corrections are used in lieu of confinement and allow offenders to rehabilitate themselves with the opportunity afforded by the criminal justice system. **Institutional corrections**, such as jail and prison, use confinement or the physical removal from society as a means of supervision.
- After conviction, there are several sentences at the judges' disposal commonly referred to as a **continuum of sanctions**, which is a range of sanctions or legal penalties that balance punishment, treatment, and supervision concerns with the seriousness of the offense and the offender's criminal convictions. The rationale of the continuum of sanctions and the variety of sentences are discussed in the next section.

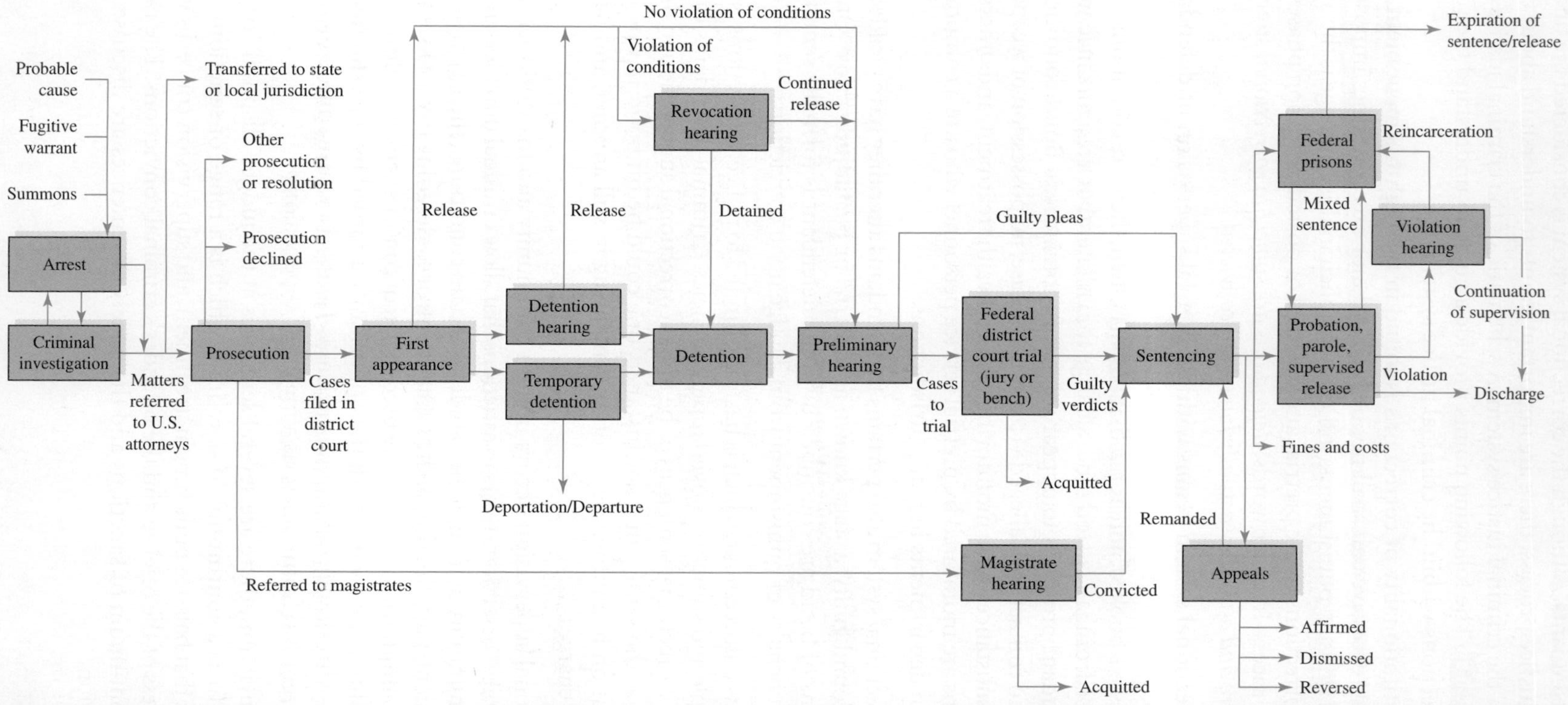

FIGURE 1–5 The Criminal Justice System. *Source*: Smith, S. K., & Motivans, M. (2006). *Compendium of federal justice statistics, 2004.* Washington, DC: U.S. Department of Justice, Office of Justice Programs, Bureau of Justice Statistics.

The Continuum of Sanctions

Criminality and Risk

How do judges decide which penalty is most appropriate for a particular criminal defendant? Which sentence is best? Should the sentencing decision be standardized according to the crime for which the defendant was convicted? Alternately, should circumstances that seem to reduce the culpability of the offenders, known as **mitigating factors**, be used to impart leniency? Or, should circumstances that seem to increase the culpability of the offenders, known as **aggravating factors**, be used to impart a harsher sentence?

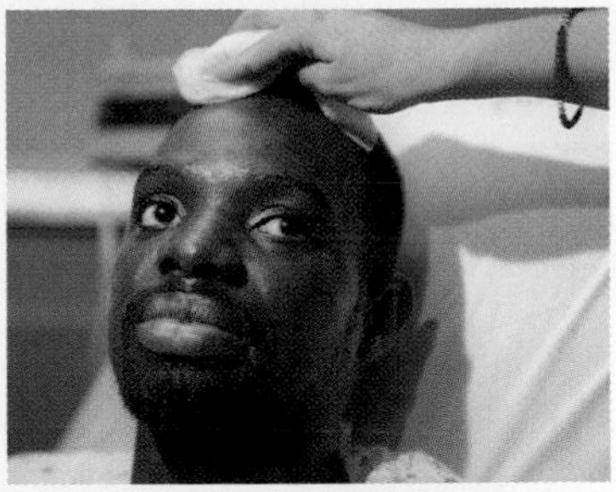

Despite the importance of legal variables, extra-legal variables, such as race and ethnicity, can influence the way the criminal justice system responds to citizens.

Several factors are used to determine which criminal cases enter the system and which cases continue on through conviction and punishment. Criminologists have investigated two types of variables that influence officer discretion: practitioner decision making and criminal justice outcomes. These are **legal variables**, such as offense severity, prior criminal record, and number of charges, and **extralegal variables**, such as demographic characteristics. Legal variables overwhelmingly explain more variation in criminal justice than extralegal variables, yet there is another important variable that is a combination of the legal and extralegal classifications: **criminality**. Criminality is the propensity towards antisocial behavior that a defendant embodies. Often, criminologists use assorted risk and protective factors as proxies of criminality. In this way, characteristics such as age, onset of criminal behavior, employment status, family structure, intelligence, or scores on diagnostic tests such as psychopathy or antisocial personality disorder are viewed as proxies of an offender's criminality.

Criminality has an important practical value because it is one of the factors used by practitioners to decide the most appropriate type of sanction to fit the treatment and punishment needs of the offender. When criminality and crime are exceedingly low, such as most traffic violations, the punishment is a fine and no treatment is needed. When criminality and crime are exceedingly high, such as capital murder, the punishment can be death and the treatment moot. Of course, most crimes fall between these two extremes and so criminal punishment attempts to offer some balance of treatment and punishment. As such, community corrections reflect a range of criminal penalties whose treatment and punishment modalities seek to match the varying criminality of correctional clients.

Alex Holsinger and Edward Latessa, criminologists who are noteworthy for evaluating correctional programs, studied the application of the sanction continuum to juvenile offenders and found that criminal justice practitioners appeared to be striking the appropriate balance between treatment and punishment of clients with varying degrees of criminality. Their study contained 544 delinquents who were sentenced to diversion, probation, special/intensive probation, a residential rehabilitation center, or the department of youth services. Sharp differences in criminality existed across the five placements. Those who received diversion were the lowest risks and had the lowest criminality, and those sentenced to confinement were the highest risks and demonstrated the most criminality. For instance, Holsinger and Latessa found that delinquents who were sent to prison had an average criminal risk index score that was 400 percent greater than youths who were diverted. In terms of average behavioral risk score, youths who were placed in a residential center and those who were placed in the department of youth services were 236 percent and 220 percent, respectively, more of a behavioral risk than youths who were diverted.[8]

The logic of the continuum of sanctions is used daily in American corrections. As shown in FIGURE 1-6, a major initiative in the federal Office of Juvenile Justice and Delinquency Prevention is the comprehensive strategy for serious, violent, and chronic juvenile offenders. The comprehensive strategy blends prevention that targets youths

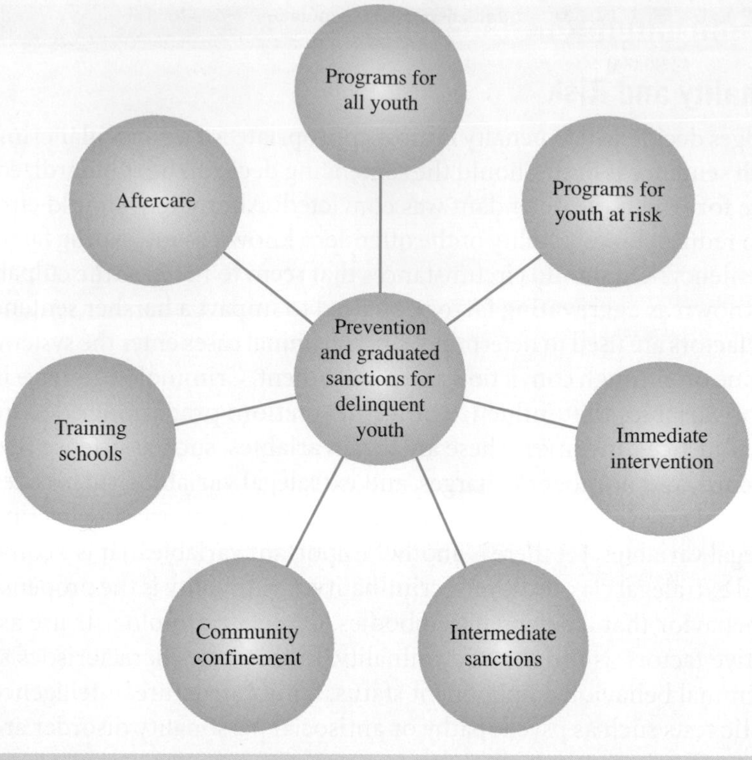

FIGURE 1–6 The Continuum of Sanctions. *Source*: Modified from Howell, J. C. (2003). Diffusing research into practice using the comprehensive strategy for serious, violent, and chronic juvenile offenders. *Youth Violence and Juvenile Justice*, 1, 219–245.

who are at risk for serious delinquency and graduated sanctions, which are used for delinquents. This approach furnishes both prevention/treatment and punishment and is tailored to the specific needs and risk factors of the offender. The most serious and violent delinquents receive the most intensive and severe penalties and pose the greatest need for rehabilitative services. Lesser offenders receive more mild forms of correctional supervision that are discussed next.

Community Corrections

Interchangeably referred to as intermediate sanctions, community corrections, or community-based corrections, intermediate sanctions is any form of correctional treatment that deals with the offender within as opposed to outside of society. Community corrections are a lenient alternative to incarceration that accords criminal offenders the opportunity to rehabilitate themselves and become functioning, noncriminal members of society while still integrated in the society. That community-correctional clients remain at large, embedded in the community, symbolically represents the opportunity that they are given. In fact, all community corrections strike a balance between protecting the community and rehabilitating the offender. This blended practice of law enforcement and social work functions can create tension because of the competing purposes of these goals. Finally, community corrections are significantly less expensive than prison in terms of the fiscal costs of administering the sanction and the punishment severity *inflicted* on the offender. For these reasons, criminal offenders and criminal justice practitioners alike often view any criminal punishment short of prison as a last resort or final opportunity for the criminal offender to reform his or her antisocial behavior.

Renowned criminologist Norval Morris argues that community corrections must serve legitimate treatment and correctional needs; otherwise they will not alleviate prison

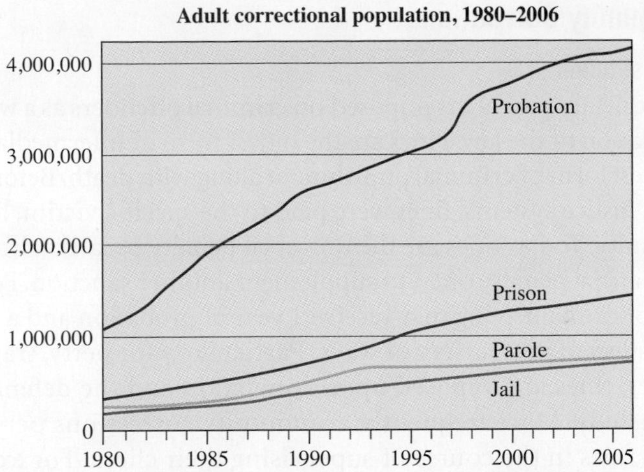

FIGURE 1–7 Adult Correctional Populations, 1980–2006. *Source*: Bureau of Justice Statistics. (n.d.). *The number of adults in the correctional population has been increasing.* Retrieved May 29, 2008, from http://www.ojp.usdoj.gov/bjs/glance/corr2.htm.

crowding. Morris articulated three principles to guide the placement of offenders on community corrections. First, the sentence should be parsimonious and provide the least restrictive punishment. Second, offenders should receive their just deserts, in that no sanction should be imposed that is greater than what is deserved. In other words, the punishment and the crime need to match. Morris was apprehensive about whether policy makers could accurately make predictions of future dangerousness. Third, sentencing should follow from observed legal characteristics like offense severity.[9] Following these principles should result in defendants being placed on the most appropriate and just intermediate sanction.

Compared to traditional punishments of confinement, community corrections are versatile criminal punishments that can fit multiple purposes. Michael Tonry, former president of the American Society of Criminology, suggests they can be viewed as punitive because they are more intrusive and burdensome than standard probation. Because of the burdensome conditions that are a part of most intermediate sanctions, violations and noncompliance rates tend to be high. Also, community corrections can be viewed as rehabilitative because programs with well-designed treatment protocols can reduce recidivism among offenders. Community corrections reduce money and prison-bed costs without sacrificing public safety.[10] For instance, probation and parole receive about 15 percent of state expenditures for corrections, yet they account for the supervision of 70 percent of correctional clients.

The main criticism of intermediate sanctions is that they are responsible for the dramatic growth in the American correctional population. As shown in **FIGURE 1–7**, the probation population increased more than 400 percent since 1980. Today, the total correctional population in the United States exceeds 7 million, with nearly 5 million on probation or parole. Approximately 1 in 30 adults today is under the supervision of the correctional system.[11] The growing of the correctional population via the proliferation of community corrections or intermediate sanctions is referred to as **net widening.** Although intermediate sanctions provide the opportunity for offenders to avoid prison and taxpayers to avoid paying for them to go to prison, the offenders must go somewhere. That somewhere is the community.

Types of Community Corrections

Fines and Restitution

Fines are monetary payments imposed on criminal offenders as a way to repay society for their violation of the law. Fines are the oldest form of intermediate sanction, and arguably the oldest form of criminal punishment along with death. Before the formalization of criminal justice systems, fines were paid to the specific victim, his or her family, and the community. Today, fines are the universal penalty because virtually all statutes denote some financial penalty often to supplement another sanction. For example, persons convicted of drunk driving may receive 1 year of probation and a $500 fine.

Fines are collected in a variety of ways. Particularly for petty, traffic, and misdemeanor offenses, fines are imposed upon conviction and the defendant pays upon release from custody. More frequently, community corrections personnel monitor the payment of fines in the course of supervising their client. For example, the correctional officer interviews the defendant to ascertain his or her financial situation, income, and ability to pay to arrange the schedule for repayment. Failure to pay the fine within the time span specified by the court or administrating agency could result in a warrant for noncompliance—technically, failure to pay. Other jurisdictions employ day fines that are geared to the average daily income of the offender. Day fines help to ensure payment because of the daily responsibility placed on the offender. Other jurisdictions garnish a defendant's wages to ensure payment of fines and restitution. Finally, jail inmates and prisoners often work for wages while incarcerated. That income can similarly be garnished to pay fines, court costs, restitution, and outstanding child support.

The monetary amount of fines varies greatly to match the legal seriousness of the crime. For instance, fines for petty and misdemeanor crimes are often less than $100, whereas fines for individuals or corporations convicted of securities, fraud, or other white-collar crimes can be hundreds of millions of dollars. It has been argued that affluent white-collar offenders should be forced to pay exorbitant fines that would impose the same level of hardship as prison.[12] Another positive consequence would be increased local, state, or federal revenue depending on the jurisdiction that imposed the fine. Whatever the fiscal potential of fines, they do not generally affect recidivism. Criminologists have found that fines were not helpful in reducing recidivism among offenders forced to pay them primarily because fines were viewed as such an indirect, almost incidental, form of punishment.[13,14]

Whereas fines are paid to the state, **restitution** is paid to the crime victim to recoup some of the harm caused by the offender's wrongful acts. All criminal courts have the authority to order convicted offenders to pay restitution to victims as part of their sentences. In many states, courts are required to order restitution to victims in cases involving certain types of crimes, typically violent felony offenses.

Restitution can cover any out-of-pocket losses directly relating to the crime, including medical expenses, therapy costs, prescription charges, counseling costs, lost wages, expenses related to participating in the criminal justice process, lost or damaged property, insurance deductibles, crime-scene cleanup, or any other expense that resulted directly from the crime.[15]

When courts order restitution, they look not only at the victim's losses, but also at the offender's ability to pay. In some states, the court may reduce the total amount of restitution ordered if the offender is unlikely to be able to pay that amount. In other states, courts will order the offender to pay for the full amount of the loss, but then set a payment schedule based on the offender's finances, which may only be a minimal amount per month. Maureen Outlaw and Barry Ruback report that offenders who have greater resources, more protective factors, and minimal criminal record are most likely to pay restitution on time.[16] Unfortunately, many victims wait years before they receive any restitution because of the assorted deficits of the average criminal offender. To help ensure the payment of restitution, it is often an explicit condition of probation such that failure to pay restitution can result in revocation of the probation sentence.

Forfeiture

Another financial-based intermediate sanction is **forfeiture.** Forfeiture is the loss of ownership for the illegal use of some property or asset. Criminal forfeiture is in personam, which means that the criminal defendant is the target of the forfeiture that can only occur after criminal conviction. Civil forfeiture is in rem, which means that it targets property, and it does not require formal adversarial proceedings, and adjudication of guilt is not needed. Criminal forfeiture became part of contemporary criminal justice in 1970 with the enactment of the Racketeer Influenced and Corrupt Organizations (RICO) statutes that targeted the operations of organized crime activities, such as racketeering, extortion, drug trafficking, or money laundering. The RICO statutes provided the legal justification to seize any assets associated with or produced by criminal enterprises. Many states have similarly developed RICO statutes based on the federal model.

Although developed to tackle organized crime, forfeiture has increasingly been used to target drug violators. Criminal justice system agents employed both criminal and civil forfeiture as a way to cripple the resources of drug offenders (that were comparable to organized crime networks) and utilize proceeds from the seized assets. Because civil forfeiture did not depend on adversarial criminal prosecution, it was viewed as a violation of the due process rights of criminal defendants. The passage of the Civil Asset Forfeiture Reform Act (CAFRA) of 2000 rectified this by providing the procedural protections available to criminal defendants to those whose assets were seized. Moreover, the prosecutor was charged with the burden of proving that particular crimes had occurred and that the seized assets were the fruits of criminal activity, had facilitated criminal activity, or was contraband in itself.[17]

Criminologists have produced mixed findings regarding the prevalence of forfeiture and the reliance of the criminal justice system on the sanction. John Worrall surveyed 1,400 municipal and county law enforcement agencies to examine their use of civil forfeiture against drug violators. Worrall found that law enforcement agencies commonly used civil forfeiture and that 40 percent of agencies reported that forfeiture was a necessary way to supplement the departmental budget.[18] James Clingermayer, Jason Hecker, and Sue Madsen surveyed 70 law enforcement agencies in Ohio and Kentucky and found a much different situation regarding forfeiture. Although they found that virtually all jurisdictions used forfeitures, the forfeitures were overwhelmingly of the criminal variety following a criminal prosecution. Most agencies never used civil forfeiture. Moreover, agencies received a very small part of their budgets from seizures and the sanction had little impact on police procedures and policies.[19] Nevertheless, forfeiture is a useful and potentially lucrative intermediate sanction used to cost-effectively punish criminal offenders.

Research is mixed about how widespread the use of forfeiture of drug assets to subsidize criminal justice systems is.

Day Reporting

Day reporting is a multifaceted intermediate sanction that serves both pretrial and postconviction criminal defendants. The sanction requires that defendants report to an official criminal justice facility on a daily basis to check in and demonstrate to correctional staff that they are complying with the conditions of their current legal status. For pretrial defendants who have been released on bond, day reporting usually occurs at the county jail or a community corrections facility. Depending on the conditions of their bond, defendants may submit to Breathalyzer tests or provide proof that they worked or attended counseling. Because clients must daily interact with correctional staff, day reporting theoretically reduces the incentive to engage in criminal behavior that would violate the conditions of bond. Day reporting allows defendants to remain in the community to work toward their own rehabilitation. Pretrial day reporting also saves on jail space and costs and is one of the most widely used alternatives to incarceration.

Day reporting is also used for postconviction groups, especially probationers and parolees. Day reporting centers provide an assortment of services, such as substance abuse treatment, cognitive restructuring, anger management classes, batterer education classes, parenting skills education, mental health treatment, and others that are designed to reduce antisocial attitudes and behaviors that lead to crime. Day reporting is an explicit condition of their supervision and provides greater supervision than traditional probation because of the frequency of contact. Day reporting centers also refer correctional clients to services in the community not provided by the center.

Several evaluations of day reporting indicated that the sanction is a promising way to reduce recidivism and increase the prosocial functioning of criminal offenders. D. J. Williams and Tiffany Turnage conducted a 1-year follow-up study of 92 day reporting clients in Utah and found that 67 percent had no postdischarge problems and 78 percent of the offenders remained out of jail or prison.[20] Based on data from offenders in Indiana, Sudipto Roy and Jennifer Grimes found that 69 percent of clients successfully completed the day reporting program compared to 31 percent who did not.[21] An evaluation of nearly 1,400 day reporting clients in Illinois found that clients who utilized more services offered by the day reporting center had lower recidivism rates than clients who did not take advantage of the resources provided.[22]

Who succeeds and fails in a day reporting program depends primarily on the criminality and risk factors that the individual offender possesses. Indeed, habitual criminals have been found to be 400 percent more likely to violate the conditions of day reporting than first-time offenders.[23] Nevertheless, day reporting has proven to be a viable, cost-effective intermediate sanction that can serve the needs of all but the most recalcitrant offenders.[24,25]

Community Service

Community service is a form of restitution that involves civic participation toward the improvement of the community. Examples of community service are working with social service providing agencies, such as the Boys and Girls Club, cleaning public parks or roadways, and any activity that constitutes a donation of time to the public good. Community service is usually ordered in conjunction with other intermediate sanctions. For example, a defendant is sentenced to 1 year of probation in which he or she must pay $500 in fines, court costs, and restitution, and perform 100 hours of community service. Depending on the sentence, community service is monitored by a probation officer or community corrections specialist. In most jurisdictions, a network of social service providers are approved by the courts and defendants select the agencies with which they want to collaborate. Sometimes, defendants are ordered to donate their time to a specific social service agency especially if the agency is in some way related to the crime. For instance, a person convicted of driving while intoxicated may be ordered to work with practitioners in youth prevention programs that target alcohol use.

Unlike other intermediate sanctions, the criminal justice system does not expect significant reductions in recidivism because of community service. Because it is usually ordered in conjunction with other penalties, it is somewhat difficult to separate the potential independent effects of performing a public good on reducing crime rates. Depending on their criminal history and other social characteristics, offenders view community service as an annoying, even onerous time commitment; a welcome opportunity in lieu of jail; or an empowering experience that will likely deter future crime. Irrespective of what offenders feel about it, community service allows the criminal justice system to mandate civic activity that improves the community, and many courts permit indigent defendants to perform community service to work off fines.[26,27]

Deferred Prosecution, Judgment, or Sentence

Variously referred to as a **deferred prosecution, judgment, or sentence**, deferring a defendant's sentence is one of the most widespread and cost-effective ways to control the correctional population. Here is a hypothetical case illustrating how it generally works. Suppose a defendant, with minimal criminal history, is arrested for theft. He or she pleads guilty to the crime in exchange for a deferred judgment period, usually ranging from 6 months to 2 years. Unlike probation, deferred sentences entail no conditions and do not require the defendant to check in with correctional personnel. Instead, clients who received a deferred sentence must simply not get arrested during the specified time period and theoretically abstain from committing crimes. If the defendant remains crime-free for the specified period, the guilty plea is voided and the entire event expunged from the defendant's record.

Deferred sentences are used for both misdemeanor and felony crimes. Because of the possibility of **expungement**, which is the complete removal of a criminal record from existence, deferred sentences offer one of the best incentives for offenders to reform their criminal ways. If defendants are rearrested during the deferred sentence, two courses of action are pursued. First, the deferred period is extended, for example from 6 months to 1 year, and the defendant is provided another opportunity on the deferred sentence. Second, the deferred sentence is revoked and the client is placed on probation. Importantly, a guilty plea that results in probation will not be dismissed and expunged regardless of how well the client complies while under supervision.

Conrad Printzlien originally devised deferred prosecution. Printzlien noted the differences in criminality among juvenile offenders and hoped to divert nonserious offenders from the criminal justice system and reserve punishment resources for the most serious offenders. Printzlien conducted a background investigation on his clients. Those with stable community ties and minimal prior record had their criminal charges held in abeyance for a specific time frame contingent on the defendant's good behavior. If the juvenile delinquent did well on the deferred sentence, the case was closed and expunged. Youths who did not comply faced the original complaint or prosecution. This early form of deferred sentencing was known as the Brooklyn Plan.[28]

Home Detention, House Arrest, and Electronic Monitoring

Home detention, variously referred to as **house arrest** or home confinement, and **electronic monitoring** are distinct intermediate sanctions that are routinely combined for use in the same sentence. House arrest is a sanction in which the offender must not leave his or her home with the exception of court-approved times for work and treatment. For instance, a person may be permitted to leave the house during business hours Monday through Friday. When not working or traveling to work, the client must remain in the home. Offenders can be monitored by telephone, work visits, or more commonly

CORRECTIONS FOCUS

Tracking Prisoners

There are global positioning systems (GPS). There's radio frequency identification (RFID). For those who want to go completely high tech, there's biometrics. So how do these systems work?

Have you ever been lost? Worse yet, have you ever lost track of someone you were supposed to be watching? Now imagine what the consequences might be if the person you were assigned to watch also happened to be a convicted sexual predator or murderer. Keeping track of prison inmates is a full-time job, but there are tools that can make this job manageable. Some of these tools are as simple as closed-circuit TVs. Others are more sophisticated and costly. These options include GPS, RFID, and even biometrics.

Most of us are familiar with GPS. They are a feature common in cell phones, automobiles, and even children's toys. In a nutshell, here's how these instruments work. GPS use a triangulation process that is linked to three satellites. The GPS receiver measures the travel time of radio signals and determines the location of the signal's origin by measuring the distance from the signal to each of the three satellites. But it's not just the distance that is used to determine location—velocity is also used. The velocity of a radio frequency is commonly referred to as the speed of light, which is approximately 186,000 miles per second. Using three satellites, three different distances, and one constant speed, the location of the signal is calculated using basic math, and from it the signal's position can be determined.

Manufacturers strongly recommend both guards and inmates wear RFID transmitters. Guards wear them for reasons of safety and welfare, while inmates wear them for reasons of tracking and surveillance. Each transmitter emits an assigned radio frequency that identifies the wearer every 2 seconds. The radio frequencies are received by multiple antennas strategically located throughout the facility. The signal is routed to a server and the data is translated by computer program providing detailed information on the location of the device and the person wearing it. Tracking made simple!

Biometrics refers to a system of identification that uses physiological and/or behavioral characteristics. You've seen it used in the movies and on TV. Identification is verified by examining a person's iris, retinal, and facial characteristics, but biometrics can also include fingerprint and voice identification as well as a dynamic signature to verify an individual's identity. All of these types of biometric techniques have advantages and disadvantages. In a recent study, corrections officials for the navy tested these various methods and found that in a prison environment, facial recognition technology has a higher than acceptable false positive rate and voice recognition is far too unreliable. Fingerprint readers, based on an identification process that some say originated in Persia during the 1400s, and possibly even earlier in Nova Scotia, ancient Babylon, and China, works the best and is far less costly than the other methods.

Sources: The history of fingerprints. (2008). Retrieved August 9, 2008, from http://www.onin.com/fp/fphistory.html; Harris, T., & Brain, M. (n.d.). *How GPS works.* Retrieved May 12, 2007, from http://www.howstuffworks.com/gps3.htm; *Wi-Fi active RFID system: TSI PRISM system* (n.d.). Retrieved May 12, 2007, from http://www.morerfid.com/details.php?subdetail=Product&action=details&product_id=144; Swedberg, C. (2005). *L.A. County jail to track inmates.* Retrieved October 1, 2008, from http://www.rfidjournal.com/article/articleprint/1601/-1/1.

via electronic surveillance devices that are attached to the body of the offender. The electronic monitoring device, known in popular culture as an ankle bracelet, sends a signal that notifies correctional personnel if the client leaves the house and thus violates the sentence.

Home detention and electronic monitoring are appealing intermediate sanctions for a variety of reasons. First, they permit convicted offenders to remain in the community and continue to be contributing members of society. Since their freedom is curtailed to work and treatment, the sanctions force offenders into a concentrated commitment to conventional behavior. In the same way, offenders are not permitted to go to bars or other places with high potential for criminal opportunities. Randy Gainey and Brian Payne interviewed offenders who had been placed on home detention with electronic monitoring and found that most offenders viewed the intermediate sanction as a positive experience that was certainly better than jail.[29]

Second, house arrest and electronic monitoring address offenders who ordinarily would have been sentenced to jail. Consequently, the sanctions offer significant savings in terms of jail space, jail operating costs, and jail crowding.[30–33] Third, evaluation studies from several states, including California, Georgia, and Virginia found evidence that offenders on house arrest/electronic monitoring had lower recidivism rates than comparable offenders.[34–36]

There are also deficiencies. First and foremost is that the sanctions cannot address criminal behaviors that occur within the home. Offenders may successfully comply with their sentence while engaging in domestic violence, child abuse, or using drugs within their home. Second, the crime-saving effects of house arrest and electronic monitoring are equivocal. Kevin Courtright, Bruce Berg, and Robert Mutchnick studied offenders in Pennsylvania and found that these offenders were as likely as jail inmates to get rearrested or have their probation revoked.[37,38] Similarly, James Bonta and his colleagues found that electronic monitoring was ineffective at reducing recidivism, added little value as an intermediate sanction, and only served to widen the net of the correctional apparatus.[39,40]

Probation

Probation is a sanction for criminal offenders who have been sentenced to a period of correctional supervision in the community in lieu of incarceration. Probation offers conditional freedom to offenders who must abide by a variety of conditions that are imposed to facilitate their rehabilitation. Common probation conditions are substance abuse counseling and urinalysis, no contact with victims in the case, psychiatric counseling, restitution, community service, maintenance of employment, and regular communication with one's probation officer. Standard conditions refer to universal mandates that apply to all probationers, such as regularly reporting to their probation officer. Treatment conditions address a problem or issue that if resolved will help the offender remain crime free; punitive conditions are burdens placed on probationers convicted of the most serious crimes.

A **probation officer** is the practitioner who oversees and monitors a probationer's case to determine that the defendant is complying with all conditions of probation. When probationers do not comply with their sentence, their probation officer can pursue two courses of action. Unless there is a grievous violation, such as an arrest for a new violent felony, the probation officer will warn the probationer and potentially seek to impose new conditions or extend the period of probation. Both of these actions must be court approved before the probation department may act. Other times, the probation officer arrests the probationer for violating the terms of the sentence. At court, the probation sentence can be terminated, usually resulting in a prison sentence, or made more restrictive. Persons who are performing exceptionally well can also have their probation terminated early. Violations of probation that are based on relatively minor conditional violations are oftentimes referred to as technical violations.

Probation is the jack of all trades sanction because it touches virtually all aspects of criminal justice. Upon arrest, it is usually the department of probation that conducts a **presentence investigation (PSI)** that is the primary source of information that the court uses to determine which cases will be deferred from formal prosecution. The criminal and social history information in the PSI can affect bond and pretrial release, adjudication, sentencing, correctional placement, and supervision. Joan Petersilia, a well-known correctional expert, expressed that, "No other justice agency is as extensively involved with the offender and his case as is the probation department."[41, p. 159]

Probation also plays a major part in deflecting or diverting crimes from the criminal justice system and thus provides great savings on court and correctional expenditures. Aside from nominal criminal offenders, recidivism rates are relatively high. This means that offenders already on probation commit many new crimes. Once this happens, the courts have a decision to make. They can either initiate prosecution for the new crimes or simply use the new arrest as the basis for a violation or revocation of probation. Prosecutors favor the latter approach. Rodney Kingsnorth and his colleagues found that prosecutors believed that case disposition by means of a probation violation hearing and revocation was preferable to filing new charges. Because probation violations could readily result in jail or prison sentences, new charges were often rejected or dismissed to streamline the case against the offender.[42] In this way, probation and its violation can serve a quasi-judicial function.

Parole

Parole is a method of completing a prison sentence in the community rather than in confinement. A paroled offender can legally be recalled to prison to serve the remainder of the sentence if he or she does not comply with the conditions of parole. Parole conditions are similar to probation conditions as parolees are expected to seek or maintain employment, attend mental health counseling or therapy, participate in substance abuse treatment, submit to drug tests, avoid contact with victims in their case, and avoid contact with other negative influences such as felons or fellow gang members. More than 80 percent of parolees have various conditions by which they must abide. Two types of parole exist. **Discretionary parole** occurs when parole boards have the discretionary authority to conditionally release prisoners based on a statutory or administrative determination of eligibility. **Mandatory parole** occurs in jurisdictions using determinate sentencing statutes (e.g., conviction for Class B felony is 25 years) in which inmates are conditionally released from prison after serving a portion of their original sentences minus any good time earned.[43]

Parole plays the following three critical roles in the criminal justice system:

1. Parole boards determine the actual length of prison sentences once an offender has served the minimum term of his or her sentence. On a case-by-case basis, the parole board determines whether a prisoner is ready to be released into the community. Because of this, the parole board, an executive branch agency, has considerable oversight on the judiciary.
2. Parole agencies supervise probationers and therefore oversee the reintegration of returning prisoners.
3. Parole boards and parole officers are authorized to revoke parolee sentences if they are not in compliance. In this sense, parole serves an important crime control function by removing high-risk criminal offenders from the community once it is clear that they are recidivistic and noncompliant.[44]

The primary distinction between parole and all of the other forms of community corrections is that parolees are placed in the community after serving time in prison. Conversely, other intermediate sanctions place offenders in the community in lieu of prison. Parole shares the same nomenclature as probation. For instance, parole officers supervise parolees, monitor them for parole violations, and have the authority to revoke parole. There is one important difference: parole is always a state function that is administered by one executive department per state.

To many, parole is the most serious form of community corrections because of the criminality of the population. Unlike probationers, half of whom were simply convicted of misdemeanors, parolees are all convicted felons who have served time in prison. Parolees

CORRECTIONS BRIEF

Adult Correctional Supervision: Probation and Parole

Just over 7 million persons make up the adult correctional supervision population. This population is comprised of two groups—those convicted of a crime and sentenced to a correctional facility but placed directly on probation by the court without serving time and those convicted offenders who served time in a correctional institution but are eligible for release plus a period of conditional supervision in the community.

In 2006, the adult probation population increased by 0.5 percent to more than 4,237,000 clients. The adult parole population grew by 1.6 percent to more than 798,000 clients. Nearly 50 percent of the probationers had been convicted of a felony, and 49 percent had been convicted of a misdemeanor. About 28 percent were on probation for a drug offense violation, while 15 percent were on probation for driving while under the influence of alcohol.

Probationers account for more than half of the growth in the adult correctional population. The increase in correctional population from 1990 to 2006 was nearly 2.5 million convicted offenders. Probationers were responsible for 53 percent of this increase in population. The growth in probation population is most noticeable in California and Pennsylvania while New York and Washington experienced the greatest decrease in probationer populations.

Data indicate that nearly 25 percent of probationers are female and that 57 percent of probationers receive a direct sentence from the court to supervised probation under the department of corrections. Records also indicate that half of all probationers have been convicted of a felony, that 28 percent of probationers were convicted on a drug charge, compared to 40 percent of parolees, and that 15 percent had been convicted of driving while intoxicated (DWI). Of these probationers, nearly 60 percent successfully satisfy the conditions set forth by the courts and complete their probationary period.

One in every 286 adults is under parole supervision in the United States. One in eight adult parolee is female. The population of adult parolees is comprised of inmates eligible for mandatory release in compliance with state and federal statutes and those who earned credit for good time and are eligible for early release in accordance with new release policies passed by state legislatures after 1980. As a result, from 1980 to 2004, the number of discretionary releases granted by parole boards decreased from 55 percent to 22 percent. Consequently, from 1980 to 1995, mandatory parole release jumped from 19 percent to 39 percent. From 1995 to 2004, the number of mandatory releases remained stable. Forty-five percent of parolees successfully complete their period of supervision. Successful completion rates for parolees are consistently lower than the completion rates of probationers. Approximately 40 percent of parolees find their way back to prison prior to completing the program.

Source: Glaze, L. E., & Bonczar, T. P. (2007). *Probation and parole in the United States, 2006*. Washington, DC: U.S. Department of Justice, Office of Justice Programs, Bureau of Justice Statistics.

are the most high-risk group of correctional clients. Because of this, the parole board, the administrative board that is empowered to grant parole, must be mindful of crime control when deciding which inmates to grant another opportunity for redemption.

Institutional Corrections

When most people think of corrections, they envision **institutional corrections** in which criminal offenders are confined, locked up, removed from society, and kept away or incapacitated from other members of society. Other than capital punishment, institutional corrections are the harshest form of criminal punishment and are reserved for offenders convicted of felonies, especially serious crimes including murder, rape, robbery, kidnapping, child molestation, and the like, and generally for offenders with extensive criminal histories. The various forms of institutional corrections are explored next.

Jail and Prison

Jail is a local correctional facility usually operated by a county sheriff's department and used for the short-term confinement of petty offenders, misdemeanants, persons convicted of low-level felonies, and persons awaiting transport to some other criminal justice or social service agency. Jails confine persons before and after adjudication, and those who have been sentenced typically serve sentences of usually no more than 1 year. Jails house a diverse group of inmates and also:

- Receive those pending arraignment and hold them pending trial, conviction, or sentencing.
- Readmit probation, parole, and bail-bond violators and absconders.
- Temporarily detain juveniles pending transfer to juvenile authorities.
- Hold mentally ill persons pending their movement to appropriate mental health facilities.
- Hold individuals for military, for protective custody, for contempt, and for the courts as witnesses.
- Release convicted inmates to the community upon completion of sentence.
- Hold inmates pending transfer to federal, state, or other authorities.
- House inmates for federal, state, or other authorities because of crowding of their facilities.
- Operate community-based programs as alternatives to incarceration.[45]

Although the general public and television crime dramas often use *jail* and *prison* interchangeably, there are important differences. Michael Harrington and Cassia Spohn identified several differences between the facilities. First, the quality of life in jail is generally much better than in prison because of the shorter duration and the less serious types of offenders with whom one is to be housed. Second, jails are closely located to where offenders live; prisons are often located in remote areas, often far away from the cities in which offenders disproportionately lived before they were incarcerated. Third, whereas prisons are isolating, jails facilitate community ties with the continuation of employment, treatment, and family opportunities.[46] As such, as far as institutional corrections go, jails are preferable to prisons.

A **prison** is a correctional facility used to confine persons convicted of serious crimes and serving sentences of usually more than 1 year. Most prisons are state-administered facilities, although the federal criminal justice system (discussed later in this chapter) also operates a separate prison system known as the Federal Bureau of Prisons (BOP). State prisons can also be administered by private correctional organizations. A defendant who has been sentenced to prison is known as an **inmate** or **prisoner**.

Although confinement has existed in Western societies for centuries, prisons as they are understood today are an American invention. In the early 19th century, prisons, then symbolically known as penitentiaries, were hailed as an outgrowth of the Enlightenment, during which criminal offenders were confined and expected to contemplate their criminal behavior and work toward their rehabilitation and ultimate redemption. Inmates were expected to be penitent, defined as feeling or expressing remorse for one's misdeeds or sins; as such, the penitentiary was designed as a place for criminals to repent. Throughout American history, prisons have reflected the social conditions of the day. Early prisons reflected the intense religiosity of the colonial era. Modern prisons reflect the pragmatic goals of incapacitation, crime control, and due process. Prisons have always been controversial and marked by periods of reform.

Halfway Houses/Residential Treatment

The term **halfway house** describes the status of a criminal defendant that is partially confined and partially integrated into the community. Traditionally, halfway houses served postconviction offenders as they transitioned from prison confinement to a period of aftercare or parole. However, for a variety of reasons, such as alcohol or drug treatment, mental health counseling, or some other risk factor, halfway house clients were viewed as too risky to be entirely released to the community. Unlike prisons, which are absolutely secured, halfway houses are correctional facilities from which residents are regularly permitted to leave the facility, unaccompanied by a correctional official, to attend treatment, use community resources (pertaining to their rehabilitation), attend school or some educational program, work, or seek employment. Halfway house residents generally sleep at the facility and are free to participate in their structured activities during specified times, usually normal business hours.

Today, halfway houses are often referred to as residential communities, residential community corrections, or **residential treatment** facilities. Halfway houses are advantageous as an intermediate sanction for two reasons. They are more cost-effective than

Residential communities assist correctional clients in their transition to conventional society.

prison and many jurisdictions utilize private halfway houses that offer even greater cost savings. For instance, Travis Pratt and Melissa Winston analyzed a nationwide census of public and private correctional facilities and found that private halfway houses were among the most cost-efficient forms of community supervision.[47]

Similar to most intermediate sanctions, halfway houses now serve both pretrial and postconviction offenders. Depending on the jurisdiction, parolees or probationers can reside in halfway houses. In some places, high-risk defendants on bond can reside in halfway houses or even county jails in special work release or work-ender units in which offenders reside in the facility when not working or attending treatment. Using various data sources and types of offenders, residential treatment has been found to be fairly effective at reducing recidivism and violence among criminal offenders.[48] Even more importantly from an administrative perspective, halfway houses provide another inexpensive opportunity to supervise criminal offenders for whom prison would be too expensive and perhaps too severe a sanction.[49]

Boot Camps/Shock Incarceration

Correctional **boot camps**, sometimes referred to as **shock incarceration** or intensive incarceration, are short-term incarceration programs that incorporate the strict discipline, hard labor, and physical training of military basic training followed by an aftercare program, parole, or probation (depending on the state and the legal classification of the offender) that contains conditions and treatment. A major advantage of boot camps is that they are significantly less expensive than placing felons in traditional prison.[50]

Boot camp participants are young convicted felons without extensive criminal histories for whom boot camp is an opportunity for rehabilitation in lieu of prison confinement. Boot camps were first introduced in 1983 in Georgia and Oklahoma to tremendous public and political fanfare. Citizens appreciated the harsh discipline, physical coercion, and tough-love approach to simultaneously treating and punishing youthful criminals. Some academic criminologists detested boot camps for these same reasons.[51,52]

Evaluations of boot camps in many states have produced conflicting findings about the overall effectiveness of boot camps as an intermediate sanction depending on the study outcome. Faith Lutze found that boot camps were successful in providing an environment of safety and discipline, which offenders felt was more conducive to rehabilitation than what a minimum-security prison could offer.[53] Even if boot camps offer an environment that seems conducive to rehabilitation, offenders do not always take advantage. For instance, a variety of criminologists have found that offenders who attended boot camp were no better than traditional prisoners in terms of reducing their antisocial attitudes, delinquent cognitions, or recidivism.[54–56] The effectiveness of boot camps is also contingent on the legal classification and even criminality of the participants. Boot camps were designed for offenders with little to no criminal history and tend to be most effective for such clients. When offenders with more extensive criminal records are placed in boot camp, the results are less impressive.[57]

After 20 years of research on boot camps, the following three important conclusions should be drawn:

1. The ultimate effectiveness of boot camps (and any sanction for that matter) depends greatly on the criminality of the clients. To illustrate, Brent Benda and his colleagues have consistently found that boot camp graduates who have low self-control, deficits in social skills, and frequent associations with criminal peers are significantly more likely to recidivate when followed for 5 years. Boot camp alumni with gang, drug, and weapons histories were also more problematic than clients who did not have this criminal baggage.[58–60]

2. The overall effects of boot camps on recidivism and related outcomes are modestly positive. Doris Layton MacKenzie, David Wilson, and Susanne Kider conducted an

exhaustive meta-analysis of 29 studies that used 44 samples of boot camp offenders. In nine studies, boot camp participants had lower recidivism than comparison groups who either did not participate in the boot camp or were simply sentenced to prison. In eight studies, boot camp clients were worse than their counterparts. In 12 studies, no significant differences emerged.[61] Boot camps that were most effective offered more rehabilitation components, such as drug treatment and education programs, and targeted prison-bound offenders.[62,63]

3. Even if boot camps modestly affect recidivism, they are important because they cost significantly less money than sending the same offenders to prison. These short-term cost savings will likely continue to justify the use of boot camps.

Although they receive great publicity and public support, boot camps are mostly ineffective at reducing recidivism among correctional clients.

This was but a snapshot of the various sentences that are part of the correctional system. Each is discussed in greater detail later in the book. Next, the correctional system is viewed by the numbers in terms of the statistical size of the various correctional populations, expenditures and employment information, and collateral issues that give corrections a broader societal relevance, such as its impact on popular culture, the media, and public health. Finally, the chapter concludes with a profile of federal corrections, which are distinct from the assorted local and state correctional systems.

Corrections by the Numbers

Today, the correctional population exceeds 7.2 million adults, which equates to about 3.2 percent of the United States adult population. In other words, 1 in every 31 adults is either incarcerated, on probation, or on parole. Among the persons under correctional supervision:

- More than 4.2 million are on probation.
- More than 825,000 are on parole.
- More than 1.6 million are in state or federal prison.
- Nearly 770,000 are in jail.
- Nearly 16,000 are in territorial prisons.
- More than 10,000 are in facilities under the authority of the Bureau of Immigration and Customs Enforcement.
- More than 2,300 are in military facilities.
- Nearly 2,000 are in jails on Native American reservations.
- Nearly 100,000 are in juvenile facilities.[64,65]

The correctional population varies greatly between states. A good rule of thumb is that if a state has many electoral votes, it also has large probation, parole, and prisoner populations. For example, nearly 700,000 inmates are concentrated within the BOP, California, Texas, Florida, and New York. California and Texas have roughly 170,000 prisoners, whereas less populated states, such as North Dakota, Maine, Wyoming, Vermont, and New Hampshire have between 1,000 and 2,000 inmates. More than 107,000 inmates representing 7 percent of all inmates are supervised in privately operated prisons.

Because social groups have dramatically different rates of criminal behavior, the effects of the correctional system on gender, racial, and ethnic groups varies. There are sharp offending differences by gender, race, and ethnicity. For gender, about 1 in every 108 men and 1 in every 1,538 women were under the jurisdiction of correctional authorities. In other words, men are more than 14 times as likely as women to be in the system. Women comprise just 7 percent of the total prison population. Racial and

TABLE 1-1 Prevalence of Imprisonment by Gender and Race

U.S. Residents Ever Incarcerated	Number 1974	Number 1991	Number 2001	Percent of Adult U.S. Residents 1974	Percent of Adult U.S. Residents 1991	Percent of Adult U.S. Residents 2001
Total	1,819,000	3,437,000	5,618,000	1.3	1.8	2.7
Male	1,677,000	3,142,000	5,037,000	2.3	3.4	4.9
White	837,000	1,395,000	1,978,000	1.4	1.9	2.6
Black	595,000	1,181,000	1,936,000	8.7	12.0	16.6
Hispanic	94,000	392,000	911,000	2.3	4.9	7.7
Female	142,000	295,000	581,000	0.2	0.3	0.5
White	86,000	139,000	225,000	0.1	0.2	0.3
Black	51,000	109,000	231,000	0.6	0.9	1.7
Hispanic	8,000	30,000	86,000	0.2	0.4	0.7

Source: Bonczar, T. P. (2003). *Prevalence of imprisonment in the U.S. population, 1974–2001*. Washington, DC: U.S. Department of Justice, Office of Justice Programs, Bureau of Justice Statistics.

ethnic minorities are disproportionately sentenced to probation and parole and comprise 60 percent of the state and federal prison population.[66]

Thomas Bonczar estimated that over 5.6 million American adults currently residing in conventional society had previously served time in prison. As shown in TABLE 1-1, the rate of ever having gone to prison among adult African American males (16.6 percent) was double the rate of Hispanic males (7.7 percent) and over six times the rate of white males (2.6 percent). Bonczar also reported that *if* incarceration rates remain unchanged, 6.6 percent of U.S. residents born in 2001 will go to prison in their lifetime. This included about 1 in 3 African American males, 1 in 6 Hispanic males, and 1 in 17 white males. For women, the rates were 5.6 percent for African Americans, 2.2 percent for Hispanics, and less than 1 percent for whites.[67]

American justice is also big business, and the correctional system comprises the bulk of public spending for crime control. For instance, the California prison system operates at approximately 175 percent above capacity and costs billions to operate. In 2007, California legislators passed a $7.3 billion plan to add more than 53,000 additional beds for inmates and more rehabilitation programs.[68] On a national level, Kristen Hughes reports that more than $185 billion was spent on the criminal justice system, an increase of more than 400 percent since 1982. Total justice system expenditures comprised more than 7 percent of all state and local public expenditures—approximately as much as expenditures on hospitals and health care. According to the most recent available data, nearly 2.4 million Americans work in the criminal justice system, resulting in a monthly payroll of $9 billion.[69]

Per capita expenditures on criminal justice increased more than 300 percent between 1982 and 2003. On average, each resident of the United States expends $209 on the correctional system, an increase of 423 percent in that time frame. Total direct expenditures (FIGURE 1-8) on corrections increased a whopping 619 percent in that time frame. The increases for policing and courts were 396 percent and 474 percent, respectively. The federal criminal justice system (discussed later in this chapter) experienced even greater growth. Between 1982 and 2005, the federal government increased expenditures on policing by 708 percent, legal services by 573 percent, and corrections by 925 percent.[70]

Within the correctional system, prisons are far and away the costliest to run. James Stephan estimated that more than $38 billion are spent to maintain the nation's state prison systems. Daily operating expenses exceed $28 billion. About 77 percent of a state's

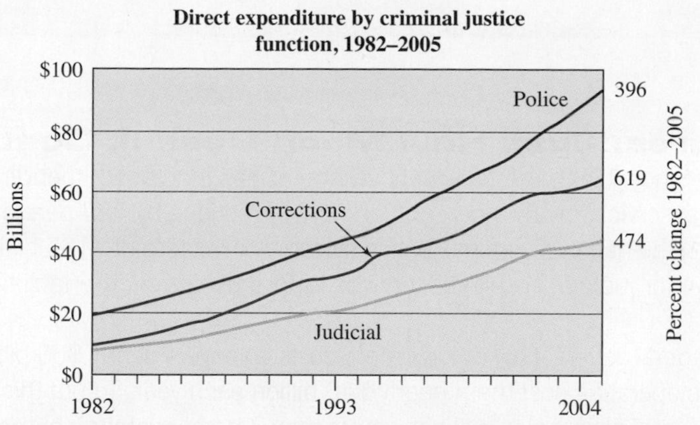

FIGURE 1–8 Per Capita Justice Expenditures, 1982–2005. *Source*: Hughes, K. A. (2008). *Justice expenditures and employment in the United States, 2005*. Washington, DC: U.S. Department of Justice, Office of Justice Programs, Bureau of Justice Statistics.

correctional costs are spent on prison operations, with the remaining 23 percent devoted to juvenile justice, probation and parole, other community corrections, and administration. Medical care for state prisoners totaled more than $3 billion each year—which is 12 percent of operating expenditures. According to the most recent data, one state prisoner costs taxpayers $22,650 per year or $62.05 per day to incarcerate. In the federal Bureau of Prisons, the figures are $22,632 per year or $62.01 per day.[71]

In addition to its monetary costs, the American correctional system creates collateral problems for American society. In some cases, corrections achieved cultural significance. For instance, cultural icon Oprah Winfrey has devoted time on her talk show to educate parents about the dangers of sex offenders, which has resulted in multiple arrests, including a pedophile who was on the FBI's most wanted fugitive list.[72] In 2007, a 90-year-old former member of the Colombo crime family was arrested for violating his parole. John "Sonny" Franzese was a long-time patron of the Copacabana nightclub where he spent time with entertainers Frank Sinatra and Sammy Davis Jr.[73] Corrections news is not always negative, however. After severe flooding in the Great Plains, inmates from Missouri prisons helped National Guard members fill sandbags to protect a water treatment plant, schools, and an ethanol plant.[74]

The correctional system and correctional clients create three important problems for mainstream society: crime, family disruption, and public health.

1. The most obvious collateral consequence of the correctional system is the inability to reduce crime. Community corrections clients remain free and thus have ample opportunity to recidivate. Prisoners bring antisocial behaviors home after their release, thus increasing crime rates in their communities.[75,76] For instance, Ingrid Binswanger and her colleagues found that in the first 2 weeks after release from prison, ex-cons have a death rate (mostly from drug overdoses or homicide) that is 1,270 percent higher than other residents.[77] This suggests that correctional clients and the difficulty of the correctional system in adequately supervising them can jeopardize public safety.
2. Institutional corrections disrupt family structures and place exceptional burdens on the spouses, children, and other relatives of prisoners. These burdens often reduce the life chances of those affected, especially children of inmates. For instance, Christopher Mumola reports that African American children are nine times and Hispanic children three times more likely than white children to have a parent in prison.[78] These disparities partially reflect race differences in social

CORRECTIONS FOCUS

Justice System Expenditures: Just How Much Does It Cost?

Juvenile system expenditures are not cheap! Since 1982, the federal government has increased spending on police protection by 708 percent, on judicial and legal services by 573 percent, and on corrections by 925 percent. In dollars and cents, this means that the cost of operating the nation's criminal justice system is in excess of $185 billion per year. This money funds police protection, also pays for judicial and legal services, and provides secure facilities for those convicted of all types and levels of crimes.

These funds come from local, state, and federal coffers. Law enforcement costs taxpayers nearly $60 billion per year and efforts at keeping our correctional facilities operating cost them nearly $40 billion each year. To put this in perspective, the criminal justice system costs state and local governments slightly more than 7 percent of their entire operational budgets. Spending on education is somewhere around four times that spent on the nation's justice system. Public welfare figures are roughly twice the expenditure and the money spent on health care and hospitals is nearly equal to that spent on the entire justice system.

From 1982 to 2003, expenditures for corrections increased 423 percent. This percentage represents an increase in cost from $40 per U.S. resident in 1982 to $209 per U.S. resident in 2003. In 1982, judicial and legal services cost $34 per U.S. resident. By 2003 this figure was $143. The resulting increase in expenditure for judicial and legal services was 321 percent. The costs for police protection increased by 241 percent, from $84 to $286 per U.S. resident. It is predicted that the average annual cost to operate the nation's criminal justice system will increase on average 8 percent each year.

The nation's criminal justice system employs over 2.3 million persons. This employment figure represents approximately 2 percent of the nation's workforce. State and local governments employ nearly 90 percent of all criminal justice system employees. Fifty-eight percent of these employees work for local governments. The 2.3 million employees working for the system generate an annual payroll in excess of $9 billion. It is without question that the nation's criminal justice system will continue to grow and with this growth will come an ever-increasing cost to operate. Indicators based on police workload alone reveal that FBI arrest estimates grew from 12 million arrests in 1982 to 13.6 million arrests in 2003. And of course with an increase in workload comes an increase in the number of police. During this same time period, the number of police employees grew from 724,000 to 1.1 million. More police officers, deputies, and special agents means more arrests, and with more arrests come more convictions. Ultimately, convicted offenders need to be housed in a secure facility. Job security is a given when working for the U.S. criminal justice system.

Source: Hughes, K. A. (2006). *Justice expenditures and employment in the United States, 2003*. Washington, DC: U.S. Department of Justice, Office of Justice Programs, Bureau of Justice Statistics.

development and delinquency among adolescents. Mark Berg and Matt DeLisi suggested a connection between community-level violence and prison violence among racial and ethnic minorities that contributed to social problems within minority neighborhoods.[79]

3. The correctional system poses serious public health risks. Approximately 40 percent of the prisoners in the United States are infected with hepatitis C, a serious disease that causes liver failure and liver cancer. Many inmates are unaware they have the disease. Hepatitis C is transmitted much like the HIV virus that causes AIDS, mainly via intravenous drug use and unprotected sexual contact. The prevalence of hepatitis C among prisoners is 20 times the rate among the general population, thus the reentry of correctional clients to the community poses health risks (see FIGURE 1-9). Unfortunately, the correctional system is only beginning to recognize the seriousness of the hepatitis C epidemic, and health care is lagging.[80]

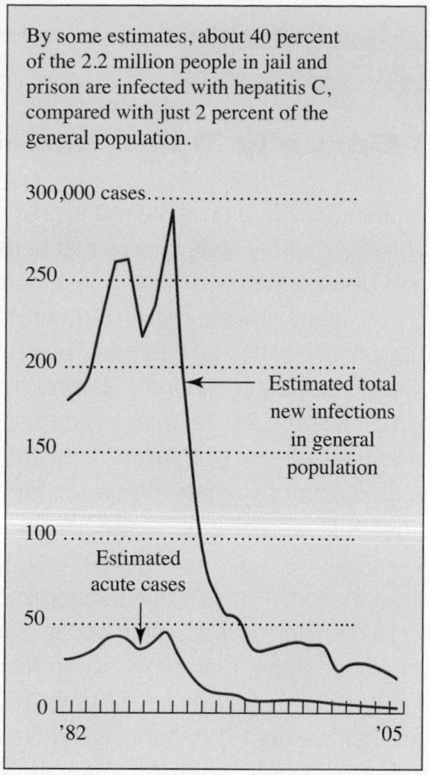
By some estimates, about 40 percent of the 2.2 million people in jail and prison are infected with hepatitis C, compared with just 2 percent of the general population.
300,000 cases
250
200
150
100
50
0
Estimated total new infections in general population
Estimated acute cases
'82
'05

FIGURE 1-9 Hepatitis C Among Prisoners, 1982–2005. *Source*: Centers for Disease Control and Prevention. (2008). *Viral hepatitis C fact sheet*. Washington, DC: U.S. Department of Health and Human Services.

The Federal Criminal Justice System

While the term *criminal justice system* is understood to represent the total set of agencies and organizations relating to police, courts, and corrections, the system is of course fragmented by jurisdiction. Towns, cities, counties, and states have their own police, courts, and corrections. The same holds for the United States. The federal criminal justice system contains many agencies that arrest, prosecute, and detain criminal defendants. Some federal criminal justice agencies include:

- Federal Bureau of Investigation (FBI)
- U.S. Marshals
- U.S. Immigration and Customs Enforcement (ICE)
- Federal Bureau of Prisons (BOP)
- Drug Enforcement Administration (DEA)
- U.S. Customs and Border Protection
- U.S. Postal Inspectors
- U.S. Attorneys
- U.S. Probation and Pretrial Services
- U.S. Parole Commission

Like the states, the federal criminal justice system processes hundreds of thousands of cases per year. And like the states, the federal system diverts most cases from the system as it works from law enforcement through the courts and terminates in corrections (see

CORRECTIONS RESEARCH

Drug Use and Sexually Transmitted Infections in Prison

The likelihood of being incarcerated on a drug offense is greater today than it has ever been. Statistical data on prisoner populations reveals that between 60 and 80 percent of state and federal inmates use or have used illegal substances. Records indicate that over a quarter of a million prisoners in state facilities report having used intravenous drugs, half of whom also report having shared needles. The number of substance users increases significantly when including those inmates who have smoked substances such as crack cocaine. With this use of illegal drugs comes the risk of contracting and/or transmitting infectious diseases. Not surprisingly, the infectious disease rate for prison inmates is five to six times greater than rates for the general population. Researchers blame this high-risk behavior on the social demographics of the prison population.

Many prison inmates come from a socially and economically disadvantaged population. These inmates tend to lack formal education and generally do not have access to adequate medical care. In addition, many of these inmates suffer from personal trauma such as physical and/or sexual abuse. A substantial number were unemployed prior to being arrested for their crimes. This population also has an affinity for high-risk behavior that places them at risk for contracting an infectious disease. Generally speaking, those who use illegal substances practice a variety of high-risk behaviors, not the least of which is sexual intercourse with concurrent partners.

Female inmates are at particularly high risk for contracting sexually transmitted infections—especially female inmates who abuse drugs and/or alcohol. The infection rate among female prisoners has been tied to intravenous drug use and prostitution for drugs. Sexually transmitted infections (STIs) pose an even bigger risk for this population since many of the STIs are asymptomatic in women. As a result, female inmates find themselves living with STIs for a much longer period of time before seeking treatment.

Why is drug use and the spread of sexually transmitted infections a problem worth addressing? There are over 2.3 million inmates in the U.S. correctional system (prison and jail). The group of prisoners who are at highest risk for contracting and transmitting a sexually infectious disease are those housed for short periods of time in local jails—typically no more than 48 hours, but the sentence can be for as long as 1 year. Because their time in the facility is short, very few offenders in these facilities are screened for infectious diseases despite federal guidelines and recommendations to do so. Even more problematic is the system's resistance to steps that could prevent the spread of sexually transmitted infections in these facilities.

Local, state, and federal correctional facilities restrict sexual activity among inmates and thus resist the idea of distributing condoms even though officials acknowledge inmates do participate in sexual relationships in a variety of settings. Inmates improvise by using portions of latex gloves and plastic wrap. The outcome is the continued likelihood of the transmission of sexually infectious diseases.

Source: Wolfe, M. I., et al. (2001). An outbreak of syphilis in Alabama prisons: Correctional health policy and communicable disease control. *American Journal of Public Health, 91,* 1220–1225.

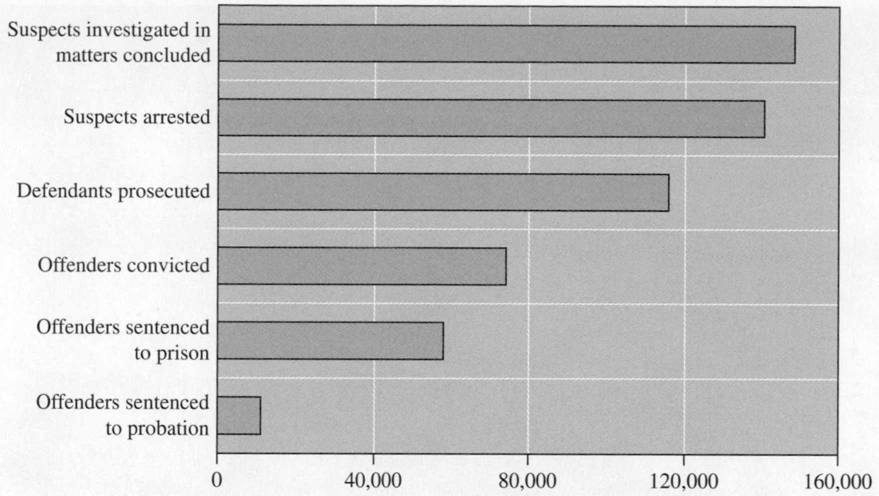

FIGURE 1–10 Annual Case Processing in the Federal Criminal Justice System. *Source*: Smith, S. K., & Motivans, M. (2006). *Compendium of federal justice statistics, 2004*. Washington, DC: U.S. Department of Justice, Office of Justice Programs, Bureau of Justice Statistics.

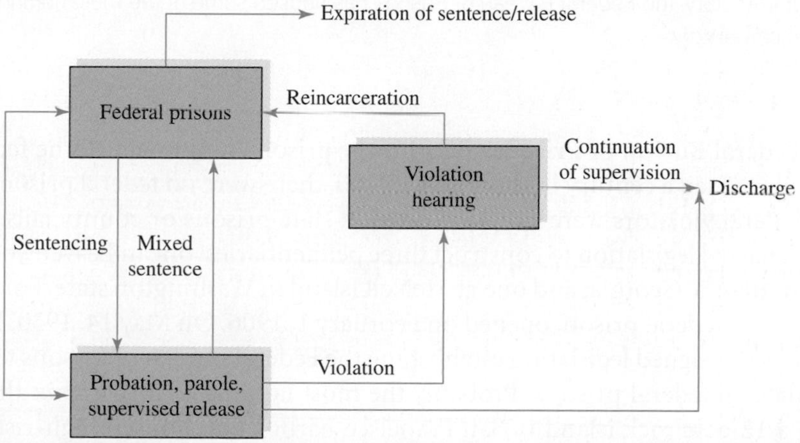

FIGURE 1–11 Structure of Federal Criminal Justice System. *Source*: Smith, S. K., & Motivans, M. (2006). *Compendium of federal justice statistics, 2004*. Washington, DC: U.S. Department of Justice, Office of Justice Programs, Bureau of Justice Statistics.

FIGURE 1–10 and FIGURE 1–11). According to the most recent Compendium of Federal Justice Statistics, which contained data from 2004, more than 148,229 suspects were investigated by federal law enforcement each year, of whom 141,212 were arrested. Unlike local and state criminal justice systems where suspects are routinely investigated but less likely to be arrested, the federal system is more judicious. Defendants who are investigated are also more likely to be arrested by federal authorities. U.S. attorneys prosecuted 116,363 defendants resulting in 74,782 convictions. Based on these convictions, 58,106 offenders were sentenced to prison and 11,067 to probation.[81]

As shown in Figure 1–11, federal correctional clients follow an admittedly confusing route through the correctional system. Depending on their sentence, defendants can serve community corrections, institutional corrections, or both. If an offender violates the conditions of his or her sentence, supervised release can be violated and result in reincarceration.

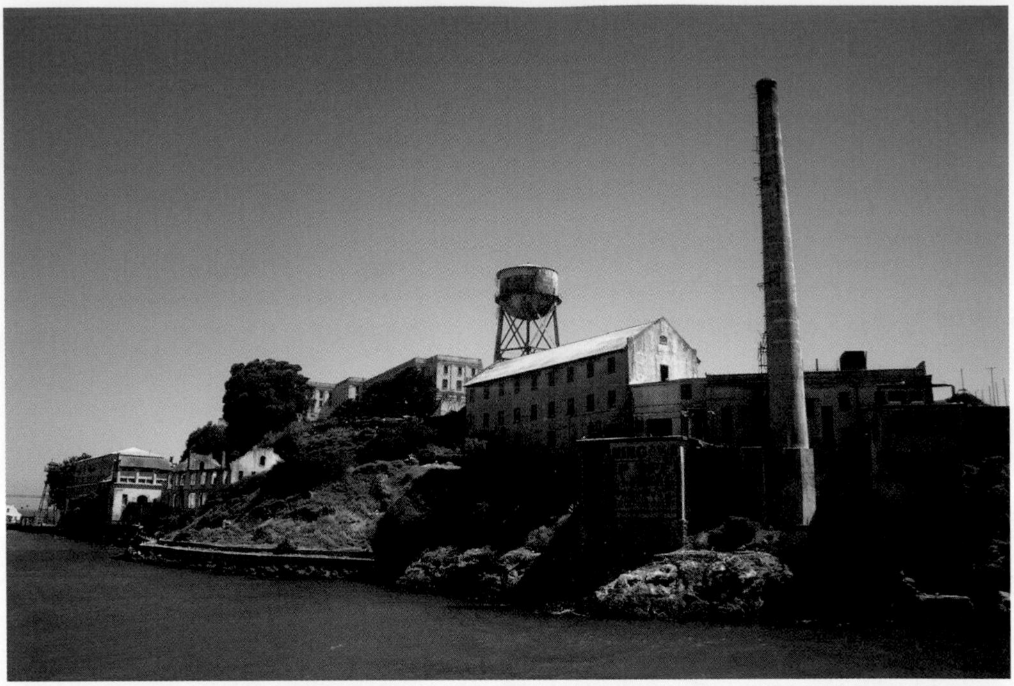

Throughout its history, the Federal Bureau of Prisons has housed some of the most notorious prisoners in American history.

The **Federal Bureau of Prisons** (**BOP**) is the prison component of the federal system. For more than a century in the United States, there were no federal prison facilities because federal violators were simply housed in state prisons or county jails. In 1891, Congress enacted legislation to construct three penitentiaries: one in Leavenworth, Kansas; one in Atlanta, Georgia; and one at McNeil Island in Washington state. Fort Leavenworth, the first federal prison, opened on February 1, 1906. On May 14, 1930, President Herbert Hoover signed legislation establishing the Federal Bureau of Prisons to manage and regulate all federal prisons. Probably the most famous facility within the BOP is Alcatraz, a 12-acre rock island in San Francisco harbor that housed high-risk prisoners from other facilities between 1934 and 1963. By October 2008, more than 202,000 inmates were in the BOP.[82]

The BOP operates institutions at five different security levels based on the presence of external patrols, towers, security barriers, or detection devices; the type of housing within the institution; internal security features; and the staff-to-inmate ratio. Each facility is designated as minimum, low, medium, high, or administrative.

- Minimum-security institutions, also known as federal prison camps (FPCs), have dormitory housing, a relatively low staff-to-inmate ratio, and limited or no perimeter fencing. These institutions are work and program oriented. Many are located adjacent to larger institutions or on military bases where inmates help serve the labor needs of the larger institution or base.
- Low-security federal correctional institutions (FCIs) have double-fenced perimeters, mostly dormitory or cubicle housing, and strong work and program components. The staff-to-inmate ratio in these institutions is higher than in minimum security facilities.
- Medium-security FCIs have strengthened perimeters, mostly cell-type housing, a wide variety of work and treatment programs, an even higher staff-to-inmate ratio than low-security FCIs, and even greater internal controls.

- High-security institutions, also known as United States penitentiaries (USPs), have highly secured perimeters featuring walls or reinforced fences, multiple- and single-occupant cell housing, the highest staff-to-inmate ratio, and close control of inmate movement.
- Administrative facilities are institutions with special missions, such as the detention of pretrial offenders; the treatment of inmates with serious or chronic medical problems; or the containment of extremely dangerous, violent, or escape-prone inmates. Administrative facilities include Metropolitan Correctional Centers (MCCs), Metropolitan Detention Centers (MDCs), Federal Detention Centers (FDCs), Federal Medical Centers (FMCs), Federal Transfer Centers (FTC), Medical Center for Federal Prisoners (MCFP), and the Administrative-Maximum (ADX). U.S. Penitentiary Administrative facilities are capable of holding inmates in all security categories. A number of BOP institutions also have a small, minimum-security camp adjacent to the main facility known as satellite camps.[83]

The objectives of federal supervision are to (1) enforce compliance with the conditions of release, (2) minimize risk to the public, and (3) reintegrate the offender into a law-abiding lifestyle. There are more than 109,712 active offenders under federal supervision in the United States, 91 percent of whom are felons. More than 77,332 are on **supervised release**, which is a term of supervision that the court imposes to follow a period of imprisonment. Nearly 30,000 offenders are on probation.[84]

About 3,000 people are on parole. Federal parole has an interesting and convoluted history. Federal parole was enacted in 1910 along with three parole boards consisting of the warden of the federal institution (three federal penitentiaries existed in 1910), the physician in the institution, and the Superintendent of Prisons of the Department of Justice. A single federal board of parole was created in 1930. In 1976, the United States Parole Commission was established after the passage of the Parole Commission and Reorganization Act. The Comprehensive Crime Control Act of 1984 created the United States Sentencing Commission to establish sentencing guidelines for the federal courts and a regime of determinate sentences. These sentencing guidelines went into effect on November 1, 1987, thus defendants sentenced on or after that date served determinate terms and were not eligible for parole consideration. For all intents and purposes, federal parole was abolished in 1987, and federal correctional clients who were not in a Bureau of Prison facility and their status was dubbed supervised releases as described earlier in the chapter.

Due to federal offenders who were sentenced prior to November 1, 1987, the United States Parole Commission has been unable to be legally phased out. Federal parole has been extended via the Judicial Improvements Act of 1990, the Parole Commission Phaseout Act of 1996, and the 21st Century Department of Justice Appropriations Authorization Act of 2002. Once the final federal offender sentenced before November 1, 1987, terminates his or her case, federal parole will end. Ultimately, the United States Probation and Pretrial Services System monitor all federal supervised release clients.[85]

WRAP UP

CASE STUDY CONCLUSION

What Hilton Could Expect Behind Bars—It's Not Just Another Gated Community!

The Los Angeles County jail for women is home to approximately 2,200 female inmates. Celebrity inmates are typically segregated from the general population and are usually assigned either a one- or two-person cell. The jail cell is no larger than 12 by 8 feet. But otherwise it's almost like home. There's a toilet, a sink, a polished steel mirror, and a window that measures six inches across. Inmates are allowed 1 hour a day outside of their cells. During this time they are allowed to watch TV, exercise, or shower. Prisoners can even call home using a bank of telephones and drawing on their prepaid phone cards; cell phones are not allowed. But it gets worse. Paris Hilton was required to wear a standard issue orange prison jumpsuit. And as she soon learned, personal hygiene products lacked a designer label and additional hair products and cosmetics had to be purchased from the jail commissary. The good news is there was plenty of time to read. Jail policy allows each inmate three books or combination of three books and magazines per week. Photos of family and friends are also allowed, provided the photographs are no larger than four by six inches.

What About the Food?

Breakfast is served between 6:00 a.m. and 7:30 a.m. There is no room service—it's more of a buffet style, serve yourself, clear your table when finished type of setting. No beef! No pork! And it's all low sodium. That's right, prison dieticians have decided on a low-sodium poultry diet for all inmates. The only hot meal is dinner.

Here's the Deal—Time Served

California law allows for good time, which means inmates receive time off for good behavior. Each day of good time decreases actual time served. Here's the deal—persons sentenced to 45 days in jail with good time can expect to be released after serving 23 days of their 45-day sentence. Hilton had pleaded no contest to the original reckless driving case in January 2007, and was sentenced to 36 months' probation and a $1,500 fine. She was sentenced to 45 days in county jail for violating her probation and ultimately served 22 days in detention.

Sources: Ventre, M. (2007). *Jail bad? It's just another way to get publicity.* Retrieved June 1, 2007, from http://www.msnbc.msn.com/id/18680783/print/1/displaymode/1098/; Associated Press. (2007). *Paris Hilton sentenced to 45 days in jail.* Retrieved June 1, 2007, from http://www.msnbc.msn.com/id/18472845/print/1/displaymode/1098/; Associated Press. (2007). *What Paris can expect behind bars.* Retrieved June 1, 2007, from http://www.msnbc.msn.com/id/18497580/print/1/displaymo

Chapter Summary

- The correctional system spans the pretrial and posttrial phases and supervises defendants throughout the criminal justice process.
- Like all components of the criminal justice system, offenders are diverted from the correctional system to facilitate rehabilitation, ensure public safety, and balance costs.
- An individual's criminality and risk are the fundamental determinants of placement along the continuum of sanctions.
- Correctional supervision occurs in the community, such as fines, community service, deferred sentences, home detention, probation, and within institutions, such as jail and prison.

- More than 7 million defendants are under correctional supervision, more than 2 million are incarcerated, and tens of billions of dollars are spent annually to operate the correctional system.
- Correctional clients create assorted social problems, including crime and recidivism, family disruption, and public health risks.
- The federal correctional system maintains its own system just as cities, counties, and states operate independent correctional systems.

Key Terms

aggravating factors Circumstances that seem to increase the culpability of the offenders.

bond A pledge of money or some other assets offered as bail by an accused person or his or her surety (bail bondsman) to secure temporary release from custody.

boot camps/shock incarceration Short-term incarceration programs that incorporate the strict discipline, hard labor, and physical training of military basic training followed by an aftercare program that contains conditions and treatment.

community corrections Sanctions that allow criminal offenders to remain in the community as long as they abide by certain conditions, such as maintaining employment, participating in drug treatment, or undergoing psychological treatment.

community service A form of restitution that involves civic participation toward the improvement of the community.

continuum of sanctions A range of sanctions or legal penalties that balance punishment, treatment, and supervision concerns with the seriousness of the offense and the offender's criminal convictions.

corrections The collection of local, state, and federal agencies that supervise and treat criminal defendants.

courts A major component of the criminal justice system comprised of prosecutors, defense counsel, and judges that perform a variety of functions, foremost of which is to serve as a check and balance on the police.

criminality The propensity towards antisocial behavior that a defendant embodies.

day reporting Sanction that requires defendants to report to an official criminal justice facility, such as a jail, on a daily basis to check in and demonstrate to correctional staff that they are complying with the conditions of their current legal status.

defendant The person accused of a criminal violation.

deferred prosecution, judgment, or sentence A sentence whereby the defendant pleads guilty in exchange for a suspended sentence that will be voided and expunged if the defendant complies with certain conditions.

discretion The latitude to choose one course of action or another.

discretionary parole Release that occurs when parole boards have the discretionary authority to conditionally release prisoners based on a statutory or administrative determination of eligibility.

Eighth Amendment Amendment to the Bill of Rights of the United States Constitution that states that "excessive bail shall not be required, nor excessive fines imposed, nor cruel and unusual punishments inflicted."

electronic monitoring (EM) The use of surveillance technology to monitor offenders in the community. *Also see* home detention and house arrest.

expungement The complete removal of a criminal record from existence.

extralegal variables Factors that influence criminal justice discretion but are not legally relevant, such as demographic characteristics.

Federal Bureau of Prisons (BOP) The prison component of the federal system.

fines Monetary payments imposed on criminal offenders as a way to repay society for the offenders' violations of the law.

forfeiture The loss of ownership of some property or asset for its illegal use.

halfway houses/residential treatment Describes the confinement status of a criminal defendant who is partially confined and partially integrated into the community.

home detention, house arrest, and electronic monitoring Community corrections that permit offenders to serve sentences in their homes while maintaining employment and community ties.

house arrest A sanction where the offender must not leave his or her home with the exception of court approved times for work and treatment. *Also see* home detention and electronic monitoring.

inmate (or prisoner) A defendant who has been sentenced to jail or prison.

institutional corrections Confinement or the physical removal from society as a means of supervision.

jail A local correctional facility usually operated by a county sheriff's department and used for the short-term confinement of petty offenders, misdemeanants, persons convicted of low-level felonies, and persons awaiting transport to some other criminal justice or social service agency.

legal variables Legally relevant factors, such as offense severity, prior criminal record, and number of charges.

mandatory parole Type of parole that occurs in jurisdictions using determinate sentencing statutes where inmates are conditionally released from prison after serving a portion of their original sentences minus any good time earned.

mitigating factors Circumstances that seem to reduce the culpability of the offender.

net widening The growing of the correctional population by supervising an increasing number of offenders in the community.

parole Form of correction in which the convicted person completes a prison sentence in the community rather than in confinement.

police Also known as law enforcement, the part of the criminal justice system that responds to citizen complaints, provides basic services such as traffic control, enforces the criminal law, and in doing so, initiates criminal cases.

posttrial or postadjudication The stage of the criminal justice system after defendants have pleaded guilty or been found guilty.

presentence investigation (PSI) report A report prepared for the court that summarizes the defendant's social and criminal history for the purpose of sentencing.

pretrial supervision The correctional supervision of a defendant who has been arrested, booked, and bonded out of jail.

prison A correctional facility used to confine persons convicted of serious crimes and serving sentences of usually more than 1 year.

prisoner *See* inmate.

probation A sanction for criminal offenders who have been sentenced to a period of correctional supervision in the community in lieu of incarceration.

probation officer The practitioner who oversees and monitors a probationer's case to determine that the defendant is complying with all conditions of probation.

residential treatment *See* halfway houses/residential treatment.

restitution Money paid to the crime victim to recoup some of the harm caused by the offender's wrongful acts.

shock incarceration *See* boot camps/shock incarceration.

supervised release In the federal system, a term of supervision that the court imposes to follow a period of imprisonment.

Critical Thinking Questions

1. What is the reputation of the American correctional system? Is it too big? Costly? In what ways do the American media portray the correctional system?
2. What should be the overriding goal of the criminal justice system? Does public safety currently take precedence over individual rights? Does the balance between protecting the public and protecting the defendant vary by state?
3. Should offenders convicted of certain crimes only be punished by confinement? Should community corrections opportunities be afforded to all offenders, or do some correctional clients pose too great a risk?
4. What typifies dangerousness in a correctional client? Which behavioral and attitudinal factors come to mind?
5. Is it okay that people receive differential treatment in the justice system? Is it naïve to think otherwise?

Notes

1. Seiter, R. P., & Kadela, K. R. (2003). Prisoner reentry: What works, what does not, and what is promising. *Crime & Delinquency, 49,* 360–388.
2. Kleiman, M. (1999). Community corrections as the front line in crime control. *UCLA Law Review, 46,* 1909–1925.
3. Petersilia, J. (2002). Community corrections. In J. Q. Wilson & J. Petersilia (Eds.), *Crime: Public policies for crime control* (pp. 483–508). Oakland, CA: Institute for Contemporary Studies Press.
4. Pettit, B., & Western, B. (2004). Mass imprisonment and the life course: Race and class inequality in U.S. incarceration. *American Sociological Review, 69,* 151–169.
5. Flanagan, T. J., Marquart, J. W., & Adams, K. G. (1998). *Incarcerating criminals: Prisons and jails in social and organizational context.* New York: Oxford University Press.
6. Durose, M. R., & Langan, P. A. (2007). *Felony sentences in state courts, 2004.* Washington, DC: U.S. Department of Justice, Office of Justice Programs, Bureau of Justice Statistics.
7. Baumer, T. L. (2007). Reducing lockup crowding with expedited initial processing of minor offenders. *Journal of Criminal Justice, 35,* 273–281.

8. Holsinger, A. M., & Latessa, E. J. (1999). An empirical evaluation of a sanction continuum: Pathways through the juvenile justice system. *Journal of Criminal Justice, 27,* 155–172.

9. Morris, N. (1974). *The future of imprisonment.* Chicago: University of Chicago Press.

10. Tonry, M. (1998). Intermediate sanctions in sentencing guidelines. *Crime & Justice, 23,* 199–254.

11. Glaze, L. E., & Bonczar, T. P. (2007). *Probation and parole in the United States, 2006.* Washington, DC: U.S. Department of Justice, Office of Justice Programs, Bureau of Justice Statistics.

12. Posner, R. A. (1980). Optimal sentences for white-collar criminals. *American Criminal Law Review, 17,* 409–418.

13. Critelli, J. W., & Crawford, R. F. (1980). The effectiveness of court-ordered punishment: Fines versus no punishment. *Criminal Justice & Behavior, 7,* 465–470.

14. Gordon, M. A., & Glaser, D. (1991). The use and effects of financial penalties in municipal courts. *Criminology, 29,* 651–676.

15. Gillis, J. W. (2002). *Ordering restitution to the crime victim.* Washington, DC: U.S. Department of Justice, Office of Justice Programs, Office for Victims of Crime.

16. Outlaw, M. C., & Ruback, R. B. (1999). Predictors and outcomes of victim restitution orders. *Justice Quarterly, 16,* 847–869.

17. Clingermayer, J. C., Hecker, J., & Madsen, S. (2005). Asset forfeiture and police priorities: The impact of program design on law enforcement activities. *Criminal Justice Policy Review, 16,* 319–335.

18. Worrall, J. L. (2001). Addicted to the drug war: The role of civil asset forfeiture as a budgetary necessity in contemporary law enforcement. *Journal of Criminal Justice, 29,* 171–187.

19. Clingermayer, Hecker, & Madsen.

20. Williams, D. J., & Turnage, T. A. (2001). The success of a day reporting center program. *Corrections Compendium, 26,* 1–3, 26.

21. Roy, S., & Grimes, J. N. (2002). Adult offenders in a day reporting center: A preliminary study. *Federal Probation, 66,* 44–50.

22. Martin, C., Lurigio, A. J., & Olson, D. E. (2003). An examination of re-arrests and re-incarcerations among discharged day reporting center clients. *Federal Probation, 67,* 24–30.

23. Roy & Grimes.

24. Craddock, A. (2004). Estimating criminal justice system costs and cost-saving benefits of day reporting centers. *Journal of Offender Rehabilitation, 39,* 69–98.

25. Craddock, A., & Graham, L. A. (2001). Recidivism as a function of day reporting center participation. *Journal of Offender Rehabilitation, 34,* 81–97.

26. Caputo, G. A. (1999). Why not community service? *Criminal Justice Policy Review, 10,* 503–519.

27. Harris, R. J., & Lo, T. W. (2002). Community service: Its use in criminal justice. *International Journal of Offender Therapy and Comparative Criminology, 46,* 427–444.

28. Rackmill, S. J. (1996). Printzlien's legacy, the "Brooklyn Plan," A.K.A. deferred prosecution. *Federal Probation, 60,* 8–15.

29. Gainey, R. R., & Payne, B. K. (2000). Understanding the experience of house arrest with electronic monitoring: An analysis of quantitative and qualitative data. *International Journal of Offender Therapy and Comparative Criminology, 44,* 84–96.

30. Vollum, S., & Hale, C. (2002). Electronic monitoring: A research review. *Corrections Compendium, 27,* 1–4, 23–27.

31. Glaser, D., & Watts, R. (1993). The electronic monitoring of drug offenders on probation. *Journal of Offender Monitoring, 6,* 1–10, 14.

32. Courtright, K. E., Berg, B. L., & Mutchnick, R. J. (1997). The cost effectiveness of using house arrest with electronic monitoring. *Federal Probation, 61,* 19–22.

33. Papy, J., & Nimer, R. (1991). Electronic monitoring in Florida. *Federal Probation, 55,* 31–33.

34. Glaser & Watts.

35. Finn, M. A., & Muirhead-Steves, S. (2002). The effectiveness of electronic monitoring with violent male parolees. *Justice Quarterly, 19,* 293–312.

36. Gainey, R. R., Payne, B. K., & O'Toole, M. (2000). The relationships between time in jail, time on electronic monitoring, and recidivism: An event history analysis of a jail-based program. *Justice Quarterly, 17,* 733–752.

37. Courtright, K. E., Berg, B. L., & Mutchnick, R. J. (1997). The effects of house arrest with electronic monitoring on DUI offenders. *Journal of Offender Rehabilitation, 24,* 35–51.

38. Courtright, K. E., Berg, B. L., & Mutchnick, R. J. (2000). Rehabilitation in the new machine? Exploring drug and alcohol use and variables related to success among DUI offenders under electronic monitoring: Some preliminary outcome results. *International Journal of Offender Therapy and Comparative Criminology, 44,* 293–311.

39. Bonta, J., Wallace-Capretta, S., & Rooney, J. (2000). Can electronic monitoring make a difference? An evaluation of three Canadian programs. *Crime & Delinquency, 46,* 61–75.

40. For more criticisms of this sanction, see Schmidt, A. (1991). Electronic monitors: Realistically, what can be expected? *Federal Probation, 55,* 49–57; and Corbett, R., & Marx, G. T. (1991). No soul in the new machine: Technofallacies in the electronic monitoring movement. *Justice Quarterly, 8,* 399–414.

41. Petersilia, J. (1997). Probation in the United States. *Crime & Justice, 22,* 149–200.

42. Kingsnorth, R. F., MacIntosh, R. C., & Sutherland, S. (2002). Criminal charge or probation violation? Prosecutorial discretion and implications for research in criminal court processing. *Criminology, 40,* 553–578.

43. Hughes, T. A., Wilson, D. J., & Beck, A. J. (2001). *Trends in state parole, 1990–2000.* Washington, DC: U.S. Department of Justice, Office of Justice Programs, Bureau of Justice Statistics.

44. Travis, J., & Lawrence, S. (2002). *Beyond the prison gates: The state of parole in America.* Washington, DC: The Urban Institute, Justice Policy Center.

45. Harrison, P. M., & Beck, A. J. (2007). *Prison and jail inmates at midyear 2006.* Washington, DC: U.S. Department of Justice, Office of Justice Programs, Bureau of Justice Statistics.

46. Harrington, M. P., & Spohn, C. (2007). Defining sentence type: Further evidence against use of the total incarceration variable. *Journal of Research in Crime and Delinquency, 44,* 36–63.

47. Pratt, T. C., & Winston, M. R. (1999). The search for the frugal grail: An empirical assessment of the cost-effectiveness of public versus private correctional facilities. *Criminal Justice Policy Review, 10,* 447–471.

48. For examples, see Hartman, D. J., Friday, P. C., & Minor, K. I. (1994). Residential probation: A seven-year follow-up study of halfway house discharges. *Journal of Criminal Justice, 22,* 503–515; and Dowell, D. A., Klein, C., & Krichmar, C. (1985). Evaluation of a halfway house for women. *Journal of Criminal Justice, 13,* 217–226. For more equivocal findings, see Dowdy, E. R., Lacy, M. G., & Unnithan, N. P. (2002). Correctional prediction and the level of supervision inventory. *Journal of Criminal Justice, 30,* 29–39; and Latessa, E. J., & Travis III, L. F. (1991). Halfway house or probation: A comparison of alternative dispositions. *Journal of Crime and Justice, 14,* 53–75.

49. On the overuse of prison to serve minimum- and medium-risk felons, see Bonta, J., & Motiuk, L. L. (1990). Classification to halfway houses: A quasi-experimental evaluation. *Criminology, 28,* 497–506.

50. MacKenzie, D. L., & Piquero, A. (1994). The impact of shock incarceration programs on prison crowding. *Crime & Delinquency, 40,* 222–249.

51. Lutze, F. E., & Brody, D. C. (1999). Mental abuse as cruel and unusual punishment: Do boot camp prisons violate the Eighth Amendment? *Crime & Delinquency, 45,* 242–255.

52. Welch, M. (1997). A critical interpretation of correctional boot camps as normalizing institutions. *Journal of Contemporary Criminal Justice, 13,* 184–205.

53. Lutze, F. E. (1998). Are shock incarceration programs more rehabilitative than traditional prisons? A survey of inmates. *Justice Quarterly, 15,* 547–563.

54. MacKenzie, D. L. (1991). The parole performance of offender released from shock incarceration (boot camp prisons): A survival time analysis. *Journal of Quantitative Criminology, 7,* 213–236.

55. MacKenzie, D. L., & Brame, R. (1995). Shock incarceration and positive adjustment during community supervision. *Journal of Quantitative Criminology, 11,* 111–142.

56. Mitchell, O., MacKenzie, D. L., & Perez, D. M. (2005). A randomized evaluation of the Maryland correctional boot camp for adults: Effects on offender antisocial attitudes and cognitions. *Journal of Offender Rehabilitation, 40,* 3–4, 71–86.

57. Stinchcomb, J. B., & Terry III, W. C. (2001). Predicting the likelihood of re-arrest among shock incarceration graduates: Moving beyond another nail in the boot camp coffin. *Crime & Delinquency, 47,* 221–242.

58. Benda, B. B. (2003). Survival analysis of criminal recidivism of boot camp graduates using elements from general and developmental explanatory models. *International Journal of Offender Therapy and Comparative Criminology, 47,* 89–110.

59. Benda, B. B., Toombs, N. J., & Peacock, M. (2003). Discriminators of types of recidivism among boot camp graduates in a five-year follow-up study. *Journal of Criminal Justice, 31,* 539–551.

60. Benda, B. B., Toombs, N. J., & Peacock, M. (2006). Distinguishing graduates from dropouts and dismissals: Who fails boot camp? *Journal of Criminal Justice, 34,* 27–38.

61. MacKenzie, D. L., Wilson, D. B., & Kider, S. B. (2001). Effects of correctional boot camps on offending. *Annals of the American Academy of Political and Social Science, 578,* 126–143.

62. MacKenzie, D. L., Brame, R., McDowall, D., & Souryal, C. (1995). Boot camp prisons and recidivism in eight states. *Criminology, 33,* 327–357.

63. MacKenzie, Wilson, & Kider.

64. West, H. C., & Sabol, W. J. (2008). *Prisoners in 2007.* Washington, DC: U.S. Department of Justice, Office of Justice Programs, Bureau of Justice Statistics.

65. Glaze & Bonczar.

66. West & Sabol.

67. Bonczar, T. P. (2003). *Prevalence of imprisonment in the U.S. population, 1974–2001.* Washington, DC: U.S. Department of Justice, Office of Justice Programs, Bureau of Justice Statistics.

68. Associated Press. (2007). *Calif. OKs big boost in prison funding.* Retrieved April 26, 2007, from http://www.msnbc.msn.com/id/18340802/print/1/displaymode/1098/.

69. Hughes, K. A. (2006). *Justice expenditures and employment in the United States, 2003.* Washington, DC: U.S. Department of Justice, Office of Justice Programs, Bureau of Justice Statistics.

70. Hughes.

71. Stephan, J. J. (2004). *State prison expenditures, 2001.* Washington, DC: U.S. Department of Justice, Office of Justice Programs, Bureau of Justice Statistics.

72. Associated Press. (2005). *Oprah helps nab fugitive sex offender.* Retrieved October 7, 2005, from http://www.cnn.com/2005/US/10/07/oprah.offender.ap/index.html.

73. Associated Press. (2007). *Mobster, 90, accused of parole violation.* Retrieved May 10, 2007, from http://msnbc.msn.com/id/18596394/print/1/displaymode/1098/.

74. Associated Press. (2007). *Inmates, guard join Missouri effort to keep flood waters out.* Retrieved May 11, 2007, from http://www.kansascity.com/116/v-print/story/103108.html.

75. Clear, T. R., Rose, D. R., & Ryder, J. A. (2001). Incarceration and the community: The problem of removing and returning offenders. *Crime and Delinquency, 47,* 335–351.

76. Clear, T. R., Rose, D. R., Waring, E., & Scully, K. (2003). Coercive mobility and crime: A preliminary examination of concentrated incarceration and social disorganization. *Justice Quarterly, 20,* 33–64.

77. Binswanger, I. A., Stern, M. F., Deyo, R. A., Heagerty, P. J., Cheadle, A., Elmore, J. G., et al. (2007). Release from prison: A high risk of death for former inmates. *New England Journal of Medicine, 356,* 157–165.

78. Mumola, C. J. (2000). *Incarcerated parents and their children.* Washington, DC: U.S. Department of Justice, Office of Justice Programs, Bureau of Justice Statistics.

79. Berg, M. T., & DeLisi, M. (2006). The correctional melting pot: Race, ethnicity, citizenship, and prison violence. *Journal of Criminal Justice, 34,* 631–642.

80. Associated Press. (2007). *Prison's deadliest inmate, hepatitis C, escaping.* Retrieved May 21, 2007, from http://www.msnbc.msn.com/id/17615346/print/1/displaymodel/1098/.

81. Smith, S. K., & Motivans, M. (2006). *Compendium of federal justice statistics, 2004.* Washington, DC: U.S. Department of Justice, Office of Justice Programs, Bureau of Justice Statistics.

82. Rush, G. E. (2004). *The dictionary of criminal justice* (6th ed.). New York: Dushkin/McGraw-Hill.

83. Federal Bureau of Prisons. (n.d.). *Prison types and general information.* Retrieved May 27, 2007, from http://www.bop.gov/locations/institutions/index.jsp#.

84. Smith & Motivans.

85. DeLisi, M. (2006). *Criminal justice: Balancing crime control and due process.* Dubuque, IA: Kendall/Hunt.

CHAPTER

2

The Philosophy and History of Corrections

"The respect for the law is the obverse side of our hatred for the criminal transgressor." [1, pp. 585–586]

OBJECTIVES

- Understand natural law and the philosophical reasons why societies develop criminal justice and correctional systems.
- Compare deterrence, retribution, incapacitation, rehabilitation, and restoration as punishment philosophies and sentencing rationales.
- Trace the history of corrections to ancient societies and throughout various religious traditions.
- Follow the development of corrections in colonial America.
- Understand the penitentiary and reformatory movements and their relationship to social conditions and crime rates.
- Recognize key figures in correctional history, such as John Howard, Alexander Maconochie, Walter Crofton, Zebulon Brockway, John Augustus, and others.
- Identify the eras of correctional and prison history in the 20th and 21st centuries.
- Understand the current state of correctional philosophy and practice.

CASE STUDY

So She Killed Him: She Was Abused!

Domestic abuse is not a new social phenomenon. History reveals men have generated reasons and justifications for physically dominating women for centuries. But do a history of physical abuse and the anticipation of yet another assault justify murder? Do cases with potentially sympathetic victims undermine the philosophy and spirit of the law?

From the perspective of the defense, Mary Winkler was a battered spouse. As a direct result of the physical, sexual, and emotional abuse, she suffered from posttraumatic stress disorder. Under these conditions it would be impossible for Mary Winkler to form the intent to kill her husband, Matthew Winkler. Arguably, she was too upset, helpless, and battered to consciously form the intent and develop a plan to murder her husband. The court should also consider the possibility that the weapon was discharged accidentally. Mary even claimed that the gun had gone off by accident. Her action that ended the life of her abuser was not her own. This decision had been made by the batterer through his actions that long tormented her life.

Defense attorneys for Mary Winkler also asked the court to disallow statements made by their client to law enforcement claiming the statements were made while she was being held illegally because Orange Beach, Alabama, police lacked the probable cause to detain Mary.

The defense asked the court to consider that according to Mary Winkler, Matthew Winkler had previously punched and kicked her, had refused to allow a divorce, and had "forced her to perform sex acts she thought were unnatural." The night before the incident, Matthew had placed his hand over the mouth and nose of their 1-year-old child in an attempt to quiet the child, causing Mary to fear for the safety and physical well-being of her daughter.

1. Why did she shoot him?
2. Were Mary's actions deliberate?
3. But was it self-defense or could it be considered reasonable force?
4. What penalties should she face?

"Penitentiaries were little more than holding bins for the dregs of society."[2, p. 862]

The Philosophy of Corrections

Throughout history, people and cultures have varied greatly in their beliefs about what is an appropriate response to violations of law. Of course, responding to violations of the law depends on what law is violated (presumably murder and shoplifting will elicit different responses) and the circumstances surrounding the offense, such as the age of the offender, whether the person acted purposely or negligently, and whether the person acted aggressively or in self-defense; however, different value systems result in different responses to crime. Some people and cultures are bleeding hearts and lenient, others are cold-hearted and harsh. Some are seemingly unable and unwilling to punish, others punish with zeal. Throughout this chapter, you will recognize that the history of corrections reflects ongoing changes in beliefs and practices about the best way to punish criminal offenders.

If corrections or punishment has vacillated between these poles of harshness and leniency, a more basic question is what do societies do to punish criminal offenders in the first place? Why do we punish? When do societies develop correctional systems to respond to law violators? A good place to start is natural law. **Natural law** is the belief that the human world is organized by a positive or good natural order that should be obeyed by all humans. First described by the Greek writer Sophocles, natural law is most famously attributed to Aristotle and its revival in the 13th century by philosopher St. Thomas Aquinas. Unlike the codified laws that we follow today, natural law is unwritten. Instead, it is tacitly understood and appreciated by human reason. As Aristotle indicated in *Politics*, "Just punishments and chastisements do indeed spring from a good principle, but they are good only because we cannot do without them—it would be better that neither individuals nor states should need anything of the sort."[8, p. 13]

Natural law is authoritative or binding over human conduct and the good of the order (referred to generally as "the good") takes primacy over individual rights and concerns. In short, natural law is obvious and unequivocal that certain behaviors are wrong and intolerable and therefore must be punished. Evidence for natural law can be found in the universal human revulsion against specific negative behaviors or crimes. You would be hard pressed to find a society or group of people that did not morally condemn behaviors such as murder, incest, or even theft. These behaviors appear to be intrinsically wrong, or ***mala in se***. Because of their severity, *mala in se* offenses have historically been punished in the most severe way, by a sentence of death. As human organizations became more complex and societies became more modern, the mode of punishment evolved.[9] The range of behaviors that were defined as crimes broadened and included many acts that were deemed illegal. ***Mala prohibita*** offenses are crimes made illegal by legislation, not by natural law, and are punished in a variety of ways, such as fines or detention.

"Of all the justifications of criminal punishment, the desire to incapacitate is the least complicated, the least studied, and often the most important."[3, p. v]

Along with evolving modes of punishment, different punishment philosophies have also ebbed and flowed throughout history and to the present. For instance, consider the following quotation:

> We conclude that the present prison system is antiquated and inefficient. It does not reform the criminal. It fails to protect society. There is reason to believe that it contributes to the increase of crime by hardening the prisoner. We are convinced that a new type of penal institution must be developed, one that is new in spirit, in method, and in objective.[10, p. 562]

While this seems like an editorial from a newspaper in the 21st century, it comes from an article by Sanford Bates, the original director of the Bureau of Prisons. Bates was echoing the conclusions of the Wickersham Commission, which convened in 1931 to assess the state of criminal justice in the United States. Then and now there is dissatisfaction with correctional policies and the inability of the correctional system to reduce crime and reform offenders. Because of this, different punishment philosophies have appeared in correctional history. The main punishment philosophies are deterrence, retribution, incapacitation, rehabilitation, and the newest one, restoration.

- **Deterrence** is the act of frightening the potential actor with the use of the threats of punishment. It is the discouragement of crime because of fear of its consequences. There are two general types of deterrence. **Specific deterrence** pertains to the individual offender being sentenced and punished. **General deterrence** pertains to the large number of potential criminals who might be discouraged from committing crime because of the punishments received by others. In short, deterrence is the use of punishment to send a message and speaks to the rationality of crime. If the correctional system is tough enough, people will decide that crime is too risky to commit for fear of the punishment. The spirit and logic of general deterrence is captured by the Chinese proverb: It is better to hang the wrong fellow than no fellow.

- **Retribution** is the payment of a debt to society and the expiation of one's criminal offense. **Expiation** is based upon the belief that crime arouses the anger of the gods against the entire community, and the only way to reduce the anger is to destroy the offender. Retribution is inherent in the biblical message of "an eye for an eye, tooth for tooth" and is utilized when offenders are punished harshly, such as with death or life imprisonment sentences. Those punished for retributive reasons are commonly described as getting their just deserts, meaning they get what they deserved because of their criminal violation. To the general public, the sense of vengeance or revenge directed at a criminal offender is consistent with the theory of retribution. However, retribution does seek to match severe punishment to the severity of the original offense. Revenge is simply bloodlust to punish a hated

"Squandering our scarce correctional treatment program resources on low-risk offenders that do not need them is a waste of those resources."[4, p. 522]

criminal. Walter Berns's statement that "anger is the passion that recognizes and cares about justice" conveys the sentiment of retribution.[11, p. 152]

- **Incapacitation** is the inability to act. In corrections, incapacitation refers to the use of imprisonment to preclude the ability of an offender to victimize members of society. Without question, American prisons are in the business of incapacitation, simply removing offenders from circulation so they cannot victimize members of mainstream society, a general process known as **collective incapacitation**. It is well known that less than 10 percent of criminals commit more than 50 percent of crimes and even higher percentages of violent crimes. The policy designed to specifically target this group of habitual offenders for imprisonment is known as **selective incapacitation**.[12]
- **Rehabilitation** means to restore an offender to a law-abiding lifestyle. In corrections, the purpose of sentencing is to help the offender live a crime-free life in the community via mandated participation in programs, such as drug and alcohol treatment, psychiatric counseling, anger management training, life skills training, and other treatment modalities. Toward that end, correctional officials, such as a probation officer or parole officer, supervise clients to improve the offender's chances of being a productive and law-abiding citizen.
- **Restoration** is a theory of justice that emphasizes repairing the harm caused by crime. Restorative justice is accomplished through cooperative processes that include offenders, victims, and community residents. Restoration transforms the traditional relationship between communities and government in responding to crime by including all parties in an interactive, mediation-style process as opposed to the punitive, bureaucratic approaches of the courts. Examples of restorative justice are victim offender mediation, offender reintegration, restitution, community service, and offender–victim–family conferencing.[13] Restorative justice is ideologically similar to rehabilitation and dissimilar to retribution and incapacitation.

The next section provides a brief historical overview that showcases early approaches to corrections as a means to respond to criminals and crime.

Historical Approaches to Corrections

Throughout history, corrections and criminal justice generally were largely one and the same. To be suspected or accused of a crime was to be considered guilty of a crime, and summary punishment was often the outcome. Punishment has historically been swift and brutal and victims of crime were encouraged and even expected to exact personal retaliation against criminals. Even families or kin groups engaged in this type of retributive justice in *blood feuds* with other families.

Fortunately, corrections and criminal justice has evolved in the following three important ways:

1. The ways that justice and punishment are administered have evolved from informal to formal or bureaucratic means. In earlier epochs, the criminal justice system did not exist. Instead, family and community members responded to, sanctioned, and judged crimes and other behaviors that were deemed inappropriate. This is called **informal social control**. Informal social control still exists today. The ways that parents, friends, and coworkers correct one's behavior are informal means of social control. Being grounded for 2 weeks by one's parents, lectured to by one's boss, or given a stern gaze by one's friends are just some methods that we use to police, judge, and punish others in everyday life.

2. Criminal justice and punishment have also evolved from a personal to an impersonal process, which is related to the first way corrections has evolved. Although informal social control can be effective, it is also susceptible to biases and abuses because of the emotional connections between offender and victim. If the judge and the judged are members of the same family, then it is likely that evaluations of criminal conduct will be subjective. Subjectivity can compromise the lawful, equitable, and proportional goals of justice. It is thought that objectivity better serves the pursuit of justice since it is based on fact, evidence, and procedure instead of raw emotion. This is an exceedingly important point. A dispassionate, formal, professional system of criminal justice has evolved from the visceral, informal, and personal methods of the past. This raises important questions about the ability of the modern, formal criminal justice system to harness and address the emotions elicited by criminal wrongdoing. Can formal criminal justice be as personally satisfying as former, informal methods?
3. There has also been a dramatic change from brutal, barbaric forms of punishment to what are thought to be civilized measures of reasoned punishment. A hallmark of the progression of civilization has been the diminution of violence as punishment. For example, although the United States still employs capital punishment, the ultimate sanction is rarely imposed and is administered in what is supposed to be a humane, medical procedure. By comparison, historical approaches to criminal justice were draconian and used the penalty of death for scores of crimes, even minor ones. In short, a hallmark of civilization has been the transformation of justice from something that was retributive and repressive to something that is more rehabilitative and restitutive. By and large, the personal vengeance inherent in justice was replaced by an impersonal bureaucracy.

"When Sodom and Gomorrah flouted God's will, his anger laid them waste."[5, p. 34]

Code of Hammurabi

Arguably the earliest important date in correctional history was the establishment of the **Code of Hammurabi** by the Babylonian King Hammurabi in 1780 BCE. The Code of Hammurabi was fairly sophisticated and contained 282 clauses or case laws pertaining to a variety of social and legal issues. The Code of Hammurabi was guided by the doctrine of ***lex talionis***, meaning an eye for an eye, a tooth for a tooth. The *lex talionis* embodied three principles that are applicable to the present day. First, law and criminal punishment should be punitive and in part driven by vengeance. Second, crime and its punishment aimed to be proportionate. Hence, a person convicted of murder would be executed because the punishment equals the severity of the underlying criminal conduct. Unfortunately, because many nonlethal behaviors were punishable by death, the Code of Hammurabi often was excessive and not proportionate. Third, punishment was inflicted in the name of the community or city-state, not the specific victim. The idea that all societal members suffer from crime, thus making it a social problem, is certainly salient to us today and is a basis of the restorative justice movement.

The Code of Hammurabi from 1780 BCE contains some of the earliest tenets of the punitive philosophy that underlies criminal punishment. In what ways do American correctional systems continue to embody the spirit of the Code of Hammurabi?

Judeo-Christian Traditions

Between the 16th and 13th centuries BCE, the Judeo-Christian traditions weighed in on criminal justice. According to religious tradition, Moses received the Ten Commandments from God. Containing most famously the proscription against murder, the Ten Commandments have heavily influenced cultures and legal systems within the Judeo-Christian tradition, such as the United States. A noteworthy contribution during this era was the book of Deuteronomy attributed to Moses. Deuteronomy is essentially a legal book containing the rights, laws, penalties, and protocriminal justice system of Israel.

"To establish a prison environment which will not be a welcome asylum to the man who has lived in squalor and degradation and yet not be a place of continual torture and deprivation to a man of finer sensibilities, is considerable of a task in itself."[6, p. 570]

Like the Babylonians, the Judaic and Christian traditions of criminal justice were punitive and viewed death as an appropriate penalty for many transgressions. Consider two verses from Deuteronomy 17:6–7, "At the mouth of two witnesses, or three witnesses, shall he that is worthy of death be put to death; but at the mouth of one witness he shall not be put to death. The hands of the witnesses shall be first upon him to put him to death, and afterward the hands of all the people. So thou shalt put the evil away from among you."[14] An interesting side note is the reference to the notion of evil, and by extension, evil people. From the law of Moses to our modern concern about serial killers and other infamous criminals, people have struggled with the proper conceptualization and handling of criminals.

Greek and Roman Traditions

The Greek and Roman societies also made significant early contributions to criminal justice. In 621 BCE, the Athenian politician and magistrate Draco compiled the first comprehensive set of laws in Greece. Prior to this time, criminal matters were viewed as private matters and were resolved by the injured party or victim's family. Draco's laws were noteworthy for their severity as the penalty for many offenses was death. Poisoning, starvation, death by exposure, and banishment were just some of the sanctions employed during Draco's time. Indeed, the contemporary term **draconian**, often used to describe tough criminal justice policies, is derived from Draco and his legacy. Over the next century, as Greek society was plagued by dissent, the harsh criminal justice code of Draco was softened by reformists such as Solon and Cleisthenes. These progressive Greeks made only homicide a capital crime and instituted the widespread use of fines as a form of punishment. Fines served two purposes or constituencies. They were a form of restitution to the victim and served as a tax for the public good. By paying both victim and community, Solon's use of fines helped bridge the private and public interests of criminal justice.

From the founding of Rome in 750 BCE to 450 BCE, criminal justice was administered according to tradition of Roman patricians. Unfortunately, this informal, top-down form of justice was unfairly administered to nonelites. In 450 BCE, Roman magistrates created the **Law of the Twelve Tables**, a comprehensive and codified legal code to replace the oral, informal, and largely unfair prior tradition. The Twelve Tables remained in effect for nearly 1,000 years until the fall of Constantinople and the eastern Roman Empire. An interesting facet of the Twelve Tables was the establishment of two sets of laws, one exclusively for Roman citizens and the other for noncitizens. The idea that law and criminal justice are applied differently based on individual characteristics exists to the present day.

Magna Carta

A centerpiece historical contribution to criminal justice and the rights of criminal defendants is the **Magna Carta** or Great Charter. Signed by King John of England on June 15, 1215, the Magna Carta was a codified set of laws that both delineated the set of behaviors that citizens could not engage in and limited the powers of the throne. In many respects, the Magna Carta was the forerunner of the United States Constitution with its dual goals of cautiously empowering the state and granting rights and protections to the public.

In fact, the United States owes its entire criminal justice system and common law tradition to England. Common law is based on customs, traditions, unwritten norms, and general principles that ultimately find their way into codified or statutory law. Common law would characterize the burgeoning American colonies from the arrival of Columbus in 1492 to the Declaration of Independence in 1776 and the drafting of the United States Constitution from 1787 to 1789 to the ratification of the Bill of Rights in 1791. Colonial justice is described in greater detail later in this chapter.

On Crimes and Punishments

"It is revolting to have no better reason for a rule of law than that so it was laid down in the time of Henry IV."[7]

American justice also owes a tremendous debt to **Cesare Beccaria**'s masterpiece *Dei delitti e Delle Pene,* or *On Crimes and Punishments,* published in 1764. An Italian nobleman and jurist, Beccaria was disgusted with the arbitrary, discriminatory, and largely barbaric system of justice that typified 18th-century Italy. Beccaria believed in the Enlightenment idea that people were rational and thus their behavior followed an almost economic weighing of the costs and benefits or pains and pleasures of action. Commensurately, punishment should be swift, certain, and severe (but proportionate) to hopefully deter or dissuade people from choosing to engage in crime. According to Beccaria, "in order for punishment not to be, in every instance, an act of violence of one or of many against a private citizen, it must be essentially public, prompt, necessary, the least possible in the given circumstances, proportionate to the crimes, dictated by the laws."[15, p. 284]

On Crimes and Punishments contained a variety of ideas that seem obvious today but were revolutionary for their time. Some of these ideas were that laws should be rational, punishments should be in degree to the severity of the crime (thus capital punishment should not be widely applied), the presumption of innocence, that the law should apply equally to all people regardless of social class or other status, and that long imprisonment is a more powerful deterrent than condemnation.[16]

Corrections in Colonial America

In many respects, the colonial United States continued the historical approach to criminal justice by relying heavily on punishment. However, there were also signs of other forms of correction and punishment, some of which are used in today's criminal justice system. For instance, the American colonies relied extensively on informal social controls including public shaming and ridicule. Because communities were small and close-knit, the proclivity for gossip actually helped serve the purposes of keeping people in line and publicly humiliating them when they transgressed social norms.

The colonists also used fines for minor offenses, such as flirting or engaging in sexual contact that was considered improper, such as premarital kissing. For slightly more serious violations, **corporal punishment**, or the infliction of pain to correct and punish deviant behavior was used. *Pillories* were wooden frames with holes for an offender's head and hands. Offenders would stand attached to the pillory for hours as villagers ridiculed and at times threw rocks and garbage at them. *Stocks* were wooden frames with holes for the person's hands and feet and were basically a seated version of the pillory. Other accused persons were publicly whipped, receiving various numbers of lashes or whippings depending on the severity of the offense. Those who swore, engaged in questionable sexual conduct, were intemperate, associated with servants or slaves, or disrespected parents or village leaders received mutilation (cutting ears off was a common practice), water torture, whippings, beating, or even *brandings.* In addition to the extreme physical pain inflicted by branding, the brands also served the purpose of notifying the community what the criminal had done. Thieves were branded with *T* on their forehead, burglars and persons accused of blasphemy received a *B*, and as immortalized in the Nathaniel Hawthorne classic *The Scarlet Letter*, adulterers were branded or forced to wear an *A*. Noted legal historian and scholar Lawrence Friedman suggests that

> It was a paternal society—a society built on the model of a patriarchal house. Like a stern father, the authorities did not believe in sparing the rod. The courts enforced discipline. In a way, it was a crime just to be a bad citizen: not to conform to standards of good virtue and respectability.[17, p. 38]

An early form of incapacitation practiced by the colonists was **banishment**, in which wrongdoers were excommunicated or excluded from the community entirely. Repeat

Transportation is a form of banishment in which criminals were sent away, such as the British practice of placing criminals on ships and sending them to colonial America and colonial Australia.

Torture has historically been used to punish persons accused of crimes and was common on transportation ships.

criminal offenders were a group commonly subjected to banishment (the same logic is used today). The colonial use of banishment is somewhat ironic because the bourgeoning United States received thousands of English criminals who had been banished or transported from England. *Transportation* was used by England to export criminals since at least 1615, when James I ordered that clemency could be granted to lesser criminals, such as thieves, swindlers, and prostitutes, as long as they were banished to what is today the United States and Australia. The English Transportation Act of 1718 instituted banishment as the usual punishment for property offenders (violent offenders were simply executed), and it is estimated that between 50,000 and 100,000 criminals were banished to colonial America.[18] The ships used for transportation, which were little more than floating jails, were known as *hulks*.

It wasn't all physical punishment in the American colonies, however. As early as the 17th century, there was the beginning of what would today be called pretrial supervision. (Bail was used in Roman law as early as 700 BCE.) Lawbreakers and other suspects had to post money or some other form of collateral as an enticement to obey the law while on "bond." This early type of bail release was known as the *fee system*. There were also local jails based on the **Common Law** tradition—the customary criminal justice and legal traditions or doctrines that the United States inherited from England. These early jails, known as *gaols*, held persons awaiting execution, whipping, or some other punishment. Gaols had been in

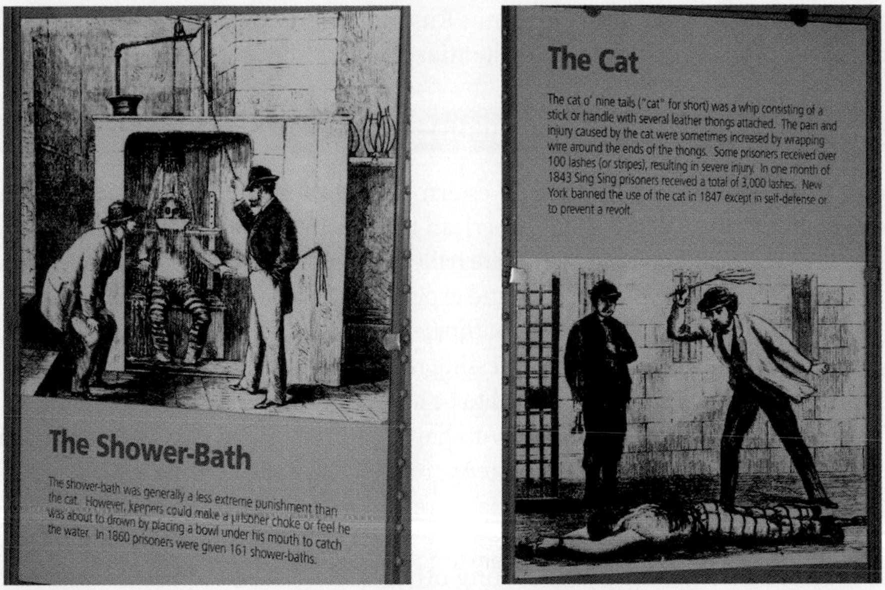

Various forms of corporal punishment, such as the shower bath and flogging were common in early American prisons, such as Sing Sing. Over time, sheer confinement replaced the physical infliction of pain on prisoners.

place in English Common Law since the reign of King Henry II in 1166. It is interesting to note that the function, varied population, and overall squalor of jails changed little since the 12th century. For nearly 1,000 years, jails have housed persons accused of crimes and awaiting trial, prisoners, the poor, displaced persons, the mentally ill, and others who could not be accommodated by some other party of social service agency.[19]

The colonial approach to corrections was effective for awhile and worked because the colonies were relatively small and homogenous. Matthew Meskell suggests that three social forces created an inevitable decline in colonial corrections and necessitated reforms. First, as the 18th century progressed, the populations increased dramatically in places, such as New York, Massachusetts, and Pennsylvania. Punishments that worked well in small villages were almost totally ineffective in large, expansive settings where residents were more mobile. Second, Americans were repulsed by the violent harshness of English Common Law and in turn disliked the use of corporal and capital punishments in their own society. The following description of Pennsylvania jails in 1776 captures the colonial dissatisfaction with too tough a correctional system:

> In one corrupt and corrupting assemblage were to be found the disgusting objects of popular contempt, besmeared with filth from the pillory—the unhappy victims of the lash … the half naked vagrant—the loathsome drunkard—the sick suffering from various bodily pains, and too often the unaneled malefactor.[20, p. 839]

Third, there was an intellectual movement away from corporal and capital punishments (recall the contributions of Beccaria described earlier in this chapter). A major figure in this intellectual ferment was **John Howard**, who was appointed sheriff of Bedfordshire, England, in 1773. Howard had once been imprisoned in a French facility and was horrified at the conditions of confinement that characterized European jails. In 1777, Howard published *The State of Prisons in England and Wales*, a work that publicized the appalling conditions of English jails, the unfair use of the bail/fee system, and generally, an uncivilized correctional system. His work resulted in the passage of the Penitentiary Act in 1779, which required English prisons and jails to provide safe, sanitary facilities; conduct systematic inspections to ensure compliance with appropriate procedures; abolish charging fees to inmates; and oversee a healthy lifestyle regimen for prisoners. Howard is credited with coining the term *penitentiary*, and his work heavily influenced colonial intellectuals including Benjamin Rush and Benjamin Franklin and would lay the groundwork for the American penitentiary.[21]

The Invention of the Penitentiary

Although confinement has existed in Western societies for centuries, prisons as they are understood today are considered an American invention. At their inception, prisons, then symbolically known as **penitentiaries**, were hailed as an outgrowth of the Enlightenment in which criminal offenders were confined and expected to contemplate their criminal behavior and work toward their rehabilitation and ultimate redemption. Indeed, inmates were expected to be **penitent**, defined as feeling or expressing remorse for one's misdeeds or sins. As such, the penitentiary was specifically designed to be a place for criminals to be penitent.

Throughout American history, prisons have reflected the social conditions of the day and early penitentiaries reflected the intense religiosity of the colonial era. The Pennsylvania Quakers led by William Penn initiated reforms of the colonial approach to correction in which physical punishment would be replaced by isolation. In 1787, Benjamin Franklin and Dr. Benjamin Rush (among other distinguished citizens) organized the Philadelphia Society for Alleviating the Miseries of Public Prisons, which mobilized the Commonwealth of Pennsylvania to set the international standard in prison design. In 1790, the Philadelphia Society established what is often credited as the first penitentiary or prison in the United States at the Walnut Street Jail (see the following box for a profile of the first American prison). It took decades to convince state leaders of the superiority of the penitentiary approach, but would culminate in the Western State Penitentiary in Pittsburgh in 1826 and the more famous Eastern State Penitentiary in Cherry Hill just outside Philadelphia in 1829.

Eastern State Penitentiary was the most expensive American building of its day (it had running water and central heat before the White House had such amenities), was one of the most famous buildings in the world, and was a major tourist attraction. As described earlier, the function of the penitentiary was not to simply punish, but move the criminal toward spiritual reflection and change. The Quaker-inspired **Pennsylvania system** involved the following:

- Total isolation from other prisoners
- Labor in solitary confinement
- Strictly enforced silence

In early American prisons, inmates walked in lockstep as shown in this historical photo from Sing Sing Prison in New York. Are inmate movements within facilities similar or different from lockstep approaches?

CORRECTIONS FOCUS

Newgate of Connecticut

The Walnut Street Jail in Philadelphia is often referred to as being the first prison in American history when it opened in 1790. However, the Connecticut General Assembly authorized the creation of Newgate in Connecticut in 1773 nearly 20 years before the founding of the Walnut Street Jail. Newgate was a colonial prison that was built in an abandoned copper mine and used to confine five specific types of offenders: robbers, burglars, forgers, counterfeiters, and horse thieves. The use of a prison for confinement purposes was a departure from the use of corporal punishment. Newgate received its first prisoner in December 1773 and housed political prisoners during the Revolutionary War. Beginning in 1824, Newgate also housed female inmates. Newgate was noteworthy for inmate escapes and generally inhumane conditions and was closed in 1827.

Several factors have been cited for the general anonymity of Newgate compared to more famous prisons and prison systems in Pennsylvania and New York. For instance, Newgate was not administered by a progressive penologist who sought to rehabilitate prisoners into law-abiding citizens. Instead, Newgate was simply a confinement facility—one that was characterized by inefficiency and by what would today be considered barbaric conditions and treatment by correctional officials. Nevertheless, Newgate deserves its place in the history of the American prison.

Sources: Durham, A. M., III. (1989). Newgate of Connecticut: Origins and early days of an early American prison. *Justice Quarterly, 6,* 89–116. Retrieved May 29, 2008, from http://www.cultureandtourism.org/cct/cwp/view.asp?a=2127&q=302258.

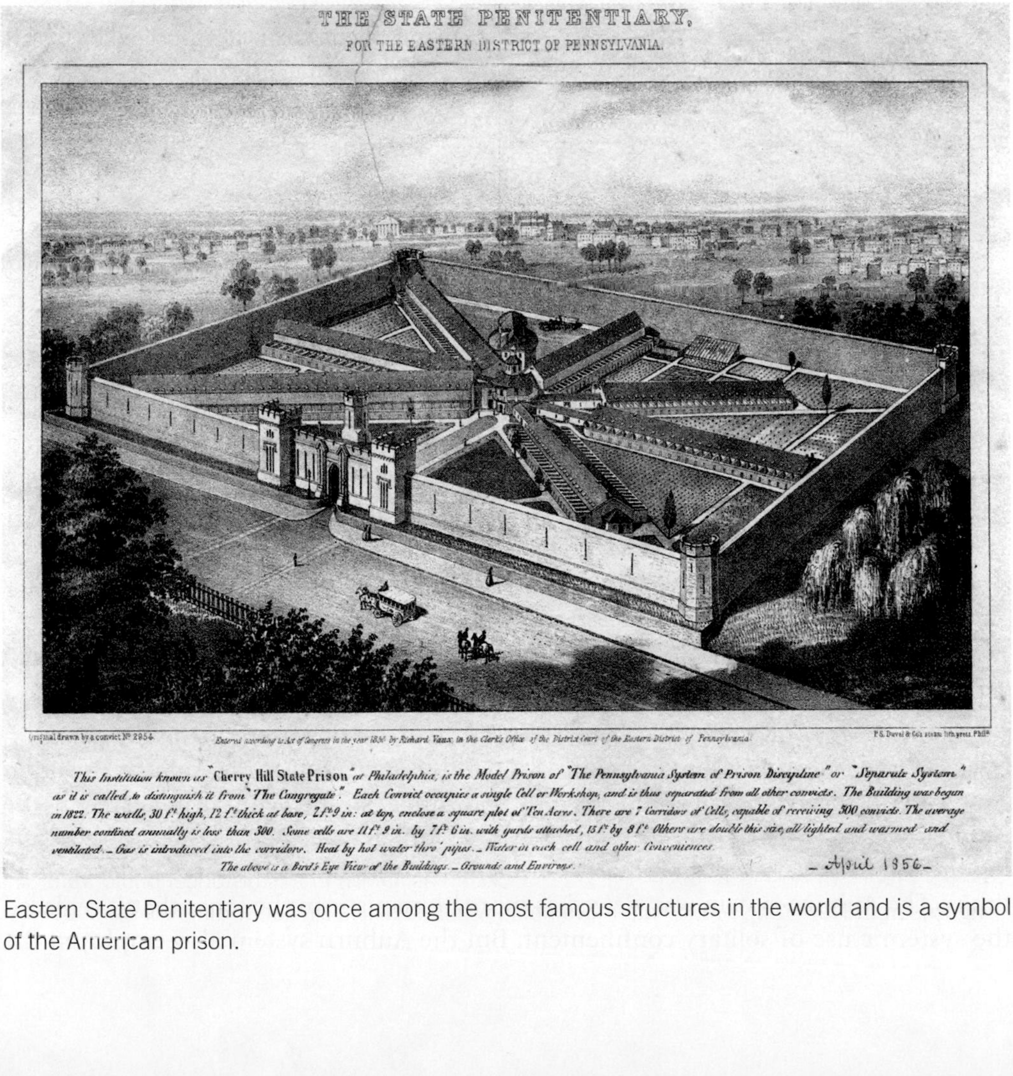

Eastern State Penitentiary was once among the most famous structures in the world and is a symbol of the American prison.

CORRECTIONS BRIEF

How Would You Design a Prison?

Did you ever wonder how a prison operates or what it looks like on the inside? Correctional facilities are categorized as either direct or indirect supervision facilities. The more traditional facility is referred to as an indirect supervision facility. In this type of facility, correctional officers are stationed in a centrally located control room from which they can view the activities of inmates allowed into the inner perimeter, or dayroom, of the cell confinement area. The outer perimeter is lined with cells or pods and, depending on the size of the facility, may consist of from 40 to 60 beds in each pod. Indirect supervision facilities are also characterized by fixtures and furniture that resist vandalism. These facilities rely on a considerable amount of technology used primarily to facilitate the movement of inmates by correctional officers, when communication between officers is necessary, as well as when directing the activities of inmates.

Direct supervision facilities have some of the same vandal-resistant furnishings. These facilities also rely heavily on technology. But direct supervision facilities take a different approach to handling and working with prisoners. Inmates in a direct supervision facility are expected to conform to the expectation of acceptable behavior. In other words, this is not the street—so prisoners are not expected to act like it is! The difference is in the expectations. Because direct supervision institutions expect more from their clients, they offer certain additional amenities not found in the more traditional, indirect supervision facility. These little extras include carpeting, upholstered furniture, television, game tables, and exercise equipment. The relationship between the correctional officers and the inmates also differs. Officers are stationed inside the living quarters—not in a control booth. Officers are also required to interact with prisoners. In fact, this is one of the officers' primary duties. Control of the institution depends on the ability of the officers to detect and diffuse potential problems.

- What is the ratio of indirect supervision facilities to direct supervision facilities? What accounts for this difference?
- What has caused the shift in philosophy toward a direct supervision management system?
- Which type of facility is most likely to benefit both inmate and society?

Sources: J. Farbstein and Associates, Inc., with Wener, R. *A comparison of, "direct" and "indirect" supervision correctional facilities.* Retrieved May 7, 2007, from http://www.nicic.org/pubs/pre/007807.pdf; Ard, L. R. (2007). *The fifth generation jail: Contra Costa's West County justice facility.* Retrieved May 2, 2007, from http://nicic.org/Library/period87.

- Extraordinarily strict social control in which inmates were hooded whenever they were outside their cells
- Extreme isolation that would cause criminals to think about the wrongfulness of their crimes and become genuinely penitent[22–23]

As a punishment philosophy, the Pennsylvania system was developed in the 18th century; however, the **Auburn system** began in 1816 with the opening of the Auburn Prison in New York. Although heavily influenced by and similar to the Pennsylvania system, the Auburn system was a *congregate system* in which inmates ate and worked together during the day and were kept in solitary confinement at night with enforced silence at all times. The Auburn system was viewed as more humanistic in the sense that it replaced the systemic use of solitary confinement. But the Auburn system also employed the *lockstep* (inmates marching in single file, placing the right hand on the shoulder of the man ahead, and facing toward the guard), the striped suit, 2-foot extensions of the walls between cells, and special seating arrangements at meals to ensure strict silence. Auburn also introduced the tier system with several floors or wings that have stacked cells over another and classified (and punished) inmates by their level of compliance. By the 1830s, the Auburn system generally replaced the Pennsylvania system, which was discontinued as a prison approach by 1913.

The goal of the Pennsylvania and Auburn systems was to reform inmates, but they used different methods. It is difficult to say which model was more effective. In fact, neither rehabilitated inmates very well. The reasons for their respective failures are many. Critics of the Pennsylvania system held that its prisons were too expensive to build and operate and that separate confinement led to widespread insanity within the prison population. Opponents of the Auburn system argued that the system was too cruel and inhumane to affect people's lives positively. According to de Beaumont and de Tocqueville:

> The Philadelphia [*sic*] system being also that which produces the deepest impressions on the soul of the convict, must effect more reformation than that of Auburn. The latter, however, is perhaps more conformable to the habits of men in society, and on this account effects a greater number of reformations, which might be called "legal," inasmuch as they produce the external fulfillment of social obligations. … the Philadelphia system produces more honest men, and that of New York more obedient citizens.[24, p.374]

Although the Pennsylvania system lost favor in the United States, it became widely imitated throughout the rest of the world. For instance, correctional systems in Belgium, China, England, France, Germany, Holland, Italy, Japan, and Spain adopted various methods of the two systems. Ultimately, the Auburn system was more widely adopted in the United States for one principal reason: it reinforced the emerging industrial philosophy that allowed states to use convict labor to defray prison costs.

The Invention of the Reformatory

During the Jacksonian era spanning the first several decades of the 19th century, there was widespread dissatisfaction with American prisons. In their 1833 masterwork, Gustave de Beaumont and Alexis de Tocqueville opined that "while society in the United States gives the example of the most extended liberty, the prisons of the same country offer the spectacle of the most complete despotism."[25, p. 381 note 22] Upon visiting Eastern State Penitentiary in 1842, Charles Dickens wrote, "I hold this slow and daily tampering with the mysteries of the brain to be immeasurably worse than any torture of the body."[26] In other words, the methods of correction inherent in the Pennsylvania and Auburn systems were viewed as cruel, counterproductive, and flagrantly in violation of basic tenets of human, civil, and due process rights.[27]

Over time, American penologists were also influenced by the innovations of foreign correctional administrators, most notably **Alexander Maconochie** and **Sir Walter Crofton**. As a consequence of the Revolutionary War, England stopped transporting criminals to the American colonies and instead shipped them to what is now Australia. Between 1840 and 1844, Captain Alexander Maconochie was placed in charge of one of the worst British penal colonies, located about 1,000 miles off Australia's coast on Norfolk Island. This was where twice-condemned criminals—offenders who had committed felonies in England, been transported to Australia, and committed additional crimes there—were sent.

Like John Howard, Maconochie had previously been a prisoner—he was captured by the French while serving as a British naval officer, and was thus sensitive to the often deplorable conditions of confinement. Upon seeing the conditions under which most inmates lived, Maconochie introduced humane reforms that would give prisoners some degree of hope for their future. He proposed the following changes:

- Criminal sentences should not be for a specific period of time; rather release would be based on the performance of a specified quantity of labor. In brief, fixed-time sentences should be abolished in favor of task sentences.
- The quantity of labor prisoners must perform should be expressed in a number of marks (see the discussion of the mark system that follows this list) that must be earned before release was possible.
- While in prison, inmates should earn everything they receive; all sustenance and indulgences should be added to their debts of mark.
- Prisoners would be required to work in groups of six or seven people, and the entire group should be held accountable for the behavior of each of its members.
- Prisoners, while still obliged to earn their daily tally of marks, should be given proprietary interest in their own labor and be subject to a less rigorous discipline in order to prepare them for release into society.[28]

Maconochie developed a **mark system**, which were credits against a sentence that allowed inmates to be released once they earned the required number of marks through good behavior. The mark system consisted of four stages. First, the penal stage was the harshest form of punishment and was typified by solitary confinement and meager living conditions. Second, the associated stage permitted inmates to associate with others and begin to earn marks by participating in programs, working, and abstaining from continued criminal behavior. The worse the inmate's behavior during this initial adjustment, the more marks were required for release. Third, the social stage approximated community living so inmates could better function upon release. Fourth, the final stage of *ticket of leave* was achieved when all marks were earned and the offender was conditionally released to the community.[29–30] Today, the use of good time toward an inmate's sentence and parole are familiar concepts; however, they were revolutionary in Maconochie's era. His progressive ideas were denigrated as coddling of criminals, and Maconochie was relieved of duty in 1844.

A disciple of Maconochie, Sir Walter Crofton was the chairman of the board of directors of the Irish prisons. Crofton instituted very similar protocols in Ireland, which were based on Maconochie's mark system. Under Crofton's direction, Irish prisons were characterized by:

- Reward, in which all advantages, including ultimate release, were dependent on industry and good conduct, as shown by daily records.
- Individuality, in which prisons were not permitted to house more than 300 inmates, thus avoiding the problems associated with overcrowding.
- Gradual approximation to freedom, in which every successive stage of discipline (like the mark system) was characterized by less restraint.
- Strict supervision after discharge and certain revocation of ticket to leave on any appearance of a relapse.

Despite these innovations, there was still the widespread public belief that crime threatened the stability and order of society, and prisons appeared to be doing little to reduce the crime rate. Even in the middle 19th century, the general public considered prisons as mere holding stations, regardless of how innovative their design, until criminals were released to offend again.

CORRECTIONS HISTORY

Principles from the 1870 National Congress on Penitentiary and Reformatory Discipline

- Punishment is inflicted on the criminal in expiation of the wrong done, and especially with a view to prevent his relapse by reformation.
- Treatment is directed at the criminal and his new birth to respect for the laws.
- Practice shall conform to theory and the process of public punishment be made in fact, as well as pretense, a process of reformation.
- A progressive classification should be established and include at least three stages: a penal stage, a reformatory stage, and a probationary stage worked on some mark system where they earn promotion, gaining at each successive step, increased comfort and privilege.
- Since hope is a more potent agent than fear, rewards more than punishments are essential to every good prison system.
- The prisoner's destiny during his incarceration should be put in his own hands.
- The two master forces opposed to the reform of the prison systems are political appointments and instability of administration.
- Prison officers need a special education for their work, special training schools should be instituted for them and prison administration should be raised to the dignity of a profession.
- Sentences limited only by satisfactory proof of reformation should be substituted for those measured by mere lapse of time.
- Of all the reformatory agencies religion is the first in importance.
- Education is a matter of primary importance in prisons.
- No prison can be made a school of reform until there is, on the part of officers, a hearty desire and intention to accomplish this effect.
- There must be a serious conviction in the minds of prison officers that the imprisoned criminals are capable of being reformed.
- A system of prison reform must gain the will of the convict.
- The interest of society and the interest of the convicted criminal are really identical. Society is best served by saving its criminal members.
- The prisoner's self respect should be cultivated.
- In prison administration moral forces should be relied upon with as little mixture of physical force as possible.
- Steady honorable labor is the basis of all reformatory discipline. It not only aids information it is essential to it.
- It is important that criminals be trained while in prison to the practice and love of labor.
- We regard the contract system of prison labor as prejudicial—alike to discipline, finance, and reformation.
- The stage of conditional leave is problematic to administer but we believe Yankee ingenuity is competent to devise some method of practical application among separate jurisdictions and the vast reach of our territory.
- Prisons, as well as prisoners, should be classified or graded. There shall be prisons for the untried; prisons for young criminals; prisons for women; for misdemeanants; male felons; and the incorrigible.

(continued)

CORRECTIONS HISTORY—CONTINUED

- It is believed that repeated short sentences are worse than useless.
- Greater use should be made of the social principal in prison discipline than is now. The criminal must be prepared for society in society.
- Public preventative institutions for the treatment of children constitute a true field of promise in which to labor for the repression of crime.
- More systematic and comprehensive methods should be adopted to serve discharged prisoners. Having raised him up, it has the further duty to aid in holding him up.
- The successful prosecution of crime requires the combined action of capital and labor.
- It is plainly the duty of society to indemnify the citizen who has been unjustly imprisoned.
- Our laws regarding insanity and its relationship to crime need revision.
- Does society take all the steps it easily might to change, or at least improve, the circumstances in our social state that thus lead to crime?
- The exercise of executive clemency is one of grave importance, and at the same time of great delicacy and difficulty.
- The proper duration for imprisonment for a violation of the laws of society is one of the most perplexing questions in criminal jurisprudence.
- The establishment of a National Prison Bureau or a National Prison Discipline Society is recommended.
- We declare our belief that the education and self-respect of the convict would be served by the establishment of a weekly newspaper to enable him to keep pace with passing events.
- Prison architecture is a matter of grave importance. The proper size of prisons is a point of much interest. In our judgment 300 inmates are enough to form the population of a single prison; and, in no case, would we have the number exceed five or six hundred.
- The organization and construction of prisons should be by the state.
- As a general rule, the maintenance of all penal institutions, above the county jail, should be from the earnings of their inmates, and without cost to the state.
- A right application of the principles of sanitary science in the construction and arrangements of prisons is another point of vital importance.
- The principle of the pecuniary responsibility of parents for the full or partial support of their criminal children in reformatory institutions, extensively applied in Europe, has been found to work well in practice.
- It is our intimate convictions that one of the most effective agencies in the repression of crime would be the enactment of laws, by which the education of all the children of the state should be made obligatory.
- It is our conviction that no prison system can be perfect or successful to the most desirable extent, without some central and supreme authority to sit at the helm, guiding, controlling, unifying, and vitalizing the whole.

Source: American Correctional Association. (1970). *National congress on penitentiary and reformatory discipline, 1970 proceedings.* Alexandria, VA: American Correctional Association.

Edgardo Rotman described the state of American prisons as follows:

> The elements of the original penitentiary designed, based on regimentation, isolation, religious conversion, and stead labor, had been subverted by a pervasive overcrowding, corruption, and cruelty. Prisoners were often living three and four to a cell designed for one, and prison discipline was medieval-like in character, with bizarre and brutal punishments commonplace in state institutions. Wardens did not so much deny this awful reality as explain it away, attributing most of the blame not to those who administered the system but to those who experienced it. Because the prisons were filled with immigrants who were ostensibly hardened to a life of crime and impervious to American traditions, those in charge had no choice but to rule over inmates with an iron hand.[31, p. 152]

These concerns did not go unnoticed. The New York Prison Association commissioned Enoch Cobb Wines and Theodore Dwight to conduct a national survey of prisons and correctional methods. Their findings were grim. Wines and Dwight suggested an almost complete reconstruction of American prisons, including barring prison administration appointments based on politics, granting wardens the power to remove guards at will, abolishing prison labor for profit, increasing religious and academic training, and even redesigning the basic prison buildings.[32] Inspired by their report, the National Congress on Penitentiary and Reformatory Discipline (a forerunner of the contemporary American Correctional Association) met in October 1870 in Cincinnati, Ohio, and established principles of modern, humanistic correctional theory and practice.[33]

One of the most famous practitioners who placed the **reformatory** theory into practice was Zebulon Brockway. As warden of the Elmira (New York) Reformatory, Brockway infused educational programs, vocational training, an administrative and operating system based on military discipline, and a humanistic orientation into American corrections. In 1876, the Elmira Reformatory began receiving inmates. Elmira was built like Auburn with inside cell blocks for solitary confinement at night and communal workshops. Ten percent of Elmira's cells were built with outside courtyards, similar to those at Cherry Hill. This modified design allowed natural light to penetrate the building. Elmira also used more artificial light than the Auburn or Cherry Hill prisons and had more modern sanitary facilities.

The Elmira Reformatory was the quintessential reformatory under the guidance of Warden Zebulon Brockway. In many respects, Brockway advanced the rehabilitative capacity of American corrections.

Elmira also differed from the typical prison of this period in one other respect. Indeterminate sentencing meant that prisoners received a maximum sentence with early release on parole if they exhibited good behavior. At entry, all prisoners were placed in the second grade. After six months of good conduct, they were promoted to the first grade, and six months of continued good conduct entitled them to parole. Prisoners who misbehaved were demoted to the third level, where a month's good conduct was required to restore them to the second grade. Inmates who regularly misbehaved were obliged to serve their maximum sentence.

Brockway believed that prisoners could be reformed only in an atmosphere conducive to rehabilitation. It was in that spirit that Brockway developed what became known as the Elmira model:

- Clothing that was not degradingly distinctive but uniform, and represented the respective grades or standing of the inmates
- A liberal prison diet designed to promote vigor
- A gymnasium completely equipped with baths and exercise equipment and facilities for field athletics
- Facilities for training about one third of the population in mechanical and free-hand drawing, wood- and metalworking, cardboard constructive form work, clay modeling, cabinet making, and iron molding
- Trade or vocational instruction based on the needs and capacities of individual prisoners
- A school with a curriculum from an adaptation of the kindergarten to the usual high school course, and special classes in college subjects
- A library for circulation, consultation, and occasional social use
- A weekly institutional newspaper, in lieu of all outside newspapers, edited by prisoners
- Recreation and entertainment for the inmates
- Nondenominational religious opportunities

Between 1876 and 1901, the Elmira model was adopted in correctional systems in 12 states across the United States. However, by the time Brockway retired, the enthusiasm that had inspired the reformatory movement began to decline mainly because crime continued to be widespread. The reformatory did not appear to work. As a result, the enlightened concepts of the reformers gave way once more to a more control-oriented approach to corrections.

An inherent limitation of the Elmira system was that guards were unwilling to adjust to a correctional philosophy that provided inmates with autonomy. Emphasis on security remained their first priority, especially with the increasing populations of the institutions. Administrators were forced to create holding areas for more violent offenders, thus making reform programs available only to a few. At Elmira and elsewhere, simple custody reemerged as the primary goal and punishment as the method for controlling prisoners.[34]

Probation and Parole

While confinement tends to dominate the discussion (and budget) of corrections, there were also interesting developments of community corrections. Like the various eras of prison history, the historical development of sanctions, such as probation and parole, responded to social conditions, crime rates, and the philosophical movement of the era. For instance, *probation*, which is Latin for a period of proving or trial, began in 1841 and is credited as the invention of **John Augustus**. Augustus was a Bostonian shoemaker of financial means who secured the release of a confirmed alcoholic arrested for being a common drunk by acting as surety for him. At sentencing, Augustus asked the judge to defer sentencing for 3 weeks and release the defendant to his custody. After 3 weeks, the offender convinced the judge of his rehabilitation and received a fine. The period of community correction alleviated the need for jail, and probation was born. Until his death in 1859, Augustus bailed out 1,800 persons and was liable for nearly $250,000 in secured bonds.

Augustus was selective as to who could be on his probationary caseload. The ideal candidate was a first-time offender for a nonserious charge who had moral character and demonstrated potential for reforming his or her criminal behavior. Augustus also developed the basic operating procedure of the modern probation system, which is:

- Conducting a presentence investigation
- Mandating probation conditions
- Developing a caseload
- Reporting to the court
- Revoking the sentence, if necessary

In 1878, Massachusetts became the first state to formally adopt probation for juveniles. All states followed between 1878 and 1938. By 1956, all states and the federal system had adult probation.[35]

The 19th century also saw the development of parole (in addition to the work of Maconochie and Crofton). The history of parole in the United States can be understood by following the penal history of New York State. In the early 19th century, judges sentenced inmates to flat, determinate sentences, such as 30 years. Due to the inflexibility of these sentences, governors were forced to grant mass pardons to alleviate prison crowding. In 1817, New York introduced the nation's first good time law that rewarded prison inmates with time off their period of imprisonment for good behavior. In 1876, Zebulon Brockway, who was mentioned earlier in the chapter, created parole and the indeterminate sentence whereby judges set a minimum and maximum term and permitted parole release of those who had served the minimum. Both of Brockway's innovations were predicated on the belief that criminals could be reformed and that their punishment and correction should be individualized to fit the heterogeneity of the criminal population.

In 1930, the Division of Parole was established. In addition, a board of parole was created within the division and given the responsibility, formerly held by the New York Department of Corrections, for decisions on parole releases from prisons.[36] From the late 19th century through the first decades of the 20th century, the other states followed the lead of New York and revamped their own sentencing structure and correctional approach to include indeterminate sentencing and parole.

Perhaps more than any other form of criminal punishment, parole has been the most susceptible to fluctuations in public opinion regarding crime control. From its inception, parole was hailed as a mechanism to both permit criminal offenders an opportunity for reform and cost-effectively reduce the prison population. Over time, however, the general public grew tired of parole because the sanction was neither providing the necessary treatment or correction to reform criminals, nor were criminals serving meaningful terms behind bars. Due to indeterminate sentencing and parole, there was little truth in sentencing. Indeed, the recent changes in how parole is administered demonstrate how susceptible it is to political pressure. For instance, between 1980 and 2000, the discretionary parole release rate remained relatively constant. During the same period, mandatory parole releases increased 500 percent.[37] In other words, the discretionary freedom of parole boards has been severely curtailed, and these tensions continue to surround parole to the present day.

Recent Developments

The first decades of the 20th century lacked the philosophical and intellectual power of the reformatory movement. Instead, the correctional system was pragmatic and not particularly designed, or perhaps even interested, in the rehabilitation of the offender. While the imprisonment rate remained steady for several decades, the absolute number of inmates increased substantially during this era, prompting the need for additional prison facilities. For instance, beginning with the enactment of the **Three Penitentiary Act** in 1891, which authorized the building of the first three federal prisons at Leavenworth, Atlanta, and McNeil Island, Washington, the federal government developed a formalized federal prison system. In 1930, the Bureau of Prisons (BOP) was established within the Department of Justice and charged with the management and regulation of all federal penal and correctional institutions. This responsibility covered the administration of the 11 federal prisons containing over 13,000 inmates in operation at the time. By 1940, the BOP had grown to 24 facilities with 24,360 inmates. Except for a few fluctuations, the number of inmates did not change significantly between 1940 and 1980, when the population was 24,252. However, the number of facilities almost doubled (from 24 to 44) as the BOP gradually moved from operating large facilities confining inmates of many security levels to operating smaller facilities that each confined inmates with similar security needs.

As a result of federal law enforcement efforts and new legislation that dramatically altered sentencing in the federal criminal justice system, the 1980s brought a significant increase in the number of federal inmates. The Sentencing Reform Act of 1984 established determinate sentencing, abolished parole, and reduced good time; additionally, several mandatory minimum sentencing provisions were enacted in 1986, 1988, and 1990. From 1980 to 1989, the inmate population more than doubled, from just over 24,000 to almost 58,000. During the 1990s, the population more than doubled again. The explosive growth in the BOP is discussed in greater detail later in this chapter.[38]

During the first decades of the 20th century, the correctional system was swifter, tougher, and unquestionably interested more in crime control than the treatment of inmates. A way to evaluate this era of correctional toughness is the speed with which condemned offenders were not only executed but also processed on death rows across the United States. As shown in FIGURE 2-1 and FIGURE 2-2, it was once routine procedure for

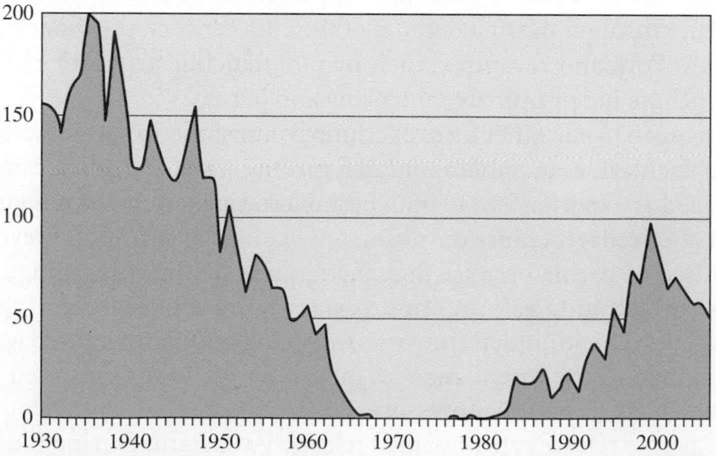

FIGURE 2-1 United States Executions, 1930–2007. *Source*: Snell, T. L. (2007). *Capital punishment, 2006.* Washington, DC: U.S. Department of Justice, Office of Justice Programs, Bureau of Justice Statistics.

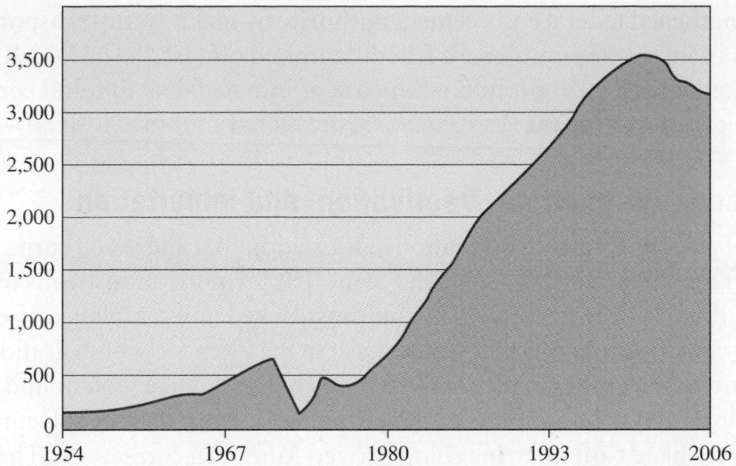

FIGURE 2-2 Prisoners on Death Row, 1954–2006. *Source*: Snell, T. L. (2007). *Capital punishment, 2006*. Washington, DC: U.S. Department of Justice, Office of Justice Programs, Bureau of Justice Statistics.

the states to execute between 100 and 200 inmates each year. Moreover, once sentenced to death, offenders were executed with considerable dispatch, unlike in the prolonged appeal process that exists today.

Industrial Prison Era

In addition to being crowded, prisons of this era were characterized as harsh, and inmates were utilized as free labor. The **Industrial Prison Era** spanning approximately 1900–1935 placed an emphasis on inmate labor and commerce to such a degree that prisons were self-sustaining and even profitable. Five types of inmate labor systems were used:

- *Contract labor system*. Private contractors provide prisons with machinery and raw materials in exchange for the inmate labor to produce finished products.
- *Piece-price system*. Contractors give raw materials to prisons, which use convict labor to produce finished products. Once the goods are manufactured, they are sold by the piece to the contractor, who resells them on the open market.
- *Lease system*. Contractors bid against each other to own the rights to inmate labor. Inmates work outside the prison facility, under the supervision of a private contractor, who is responsible for the inmates' food, shelter, and clothing.
- *Public account system*. The state retains control of inmate labor and provides convicts with the machinery and raw materials to produce finished products. The state sells the products on the open market and uses the profits to defray the cost of prison operations.
- *State-use system*. Prison labor is used to produce goods for state-supported institutions, such as schools and hospitals.[39]

During the Great Depression, prison labor and commerce came under scrutiny from organized labor. On January 29, 1929, the **Hawes-Cooper Act** enabled states to implement laws regarding the acceptance or prohibition of prison-made goods coming within its borders. It did not prohibit interstate transportation of prison-made goods, but made prison-made goods subject to the laws of any state just like other commercial goods.[40] In 1935, the **Ashurst-Sumners Act** authorized federal prosecution of violations of state laws enacted pursuant to the Hawes-Cooper Act, and subsequent amendments to this law in 1940 strengthened federal enforcement authority by making any transport of prison-made goods in interstate commerce a federal criminal offense.[41] The **Walsh-Healey Act** passed by Congress in 1936 prohibited the use of inmate labor to fulfill certain federal contracts in excess of $10,000.[42]

The Hands-Off Doctrine, Deprivation, and Importation

One result of all of the previously mentioned legislation that addressed correctional labor was the swift end to inmate labor, which meant that formerly industrious inmates were mostly idle. Prisons were overcrowded and most lacked any semblance of educational, trade, or therapeutic programs that would assist in the offender's reintegration to society. It was not uncommon for correctional facilities to experience violent and costly riots as inmates protested their conditions of confinement. From the Great Depression until the late 1960s, a **hands-off doctrine** characterized American corrections. There was little judicial oversight of the practices and operations of prisons and other sanctions, and they were largely shut off from the press and academia. In short, what went on in American prisons stayed in American prisons. Gradually, the Supreme Court recognized inmate grievances pertaining to the application of the Eighth Amendment to state prisoners in *Robinson v. State of California* (1962), whether an inmate could bring action under the Civil Rights Act in *Cooper v. Pate* (1964), the case that effectively ended the hands-off era, and others.[43–45]

Another result was the entrenchment of antisocial attitudes, values, and behaviors by prisoners. By approximately 1940, academic criminologists began to gain entrée into American prisons and what they described was unsettling. Donald Clemmer's *The Prison Community*, published in 1940, showed that prisons were wholly separate microsocieties that contained their own language or argot, values, beliefs, and norms, and expectations of behavior. Clemmer developed the idea of **prisonization** defined as the socialization process whereby inmates embrace the oppositional and antisocial culture of the prisoner population. A variety of circumstances made prisonization more likely, such as:

- Serving a lengthy sentence
- Having an unstable personality
- Associating with similarly disturbed inmates
- Having few positive relations with those on the outside
- Readily integrating into prison culture
- Blindly accepting prison dogma
- Associating with hardened offenders or career criminals
- Continuing to engage in antisocial behavior while imprisoned.[46–47]

Norman Hayner and Ellis Ash, two contemporaries of Clemmer, depicted prison conditions in the following way, "a clear realization of the degenerating influence of our present prison system should encourage more experiments aiming to devise a community for offenders that will actually rehabilitate."[48, p. 583]

In 1958, Gresham Sykes' *The Society of Captives* portrayed the prison as a despotic, punitive, inhumane social organization designed purely for punishment, retribution, and retaliation, and not rehabilitation. This became known as the **deprivation model** of inmate behavior in which guards created a regime or social order that forced inmates to conform. The regime was totalitarian, not because guards felt this was the best way to proceed, but rather because of society's desire to prevent escape and disorder. Sykes highlighted the deficiencies of this approach, including the lack of a sense of duty among those who were held captive, the obvious fallacies of coercion, the pathetic collection of rewards and punishments to induce compliance, and the strong pressures toward the corruption of the guard in the form of friendship, reciprocity, and the transfer of duties into the hands of trusted inmates.

According to Sykes, the deprivation resulted in five *pains of imprisonment*, which were (1) deprivation of liberty, (2) deprivation of goods and services, (3) deprivation of heterosexual relationships, (4) deprivation of autonomy, and (5) deprivation of security. To adjust to this new environment, Sykes identified archetypal inmate roles, such as rats, center men (those who aligned with guards), gorillas, merchants, wolves, punks, real men, toughs, etc.[49] Over time, criminologists have found that the deprivation model of inmate behavior is still relevant to the present day and that correctional facilities characterized by regimes of rigid social control tended to experience more inmate-related problems than facilities with a treatment or less repressive form of administrative control.[50–56]

Early critiques of prison centered on the deplorable conditions of confinement and the unjust and unconstitutional treatment of inmates and criminal offenders generally. Academic penologists usually attributed blame for the appalling state of American prisons toward the criminal justice system, such as wardens, prison administrators, and correctional officers, not the inmates. Ironically, it was a former prisoner turned academic named John Irwin, who, along with Donald Cressey, advanced a new explanation of prisoner behavior in 1962.[57] The **importation model** argued that prisoner behavior and the conditions of prisons were mostly a function of the characteristics, values, beliefs, and behaviors that criminals employed on the outside of prison. In other words, inmates of varying degrees of criminality imported their behavioral repertoire and behaved accordingly. To connect to the earlier point, prison conditions were often horrendous because of the commensurate behavior that offenders brought to the facility. The importation model has received substantial empirical support evidenced by the continuity in criminal behavior among the most hardened offenders.[58–63]

During the late 1960s, the link between prisons and conventional society achieved its greatest synergy since the initial design of the penitentiary. The 1960s and 1970s were decades of great turmoil, malaise, and revolution that centered on civil rights, minority rights, women's rights, worker's rights, and overall a broadening liberalization of society. This social turmoil produced a different type of correctional client. The loosely bounded offender and inmate subcultures of the deprivation era were replaced by young, politicized, often gang-affiliated offenders.[64]

Also occurring between 1965 and 1993 was an unprecedented increase in the crime rate.[65] Rising crime rates, particularly for violent crimes such as murder, rape, and robbery, became a primary concern of the general public and an increasingly important political item. As the nation's criminal justice philosophy shifted to the right, so, too, did its thoughts on how to best supervise criminal offenders. Lawrence Sherman noted that during this era, "[conservatism] helped fuel a sea change from treating criminals as victims of society to treating society as the victim of criminals."[66, p. 126] To appear soft on crime was to virtually guarantee a loss at election polls. American society generally shifted to the political right during the 1980s and 1990s, and correctional policy followed suit. As the 1980s arrived, the American correctional system was poised to explode in unprecedented ways.

There are many ways to understand the explosive growth of corrections in American society during the later part of the 20th century (recall the figures on growth in various correctional populations in Chapter 1). FIGURE 2-3 illustrates the dramatic increases in prisons and inmate population over the past century. The growth since about 1980 has been the sharpest.

Glenn Walters, a prominent criminologist and forensic psychologist, has worked at the BOP for nearly 25 years. In 1984, the BOP consisted of 32,000 inmates, 12,000 staff, and 44 different institutions. By 2007, the BOP had grown to 190,000 inmates,

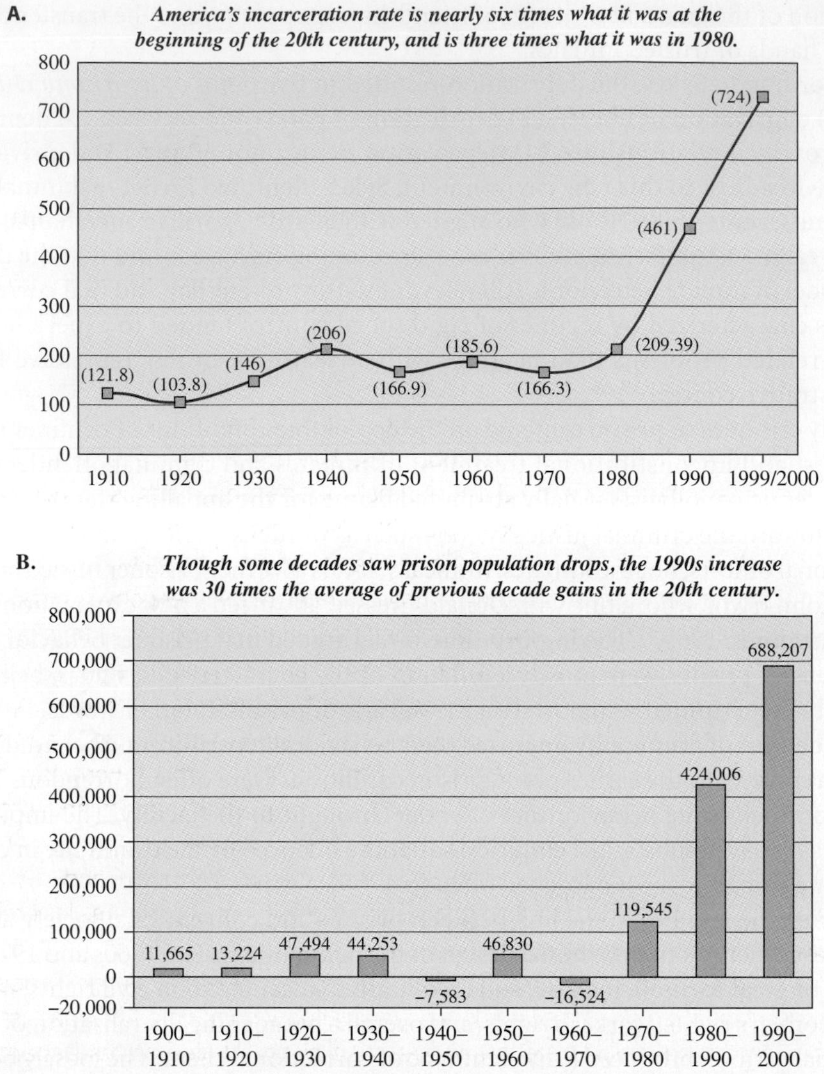

FIGURE 2-3 Incarceration, 1910–2000. A. Incarceration, 1910–2000. B. Change in Prison Population Each Decade, 1900–2000. *Source*: Ziedenberg, J., & Schiraldi, V. (1999). *The punishing decade: Prison and jail estimates at the millennium.* Washington, DC: Justice Policy Institute.

35,000 staff, and 113 institutions. During this span, there was a 494 percent increase in the inmate population of the BOP, but only a 192 percent increase in staffing and a 157 percent increase in institutions. The density of institutions and the inmate–staff ratio have more than doubled in the past 23 years, from 727 inmates per institution in 1984 to 1681 inmates per institution in 2007 and from 2.69 inmates per staff member in 1984 to 5.43 inmates per staff member in 2007.

What might account for the dramatic increase in the BOP inmate population over this span? The **Sentencing Reform Act of 1984**, which established determinate sentencing, abolished parole, and reduced the amount of good time inmates could earn, and mandatory sentencing charters enacted in 1986, 1988, and 1990 both raised the number of inmates entering prison and reduced the number of inmates leaving prison. However, these were not the only factors responsible for the rapid growth of the federal prison population between 1984 and 2007. America has been engaged in a war on drugs since

CORRECTIONS RESEARCH

What if They Can't Read?

State prison budgets exceed money allocated to state and community colleges. So why allocate a portion of state and federal funding to educate inmates? Research reveals college-in-prison programs decrease recidivism rates and this alone decreases reincarceration rates. Long term, this type of program may very well be the most cost-effective crime prevention tool available to the criminal justice system. After all, recidivism rates in the United States range from 41 percent to 71 percent. Nothing else seems to be working.

It has long been known that social, psychological, and demographic factors contribute to crime and ultimately recidivism. One such factor is education. It is estimated that 19 percent of adult inmates cannot read. The functional literacy rate among prison inmates stands at 23 percent—and the average inmate released from prison is described as uneducated and unemployable. According to the National Institute of Justice Report to Congress, simply allowing inmates the opportunity to earn an education is much more effective at lowering recidivism rates than other conventional forms of deterrence including boot camps, shock incarceration, or vocational training.

The state of Texas found an inverse relationship between recidivism and postsecondary education. What's even more interesting is that these recidivism rates could be differentiated by the type of degree. Researchers found former inmates who had earned an associate's degree had a recidivism rate of 13.7 percent. Former inmates who earned a baccalaureate degree had a recidivism rate of 5.6 percent, and for those few ex-inmates who earned a master's degree, the recidivism rate was 0 percent. Similar findings exist for Maryland, Ohio, Indiana, Alabama, Wisconsin, and New York. The Federal Bureau of Prisons found completion of educational programs lowered the recidivism rates for federal prisons as well.

This initiative ground to a screeching halt in 1995. Elected state officials, concerned with appearing tough on crime, introduced legislation to eliminate tuition assistance opportunities to inmates. This effort was resisted by the United States Department of Education, which continued to support the availability of Pell Grants for inmates. However, in 1995 the Violent Crime Control and Law Enforcement Act put an end to Pell Grants for prisoners, ending a 30-year-old practice of funding education opportunities for prison inmates.

Not much funding was allocated prisoners prior to the Violent Crime Control and Law Enforcement Act. The annual Pell Grant award for a prison inmate was less than $1,300—money that went directly to the college or university providing the education and not to the inmate. Total funding represented one tenth of 1 percent of the annual Pell Grants handed out to college students throughout the United States.

Sources: Karpowitz, D., & Kenner, M. (2007). *Education as crime prevention: The case for reinstating Pell Grant eligibility for the incarcerated.* Retrieved May 9, 2007, from http://www.bard.edu/bpi/pdfs/crime_report.pdf.

the early 1900s, but the war gained new momentum in the late 1980s and early 1990s with the advent of several presidential initiatives. The drug war not only increased the BOP inmate population but also changed the population's composition. In 1984, 29 percent of the BOP inmate population was serving time for drug law violations; by 2008, the percentage had risen to 53 percent.

Federal statutes on gun control, immigration, child pornography, and carjacking as well as the Revitalization Act of 1997, in which the BOP took custody of all District of

CORRECTIONS IN THE NEWS

Gender-Responsive Facilities to Accommodate the Increasing Female Inmate Population

The number of female inmates in this country is increasing. In fact, there has been a 468 percent increase in the female inmate population since 1983. In 1983, there were 15,330 female inmates in U.S. correctional facilities. By 2004, there were 86,999 female inmates housed in jails and prisoners across the country. With this increase comes the demand for new gender-specific structures that take into account sight lines, the need for housing classifications, modesty, and visitation.

Developing a master plan is the first step in the process of constructing new jail and prison facilities. This plan should include information on historical trends of inmate populations, profiles of male and female prisoners, inmate population forecasts, annual number of bookings, average length of stay, variation in daily count or peaking factor, and special focus program delivery. This information will provide planners, developers, and builders with the details of how to effectively design a gender-responsive facility. In the past, jails and prisons were built based on forecasts of at-risk populations. The at-risk population was defined as males aged 18 to 28. This figure did not account for females. In addition, with the advent of mandatory sentencing and the aging of male offenders in general, this at-risk calculation is no longer as reliable as it once was.

Information on inmate profiles reveals only 12 percent of female inmates are charged with violent offenses—many of these offenses involved an intimate partner. Typically, women find themselves involved in the criminal justice system as the result of their exposure to domestic abuse or family conflict, poverty, and substance use. They are also more likely to be involved in crimes as a result of an intimate relationship with a male offender. Overall, female offenders are generally charged with property crimes, drug offenses, or public order offenses. Essentially, female offenders are much less likely to require maximum-security housing than are their male counterparts. Female offenders tend to be better educated than are male prisoners. And women inmates also are much more likely to have mental health needs than are male offenders.

Those responsible for designing, developing, building, and operating the facility must consider that women have different needs than do men—safety, respect, and dignity must be primary considerations. But there are other concerns. Female prisoners are more likely to be the primary care givers for young children and in some instances aging parents. Correctional facilities must take into account the needs of the family as well as the need for security and detention. The safe and secure delivery of special needs programs for female offenders with mental health issues, substance use problems, and/or for those who suffer from physical abuse can be facilitated by proper design.

Sources: Elias, G. (2007). *Facility planning to meet the needs of female inmates*. Washington, DC: U.S. Department of Justice, Office of Justice Programs, National Institute of Corrections; Bloom, B., Owen, B., & Covington, S. (2005). *A summary of research, practice, and guiding principles for women offenders*. Washington, D.C.: U.S. Department of Justice, Office of Justice Programs, National Institute of Corrections.

Columbia code felony offenders, not only increased the overall prison population but also introduced a new class of violent offender to the BOP. In 1984, the only violent crime the United States Attorney's office was prosecuting to any extent was bank robbery; by 2008 murderers, rapists, assaulters, burglars, and child molesters were entering the system in record numbers. Changes in both the size and composition of the federal prison population may have contributed to a rise in violence within the BOP as exemplified by a 155 percent increase in the rate of inmate assaults on staff and a 206 percent increase in the rate of inmate assaults on other inmates between 1984 and 2008.[67]

The New Penology and Beyond

As shown in FIGURE 2-4, the incarceration rate increased approximately 500 percent since 1980, making it clear that imprisonment had become the standard method of punishing criminal offenders with incapacitation the assumed rationale for confinement. Malcolm Feeley and Jonathan Simon dubbed this approach the **new penology**, defined as the

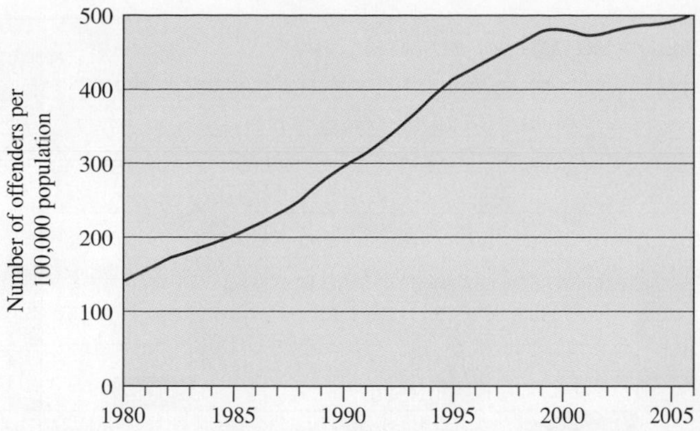

FIGURE 2–4 Incarceration Rate, 1980–2006. *Source*: Sabol, W. J., Couture, H., & Harrison, P. M. (2007). *Prisoners in 2006*. Washington, DC: U.S. Department of Justice, Office of Justice Programs, Bureau of Justice Statistics.

management of groups or subpopulations of offenders based on their actuarial risk to society. The new penology involves shifts in the following three distinct areas:

1. The emergence of new discourses. In particular, the language of probability and risk increasingly replaces earlier discourses of clinical diagnosis and retributive judgment.
2. The formation of new objectives for the system as increasing primacy is given to the efficient control of internal system processes in place of the traditional objectives of rehabilitation and crime control.
3. The deployment of new techniques. These techniques target offenders as an aggregate in place of traditional techniques for individualizing or creating equity.[68]

According to Feeley and Simon, the new penology emphasized control and surveillance of offenders, considered rehabilitation to be largely idealistic, and de-emphasized the likelihood of offender reintegration. In this sense, the new penology is portrayed negatively. Among academics and some elites, the increased reliance on imprisonment is seen as unjust and discriminatory. Nevertheless, it was *the* approach to corrections.

While it is true that in the public eye, American corrections is today more than ever dominated by confinement and control, there have also been progressive advancements at supervising offenders in the community. Evaluation researchers Edward Latessa and Christopher Lowenkamp suggest that evidence-based practices demonstrate empirically that recidivism rates can be significantly reduced through theoretically sound, well-designed programs that appropriately apply the principles of effective intervention. The principles of effective intervention are risk, need, treatment, and fidelity.

- *The risk principle is the who to target.* The most intensive correctional treatment and intervention sentence or program should be reserved for high-risk offenders, such as chronic or violent criminals. For low-risk offenders, simply holding them accountable for their actions and imposing minimal sanctions is usually sufficient to prevent recidivism.
- *The need principle is the what to target.* Programs should target crime-producing needs, such as antisocial peer association, antisocial personality, drug use, alcoholism, self-control skills, and other factors that are highly correlated with crime.
- *The treatment principle addresses how to target offenders' needs.* The most effective programs are behavioral and center on present circumstances and risk

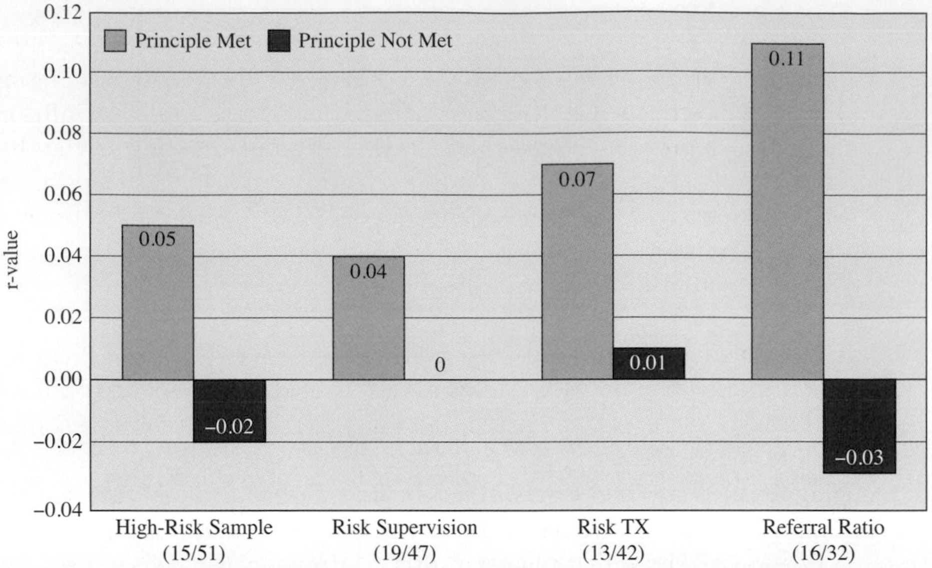

FIGURE 2–5 The Risk Principle in Practice. *Source*: Lowenkamp, C. T., Pealer, J., Smith, P., & Latessa, E. J. (2006). Adhering to the risk and need principles: Does it matter for supervision-based programs? *Federal Probation, 70*, 3–8.

factors that are responsible for the offender's behavior. Behavioral interventions are action- rather than talk-oriented and teach offenders new, prosocial skills to replace antisocial ones.

- *The fidelity principle pertains to the integrity and quality of the program, intervention, or sentence.* These include making sure that the program has well-trained staff, close monitoring of offenders, assisting with other needs of the offender, ensuring the program is delivered as designed through quality-assurance processes, and structured aftercare.[69]

As shown in FIGURE 2–5, when the principles of effective intervention are met, correctional clients of varying criminality serving various sentences respond better to the intervention. There is less recidivism and their antisocial behavior is more likely to be corrected.

After centuries of innovation and practice, what do contemporary American prisons generally look like? Michael Tonry and Joan Petersilia assessed them as follows:

- Compared with earlier eras, prisons are larger in terms of the number of inmates they house.
- Inmate populations and staffs are more diverse and disproportionately African American and Hispanic.
- Many more line and management staff are women.
- Gangs are larger and their influence more pervasive.
- More prison staff are unionized.
- A large and growing fraction of prisons (and sanctions generally) are under private management.
- The possibility of judicial oversight and intrusion is greater.
- Inmates serve increasingly lengthy sentences, which brings increased demands for medical care and other services for the aging and elderly.[70]

Overall, compared to penitentiaries, reformatories, and prisons from any other era in American history, the correctional system in the 21st century is the most scientifically informed, safe, humane, treatment and program oriented, and transparent in terms of its openness to outside scrutiny. Contemporary corrections uses scientifically influenced actuarial methods to appropriately classify, supervise, treat, and manage prisoners based on their level of risk. For instance, many states use the client management classification system (CMC) to supervise correctional clients. The CMC addresses the treatment and supervision needs in five ways. In ascending order of seriousness, these are (1) selective intervention-situational, (2) selective intervention-treatment, (3) casework/control, (4) environmental structure, and (5) limit setting classifications.[71] More than ever, the correctional system knows what it is doing when dealing with correctional clients.

Still, there are vestiges of previous punishments and old motivations to punish ebb and flow. For instance, there is a cadre of criminal offenders who are thoroughly opposed to quitting crime and for whom there is no realistic chance of effective supervision, let alone rehabilitation.[72] Many of the most serious criminals are intractably antisocial and are increasingly punished via solitary confinement. Unfortunately, the continual use of solitary confinement carries with it collateral costs in terms of psychologically damaging inmates.[73] In this sense, the American prison has harkened to the methods of the Pennsylvania system to—if not force penitence—at least punish noncompliant prisoners.

WRAP UP

CASE STUDY CONCLUSION

According to the perspective of the prosecution, Mary Winkler committed premeditated first-degree murder. According to Tennessee state law, for a murder to be premeditated, the offender must have committed the act after "the exercise of reflection and judgment." In other words, intent is a critical element of this charge. Forming intent occurs prior to the commission of the crime. Intent could have been formed moments before the act was committed, or it may have existed in the mind of the accused for an extended period of time. Mary's actions of taking the shotgun from the closet, then going to the bedroom, pointing the loaded weapon at her husband who was sleeping in their bed, and finally pulling the trigger were a series of events that could have been halted at any time had she not intended to kill her husband. According to the Tennessee Bureau of Investigation, Mary Winkler and her husband, Matthew Winkler, had been arguing the night before "over finances and other family problems."

Matthew Winkler did not die instantly. In fact, he was alive when Mary left the house. She even apologized, according to her statement, to her husband for having shot him. She did not, however, seek medical attention for her fatally wounded husband. Instead, knowing that she was committing murder, Mary took her children and fled the state. He eventually bled to death. The next day, Mary took her kids to the beach. On April 19, 2007, Winkler was ultimately found guilty of voluntary manslaughter and was later sentenced to 210 days in confinement—a sentence Winkler herself believes was too brief. By August 14, 2007, Winkler was released and one year later she received custody of her three children.

Sources: Filan, S. (2007). *Is abuse a legal justification for murder? A jury will decide if Mary Winkler is guilty of first-degree murder.* Retrieved June 4, 2007, from http://www.msnbc.msn.com/id/18202905/print/1/displaymode/1098/; Baird, W. (2007). *Pastor's wife wants statements tossed.* Retrieved August 28, 2008, from http://www.trutv.com/library/crime/notorious_murders/family/mary_winkler/1.html.

Chapter Summary

- Throughout history, correctional systems have struggled with balancing the needs of punishment and correction.
- Depending on the severity of the offense and the seriousness of the offender, different punishment philosophies are utilized.
- The penitentiary of the Pennsylvania system was designed to force offenders to reflect in complete silence and isolation for their crimes.
- The reformatory of the Auburn system was a congregate system that entailed many progressive features to rehabilitate offenders.
- Correctional approaches, especially prisons, are susceptible to social conditions and perceptions about whether they correct behavior.
- The deprivation model suggests that the structures of the prison mold inmate behavior.

- The importation model suggests that offender characteristics determine inmate behavior.
- The imprisonment rate increased 500 percent since 1980 due to sentencing changes and reflects a punitive correctional paradigm called the new penology.
- While the American correctional system is considered tough, it also uses scientific principles to provide the best supervision and treatment of criminal offenders.

Key Terms

Ashurst-Sumners Act Law that authorized federal prosecution of violations of state laws enacted pursuant to the Hawes-Cooper Act, and subsequent amendments to this law in 1940 strengthened federal enforcement authority by making any transport of prison-made goods in interstate commerce a federal criminal offense.

Auburn system Response to the Pennsylvania system; used congregate inmate organization.

Augustus, John Founder of probation in the United States.

banishment Penalty in which wrongdoers were excommunicated or excluded from the community entirely.

Beccaria, Cesare Philosopher who wrote *On Crimes and Punishments*, which liberalized criminal justice.

Code of Hammurabi Ancient body of laws during the reign of the Babylonian King Hammurabi in 1780 BCE.

collective incapacitation Criminals are prevented from committing crime because they are incarcerated.

Common Law The customary criminal justice and legal traditions or doctrines that the United States inherited from England.

corporal punishment Sanctions that inflict physical pain on the offender.

Crofton, Sir Walter Disciple of Maconochie who employed similar reforms in Irish prisons.

deprivation model Inmate behavior model that proposes that inmate behavior is primarily a function of the oppressive structural features posed by the prison facility itself.

deterrence The punishment philosophy that rests on the idea that people are rational thinkers endowed with free will who weigh the costs and benefits of each course of action in their lives and then choose to act.

draconian Tough criminal justice policies.

expiation Based upon the belief that crime arouses the anger of the gods against the entire community, and the only way to reduce the anger is to destroy the offender.

general deterrence The large number of potential criminals who might be discouraged from committing crime because of the punishments received by others.

hands-off doctrine Little judicial oversight of the practices and operations of prisons and other sanctions, which were largely shut off from the press and academia.

Hawes-Cooper Act Enabled states to implement laws regarding the acceptance or prohibition of prison-made goods coming within its borders.

Howard, John English sheriff who caused reforms of English jails and prisons.

importation model Argued that prisoner behavior and the conditions of prisons were mostly a function of the characteristics, values, beliefs, and behaviors that criminals employed on the outside of prison.

incapacitation The inability to act; refers to the use of imprisonment to preclude the ability of an offender to victimize members of society.

Industrial Prison Era Time that spanned approximately 1900–1935 during which an emphasis was placed on inmate labor and commerce.

informal social control Unofficial sanctions that arise from informal family and friendship networks.

Law of the Twelve Tables A comprehensive and codified legal code to replace the oral, informal, and largely unfair prior tradition.

lex talionis The law of retaliation such that punishment must be inflicted with an eye for an eye and a tooth for a tooth.

Maconochie, Alexander Administrator of Norfolk Island (Australia) penal colony who devised the mark system and other innovations that influenced American penology.

Magna Carta Codified set of laws from England in 1215 that was the forerunner of the United States Constitution with its dual goals of cautiously empowering the state and granting rights and protections to the public.

mala in se Acts that are intrinsically wrong and violations of natural law.

mala prohibita Offenses are crimes made illegal by legislation, not by natural law.

mark system System devised by Maconochie in which credits (marks) against a sentence allowed inmates to be released once they earned the required number of marks through good behavior.

natural law The belief that the human world is organized by a positive or good natural order that should be obeyed by all humans.

new penology The management of groups or subpopulations of offenders based on their actuarial risk to society.

penitent Feeling or expressing remorse for one's misdeeds or sins.

penitentiaries Early prison that used silence and isolation to force inmates to be penitent.

Pennsylvania system Quaker-inspired system that created the penitentiary.

prisonization The socialization process whereby inmates embrace the oppositional and antisocial culture of the prisoner population.

reformatory Response to penitentiary movement, popularized by the reforms of Zebulon Brockway.

rehabilitation Restoration of an offender to a law-abiding lifestyle.

restoration A theory of justice that emphasizes repairing the harm caused by crime.

retribution The philosophical rationale that implies the payment of a debt to society and the criminal offender's expiation and atonement for his or her crime.

selective incapacitation The use of prison to selectively target high-rate, career criminals.

Sentencing Reform Act of 1984 Legislation that established determinate sentencing, abolished parole, and reduced the amount of good time inmates could earn.

specific deterrence The individual offender being sentenced and punished.

Three Penitentiary Act Legislation in 1891 that authorized the building of the first three federal prisons at Leavenworth, Kansas; Atlanta, Georgia; and McNeil Island, Washington.

Walsh-Healey Act Legislation passed by Congress in 1936; prohibited the use of inmate labor to fulfill certain federal contracts in excess of $10,000.

Critical Thinking Questions

1. Arguments for capital punishment usually center on deterrence. Is there an effective argument against retribution? Why is retribution not used as the philosophical basis for the death penalty?
2. How has religion shaped prisons since their inception and through today? What constitutional issues are raised by having religious or faith-based programs in prison? If the programs are effective, should concerns about church and state be ignored?
3. Is the new penology a positive or negative development in corrections?
4. Have people really evolved beyond the barbaric methods of early correctional systems? What elements of the current correctional system seem to represent retributive intentions?
5. In terms of inmate classification, correctional administration is fairly scientific. Does the field of corrections have a reputation for being scientifically rigorous?

Notes

1. Mead, G. H. (1918). The psychology of punitive justice. *American Journal of Sociology, 23*, 577–602.
2. Meskell, M. W. (1999). An American resolution: The history of prisons in the United States from 1777 to 1877. *Stanford Law Review, 51*, 839–865.
3. Zimring, F. E., & Hawkins, G. (1995). *Incapacitation: Penal confinement and the restraint of crime*. New York: Oxford University Press.
4. Latessa, E. J., & Lowenkamp, C. (2006). What works in reducing recidivism. *University of St. Thomas Law Journal, 3*, 521–525.
5. Friedman, L. M. (1993). *Crime and punishment in American history.* New York: Basic Books.
6. Bates, S. (1932). Have our prisons failed? *Journal of Criminal Law and Criminology, 23*, 562–574.
7. Quotation taken from Supreme Court Justice Oliver Wendell Holmes Jr. in an address delivered at the dedication of the new hall at the Boston University School of Law, Boston, Massachusetts, on January 8, 1897.
8. Aristotle, *Politics VII*, 13, from Aristotle.(1998). *Politics: Books VII and VII.* New York: Oxford University Press.
9. DeLisi, M. (2006). *Criminal justice: Balancing crime control and due process.* Dubuque, IA: Kendall/Hunt.
10. Bates, p. 562.
11. Berns, W. (1979). *For capital punishment: Crime and the morality of the death penalty.* New York: Basic Books.
12. Zimring & Hawkins.
13. Restorative Justice Online web site. Retrieved June 8, 2007, from http://restorativejustice.org/intro.
14. Deuteronomy 17:6–7 selected from Carroll, R., & Prickett, S. (Eds.). (2008). *The Bible: Authorized King James Version (Oxford World's Classics).* New York: Oxford University Press.
15. Beccaria, C. (1994). On crimes and punishments. In J. E. Jacoby (Ed.), *Classics of criminology* (pp. 277–286). Prospect Heights, IL: Waveland Press.

16. DeLisi.

17. Friedman, p. 38.

18. Wadman, R. C., & Allison, W. T. (2004). *To protect and to serve: A history of police in America.* Upper Saddle River, NJ: Pearson/Prentice Hall.

19. Goldfarb, R. (1976). *Jails: The ultimate ghetto of the criminal justice system.* New York: Doubleday.

20. Vaux, R., cited in Meskell, p. 839.

21. For an overview of correctional history, see Blomberg, T. G., & Lucken, K. (2000). *American penology: A history of control.* Hawthorne, NY: Aldine de Gruyter.

22. Eastern State Penitentiary. (n.d.). *Six page history.* Retrieved August 29, 2008, from http://www.easternstate.org/history/sixpage.html.

23. The History Channel. (1996). The big house: Eastern State Penitentiary. New York: A&E Television Networks.

24. de Beaumont, G., & de Tocqueville, A.(1994). On the penitentiary system in the United States and its application in France. In J. E. Jacoby (Ed.), *Classics of criminology* (pp. 372–386). Prospect Heights, IL: Waveland Press.

25. de Beaumont & de Tocqueville.

26. The History Channel. (1996). *The big house: Eastern State Penitentiary.* New York: A&E Television Networks.

27. See Skidmore, R. A. (1948). Penological pioneering in the Walnut Street Jail, 1789–1799. *Journal of Criminal Law and Criminology, 39,* 167–180.

28. Barry, J. V. (1956). Alexander Maconochie. *Journal of Criminal Law, Criminology, and Police Science, 47,* 84–106.

29. Barry, J. V. (1958). *Alexander Maconochie of Norfolk Island: A study of a pioneer in penal reform.* London: Oxford University Press.

30. Morris, N. (2002). *Maconochie's gentlemen: The story of Norfolk Island and the roots of modern prison reform.* New York: Oxford University Press.

31. Rotman, E. (1998). The failure of reform: United States, 1865–1965. In N. Morris & D. J. Rothman (Eds.). *The Oxford history of the prison: The practice of punishment in Western society* (pp. 151–177). New York: Oxford University Press.

32. Meskell, p. 839.

33. Wines, E. C., & Dwight, T. W. (1867). *Report on the prisons and reformatories of the United States and Canada,* to the New York legislature, January 1867.

34. Brockway, Z. R. (1994). The American reformatory prison system. In J. E. Jacoby (Ed.), *Classics of criminology* (pp. 387–396). Prospect Heights, IL: Waveland Press.

35. Petersilia, J. (1997). Probation in the United States. *Crime and Justice, 22,* 149–200.

36. Petersilia, J. (1998). Probation and parole. In M. Tonry (Ed.), *The handbook of crime and punishment* (pp. 563–588). New York: Oxford University Press.

37. Travis, J., & Lawrence, S. (2002). *Beyond the prison gates: The state of parole in America.* Washington, DC: The Urban Institute, Justice Policy Center.

38. Federal Bureau of Prisons. (2006). *A brief history of the Bureau of Prisons.* Washington, DC: U.S. Department of Justice, retrieved June 27, 2007, from http://www.bop.gov/about/history.jsp.

39. Regoli, R. M., & Hewitt, J. D. (2008). *Exploring criminal justice.* Sudbury, MA: Jones & Bartlett.

40. Hawes-Cooper Act, 49 U.S.C. § 11507 (1929).

41. Ashurst-Sumners Act, 18 U.S.C. § 1761 (1935).

42. Walsh-Healey Act, 41 U.S.C. §§ 34–35 (1936).

43. Useem, B., & Kimball, P. (1991). *States of siege: U. S. prison riots, 1971–1986.* New York: Oxford University Press.

44. *Robinson v. State of California,* 370 U.S. 660 (1962).

45. *Cooper v. Pate,* 378 U.S. 546 (1964).

46. Clemmer, D. (1940). *The prison community.* New York: Holt, Rinehart, and Winston.

47. Clemmer, D. (1950). Observations on imprisonment as a source of criminality. *Journal of Criminal Law and Criminology, 41,* 311–319.

48. Hayner, N. S., & Ash, E. (1940). The prison as a community. *American Sociological Review, 5,* 577–583.

49. Sykes, G. M. (1958). *The society of captives: A study of a maximum-security prison.* Princeton, NJ: Princeton University Press.

50. Akers, R., Hayner, N., & Gruninger, W. (1977). Prisonization in five countries: Type of prison and inmate characteristics. *Criminology, 14,* 527–554.

51. Huebner, B. M. (2003). Administrative determinants of inmate violence: A multilevel analysis. *Journal of Criminal Justice, 31,* 107–117.

52. Jiang, S., & Fisher-Giorlando, M. (2002). Inmate misconduct: A test of the deprivation, importation, and situational models. *The Prison Journal, 82,* 335–358.

53. Poole, E. D., & Regoli, R. M. (1983). Violence in juvenile institutions: A comparative study. *Criminology, 21,* 213–232.

54. Reisig, M. D., & Lee, Y. (2000). Prisonization in the Republic of Korea. *Journal of Criminal Justice, 28,* 23–31.

55. Walters, G. D. (2003). Changes in criminal thinking and identity in novice and experienced inmates: Prisonization revisited. *Criminal Justice and Behavior, 30,* 399–421.

56. Wheeler, S. (1961). Socialization in correctional communities. *American Sociological Review, 26,* 697–712.

57. Irwin, J., & Cressey, D. (1962). Thieves, convicts, and the inmate culture. *Social Problems, 10,* 142–155.

58. DeLisi, M. (2003). Criminal careers behind bars. *Behavioral Sciences and the Law, 21,* 653–669.

59. DeLisi, M., Berg, M. T., & Hochstetler, A. (2004). Gang members, career criminals, and prison violence: Further specification of the importation model of inmate behavior. *Criminal Justice Studies, 17,* 369–383.

60. Cao, L., Zhao, J., & Van Dine, S. (1997). Prison disciplinary tickets: A test of the deprivation and importation models. *Journal of Criminal Justice, 25,* 103–113.

61. Gaes, G. G., Wallace, S., Gilman, E., Klein-Saffran, J., & Suppa, S. (2002). The influence of prison gang affiliation on violence and other prison misconduct. *Prison Journal, 82,* 359–385.

62. Gendreau, P., Goggin, C. E., & Law, M. A. (1997). Predicting prison misconducts. *Criminal Justice and Behavior, 24,* 414–431.

63. Schrag, C. (1954). Leadership among prison inmates. *American Sociological Review, 19,* 37–42.

64. Jacobs, J. B. (1977). *Stateville: The penitentiary in mass society.* Chicago: University of Chicago Press.

65. Wilson, J. Q. (1983). *Thinking about crime* (Revised ed.). New York: Vintage Books.

66. Sherman, L. W. (2005). The use and usefulness of criminology, 1751–2005: Enlightened justice and its failures. *Annals of the American Academy of Political and Social Science, 600,* 115–135.

67. Walters, G. D. (2008). Criminal predatory behavior in the Federal Bureau of Prisons. In M. DeLisi & P. J. Conis (Eds.), *Violent offenders: Theory, research, public policy, and practice.* Sudbury, MA: Jones & Bartlett.

68. Feeley, M. M., & Simon, J. (1992). The new penology: Notes on the emerging strategy of corrections and its implications. *Criminology, 30,* 449–474.

69. Latessa & Lowenkamp.

70. Tonry, M., & Petersilia, J. (1999). American prisons at the beginning of the 21st century. *Crime and Justice, 26,* 1–16.

71. Harris, P. M., Gingerich, R., & Whittaker, T. A. (2004). The 'effectiveness' of differential supervision. *Crime & Delinquency, 50,* 235–271.

72. DeLisi, M. (2005). *Career criminals in society.* Thousand Oaks, CA: Sage.

73. On the deleterious effects of solitary confinement, see Andersen, H. S., Sestoft, D., Lillebaek, T., Gabrielsen, G., & Hemmingsen, R. (2003). A longitudinal study of prisoners on remand: Repeated measures of psychopathology in the initial phase of solitary versus non-solitary confinement. *International Journal of Law and Psychiatry, 26,* 165–177.

CHAPTER

3

The Law and Corrections

"The basic concept underlying the Eighth Amendment is nothing less than the dignity of man. While the State has the power to punish, the Amendment stands to assure that this power be exercised within the limits of civilized standards."[1]

OBJECTIVES

- Understand how prisoners gain access to the courts and the purpose of habeas corpus.
- Identify statutes and case law pertaining to civil rights and mandamus petitions brought by prisoners.
- Specify the First Amendment rights of prisoners regarding religion, free speech and mail, and free association visitation.
- Apply the Fourth Amendment to inmate privacy rights.
- Recognize the due process considerations and case law expressed in the Fifth and Fourteenth Amendments.
- Describe the Eighth Amendment and the case law relevant to capital punishment, conditions of confinement, and habitual offender statutes.

CASE STUDY

There is no statute of limitation when the case involves murder. Charles E. Moore and Henry Hezekiah died in May 1964. Both men had been part of an effort to register Black voters in Mississippi during the civil rights movement. Police reports indicated both young men had been kidnapped, beaten, whipped, tied to old jeep parts, and dumped alive and still breathing into the Mississippi River. Confessions from Klan informants identified James Ford Seale as the man who stopped to pick up the two men as they were hitchhiking in the town of Meadville. FBI reports from the time of the crime indicate that Seale and another man beat Moore and Hezekiah nearly to death as they questioned them about rumors Blacks were importing firearms into the county. Forty-three years later, former sheriff's deputy and reputed Ku Klux Klansman Seale was charged with the crime of kidnapping.

Years later, Seale was located by Thomas Moore, Charles Moore's brother, when he returned to Roxie, Mississippi, to film a documentary about his brother's death. Thomas learned from a local resident that James Seale was still living in the area and that although there had been reports of his death, the reports were false; the reports had been verified by family members and published in several newspapers, including the Los Angeles *Times*.

1. Why wasn't Seale charged and prosecuted years ago?
2. What made this a federal case?
3. Were there others involved in this case?
4. Is physical evidence tying the defendant to a crime always necessary for a conviction?
5. Are there other cases stemming from the civil rights movement similar to this one?

"No longer can a jury wantonly and freakishly impose the death sentence; it is always circumscribed by the legislative guidelines."[2]

The rule book of the criminal justice system is the United States Constitution, which contains the procedures or rules by which criminal justice agents must comply while performing their duties. For criminal justice to be lawful, it must be in compliance with the U.S. Constitution, the supreme law of the land and the set of laws that supersedes all other laws in the country. No law or any jurisdiction can conflict with the expressed or understood doctrines of the U.S. Constitution. More precisely, the guidelines that the police, courts, and corrections must abide by are the first 10 amendments to the U.S. Constitution, also known as the **Bill of Rights**, which was ratified in 1791. (The Fourteenth Amendment also figures prominently in criminal justice because it pertains to the equal applicability and protection of the law). These amendments and the rights inherent to them are:

Amendment I: Congress shall make no law respecting an establishment of religion, or prohibiting the free exercise thereof; or abridging the freedom of speech, or of the press; or the right of the people peaceably to assemble, and to petition the government for a redress of grievances.

Amendment II: A well-regulated militia, being necessary to the security of a free state, the right of the people to keep and bear arms, shall not be infringed.

Amendment III: No soldier shall, in time of peace be quartered in any house, without the consent of the owner, nor in time of war, but in a manner to be prescribed by law.

Amendment IV: The right of the people to be secure in their persons, houses, papers, and effects, against unreasonable searches and seizures, shall not be violated, and no warrants shall issue, but upon probable cause, supported by oath or affirmation, and particularly describing the place to be searched, and the persons or things to be seized.

Amendment V: No person shall be held to answer for a capital, or otherwise infamous crime, unless on a presentment or indictment of a grand jury, except in cases arising in the land or naval forces, or in the militia, when in actual service in time of war or public danger; nor shall any person be subject for the same offense to be twice put in jeopardy of life or limb; nor shall be compelled in any criminal case to be a witness against himself, nor be deprived of life, liberty, or property, without due process of law; nor shall private property be taken for public use, without just compensation.

Amendment VI: In all criminal prosecutions, the accused shall enjoy the right to a speedy and public trial, by an impartial jury of the state and district wherein the crime shall have been committed, which district shall have been previously ascertained by law, and to be informed of the nature and cause of the accusation; to be confronted with the witnesses against him; to have compulsory process for obtaining witnesses in his favor, and to have the assistance of counsel for his defense.

Amendment VII: In suits at common law, where the value in controversy shall exceed twenty dollars, the right of trial by jury shall be preserved, and no fact tried by a jury, shall be otherwise reexamined in any court of the United States, than according to the rules of the common law.

Amendment VIII: Excessive bail shall not be required, nor excessive fines imposed, nor cruel and unusual punishments inflicted.

Amendment IX: The enumeration in the Constitution, of certain rights, shall not be construed to deny or disparage others retained by the people.

Amendment X: The powers not delegated to the United States by the Constitution, nor prohibited by it to the states, are reserved to the states respectively, or to the people.

Amendment XIV: Section 1: All persons born or naturalized in the United States, and subject to the jurisdiction thereof, are citizens of the United States and of the state wherein they reside. No state shall make or enforce any law which shall abridge the privileges or immunities of citizens of the United States; nor shall any state deprive any person of life, liberty, or property, without due process of law; nor deny to any person within its jurisdiction the equal protection of the laws.[7]

"Impairment of any other litigating capacity is simply one of the incidental and perfectly constitutional consequences of conviction and incarceration."[3]

CORRECTIONS IN THE NEWS

Sex Traffickers

Prior to 2000, no comprehensive federal law existed to prevent individuals or groups from human trafficking. No law, no federal prosecution! It was just that simple. How things have changed! Today the Trafficking Victims Protection Act of 2000 (TVPA) provides federal penalties for persons convicted of trafficking humans. Traffickers risk life in prison for a trafficking crime that results in death or if the commission of the crime involves kidnapping, attempted kidnapping, aggravated sexual assault, attempted aggravated assault, or an attempt to murder the victim. If the trafficker exploits a child under the age of 14 through force, fraud, or coercion for the purposes of sex trafficking, the trafficker again risks life in prison. The act or acts of coercion include psychological coercion, trickery, and the seizure of documents.

There are an estimated 18,000 to 20,000 human trafficking victims trafficked into the United States each year. From 2001 to 2005, U.S. Attorney's offices across the country were involved in 555 investigations involving acts outlawed by the TVPA. More than 58 percent of these cases involved forced labor (24 percent), sex trafficking of children (23 percent), trafficking slaves (9 percent), and unlawful conduct or a violation of other provisions (2 percent). The highest concentration of cases occurred in just four states: California (17 percent), Florida (14 percent), Texas (9 percent), and New York (8 percent).

From 2001 to 2005, 146 suspects were prosecuted under TVPA statutes. The largest number of cases prosecuted involved suspects charged with the sex trafficking of children. In 85 percent of the cases where the defendant was convicted, prison sentences were the penalty. In only 7 percent of the cases was probation the sentence. In 8 percent of the cases the defendant was ordered by the court to pay a fine and included in this percentage were those defendants who received suspended sentences. U.S. Attorneys declined to prosecute 222 cases during this period. Their main reasons included lack of evidence, weak or insufficient admissible evidence, and prosecution by other authorities.

Sources: *Trafficking Victims Protection Act of 2000 fact sheet.* Retrieved May 9, 2007, from http://www.acf.hhs.gov/trafficking/about/TVPA_2000.pdf; Motivans, M., & Kyckelhahn, T. (2006). *Federal prosecution of human trafficking, 2001–2005.* Washington, DC: U.S. Department of Justice, Office of Justice Programs, Bureau of Justice Statistics.

"From the correctional point of view, conviction of crime does not render anyone hopelessly unfit."[4, p. 35]

Clearly, some of the amendments have more to do with criminal justice than others. For instance, the Fourth Amendment is commonly known as the police amendment because it addresses search and seizure, probable cause, and warrants. The Fifth and Sixth Amendments apply broadly to the courts and contain hallowed due process concepts, such as the protection against double jeopardy, the use of grand jury indictment, fair and speedy trial, right to counsel, and others. The **Eighth Amendment** can be understood as the corrections amendment because it addresses both pretrial detention via the proscription of excessive bail and punishment via the proscription against cruel and unusual punishment. As indicated in Chapter 2, the American criminal justice system and legal system was influenced by several progressive ideas, including a more humane, less bloody means of criminal punishment.

Because corrections is the end of the line of the criminal justice process since defendants had been adjudicated and are serving some sentence, casual observers think that the law has little relevance to corrections beyond the obvious concern about cruel and unusual punishment. In practice, offenders, especially those serving jail or prison sentences, continuously challenge their conviction and utilize the criminal courts to revisit their case. As a county attorney once indicated to the current authors, most of his time was spent keeping inmates in prison as opposed to prosecuting new offenders. This chapter explores the law and corrections as well as the many ways that the criminal courts serve as a check on the correctional system. The legal doctrines that empower criminal defendants to even gain access to the criminal courts is examined next.

Why are nominations to the United States Supreme Court so controversial and often bitterly contested? What is at stake when the president seeks to appoint justices? On which issues do conservatives and liberals most disagree?

Access to Courts

There are three general scenarios by which inmates access the federal courts: (1) they can challenge the constitutionality of their imprisonment (writ of habeas corpus); (2) they can seek redress of civil rights violations by government officials (42 U.S.C. § 1983, also known as Section 1983 lawsuits); and (3) they can compel a government official to perform a duty (writ of mandamus). For general trends in prisoner petitions between 1980 and 2000, see TABLE 3–1 and FIGURE 3–1.

Habeas Corpus

The legal doctrine that grants correctional clients access to the courts to challenge the legality of their sentence is **habeas corpus**, Latin for "to have the body." Habeas corpus is mentioned in Article I, Section 9 of the U.S. Constitution, "The Privilege of the Writ of Habeas Corpus shall not be suspended, unless when in Cases of Rebellion or Invasion and public Safety may require it." Also known as the *great writ of liberty*, habeas corpus is an order for correctional authorities, known as the respondent, to bring the defendant who requested filing the paper or writ, known as the petitioner, to court. There are three main purposes of habeas corpus: (1) to provide release from illegal confinement (habeas corpus ad subjiciendum), (2) to order the prisoner to the court for prosecution (habeas corpus *ad prosequendum*), and (3) to order the prisoner before the court to give evidence (habeas corpus *ad testificandum*).[8]

Inmates pursue habeas filings for several reasons. The most common reason that inmates cite for the illegality of their sentence stems from ineffective defense counsel. In other words, prisoners believe that because their defense attorney was bad, their sentence is illegal. Other commonly cited reasons include errors by the trial court, due process concerns, and self-incrimination (**Fifth Amendment** violations), which resulted in the perceived illegal sentence. According to the most recent data from the Bureau of Justice Statistics, nearly 60,000 prisoner petitions are filed each year, 80 percent of which are from state prisoners and 20 percent from BOP inmates. More than 54 percent are habeas corpus filings.[9]

"The Fourth Amendment proscription against unreasonable searches does not apply within the confines of the prison cell."[5]

TABLE 3-1 **Prisoner Petitions in Federal District Court, 1980–2000**

	Jurisdiction and Type of Petition									
		Federal					State			
Year	Total	Total	Vacate Sentence	Habeas Corpus	Mandamus	Civil Rights	Total	Habeas Corpus	Mandamus	Civil Rights
1980	23,230	3,661	1,322	1,413	323	603	19,569	7,029	145	12,395
1981	27,655	4,053	1,248	1,629	342	834	23,602	7,786	177	12,639
1982	29,275	4,328	1,186	1,927	381	834	24,947	8,036	172	16,739
1983	30,765	4,354	1,311	1,914	339	790	26,411	8,523	202	17,686
1984	31,093	4,526	1,427	1,905	372	822	26,567	8,335	198	18,034
1985	33,452	6,262	1,527	3,405	373	957	27,190	8,520	180	18,490
1986	33,758	4,432	1,556	1,679	427	770	29,326	9,040	215	20,071
1987	37,279	4,507	1,664	1,808	313	722	32,772	9,524	276	22,972
1988	38,825	5,130	2,071	1,867	330	862	33,695	9,867	270	23,558
1989	41,472	5,577	2,526	1,818	315	918	35,895	10,545	311	25,039
1990	42,623	6,611	2,970	1,967	525	1,149	36,012	10,817	352	24,843
1991	42,452	6,817	3,328	2,112	378	999	35,635	10,325	267	25,043
1992	48,417	6,997	3,983	1,507	597	910	41,420	11,296	479	29,645
1993	53,436	8,456	5,379	1,467	695	915	44,980	11,574	388	33,018
1994	57,928	7,700	4,628	1,441	491	1,140	50,228	11,908	395	37,925
1995	63,634	8,951	5,988	1,343	510	1,110	54,593	13,627	397	40,569
1996	68,235	13,069	9,729	1,703	418	1,219	55,166	14,726	444	39,996
1997	62,966	14,952	11,675	1,902	401	974	48,011	19,956	397	27,658
1998	54,715	9,937	6,287	2,321	346	983	44,777	18,838	461	25,478
1999	56,603	10,859	5,752	3,590	555	962	45,738	20,493	513	24,732
2000	58,257	11,880	6,341	3,870	628	1,041	46,371	23,345	563	24,463

Note: Detail does not add to total, which includes jurisdiction cases from outlying territories. Data source: Administrative Office of the U.S. Courts, Report of the Proceedings of the Judicial Conference of the United States, annual (Table C–2).

Source: Scalia, J. (2002). *Prisoner petitions filed in U.S. district courts, 2000, with trends 1980–2000.* Washington, DC: U.S. Department of Justice, Office of Justice Programs, Bureau of Justice Statistics.

Habeas corpus is also the legal doctrine used by condemned offenders to challenge the propriety of their death sentence. Over the years, the ability or ease with which offenders can invoke the habeas corpus doctrine has evolved. For instance, Andrew Hammel suggests that during the tenure of Chief Justice Earl Warren, federal courts actively monitored state courts to ensure the liberal use of habeas. During the more conservative tenure of Chief Justice Warren Burger, federal courts permitted states to restrict inmate access to the courts via habeas requests.[10] Since 1996, Congress attempted to curtail the ability of prisoners to file petitions in federal court with the passage of the Antiterrorism and Effective Death Penalty Act, which contains amendments to habeas corpus requirements. For example, Section 2254 provides that federal habeas corpus relief is only available to a state prisoner if the petitioner has exhausted the remedies that are available at the state level. Section 2255 contains a 1-year period of limitation for a federal prisoner to file a motion attacking the illegality of his or her sentence.[11–12] Although the Antiterrorism and Effective Death Penalty Act was expected to reduce prisoner petitions, it actually increased the filing rate and the number of habeas corpus petitions originating from state

"Simply because an execution method may result in pain, either by accident or as an inescapable consequence of death, does not establish the sort of 'objectively intolerable risk of harm' that qualifies as cruel and unusual."[6, p. 11]

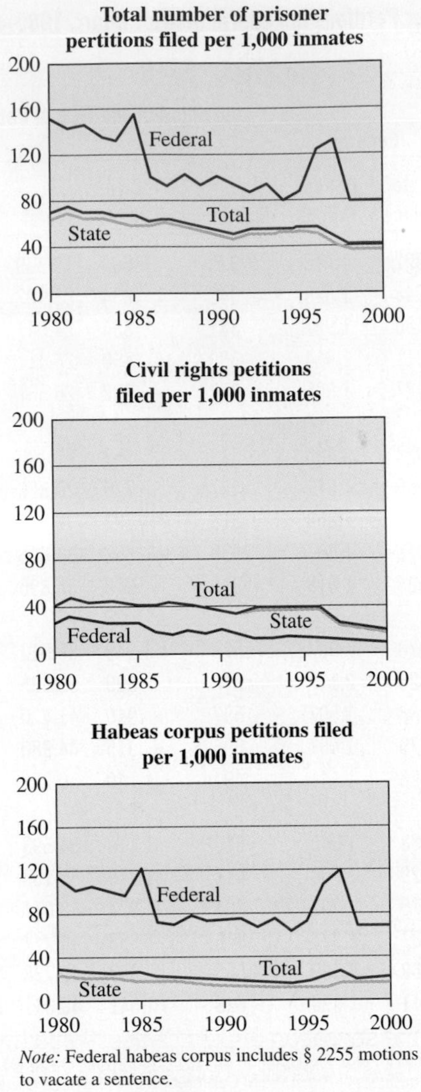

FIGURE 3–1 Petitioner Filings per 1,000 Inmates, 1980–2000. *Source*: Scalia, J. (2002). *Prisoner petitions filed in U.S. district courts, 2000, with trends 1980–2000.* Washington, DC: U.S. Department of Justice, Office of Justice Programs, Bureau of Justice Statistics.

prisoners. Between 1996 and 2000, state prison inmates filed 50 percent more habeas petitions (see **FIGURE 3–2**).[13]

Civil Rights and Mandamus

The purpose of habeas corpus is narrow; it only allows inmates to challenge the legality of their confinement/sentence. However, inmates have many complaints about their involvement in the correctional system, such as allegations of violations of their constitutional and civil rights. These allegations and petitions for money damages or injunctive relief from their sentence are covered by **Section 1983** of the United States Code. The foundation for these petitions originates in the Fourteenth Amendment, which prohibits violations of due process. The Civil Rights Act of 1871 provided the mechanism for correctional clients to seek relief from constitutional deprivations at the state level.[14] This was applied to include federal violations in *Bivens v. Six Unknown Agents of the Federal Bureau of Narcotics* in 1971.[15]

CORRECTIONS HISTORY

Death by Lethal Injection

Courts have been sentencing defendants convicted of their crimes to death for centuries. Is there a method that is completely painless? The answer to this question is probably not. Is death by lethal injection less painful than the other methods used by departments of correction in this country? You decide . . . .

Let's begin this discussion at the point where the inmate who is sentenced to death has been strapped to the gurney. Trained prison personnel are tasked with establishing an intravenous line that will be used to administer each of three different drugs that will ultimately end the life of the inmate. The first drug used is an anesthetic, commonly sodium thiopental. The next drug that is administered is a paralytic agent such as pancuronium bromide. The last drug in this series is usually potassium chloride, which causes the heart to stop beating. According to claims made by condemned offenders and their attorneys, this is not a painless procedure and there is ongoing public debate whether it is more humane than electrocution, lethal gas, hanging, or firing squad.

The sequence of drugs used in an execution by lethal injection was developed in 1977 by an Oklahoma medical examiner. It sounds reasonable and sure, but the medical examiner had little training in pharmacology, basing the development of this protocol on personal experience having been subjected to anesthesia himself. Nonetheless, the procedure was soon adopted by Oklahoma and eventually by Texas and other states with the death penalty. In 1982, Texas was the first state to execute a prisoner using lethal injection. Within 10 years, Texas had executed 53 prisoners by means of lethal injection.

It is interesting to note that each of the drugs, and the massive quantities dictated by protocol, are themselves lethal. Pancuronium bromide is a neuromuscular blocking agent capable of causing death by asphyxiation—but this drug does not affect consciousness or block the sensation of pain. It does keep the prisoner from moving or thrashing about during the procedure. Consequently, if the prisoner is not anesthetized sufficiently prior to the administering of pancuronium bromide, the inmate will experience the pain of suffocating. Because of this, 30 states have banned the use of neuromuscular blocking agents due to the potential risk of suffering. Sodium thiopental alone, at the dose prescribed by the state, some 5 to 20 times the dose used during surgery, will cause the inmate to go limp, stop breathing, and lose consciousness within a minute of the drug being administered.

So far, and after approximately 40 cases, heard both by state and federal courts, none of the courts have ruled lethal injection to be unconstitutional. Times are changing; courts are beginning to express some concern over the procedures used in an execution by lethal injection. However, on April 16, 2008, in *Baze v. Rees*, the United States Supreme Court upheld lethal injection as a constitutional form of capital punishment. In the words of Chief Justice John Roberts, "Simply because an execution method may result in pain, either by accident or as an inescapable consequence of death, does not establish the sort of 'objectively intolerable risk of harm' that qualifies as cruel and unusual."

Sources: Human Rights Watch (2006). *So long as they die: Lethal injections in the United States.* Retrieved May 24, 2007, from http://hrw.org/reports/2006/us0406/; Human Rights Watch. (2006). *U.S.: States negligent in use of lethal injections*, Retrieved May 24, 2007, from http://hrw.org/english/docs/2006/04/24/usdom13241.htm; *Baze v. Rees* (553 U.S. XXXX) (2008).

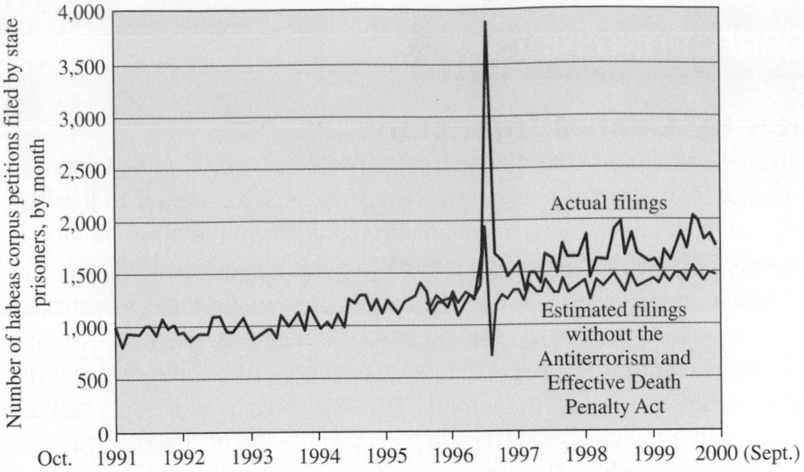

FIGURE 3–2 Habeas Petitions and the Antiterrorism and Effective Death Penalty Act. *Source*: Scalia, J. (2002). *Prisoner petitions filed in U.S. district courts, 2000, with trends 1980–2000*. Washington, DC: U.S. Department of Justice, Office of Justice Programs, Bureau of Justice Statistics.

An unseen part of the correctional experience is the attempts by prisoners to challenge the legality of their sentence in the courts. It is commonly recognized that the courts serve as a check and balance on the police power, but do the courts similarly check the correctional system?

A variety of legislative initiatives have been advanced to limit frivolous and malicious prisoner litigation against correctional systems. For instance, the Civil Rights of Institutionalized Persons Act of 1980 was enacted to reduce the number of civil rights petitions filed in the federal courts. According to the legislation, state prisoners were required to exhaust state-level administrative remedies before filing their petitions in federal court. In this way, Congress attempted to reserve federal courts for more serious civil rights violations or other significant constitutional issues.[16] The Prison Litigation Reform Act of 1996 attempted to reduce the number of petitions filed by inmates who claimed civil rights violations in three ways:

1. Inmates were required to exhaust all administrative remedies before filing in federal courts.
2. Inmates who filed as indigent persons (in forma pauperis) nevertheless required the payment of filing fees and court costs.
3. Inmates are prohibited from filing as indigent if they had prior petitions dismissed as frivolous or malicious.[17]

Civil rights petitions declined 40 percent as a result of the Prison Litigation Reform Act of 1996 (see FIGURE 3–3).

Finally, a **writ of mandamus** is an extraordinary remedy used when the plaintiff has no other way to access the courts for relief and he or she seeks to compel a governmental duty. Writs of mandamus are rare, with slightly over 1,000 filed in the most recent year where data are available.[18] The relevant case law that speaks to the ability of correctional clients to access the courts is explored next.

Case Law

Among the most important and the earliest Supreme Court decisions regarding inmate access to courts is ***Ex parte Hull***. In 1941, the Court held that states could not impair a petitioner's right to apply to a federal court for a writ of habeas corpus. The case arose in Michigan where correctional officials required inmates to submit their legal mailings for review prior to being sent to the courts. Only papers that met the guidelines of correctional staff were forwarded, suggesting that prison officials and prison administrative

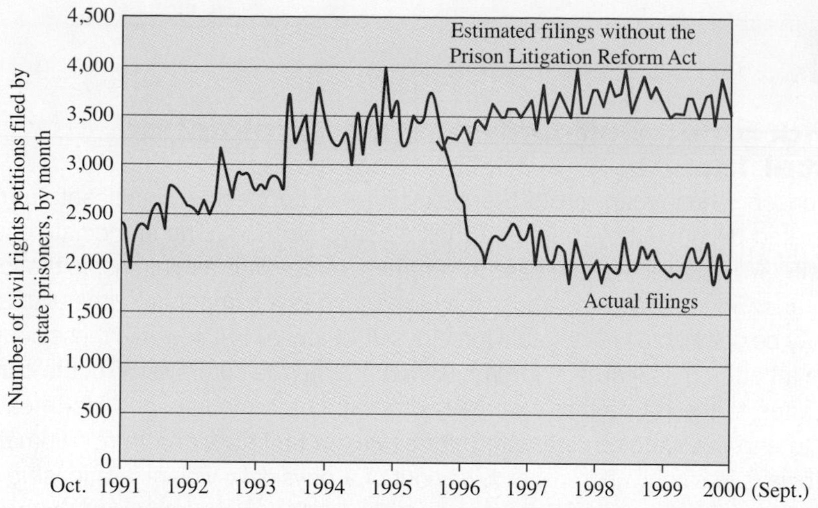

FIGURE 3-3 Civil Rights Petitions and the Prison Litigation Reform Act. *Source*: Scalia, J. (2002). *Prisoner petitions filed in U.S. district courts, 2000, with trends 1980–2000.* Washington, DC: U.S. Department of Justice, Office of Justice Programs, Bureau of Justice Statistics.

guidelines effectively abridged habeas rights.[19] *Ex parte Hull* is important on two fronts. First, is established **precedent**, a decision by the appellate court (usually the Supreme Court) that serves to guide all future legal decisions that encompass a similar topic, for inmates to apply for habeas corpus. Second, it loosened the hands-off doctrine that characterized American corrections, especially prisons, for most of the first half of the 20th century.

The spirit of *Hull* can be seen in several cases from the 1960s. In *Smith v. Bennett* (1961), the Court held that states cannot limit writ applications only to prisoners who can pay a filing fee.[20] On the issue of indigent inmates, the Court held in *Long v. District Court* (1966) that states must also furnish a transcript of court proceedings when the inmate cannot afford it if the court transcript is needed to pursue subsequent legal action.[21] In 1969, a landmark case, ***Johnson v. Avery***, affirmed the *Hull* decision, furthered the decline of the hands-off approach to corrections, and addressed the First Amendment protection of free speech and association. The issue at hand centered on the rightfulness of inmates to provide legal assistance or serve as a jailhouse lawyer to their peers. Johnson, a Tennessee inmate, had been cited for helping another inmate prepare to submit a writ of habeas corpus—an action that was in direct violation of prison policy. Upon review, the Supreme Court held that the policy was invalid and that inmates *are* able to provide legal assistance to other inmates if no other legal assistance is available. Like the *Hull* decision 28 years prior, *Johnson v. Avery* established that access to the courts for prisoners to present their legal complaints cannot be denied or obstructed.[22]

Like all legal doctrines, access to the courts evolves and is subject to the criminal justice mood of the country and, more specifically, the Supreme Court. During the 1960s, many legal decisions reflected a liberalization of inmate rights, greater access to the courts, and the decline of the hands-off approach to corrections. For instance, access to the courts was bolstered in 1977 with the *Bounds v. Smith* decision. In *Bounds*, the Court held that prisoners must have access to an adequate law library if no adequate form of legal assistance was provided for them.[23] Approximately 20 years later, the Supreme Court did an about-face on the *Bounds* decision. In ***Lewis v. Casey*** (1996), the Court held that prisoners who claim that they have been denied access to the courts and that the prisons failed to comply with *Bounds v. Smith* must show that their rights were prejudiced as a

CORRECTIONS FOCUS

Battered Woman's Syndrome: Self-Defense or Diminished Capacity to Form Mental Intent

It's simple, you kill someone—you go to prison. And in many cases that's exactly what happens. A significant number of women in prison for murder are incarcerated because they murdered their abusive partners. The immediate cause of the crime is in many situations case specific. What these women have in common, however, is a relationship that can be characterized by years of abuse, threats, and violence. Was the abuse they experienced the impetus for the ultimate act of revenge? Could their behavior in any way be deemed as reasonable force or self-defense? Is it possible these convicted female homicide offenders suffered from a battered woman's syndrome (BWS) prior to the commission of the crime?

In the 1970s, legal advocates suggested to the courts that a woman who, without immediate and life-threatening provocation, made a conscious choice to end the life of an intimate partner was in fact suffering from traumatic life experiences that, void of illegitimate pathways to safety, offered her a way out of a physically violent relationship and a life free from abuse. For a short time and in a limited number of court rooms, the BWS defense answered the question everyone was asking—why did she kill him? Was it enough for an acquittal? Only in a limited number of cases did this defense convince the jury that the alleged female homicide offender deserved to be set free.

Typically, the use of the BWS claim varied with the facts of each case in which it was employed. In some criminal cases, the BWS claim was used to convince the jury that the defendant truly believed her life was in danger and that she acted in self-defense using reasonable force to save her life and/or the lives of her children. In other cases, the BWS defense was used to persuade the jury of the woman's incapacity to form the intent to commit the murder. Unfortunately, to date, no empirical evidence has been found to support this defense. This does not mean that BWS is not a true syndrome. It only means that no empirical evidence supports the BWS contention, and until there is such evidence, other pathways to a life free from abuse need to be made available.

Source: Dixon, J. W. (2002). *Battered woman syndrome.* Retrieved May 16, 2007, from http://www.expertlaw.com/library/domestic_violence/battered_women.html; DeHart, D. D. (2005). *Pathways to prison: Impact of victimization in the lives of incarcerated women.* Washington, DC: U.S. Department of Justice, Office of Justice Programs, National Institute of Justice.

result of the denial of these rights in order to recover in a Section 1983 suit. In an opinion led by Justice Antonin Scalia, arguably the court's most ardent conservative, the *Lewis* decision blasted earlier precedents for their overly liberal interpretation of the access to courts doctrine:

> Several statements in *Bounds* went beyond the right of access recognized in the earlier cases on which it relied. . . . To demand the conferral of such sophisticated legal capabilities upon a mostly uneducated and indeed largely illiterate prison population is effectively to demand permanent provision of counsel, which we do not believe the Constitution requires.[24]

Similarly, the expectation that inmates are entitled to associate with other inmates for habeas or other legal reasons also has been curtailed. *Turner v. Safley* (1987) held that the test of reasonable relationship to legitimate penal objectives, not strict scrutiny, is used to determine if prison rules that affect only inmates are constitutional. A rule prohibiting inmate-to-inmate correspondence was upheld because it was neutral and logically advanced the goals of institutional security and safety.[25] In other words, inmates do not have a right to free association for legal discourse because inmate free association can lead to violence or rioting. A similar decision was reached in 1989 in *Thornburgh v Abbot*, where the Court held that the Federal Bureau of Prisons can reject incoming publications that potentially threaten institutional safety because it is a reasonable and legitimate penological concern.[26] In *Shaw v. Murphy* (2001), the Court held that inmates do not have a First Amendment right to provide legal assistance to other inmates.

In sum, inmates have a constitutional right to access the courts to directly appeal their sentence, file civil rights lawsuits under Section 1983, request a writ of mandamus, and request a writ of habeas corpus. In fact, habeas corpus is a fundamental right of American jurisprudence and is the primary reason that correctional clients are not finished contesting their legal case simply because they have been convicted and sentenced. The access to courts doctrine is a hallmark of American justice because it permits a check and balance to ensure that every sentence of confinement is legal.

First Amendment

Constitutionally speaking, correctional clients appear to be in a gray area as to their legal rights. An essential part of any criminal punishment is the deprivation of liberty or freedom. There are many examples of this. Defendants on house arrest cannot leave their own home except as specified by the courts. Probationers must report to their probation officer at certain dates and times, abstain from using alcohol, refrain from contacting specific individuals, and the like. Parolees can be barred from living less than 2,000 feet from a school, must attend counseling and treatment regardless of their interest in doing so, and avoid fraternizing with felons, gang members, and other undesirable characters.

Because of this, it is common for correctional clients to perceive that their sentence is infringing on their constitutional rights and prisoners tend to gravitate to the "to petition the government for a redress of grievances" clause of the First Amendment. Many types of complaints are cited as infringements on constitutional rights, and the First Amendment is often viewed as the most important amendment, and the one containing the most sacred rights, such as freedom of speech, religion, press, and assembly. Legally speaking, prisoners retain their **First Amendment** rights while incarcerated unless those rights are (1) inconsistent with their status as prisoner or (2) inconsistent with the legitimate penological goals of the institution. This balance of rights is known as the **balancing test** decision reached in ***Pell v. Procunier*** in 1974.[27]

Religion

In April 2007, a jail chaplain in Rockland County, New York, was suspended after she distributed religious booklets that condemned Islam, depicted the prophet Muhammad as a religious dictator, and generally contained offensive depictions of Muslims.[28] Although this incident is controversial because of its depiction of Islam, it also pertains to perhaps the most hallowed right within the First Amendment: religion. The seminal case for the right to religious freedom for prisoners is ***Cooper v. Pate*** (1964). In Cooper, the Court held that inmates were permitted to practice their religion provided that three basic conditions were met: (1) the religion must be an established religion (not contrived by the inmate); (2) the inmate's religious practices must conform to the tenets of the religion; and (3) the religious practices cannot pose a security risk or disrupt prison operations.[29]

Two important federal laws that address religious rights of correctional clients are the Religious Freedom Restoration Act of 1993 (RFRA) and the Religious Land Use and Institutionalized Persons Act of 2000 (RLUIPA). The RFRA established that governmental agencies may substantially burden a person's exercise of religion only if it demonstrates that the burden is (1) in furtherance of a compelling governmental interest and (2) is the least restrictive means of furthering that compelling governmental interest.[30]

However, in 1997 in *City of Boerne v. Flores*, the Supreme Court held that Congress exceeded its powers by enacting the RFRA and infringed on a judicial act, thus the Religious Freedom Restoration Act was voided. Just 3 years later, however, Congress enacted the RLUIPA, which addressed the protection of religious practices by institutionalized persons (prisoners) with basically the same language from the RFRA.[31] As of 2008, the

The courts have affirmed First Amendment religious rights among prisoners. Which types of inmate religious practices have pushed the boundaries of constitutionally permissible forms of worship?

Supreme Court has not evaluated the constitutionality of the Religious Land Use and Institutionalized Persons Act of 2000.

What constitutes an established religion is sometimes a point of contention between correctional clients and correctional administrators, and occasionally the Supreme Court is needed to resolve the matter. For instance, in *Cruz v. Beto* (1972), a Texas inmate (Cruz) filed a Section 1983 suit because correctional authorities were not allowing him to use the prison chapel, correspond with a Buddhist religious advisor, and share his Buddhist materials with other prisoners. In fact, Cruz was placed in solitary confinement after attempting to disperse Buddhist materials (correctional staff doubted the authenticity of Cruz's claim to be Buddhist). At the same time, religious services were provided to inmates of Jewish and Christian faiths. Upon appeal, the Supreme Court held that by denying Cruz a reasonable opportunity to pursue his faith when others were afforded opportunities to pursue theirs, correctional authorities were effectively discriminating against the Buddhist religion.[32]

Perhaps the outcome in *Cruz* should have been obvious since Buddhism is an official religion. In the 1970s, some inmates at the U.S. Penitentiary in Atlanta organized a "religion" called the Church of the New Song (CONS). Despite the claims made by CONS that it should receive the same amenities and services as other religions, the federal courts did not agree because CONS was not a genuine religion (for instance, its membership was restricted to those inmates).[33] Similarly, in *McCorkle v. Johnson* (1989), the federal courts upheld an Alabama correctional policy that banned Satanic materials and Satanic worship despite the protests of inmates who claimed to be Satanists because the materials and practices were inherently violent and posed security and safety risks for inmates.[34]

Essentially, correctional officials must accommodate religious practices that are based on the tenets of a genuine religion provided that the practices are not dangerous or in conflict with the reasonable operations of the facility. For example, the Court held in *O'Lone v. Shabazz* (1987) that a prison regulation that prohibited inmates on outside work details from returning to the main prison building during the day, and thereby preventing them from attending Muslim services that the Koran dictated be held during the early afternoon on Fridays, *did not* violate their First Amendment rights. Prison officials only need to show that the regulation was reasonably related to the security interest of the prison.[35] In other circumstances, federal courts have ruled in favor of inmates and their religious requests. Federal courts have decided that correctional officials provide sweat lodges for Native American inmates (*Hamilton v. Schriro*, 1996), provide special meals for Ramadan for Islamic inmates (*Walker v. Blackwell*, 1969), and offer kosher food as part of the prison menu for Jewish inmates (*Kahane v. Carlson*, 1975, and *Jackson v. Mann*, 1999).[36–39]

Free Speech and Mail

Perhaps more important than the First Amendment rights to religious expression is the right of free speech. Free speech is a hallmark of American freedom and liberty; however, the right to free speech is not absolute. There are many forms of speech that can bring censure, rebuke, or in the case of harassing language, criminal charges. Because prisoners are incapacitated from society, their speech takes the form of telephone calls, e-mail, and mail. The landmark case that established inmate rights to speech via the mail is ***Procunier v. Martinez*** (1974). In *Procunier*, the Court held that mail correspondence between inmates and outside parties was speech protected by the First Amendment. However, there were limits to that speech. Correctional officials could restrict inmate mail (and thus restrict their free speech) to further the interests of legitimate governmental interests. More specifically, inmate mail can be restricted for three reasons:

1. To preserve order and discipline
2. To maintain institutional security
3. To rehabilitate the prisoner[40]

Contraband is a serious risk to institutional safety. Cases such as *Bell v. Wolfish* limited opportunities for visitors to smuggle contraband within periodicals.

In 2006, an interesting case occurred involving a Wisconsin prisoner serving time for murder, armed robbery, and weapons possession. The inmate filed a lawsuit against correctional officials who were refusing to provide to the inmate his e-mail printouts from a personal ad he owns on the Inmate Connections service. The 7th U.S. Circuit Court of Appeals ruled in favor of the inmate and the lawsuit is going forward.[41] In addition to correctional policies limiting access to e-mail output, there are other limits on inmate speech. To guard against security breaches, inmates are prohibited from writing to inmates in other institutions except in narrow, extenuating circumstances (*Turner v. Safley*, 1987).[42] Federal courts have limited inmate access to nude photographs that are sent through the mail. The same is applied to magazines, newspapers, and other periodicals. In *Thornburgh v. Abbot* (1989), the Court held that prison regulations that permit the Federal Bureau of Prisons to reject incoming publications found to be detrimental to institutional security are valid if they are reasonably related to a legitimate penological interest.[43] Thornburgh built upon the "publisher only rule" established in *Bell v. Wolfish* (1979) in which inmates were permitted to receive periodicals exclusively from the publisher since friends and family were more likely to hide **contraband**, or materials prohibited in correctional facilities, such as drugs and weapons, in the mail.[44]

Free Association and Visitation

> The fact of confinement and the needs of the penal institution impose limitations on constitutional rights, including those derived from the First Amendment, which are implicit in incarceration. Perhaps the most obvious of the First Amendment rights that are necessarily curtailed by confinement are those associational rights that the First Amendment protects outside of prison walls.[45]

This passage comes from the landmark case in inmate right to association, *Jones v. North Carolina Prisoners' Labor Union, Inc.* (1977). In *Jones*, the Court held that prison rules prohibiting the solicitation of members for the prisoners' union, barring meetings of the union, and refusing to deliver packets of union publications that were sent to the prison in bulk mailings did not violate First Amendment freedom of speech or association or equal protection rights specified in the Fourteenth Amendment (discussed later in this chapter). The Court also decided that prison officials reserved the right to permit some organizations, such as Alcoholics Anonymous, to organize and meet in prison while depriving others. Another group that does not have a right to access or association with inmates is the news media. In *Pell v. Procunier* (1974), the Court held that prison regulations prohibiting face-to-face press interviews did not violate the First Amendment because others avenues were available to the media.[46]

Association rights extend beyond labor unions and the media. The Supreme Court has ruled on whether prisoners have a constitutional right to have contact visits, in which they can physically touch visitors. They do not. In *Block v. Rutherford* (1984), the Court held that the Los Angeles County Jail's policy of total prohibition on contact visits by pretrial detainees is a reasonable response to legitimate security concerns.[47] In *Overton v. Bazzetta* (2003), the Court held that jails can place limits on who can visit inmates, including their own children, if the limitations serve legitimate penological interests.[48] Correctional officials can also revoke visitation privileges of specific visitors who pose a threat to institutional security or the orderly operation of the visitation area, a decision reached in *Kentucky Department of Corrections, v. Thompson* (1989).[49]

Finally, perhaps the most controversial association issue pertaining to prisoners is conjugal visits, which are overnight visits between inmates and their spouses in which sexual activity is permitted. Because of security and contraband risks, most states do not allow conjugal visits for prisoners. In fact, only six states, California, Connecticut, Mississippi, New Mexico, New York, and Washington, permit conjugal visits. In 2007, California became the first state to allow gay and lesbian partners of prison inmates to participate

CORRECTIONS FOCUS

The Hands-Off Doctrine

In the early to mid-1900s, the courts were reluctant to support claims by convicted prisoners of constitutional guarantees. Public opinion, mirrored by court decisions, limited the rights of prisoners and the courts felt the power to define and enforce the constitutional rights of prisoners was not within the mandate of their authority. The general consensus was that in so doing, the court's decision would undermine state and federal correctional policy that must also consider security and the appropriate and necessary discipline of inmates.

By the 1960s, the reluctance by certain courts to apply the hands-off doctrine was increasing. In essence, the mood of the court was changing. It was not until the 1960s and 1970s that courts generally accepted the idea that prisoners have rights and that the courts are bound to protect those rights. The Supreme Court decided, in a series of opinions, that rights guaranteed by the U.S. Constitution must also be afforded prison inmates.

Sources: Cruz v. Beto, 405 U.S. 319 (1972) [freedom of religion]; *Wolf v. McDonnell*, 418 U.S. 539 (1974) [procedural due process]; *Pell v. Procunier*, 417 U.S. 817 (1974) [freedom of speech].

in conjugal visits.[50] Although the Supreme Court has yet to rule on the constitutionality of conjugal visits, lower courts have addressed the issue. In *Lyons v. Gilligan*, a federal court determined that there is no constitutional right to conjugal visits and correctional policies can lawfully proscribe them.[51] In *Mary of Oak Knoll v. Coughlin*, a New York state court upheld a policy which limited conjugal visits to inmates who could provide a valid marriage certificate to verify the authenticity of their marriage. Inmates without a valid certificate were prevented from conjugal visits.[52]

Fourth Amendment

The **Fourth Amendment** is commonly known as the police amendment, since it focuses on search and seizure, warrants, and probable cause. It would seem that the Fourth Amendment has little applicability to correctional clients; after all, there are no police officers patrolling jails and prisons. However, in correctional facilities, officers and other staff perform quasi-law enforcement functions and, as officers of the state, are bound by the Fourth Amendment. This section explores the important case law about the Fourth Amendment rights of inmates, including how closely bound to the Fourth Amendment correctional officers are and whether inmates receive the same Fourth Amendment protections as members of conventional society.

The landmark case in the application of the Fourth Amendment to inmates is ***Hudson v. Palmer*** (1984). In *Hudson*, the Court held that an inmate did not have a reasonable expectation of privacy in his cell that entitled him to Fourth Amendment protections against unreasonable searches and seizures. The Court also refused to find a due process violation where the inmate had been deprived of his property by a state employee (that had been damaged during a cell search) because state law provided for a meaningful postdeprivation remedy for the loss. Indeed, the Court was clear that the sheer differences between free society and prison make for a more narrow application of the Fourth Amendment.

> A right to privacy in the traditional Fourth Amendment terms is fundamentally incompatible with the close and continual surveillance of inmates and their cells required to ensure institutional security and internal order. We are satisfied that society would insist that the prisoner's expectation of privacy always yield to what must be considered the paramount interest in institutional security.[53]

Overall, inmates have limited privacy rights while they are in custody and the Supreme Court has ruled on this in a variety of cases. In *Bell v. Wolfish* (1979), the Court held that authorities can search an inmate's cell with him being present.[54] Also in the *Bell* decision, the Court held that body cavity and strip searches were permitted and thus not a violation of constitutional protections against illegal search and seizure.

In correctional facilities, there is also no constitutional right to privacy during visitation with family and friends. In fact, not only is there no entitlement to privacy, but also the authorities can record conversations between inmates and their visitors. This was the decision in *Lanza v. New York* (1962).[55] Moreover, authorities can turn over recorded conversations between inmates and visitors to law enforcement and prosecutors to pursue criminal charges against the inmate, a decision reached in *United States v. Hearst* (1978).[56]

Inmates have limited Fourth Amendment rights because of their status as prisoners. This suggests that within correctional facilities there is a greater emphasis on institutional safety than individual rights to privacy.

These procedures are permitted as part of the regular course of maintaining a safe prison environment, but how often do correctional facilities actually monitor inmate visits, seize their communication, and limit their privacy? Heath Hoffman, George Dickinson, and Chelsea Dunn studied trends in prison communication policies between 1971 and 2005. Overall, Hoffman and his colleagues found that prisons have become more restrictive in their policies toward inmate visits and communication. For instance, they found:

- Between 1971 and 2005, the proportion of facilities that had 365-day visitation declined from 48 percent to 19 percent.
- Almost all prison facilities routinely monitor inmate mail to check for incoming contraband.
- Inmates are afforded liberal access to telephones and 84 percent of prisons routinely monitor inmate phone calls.
- Almost 70 percent of facilities always monitor inmate phone calls.
- Inmate access to the Internet and e-mail is severely restricted.[57]

Fifth and Fourteenth Amendments

Due process is so important to American law that it is mentioned twice in the Bill of Rights, in the Fifth and Fourteenth Amendments. Generally, **due process** means that laws and criminal procedures are reasonable and applied in a fair and equal manner. Due process guarantees that people have a right to be fairly heard before they can be deprived of life, liberty, and property. Due process is a sacred legal concept derived from Article 29 of the Magna Carta, which was published in 1215.[58] Given the importance of due process to criminal justice, the case law supporting it is extensive. This section reviews landmark decisions and other case law that pertains to a variety of procedures used to supervise correctional clients.

The landmark case in due process rights of prisoners is ***Wolff v. McDonnell*** (1974), which specified the due process guidelines for major prison disciplinary proceedings. In *Wolff*, the Court held that:

- Written notice of the charges must be given to the inmate.
- The fact finder must make written statements of the evidence relied upon and reasons for the disciplinary action.
- The inmate must be allowed to call witnesses and present documentary evidence except when doing so would be unduly hazardous to institutional safety or correctional goals.
- Due process *does not* require confrontation and cross-examination of adverse witnesses or the right to counsel.
- Guards may open incoming mail from an attorney if done in the presence of the inmate.[59]

CORRECTIONS HISTORY

Reasons for Striking the Hands-Off Doctrine

1. More vocal prisoners
2. Civil rights demonstrations
3. Vietnam War protests
4. Ghetto riots
5. Prison riots
6. Attorneys' concerns about prison conditions
7. Development of a civil-liberties bar
8. More effective counsel for the defendants
9. North American Civil Liberties Union's National Prison Project
10. Expert witnesses hired to represent prisoners

Source: Branham, L. S., & Hamden, M. S. (2005). *Cases and materials on the law and policy of sentencing and corrections* (7th ed.). Belmont, CA: Thomson/West.

Two years later, in *Baxter v. Palmigiano* (1976), the Court added more conditions for disciplinary hearings. The Court held that:

1. Inmates have no due process right to retained or appointed counsel regardless of the charges.
2. The Fifth Amendment does not prohibit the drawing of adverse inferences from the inmate's failure to testify at the hearing.
3. Inmates do not have a right to confront and cross-examine the witnesses against them.
4. Authorities do not have to state reasons for denying these rights to inmates.[60]

In other words, although inmates have due process rights during disciplinary hearings, they are considerably limited especially compared to the due process rights of citizens in the noncorrectional settings.

In addition to *Wolff*, the Supreme Court has ruled on a variety of due process claims made by inmates, parolees, and probationers that pertain to their Fifth and **Fourteenth Amendment** rights. In most, but not all, cases, the Court held to restrict due process rights or to deny that a due process claim exists in the first place. For instance:

- *Morrissey v. Brewer* (1972): The Court held that due process establishes the right of a parolee to a preliminary and final hearing before parole can be revoked.[61]
- *Gagnon v. Scarpelli* (1973): The Court held that probationers are entitled to a preliminary and final revocation hearing and in special circumstances may be required to assign counsel at the hearing.[62]
- *Estelle v. Dorrough* (1975): The Court held that automatic dismissal of pending appeals if an inmate escapes from prison for more than 10 days while the appeal was pending did not violate equal protection rights.[63]
- *Meachum v. Fano* (1976): The Court held there was no due process requirement for a formal hearing prior to transferring an inmate from a medium- to maximum-security facility.[64]
- *Craig v. Boren* (1976): The Court held that disparity in treatment between male and female inmates must be justified by important government objectives and must be substantially related to advancing those objectives.[65]

- *Montanye v. Haymes* (1976): The Court held there was no due process right to a hearing prior to the transfer of an inmate from one prison to another absent state law which claims otherwise.[66]
- *Greenholtz v. Inmates of the Nebraska Penal and Correctional Complex* (1979): The Court upheld Nebraska's procedures for parole hearings, including a preliminary hearing and final hearing where the inmate can call witnesses, present evidence, and be represented by private counsel.[67]
- *Viteck v. Jones* (1980): The Court held that an involuntary transfer of a prisoner to a mental hospital required a hearing that included written notice of the transfer, an adversary hearing before an independent decision maker, written findings, and effective and timely notice of these rights. In their reasoning, the Court asserted that the stigmatizing effects of transfer to a mental hospital required a due process hearing.[68]
- *Jago v. Van Curen* (1981): The Court held that revocation of a parole date prior to the release of the inmate on parole did not require a hearing.[69]
- *Hewitt v. Helms* (1983): The Court held that an informal, nonadversary evidentiary review was sufficient for the transfer of an inmate to administrative segregation (isolation) pending a complete investigation of the alleged misconduct.[70]
- *Olim v. Wakinekona* (1983): The Court held that a Hawaiian inmate was not denied due process by a transfer to an out-of-state prison without a hearing.[71]
- *United States v. Gouveia* (1984): The Court held that inmates were not constitutionally entitled to appointment of counsel while the inmates were in administrative segregation prior to initiation of adversary judicial proceedings against them.[72]
- *Superintendent v. Hill* (1985): The Court held that due process is satisfied if the record relied on by a prison disciplinary board to revoke good time credits contains some evidence that supports the decision.[73]
- *Daniels v. Williams* (1986): The Court held that negligent acts of correctional officers that lead to unintended property loss or injury do not violate the inmates' due process rights.[74]
- *Davidson v. Cannon* (1986): The Court held procedural and substantive due process rights are not violated by a lack of due care or simple negligence on the part of prison officials.[75]

Broadly speaking, inmates and other correctional clients of course retain their constitutional rights to due process, which are expressed in the Fifth and Fourteenth Amendments. But, as the list of these cases suggests, due process rights are streamlined for correctional clients and as long as correctional officials are operating in good faith according to legitimate and sensible correctional goals, there is no rights violation.

Eighth Amendment

To be a correctional client is not fun. In addition to the curtailment on one's liberty, being on probation, parole, or incarcerated carries with it several inconveniences and privations. This is particularly true for prisoners who face the frightening reality of living with some of the most violent, disturbed, and antisocial people in society. In addition, jails and prisons are very crowded, noisy, monotonous, and generally unclean. However, they cannot be such a negative environment that it violates the Eighth Amendment prohibition against cruel and unusual punishment. The standard that is used to evaluate the overall quality of a prison environment is the **totality-of-conditions test** established in ***Pugh v. Locke*** (1976). In *Pugh*, Alabama prisons were found to be so appalling and debilitating

CORRECTIONS IN THE NEWS

Are Wrongful Convictions Isolated Cases?

In 1986, a crime of rape was committed. The victim, a 13-year-old female, was sexually assaulted at knifepoint. The young victim could not identify her assailant so the defendant's chances of impeaching her testimony were very slim. There was physical evidence, but although DNA evidence was available, the court's willingness to accept and recognize this type of evidence in criminal cases was still years away. The case against the defendant was based on a confession by one of the two other men involved in the crime who implicated the defendant as his accomplice. The defendant was arrested for the crime. The only problem was—he didn't do it.

More than 220 convicted felons have been exonerated through the proper use of DNA evidence in the United States. Fifteen of these felons had been sentenced to death. The average length of time served by these former inmates was 12 years. The actual perpetrator has been identified in only 74 of the cases. Of these exonerated felons, 120 were African American, 56 were Caucasians, 19 were Latinos, and 1 was Asian American.

Problems with witnesses' testimony, problems with the investigation, and problems with the system all explain a portion of the variance in this model. There is overlap as well. Eyewitness testimony is by far the leading cause of wrongful convictions. In 77 percent of the cases, eyewitness testimony was one of the factors used to convince the jury the defendant was guilty of the crime. Sixty-five percent of the wrongful convictions can also be attributed to errors in crime lab procedures. In the worst of these cases, crime lab analysts presented false testimony regarding the results of DNA tests. But that's not all; 25 percent of these cases also involved false confessions, which ultimately led to a wrongful conviction—35 percent of this percentage involved a confession from a suspect under the age of 18 or one who was developmentally disabled. Furthermore, information obtained from jailhouse informants aided in 15 percent of the wrongful convictions.

In the event that the courts recognize the wrongful conviction and release the inmate, 21 have a compensation statute; 29 states do not. In Iowa, for example, the first consideration is whether the defendant pleaded guilty to the crime. If so, the defendant is not entitled to file a claim for compensation against the state. If the defendant pleaded not guilty, but was found guilty in a court of law the defendant is eligible for up to $50 per day of the length the time spent in prison plus any lost wages, not to exceed $25,000 per year. The defendant is also entitled to have his attorney's fees paid if the claim is made within 2 years of his release.

Sources: *The Innocence Project.* Retrieved August 29, 2008, from http://www.innocenceproject.org; Iowa Code 633A.1 (1997).

that they worked to deteriorate the health and spirit of inmates and thus reduce the likelihood of successful rehabilitation. The totality-of-conditions test is the aggregate characteristics of the facility that are used to show an Eighth Amendment violation.[76] One example of appalling prison conditions relates to health care. In ***Estelle v. Gamble*** (1976), the Court held that deliberate indifference to a prisoner's serious medical needs constituted cruel and unusual punishment. According to the Court:

> Deliberate indifference to serious medical needs of prisoners constitutes the unnecessary and wanton infliction of pain proscribed by the Eighth Amendment. This is true whether the indifference is manifested by prison doctors in their response to the prisoner's needs or by prison guards in intentionally denying or delaying access to medical care or intentionally interfering with the treatment once prescribed.[77]

The concept of deliberate indifference was modified in 1991 in the case *Wilson v. Seiter,* with the establishment of the **deliberate indifference** standard, which states that the conditions at a prison are not unconstitutional unless it can be shown that prison administrators show deliberate indifference to the quality of life in prisons and inmates' most basic needs.[78] In 1994, the deliberate indifference doctrine was broadened in the case of *Farmer v. Brennan*. In *Farmer*, the Court held that a prison official may be liable under the Eighth Amendment for denying humane conditions of confinement only if he knows that inmates face a substantial risk of serious harm, for example, because of gang animosity, and disregards that risk by failing to take reasonable measures to abate it.[79]

A careful reading of the Eighth Amendment, which states that "Excessive bail shall not be required, nor excessive fines imposed, nor cruel and unusual punishments inflicted" describes three distinct correctional domains in which correctional clients can file grievances for purportedly unconstitutional treatment. These are (1) the pretrial period while on bail, (2) the postadjudication phase resulting in any sentence where fines were imposed, and (3) the penalty phase, especially confinement and capital punishment. Overwhelmingly, case law pertaining to the Eighth Amendment has centered on capital punishment. The remaining part of the chapter reviews the case law related to the Eighth Amendment and the various doctrines that evolved from it.

Capital Punishment

Without question, capital punishment, commonly known as the death penalty, has received the most attention from appellate courts regarding the proscription of cruel and unusual punishment. Evaluations of capital punishment have followed the "evolving standards of decency that mark the progress of a maturing society," an idea established in ***Trop v. Dulles*** in 1958. In *Trop*, the Court held that the penalty of loss of nationality for the crime of desertion was overly severe and thus violated the cruel and unusual punishment clause of the Eighth Amendment.[80]

During the 1960s, there was growing sentiment in the United States that capital punishment itself was cruel and unusual. As such, executions plummeted from earlier decades when states routinely executed more than 150 inmates annually. For instance, only three persons were executed in 1966 and 1967, and from 1968 to 1976 there was a de facto moratorium on the death penalty. From 1972 to 1976, the death penalty was officially held to be unconstitutional. In three cases (*Furman v. Georgia*, *Jackson v. Georgia*, and *Branch v. Texas*), collectively known as the *Furman* decision, the Supreme Court, in a 5–4 decision, held that the manner in which the death penalty was imposed and carried out under the laws of Georgia and Texas (famously described as arbitrary and capricious) was cruel and unusual and overall in violation of the Eighth and Fourteenth Amendments.[81–83] The ruling in ***Furman v. Georgia*** (1972) voided death penalty statutes nationwide and commuted the sentences of more than 600 death row inmates.

No sooner was capital punishment declared unconstitutional than legislatures enacted new death penalty statutes that addressed the Court's concern about the arbitrary and capricious application of the sanction. New death penalty statutes essentially describe the conditions under which a homicide is escalated into a capital crime. Two types of circumstances are considered: aggravating and mitigating circumstances. **Aggravating circumstances**, such as murder of more than one person or murder in conjunction with serious felonies like kidnapping and rape, are characteristics that make the crime seem worse in totality and thus deserving of death as the only appropriate punishment. **Mitigating circumstances**, such as youth, mental retardation, or the defendant's prior abuse and victimization history, seem to render a crime less serious and provide context that appears to reduce the overall viciousness of the behavior.

Aggravating and mitigating circumstances resuscitated the death penalty after its ban from 1972 to 1976 because they allowed states to use discretion by providing sentencing guidelines for the judge and jury when deciding whether to impose death. These guided discretion statutes were approved by the Supreme Court in five cases (***Gregg v. Georgia***, *Jurek v. Texas*, *Roberts v. Louisiana*, *Woodson v. North Carolina*, and *Proffitt v. Florida*) collectively referred to as the *Gregg* decision. This landmark decision held that the new death penalty statutes in Florida, Georgia, and Texas were constitutional, and that the death penalty itself was constitutional under the Eighth Amendment.

The *Gregg* decision resulted in the following three procedural reforms:

1. **Bifurcated trials,** in which there are separate deliberations for the guilt and penalty phases of the trial. Only after the jury has determined that the defendant is guilty of capital murder does it decide in a second trial whether the defendant should be sentenced to death or given a lesser sentence of prison time.
2. **Automatic appellate review** of convictions and sentence.
3. **Proportionality review,** which helps the state to identify and eliminate sentencing disparities by comparing the sentence in the case with other cases within the state.[84–88]

Since the landmark *Furman* and *Gregg* decisions, there have been several other important rulings on the death penalty, including three categorical exemptions, for the insane, mentally retarded, and juveniles. In ***Ford v. Wainwright*** (1986), the Court held that the Eighth Amendment prohibits a state from carrying out a sentence of death upon a prisoner who is insane.[89] In ***Atkins v. Virginia*** (2002), the Court held that the execution of the mentally retarded was cruel and unusual punishment according to the evolving standards of decency developed in *Trop*.[90] In *Atkins*, the Court drew heavily on international perspectives from the European Union to inform its decision, a rationale that drew sharp dissents from the conservative members of the court. Interestingly, the *Atkins* decision overturned the Court's decision in *Penry v. Lynaugh* (1989), which had upheld the execution of mentally retarded persons because of the absence of a national consensus or evolving standard against it.[91]

In 2005, the Court held in ***Roper v. Simmons*** that it is unconstitutional to impose the death penalty on offenders younger than 18 at the time of their capital crimes. The case centered on Christopher Simmons, who at 17 plotted and executed the crimes of burglary, abduction, and murder.[92] The Roper decision represented the culmination of a legal struggle about the appropriate minimum age for capital punishment eligibility. For example, in *Thompson v. Oklahoma* (1988), the Court held that the execution of persons under the age of 16 at the time of their crimes was cruel and unusual.[93] Just 1 year later in *Stanford v. Kentucky*, the Court held that for 16- and 17-year-olds, there is no national consensus suggesting that their execution would be cruel and unusual.[94]

The Supreme Court's rationale used in the *Atkins* and *Roper* decisions is controversial. Wayne Myers suggests that both decisions dealt with the issue of cognitive ability, intellectual development and decision making, and maturity. It is believed that mentally retarded and adolescent defendants are lacking or are so diminished in these skills that their ability to appreciate the wrongfulness of their conduct is compromised. Furthermore, in both cases, the Court used the evolving standards of decency logic to categorically bar entire groups from capital punishment. Myers argues this is a mistake because the Court is imposing a worldview or set of beliefs about when the death penalty is appropriate or lawful. This task, according to Myers, should be left to individual state courts.[95]

Conditions of Confinement

There have been assorted claims that various aspects of the correctional system are themselves examples of cruel and unusual punishment. For instance, Faith Lutze and David Brody suggested that the verbal abuse and harsh discipline used in boot camps could be characterized as cruel and unusual and could give rise to prisoner lawsuits.[96] Dwight Aarons examined whether the inordinate delays that condemned offenders serve on death row, in other words, the waiting, is itself cruel and unusual punishment.[97] Mostly, however, concerns about cruel and unusual punishment pertain to the conditions that exist in the nation's jails and prisons. One of the first cases that addressed the conditions of correctional facilities is *Wright v. McMann* (1967), which brought the appalling, inhumane, and barbaric nature of some correctional environments to the courts' attention and determined that debasing, uncivilized, and inhumane conditions violated the cruel and unusual punishment clause of the Eighth Amendment.[98]

In 1979, the Supreme Court visited the conditions of confinement, specifically crowding, in the case of *Bell v. Wolfish*. In *Bell*, the Court held that double bunking (placing two inmates in a single occupancy cell) of pretrial inmates did not violate their rights because their confinement was not technically punishment (since they were pretrial) but instead the incidental consequences of their legal status. Also, the Court also held that cell searches and visual body cavity searches after visits and without probable cause was allowed.[99]

The constitutionality of double bunking (and from the inmate's perspective, the constitutionality of crowding) was affirmed in ***Rhodes v. Chapman*** (1981). In *Rhodes*, the Court held that double celling at a prison does not constitute cruel and unusual punishment where there is no evidence that the conditions in question inflict unnecessary or wanton pain, or are disproportionate to the severity of crimes warranting imprisonment.[100] The *Rhodes* decision established a general good faith doctrine whereby correctional officials were authorized to enforce policies that nevertheless seemed cruel and unusual from the inmates' viewpoint as long as they were not gratuitously violating common sense standards of decency. This good faith doctrine can apply to cases where correctional officers assault and *even shoot* inmates. In *Whitley v. Albers* (1986), the Court held that where a prison security measure that indisputably poses significant risks to the safety of inmates (in this case, an inmate was shot during a disturbance), the inquiry must focus on whether the actions were taken in a good faith effort to maintain or restore discipline or maliciously and sadistically for the purpose of causing harm.[101] The same standard applies to the use of physical force against inmates; staff cannot maliciously assault inmates but can use physical force to maintain discipline (*Hudson v. McMillian* [1992]).[102]

Habitual Offender Statutes

Another important Eighth Amendment issue focuses on laws designed to control habitual or career criminals. Alternating and at times inconsistent decisions have been established about the constitutionality of punishing chronic criminal offenders with habitual offender laws that require increased sentencing, often life imprisonment. The spirit of these laws is to inflict a lifetime achievement penalty for criminals who simply refuse to desist from crime. The letter of the law is more problematic because they result in severe sentences that often exceed the legal seriousness of the instant offense, or the most recent crime for which the offender was arrested and convicted. Jurists have declared that life sentences constitute cruel and unusual punishment if the instant offense was relatively benign regardless of the severity of the defendant's prior criminal history.

The landmark case that addressed the constitutionality of habitual offender laws was ***Weems v. United States*** (1910). In *Weems*, the Court decided that criminal punishments must be graduated, proportionate, or commensurate to the seriousness of the underlying crime. The defendant in that case, William Weems, was sentenced to 15 years of hard labor and an assortment of other penalties for falsifying public documents—hardly a grievous offense.[103] Just 2 years later, the United States Supreme Court reviewed its first habitual offender law in *Graham v. West Virginia* (1912). The Court decided that a life sentence for a repeat property offender (e.g., burglary and grand theft) neither violated double jeopardy provisions in the Fifth Amendment nor constituted cruel and unusual punishment in violation of the Eighth Amendment.[104]

Habitual offender statutes did not appear on the state-level radar screen until the 1960s. The proportionality issue for habitual offender statues was applied to the states in *Robinson v. California* in 1962.[105] In the decades since, the judiciary has been unable to reach consensus on the legality of statutes that seek to severely punish recidivists. At issue was the fairness of administering a life sentence for minor felonies regardless of the defendant's record of recurrent convictions and incarceration. For instance, in *Rummel v. Estelle* (1980), the Court affirmed the constitutionality of a Texas law that imposed life imprisonment for defendants with three prior felony convictions. The defendant in the case had been convicted of three forgery/fraud cases that yielded meager financial gains between $25 and $125. Nevertheless, the life sentence was imposed.[106]

In *Hutto v. Davis* (1982), the Court explored additional issues in the aggravated sentencing of criminal offenders. First, they held that two consecutive 20-year prison terms and two fines of $10,000 upon conviction for the distribution of 9 ounces of marijuana did not violate the cruel and unusual punishment clause. Moreover, the Court refused to note sentencing disparities for like crimes in the same state and other states.[107] This changed a year later in *Solem v. Helm* (1983), when, in a 5–4 decision, the Supreme Court held that a life imprisonment without parole sentence given under a habitual offender law for a person convicted of check fraud for less than $100 was unconstitutional. The defendant who had seven previous nonviolent felony convictions was, in the view of the justices, treated more harshly than his in-state criminal peers who had committed more serious offenses. Also, the Court ruled that this sentence was harsher than other sentences imposed for similar crimes in other states.[108] In *Harmelin v. Michigan* (1991) the Court ruled, again in a narrow 5–4 opinion, that the Eighth Amendment *was not* violated in a noncapital case that result in a life in prison without parole sentence. The defendant was convicted of possessing 672 grams or 24 ounces of cocaine in Michigan, where possession of more than 650 grams warranted life in prison without parole.[109] In 2003, the Supreme Court reviewed two cases originating in California (*Ewing v. California* and *Lockyer v. Andrade*), where 25-years-to-life sentences were administered to chronic offenders whose instant offenses were nominal thefts. The Court affirmed the constitutionality of the sentences acknowledging that although the sentences were long, so were the criminal records of these recidivists.[110–111]

WRAP UP

CASE STUDY CONCLUSION

Federal law enforcement referred all evidence collected to local authorities and the evidence was brought to the court's attention; however, the local prosecutor had little interest in pursuing the case and a justice of the peace moved to dismiss the case without the evidence ever making it to a grand jury. As a result, other than James Seale, those involved in this incident were never tried for their crimes. The other Klansmen have since died. Had they been charged, prosecuted, and acquitted previously, Seale could not have been tried and convicted some 43 years later.

Federal law enforcement has jurisdictional restrictions and limitations. However, in this case, those limitations were removed when, after allegedly abducting the two young men, the accused drove across state lines and ultimately committed the crime in a national forest. According to FBI records from 1964, after beating the men and extracting information about the location of a stockpile of firearms, other Klansmen disposed of the two nearly dead men, dumping them in the Ole River near Tallulah, Louisiana.

Sometimes prosecutors make deals. In this case, prosecutors used the testimony of Charles Marcus Edwards, a former Klansman, to convict Seale. Edwards agreed to testify, but his agreement was based on a promise of immunity. According to Edwards, both young men were placed in the trunk of Seale's Volkswagen and transported to a nearby farm. Eventually, both men were driven across the Mississippi state line into Louisiana. Edwards also informed the court that Seale had told him the bodies had been tied to heavy weights and thrown into the river. Edwards claims that both men were alive when he left them.

Sources: PR Newswire. (n.d.). *Former Klansman, James Ford Seale found guilty for role in 1964 kidnapping and murder of two African-American men.* Retrieved June 17, 2007, from http://www.prnewswire.com/cgi-bin/stories.pl?ACCT=104&STORY=/www/story/06-14-2007/0004608813&EDATE; Associated Press. (2007). *Reputed Klansman convicted in 1964 deaths.* Retrieved June 14, 2007, from http://www.msnbc.msn.com/id/19234202/print/1/displaymode.1098/.

Chapter Summary

- Access to the courts is guaranteed in the United States Constitution and habeas corpus is a hallmark of American law.
- Although inmates are protected by the First Amendment, their speech and association rights are limited.
- Inmates have no constitutional right to privacy while incarcerated and correctional authorities may search their cells, inspect their mail, and record their visitation conversations.
- The due process doctrine in the Fifth and Fourteenth Amendments applies to correctional procedures such as parole board hearing and disciplinary proceedings.
- Capital punishment was unconstitutional between 1972 and 1976 but is constitutionally permitted today because of the use of aggravating and mitigating circumstances.
- The conditions of jails and prisons and habitual offender statutes have been cited as potential violations of prohibition of cruel and unusual punishment.

Key Terms

aggravating circumstances Characteristics that make the crime seem worse in totality and thus deserving of death as only appropriate punishment.

Atkins v. Virginia Supreme Court case that held that executing mentally retarded persons *did* constitute cruel and unusual punishment and was a violation of the Eighth Amendment, consistent with the evolving standards of decency.

automatic appellate review Automatic review of death sentences established by *Gregg v. Georgia.*

balancing test Prisoners retain their First Amendment rights while incarcerated unless those rights are inconsistent with their status as prisoner or inconsistent with the legitimate penological goals of the institution.

bifurcated trials Trials in which there are separate deliberations for the guilt and penalty phases of the trial.

Bill of Rights The first 10 amendments to the United States Constitution.

contraband Materials prohibited in correctional facilities, such as drugs and weapons.

Cooper v. Pate Case that resulted in a ruling that inmates were permitted to practice their religion provided that the following three basic conditions were met: (1) the religion must be an established religion (not contrived by the inmate); (2) the inmate's religious practices must conform to the tenets of the religion; and (3) the religious practices cannot pose a security risk or disrupt prison operations.

deliberate indifference Standard that affirms that the conditions at a prison are not unconstitutional unless it can be shown that prison administrators show deliberate indifference to the quality of life in prisons and inmates' most basic needs.

due process Laws and criminal procedures that are reasonable and applied in a fair and equal manner.

Eighth Amendment Amendment to the Bill of Rights of the United States Constitution that states that "excessive bail shall not be required, nor excessive fines imposed, nor cruel and unusual punishments inflicted."

Estelle v. Gamble Case in which the Court held that deliberate indifference to a prisoner's serious medical needs constituted cruel and unusual punishment.

Ex parte Hull Case that loosened the hands-off doctrine that characterized American corrections.

Fifth Amendment Constitutional amendment that states that no person shall be held to answer for a capital, or otherwise infamous crime, unless on a presentment or indictment of a grand jury, except in cases arising in the land or naval forces, or in the militia, when in actual service in time of war or public danger; nor shall any person be subject for the same offense to be twice put in jeopardy of life or limb; nor shall be compelled in any criminal case to be a witness against himself, nor be deprived of life, liberty, or property, without due process of law; nor shall private property be taken for public use, without just compensation.

First Amendment Constitutional amendment that states that Congress shall make no law respecting an establishment of religion, or prohibiting the free exercise thereof; or abridging the freedom of speech, or of the press; or the right of the people peaceably to assemble, and to petition the government for a redress of grievances.

Ford v. Wainwright Case that ruled that the Eighth Amendment prohibits a state from carrying out a sentence of death upon a prisoner who is insane.

Fourteenth Amendment Constitutional amendment that states in Section 1: All persons born or naturalized in the United States, and subject to the jurisdiction thereof, are citizens of the United States and of the state wherein they reside. No state shall make or enforce any law which shall abridge the privileges or immunities of citizens of the United States; nor shall any state deprive any person of life, liberty, or property, without due process of law; nor deny to any person within its jurisdiction the equal protection of the laws.

Fourth Amendment Constitutional amendment that states that the right of the people to be secure in their persons, houses, papers, and effects, against unreasonable searches and seizures, shall not be violated, and no warrants shall issue, but upon probable cause, supported by oath or affirmation, and particularly describing the place to be searched, and the persons or things to be seized.

Furman v. Georgia Supreme Court case that established that capital punishment is cruel and unusual and violates the Eighth Amendment.

Gregg v. Georgia Supreme Court case that held that the new death penalty statutes in Florida, Georgia, and Texas were constitutional, and that the death penalty itself was constitutional under the Eighth Amendment.

habeas corpus The legal doctrine that grants correctional clients access to the courts to challenge the legality of their sentences.

Hudson v. Palmer Court case in which the Court ruled that inmates do not have a reasonable expectation of privacy.

Johnson v. Avery Court case in which the Court ruled that access to courts to present legal complaints cannot be denied or obstructed.

Lewis v. Casey Court case in which the Court ruled that prisoners who claim that they have been denied access to the courts and that the prisons failed to comply with *Bounds v. Smith* must show that their rights were prejudiced as a result of the denial of these rights in order to recover in a Section 1983 suit.

mitigating circumstances Characteristics such as youth, mental retardation, or victimization that render a crime less serious or add context that seems to reduce the overall viciousness of the behavior.

Pell v. Procunier Case that established the balancing test.

precedent A decision by the appellate court (usually the Supreme Court) that serves to guide all future legal decisions that encompass a similar topic.

Procunier v. Martinez Case whose ruling set the precedent that mail correspondence between inmates and outside parties was speech protected by the First Amendment.

proportionality review Judicial review of criminal sentences which helps the state to identify and eliminate sentencing disparities by comparing the sentence in the case with other cases within the state.

Pugh v. Locke Case that established the totality-of-conditions test.

Rhodes v. Chapman Case that resulted in a ruling that double celling at a prison does not constitute cruel and unusual punishment where there is no evidence that the conditions in question inflict unnecessary or wanton pain, or are disproportionate to the severity of crimes warranting imprisonment.

Roper v. Simmons Case in which the Supreme Court ruled that it is unconstitutional to impose the death penalty on offenders younger than 18 at the time of their capital crimes.

Section 1983 Part of the United States Code that covers inmate allegations and petitions for money damages or injunctive relief from their sentence.

totality-of-conditions test The standard that is used to evaluate the overall quality of a prison environment.

Trop v. Dulles Established the evolving standards of decency doctrine.

Weems v. United States Case that established that criminal punishments must be graduated, proportionate, or commensurate to the seriousness of the underlying crime.

Wolff v. McDonnell Case in which the ruling specified the due process guidelines for major prison disciplinary proceedings.

writ of mandamus Extraordinary remedies used when the plaintiff has no other way to access the courts for relief and he or she seeks to compel a governmental duty.

Critical Thinking Questions

1. How does the meaning of intelligence as measured by IQ change depending on the legal status of the offender? If the mentally retarded are exempt from capital punishment, should they then be exempt from any punishment?
2. Did the Supreme Court rule correctly in *Roper v. Simmons*? Are adolescents different in terms of their decision making and thus not as legally responsible for their conduct as adults?
3. What are the characteristics of judges who are nominated to be Supreme Court Justices from both liberal and conservative perspectives? Are there commonalities between liberal and conservative perspectives?
4. Which aggravating factors are most effective at making a criminal event appear much worse?
5. Which mitigating factors are most effective at making a criminal event appear less serious?

Notes

1. *Trop v. Dulles,* 356 U.S. 86 (1958).
2. *Gregg v. Georgia*, 428 U.S. 153 (1976).
3. *Lewis v. Casey*, 518 U.S. 343 (1996).
4. Rubin, S. (1971). Loss and curtailment of rights. In L. Radzinowicz & M. E. Wolfgang (Eds.), *Crime and justice Volume III: The criminal in confinement* (pp. 25–40). New York: Basic Books.
5. *Hudson v. Palmer*, 468 U.S. 517 (1984).
6. Roberts, J. (2008). *Opinion* in Baze et al. v. Rees, Commissioner, Kentucky Department of Corrections et al. Retrieved June 1, 2008, from http://www.scotusblog.com/wp/wp-content/uploads/2008/04/07-5439.pdf.
7. Cornell University Law School, Legal Information Institute. (n.d.). *United States Constitution*, Retrieved July 3, 2007, from http://www.law.cornell.edu/constitution/constitution.table.html#amendments.
8. Cripe, C. A., & Pearlman, M. G. (2005). *Legal aspects of corrections management.* Sudbury, MA: Jones & Bartlett.
9. Scalia, J. (2002). *Prisoner petitions filed in U.S. district courts, 2000, with trends 1980–2000.* Washington, DC: U.S. Department of Justice, Office of Justice Programs, Bureau of Justice Statistics.

10. Hammel, A. (2002). Diabolical federalism: A functional critique and proposed reconstruction of death penalty federal habeas. *American Criminal Law Review, 39*, 1–99.
11. Antiterrorism and Effective Death Penalty Act 28 U.S.C. §§ 2241–2255.
12. Cripe & Pearlman.
13. Scalia.
14. *Civil Rights Act of 1871*, 42 U.S.C. § 1983.
15. *Bivens v. Six Unknown Agents of the Federal Bureau of Narcotics*, 403 U.S. 388 (1971).
16. *Civil Rights of Institutionalized Persons Act of 1980*, 42 U.S.C. § 1997e.
17. *Prison Litigation Reform Act of 1996*, Pub. L. No. 104-134; H.R. 3019, 104th Cong. (1996).
18. Scalia.
19. *Ex parte Hull*, 312 U.S. 546 (1941).
20. *Smith v. Bennett*, 365 U.S. 708 (1961).
21. *Long v. District Court*, 385 U.S. 192 (1966).
22. *Johnson v. Avery*, 393 U.S. 483 (1969).
23. *Bounds v. Smith*, 430 U.S. 817 (1977).
24. *Lewis v. Casey*, 518 U.S. 343 (1996).
25. *Turner v. Safley*, 482 U.S. 78 (1987).
26. *Thornburgh v. Abbot*, 490 U.S. 401 (1989).
27. *Pell v. Procunier*, 417 U.S. 817 (1974).
28. Associated Press. (2007). *Jail chaplain suspended for anti-Islam books.* Retrieved April 13, 2007, from http://www.msnbc.msn.com/id/18094396/.
29. *Cooper v. Pate*, 378 U.S. 546 (1964).
30. Religious Freedom Restoration Act of 1993 (42 U.S.C. § 2000bb).
31. Religious Land Use and Institutionalized Persons Act of 2000 (42 U.S.C. § 2000cc).
32. *Cruz v. Beto*, 405 U.S. 319 (1972).
33. *Theriault v. Carlson*, 339 F.Supp. 375 (1973) and 495 F.2d 390 (1974); *Theriault v. Silber*, 391 F.Supp 578 (1975).
34. *McCorkle v. Johnson*, 881 F.2d 993 (11th Cir. 1989).
35. *O'Lone v. Shabazz*, 482 U.S. 342 (1987).
36. *Hamilton v. Schriro*, 74 F.3d 1545 (8th Cir. 1996).
37. *Walker v. Blackwell*, 411 F.2d 23 (1969).
38. *Kahane v. Carlson*, 527 F.2d 492 (2nd Cir. 1975).
39. *Jackson v. Mann*, 196 F.3d 316 (2nd Cir. 1999).
40. *Procunier v. Martinez*, 416 U.S. 396 (1974).
41. McCullagh, D. (2007). *Police blotter: Prison inmate wants personal ad replies.* Retrieved July 10, 2007, from http://news.com.com/2102-1030_3-6134417.html.
42. *Turner v. Safley*, 482 U.S. 78 (1987).
43. *Thornburgh v. Abbot*, 490 U.S. 401 (1989).
44. *Bell v. Wolfish*, 441 U.S. 520 (1979).
45. *Jones v. North Carolina Prisoners' Labor Union, Inc.*, 433 U.S. 119 (1977).
46. *Pell v. Procunier*, 417 U.S. 817 (1974).
47. *Block v. Rutherford*, 468 U.S. 576 (1984).

48. *Overton v. Bazzetta*, 539 U.S. 126 (2003).
49. *Kentucky Department of Corrections v. Thompson*, 490 U.S. 454 (1989).
50. Associated Press. (2007). *Calif. gay, lesbian inmates get conjugal visits.* Retrieved June 4, 2007, from http://www.msnbc.msn.com/id/18994457/.
51. *Lyons v. Gilligan*, 382 F.Supp 198 (Northern District of Ohio, 1974).
52. *Mary of Oak Knoll v. Coughlin*, 475 NYS 2d 644 (N.Y. Appeals Division, 1984).
53. *Hudson v. Palmer*, 468 U.S. 517 (1984).
54. *Bell v. Wolfish*, 441 U.S. 520 (1979).
55. *Lanza v. New York*, 370 U.S. 139 (1962).
56. *United States v. Hearst*, 435 U.S. 1000 (1978).
57. Hoffman, H. C., Dickinson, G. E., & Dunn, C. L. (2007). Communication policy changes in state adult correctional facilities from 1971 to 2005. *Criminal Justice Review, 32*, 47–64.
58. Rush, G. E. (2000). *The dictionary of criminal justice* (5th ed.). New York: McGraw-Hill.
59. *Wolff v. McDonnell*, 418 U.S. 539 (1974).
60. *Baxter v. Palmigiano*, 425 U.S. 308 (1976).
61. *Morrissey v. Brewer*, 408 U.S. 471 (1972).
62. *Gagnon v. Scarpelli*, 411 U.S. 778 (1973).
63. *Estelle v. Dorrough*, 420 U.S. 534 (1975).
64. *Meachum v. Fano*, 427 U.S. 215 (1976).
65. *Craig v. Boren*, 429 U.S. 190 (1976).
66. *Montanye v. Haymes*, 427 U.S. 236 (1976).
67. *Greenholtz v. Inmates of the Nebraska Penal and Correctional Complex*, 442 U.S. 1 (1979).
68. *Viteck v. Jones*, 445 U.S. 480 (1980).
69. *Jago v. Van Curen*, 454 U.S. 14 (1981).
70. *Hewitt v. Helms*, 459 U.S. 460 (1983).
71. *Olim v. Wakinekona*, 461 U.S. 238 (1983).
72. *United States v. Gouveia*, 467 U.S. 180 (1984).
73. *Superintendent v. Hill*, 472 U.S. 445 (1985).
74. *Daniels v. Williams*, 474 U.S. 327 (1986).
75. *Davidson v. Cannon*, 474 U.S. 344 (1986).
76. *Pugh v. Locke*, 406 F.2d 318 (1976).
77. *Estelle v. Gamble*, 429 U.S. 97 (1976).
78. *Wilson v. Seiter*, 111 S.Ct. 2321 (1991).
79. *Farmer v. Brennan*, 511 U.S. 825 (1994).
80. *Trop v. Dulles*, 356 U.S. 86 (1958).
81. *Furman v. Georgia*, 408 U. S. 238, (1972).
82. *Branch v. Texas*, 408 U. S. 238 (1972).
83. *Jackson v. Georgia*, 408 U. S. 238 (1972).
84. *Gregg v. Georgia*, 428 U. S. 153, (1976).
85. *Jurek v. Texas*, 428 U. S. 262 (1976).
86. *Roberts v. Louisiana*, 428 U. S. 325 (1976).

87. *Proffitt v. Florida*, 428 U. S. 242 (1976).
88. *Woodson v. North Carolina*, 428 U. S. 280 (1976).
89. *Ford v. Wainwright*, 477 U.S. 399 (1986).
90. *Atkins v. Virginia*, 536 U.S. 304 (2002).
91. *Penry v. Lynaugh*, 492 U.S. 302 (1989).
92. *Roper v. Simmons*, 543 U.S. 551 (2005).
93. *Thompson v. Oklahoma*, 487 U.S. 815 (1988).
94. *Stanford v. Kentucky*, 492 U.S. 361 (1989).
95. Myers, W. (2006). *Roper v. Simmons*: The collision of national consensus and proportionality review. *Journal of Criminal Law and Criminology, 96*, 947–994.
96. Lutze, F. E., & Brody, D. C. (1999). Mental abuse as cruel and unusual punishment: Do boot camp prisons violate the Eighth Amendment? *Crime & Delinquency, 45*, 242–255.
97. Aarons, D. (1998). Can inordinate delay between a death sentence and execution constitute cruel and unusual punishment? *Seton Hall Law Review, 29*, 147–207.
98. *Wright v. McMann*, 387 F.2d 519 (2d Cir. 1967).
99. *Bell v. Wolfish*, 441 U.S. 520 (1979).
100. *Rhodes v. Chapman*, 452 U.S. 337 (1981).
101. *Whitley v. Albers*, 475 U.S. 312 (1986).
102. *Hudson v. McMillian*, 503 U.S. 1 (1992).
103. *Weems v. United States*, 217 U.S. 349 (1910).
104. *Graham v. West Virginia*, 224 U.S. 616 (1912). Also see *O'Neil v. Vermont*, 144 U.S. 323 (1892) and *Howard v. Fleming*, 191 U.S. 126 (1903).
105. *Robinson v. California*, 370 U.S. 660 (1962).
106. *Rummel v. Estelle*, 445 U.S. 263 (1980).
107. *Hutto v. Davis*, 454 U.S. 370 (1982).
108. *Solem v. Helm*, 463 U.S. 277 (1983).
109. *Harmelin v. Michigan*, 501 U.S. 957 (1991).
110. *Ewing v. California*, 528 U.S. 11 (2003).
111. *Lockyer v. Andrade*, 538 U.S. 63 (2003).

PART II

Corrections: The Management of Offender Risk

CHAPTER

4

Sentencing and Offender Classification

"Specialty courts are an innovative and therapeutic way to handle people who do not fit into the traditional and inflexible criminal justice model."[1, p. 348]

OBJECTIVES

- Understand criminal sentencing and the factors that inform it.
- Identify the presentence investigation (PSI) report and its uses by the criminal justice system.
- Follow changing philosophies of sentencing, trends in sentencing, and the role of the United States Sentencing Commission in sentencing policy.
- Learn the functions of specialized/problem-solving courts, such as drug courts, DWI courts, family courts, mental health courts, and community courts.
- Recognize the factors that are used to classify inmate populations.
- Assess the risk factors that contribute to inmate misconduct and violence.

CASE STUDY

The saga of Salvatore "Sammy the Bull" Gravano is one of the most fascinating and troubling instances of the philosophy and practice of criminal sentencing. Gravano was a lifelong delinquent and criminal offender who worked his way into the Colombo crime family in the New York City area. Gravano gained a reputation for his loyalty and willingness to use violence to resolve organized crime disputes, and in the mid-1970s he joined the Gambino crime family and worked as a murder-for-hire hit man. Gravano later said this about his occupation:

> Am I supposed to feel remorse? Aren't I supposed to feel something? But I felt nothing, at least nothing like remorse. If anything, I felt good. Like high. Like powerful, maybe even superhuman. It's not that I was happy or proud of myself. Not that. I'm still not happy about that feeling. It's just that killing came so easy to me.[6, p. 75]

In December 1990, Gravano was arrested along with several others, including John Gotti, the leader of the Gambino crime family. In the course of his pretrial detention, Gravano heard recordings of Gotti talking negatively about Gravano behind his back. Infuriated and feeling betrayed, Gravano agreed to testify against Gotti in exchange for full immunity. Prosecutors offered partial immunity, and Gravano confessed to 19 murders, conspiracy to murder, and multiple counts of illegal gambling, loan-sharking, and obstruction of justice. He also debriefed United States attorneys, the FBI, and other law enforcement agencies, testified in 10 separate criminal proceedings, delivered testimony to Senate subcommittees on crime, and helped to convict 40 members of the Mafia, many of them senior associates of organized crime. As a result of his plea agreement with prosecutors, Gravano was sentenced to 5 years in prison followed by 3 years of supervised release, and assessed a $50 court fine. He received sentence credit time for nearly 4 years already served in jail during the trial of John Gotti. Gravano was provided another identity and placed in the federal Witness Protection program. He reappeared in 2001 when he was arrested for operating the largest ecstasy narcotics ring in Arizona history. In 2002, he was sentenced to 20 years in federal prison for drug trafficking. Also in 2002, he was sentenced to 19 years in state court; the sentences are served concurrently.[7]

1. Why was Gravano's original plea deal so lenient?
2. Why was Gravano's subsequent drug sentence so harsh?

"Desert could be seen as the distribution of liability and punishment that follows the community's shared principles of justice—the moral intuitions of the people whom the law governs."[2, p. 19]

Sentencing

A criminal **sentence** is the penalty imposed by a court on a person convicted of a crime. There is great variation in criminal sentencing, which reflects the variation in the seriousness of criminal conduct and the extensiveness of the defendant's prior criminal record. Indeed, **offense seriousness** and defendant's **criminal history** are the two strongest determinants of sentencing outcome and severity. A criminal sentence denotes two concepts: (1) the type of sentence that the defendant must serve, such as death, prison, jail, probation, deferred sentence, etc.; and (2) the amount of time to be served, such as life imprisonment, 25 years, 5 years, 6 months, or 1 week. The longest prison sentence ever imposed is believed to be the 10,000-year sentence given to Dudley Kyzer on December 4, 1981, in Tuscaloosa, Alabama, upon conviction for three murders. The longest time served was by Paul Geidel, who was convicted of second-degree murder on September 5, 1911, and was ultimately released from prison on May 7, 1980, at age 85. The total time that Geidel served in prison was 68 years, 8 months, and 2 days.[8] Sentences usually contain a variety of **conditions**, which are the terms that the defendant must abide by to remain in compliance with the court. Typical conditions of criminal sentences include monitored sobriety via drug testing or urinalysis, no contact with the victim or witnesses to the crimes, community service, psychiatric counseling, and others.

CORRECTIONS RESEARCH

The Effect of Tougher Prison Conditions on Recidivism: Fact or Fantasy?

If you can't do the time, don't do the crime! Prisoners are released from correctional institutions in this country to the tune of nearly 600,000 persons each year. Nearly two thirds of them commit other crimes and are rearrested within 3 years of their release. Obviously, something is not working! What if prison conditions were harsher—would inmates released from prison consider the harshness of the living conditions in a state or federal prison prior to committing their next felony? If you are a proponent of specific deterrence, then your answer would be, yes—assuming of course, convicts learn from their mistakes. On the other hand, harsher conditions could cause violent retaliatory responses by the inmates and result in an eventual increase in postrelease crimes.

In the federal prison system, inmates are housed using a federal inmate classification system based on an inmate load and security designation form. The information obtained through the use of this form and the security level score based on crimes committed, the prison sentence, and the court's recommendations determine a security level that reflects the inmate's anticipated need for supervision. A higher score predicts that prisoner misconduct is likely and results in an inmate being assigned to a more secure cell block. This means that as the level of security increases, so do the restrictions on individual freedom, interaction with other inmates and staff, and personal autonomy. It also means less contact with family and/or the community.

Let's not forget to also consider that higher levels of security mean the inmate will be cohabitating with a peer group that is likely to be more dangerous as well. This means prison life under harsher conditions could very well be responsible for increasing an inmate's taste for violence, which could influence postrelease behaviors. These conditions are also likely to foster new interpersonal relationships and affiliations—both of which may induce aberrant behavioral responses by the prisoner during his stay in prison and also after his release.

For the most part, prison conditions are compliant with the demands of state and federal policy makers. Lessening existing security conditions within the prison may put others within the institution, both staff and inmates, at risk. Conversely, strict security arrangements for high-risk prisoners do decrease prison misconduct.

Source: Chen, M. K., & Shapiro, J. M. (2006). *Do harsher prison conditions reduce recidivism? A discontinuity-based approach*. Retrieved September 15, 2008, from http://sentencing.nj.gov/downloads/pdf/articles/2007/Jan2007/document08.pdf.

"Actuarial assessment methods base objective risk predictions in the observed outcome behavior of those previously assessed, whereas clinical methods rely on subjective decisions informed by the education, training, and experience of the decision maker."[3, p. 524]

Implicit in the criminal sentence is some combination of punishment philosophies, such as rehabilitation, retribution, deterrence, or incapacitation. Again, punishment philosophies are geared toward the seriousness of the criminal conduct and the seriousness of the offender's criminal past. First-time offenders are viewed as less deserving of harsh punishment than habitual criminals. Persons convicted of violent felonies deserve more severe sentences than persons convicted of traffic or more trivial misdemeanor offenses. Throughout American sentencing history, a variety of approaches to sentencing have been used to accommodate different punishment philosophies. An indeterminate sentence indicates a range of time between the minimum date of parole eligibility and a latest discharge date from prison. A completely indeterminate sentence has a minimum of 1 day and a maximum of natural life. The rationale for such indeterminacy was to

CORRECTIONS FOCUS

I Need a Job!

Imagine how difficult it must be to return to society, the community, the neighborhood, and your family after serving time for a felony conviction. Add to this a lack of job skills, poor employment history, a violent past, and you have a scenario facing many former inmates. So why is their employment, or lack thereof, such an issue? Unemployment has been consistently shown to increase the likelihood of recidivism among ex-offenders. After all, career criminals are responsible for a disproportionate amount of serious crime, so why not give them something else to do?

The Center for Employment Opportunities (CEO) in New York City believes it has a solution to this problem. This program prepares ex-offenders for locating employment opportunities but it goes even further by training these men and women how to keep their jobs. The program begins by establishing a set of enforced rules. Learning to follow these rules develops, for the ex-offender, a heightened sense of self-discipline and esteem. Learning to abide by rules is analogous to working within the context of a company's policy and procedure manual.

The CEO provides a variety of training to ex-offenders ranging from job readiness to life skills to courses that prepare the ex-offender for the job interview. Learning how to talk with a prospective employer about a criminal past is one of the skills stressed in this training. CEO serves both the potential employee as well as small business owners. Most small businesses do not have a human resources department responsible for screening and hiring applicants. CEO does this—and at no cost to the employer. Employers also benefit from the program in that CEO pays employers to train these new employees. CEO and the parole board also monitor the ex-offender's performance. CEO does the job search, the initial training, assists owners with the hiring process, and monitors performance and employer satisfaction.

- What are the potential problems, if any, with this type of program?
- Should ex-offenders be coached on how to discuss their criminal past with potential employers?
- Should this program be available to all ex-offenders?
- Could this type of job placement program trigger a complaint from unionized labor?

Sources: DeLisi, M. (2005). *Career criminals in society*. Thousand Oaks, CA: Sage; Finn, P. (2007). *Successful job placement for ex-offenders: The Center for Employment Opportunities*. Retrieved September 15, 2008, from http://www.ncjrs.gov/pdffiles/168102.pdf; Finn, P. (2007). *Washington State's corrections clearinghouse: A comprehensive approach to offender employment*. Retrieved September 15, 2008, from http://www.ncjrs.gov/pdffiles1/174441.pdf.

"From a national perspective, the 'three strikes and you're out' movement was largely symbolic. It was not designed to have a significant impact on the criminal justice system. The laws were crafted so that in order to be 'struck out' an offender would have to be convicted two or more often three times for very serious but rarely committed crimes . . . consequently, the vast majority of the targeted offender population was already serving long prison terms for these types of crimes. From this perspective, the three strikes law movement is much ado about nothing and is having virtually no impact on current sentencing practices."[4, pp. 138, 142]

allow offenders the opportunity to reform their behavior and work toward their rehabilitation. Those who appeared to be rehabilitating themselves likely received shorter sentences whereas intractable criminals faced longer terms. Due to concern about the wide range of sentences for the same crimes, sentencing philosophies moved toward **determinate sentencing**, sometimes known as flat or straight sentences, where a specific term was imposed upon conviction, for instance conviction of trespassing resulted in 1 year in prison.

Sentencing is a process that gives legitimacy to the entire criminal justice system. In fact, criminal sentencing is not merely a matter of criminal justice but affects other social institutions as well. For example, it has long been argued that persons who have been sentenced to prison, served time, and are then released face a variety of barriers that obstruct their ability to reconnect to conventional society. Devah Pager recently found that ex-prisoners were 30 to 50 percent less likely than nonoffenders to be considered for work by employers, suggesting that a prison sentence creates a major obstacle. More importantly, Pager found that African American ex-offenders are more than three times less likely than White ex-offenders to be called back by employers after an initial job interview. In fact, White ex-offenders received more favorable treatment from employers than African Americans without criminal records in her study. In other words, Pager found that race—not criminal record—was the deciding factor for a job call-back.[9] Thus, sentencing is an important facet of American society and the ability of residents to participate in it.

Presentence Investigation Report

As shown in FIGURE 4-1, one of the most important documents in the sentencing process and the criminal justice system generally is the **presentence investigation (PSI) report**, which is prepared for the court and which summarizes the defendant's social and criminal history for the purpose of sentencing. In most jurisdictions, the PSI report is prepared by a probation officer while the defendant is on bond, remains in jail custody, or is otherwise at the pretrial phase. In the course of completing the PSI report, the probation officer interviews the defendant, the alleged victim, arresting officers, correctional staff who have interacted with the offender while in custody, and other interested parties who can address the defendant's employment history, residency, family and friendship networks and supports, criminal history, confinement history, treatment and psychiatric history, and other pertinent information. The overarching purpose of the PSI report is to present a snapshot of the defendant that illustrates his or her amenability to correctional supervision and the sentence that most appropriately matches his or her criminal conduct and prior record. Although the PSI report is created during the pretrial phase, it is an important legal document that often becomes part of the offender's permanent record and is consulted not only for sentencing, but also for institutional classification, counseling plans, community agency referrals, parole decisions, and even criminological research. As described by probation expert Joan Petersilia, because of the wide usefulness of the PSI report, "No other justice agency is as extensively involved with the offender and his case as is the probation department."[10, p. 159]

"While stratification researchers typically focus on schools, labor markets, and the family as primary institutions affecting inequality, a new institution has emerged as central to the sorting and stratifying of young and disadvantaged men: the criminal justice system."[5, p. 937]

The heart of the PSI report is the evaluative summary where the probation officer (or whichever correctional official completes the report) provides an overall impression of the offender. Anthony Walsh suggests that the tone of the evaluative summary should be as objective and free of emotional responses to the offender as possible. The reason

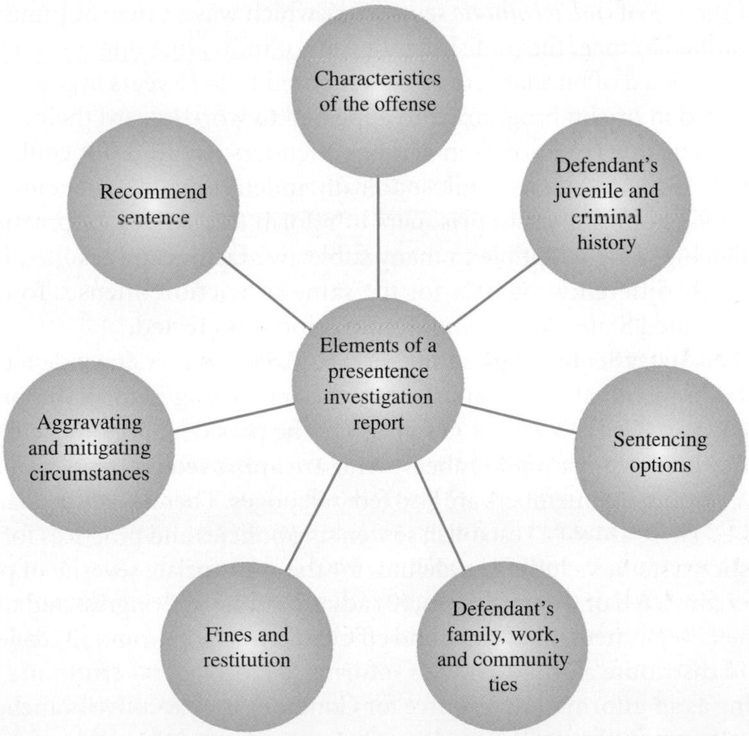

FIGURE 4-1 The Presentence Investigation (PSI). *Source: The History of the Pre-Sentence Investigation Report,* Center on Juvenile and Criminal Justice, www.cjcj.org/files/the_history.pdf.

Criminal sentencing is primarily a function of seriousness of offense and prior criminal record, but in cases such as Sammy "The Bull" Gravano, this is not always true. Gravano received just 5 years in prison despite admitting to 19 murders and other serious felonies during his career as a Mafia assassin.

is that evaluative summaries that are overly punitive, focus primarily on prior record and the offender's threat to public safety, and portray the offender as not amenable to treatment are likely to result in more severe sentencing outcomes.[11] Of course, at times this is appropriate given the serious prior records of many criminal offenders. But, an unduly harsh, cynical, or skeptical PSI report for a less serious offender can result in a criminal sentence that is unjust. In other words, a punitive PSI report can bury a criminal defendant just as an optimistic PSI report can provide greater sentencing and treatment opportunities.

Nearly 70 percent of felony cases nationwide use PSI reports for sentencing purposes and 40 states either require or allow agencies discretion to use presentence investigations. In capital cases, they are mandatory. In most incidences, defendants are permitted access to the content of their PSI report, but it is not complete access. For instance, according to the Federal Rules of Criminal Procedure rule 32(c), defendants are not granted access to (1) information that will disrupt the rehabilitation process, (2) information that was obtained under confidentiality, and (3) information that could cause potential harm to the defendant or other parties.[12] Although PSI reports have many official functions, the offender–correctional officer interview could be viewed as somewhat informal. For instance, in ***Minnesota v. Murphy*** (1984), the Supreme Court held that probation officers are not obligated to provide Miranda advisement to defendants prior to interviews.[13] And with the exception of Oregon, defendants do not have the right to an attorney during the course of a PSI interview.[14] (This should not be confused with probation revocation hearings in which defendants *do* have the right to counsel).[15–16]

United States Sentencing Commission

For many years, there was tremendous disparity in criminal sentencing where regional differences, criminal justice ideology, and even the random caprice of individual judges resulted in a wide range of sentences for the same crime. As discussed earlier, this was the result of the use of *indeterminate sentencing*, which was a range of punishment that could be modified to meet the punishment needs of individual offenders. For example, a defendant convicted of burglary could be sentenced to 1–15 years in prison. Offenders who participated in prison programs and appeared to work toward their rehabilitation could be released after 1 year or even earlier. Offenders who did not could potentially serve the entire 15-year sentence. Philosophically, indeterminate sentencing made sense because it provided incentives to prisoners to reform themselves. In practice, indeterminate sentencing was susceptible to many subjective factors and resulted in offenders serving radically different sentences for the same conviction offense. To remedy this disparity, the United States Sentencing Commission was created.

The **United States Sentencing Commission** (U.S.S.C.) is an independent commission in the judicial branch that was established by the Sentencing Reform Act provisions of the Comprehensive Crime Control Act of 1984. The president appoints eight commissioners (only seven are voting members) who are approved by the Senate. Most U.S. Sentencing Commission members are also federal judges. There are three main purposes of the U.S.S.C. These are to (1) establish sentencing policies and practices for the federal criminal justice system, including guidelines for the appropriate severity of punishment for offenders convicted of federal crimes, (2) advise and assist Congress and the executive branch in the development of effective and efficient crime policy, and (3) collect, analyze, research, and distribute a broad array of information on federal crime and sentencing issues, serving as an information resource for Congress, the executive branch, the courts, criminal justice practitioners, the academic community, and the public.

One of the primary charges of the United States Sentencing Commission was the creation of **sentencing guidelines**, which are designed to (1) incorporate philosophical purposes of punishment, such as deterrence, deserts, and incapacitation; (2) provide

CORRECTIONS BRIEF

Incarceration: Is It Just Time Away from Crime?

Offenders generally begin their delinquent careers slowly and cautiously and at a young age. As these young offenders age, their involvement with crime increases and so does their likelihood of being arrested and convicted for the offenses they commit. But at some point in their lives, their participation in aberrant behavior begins to wane. This aging out of crime curve is an accepted criminological finding. But does prison time increase the likelihood of crime desistance? Is incarceration a viable intervening variable that alters criminal trajectories? If not, should society expect its correctional institutions to provide little more than time away from crime?

Data indicate several factors are associated with crime trajectories. Past behavior has always been a reasonably reliable predictor of future behavior. Some have attempted to explain this relationship in terms of the propensity to commit crime; others believe more strongly that it is a causal relationship.

Research in support of both explanations has found that a lengthy criminal history is much more likely to predict a process whereby the individual will continue his involvement in criminal acts even after being released from prison. But even with a lengthy criminal and incarceration history, the older the inmate at the time of release, and the closer his association with past groups, the more likely the inmate is to be deterred by time spent in prison. Interestingly, prison has less of a deterrent effect if the inmate has a lengthy criminal history but was arrested later in life—and parole seems to have little if any additional deterrent effect. Thus, the findings seem to suggest prison has an incapacitation, a deterrent, and possibly even a criminogenic effect on each inmate. The extent to which one of these effects outweighs the others depends on the attributes of the inmate, including his criminal record prior to first arrest and time spent in prison.

Source: Bhati, A. S. (2006). *Studying the effects of incarceration on offending trajectories: An information-theoretic approach.* Retrieved September 15, 2008, from http://www.urban.org/UploadedPDF/411427_Effects_of_Incarceration.pdf

certainty and unfairness in sentencing by avoiding unwarranted disparity among offenders with similar characteristics while permitting sufficient flexibility to account for relevant aggravating and mitigating circumstances; and (3) reflect knowledge of human behavior as it relates to criminal justice. The sentencing guidelines went into effect on November 1, 1987.[17]

The sentencing guidelines provide federal judges with fair and consistent sentencing ranges that are based on the seriousness of the criminal conduct and the defendant's prior criminal record. As shown in TABLE 4–1, there are 43 levels of *offense seriousness* with more serious crimes receiving a higher score. Each type of crime is assigned a base offense level, which is the starting point for determining the seriousness of a particular offense. For instance, trespassing has a base offense level of 4, while kidnapping has a base offense level of 32. In addition to base offense levels, each offense type has a number of specific offense characteristics that can increase or decrease the base offense level and ultimately the sentence the offender receives. For example, robbery has a base offense level of 20. If a firearm was displayed during the robbery, there is a 5-level increase. If the firearm was actually discharged, there is a 7-level increase. Further adjustments can be made to reflect aggravating and mitigating circumstances, such as whether the offender had

TABLE 4-1 Federal Sentencing Guidelines

		Criminal History Category (Criminal History Points)					
	Offense Level	I (0 or 1)	II (2 or 3)	III (4, 5, 6)	IV (7, 8, 9)	V (10, 11, 12)	VI (13 or more)
	1	0–6	0–6	0–6	0–6	0–6	0–6
	2	0–6	0–6	0–6	0–6	0–6	1–7
	3	0–6	0–6	0–6	0–6	2–8	3–9
	4	0–6	0–6	0–6	2–8	4–10	6–12
Zone A	5	0–6	0–6	1–7	4–10	6–12	9–15
	6	0–6	1–7	2–8	6–12	9–15	12–18
	7	0–6	2–8	4–10	8–14	12–18	15–21
	8	0–6	4–10	6–12	10–16	15–21	18–24
	9	4–10	6–12	8–14	12–18	18–24	21–27
Zone B	10	6–12	8–14	10–16	15–21	21–27	24–30
Zone C	11	8–14	10–16	12–18	18–24	24–30	27–33
	12	10–16	12–18	15–21	21–27	27–33	30–37
Zone D	13	12–18	15–21	18–24	24–30	30–37	33–41
	14	15–21	18–24	21–27	27–33	33–41	37–46
	15	18–24	21–27	24–30	30–37	37–46	41–51
	16	21–27	24–30	27–33	33–41	41–51	46–57
	17	24–30	27–33	30–37	37–46	46–57	51–63
	18	27–33	33–37	33–41	41–51	51–63	57–71
	19	30–37	33–41	37–46	46–57	57–71	63–78
	20	33–41	37–46	41–51	51–63	63–78	70–87
	21	37–46	41–51	46–57	57–71	70–87	77–96
	22	41–51	46–57	51–63	63–78	77–96	84–105
	23	46–57	51–63	57–71	70–87	84–105	92–115
	24	51–63	57–71	63–78	77–96	92–115	100–125
	25	57–71	63–78	70–87	84–105	100–125	110–137
	26	63–78	70–87	78–97	92–115	110–137	120–150
	27	70–87	78–97	87–108	100–125	120–150	130–162
	28	78–97	87–108	97–121	110–137	130–162	140–175
	29	87–108	97–121	108–135	121–151	140–175	151–188
	30	97–121	108–135	121–151	135–168	151–188	168–210
	31	108–135	121–151	135–168	151–188	168–210	188–235
	32	121–151	135–168	151–188	168–210	188–235	210–262
	33	135–168	151–188	168–210	188–235	210–262	235–293
	34	151–188	168–210	188–235	210–262	235–293	262–327
	35	168–210	188–235	210–262	235–293	262–327	292–365
	36	188–235	210–262	235–293	262–327	292–365	324–405
	37	210–262	235–293	262–327	292–365	324–405	360–life
	38	235–293	262–327	292–365	324–405	360–life	360–life
	39	262–327	292–365	324–405	360–life	360–life	360–life
	40	292–365	324–405	360–life	360–life	360–life	360–life
	41	324–405	360–life	360–life	360–life	360–life	360–life
	42	360–life	360–life	360–life	360–life	360–life	360–life
	43	life	life	life	life	life	life

Source: United States Sentencing Commission. *2005 Federal Sentencing Guidelines*. Retrieved July 21, 2008, from http://www.ussc.gov/2005guid/5a.htm.

minimal participation in the crime, whether the offender obstructed justice, whether the victim was vulnerable because of age or disability, and whether the offender accepts responsibility for the crime.

The other factor in sentencing guidelines is the offender's *criminal history*. The guidelines assign each offender to one of six criminal history categories based upon the extent of the offender's prior arrests, convictions, and incarcerations and how recently these took place. First-time offenders and others with minimal and/or dated criminal history are assigned to Category I. Violent career criminals are assigned to Category VI. On the sentencing grid, the point at which criminal history category and offense level intersect determines the defendant's sentencing guideline range. The more finite sentencing range is known by a variety of terms, such as structured sentencing, guided discretion, and presumptive range sentencing.[18]

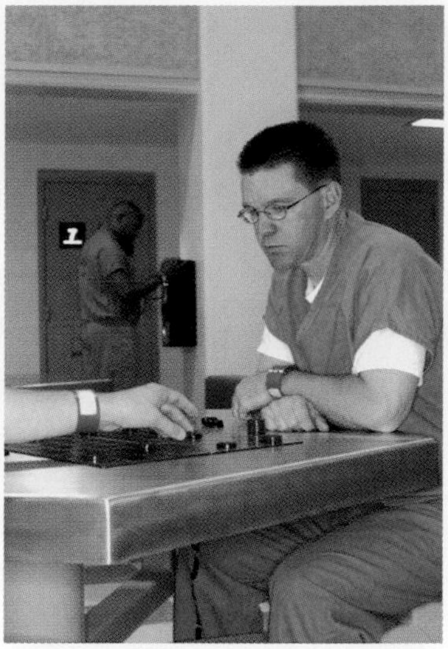

Research shows that employers treat white criminals more favorable than African Americans without criminal records. How does this relate to social inequality in the United States?

Sentencing guidelines have a provision that affords judges discretion to depart from the sentencing range in special circumstances. By statute, the court can impose a sentence outside the sentencing range if there exists an aggravating or mitigating circumstance of a kind or to a degree that is not adequately taken into consideration by the guidelines. When a judge goes outside of the specified range, this is known as a **departure** and the judge must state in writing the reason for the departure. When the judge imposes a harsher sentence, known as an upward departure, the offender may appeal. When the judge imposes a lesser sentence, known as a downward departure, the government may appeal. A special kind of departure is a substantial assistance departure, which is a downward departure for defendants who provided key assistance in the prosecution of another offender. The United States attorney files a motion for a substantial assistance departure, which must be approved by the judge and cannot depart more than four levels from the normal sentencing range.[19]

The sentencing guidelines were a major innovation for the federal criminal justice system, and since federal criminal justice policy often trickles down, they affected state judicial systems as well. The guidelines structured judicial discretion, established appellate review of sentences, abolished federal parole, introduced determinate or real time sentencing, and required that reasons for departures be placed on the record. In short, the United States Sentencing Commission's implementation of sentencing guidelines added rigor and teeth to federal sentencing. The guidelines have been challenged as unconstitutional as a violation of the separation of powers doctrine (the judicial branch performing a legislative function) but the constitutionality of U.S. sentencing guidelines has been affirmed in ***Mistretta v. United States*** (1989) and ***United States v. Booker*** (2005) although the latter case determined that a jury must determine the facts that result in an upward departure from federal sentencing guidelines.[20–21]

Sentencing Trends

According to data gathered from the National Judicial Reporting Program, criminal courts are getting somewhat tougher on sentencing over the past decade. Based on the most recent data available, nearly 1.1 million adults were convicted of felony crimes in state courts, which represented a 24 percent increase from 1994 to 2004. Approximately one in five felonies are for violent crimes, such as murder, rape, robbery, and aggravated assault (shown in FIGURE 4-2). Nationally, 94 percent of felony convictions occurred in state courts, with 6 percent occurring in federal courts. About 95 percent of convicted felons pleaded guilty and the remaining 5 percent were found guilty by a judge or jury. From 1994 to 2004, the conviction rate for violent crimes and the proportion of convicted felons that received an incarceration sentence increased.[22]

As shown in TABLE 4-2, felony sentences represented a mix of offenses. Violent offenses comprised 18 percent; property offenses comprised 29 percent; drug offenses comprised 34 percent; weapons offenses comprised 3 percent; and miscellaneous offenses comprised

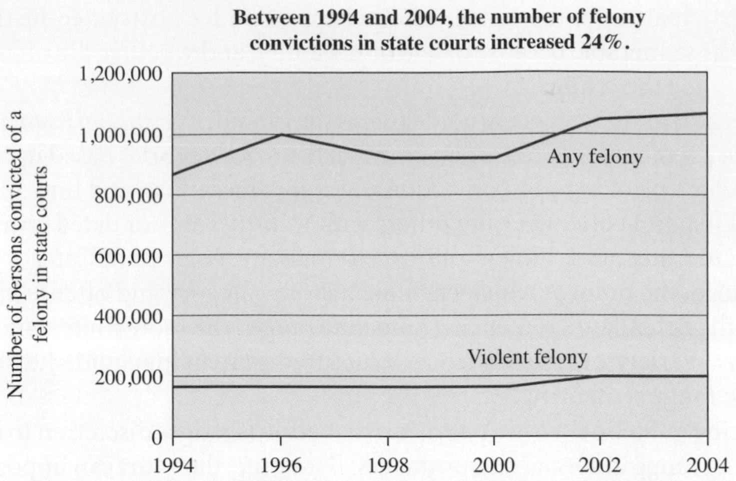

FIGURE 4–2 Felony Convictions in State Courts. *Source*: Durose, M. R., & Langan, P. A. (2007). *Felony sentences in state courts, 2004*. Washington, DC: U.S. Department of Justice, Office of Justice Programs, Bureau of Justice Statistics.

17 percent of felony convictions in state courts. Nearly one in four offenders was convicted of multiple felonies with 77 percent sentenced for a single felony.

According to researchers in the Bureau of Justice Statistics, sentences to state prison averaged 57 months, slightly less than 5 years. The average jail sentence was 6 months and the average probation sentence was 38 months.[23] The average prison sentence length was related to the seriousness of offense for which the offender was convicted. Violent offenses resulted in an average sentence of 92 months, property offenses resulted in an average sentence of 45 months, drug offenses resulted in an average sentence of

TABLE 4–2 Offense Types for Felony Convictions

Most Serious Conviction Offense	Persons Convicted of a Felony in State Courts in 2004	
	Number	Percent
All offenses	1,078.920	100
Violent offenses	194,570	18
Murder/nonnegligent manslaughter	8,400	1
Rape/sexual assault	33,190	3
Robbery	38,850	4
Aggravated assault	94,380	9
Other violent	19,750	2
Property offenses	310,680	29
Burglary	93,870	9
Larceny	119,340	11
Fraud/forgery	97,470	9
Drug offenses	362,850	34
Possession	161,090	15
Trafficking	201,760	19
Weapon offenses	33,013	3
Other offenses	177,810	17

Note: Detail may not sum to total because of rounding.

Source: Durose, M. R., & Langan. P. A. (2007) *Felony sentences in state courts, 2004*. Washington, DC: U.S. Department of Justice, Office of Justice Programs, Bureau of Justice Statistics.

TABLE 4-3 Mean Sentence Length in State Courts

Most Serious Conviction Offense	Incarceration Total	Incarceration Prison	Incarceration Jail	Straight Probation
All offenses	37 mo.	57 mo.	6 mo.	38 mo.
Violent offenses	68	92	7	44
Property offenses	29	45	6	38
Drug offenses	31	51	6	38
Weapon offenses	32	47	7	34
Other offenses	24	41	6	38

Note: Means exclude life and death sentences. Data on sentence length were reported for 89% of all cases.

Source: Durose, M. R., & Langan, P. A. (2007). *Felony sentences in state courts, 2004.* Washington, DC: U.S. Department of Justice, Office of Justice Programs, Bureau of Justice Statistics.

TABLE 4-4 Percent of Felons in State Court and Sentence Placements

Most Serious Conviction Offense	Percent of Felons Convicted in State Courts During 2004 Sentenced to—				
		Incarceration		Nonincarceration	
	Total	Prison	Jail	Probation	Other
All offenses	100	40	30	28	2
Violent offenses	100	54	24	20	2
Property offenses	100	37	31	30	2
Drug offenses	100	37	30	30	3
Other offenses	100	34	35	29	2

Note: Detail may not sum to total because of rounding. Data on sentence type were reported for 98% of all cases.

Source: Durose, M. R., & Langan, P. A. (2007). *Felony sentences in state courts, 2004.* Washington, DC: U.S. Department of Justice, Office of Justice Programs, Bureau of Justice Statistics.

51 months, weapons offenses resulted in an average sentence of 47 months, and other offenses resulted in an average of 41 months. Straight probation sentences ranged from 34 to 44 months (see TABLE 4-3).

As shown in TABLE 4-4, 70 percent of all felony convictions in state courts result in an incarceration sentence; 40 percent to state prison and 30 percent to local jails. Thirty percent of all state felony convictions result in a nonincarceration sentence, with 28 percent of those going to probation. The proportions of felony convictions resulting in incarceration were 78 percent (violent offenses), 68 percent (property offenses), 67 percent (drug offenses), 72 percent (weapons offenses), and 69 percent (other offenses). More than one in five violent felony convictions resulted in a nonincarceration sentence compared to 32 percent of property crimes, 33 percent of drug crimes, 28 percent of weapons offenses, and 31 percent of other crimes. Fewer than 1 percent of convicted felons were sentenced to life imprisonment and just 115 state offenders were sentenced to death in 2004.[23]

Three interesting trends in sentencing emerged from analysis of data from the National Judicial Reporting Program over a recent 10-year span. First, the likelihood of

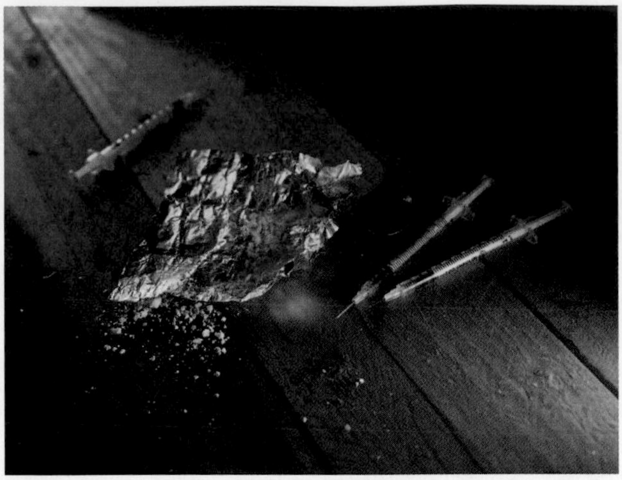

Few quibble with harsh sentences for violent and property offenders, but there is controversy over the harsh sentencing of drug violators. Should prison space be used for drug offenders? Under what circumstances should drug sentences be shorter or longer than sentences for other crimes?

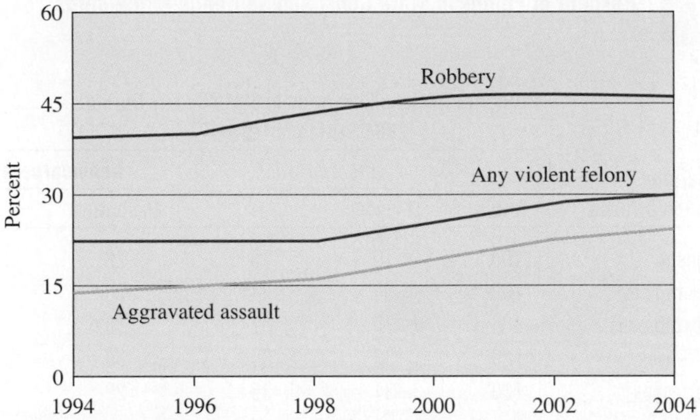

FIGURE 4–3 Percent of Felony Arrests Leading to Felony Convictions. *Source*: Durose, M. R., & Langan, P. A. (2007). *Felony sentences in state courts, 2004*. Washington, DC: U.S. Department of Justice, Office of Justice Programs, Bureau of Justice Statistics.

an arrest for a violent crime leading to a conviction has increased. As shown in FIGURE 4–3, the overall likelihood that a violent arrest would result in a conviction for a violent crime (there was no reduction for less serious crimes, such as property offenses) increased from 23 percent to 31 percent between 1994 and 2004. For robbery, the conviction rate rose from 39 percent to 46 percent, and for aggravated assault the increase was 14 percent to 25 percent.

On the other hand, the estimated average prison sentence received by violent felony offenders in state courts decreased from nearly 10 years in 1994 to 7 years in 2004. Although the average state prison sentence for violent felonies declined, the actual amount of time served remained stable (FIGURE 4–4). Since the 1970s, state legislatures have sought to reduce judicial discretion in sentencing and the determination of when the conditions of a sentence have been satisfied. Determinate sentences, mandatory minimum sentences, and guidelines-based sentencing have increased the predictability of release such that today 90 percent of state prisoners can estimate their probable release date and more than 95 percent of inmates will be released from prison (recall that very few are sentenced to death or meaningful life imprisonment). For these reasons, there tends to be little **truth in sentencing**, which is the correspondence between the sentence imposed upon those sent to prison and the time actually served prior to prison release.[24]

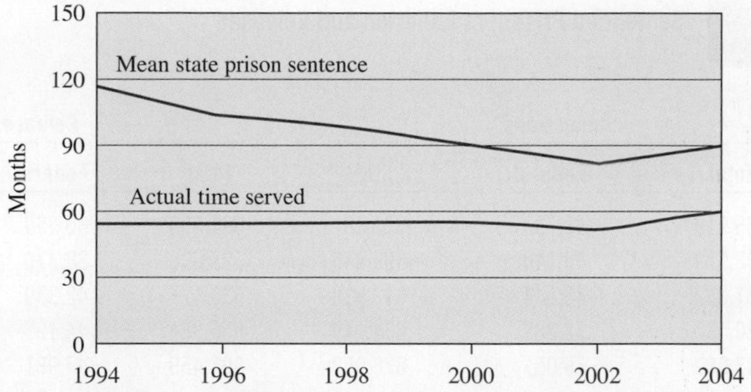

FIGURE 4–4 State Prison Sentences and Time Served. *Source*: Durose, M. R., & Langan, P. A. (2007). *Felony sentences in state courts, 2004.* Washington, DC: U. S. Department of Justice, Office of Justice Programs, Bureau of Justice Statistics.

The **Violent Crime Control and Law Enforcement Act of 1994** attempted to resolve the truth-in-sentencing problem by assuring that offenders served a larger portion of their sentences. By 1998, incentive grants were awarded to 27 states and the District of Columbia to require that violent offenders serve at least 85 percent of their sentence. Eleven additional states adopted truth-in-sentencing laws in 1995. Nationally, about 70 percent of state prison admissions for a violent offense were required to serve at least 85 percent of their sentence. Nearly one in five inmates (18 percent) served their entire prison sentence.[25] As shown in **TABLE 4–5**, 29 jurisdictions meet the federal 85 percent

TABLE 4–5 **Truth-in-Sentencing Requirements**

Meet Federal 85% Requirement		50% Requirement	100% of Minimum Requirement	Other Requirements
Arizona	Missouri	Indiana	Idaho	Alaska[c]
California	New Jersey	Maryland	Nevada	Arkansas[d]
Connecticut	New York	Nebraska	New Hampshire	Colorado[e]
Delaware	North Carolina	Texas		Kentucky[f]
District of Col.	North Dakota			Massachusetts[g]
Florida	Ohio			Wisconsin[h]
Georgia	Oklahoma[b]			
Illinois[a]	Oregon			
Iowa	Pennsylvania			
Kansas	South Carolina			
Louisiana	Tennessee			
Maine	Utah			
Michigan	Virginia			
Minnesota	Washington			
Mississippi				

[a]Qualified for Federal funding in 1996 only.
[b]Effective July 1, 1999, offenders were required to serve 85%of the sentence.
[c]Two-part sentence structure (2/3 in prison; 1/3 on parole); 100% of prison term required.
[d]Mandatory 70% of sentence for certain violent offenses and manufacture of methamphetamine.
[e]Violent offenders with two prior violent convictions serve 75%; one prior violent conviction, 56.25%.
[f]Effective July 15, 1998, offenders are required to serve 85% of the sentence.
[g]Requires 75% of a minimum prison sentence.
[h]Effective December 31, 1999, two-part sentence: offenders serve 100% of the prison term and a sentence of extended supervision and 25% of the prison sentence.

Source: Ditton, P. M., & Wilson, D. J. (1999). *Truth in sentencing in state prisons.* Washington, DC: U.S. Department of Justice, Office of Justice Programs, Bureau of Justice Statistics.

TABLE 4-6 Sentenced Prisoners Admitted and Released

	Admissions*			Releases*		
	Total	Federal	State	Total	Federal	State
2000	625,219	43,732	581,487	604,858	35,259	569,599
2001	638,978	45,140	593,838	628,626	38,370	590,256
2002	661,082	48,144	612,938	630,176	42,339	587,837
2003	686,437	52,288	634,149	656,384	44,199	612,578
2005	733,009	56,057	676,952	698,459	47,981	650,478
Percent change						
2000–2005	17.2	28.2	16.4	15.5	36.1	14.2
2004–2005	4.7	5.8	4.7	3.9	2.9	4.0

*Counts exclude escapes, AWOLs, and transfers.

Source: Sabol, W. J., Minton, T. D., & Harrison, P. M. (2007). *Prison and jail inmates at midyear 2006*. Washington, DC: U.S. Department of Justice, Office of Justice Programs, Bureau of Justice Statistics.

TABLE 4-7 State Prison Admissions by Type

Year	All*	New Court Commitments	Parole Violators
2000	581,487	350,431	203,569
2001	593,838	365,714	215,450
2002	612,938	392,661	207,961
2003	634,149	399,843	209,753
2004	646,830	411,300	219,033
2005	676,952	421,426	232,229
Percent change			
2000–2005	16.4	20.3	14.1
2004–2005	5.1	2.5	6.0

*Counts exclude escapes, AWOLs, and transfers.

Source: Sabol, W. J., Minton, T. D., & Harrison, P. M. (2007). *Prison and jail inmates at midyear 2006*. Washington, DC: U.S. Department of Justice, Office of Justice Programs, Bureau of Justice Statistics.

requirement, four states have a 50 percent requirement, three states require that 100 percent of the sentence is served, and six states have other specifications for truth in sentencing.

Nearly 750,000 prisoners were admitted to federal and state prisons in 2005, with slightly fewer than 700,000 offenders released. Between 2000 and 2005, the number of prisoner admissions increased 17.2 percent, while the prisoner releases increased 15.5 percent (TABLE 4-6). As shown in TABLE 4-7, there were 676,952 admissions to state prisons in 2005. Of these new prisoners, 421,426 were new court commitments upon conviction for new felony crimes and 232,229 were parole violators. Between 2000 and 2005, the number of new court commitments to state prisons increased more than 20 percent and the commensurate increase in parole violators increased 14 percent. From 2004 to 2005, the percent of parole violators (6 percent) was more than double the percent of new commitments (2.5 percent). Overall, state prisons are being filled with a steady stream of both new felons and former prisoners being returned for noncompliance with their parole.

Specialized/Problem-Solving Courts

Criminal defendants often have an array of problems that contribute to, interact with, and result from their crimes. In addition to their criminal behavior, serious offenders commonly have overlapping substance abuse problems, are problem drinkers or alcoholics, have psychiatric diagnoses, and are more likely to be unemployed, on public assistance, and have family problems.[26–28] For these reasons, recidivism rates for serious offenders are very high. Over time, policy makers and criminal justice practitioners recognized that a new approach to sentencing was needed if offenders were to be rehabilitated. This new approach, known as **specialized or problem-solving courts**, attempted to remedy the problems associated with criminal behavior using social services in conjunction with the justice system and not relying exclusively on punishment as traditional criminal courts have.

Drug Courts

Drug courts are specialized criminal courts that link supervision, judicial oversight, and treatment for drug-using criminal offenders. It is common for drug courts to have service components that include substance abuse treatment, public health services, psychiatric counseling, housing assistance, and information on educational, employment, and family services.[29–30] The National Association of Drug Court Professionals and the Department of Justice identified 10 key components of drug courts. These are:

1. Integration of substance abuse treatment with justice system case processing.
2. Use of nonadversarial approach.
3. Early identification and prompt placement of eligible participants.
4. Access to a continuum of treatment, rehabilitation, and related services.
5. Frequent drug testing.
6. A coordinated strategy among the judge, prosecutor, defense, and treatment providers to govern offender compliance.
7. Ongoing judicial interaction with each participant.
8. Monitoring and evaluation to measure achievements of program goals and its effectiveness.
9. Continuing interdisciplinary education to promote effective planning, implementation, and operation.
10. Partnerships with public agencies and community-based organizations to generate local support for drug courts.[31]

Drug courts were created to help the nation's courts deal with overcrowded jails and prisons, and the first drug court was established in Miami in 1989. By 2006, there were more than 1,500 drug courts with nearly 400 more being planned.[32] Overall, there have been mixed findings on the effectiveness of drug courts. John Goldkamp found that drug court participants in Miami had lower recidivism rates than correctional clients who were sentenced in traditional criminal court.[33] Gennaro Vito and Richard Tewksbury examined drug court participants in Kentucky and found that graduates had lower recidivism rates for drug and alcohol offenses than nondrug court other offenders.[34] Dale Sechrest and David Shichor found that drug court graduates in California had better prosocial outcomes than those who did not complete drug court programs.[35] Among drug court participants in a Cincinnati, Ohio, program, Shelley Johnson Listwan and her colleagues found that drug court clients generally fared better than defendants who went through traditional courts. More than 1 year after release from the program, 27 percent of drug court offenders had a new arrest, 10 percent had a new drug arrest, 37 percent had a new incarceration, and 34 percent had a new incarceration for a drug offense. The commensurate rates for nondrug court participants were 35 percent, 20 percent, 42 percent, and 40 percent, respectively.[36]

Some programs reduce recidivism for drug court graduates; however, most programs have high dropout or termination rates. Denise Gottfredson and her associates found that it is difficult to retain drug court clients in treatment programs and that greater retention would result in greater reductions in recidivism.[37] Part of the problem with keeping drug court participants in their programs is that although programs are often voluntary, many clients feel legal coercion to participate. In other words, the threat of jail is what motivates offenders, not necessarily a desire to desist from drug use. John Hepburn and Angela Harvey examined the effect of the threat of legal sanction on drug court retention and completion. They compared a group who received a 4-month suspended sentence as motivation to participate in drug court to a group of drug court participants who were statutorily prohibited from a jail sentence. Hepburn and Harvey found no differences in program retention or completion across the coerced and noncoerced groups.[38] Another important issue is the reasons certain offenders are selected for drug court. Mitchell Miller and his colleagues found that juvenile offenders with better demeanor were more likely to be selected for drug court options than juveniles with negative demeanor or poorer interpersonal traits.[39]

Although the effectiveness of drug courts is still being refined, the cost savings is impressive. Using data from Portland, Oregon, Michael Finigan and his colleagues reported that drug court offenders are $12,218 less expensive in terms of criminal justice and victimization costs than nondrug court offenders. In the 10-year follow-up, this produced savings of about $79 million.[40] These reduced costs alone are likely enough to justify continued use of drug courts. Overall, the treatment effect of drug courts is strongly related to the methodological quality of the evaluation study, the risk level of the sample, and the length of follow-up.[41]

DWI Courts

Some jurisdictions have devised **DWI courts** based loosely on the drug court sentencing model. Thomas Winfree and Dennis Giever studied one of the first DWI courts established in Las Cruces, New Mexico. The DWI court was a 1-year program consisting of individual, group, and family counseling. Participants attended several community-based treatment programs including victim impact panels. Once a month, DWI court clients appeared before a judge to discuss their progress. Clients who fell behind in their treatment or relapsed were punished with brief jail sentences. The effectiveness of the DWI court depended on the criminality of the offender. For instance, Winfree and Giever found that DWI courts were comprised of nonalcoholic first- and second-time offenders, alcoholic first- and second-time offenders, and chronic alcoholics with three or more offenses.[42]

The use of victim impact panels is particularly effective. Created by Mothers Against Drunk Driving (MADD), **victim impact panels** are interactive sessions where DWI victims tell their stories of hardship to DWI offenders. A study by Dean Rojek and his colleagues found that DWI offenders who participated in victim impact panels had lower recidivism rates through a 5-year follow-up.[43] Recent research also suggests that drug and DWI courts must pay attention to the specific substances clients use during the course of their criminal activity. For example, Jeffrey Bouffard and Katie Richardson studied specialty courts in the Midwest and found that the courts benefited offenders who had used methamphetamine, but among DWI offenders there was no evidence of reduced recidivism.[44]

Family Courts

Family courts generally handle legal matters pertaining to children and families. In recent years, several specialized courts have been developed to address various family-related problems related to child abuse and neglect, juvenile delinquency, and child custody. Often, specialized family courts are combined with drug courts and are variously referred to as dependency drug courts, family treatment drug courts, and others. Perhaps more than any other specialized court, the use of community agencies to provide services and treatment is critical for the maintenance of healthy families.

Evaluation studies provided mixed findings on the effectiveness of assorted specialized family courts. Beth Green and her colleagues conducted a national study of 250 parents who participated in family treatment drug courts (FTDC) and found that parents who entered substance-abuse treatment did so more quickly, stayed in treatment longer, and completed more treatment episodes than parents who did not participate. Also, the children of FTDC parents entered permanent placements more quickly and were more likely to be reunified with their parents compared to children of nonparticipants. All of the programs that Green and her associates examined contained intensive judicial monitoring, immediate substance abuse assessment and referral, and wraparound services provided through a collaborative drug court team.[45] In Sacramento, California, a dependency drug court was established where drug-using parents are required to submit to drug treatment, drug testing, and court monitoring with oversight from child welfare professionals. An evaluation by Sharon Boles and her colleagues found that parents who participated in dependency drug court completed more treatment and were more likely to be reunited with their children, who, in turn, were less likely to be placed in foster care.[46]

Domestic violence court is another specialized family court, and there are more than 300 currently operating in the United States. Domestic violence courts explicitly focus on the various crimes that emerge between intimate partners and families; address the co-occurring problems that domestic abusers have, such as alcoholism or drug addiction; and devote one-on-one attention to each case so that the defendants do not fall through the cracks as is frequently the case in traditional criminal courts. There have not been many evaluations of the effectiveness of domestic violence courts, and research to date is mixed. John Goldkamp and his colleagues evaluated a program in Miami and found that about half of domestic abusers were intoxicated at arrest, thus the mandatory substance abuse services was critical for enrolling the at-risk group in treatment. Recidivism rates against the same victim were more than 50 percent less among domestic violence court graduates compared to control subjects.[47]

Angela Gover and her colleagues evaluated a program in Lexington County, South Carolina, and found that defendants who were processed through domestic violence court were significantly less likely to recidivate over an 18-month follow-up.[48] Gover and her associates also found that both domestic violence court offenders and victims expressed satisfaction with the specialized court, felt that it empowered them by allowing them to express their viewpoints, and were generally supportive of the outcomes of their cases.[49] Not everyone is so pleased, however. Martha Coulter and her colleagues surveyed female victims whose cases had been processed in Florida domestic violence courts. Victims reported feeling unsafe and confused by the new procedures of the court. Victims also reported that they needed more guidance through the various steps of the legal process, and the survey revealed that domestic violence court practitioners do not necessarily have specialized training.[50]

It is critical that the perceived limitations of domestic violence courts be fixed, especially given the dismal outcomes among batterer treatment programs. Researchers with the National Institute of Justice suggest, "For more than a decade, courts have been sending convicted batterers to intervention programs rather than to prison. But do these programs work? Two studies in Florida and New York tested the most common type of

Mental health courts are increasingly used to process mentally ill offenders via treatment and supervision as opposed to punishment.

batterer intervention. Their findings raise serious questions about the effectiveness of these programs."[51, p. ii] Overall, batterers drop out of treatment programs at high rates and batterers often do not change criminogenic attitudes they hold toward women or the use of domestic violence. It is also common for victims to be displaced by the assault and to lose stability after the situation. For these reasons, it is likely that domestic violence courts will become more prevalent because of their ability to keep offenders in programs and give cases the individualized attention they need.

Mental Health Courts

Mental health courts are specialty criminal courts that address the special needs of defendants with mental illnesses. The philosophy of mental health courts is to provide treatment and other services for defendants whose problems would likely worsen if prosecuted in traditional courts. In a sense, mental health courts are reserved for defendants who appear to be less culpable and as such do not deserve harsh punishments, such as confinement. There are six general characteristics of mental health courts, which follow:

1. Mental health courts have dockets that are reserved entirely for defendants with serious and often persistent mental health problems. In most jurisdictions, a single judge presides over the mental health court.
2. Mental health courts seek to break the revolving door in and out of jail that many mentally ill criminal defendants experience. By diverting defendants from traditional courts, mental health courts link defendants with service providers that can address their psychiatric issues and hopefully reduce recidivism.
3. Mental health courts mandate community mental health treatment and often require that participants take prescribed medication and adhere to any conditions imposed by the court. This is important because mentally ill people with prior contact with the criminal justice system tend to get into trouble when they stop taking their medication.
4. Mental health courts provide continuing supervision via judicial status review hearings conducted by the court and through direct supervision in the community. Which entity conducts the judicial hearings varies by jurisdiction and can include probation officers, community treatment providers, or judicial officers.

CORRECTIONS IN THE NEWS

Inmate Mental Health

More than half of all prison inmates in the United States suffer from some type of mental health problem. This means that well over 705,000 state prison inmates, just at 78,000 federal prison inmates, and nearly 480,000 inmates serving sentences in local jails live with a mental health illness. These figures represent inmates who either reported or were diagnosed with mental health problems. These figures do not account for inmates with symptoms of a mental health disorder without a recent history or treatment.

For the purposes of this study, mental health problems were defined using two measures—a recent history of the mental health disorder and mental health symptoms that occurred within the 12 months previous to the study that included a clinical diagnosis and/or treatment for the problem. The qualifying symptoms were based on criteria from the *Diagnostic and Statistical Manual of Mental Disorders*, fourth edition (*DSM-IV*).

Inmate mental health is an important issue because inmates with mental health problems are more likely to have served time for prior offenses, to have substance use dependencies, to have been homeless in the year prior to their arrest, to report having been sexually abused early in life, and to have been involved in an altercation while in prison in which they were injured.

Mental health problems have been found to vary by the sex and age of the prisoner as well. Female inmates typically exhibit higher rates of mental health disorders than do male inmates. Age is also a factor with younger inmates having the highest rates of mental health problems. Inmates age 24 and younger have the highest rate of mental health problems. An estimated 70 percent of local jail inmates age 24 or younger were found to have mental health problems. This figure drops to 52 percent for jail inmates age 55 or older.

Inmates with mental health problems were more likely to have family members who abused drugs and/or alcohol. A majority of prison and jail inmates report family members who also have been incarcerated; one third of these prisoners report having a brother who served time as well.

For state prisoners, violent crimes by inmates with mental health problems were common. In fact, nearly half of state prisoners had committed a violent crime in the past and a violent criminal history was more prevalent among inmates with mental health disorders. Not surprisingly, state prisoners with a violent history who had a mental health disorder were more likely to recidivate.

Source: James, D. J., & Glaze, L. E. (2007). *Mental health problems of prison and jail inmates*. Washington, DC: U.S. Department of Justice, Office of Justice Programs, Bureau of Justice Statistics.

5. Mental health courts use the model of therapeutic jurisprudence, which rewards compliance with incentives such as dropping charges and sanctions noncompliance with admonitions from the judge, increased conditions, and jail confinement.
6. Mental health courts are voluntary opportunities to participate in court-supervised treatment and potentially resolve the case upon successful completion of the mandated treatment program. In this way, defendants are not stigmatized with a sentence to mental health court—they choose this option.[52–53]

Since their first use in 1997, there are nearly 100 mental health courts operating in at least 34 states and serving nearly 8,000 clients. Evaluations are showing promising outcomes for mental health courts. Merith Cosden and her colleagues studied 235 adult offenders in California who were randomly assigned to mental health court or traditional treatment. Adults who went through the mental health court had lower recidivism rates, reduced substance abuse, less stress, greater life satisfaction, and more independent living.[54] A program in Broward County, Florida, doubled the rate, which clients obtained psychiatric services, resulted in no more recidivism, and resulted in 75 percent fewer days in jail.[55] Similarly, mental health courts in Seattle have also shown lower recidivism and greater accessing of community mental health services.[56]

Community Courts

Community courts, also known as community prosecution, are a final specialized court that presents new sentencing options for criminal defendants. Community prosecution is a proactive approach to addressing crime and quality-of-life issues that brings the courts together with community residents. Like traditional criminal courts, community courts place a priority on prosecuting and punishing criminals and reducing crime; however, community courts are also focused on crime prevention and partnerships with community residents and agencies.[57]

The first community court was the Midtown Community Court in New York City, established in 1993; there are approximately 30 community courts nationwide. The innovative courts have devised a variety of legal sanctions that provide treatment while sanctioning the offender and serve the community. For example, in many large court dockets, quality-of-life offenses, such as loitering, disorderly conduct, prostitution, and the like are routinely dismissed. Community courts prosecute these low-level crimes and use community service as the sentence. At the Midtown Community Court, community service is used twice as often as criminal courts and the compliance rate for completing community service is about 75 percent. Community court clients who completed a 3-month court-ordered drug treatment program had significantly lower recidivism rates over a 3-year follow-up. At the Hartford, Connecticut, community court, defendants report great satisfaction with the courts, feel the sentences are fair, and feel that the courts empower the community.[58] Overall, community courts are an innovative way to combine criminal sentencing with community service and treatment efficacy for offenders.

The advent of specialized courts to address particular subpopulations of criminal offenders underscores the idea that sentencing is perhaps best when it is tailored to the individual circumstances of the offender. In addition, the use of specialized courts reinforces the idea that the criminal population is diverse or heterogeneous in terms of the level of risk that an offender presents. For instance, it would be foolish, wasteful, and unjust to assign the same sentence to a first-time shoplifter and a chronic offender with 100 prior arrests for theft. In terms of their criminal background and offending propensity, they are very different. The next section explores offender classification and the ways it is used to inform sentencing policy and correctional practice.

Offender Classification and Assessment

Since its inception, the American criminal justice system has evaluated differences in criminal offenders and used these differences to justify correctional practices. Distinctions between criminals were made based on the type of crime they committed (e.g., violent or property), the degree that the offender appeared to be involved in crime (e.g., first-time offender or habitual criminal), and subjective characteristics (e.g., attitude, personality, age, social class, and ethnicity). Overwhelmingly, legal relevant factors, such as criminal history and offense seriousness (which not coincidentally are the same primary factors used in contemporary sentencing) were the strongest determinants of correctional outcomes, such as sentencing and parole release. However, even though objective criteria were used to inform correctional decisions, there was still a great deal of subjectivity to **clinical assessment**, which is decision making based on the experience, education, training, and gut feeling of correctional staff. The problems with clinical assessment is that predictions about offender classification are subject to personal biases, can be based on unsubstantiated factors (e.g., the offender's attitude), and lack consistency and uniformity.

Due to the inadequacies of clinical judgments about offender risk, likelihood of recidivism, and other predictions, criminologists and practitioners developed **actuarial assessment** tools, which are offender classification and assessment instruments based on standardized, objective criteria that are used to distinguish between the criminal population to determine the most appropriate treatment and punishment modalities. Actuarial instruments are routinely tested for their ability to predict correctional outcomes, such as the likelihood of recidivism, and these statistical studies help to refine the instrument over time. As actuarial instruments get more refined, they are better able to make accurate predictions while reducing **false-negative** (serious offenders who are predicted to be nonserious offenders) and **false-positive** (nonserious offenders who are predicted to be serious offenders) predictions. Overall, actuarial instruments improve the reliability of decisions made about offenders, make correctional practice more predictable, and provide a basis for correctional personnel to justify their decision making.[59] Today, most correctional organizations use actuarial instruments to guide their decision making. Dana Jones-Hubbard and her colleagues conducted a national survey and found that nearly 80 percent of parole and probation agencies and nearly 60 percent of community corrections agencies use standardized and objective instruments. Nearly 85 percent of agencies reported that the use of actuarial instruments was critically important for effective offender classification and assessment.[60] Screening and assessment tools are also used to gauge substance abuse disorders among correctional clients. For example, a recent national survey by Faye Taxman and her colleagues found that 58 percent of adult prisons, jails, and community correctional agencies use standardized substance abuse screening tools and more than 34 percent use an actuarial risk tool.[61]

Lawrence Travis and Edward Latessa identified 10 key elements to effective offender classification and assessment. They are:

1. *Purpose*: ensure that offenders are treated differentially within a system to ensure safety and treatment appropriateness.
2. *Organizational fit*: fit the characteristics and needs of the particular organization and agency, such as pretrial, probation, parole, etc.
3. *Accuracy*: be reliable and valid in making correctional predictions.
4. *Parsimony*: be easy to use, short, and simple.
5. *Distribution*: predict across classification groups, such as gender, race, offense type, etc.
6. *Dynamism*: include risk factors that are amenable to change and allow for the measurement of change (improvement or rehabilitation) in the offender for reclassification.
7. *Utility*: achieve the purposes of offender classification and meet the goals of the agency.
8. *Practicality*: be practical and easy to implement in the field.
9. *Justice*: produce just outcomes where offender placement and service provisions are based on offender differences and yield consistent outcomes.
10. *Sensitivity*: effective classification and assessment is sensitive to the differences of offenders.[62–63]

National Trends

According to a national assessment of correctional practices in the classification of offenders, James Austin and Kenneth McGinnis found that 80 percent of national prisoner population could be classified as general population. Of these, between 35 and 40 percent are **minimum-security** inmates who require little supervision and are afforded considerable work and living opportunities in confinement; 35 to 45 percent are **medium-security** inmates who require more supervision than minimum-security inmates but still have work and programming opportunities; and 10–15 are **maximum-security** or

TABLE 4-8 Trends in Prisoner Populations by Classification

Variable	Trend (% States Reporting) Increasing	Decreasing	Unchanged	Number of States Reporting
Total prison population				
Male	66	20	14	35
Female	61	24	15	33
General population				
Male	58	26	16	31
Female	53	27	20	30
Maximum custody				
Male	46	15	39	33
Female	17	20	63	30
Special management population				
Administrative segregation				
Male	33	17	50	30
Female	28	17	55	29
Disciplinary segregation				
Male	31	19	50	32
Female	40	20	40	30
Protective custody				
Male	25	22	53	32
Female	23	3	73	31
Mental health unit				
Male	55	10	36	31
Female	48	7	45	29
Medical unit or facility				
Male	39	19	42	31
Female	31	0	69	29
Assaults				
Inmate on staff	24	53	19	42
Inmate on inmate	27	46	27	37

Source: Adapted from Austin, J., & McGinnis, K. (2004). *Classification of high-risk and special management prisoners: A national assessment of current practices.* Longmont, CO: National Institute of Corrections, p. 40.

close custody inmates who engage in misconduct and are subject to the most strict supervision and control with fewer treatment amenities. In addition, 15 percent of the prisoner population is described as **high risk** or **special management**, which includes highly aggressive prisoners, sexual predators, gang members, mentally ill inmates, and prisoners with severe medical problems and related special needs. Special management inmates are the most problematic inmates per capita and pose the greatest fiscal and staff resource costs of all prisoners.[64]

As shown in TABLE 4-8, in many states the proportion of inmates who must be removed from the general population because of administrative segregation, disciplinary segregation, protective custody, mental health needs, or medical needs is increasing. The good news, however, is that prisons are experiencing less violence in part because of improvements in inmate classification. For example, Austin and McGinnis found that 24 percent of states indicated that inmate assaults on staff were increasing but 53 percent of states indicated that such assaults were decreasing (19 percent reported no change). For inmate assaults on other inmates, 27 percent of states reported an increase, 46 percent of states reported a decrease, and 27 percent of states reported no change. Most states have

TABLE 4–9 Policies for Maximum-Security Inmates

Policy	Number of States Reporting	States with Policy in Place	
		Number	Percent
24-hour restriction	42	40	95
Contact with other high-security inmates allowed	41	28	68
Contact with visitors allowed	41	39	95
Restraints used when escorting prisoner	41	37	90
Out-of-cell time (hours/day)			
Less than 1	39	4	10
1–2	39	27	69
3 or more	39	9	23
Same policies apply to disruptive mentally ill prisoners	38	18	47

Source: Adapted from Austin, J., & McGinnis, K. (2004). *Classification of high-risk and special management prisoners: A national assessment of current practices*. Longmont, CO: National Institute of Corrections, p. 41.

policies in place to supervise maximum-security inmates. Examples of these policies include restricted out-of-cell time, the use of restraints when the prisoner is transported, limited contact with visitors, limited contact with other inmates, particularly other maximum-security inmates, and other restrictions (see TABLE 4–9).[65]

Correctional systems use an assortment of assessment systems and actuarial instruments (which are discussed later in this chapter) to appropriately classify inmates and diagnose special types of inmates, such as those most prone to violence and misconduct. Most states use one of two **internal management systems** that determine how prisoners should be housed within a particular facility or complex based upon varying levels of aggressiveness and vulnerability that are measured using a questionnaire. The **Adult Internal Management System** (AIMS) relies on two instruments to identify inmates who are likely to pose a risk to the safe and secure operation of the facility. AIMS is informed by the Life History Checklist, which focuses on the inmate's adjustment and stability in the community and the Correctional Adjustment Checklist, which creates a profile of an inmate's likely behavior in a correctional setting. The **Prisoner Management Classification (PMC) System** uses an interview to rate the inmate on 11 objective background factors that assess an inmate's social status and offense history. It is basically the inmate version of the Client Management Classification (CMC) System, which is described later.[66]

A variety of diagnostic criteria have been shown to correlate with inmate misconduct and violence (see TABLE 4–10). Most states screen inmates for these risk factors, which include membership in a **security threat group**, an organized inmate gang that engages in predatory, criminal behavior behind bars; escape risk; violence risk; suicide risk; known enemies; witness protection; mood disorders; personality disorders; psychotic disorders; and others. It is critical for correctional systems to accurately identify problem inmates because they inflict tremendous damage while incarcerated. For instance, Matt DeLisi found that 40 percent of inmates are chronic or habitual offenders while they are incarcerated; that is, they continue to amass citations and penalties for criminal behavior. In addition, a small group of extremely violent inmates were responsible for 100 percent of the murders, 75 percent of the rapes, 80 percent of the arsons, and 50 percent of the aggravated assaults that occurred during the study period.[67]

TABLE 4-10 Diagnostic Assessment Factors

	Male Inmates			Female Inmates		
Factor Assessed	Number of States Responding	States that Screen Number	States that Screen Percent	Number of States Responding	States that Screen Number	States that Screen Percent
Security threat group membership	42	37	88	40	34	85
Escape risk	42	40	95	41	39	95
Witness protection	42	36	86	41	34	83
Sexual assault protection	42	35	83	41	34	83
Potential violence in prison	42	34	81	41	33	81
Enemies	42	37	88	41	36	88
Predatory sexual behavior	42	35	83	41	34	83
Suicide risk	40	40	100	39	39	100
Mood disorders	40	40	100	40	40	100
Psychotic disorders	40	40	100	39	39	100
Personality disorder	38	32	84	37	31	84
Mental retardation	38	36	95	37	35	95

Source: Adapted from Austin, J., & McGinnis, K. (2004). *Classification of high-risk and special management prisoners: A national assessment of current practices.* Longmont, CO: National Institute of Corrections, p. 45.

The Risk Principle

Today, correctional agencies and correctional researchers use actuarial instruments under the broad term of the risk principle. Edward Latessa and Christopher Lowenkamp suggest that evidence-based practices demonstrate empirically that recidivism rates can be significantly reduced through theoretically sound, well-designed programs that appropriately apply the principles of effective intervention. The principles of effective intervention are risk, need, treatment, and fidelity.

- *The risk principle is the who to target.* The most intensive correctional treatment and intervention sentence or program should be reserved for high-risk offenders, such as chronic or violent criminals. For low-risk offenders, simply holding them accountable for their actions and imposing minimal sanctions is usually sufficient to prevent recidivism.
- *The need principle is the what to target.* Programs should target crime-producing needs, such as antisocial peer association, antisocial personality, drug use, alcoholism, self-control skills, and other factors that are highly correlated with crime.
- *The treatment principle addresses how to target offenders' needs.* The most effective programs are behavioral and center on present circumstances and risk factors that are responsible for the offender's behavior. Behavioral interventions are action rather than talk oriented and teach offenders new, prosocial skills to replace antisocial ones.
- *The fidelity principle pertains to the integrity and quality of the program, intervention, or sentence.* These include making sure that the program has well-trained staff, close monitoring of offenders, assisting with other needs of the offender, ensuring the program is delivered as designed through quality assurance processes, and structured aftercare.[68]

To date, research indicates that programs that employ these principles are among the most effective correctional programs. For example, Alex Holsinger and Edward Latessa studied the risk principle among juvenile offenders and found that criminal justice practitioners appeared to be striking the appropriate balance between treatment and punishment of clients with varying degrees of criminality. Their study contained 544 delinquents who were sentenced to diversion, probation, special/intensive probation, a residential rehabilitation center, or the department of youth services. Sharp differences in criminality existed across the five placements. Youths who received diversion were the lowest risks and had the lowest criminality, and those sentenced to confinement were the highest risks and demonstrated the most criminality. For instance, Holsinger and Latessa found that delinquents who were sent to prison had an average criminal risk index score that was *400 percent greater* than youths who were diverted. In terms of average behavioral risk score, youths who were placed in a residential center and department of youth services were 236 percent and 220 percent, respectively, more of a behavioral risk than youths who were diverted![69]

Two recent reviews confirm the importance of understanding risk principles when working with criminal offenders. Donald Andrews and Craig Dowden, two noteworthy corrections researchers, analyzed 225 studies that produced 374 statistical relationships between risk principles and sentencing/correctional outcomes. Their meta-analysis included a host of risk and protective factors, including academic background, family background, vocational skills, self-control, anger, negative affect, self-esteem, criminal thinking styles, fear of punishment, and others. Overall, Andrews and Dowden found solid support for the risk principle particularly when studies splintered their analyses by the level of offender (e.g., low, medium, or high risk). Studies that focused on females and adolescents were especially supportive of the risk principle.[70]

Similar support was shown in a study of 97 correctional programs that included 13,676 offenders conducted by Christopher Lowenkamp and his colleagues. Programs that adhered to risk principles were more likely to produce lower recidivism and noncompliance rates. Interestingly, research also shows the *costs of not applying* the risk principles particularly in the case of low-level offenders. Placing low-risk offenders in treatment or supervision settings with higher risk offenders *increases* their recidivism for three primary reasons. First, exposure to high-rate offenders provides more opportunities for low-risk offenders to associate with serious criminals and adopt more antisocial lifestyles. Second, these deviant associations tend to reduce the low-risk offenders' previously held associations with conventional peers and other prosocial support networks. Third, more strict supervision creates more opportunities for noncompliance and increases the odds that an offender will be in violation of his or her sentence. In this way, it is important to use a less-is-more strategy with low-risk offenders because treating them harshly could induce more problems.[71]

Classification and Assessment Instruments

Effective classification and assessment is dependent on understanding the individual risks and needs of offenders in order to provide appropriate treatment and supervision.

The **Client Management Classification (CMC) System** is designed to identify the level of supervision needed for individual correctional clients, their service needs, and the resources required to meet those needs. It was created in Wisconsin in 1975, evaluated as a model program by the National Institute of Corrections in 1983, and adopted by about 25 percent of probation and parole agencies across the United States. Under the CMC, offenders are initially classified as high, medium, or low security based on the risk they present and their program needs. After this initial assessment, a profiling interview is conducted to ascertain the type of supervision that will be needed and dictate the treatment relationship between the client and probation officer. In ascending order of seriousness, the four treatment modalities are selective intervention, environmental structure, casework control, and limit setting. *Selective intervention* is used for offenders who lead

CORRECTIONS RESEARCH

Co-Occurring Disorders

Data collected on male and female prisoners in the Cook County (Chicago) Department of Corrections reveal that 12.2 percent of female detainees and 6.4 percent of male detainees suffer from a severe mental disorder. At intake, 3.9 percent of male detainees met the criteria for major depression, 2.7 percent met the criteria for schizophrenia, and 1.4 percent met the criteria for mania. Figures for female detainees were 10.5 percent, 2.0 percent, and 1.4 percent, respectively.

At the time of intake, 29.1 percent of male and 53.3 percent of female detainees had a substance use disorder. The prevalence rate of alcohol use was somewhat higher than that of drug use or dependence for male detainees at the time of intake. The prevalence rate of drug abuse for female detainees, however, was nearly twice that of alcohol use with data revealing females' prevalence rate of alcohol abuse to be 22.1 percent and their prevalence rate of drug abuse to be 43.6 percent. Other research comfortably predicts that over half of all adult male arrestees at intake test positive for substance use. Findings also reveal women arrestees have significantly higher substance use problems than do women in the general population.

Researchers have found that regardless of the sex of the detainee, these individuals have a 72 percent rate of co-occurring disorders—meaning the arrestee at the time of intake is likely to be suffering from a substance use problem as well as a severe mental disorder. This condition poses significant safety and security problems for arresting officers and jailers as well as the potential for civil liability problems for jail administrators and their staff.

In addition to routine booking procedures, each detainee should be screened at the earliest possible opportunity for substance use and mental health disorders. One method is through the use of self-report questionnaires—officers can question the arrestee about his substance use history and whether he has any mental health issues. Personal observation based on a symptom checklist and supported by drug recognition training and field experience is the next and possibly the best method to identify a potential problem. Properly identifying such symptoms such as agitation, depression, and delusions or the communication of suicidal thoughts as well as signs of alcohol and drug use can alert jail staff to the potential liability or physical threat posed by a detainee meeting the criteria of a co-occurring disorder.

Sources: SAMHSA. (2002, Spring). *The prevalence of co-occurring mental illness and substance use disorders in jails.* Retrieved September 15, 2008, from http://gainscenter.samhsa.gov/pdfs/jail_diversion/gainsjailprev.pdf; Peters, R. H., & Hills, H. A. (1997). *Intervention strategies for offenders with co-occurring disorders: What works?* Retrieved September 15, 2008, from http://www.nicic.org/pubs/1997/014754.pdf.

stable, prosocial lives with the exception of their current criminal justice involvement, which is usually an isolated incident. Selective intervention is commonly divided into a situational group and a treatment group. About 40 percent of probation clients receive the selective intervention treatment modality. About 15 percent of probationers are assigned to *environmental structure*, which attempts to help offenders develop basic work and social skills, learn impulse control, and associate with conventional instead of criminal peers. *Casework control* is reserved for 30 percent of probationers, and this population consists of recidivists with more lengthy criminal records and unstable life patterns characterized by substance abuse problems and failures in domestic relationships and employment.

The most restrictive category, *limit setting*, is used for 15 percent of probationers most of whom are career criminals who show little remorse for their antisocial behavior and provide little indication that they intend to reform their behavior.

Evaluations of the CMC produced moderately favorable results. CMC probationers in Wisconsin had better employment and income outcomes and lower revocation rates than probationers who were placed on standard intensive supervised probation.[72] Among a sample of Texas parolees, high- or medium-risk CMC clients had lower rates of revocation and were less likely to be returned to prison for parole violations than non-CMC parolees.[73] A study of a version of the CMC that was used on prisoners in Washington, known as the Prisoner Management Classification (PMC) System, reported fewer major infractions among PMC inmates.[74] Overall, the CMC appears to work in that higher risk clients have higher recidivism rates and less compliance than the least risky offenders, those on selective intervention.[75] When revocation is the outcome measure, the CMC appears to accurately classify offenders and predict their criminal justice outcomes. However, when outcomes measures are less dependent on officer decision making, the CMC is less reliable. For instance, Patricia Harris and her colleagues suggest that officers trained in the principles of CMC have a heightened understanding of offender motivations and needs, which results in more lenient evaluation and thus more favorable outcomes.[76]

The construct of psychopathy, a personality disorder characterized by distinctive affective, interpersonal, and affective traits, is an important concept in correctional classification and assessment. The current understanding of psychopathy stems from Hervey Cleckley's *The Mask of Sanity*, published in 1941. Cleckley identified a set of 16 interpersonal traits and characteristics that constituted the core of the psychopath's profile and behavior. Some of these included superficial charm coupled with good intelligence, complete lack of neurotic emotions and manifestations, pathological lying, egocentricity, and incapacity for empathy, global irresponsibility, and lack of guilt or shame especially in the use of antisocial and violent behavior.[77] Since 1965, Robert Hare furthered the study of psychopathy with the creation of his **Psychopathy Checklist-Revised (PCL-R)**. The PCL-R is comprised of an interpersonal/affective traits component (Factor 1) and a social deviance component (Factor 2). Factor 1 contains the following eight items:

1. Glibness/superficial charm
2. Grandiose sense of self-worth
3. Pathological lying
4. Conning/manipulating
5. Lack of remorse or guilt
6. Shallow affect
7. Callous/lack of empathy
8. Failure to accept responsibility

Factor 2 contains the following 12 items:

1. Need for stimulation/proneness to boredom
2. Parasitic lifestyle
3. Poor behavioral controls
4. Early behavioral problems
5. Lack of realistic long-term goals
6. Impulsivity
7. Irresponsibility

8. Juvenile delinquency
9. Revocation of conditional release
10. Promiscuous sexual behavior
11. Many short-term marital relationships
12. Criminal versatility

During diagnostic interviews with professional clinicians, subjects are scored 0, 1, or 2 on the 20 items. Most scholars use 30 as the minimum threshold for psychopathy.[78–80]

The empirical support of the ability of the PCL-R to predict various offending and criminal justice outcomes is impressive, and it has been shown to be applicable to numerous groups, such as federal prisoners; psychiatric patients; incarcerated juvenile offenders; hospital inmates; child molesters; rapists; incarcerated and outpatient sex offenders; schizophrenic offenders; jail inmates; civilly committed patients; minimum-, medium-, and maximum-security inmates; and high school students. Several studies and meta-analysis, which are studies of the empirical strength of research findings, support the validity and reliability of the PCL-R and its related versions.[81–83]

The PCL-R is so influential that it is contained within additional offender classification and assessment tools. The **Historical, Clinical, and Risk Scales (HCR-20)** developed by Christopher Webster, Kevin Douglas, Derek Eaves, and Stephen Hart includes 10 items of behavioral history, including previous violence, early onset, psychopathy, personality disorder, and others; 5 items of clinical information, including lack of insight, negative attitudes, active symptoms of major mental illness, impulsivity, and unresponsiveness to treatment; and 5 items of risk management, including plan's lack of feasibility, exposure to destabilizers, lack of personal support, noncompliance to remediation attempts, and stress. Richard Lusignan and Jacques Marleau recently applied the HCR-20 to two groups of adolescent offenders, those who committed crimes against family members and those who victimized strangers. As theorized, they found that youths who scored higher on the HCR-20, indicating greater risk for violent behavior, were significantly more likely to victimize strangers and have more extensive delinquent careers.[84]

The **Violence Risk Appraisal Guide (VRAG)** and the **Sex Offender Risk Appraisal Guide (SORAG)** are 12- and 14-item actuarial tools that assess violence and sexual violence among male offenders. Developed by Grant Harris, Marnie Rice, and Vernon Quinsey, the VRAG and SORAG contain psychopathic traits from the PCL-R indicating that psychopathy figures prominently into the assessment of violence or sex offender risk. In a series of studies, Harris, Rice, and their colleagues found that the VRAG and SORAG are accurate predictors of violent recidivism among a range of offender groups, such as mentally disordered offenders, rapists, child molesters, forensic patients, and prisoners.[85–88] In a head-to-head test between 10 actuarial instruments, Anthony Glover and his colleagues reported that the VRAG correlated most strongly with violent recidivism and general recidivism among a sample of 106 federal prisoners.[89]

The **Level of Service Inventory-Revised (LSI-R)** is an interview-based instrument developed by Donald Andrews and James Bonta that contains 54 items that span 10 broad topical areas that are related to offender risk and criminal behavior. The topical areas are:

1. Criminal history
2. Education and employment
3. Financial
4. Family and marital
5. Accommodations
6. Leisure and recreation

7. Companions
8. Alcohol and drugs
9. Emotional and personal
10. Attitudes and orientation

The LSI-R is the most widely used correctional instrument in the United States and Canada. The LSI-R has also been modified for use as a screening version and an instrument specifically for juveniles. Interviews with offenders are supplemented with arrest, court, and correctional data, which are used to verify the information in the self-report.[90] The LSI-R is particularly useful as a prediction instrument when used by correctional officials who received formal training on the appropriate use of the instrument.

The LSI-R has been extensively validated by criminologists. A meta-analysis of 131 studies published between 1970 and 1994 indicated that the LSI-R was the most useful actuarial measure of adult offender recidivism.[91] Similarly, Paul Gendreau and his colleagues examined the predictive validity of the LSI-R compared to the Psychopathy Checklist Revised (PCL-R), an instrument that has been referred to as the "unparalleled measure of offender risk." Interestingly, Gendreau and his associates reported that the LSI-R was a better predictor of general recidivism and violent recidivism compared to the PCL-R.[92] Daryl Kroner and Jeremy Mills also found the LSI-R was a stronger predictor of total, violent, nonviolent, and revocation convictions than the PCL-R.[93] It has been argued that the LSI-R only works for white male offenders and that the instrument is less useful among women and minorities. For instance, Kevin Whiteacre found that depending on the cutoff score on the LSI-R, African Americans were more likely than Whites to be underclassified and overclassified as high risk depending on the outcome measure.[94] Research also indicates that it is a valid and reliable assessment tool that is applicable across groups that vary by race and ethnicity,[95–96] gender,[97] and criminality.[98–99] A recent meta-analysis by Glenn Walters revealed that the LSI-R is among the best prediction instruments currently in use.[100]

The **Lifestyle Criminality Screening Form** (LCSF) was designed by Walters, who is a researcher and clinical psychologist who works in the Federal Bureau of Prisons. Walters developed a theory of chronic antisocial behavior that centers around the following 10 principles:

1. Crime can be understood as a lifestyle characterized by a global sense of irresponsibility, self-indulgent interests, an intrusive approach to interpersonal relationships, and chronic violations of societal rules, laws, and mores.
2. Conditions impact on the development of the criminal lifestyle through physical, social, and psychological domains.
3. Conditions may limit one's options but they do not determine one's choices.
4. The behavior of the lifestyle criminal is directed toward losing in dramatic and destructive ways.
5. A distinctive thinking style derives from the lifestyle criminal's decision to engage in delinquent acts.
6. The content and process of criminologic thought are reflected in eight primary cognitive patterns—mollification, cutoff, entitlement, power orientation, sentimentality, superoptimism, cognitive indolence, and discontinuity.
7. For a criminal event to transpire, a criminal opportunity must be present.
8. The motivation for specific criminal events is derived through the process of validation, which is comprised of four secondary organizing motives: anger/rebellion, power/control, excitement/pleasure, and greed/laziness.

9. Criminal events can be understood as incorporating a complex interlinking of thoughts, motives, and behaviors.
10. Since behavior is a function of the attitude and thoughts one adopts toward a particular situation, criminal behavior will not change unless the offender first changes his thinking.[101]

The LCSF contains 14 items that encompass the four behavioral dimensions of the first postulate, irresponsibility, self-indulgence, interpersonal intrusiveness, and social rule breaking. Walters applied the LCSF to two validation groups: 25 high-risk and 25 low-risk inmates. As expected, the high-risk inmates scored significantly higher on the scale than low-risk inmates on individual items, section scores, and the total LCSF instrument.[102] The usefulness and accuracy of the LCSF is comparable to the Psychopathy Checklist-Revised (PCL-R). Walters also conducted a meta-analysis that compared 49 studies that employed these measures and found they were nearly identical in their ability to predict institutional maladjustments such as prison violence and misconduct and general recidivism. However, an impressive advantage of the LCSF is that it takes only 10 minutes to administer and can be completed with extant files. Comparatively, the PCL-R must be administered by a clinician during an interview that lasts 2 to 3 hours.[103]

In addition to the LCSF, Walters created the **Psychological Inventory of Criminal Thinking Styles (PICTS)** designed to assess the eight criminal thinking styles in his theory: mollification, cutoff, entitlement, power orientation, sentimentality, superoptimism, cognitive indolence, and discontinuity. Respectively, these thinking styles correspond to the lifestyle criminal's tendency to place blame on others and frame oneself as the victim of social circumstances; reject common deterrents to crime; believe one has license or ownership of situations and others; engage in interpersonal deception; and be shortsighted and irresponsible. As was the case with the LCSF measure, more severe criminals such as those incarcerated in maximum-security facilities scored higher on the PICTS instrument than minimum- and medium-security inmates and evidenced greater behavioral problems.[104–106] A recent meta-analysis supports the reliability and validity of the PICTS and supports its use as an actuarial instrument particularly in the way that it sheds light on the life patterns and thinking styles of the most problematic criminal offenders.[107]

The U.S. Parole Commission uses the **salient factor score**, which is the offender risk based on recidivism rates for offenders released from federal prisons, offense seriousness, and the likelihood of success under supervised release. The salient factor score is based on six items: prior convictions/adjudications, prior commitments of more than 30 days, age at current offense and prior commitments, recent commitment-free period, criminal justice status at time of arrest, and age. The instrument is reverse scored, which means that higher scores indicate lower risk. Those scoring 8–10 are considered very good risks, 6–7 are good risks, 4–5 are fair risks, and those scoring 0–3 are poor risks—that is, they are likely to recidivate. The salient factor score has been empirically validated.[108–109]

WRAP UP

CASE STUDY CONCLUSION

Gravano's legal outcomes have everything to do with the larger interests of federal prosecutors. In the Gotti case, Gravano was the star witness, who, despite the 19 homicides by his own admission was still—in the interests of justice—a smaller villain than Gotti. It was obvious to everyone including the prosecutors that the sentence that Gravano originally received was not just—it was simply expedient. Although his subsequent drug crimes were themselves serious, one gets the sense that the harsh sentence for those drug crimes not only reflected their seriousness but also a sense of catch-up for the earlier murders.

Chapter Summary

- A criminal sentence is the penalty imposed upon conviction for a crime and is primarily a function of offense seriousness and criminal record.
- A variety of approaches to sentencing have been used that change according to the prevailing philosophy of punishment and crime trends.
- More than 1 million felons are sentenced in state courts each year.
- Seventy percent of felons in state courts are sentenced to incarceration and 30 percent are sentenced to other penalties, such as probation.
- To address the specialized needs and problems of subpopulations of offenders, specialized courts have been developed to incorporate treatment, problem solving, and punishment.
- Prisoners are placed in facilities that are a function of standardized, actuarial measures of their risks of misconduct and recidivism.
- A variety of actuarial devices are in use to target sex offenders, violent offenders, psychopaths, and other offender groups.

Key Terms

actuarial assessment Tools that are offender classification and assessment instruments based on standardized, objective criteria that are used to distinguish the criminal population to determine the most appropriate treatment and punishment modalities.

Adult Internal Management System (AIMS) Classification system that relies on two instruments to identify inmates who are likely to pose a risk to the safe and secure operation of the facility.

Client Management Classification (CMC) System System designed to identify the level of supervision needed for individual correctional clients, their service needs, and the resources required to meet those needs.

clinical assessment Decision making based on the experience, education, training, and gut feeling of correctional staff.

close custody *See* maximum-security.

community courts Specialized courts that address community problems in addition to prosecuting offenders.

conditions The terms that the defendant must abide by to remain in compliance with the court.

criminal history An offender's prior arrests and convictions, which are used for sentencing decisions.

departure The judge's act of going outside the sentencing guidelines when imposing a sentence.

determinate sentencing Sometimes known as flat or straight sentencing, where a specific term is imposed upon conviction.

drug courts Specialized criminal courts that link supervision, judicial oversight, and treatment for drug-using criminal offenders.

DWI courts Specialized courts that target drunk driving offenders using the drug court model.

false-negative Label applied to serious offenders who were predicted to be nonserious offenders.

false-positive Label applied to nonserious offenders who were predicted to be serious offenders.

family courts Specialized courts that handle legal matters pertaining to children and families.

high risk Security level that applies to costly inmates, including highly aggressive prisoners, sexual predators, gang members, mentally ill inmates, and prisoners with severe medical problems and related special needs.

Historical, Clinical, and Risk Scales (HCR-20) A popular violence risk assessment tool.

internal management system System used to determine how prisoners should be housed within a particular facility or complex based upon varying levels of aggressiveness and vulnerability that are measured using a questionnaire.

Level of Service Inventory-Revised (LSI-R) The most widely used actuarial tool in corrections.

Lifestyle Criminality Screening Form (LCSF) Actuarial instrument that measures the criminal lifestyle.

maximum-security Security level for inmates who engage in misconduct and are subject to the strictest supervision and control with fewer treatment amenities.

medium-security Security level for inmates who require more supervision than minimum-security inmates but still have work and programming opportunities.

mental health courts Specialty criminal courts that address the special needs of defendants with mental illnesses.

minimum-security Security level of inmates who require little supervision and are afforded considerable work and living opportunities in confinement.

Minnesota v. Murphy A 1984 Supreme Court decision that held that probation officers are not obligated to provide Miranda advisement to defendants prior to interviews.

Mistretta v. United States A 1989 Supreme Court decision that upheld the constitutionality of sentencing guidelines.

offense seriousness The level of legal seriousness and harm in criminal conduct that is used for sentencing decisions.

presentence investigation (PSI) report A report prepared for the court that summarizes the defendant's social and criminal history for the purpose of sentencing.

Prisoner Management Classification (PMC) System Classification system based on an interview to rate the inmate on 11 objective background factors that assess an inmate's social status and offense history.

problem-solving courts *See* specialized courts.

Psychological Inventory of Criminal Thinking Styles (PICTS) Actuarial device designed to assess the eight criminal thinking styles.

Psychopathy Checklist-Revised (PCL-R) The most widely used measure of psychopathy.

salient factor score An actuarial risk assessment instrument used by federal parole officials to determine parole readiness.

security threat groups (STGs) An organized inmate gang that engages in predatory, criminal behavior behind bars.

sentence The penalty imposed by a court on a person convicted of a crime.

sentencing guidelines Federal guidelines designed to (1) incorporate philosophical purposes of punishment, such as deterrence, deserts, and incapacitation; (2) provide certainty and fairness in sentencing by avoiding unwarranted disparity among offenders with similar characteristics while permitting sufficient flexibility to account for relevant aggravating and mitigating circumstances; and (3) reflect knowledge of human behavior as it relates to criminal justice.

Sex Offender Risk Appraisal Guide (SORAG) An actuarial tool that assesses violence and sexual violence among male offenders.

special management *See* high risk.

specialized courts Courts that attempt to remedy the problems associated with criminal behavior using social services in conjunction with the justice system and not relying exclusively on punishment.

truth in sentencing The correspondence between the sentence imposed upon those sent to prison and the time actually served prior to prison release.

United States Sentencing Commission (U.S.S.C.) An independent commission in the judicial branch that was established by the Sentencing Reform Act provisions of the Comprehensive Crime Control Act of 1984 to establish sentencing guidelines for federal courts and install a formal system of determinate sentences.

United States v. Booker A 2005 Supreme Court decision that determined that a jury must determine the facts that result in an upward departure from federal sentencing guidelines.

victim impact panels Interactive sessions where DWI victims tell their stories of hardship to DWI offenders.

Violence Risk Appraisal Guide (VRAG) A popular risk assessment tool for violence risk; related to the Sex Offender Risk Appraisal Guide (SORAG), which measures risk for sexual recidivism.

Violent Crime Control and Law Enforcement Act of 1994 Federal legislation that attempted to rectify the lack of truth-in-sentencing by assuring that offenders served a larger portion of their sentences.

Critical Thinking Questions

1. What is the most important information on a PSI in terms of understanding how dangerous and criminal an offender is? Are lifestyle factors an important part in understanding the types of risk an offender poses?
2. Based on the prior question, do instruments such as the LSI-R make considerations of lifestyle seem more objective? Should actuarial instruments only be used to make correctional assessments?
3. Has the development of specialized courts been a good thing? Should criminal defendants be treated differently based on certain statuses? Does that invite discriminatory treatment?
4. Other than victim impact statements and panels, are victims ignored by the criminal justice system? Provide evidence to support your answer.

Notes

1. Redlich, A. D., Steadman, H. J., Monahan, J., Robbins, P. C., & Petrila, J. (2006). Patterns of practice in mental health courts: A national survey. *Law and Human Behavior, 30,* 347–362.
2. Robinson, P. H., & Cahill, M. T. (2006). *Law without justice: Why criminal law doesn't give people what they deserve.* New York: Oxford University Press.
3. Flores, A. W., Lowenkamp, C. T., Holsinger, A. M., & Latessa, E. J. (2006). Predicting outcome with the Level of Service Inventory-Revised: The importance of implementation integrity. *Journal of Criminal Justice, 34,* 523–529.
4. Austin, J., Clark, J., Hardyman, P., & Henry, D. A. (1999). The impact of 'three strikes and you're out.' *Punishment and Society, 1,* 131–162.
5. Pager, D. (2003). The mark of a criminal record. *American Journal of Sociology, 108,* 937–975.
6. Robinson & Cahill, p. 75.
7. Robinson & Cahill.
8. Rush, G. E. (2000). *The dictionary of criminal justice* (5th ed.). New York: Dushkin/McGraw-Hill, p. 295.
9. Pager.
10. Petersilia, J. (1997). Probation in the United States. *Crime & Justice, 22,* 149–200.
11. Walsh, A. (2001). Presentence investigation reports (PSI). In A. Walsh (Ed.), *Correctional assessment, casework, and counseling* (3rd ed., pp. 97–120). Lanham, MD: American Correctional Association.

12. Macallair, D. (2002). *The history of the presentence investigation report.* San Francisco, CA: Center on Juvenile and Criminal Justice.

13. *Minnesota v. Murphy,* 465 U.S. 420 (1984).

14. Macallair.

15. *Gagnon v. Scarpelli,* 411 U.S. 778 (1973).

16. *Morrisey v. Brewer,* 408 U.S. 471 (1972).

17. United States Sentencing Commission. (2005). *An overview of the U.S.S.C.* Retrieved September 15, 2008, from http://www.ussc.gov/general/USSCoverview.pdf.

18. United States Sentencing Commission. (2004). *An overview of federal sentencing guidelines.* Retrieved September 15, 2008, from http://www.ussc.gov/TRAINING/GLOverview04.pdf.

19. 18 U.S.C.§ 3553(b).

20. *Mistretta v. United States,* 488 U.S. 361 (1989).

21. *United States v. Booker,* 543 U.S. 220 (2005).

22. Durose, M. R., & Langan, P. A. (2007). *Felony sentences in state courts, 2004.* Washington, DC: U.S. Department of Justice, Office of Justice Programs, Bureau of Justice Statistics.

23. Durose & Langan.

24. Greenfield, L. A. (1995). *Prison sentences and time served for violence.* Washington, DC: U.S. Department of Justice, Office of Justice Programs, Bureau of Justice Statistics.

25. Ditton, P. M., & Wilson, D. J. (1999). *Truth in sentencing in state prisons.* Washington, DC: U.S. Department of Justice, Office of Justice Programs, Bureau of Justice Statistics.

26. DeLisi, M. (2005). *Career criminals in society.* Thousand Oaks, CA: Sage.

27. Loeber, R., & Farrington, D. P. (Eds.). (1998). *Serious and violent juvenile offenders: Risk factors and successful interventions.* Thousand Oaks, CA: Sage.

28. Loeber, R., & Farrington, D. P. (Eds.). (2001). *Child delinquents: Development, intervention, and service needs.* Thousand Oaks, CA: Sage.

29. Wenzel, S. L., Longshire, D., Turner, S., & Ridgely, M. S. (2001). Drug courts: A bridge between criminal justice and health services. *Journal of Criminal Justice, 29,* 241–253.

30. Wenzel, S. L., Turner, S. F., & Ridgely, M. S. (2004). Collaborations between drug courts and service providers: Characteristics and challenges. *Journal of Criminal Justice, 32,* 253–263.

31. Huddleston, C. W., Freeman-Wilson, K., & Boone, D. L. (2004). *Painting the current picture: A national report card on drug courts and other problem solving court programs* in the United States. Alexandria, VA: National Drug Court Institute.

32. Schmitt, G. R. (2006). *Drug courts: The second decade.* Washington, DC: U.S. Department of Justice, Office of Justice Programs, National Institute of Justice.

33. Goldkamp, J. S. (1994). Miami's treatment drug court for felony defendants: Some implications of assessment findings. *Prison Journal, 74,* 110–157.

34. Vito, G., & Tewksbury, R. A. (1998). The impact of treatment: The Jefferson County (Kentucky) Drug Court Program. *Federal Probation, 62,* 46–52.

35. Sechrest, D. K., & Shicor, D. (2001). Determinants of graduation from a day treatment drug court in California: A preliminary study. *Journal of Drug Issues, 31,* 129–148.

36. Johnson Listwan, S., Sundt, J. L., Holsinger, A. M., & Latessa, E. J. (2003). The effect of drug court programming on recidivism: The Cincinnati experience. *Crime & Delinquency, 49,* 389–411.

37. Gottfredson, D. C., Najaka, S. S., Kearley, B. W., & Rocha, C. M. (2006). The long-term effects of participation in the Baltimore City Drug Treatment Court: Results from an experimental study. *Journal of Experimental Criminology, 2,* 67–98.

38. Hepburn, J. R., & Harvey, A. N. (2007). The effect of the threat of legal sanction on program retention and completion: Is that why they stay in drug court? *Crime & Delinquency, 53,* 255–280.

39. Miller, J. M., Miller, H. V., & Barnes, J. C. (2007). The effect of demeanor on drug court admission. *Criminal Justice Policy Review, 18,* 246–259.

40. Finigan, M. W., Carey, S. M., & Cox, A. (2007). *The impact of a mature drug court over 10 years of operation: Recidivism and costs.* Washington, DC: U.S. Department of Justice, Office of Justice Programs, National Institute of Justice.

41. Lowenkamp, C. T., Holsinger, A. M., & Latessa, E. J. (2005, Fall). Are drug courts effective: A meta-analytic review. *Journal of Community Corrections,* 5–28.

42. Winfree, L. T., & Giever, D. M. (2000). On classifying driving-while-intoxicated offenders: The experiences of a citywide DWI drug court. *Journal of Criminal Justice, 28,* 13–21.

43. Rojek, D. G., Coverdill, J. E., & Fors, S. W. (2003). The effect of victim impact panels on DUI rearrest rates: A 5-year follow-up. *Criminology, 41,* 1319–1340.

44. Bouffard, J. A., & Richardson, K. A. (2007). The effectiveness of drug court programming for specific kinds of offenders. *Criminal Justice Policy Review, 18,* 274–293.

45. Green, B. L., Furrer, C., Worcel, S., Burrus, S., & Finigan, M. W. (2007). How effective are family treatment drug courts? Outcomes from a four-site national study. *Child Maltreatment, 12,* 43–59.

46. Boles, S. M., Young, N. K., Moore, T., & DiPirro-Beard, S. (2007). The Sacramento dependency drug court: Development and outcomes. *Child Maltreatment, 12,* 161–171.

47. Goldkamp, J. S., Weiland, D. Collins, M., & White, M. D. (1996). *The role of drug and alcohol abuse in domestic violence and its treatment: Dade County's Domestic Violence Court Experiment.* Washington, DC: U.S. Department of Justice, Office of Justice Programs, National Institute of Justice.

48. Gover, A. R., MacDonald, J. M., & Alpert, G. P. (2003). Combating domestic violence: Findings from an evaluation of a local domestic violence court. *Criminology & Public Policy, 3,* 109–132.

49. Gover, A. R., Brank, E. M., & MacDonald, J. M. (2007). Specialized domestic violence court in South Carolina: An example of procedural justice for victims and defendants. *Violence Against Women, 13,* 603–626.

50. Coulter, M. L., Alexander, A., & Harrison, V. (2005). Specialized domestic violence courts: Improvement for women victims? *Women & Criminal Justice, 16,* 91–106.

51. National Institute of Justice. (2003). *Do batterer intervention programs work? Two studies.* Washington, DC: U.S. Department of Justice, Office of Justice Programs, National Institute of Justice.

52. Redlich, A. D., Steadman, H. J., Monahan, J., Robbins, P. C., & Petrila, J. (2006). Patterns of practice in mental health courts: A national survey. *Law and Human Behavior, 30,* 347–362.

53. Bureau of Justice Assistance. (2005). *Mental health courts program.* Washington, DC: U.S. Department of Justice, Office of Justice Programs, Bureau of Justice Assistance.

54. Cosden, M., Ellens, J., Schnell, J., Yasmeen, Y., & Wolfe, M. (2003). Evaluation of a mental health treatment court with assertive community treatment. *Behavioral Sciences and the Law, 21,* 415–427.

55. Boothroyd, R., Poythress, N., McGaha, A., & Petrila, J. (2003). The Broward mental health court: Process, outcomes, and service utilization. *International Journal of Law and Psychiatry, 26,* 55–71.

56. Trupin, E., & Richards, H. (2003). Seattle's mental health courts: Early indicators of effectiveness. *International Journal of Law and Psychiatry, 26,* 33–53.

57. Nugent, M. E., Fanflik, P., & Bromirski, D. (2004). *The changing nature of prosecution: Community prosecution vs. traditional prosecution approaches*. Alexandria, VA: American Prosecutors Research Institute.

58. Kralstein, D. (2005). *Community court research: A literature review*. New York: Center for Court Innovation.

59. Clear, T. (1988). Statistical prediction in corrections. *Research in Corrections, 1,* 1–39.

60. Jones-Hubbard, D., Travis, L. F., & Latessa, E. J. (2001). *Case classification in community corrections: A national survey of the state of the art.* Washington, DC: U.S. Department of Justice, Office of Justice Programs, National Institute of Justice.

61. Taxman, F. S., Cropsey, K. L., Young, D. W., & Wexler, H. (2007). Screening, assessment, and referral practices in adult correctional settings: A national perspective. *Criminal Justice and Behavior, 34,* 1216–1234.

62. Travis, L. F., & Latessa, E. J. (1996). Classification and needs assessment. In *Managing violent youthful offenders in adult institutions.* Longmont, CO: National Institute of Corrections.

63. Latessa, E. (2004, Winter). Best practices of classification and assessment. *Journal of Community Corrections,* 4–30.

64. Austin, J., & McGinnis, K. (2004). *Classification of high-risk and special management prisoners: A national assessment of current practices.* Longmont, CO: National Institute of Corrections.

65. Austin & McGinnis.

66. Austin & McGinnis.

67. DeLisi, M. (2003). Criminal careers behind bars. *Behavioral Sciences and the Law, 21,* 653–669.

68. Latessa, E. J., & Lowenkamp, C. (2006). What works in reducing recidivism. *University of St. Thomas Law Journal, 3,* 521–525.

69. Holsinger, A. M., & Latessa, E. J. (1999). An empirical evaluation of a sanction continuum: Pathways through the juvenile justice system. *Journal of Criminal Justice, 27,* 155–172.

70. Andrews, D. A., & Dowden, C. (2006). Risk principle of case classification in correctional treatment: A meta-analytic investigation. *International Journal of Offender Therapy and Comparative Criminology, 50,* 88–100.

71. Lowenkamp, C. T., Latessa, E. J., & Holsinger, A. M. (2006). The risk principle in action: What have we learned from 13,676 offenders and 97 correctional programs? *Crime & Delinquency, 51,* 1–17.

72. Lerner, K., Arling, G., & Baird, S. C. (1986). Client management classification strategies for case supervision. *Crime & Delinquency, 32,* 254–271.

73. Eisenberg, M., & Markley, G. (1987). Something works in community corrections. *Federal Probation, 51,* 28–32.

74. Baird, C., & Neuenfeldt, D. (1990). The Client Management Classification System. *NCCD Focus, 1990,* 1–7.

75. Harris, P. M. (1994). Client management classification and prediction of probation outcome. *Crime & Delinquency, 40,* 154–174.

76. Harris, P. M., Gingerich, R., & Whittaker, T. A. (2004). The "effectiveness" of differential supervision. *Crime & Delinquency, 50,* 235–271.

77. Cleckley, H. (1941). *The mask of sanity*. St. Louis, MO: Mosby.

78. Hare, R. D. (1991). *The Hare Psychopathy Checklist-Revised.* Toronto, Canada: Multi-Health System.

79. Hare, R. D. (1993). *Without conscience: The disturbing world of the psychopaths among us.* New York: The Guilford Press.

80. Hare, R. D. (1996). Psychopathy: A clinical construct whose time has come. *Criminal Justice & Behavior, 23,* 25–54.

81. Walters, G. D. (2003). Predicting institutional adjustment and recidivism with the PCL factor scores: A meta-analysis. *Law and Human Behavior, 27,* 541–558.

82. Loza, W. (2003). Predicting violent and nonviolent recidivism of incarcerated male offenders. *Aggression and Violent Behavior, 8,* 175–203.

83. Caldwell, M. F., McCormick, D. J., Umstead, D., & Van Rybroek, G. J. (2007). Evidence of treatment progress and therapeutic outcomes among adolescents with psychopathic features. *Criminal Justice and Behavior, 34,* 573–587.

84. Lusignan, R., & Marleau, J. D. (2007). Risk assessment and offender-victim relationship in juvenile offenders. *International Journal of Offender Therapy and Comparative Criminology, 51,* 433–443.

85. Harris, G. T., Rice, M. E., & Quinsey, V. L. (1993). Violent recidivism of mentally disordered offenders: The development of a statistical prediction instrument. *Criminal Justice and Behavior, 20,* 315–335.

86. Rice, M. E., & Harris, G. T. (1997). Cross validation and extension of the VRAG for child molesters and rapists. *Law and Human Behavior, 21,* 231–241.

87. Harris, G. T., Rice, M. E., & Cormier, C. A. (2002). Prospective replication of the VRAG in predicting violent recidivism among forensic patients. *Law and Human Behavior, 26,* 377–394.

88. Harris, G. T., & Rice, M. E. (2007). Adjusting actuarial violence risk assessments based on aging and the passage of time. *Criminal Justice and Behavior, 34,* 297–313.

89. Glover, A. J. J., Nicholson, D. E., Hemmati, T., Bernfeld, G. A., & Quinsey, V. L. (2002). A comparison of predictors of general and violent recidivism among high-risk federal offenders. *Criminal Justice and Behavior, 29,* 235–249.

90. Andrews, D. A., & Bonta, J. L. (1995). *The Level of Service Inventory-Revised.* Toronto, Canada: Multi-Health Systems.

91. Gendreau, P., Little, T., & Goggin, C. (1996). A meta-analysis of the predictors of adult offender recidivism: What works! *Criminology, 34,* 575–607.

92. Gendreau, P., Goggin, C., & Smith, P. (2002). Is the PCL-R really the "unparalleled" measure of offender risk? A lesson in knowledge cumulation. *Criminal Justice and Behavior, 29,* 397–426.

93. Kroner, D. G., & Mills, J. F. (2001). The accuracy of five risk appraisal instruments in predicting institutional misconduct and new convictions. *Criminal Justice and Behavior, 28,* 471–489.

94. Whiteacre, K. W. (2006). Testing the LSI-R for racial/ethnic bias. *Criminal Justice Policy Review, 17,* 330–342.

95. Holsinger, A. M., Lowenkamp, C. T., & Latessa, E. J. (2003). Ethnicity, gender, and the Level of Service Inventory-Revised. *Journal of Criminal Justice, 31,* 309–320.

96. Schlager, M. D., & Simourd, D. J. (2007). The validity of the LSI-R among African American and Hispanic male offenders. *Criminal Justice and Behavior, 34,* 545–554.

97. Coulson, G., Ilacqua, G., Nutbrown, V., Giulekas, D., & Cudjoe, F. (1996). Predictive utility of the LSI for incarcerated female offenders. *Criminal Justice and Behavior, 23,* 427–439.

98. Loza, W., & Simourd, D. J. (1994). Psychometric evaluation of the LSI among male Canadian federal offenders. *Criminal Justice and Behavior, 21,* 468–480.

99. Flores, A. W., Lowenkamp, C. T., Smith, P., & Latessa, E. J. (2006). Validating the LSI-R on a sample of federal probationers. *Federal Probation, 70,* 44–48.

100. Walters, G. D. (2006). Risk-appraisal versus self-report in the prediction of criminal justice outcomes. *Criminal Justice and Behavior, 33,* 279–304.

101. Walters, G. D. (1990). *The criminal lifestyle: Patterns of serious criminal conduct.* Thousand Oaks, CA: Sage.

102. Walters, G. D., White, T. W., & Denney, D. (1991). The lifestyle criminality screening form: Preliminary data. *Criminal Justice & Behavior, 18,* 406–418.

103. Walters, G. D. (2003). Predicting criminal justice outcomes with the psychopathy checklist and lifestyle criminality screening form: A meta-analytic comparison. *Behavioral Sciences & the Law, 21,* 89–102.

104. Walters, G. D. (1995). The psychological inventory of criminal thinking styles: Reliability and preliminary validity. *Criminal Justice & Behavior, 22,* 307–325.

105. Walters, G. D. (1996). The psychological inventory of criminal thinking styles: Part III predictive validity. *International Journal of Offender Therapy and Comparative Criminology, 40,* 105–112.

106. Walters, G. D., Trgovac, M., Rychlec, M., Di Fazio, R., & Olson, J. R. (2002). Assessing change with the psychological inventory of criminal thinking styles: A controlled analysis and multisite cross-validation. *Criminal Justice & Behavior, 29,* 308–331.

107. Walters, G. D. (2002). The Psychological Inventory of Criminal Thinking Styles (PICTS): A review and meta-analysis. *Assessment, 9,* 278–291.

108. Hoffman, P. B. (1994). Twenty years of operational use of a risk prediction instrument: The United States Parole Commission's Salient Factor Score. *Journal of Criminal Justice, 22,* 477–494.

109. Hoffman, P. B., & Beck, J. L. (1985). Recidivism among released federal prisoners: Salient Factor Score and five-year follow-up. *Criminal Justice and Behavior, 12,* 501–507.

CHAPTER

5

The Pretrial Period and Jails

"The frequent exposure to the jail setting among repeat street criminals makes the jail an important place for the periodic reinforcement of subcultural values as the inmate re-experiences confinement and renews acquaintances with similarly situated people."[1, p. 431]

OBJECTIVES

- Understand bail/bond and the ways that it is used to release criminal defendants to the community or keep them in custody.
- Learn the various types of bond and the risk factors used in assigning them.
- Identify the ways that pretrial services operate in the United States and the factors that determine pretrial outcomes.
- Explore the consequences and effects of pretrial detention as part of the correctional process.
- Learn the place of jail in the criminal justice system.
- Recognize the characteristics, social and criminal histories, and special needs of the jail population.
- Learn ways that reforms and programming have modernized the design and function of contemporary jails.

CASE STUDY

As shown in the figure, pretrial misconduct is relatively common among felony defendants released from the 75 largest counties in the United States. About 35 percent of felons have some type of pretrial misconduct and 20 percent fail to appear in court. About 20 percent are rearrested—many for new felonies—and less than 10 percent of felons remain fugitives after 1 year. Based on these estimates of misconduct, it is clear that the pretrial period can be risky for the courts and correctional systems.

1. Which factors do courts use to set bond on felony defendants?
2. How can felony defendants get released from jail pending their appearance in court?

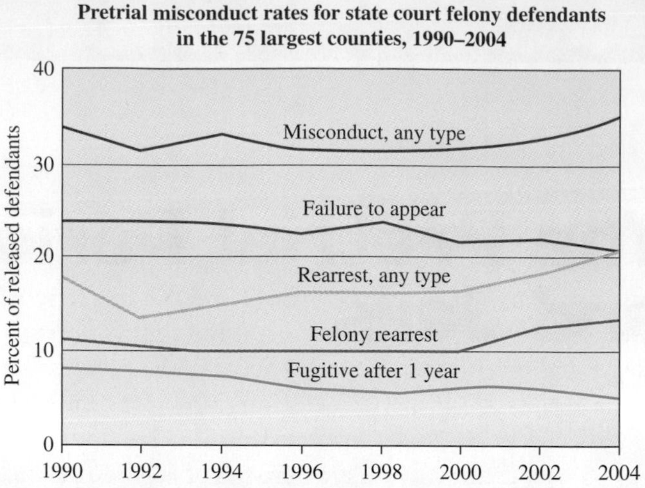

Nationwide, one in five felons fails to appear in court and 35 percent have some type of pretrial misconduct.

Source: Sabol, W. J., & Minton, T. D. (2008). *Jail inmates at midyear 2007.* Washington, DC: U.S. Department of Justice, Office of Justice Programs, Bureau of Justice Statistics.

"It is at the pretrial stage that one's freedom is so often intertwined with one's money."[2, p. 240]

What happens between a defendant's arrest and his or her first appearance in court is probably the least understood area of the criminal justice system. Criminal defendants and their families often have many questions. Where do arrestees go after they are placed in police cars and driven away? Can they be released? What is bail? What is bond? What are the differences between bail and bond? What does own recognizance mean? Do they have to pay money in order to be released? Who has jurisdiction over arrestees once police officers bring them to municipal holding stations or county jails? How much time transpires before arrestees appear in court? Do arrestees receive due process even without appearing in court?

The answers to these questions occur during the pretrial period. Once the police officer completes the arrest report and terminates discussions (if any) with the defendant, judicial personnel assume responsibility for the case. Most large jurisdictions have judicial officers, variously referred to as pretrial service interviewers, pretrial officers, bond commissioners, and the like. **Pretrial service officers** interview criminal defendants and gather information about the offender's social and criminal history, such as residency, family contacts, employment status, substance abuse and psychiatric history, and criminal history. Importantly, they do not interview defendants about their current charges as a way to influence guilt or innocence. Once the information is gathered, the judicial officer writes a report that summarizes the social and criminal history for the court and makes a bond recommendation. This is the other important purpose of pretrial service personnel—they decide the type of bond that a defendant should receive and serve as the primary way to alleviate jail crowding.

Typically, this activity transpires at a county jail. Jail is a local correctional facility that houses persons who have been convicted of crimes and sentenced to less than 2 years' confinement, as well as those awaiting trial. Operated by the county sheriff's department, jails are a temporary form of incarceration, thus they are much different than prison. Those who are unable to post bond or be released on their own recognizance are detained

"The system is lax with those whom it should be stringent, and stringent with those with whom it could safely be less severe."[3, p. 3]

until their case reaches a resolution in court, such as dismissal or conviction. This creates a sort of paradox in American due process. The **presumption of innocence** ensures that defendants are considered innocent until proven guilty, yet tens of thousands of criminal defendants each day are detained during the pretrial phase. Think of it this way. Imagine you didn't have a permanent address and you were arrested for drunk driving while traveling through a state. You technically would be transient or passing through town, and would likely be required to post bail before being released. Imagine that you cannot pay the bond amount. Two weeks later, you meet with the district attorney and a public defender and they indicate that charges against you are going to be dismissed. You are free to go. You have not been convicted of a crime, yet you were in custody for 2 weeks.[6]

This chapter explores the pretrial period, the misunderstood time during which police, court, and correctional entities meet and the correctional process begins. Three broad areas are examined. First, the historical and contemporary use of bail as a means of pretrial release and detention is explored. Second, the progression of a criminal case during the pretrial period from charging to arraignment to dismissal or conviction is reviewed. The various legal and extralegal factors that are used to determine bond are discussed. Third, the history, function, and characteristics of jails and jail inmates are described. As you will discover, jail is distinct from prison despite their common interchangeable usage.

Bail/Bond

Bail is a form of pretrial release in which a defendant enters a legal agreement or promise that requires his or her appearance in court. The bail amount is statutory, which means that legislatures establish monetary bails based on the legal seriousness of the charge. For example, class A or class I felonies, which are the most serious crimes, such as murder, may be no-bond offenses. Magistrates or judges may increase or decrease the statutory bail amount based on aggravating and mitigating factors of the case. Pretrial service officers do not set bail amounts; they simply follow the statutory schedule of bail amounts. Even though defendants are released from jail custody, they are still under the supervision of the courts. If defendants do not comply with the conditions of their bail, such as abstaining from alcohol use or having no contact with the alleged victim in the case, the court can withdraw the defendant's previously granted release. This is known as **bail revocation.**

Bond is a pledge of money or some other assets offered as bail by an accused person or his or her surety (bail bondsman) to secure temporary release from custody. Bond is forfeited if the conditions of bail are not fulfilled. The best way to understand how the bail/bond process works is with an example. A person is arrested for felony theft and assigned a bail of $1,000. The defendant can pay $1,000 to the court in exchange for release from jail. The $1,000 is essentially collateral to entice the defendant to appear in court. If the defendant misses any court dates, he or she could lose the $1,000. However, if the defendant makes all scheduled court appearances, he or she will receive the money back net any fees or fines that are imposed. If the defendant cannot afford $1,000, he can utilize the services of a bonding agent or bondsperson. A **bondsperson** is a social service professional who is contractually responsible for a criminal defendant once he or she is released from custody. Bondspersons typically charge a 15 percent fee for their services. Thus, the defendant would pay the bondsperson $150 to be released; in turn the bondsperson is potentially liable for the entire $1,000 bond if the defendant misses any court dates or absconds. Bondspersons often have close working relationships with the criminal justice system and utilize many of the same criteria that are used to set bond, such as employment, residency, and criminal history. If defendants indeed abscond while on bond, bondspersons sometimes hire a third party, known as a bail recovery agent or bounty hunter, to find the escapee.

"Jail inmates may be serious repeat offenders, novices in crime, or even naïve traffic violators."[4, p. 69]

Defendants, bondspersons, and bounty agents are bound by financial relationships. Of course, bondspersons and bounty hunters employ law enforcement-like tactics to facilitate their financial arrangements with criminal defendants. However, they are not law enforcement agents per se, thus constitutional safeguards that apply to police officers do not apply to them.

Strictly speaking, the term *bail* usually refers to the monetary value needed for release and the term *bond* refers to the type of release that the defendant was awarded. However, once released defendants are synonymously referred to as "being on bond" or "released on bail." Bail and bond are often used interchangeably even by criminal justice professionals and there is no great distinction made here either. Whichever term is used, bail/bond attempts to ensure an accused person's appearance in court. Depending on the risks that he or she poses and the circumstances of the current charges, a promise, property, money, or some other assets are posted for release. If the defendant misses court appearances, the posted security (or liability in the event of a recognizance release) is forfeited.

Types of Bond

The best type of bond that a defendant can hope for is to be released on his or her own recognizance. A **recognizance bond** is a written promise to appear in court, in which the criminal defendant is released from jail custody without paying or posting cash or property. Variously referred to as personal recognizance (PR), own recognizance (OR), or release on recognizance (ROR), these bonds are reserved for arrestees with minimal or no prior criminal record; strong community ties, such as employment and long-term residency; and relatively nonserious charges. Persons who are released on recognizance bonds are considered to be low risk in terms of reoffending, dangerousness, and failing to appear in court.

Sometimes the defendant does not have the extensive community ties or minimal prior record to justify a recognizance release, but otherwise poses little risk to the community. In these types of cases, defendants are commonly released on **cosigned recognizance bond**, where a family member, close friend, or business associate signs his or her name on the bond to guarantee the defendant's appearance in court. Other jurisdictions employ a third-party custody bond that works the same way. Sometimes, attorneys are granted third-party custody of their clients to ensure their appearance in court.

Other criminal defendants pose greater risks of missing court appearances and recidivating. Still others are too dangerous to release because they might be actively homicidal or suicidal. For riskier defendants, a variety of secured bonds are used. **Secured bonds** require the payment of cash or other assets to the courts in exchange for release from custody. In the event that the defendant misses court dates or **absconds,** which is to escape or otherwise elude legal responsibility, the cash or other assets are forfeited to the court. Various jurisdictions across the country employ various forms of secured bonds. **Cash-only bonds** mean that the defendant must post 100 percent of the bond in cash to be released. **Property bonds** are houses, real estate, or vehicles that may be cosigned to the court as collateral against pretrial flight. Absconding on a property bond could result in losing one's home. Many criminal defendants pay 10–15 percent of their bond to professional bondspersons for release. In these cases, bondspersons act as sureties and are responsible for the total bond if the defendant absconds. Other jurisdictions use a **deposit bail system** where the court acts as bondsperson and the defendant posts a percentage of their total bond. *Court-run deposit bail systems* return the bond money to the defendant, net minor administrative fees, unlike bondspersons. Researchers have found that deposit bail systems produce comparable failure to appear rates as commercial bondspersons.[7]

History and Reform

The concept of bail has a long and interesting history. Processes resembling modern day bail practices appeared as early as 2500 BCE, and in Roman law as early as 700 BCE. For example, the concept known as **hostageship** involved a person who volunteered to be prosecuted and punished in the place of the actual suspect in the event that the suspect failed to appear for court proceedings.[8] In medieval Germany and England, **wergeld** was the assessed value of a person's life and considered their bail value. Trials by compurgation whereby criminal defendants established their innocence by taking an oath and have various witnesses swear or testify to the veracity of their oath also used wergeld. Both practices apply the concept of real or human assets to use as collateral for court proceedings.

"Jails may be in the worst possible situation as they typically are the default mechanism for failures in other economic, social, and health systems."[5, p. 258]

Under English common law, sheriffs appointed their acquaintances who were often prominent members of the community called sureties. Sureties promised to pay money or land in the event that released defendants absconded. In this way, a **surety** is a guarantor that defendants will appear in court, and over time sureties became de facto sheriffs because of their power of revocation. It is because of their financial investment that sureties and modern-day bondspersons employ enforcement-like methods to guarantee that defendants appear in court. There is an important distinction. Bondspersons have contractual power, not law enforcement power; thus they are not bound to the same degree by the same constitutional constraints as police officers.

The English common law surety system was difficult to replicate in the burgeoning United States because of its sheer geographic size and the newness of community ties. Instead, pretrial release relied on the use of bondspersons. The concept of bail appears sporadically in colonial America. For example, the Eighth Amendment of the United States Constitution proscribes the requirement of excessive bail. The Judiciary Act of 1789 established bail as an absolute right in detainable criminal charges with the exception of capital offenses, or those potentially punishable by death.[9] The bail business grew with increasing numbers of bondspersons, bail recovery or enforcement agents, and bounty hunters operating at the periphery of American justice.

Due to concern about the constitutionality of pretrial release and supervision and bail enforcement, the courts addressed the issue. In New York State, *Nicolls v. Ingersoll* (1810) established that bounty hunters have same rights of capture as bonding agents when authorized by those bonding agents.[10] The United States Supreme Court weighed in on ***Reese v. United States*** (1869), which established that bounty hunters were proxy pretrial officers who had complete control of returning absconders to the court.[11] Similarly, ***Taylor v. Taintor*** (1873) clarified that bounty hunter behavior must conform to law, but bounty hunters were not bound by Fourth Amendment as are the police.[12]

The for-profit bondsperson business steamed along throughout the 19th and 20th centuries. Criminal defendants who had the monetary resources to post bail were released. Otherwise, criminal defendants waited in jail until their court appearances. However, many criminal cases are dismissed, meaning that many jail detainees are confined for criminal charges for which they are never convicted. Increasingly, the plight of persons detained prior to trial became publicized and a strictly monetary bail system came under attack.

Prior to the landmark Manhattan Bail Project, criminal defendants were kept in jail primarily because of their socioeconomic status or inability to pay bail.

Six decades into the 20th century, criminal defendants who were unable to pay their bail remained in jail custody. For all intents and purposes, ability to pay was the sole criterion for pretrial release from jail. This changed dramatically in 1961 when the Vera Institute of Justice became a driving force in the area of pretrial supervision of criminal defendants. The Vera Institute of Justice initiated the **Manhattan Bail Project** in New York City. For the project, Vera staff interviewed defendants to ascertain their community ties including their family connections in the city and employment history. After third-party verification of the information, the defendants were assigned a numerical score that represented their likelihood of absconding. Persons with weak community ties were considered high risk and persons with strong community ties were considered low risk. Judges were presented with recommendations based on these risks and released criminal defendants accordingly. The results were compelling. Releasing defendants with attendant strong community ties on promise to appear in court was more effective than requiring money bail to assure court appearances. In fact, the experimental group that was released merely on their promise to appear had twice the appearance rate of those released on bail. The project saved more than $1 million in correctional costs for defendants who otherwise would have languished behind bars.[13]

In 1965, Ronald Goldfarb published *Ransom*, a scathing critique of the due process problems inherent in the American bail system. Goldfarb argued that defendants who remain in custody face a variety of risks for further criminal punishment compared to arrestees who are released on bond. For instance, detained persons are more likely to be indicted, more likely to plead guilty, have greater trial conviction rates, and receive more punitive sentences.[14] Goldfarb's work and the Manhattan Bail Project prompted institutional change in pretrial services across the country and culminated in the **Bail Reform Act of 1966**, which authorized the use of releasing defendants on their own recognizance in noncapital federal cases when appearance in court can be shown to be likely. This effectively ended the de facto discrimination against indigent defendants. The **Bail Reform Act of 1984** reinforced the community ties clause of the 1966 act, but also provided for the preventive detention of defendants deemed dangerous or likely to abscond.

In 1967, the Vera Institute of Justice launched the Manhattan Bowery Project that aimed to remove alcoholic defendants in jail on nuisance offenses, such as public drunkenness, disorderly conduct, and vagrancy, and place them in detoxification centers. Proactive police patrols identified visibly intoxicated individuals and encouraged them to enter treatment facilities. The project resulted in an 80 percent decline in the arrests of transient alcoholics, which saved inordinate monies for jail detention and court costs. Today, the program is called Project Renewal and serves more than 20,000 alcoholic and homeless persons annually.[15]

Another innovative Vera project was its nonprofit bail bond agencies in the Bronx, New York; Nassau County, Long Island; and Essex County (Newark), New Jersey, which were launched in 1987. Vera paid defendants' bail if they agreed to submit to supervision and treatment that included a 24-hour observational period, drug testing, curfews, home visits, and employment monitoring. Defendants entered into agreement with Vera that they could be returned to jail for failing to comply with any conditions of their release. Vera encountered severe problems with its Bronx operations because defendants tended to have overlapping problems such as weak community ties and family support and crippling drug addiction. Many released defendants absconded and Vera closed the operation in 1994. The operations in Nassau County and Essex County were far more successful. Defendants were highly compliant with conditions of their release, and recidivism and absconding rates were low. Both were incorporated into independent nonprofit organization with county contracts at the conclusion of the Vera Project.[16]

Prior to innovations such as the Homeless Release Project, there was little chance that a transient person could receive supervised release from jail.

Inspired by the innovations of the Vera Institute of Justice, municipalities across the country have devised creative ways to supervise defendants during the pretrial period. For instance, officials in San Francisco developed the Homeless Release Project (HRP), which is a pretrial release program that attempts to reduce jail crowding by releasing homeless nuisance offenders and providing them supervision and individualized care. Alissa Riker and Ursula Castellano found that 85 percent of the HRP clients had substance abuse problems and 50 percent had co-occurring mental illness. These clients were interviewed to determine their treatment needs and service history and to establish temporary housing and assign a case manager. Clients are monitored to ensure that treatment and court appointments are kept. Approximately 76 percent of HRP clients complied with the conditions of the program and participants were 50 percent less likely to be rearrested than similar offenders who were not in the program.[17]

The bail reform movement also sparked federal initiatives to modernize American bail practices. In 1978, the United States Department of Justice awarded grants to the National Association of Pretrial Services Agencies (NAPSA) to develop national professional standards and the Pretrial Services Resource Center (PSRC) to assess the status of the pretrial field. The Bureau of Justice Assistance program then conducted national surveys of pretrial services programs in 1979, 1989, and 2001. The results from the most recent survey are discussed later in this chapter.

Bounty hunters have always been a sensationalistic and controversial part of the criminal justice process as exemplified by television personality Duane Chapman, also known as Dog the Bounty Hunter.

Bail Recovery/Enforcement

A sensationalistic part of criminal justice lore has been popularized by the television program *Dog: The Bounty Hunter*. A **bounty hunter** is a person hired by bondspersons to enforce the conditions of bail and recover the investment asset of the bondsperson. In other words, bounty hunters track down bail absconders and return them to jail. Afterward, bail agents will commonly revoke their bonds and pay the bounty hunter a fee for returning the absconder. Bounty hunters serve two important purposes including helping prevent insurance companies from raising premiums that they charge to insure bonds and preserving the bonding agent's reputation, power, and influence as an informal member of the criminal justice system by keeping absconding rates down.

Bounty hunters are often stigmatized because of their direct contact with criminal offenders and the enforcement aspects of their work. To some, bounty hunters are rogues operating on the fringes of due process. Brian Johnson and Greg Warchol studied contemporary bounty hunters and found that these bail recovery/enforcement agents strive to mirror the professionalism, education, and experience of the courtroom work group. Johnson and Warchol found that bounty hunters have uneven working relationships with local police. In terms of their working relationship with bounty hunters, police officers have been characterized as (1) accepting and motivated, (2) cautious but accommodating, and (3) cold and rejecting. The working relationships between law enforcement and bounty hunters is influenced by ideological worldviews of the officers, their level of understanding of bounty hunter function, and acknowledgement of the legitimacy of the bounty hunter's role in the criminal justice system.[18]

Ronald Burns and his colleagues conducted interviews with bounty hunters and examined their backgrounds and demographic characteristics, training and skills, professional motivation, perceptions of the profession, and bail enforcement practices. The average bounty hunter was a 51-year-old, conservative, White male. Nearly 90 percent of the bounty hunters they interviewed were male and more than 80 percent were White. Nearly 30 percent had bachelor's degrees and nearly 10 percent had master's or law degrees. In terms of training and skills, bounty hunters frequently had military, private detection, security, and law enforcement backgrounds. About 92 percent had training in bail law, 63 percent had a formal bail certification, and 75 percent had formal bail training. Money and autonomy were the primary motivations for bounty hunter careers and most reported that bounty hunters were underappreciated and misunderstood by the criminal justice system. Bounty hunters use a variety of resources to locate absconders, including informants, paid information, local police, and the Internet. Most bounty hunters carried an array of sublethal weapons and law enforcement equipment, such as mace and handcuffs. Fewer than 20 percent carried firearms or used weapons to affect an arrest, although the level of risk and physical danger was perceived to be high.[19]

Contemporary Pretrial Services

John Clark and Alan Henry, researchers within the Bureau of Justice Assistance, analyzed data based on the national survey of more than 200 pretrial services programs across the United States. Their report is a comprehensive look at contemporary pretrial services nationwide and includes important findings pertaining to administrative issues, bond interviews and assessments, and special populations and monitoring.

Administrative Issues

Nationwide, Clark and Henry found:

- The average pretrial service unit is staffed by 18 persons, receives funding from county and state sources, and interviews more than 5,000 defendants annually.
- About 40 percent of agencies have from two to five staff members.
- Programs serving large metropolitan areas, about 2 percent of all programs, interview more than 50,000 defendants annually.
- More than half of pretrial service programs operate during normal business hours; however some offer 24-hour, 7-day operations.
- About 21 percent of programs have delegated release authority. Of those units with release authority, officers can release some felonies and most misdemeanor offenses.
- The administrative location of pretrial service units varies greatly. Probation controls 31 percent of pretrial service programs, courts operate 29 percent, sheriff's departments operate 19 percent, and private, nonprofit firms control 8 percent.[20]

Bond Interviews and Assessments

One of the most critical parts of the pretrial process is the interaction between criminal defendants and criminal justice practitioners that assess offender risk and determine bond.

- About 75 percent of agencies interview arrestees prior to their first appearance in court.
- Agencies gather an array of information from the defendant on the social and criminal history.
- Self-reported criminal history is validated using a variety of data sources such as local police records, local judicial records, jail records, and the National Crime Information Center computer, which can access a database with over 25 million criminal histories.
- Bond recommendations are based on objective risk scales, more than half of which have been validated, subjective or expert judgments of pretrial service staff, or a combination of objective and subjective approaches.
- About 42 percent of pretrial service units employ both, 35 percent use subjective criteria only, and 23 percent rely exclusively on a risk assessment instrument.[20]

Special Populations and Monitoring

Because of the high prevalence of substance abuse and mental health disorders among the criminal population, early detection of psychiatric problems is an important part of the pretrial process.

- Nearly 75 percent of pretrial service programs ask questions about mental health and psychiatric history, and many of these refer clients with mental health needs to appropriate agencies.

- About 25 percent have developed specialized protocols for dealing with clients arrested for domestic violence. Other special programs have been devised to assist homeless arrestees.
- Nearly 70 percent of agencies administer drug testing while defendants are on bond and 50 percent conduct alcohol testing. Substance abuse monitoring is done in conjunction with general counseling services.
- Approximately 54 percent of pretrial service units are servicing jails that operate at greater than 100 percent capacity. Given the problem of jail crowding, pretrial service units are viewed as both a valuable service for the courts and correctional systems, but also an important release valve for the jail population.[21]

Pretrial Release of Felony Defendants

The **National Pretrial Reporting Program** is a national initiative sponsored by the Bureau of Justice Statistics, which collects detailed information about the criminal history, pretrial processing, adjudication, and sentencing of felony defendants in state courts in the 75 largest counties in the United States. A sample of 13,206 cases was representative of the more than 55,000 felony cases filed in these jurisdictions per month. The 75 largest counties in the country accounted for 50 percent of the total crime occurring in the United States. Based on these data, Bureau of Justice statisticians Brian Reaves and Jacob Perez produced a number of important findings about felony defendants during the pretrial period of the criminal justice system, such as:

- 63 percent of felony defendants are released from jail prior to the resolution of their case. This includes:
  - 24 percent of murder defendants
  - 48 percent of rape defendants
  - 50 percent of robbery defendants
  - 68 percent of assault defendants
- The most common form of release was personal recognizance, which 38 percent of all felony defendants received.
- About 25 percent of persons released on felony bond fail to appear in court and have warrants issued for their arrest.
- Overall, 33 percent of felons released on bond are either rearrested for a new offense, fail to appear in court, or commit some other violation that results in revocation of their bond.
- Among defendants already on pretrial release when arrested for their current felony, 56 percent were released again.
- Of those released again, 32 percent were released while on parole and 44 percent were on probation.
- Bail amount varied by type of release. The type of release bond with average bail amount was:
  - Surety $ 7,100
  - Deposit $15,200
  - Full cash $ 3,300
  - Property $10,900
  - Unsecured $10,100
- Approximately 52 percent of all felony releases occurred the day of arrest.

- Of persons released from jail on felony charges, 55 percent had no prior convictions; 45 percent did have prior convictions.
- About 53 percent of felony releases had prior arrests, 27 percent had prior felony convictions, and 9 percent had a prior violent felony conviction.
- Among those who were released and rearrested, about 8 percent were arrested within 1 week, 37 percent within 1 month, 71 percent within 3 months, and 91 percent within 6 months.[22–23]

Federal Pretrial Release and Detention

Pretrial services are not just a state function, but also occur in the federal criminal justice system. Recall that the landmark Bail Reform Act of 1966 was the federal initiative that de-emphasized monetary bail and required the courts to release any defendant charged with noncapital crimes on his or her recognizance or an unsecured appearance bond unless the court determined that the defendant posed significant risks to the community. Pretrial release facilitated due process in three important ways. First, it furthered the presumption of innocence by avoiding undue jail detention. Second, it enabled criminal defendants to better participate in their defense. Third, it reduced the possibility that defendants would be detained longer than otherwise appropriate for the offense committed. In other words, they would not serve weeks or months for trivial charges, such as shoplifting.

The **Federal Pretrial Services Act of 1982** established pretrial services for defendants in the United States district courts. Forty-two federal districts are served by a federal pretrial service agency. United States Probation serves the remaining 52 districts. Federal pretrial services officers conduct investigations and supervise clients released into their custody. Like state pretrial service staff, federal officers conduct extensive criminal history checks and assess community ties. Together this information is used to assess risks of flight, recidivism, and danger.[24]

Like criminal defendants facing state charges, the preponderance of federal defendants are released from custody on some type of bond. John Scalia of the Bureau of Justice Statistics found that about 53 percent of the 56,982 defendants charged with a felony offense were released from custody. Nearly 60 percent of these were released on their own recognizance on an unsecured bond. More than 34 percent of federal defendants were detained pending adjudication of their charges, including roughly half of persons charged with violent crimes, immigration violations, and drug trafficking. Noncitizen and homeless defendants were also significantly less likely to be released due to their weaker ties to the community.[25]

Compared to state pretrial service units, federal authorities are more stringent in detaining defendants. In accordance with the Bail Reform Act of 1984, federal authorities conduct a detention hearing within 3 to 5 days of the defendant's arrest. At the detention hearing, federal authorities must present clear and convincing evidence that detention is the sole way to ensure not only the defendant's appearance in court, but also to reduce the risks of danger and recidivism that he or she posed. Certain conditions, such as if the defendant's current charges involve firearms, they are already on a criminal justice status, or are a violent recidivist automatically mandate pretrial detention.

Determinants of Pretrial/Release Detention

Whether a criminal defendant is released from custody constitutes two sides of the same discretionary coin. Essentially, pretrial service personnel assess three basic types of risk when deciding whether to release a defendant from custody and how they should release the defendant, such as via recognizance or a more restrictive secured bond. The three risks for consideration are (1) danger risk, (2) recidivism risk, and (3) flight or failure to appear (FTA) risk.

Danger risk is the level of danger that the defendant poses toward himself or herself, the specific victim in the current case, or society at large. Danger risk is comprised of several factors, such as the level of injury that the current victim sustained; the seriousness of the current charges; whether the victim is actively homicidal, suicidal, or expresses homicidal or suicidal ideation; and the extent of the defendant's criminal history. Defendants that meet a variety of criteria related to the seriousness of their current charges or the magnitude of their criminal record can be statutorily prohibited from recognizance release. In the event that defendants are charged with capital crimes, criminal suspects can be denied bail altogether.

Recidivism risk refers to the likelihood, assessed by diagnostic instrument, pretrial officer expertise, or both, that the criminal defendant, if released, would immediately engage in criminal behavior. Obviously, pretrial staff cannot see the future and predict future behavior. However, one's criminal history is a relatively reliable predictor of one's future conduct. Thus, defendants with lengthy prior records containing numerous arrests, convictions, and previous involvements with the criminal justice system are viewed as high risk for reoffending. Conversely, persons with no prior record or great intervals of time between arrests—for example, a defendant who was arrested once, 20 years ago—are viewed as low risks for recidivism. Another important indicator of recidivism is current legal status. Many criminal defendants are already on parole, probation, bond, or summons for other charges in other or the same jurisdictions. Since these defendants are already in legal trouble, the current charges, even if minor, are seen as illustrative that the defendant is a recidivist.

Flight risk is assessed primarily by three factors. First, prior history of missing court appearances, bond revocations, and failing to comply with conditions of probation are viewed as indicators that the defendant would likely miss immediate court dates. Since criminal records contain arrests for failing to appear in court (FTA), a defendant's flight risk is a function of his criminal record. Second, in addition to their current charges, some criminal defendants are also found to have active warrants for their arrest because of previous incidents of failing to appear in court. Thus, defendants with one or more current FTA warrants are considered high risk for future missed court appearances. Third, flight risk is related to the community ties of a criminal defendant. Persons with long-term residency in the area, homeowners, currently employed, and persons with extensive family and friendship networks are low risks to miss court dates, flee the jurisdiction, or flee. Conversely, persons who are transient, have little to no financial investment in the community, are unemployed, and have little to no social support have little binding them to the community; as such, there is little incentive to remain in town and handle legal responsibilities. Those with weak community ties are viewed as high risks to leave the area, or at a minimum, miss court.

Protective and Risk Factors

In determining the risks of recidivism, danger, and flight, pretrial service personnel weigh an assortment of characteristics of the defendant. Some of these factors present the defendant in a positive light and indicate that he or she poses little risk to the community. These are known as *protective factors*. Conversely, *risk factors* are damaging or aggravating circumstances that indicate that the defendant will pose some risk if released from custody. Protective and risk factors for pretrial release or detention are specified in the United States Code Title 18. Protective factors include benign current charges, strong employment record, homeowner, entrenched community ties, strong family and friendship networks, and no or minimal criminal history. Risk factors include already on bond, probation, or parole, awaiting sentencing in another criminal matter, homeless or transient, unemployed, substance abuse problem, serious or violent charges, and lengthy criminal history.[26]

Criminologists have studied the protective and risk factors that influence the assignment of bail and the types of release accorded to criminal defendants.[27] The balance of research on pretrial decision making and bail outcomes indicates that legal factors that influence flight, recidivism, and dangerousness risks are the strongest determinants of pretrial release and detention. By and large, pretrial detention and financially punitive bails are applied to defendants with lengthy criminal records, the most serious current charges, and poor community ties. On the other hand, pretrial release, recognizance bonds, and unsecured bonds are the norm for arrestees with little prior record and strong community ties.[28–32] A large-scale study of more than 21,000 inmates in the Los Angeles County jail illustrates differences in criminality between those who are freed on bond and those who remain in custody. Joan Petersilia and her colleagues found that Los Angeles jails were comprised almost entirely of persons charged with or convicted of serious felonies and/or persons with extensive criminal records. In fact, between the seriousness of their current charges and the length of their criminal records, few inmates residing in large urban jails were deemed appropriate for pretrial release or intermediate sanctions. Instead, confinement appeared to be the most appropriate placement.[33]

Discretionary Outcomes

Conceptually, protective and risk factors should inversely predict release on recognizance and mandatory detention. However, this is not always the case. For example, Sheila Royo Maxwell examined the congruence between predictors of release on recognizance (ROR) and failure to appear (FTA) violations. Expectedly, Maxwell found that defendants with lengthier records, prior crimes of violence, and current serious charges were both less likely to receive an ROR release and more likely to fail to appear. But, certain demographic characteristics also influenced the decision making of pretrial officers. Women, persons with prior misdemeanor convictions, and property offenders were more likely to be released on recognizance although they had higher rates of missing court. White defendants were more likely than African Americans to be denied ROR even though race was not a significant predictor of absconding.[34]

At the federal level, researchers have found that nonlegal considerations also influence pretrial release and bail outcomes. Based on data from 5,660 defendants in 10 federal courts, Celesta Albonetti and her colleagues found that those with lengthy prior records, current or past crimes of violence, and weak community ties were less likely to be released before trial. They also found that offense seriousness and dangerousness risks negatively affected White, not minority, defendants.[35]

That defendant demographic factors influence pretrial decision making is a troubling threat to due process. Prior to the Manhattan Bail Project, bail was explicitly detrimental to lower income persons. Unfortunately, criminologists continue to unearth different pretrial treatment for different types of people.[36–38] Because of real or perceived weaker community ties, Hispanic arrestees are especially likely to receive more punitive bonds and remain in custody. Importantly, there is a silver lining. Even in studies that found significant differences in the types of bond afforded to various racial and ethnic groups, the size of these effects was negligible compared to the influence of legal factors. For example, Stephen Demuth and Darrell Steffensmeier analyzed the pretrial release process of nearly 40,000 felony defendants from the 75 largest counties in the United States and found that African American and Hispanic defendants were more likely to be detained and held on bail net the effect of legal factors. Yet, offense seriousness, for crimes like murder, rape, and robbery, ranged from *200 percent to 2,000 percent* more powerful of a predictor than race/ethnicity. Several criminal history indicators, such as multiple charges, FTA history, active criminal justice status, prior felony convictions, prior jail detention, and prior imprisonment were as important or usually far more significant predictors than demographics.[39–40]

Conditional release on bond does not necessarily ensure that criminal defendants will either appear in court or desist from criminal offending. John Goldkamp and Peter Jones evaluated pretrial drug testing projects in Wisconsin and Maryland in 1983 and 1989 and tested the assumption that intensive monitoring of drug use during pretrial release would reduce FTA and recidivism rates. The results were counterintuitive. Although fewer than 10 percent of defendants produced positive drug tests, between 50 and 70 percent of clients recorded more than five violations of the drug program. Moreover, substance abuse monitoring did not improve the rates by which defendants appeared in court or reoffended. In short, they found substantial noncompliance and continued criminal behavior among drug-using defendants released on bond.[41–42] Subsequent replications of this approach in Florida and Arizona yielded similarly dismal results of continued noncompliance and criminal offending while on bond.[43–44]

To summarize, a defendant's risks of flight, recidivism, and danger are the primary determinants of whether he or she is released on bond and how punitive or lenient the bail process is. Strong community ties entail long-term residency, stable employment, and strong familial networks. Weak community ties entail transience, unemployment, and little social and personal connection to the local community. Although researchers still find that demographic characteristics, such as gender and race, significantly affect pretrial outcomes, the effects are negligible compared to legal considerations like offense seriousness and criminal record.

The Effects of Pretrial Detention

Administrative Issues

Despite the advances in the bail process in American justice, there remain unresolved issues about the ultimate due process of pretrial detention. John Goldkamp, Michael Gottfredson, Peter Jones, and Doris Weiland conducted a national assessment of the pretrial process. Their observations were based on analyses of three very different approaches to pretrial service. In Dade County, Florida, the department of corrections supervised the pretrial staff; however an individual judge made the preponderance of bond decisions. In Boston, rotating judges determined bail without the assistance of a pretrial staff. In Arizona, a modern pretrial service unit handled the pretrial release duties as officers of the court. Goldkamp and his colleagues offered this somewhat grim five-point conclusion:

1. There is a continued reliance on financial bail as a major emphasis on release decisions. Of course, protective and risk factors influence the assignment of bail; however, cold hard cash or other fiscal resources are still needed for release. Similarly, the presence of profiteering bondspersons remains a visible and dubious part of the pretrial process.
2. The judiciary must assume a leadership role in bringing consistency to the organization, administration, and release policies of bail.
3. It is incumbent that pretrial services move to the adoption of guidelines-based decision making.
4. The judiciary must appropriately staff pretrial service units to meet the pressing problems of jail crowding and unfair or unjust pretrial detention.
5. Pretrial supervision agencies must serve as the gatekeepers of information for the criminal process as well as for pretrial release and detention.[45]

Malcolm Feeley's landmark book *The Process Is the Punishment* conveyed the hassles and uncertainty that defendants face during the pretrial period.

Procedural Justice Issues

The masterwork exploring the procedural justice issues occurring at the pretrial period is legal scholar Malcolm Feeley's aptly titled *The Process Is the Punishment: Handling Cases in a Lower Criminal Court*. Based on his observations of the pretrial court processes in New Haven, Connecticut, Feeley argued that the real punishment for many people is the pretrial process itself, which is burdensome, uncomfortable, bewildering, and seemingly based on the subjective judgments of various criminal justice practitioners. For example, upon arrest, defendants must interact with police officers, sheriff's officers, booking deputies, detention officers at the police station, pretrial service officers, bonding agents, defense counsel, private counsel, and the like. These interactions must be accomplished while the defendant is detained and without many of the resources that he or she would need. Court appearances are set in accordance with the court schedule, not the defendant's personal calendar. In this way, the contingencies of being arrested and being released on bond can and often do interfere with work and family obligations. By and large, these officials or supportive figures have conflicting responsibilities and duties and their lack of coordination creates logistical problems for defendants.

Upon intake to the criminal justice system, these supportive figures define issues and label defendants for all those who subsequently handle them. Although they may possess limited discretion, their decision making can have significant consequences at later stages of the process. Because the process is so informal and depends so heavily on oral communications, decisions made by the courtroom workgroup are based heavily on the impressions, information, and recommendations passed on by these supportive figures. The sanctions imposed on defendants are heavily influenced by these people's initial impressions.

According to Feeley, due process concerns are subordinated to the profound short-term impressions of arrest and pretrial behavior and demeanor, arrest record (regardless of conviction record), and professional assessments of whether an individual is worthy of prosecution or dismissal, intervention, or a break, entered into the system, or thrown back. Crime control is also not achieved because the courts are structured to offer rapid, informal justice that invites carelessness and error. Because the pretrial period is such a disorganized mess, the majority of criminal defendants prefer to accept plea bargains simply to end their involvement in the process. Since the punishment is in the process, defendants invoke few adversarial options available to them. The defendant's goal is to end the case as quickly as possible. In return, the state produces perfunctory convictions for reduced criminal charges and justifies the troubling practices of the pretrial period.[46]

Substantive Justice Issues

Enduring the pretrial punishment process carries several legal implications. By and large, two classes of criminal defendants emerge at the pretrial period—those who are released from custody and those who remain in custody. The latter group are purported to suffer deleterious legal outcomes as a function of their remaining in jail prior to court. These negative outcomes can include a greater likelihood of imprisonment, longer sentences, and more punitive sentencing recommendations from the prosecution.[47] Unfortunately, some early research did not adequately control for legally relevant factors that explained pretrial detention. As such, the effects of pretrial detention on subsequent legal outcomes were somewhat cloudy.

Marian Williams conducted a methodologically more sophisticated examination of the effects of pretrial detention on legal outcomes. Using data from 412 Florida cases, Williams explored the effects of detention on likelihood of incarceration and length of sentence while controlling for a host of important variables, such as offense seriousness, number of felony charges, prior felony convictions, whether the defendant had a private attorney, length of disposition, age, race, and gender. She found that defendants who were held in jail prior to court were *six times* more likely than released arrestees to be sentenced to incarceration and for lengthier terms. Importantly, Williams noted that pretrial detention can be viewed as either a legal variable or proxy for criminal history, or as an extralegal variable that relates to social class and therefore ability to pay bond.[48] Irrespective of how it is framed, pretrial detention had meaningfully negative impacts on subsequent criminal justice system outcomes.

Jails

Being detained in jail is the flip side to being released on bond. **Jail** is a local correctional or confinement facility that is typically administered by a county-level sheriff's department or a municipal-level law enforcement agency. Jails are utilized to control two general populations of offenders, defendants awaiting trial and persons who have already been convicted and sentenced for their crimes. In addition, jails house a multitude of individuals and are frequently used as a waiting station until persons can be transported to a more appropriate venue or social service provider. At any moment, a jail population might contain:

- Persons who have absconded from military service.
- Persons wanted by probation or parole officers.
- Persons awaiting placement in a psychiatric facility.
- Persons awaiting transport to the hospital or some other medical facility.
- Juveniles who are being held (in isolation from adult inmates) until their age is ascertained for appropriate placement.
- Jails are also used by law enforcement as a last resort to detain transients, noncitizens or illegal aliens, people who are highly intoxicated on drugs or alcohol, and anyone else who poses risks to their own and public safety.

Jail Population

As shown in FIGURE 5-1, nationally, more than 3,365 American jails supervise 766,010 persons, which is a jail incarceration rate of 256 inmates per 100,000 residents.[49] The jail incarceration rate varies greatly by race and ethnicity. For Whites, the jail

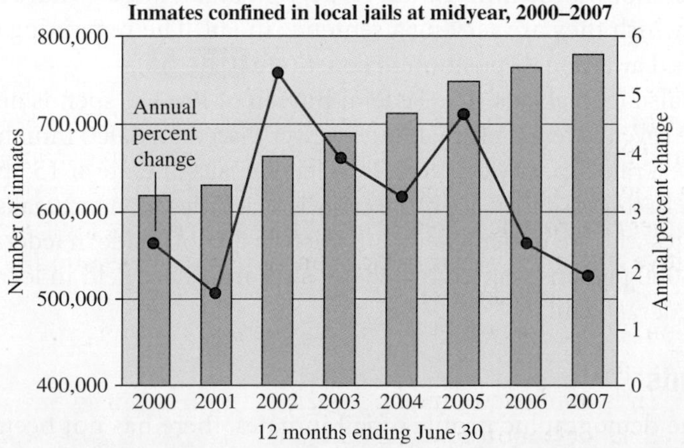

FIGURE 5-1 Jail Population. *Source*: Sabol, W. J., & Minton, T. D. (2008). *Jail inmates at midyear 2007*. Washington, DC: U.S. Department of Justice, Office of Justice Programs, Bureau of Justice Statistics.

TABLE 5-1 Jail Inmate Demographics

	Percent of Jail Inmates			
Characteristic	**2000**	**2005**	**2006**	**2007**
Gender				
Male	88.6	87.3	87.1	87.1
Female	11.4	12.7	12.9	12.9
Age				
Adult	98.8	99.1	99.2	99.1
Male	87.4	86.5	86.3	86.3
Female	11.3	12.6	12.9	12.8
Juvenile	1.2	0.9	0.8	0.9
Held as adults	1.0	0.8	0.6	0.7
Held as juveniles	0.2	0.1	0.2	0.2
Race/Hispanic Origin				
White	41.9	44.3	43.9	43.3
Black/African American	41.3	38.9	38.6	38.7
Hispanic/Latino	15.2	15.0	15.6	16.1
Other	1.6	1.7	1.8	1.8
Two or more races	—	0.1	0.1	0.1

Source: Sabol, W.J., & Minton, T.D. (2008). *Jail inmates at midyear 2007*. Washington, DC: U.S. Department of Justice, Office of Justice Programs, Bureau of Justice Statistics.

incarceration rate is 170 per 100,000 residents. The comparable rates for African Americans and Hispanics are 815 and 283 per 100,000 residents, respectively. Overall, the jail population constitutes about one third of the nation's correctional population.

The majority of the jail population is male, with men comprising 87 percent and women 13 percent of all inmates. About 44 percent of jail inmates are White, nearly 39 percent are African American, nearly 16 percent are Hispanic, and the remaining inmates are other or multiethnic. About 38 percent of jail inmates have been convicted of crimes for which they are serving a sentence in jail. The remaining 62 percent are unconvicted and awaiting disposition in court (see TABLE 5-1).

There are also federal jails. The Federal Bureau of Prisons spends nearly $170 million to operate seven federal jails that house fewer than than 6,000 inmates. Federal jails combined have a rate capacity of 3,810, thus federal jails operate at 155 percent of their rated capacity. In this way, they are more crowded facilities than local jails. Interestingly, most jail inmates who are under federal jurisdiction do not reside in federal jails. Instead, more than 12,000 persons wanted by federal authorities are held in local jails to await transfer to a federal facility.[50]

Jail Trends

In terms of the demographic profile of jail inmates, there has not been much change since 1990. Slightly more than 6,000 juveniles were housed in jails in 2006, which represents little change from 1990. There were nearly seven times as many men than women incarcerated in American jails—and the gender gap among jail inmate status widened between 1990 and 2006 (see FIGURE 5-2).

CORRECTIONS RESEARCH

How Effective Are Supermax Prisons?

According to the National Institute of Corrections, a supermax prison is a stand-alone unit specifically designed to accommodate violent and disruptive inmates and 44 states have fully functional supermax facilities.

Inmates housed in supermax facilities are locked away in their individual cells for up to 23 hours each day. Contact with staff and/or other inmates is minimal. These facilities have been designed to achieve specific goals, which include increased safety for staff and other prisoners, order among inmates, control throughout the prison system, and the incapacitation of violent and disruptive inmates. These are the manifest functions of a supermax system, but there are unintended effects—both positive and negative. An increase in mental health disorders is one easily identified negative outcome of the supermax prison system. On the other hand, a positive effect is the improvement of living conditions for other inmates in the general population after the violent and disruptive inmate is removed and reassigned to a supermax facility.

The actual impact of supermax prisons on prisoners varies. Some supermax prisoners report a positive change in their behavior. Supermax inmates also report a greater sense of safety and calm and reduced levels of stress and fear. Upon reassignment from a supermax facility, former supermax prisoners exhibit greater compliance with rules and less violent and disruptive behavior when returned to the general prison population. Another unintended, but very positive effect of the supermax prison is the high-quality health care, both medical and psychiatric, available to supermax prisoners.

There are unintended negative effects as well. Some supermax prisoners are more frequently involved in disciplinary infractions. There is an increased level of tension between inmates and correctional staff, and in some prisoners there is a tendency toward an increase in violent behavior. There have also been reports by supermax prisoners of alleged human rights violations.

Unfortunately, very little data exists to adequately address the question of whether former supermax prisoners are more likely to recidivate once they are released from prison. The information that is available indicates former supermax inmates have increased rates of recidivism once they are released from prison and return to society.

Ninety-five percent of wardens polled agree that supermax prisons serve to increase safety, order, and control. Eighty percent felt supermax prisons worked to improve inmate behavior while in the system. Nearly 50 percent believed supermax prisons were used to punish prisoners and reduce recidivism. Only one third of wardens surveyed agreed that supermax prisons serve a rehabilitative function. Less than 25 percent felt supermax prisons reduced crime in society.

Source: Mears, D. P. (2008). An assessment of supermax prisons using an evaluation research framework. *Prison Journal, 88,* 43–68.

According to the most recent data, approximately 350,000 jail inmates were African American, 300,000 were White, and more than 100,000 were Hispanic (see FIGURE 5–3). In terms of raw numbers, there were more Whites than African Americans in jail; however, once racial data and their proportion of the total population are considered, a different picture emerged (FIGURE 5–4). The jail incarceration rate varies significantly by race and ethnicity. At all points from 1990 to 2006, African Americans had the highest jail incarceration rate, more than twice the rate of Hispanics. In turn, the Hispanic jail

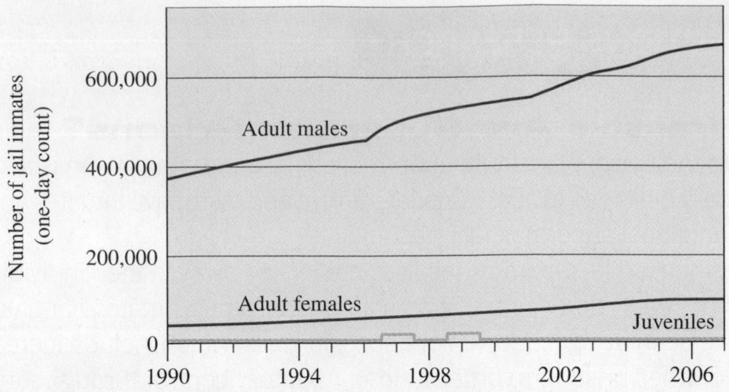

FIGURE 5–2 Jail Populations by Age and Gender, 1990–2007. *Source*: Bureau of Justice Statistics. (n.d.) *Almost nine out of every ten jail inmates were adult males.* Retrieved June 6, 2008, from http://www.ojp.usdoj.gov/bjs/glance/jailag.htm.

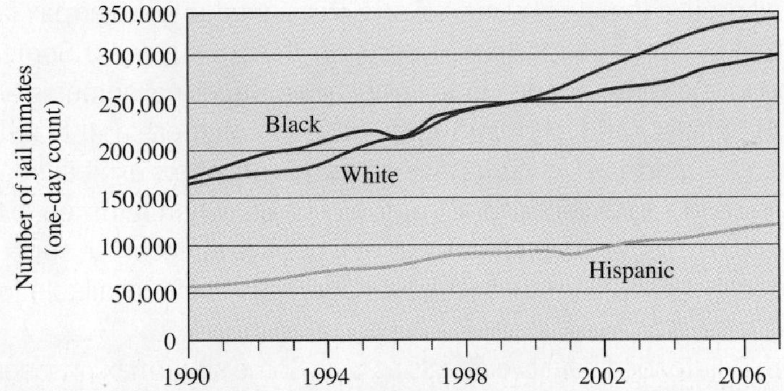

FIGURE 5–3 Jail Populations by Race and Ethnicity, 1990–2007. *Source*: Bureau of Justice Statistics. (n.d.) *Between 1990 and 2007, the number of white and Hispanic jail inmates increased at the same average annual rate. The number of black inmates increased at a slower pace.* Retrieved June 6, 2008, from http://www.ojp.usdoj.gov/bjs/glance/jailag.htm.

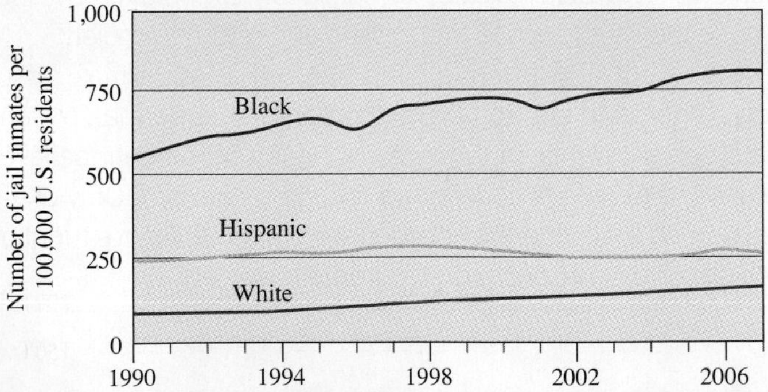

FIGURE 5–4 Jail Incarceration Rates by Race and Ethnicity, 1990–2007. *Source*: Bureau of Justice Statistics. (n.d.) *Blacks were almost three times more likely than Hispanics and five times more likely than whites to be in jail.* Retrieved June 6, 2008, from http://www.ojp.usdoj.gov/bjs/glance/jailag.htm.

incarceration rate is nearly double the rate for Whites. The respective jail incarceration rates were 815 for African Americans, 283 for Hispanics, and 170 for Whites.[51]

An indicated earlier, 62 percent of the nation's jail inmates were awaiting court action on their current charge. In other words, more than half of the American jail population had not yet been convicted for what they were currently charged. The remaining 38 percent were postadjudication defendants serving time for various convictions, probation violations, and parole violations pending transfer to a state department of corrections.

Time Served and Capacity

Jail confinement is usually a temporary experience. When considering pre- and post-adjudication inmates, the average length of stay is a mere 3 days. Many defendants are detained for less than 24 hours, remaining in custody until they are able to mobilize resources for release.[52] Based on the most recent data, 33 percent of jail inmates who have been convicted of crimes serve less than 30 days in jail. For unconvicted offenders, more than 44 percent serve less than 30 days in jail. Almost 25 percent of inmates serve less than 2 weeks in jail.[53]

The total rated capacity of jails is 810,863 beds. **Rated capacity** is the maximum number of beds of inmates allocated by rating officials to each jail facility. Nationwide, jails operated at an average of 94 percent of rated capacity. Jail facilities vary tremendously in their size and capacity. As shown in FIGURE 5–5, smaller jails are less occupied than larger facilities. In jails with fewer than 50 inmates, the average percent occupied is about 65 percent. However, smaller jails are also more susceptible to local criminal justice and political factors that can unpredictably increase or decrease the jail population.[54] On the other hand, jails with 500 or more inmates are 100 percent occupied.

As shown in FIGURE 5–6, local jail officials added jail capacity at a rate about equal to the growth in the jail inmate population in recent years. Between 1995 and 2006, the jail population and rated capacity both increased steadily, although during some periods the rates of increase in population and capacity varied. For instance, between 1998 and 2001, capacity expanded more quickly than the jail population and the average percentage of rated capacity declined from 97 percent to 90 percent. After 2002, jail populations increased at a slightly faster rate than rated capacity and the percentage of rated capacity increased to its current level of 94 percent.[55] Overall, researchers found that available jail capacity results in increases in jail population regardless of the local crime rate. In other words, if space becomes available in jail, it will be quickly filled.[56]

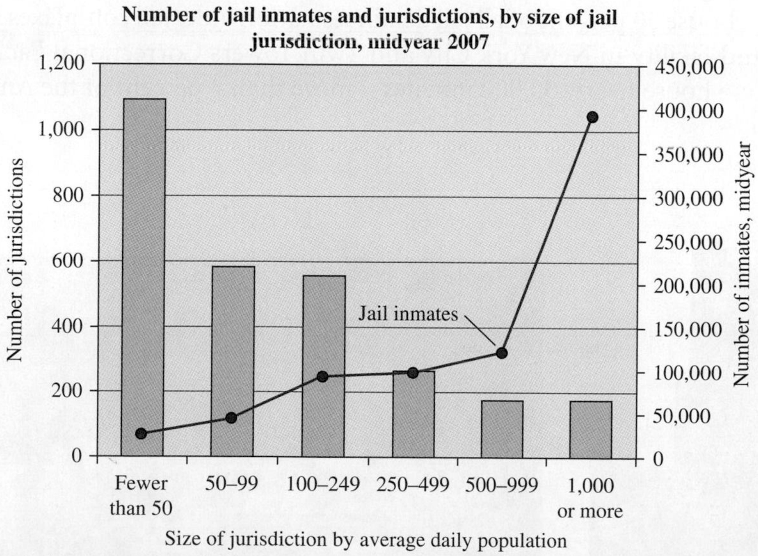

FIGURE 5–5 Percent of Capacity Occupied by Jail Size. *Source*: Sabol, W. J., & Minton, T. D. (2008). *Jail inmates at midyear 2007*. Washington, DC: U.S. Department of Justice, Office of Justice Programs, Bureau of Justice Statistics.

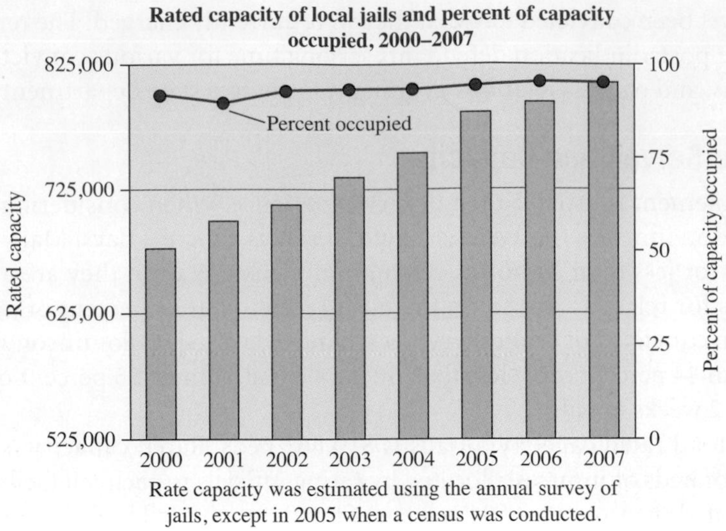

FIGURE 5–6 Rated Capacity and Jail Population. *Source*: Sabol, W. J., & Minton, T. D. (2008). *Jail inmates at midyear 2007.* Washington, DC: U.S. Department of Justice, Office of Justice Programs, Bureau of Justice Statistics.

Law enforcement and jail administrators have devised innovative ways to control local jail populations. One approach is to summons and release offenders for misdemeanor and low-level felony offenses. The way that a **summons and release** (also known as a book and release) works is that defendants are taken to jail, interviewed by police, booked and processed by sheriff's deputies, and issued a summons or ticket with a court date. No bond is used; defendants are simply given a ticket and released. This approach can be effective. Terry Baumer and Kenneth Adams found that by issuing summonses for defendants accused of possession of marijuana, possession of drug paraphernalia, driving with a suspended license or without having received a license, prostitution, patronizing a prostitute, and shoplifting, the number of inmates booked into jail declined by 30 percent.[57]

The 50 largest jails in the United States account for less than 2 percent of all jurisdictions but house 30 percent of all jail detainees nationwide. Jail complexes such as the Riker's Island facility in New York City and Twin Towers Correctional Facility in Los Angeles alone house nearly 33,000 inmates—more than 4 percent of the American jail population.

(a) Rikers Island Jail Complex in New York City and **(b)** the Twin Towers Correctional Facility in Los Angeles are among the largest correctional settings in the world.

Social and Criminal Histories of Jail Inmates

Jail and prison are often used interchangeably in the mainstream media; however there are vital differences between these facilities. Jails are local, administered usually by the sheriff's department, and entail brief lengths of stay. More than half of the jail population has not yet been convicted. Prisons are remote, state-administered correctional facilities used to confine convicted felons. Many people who are in jail will never be in prison, such as persons arrested for traffic violations and misdemeanors; however, almost all prisoners have at some point been detained in jail.

Because jails detain both those who will not be convicted and those who already have been convicted, the population is diverse in terms of the social and criminal history of the inmates. A national study of 134 jails in 39 states indicated that nearly 15 percent of jail inmates nationally are actively involved in street gangs.[58] Many jail inmates have chronic criminal careers characterized by an early onset of antisocial behavior, generalized involvement in diverse forms of crime, and recurrent cycling in and out of the correctional system.[59–61] Using data from the national Survey of Inmates in Local Jails, Doris James discovered extensive criminality among some jail detainees. About 46 percent of all jail inmates were already on probation or parole at the time of their most recent arrest. Nearly 40 percent had served three or more separate commitments to state or federal prison. Seventy percent of jail inmates had some sort of prior criminal record and 41 percent of jail inmates had a current or past arrest for violent crimes, such as murder, rape, robbery, or aggravated assault. As shown in TABLE 5-2 and TABLE 5-3, it is common for jail inmates to not only have an active criminal justice involvement, such as bond, probation, or parole, but also to have prior sentences to probation, incarceration, or both.[62]

Nearly 60 percent of jail inmates were raised in single-parent households and one in nine was raised in a foster home or institution. Forty-six percent of jail inmates had an immediate family member who had been incarcerated. More than 50 percent of female and 10 percent of male jail inmates reported that they had suffered from past sexual or physical abuse.[63]

In addition to criminal behavior, jail inmates also have often serious histories of substance abuse. Nearly 70 percent of jail inmates report symptoms in the year before their admission to jail that met substance dependence or abuse criteria. Forty percent of jail inmates are dependent or addicted to alcohol or drugs and another 25 percent of

TABLE 5-2 Criminal Justice Status of Jail Inmates

Criminal Status	Percentage
None	46.8
Any Status	53.2
On probation	33.6
On parole	12.6
On bail/bond	6.9
On other pretrial release	2.3
On alcohol/drug diversion counseling	2.0
On other release	2.3
On escape	0.6

Source: James, D.J. (2004). *Profile of jail inmates, 2002.* Washington, DC: U.S. Department of Justice, Office of Justice Programs, Bureau of Justice Statistics.

TABLE 5-3 Prior Sentences of Jail Inmates

Probation	
0	38.9%
1	32.6
2	14.8
3–5	11.2
6–10	2.0
11 or more	0.6
Incarceration	
0	42.1%
1	23.7
2	10.3
3–5	14.3
6–10	6.8
11 or more	2.8
Incarceration or Probation	
0	26.9%
1	17.5
2	16.8
3–5	21.9
6–10	11.0
11 or more	5.9

Source: James, D.J. (2004). *Profile of jail inmates, 2002.* Washington, DC: U.S. Department of Justice, Office of Justice Programs, Bureau of Justice Statistics.

inmates abused alcohol and drugs but did not meet diagnostic criteria for dependence. Among inmates who met substance dependence or abuse criteria, 63 percent had participated in substance abuse treatment. These are staggeringly high prevalence estimates of substance abuse. As a point of reference, only 9 percent of Americans in the resident population were found to be dependent on alcohol or drugs.[64]

Jail inmates who are addicted to drugs and alcohol fare significantly worse than nonaddicted jail inmates on nearly every measure of social and behavioral measure. Compared to nonaddicted inmates, jail inmates who are dependent on drugs and alcohol are:

- More likely to have been homeless.
- Less likely to have been employed.
- More likely to have been physically abused.
- More likely to have been sexually abused.
- More likely to have ever received public assistance.
- More likely to have lived in foster care.
- More likely to have depended on parents for supported living.
- More likely to have parents who abused alcohol, drugs, or both.
- More likely to have had their mother, father, brother, sister, or spouse incarcerated in the past.

Chemically dependent jail inmates have more extensive criminal histories than nonaddicted inmates. About 16 percent of jail inmates committed their recent crimes to get money for drugs and nearly 30 percent were on drugs at the time of their current offense.

CORRECTIONS IN THE NEWS

Prisons and the Spread of HIV

Prisoners are at added risk for the contraction of HIV while in prison. Few prisoners remain in prison the remainder of their lives. The incarceration rate for the United States is the highest of any developed country. Figures indicate that the rate of incarceration was 724 per 100,000 persons in 2004. Currently there are more than 2 million inmates in local, state, and federal facilities who have committed crimes ranging from misdemeanor acts of prostitution to felony possession, distribution, and manufacture of controlled substances to murder. The criminal justice system is not entirely to blame—after all, it is made up of people who are just doing their jobs. Politicians have unknowingly placed the general population at risk as well. Get tough on crime policies sell well to the voter but by their nature are superficial remedies. The consequence—by using this tactic to control drug use, more and more first time offenders arrested on drug charges are incarcerated and subsequently are exposed to HIV. With the AIDS prevalence three times higher in prison populations than in the general population, the chances of incurring a significant exposure to this disease is reasonably great.

Female inmates account for anywhere from 5 to 10 percent of the prison population in any given year. Female prisoners also have a higher rate of HIV infection than do male prisoners. Since many women with substance use problems also find themselves, willingly and unwillingly, involved in the sex for hire industry, this should not come as a surprise. As a result, women are exposed to HIV/AIDs at higher rates than are males. In fact, two states, New York and Maryland, have female prison populations in which 10 percent of the inmates are HIV positive. In only one state, New York, is the rate of infection for HIV greater than 5 percent of the male inmates.

Traditionally, efforts to prevent the spread of the virus have involved isolating the prisoners with HIV from the general prison population. As of 2005, Alabama was the only state that placed all HIV positive inmates in separate housing units. Other correctional facilities elect to segregate infected prisoners on a case-by-case basis. Several other relevant options exist. First, the department of corrections could increase staff-to-prisoner ratios. A second option might be that of evaluating, classifying, and scheduling inmates for reexaminations on a regular time interval and prior to release. The answer also might be to decrease crowding, prison violence, and sexual assault.

Sources: Maruschak, L. M. (2004). *HIV in prisons and jails, 2002*. Washington, DC: U.S. Department of Justice, Office of Justice Programs, Bureau of Justice Statistics.

Medical Problems, Suicide, and Homicide in Jails

According to the most recent data from the national Survey of Inmates in Local Jails, nearly 230,000 jail inmates or 37 percent reported having a current medical problem other than a cold or common flu virus. Some of the most common medical ailments are arthritis, hypertension, asthma, and heart problems. Fewer than 5 percent of inmates reported more serious medical problems, such as cancer, paralysis, stroke, diabetes, liver failure, hepatitis, tuberculosis, or HIV. Between 40 and 60 jail inmates die from AIDS-related causes annually. Nearly 25 percent of jail inmates reported having a learning impairment, such as dyslexia or attention deficit disorder. One in eight inmates reported being injured since admission to jail and injuries are equally likely to stem from an assault by another inmate or due to an accident.[65]

After the passage of the Death in Custody Reporting Act of 2000, the Bureau of Justice Statistics began collecting inmate death records from all local jails and state prisons. According to the most recent data, 978 inmates died in American jails in the most recent reporting year. The most common causes of death were medical illness (48 percent) and suicide (32 percent). Slightly more than 2 percent of jail inmate deaths representing 20 deaths were homicides. The national suicide rate in American jails is 47 per 100,000 inmates, which is more than three times the suicide rate in state prisons (14 per 100,000 inmates). Interestingly, jail suicide rates are twice as low in the 50 largest jail systems than in other jails. Violent offenders have significantly higher suicide rates (92 per 100,000 inmates) and homicide rates (5 per 100,000) in jails than nonviolent offenders (31 per 100,000 and 2 per 100,000, respectively).

Nearly 50 percent of jail suicides occurred within the first week of custody, and 14 percent of jail suicides occurred within 24 hours of admission to jail. The median time served in jail prior to committing suicide was 9 days. More than 80 percent of jail suicides occurred in the inmate's cell. Homicide followed a similar temporal pattern. Nearly 30 percent of jail homicides occurred during the first week of jail confinement and 54 percent occurred after 2 weeks.[66]

Trend data indicate that American jails are significantly safer than in prior decades particularly in terms of suicide (see FIGURE 5-7). For instance, the suicide rate was approximately 130 per 100,000 in 1985, which is nearly three times the jail suicide rate in 2000. The homicide rate in American jails has remained relatively stable at about 5 per 100,000 (FIGURE 5-8).

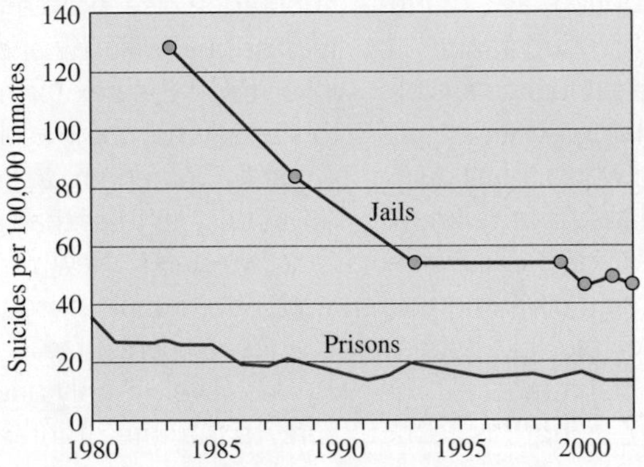

FIGURE 5-7 Suicide Rate in American Jails, 1980–2000. *Source*: Mumola, C. J. (2005). *Suicide and homicide in state prisons and local jails.* Washington, DC: U.S. Department of Justice, Office of Justice Programs, Bureau of Justice Statistics.

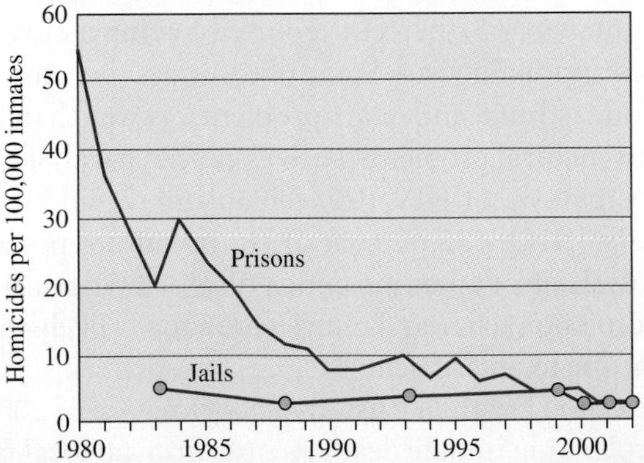

FIGURE 5-8 Homicide Rate in American Jails, 1980–2000. *Source*: Mumola, C. J. (2005). *Suicide and homicide in state prisons and local jails.* Washington, DC: U.S. Department of Justice, Office of Justice Programs, Bureau of Justice Statistics.

History and Reform

American criminal justice owes an enormous debt to English common law and the jail tradition is no exception. Unfortunately, jail history in the United States is overwhelmingly negative and these facilities have been referred to as the "sewers" and "ghettos" of the criminal justice system. In the colonial era, jails served no correctional function but instead were used to detain persons who were wanted in the interests of justice and debtors who could not meet their financial obligations. In lieu of jail confinement, those convicted of crimes were banished, branded, pilloried, maimed, or executed. Jails were then used as last-resort holding bins for groups of people considered outside the mainstream society, namely the mentally ill, alcoholics, and the poor.

As the United States expanded and became more modernized, jails also increased in number so that nearly every county and/or municipality had one. However, for most of its history, jails were not appreciably different in their fundamental form and function from those of the 18th century—that is, as catchall asylums for the poor and disaffected.[67–71] For example, Rick Ruddell and Larry Mays surveyed 213 jail administrators from small jails and found that jails were often viewed as the facility that cannot turn away people in need. Because of this, jails in small towns and rural areas disproportionately house inmates with special needs and, unfortunately, do not have the resources to provide services to address these needs. The breakdown of the special needs population included:

- Nearly 9 percent of inmates with mental illnesses.
- Approximately 32 percent of inmates who are chronic offenders.
- Less than 4 percent of inmates who are gang members.
- Nearly 2 percent of inmates who are elderly.
- More than 4 percent of inmates who are seriously ill.
- Nearly 14 percent of inmates who are considered long term and serving a sentence of 1–2 years.[72]

Recently however, there has been progress. As this chapter has detailed, federal legislation and state and federal criminal justice initiatives have tremendously improved the pretrial phase of the criminal justice system and made pretrial corrections more impartial and fair. Professional and efficient pretrial service units utilize community ties and criminal history, not just financial resources, as the determinants of pretrial release.

Jail facilities themselves have been redesigned in terms of their physical environment and approach to inmate supervision. **New generation jails** were introduced in 1974 and featured podular design and **direct supervision** whereby inmates were housed in single-occupancy cells that adjoined a larger communal area. Inmates interacted in the self-contained living unit or pod for most of the day. Unlike the traditional jail structure that employed **linear supervision** or simply a corridor of separate cells, direct supervision facilities allowed correctional staff to constantly observe all aspects of the inmate's living space. The living space itself contained modern amenities, such as carpeting and basic features that one might find in a dormitory. The differences between traditional and new generation jails are important. According to Linda Zupan:

> Traditional facilities are those where there is no continuous supervision of inmates by staff. Inmates are not directly viewed by staff for extended periods and the underlying basis for supervision is a reliance on bars and security to prevent inmate escapes and assaults on one another and staff. The physical design tends to be linear in that cells are extended off an officer patrol corridor. On the other hand podular/direct jails are designed to reduce inmate opportunities for aberrant behavior. Correctional officers are placed in the inmate areas and are

expected to freely interact with inmates. Officers are expected to directly and continuously supervise the inmates. The physical design of podular/direct jails is more open with cells positioned at the perimeter of the cell block where inmates and staff can interact in the center day room area.[73]

New generation jails are designed around the following seven correctional principles:

1. Effective control and supervision, including easily surveillable areas, population divided into controllable groups, and having an officer in control of the unit.
2. Competent and professional staff.
3. Facility safety for staff and inmates.
4. Manageable and cost-effective operations.
5. Effective staff–inmate communication.
6. Inmate classification, screening, and orientation, including maximum supervision during the inmate's initial hour of confinement and knowing with whom they are dealing.
7. Just and fair treatment of inmates.[74]

New generation jails are theorized to serve two important interrelated purposes. First, they are more humane facilities compared to the traditional jail in which inmates live in small cells for most of their detention. Since a jail stint is itself very brief, it makes sense to create a correctional atmosphere that promotes rehabilitation and facilitates the offender's reintegration into the community. Second, the increased amenities offer jail inmates an incentive to obey jail regulations. Noncompliant inmates lose their status in podular modules and go back to traditional cells. In this way, serving inmate needs and ensuring inmate and staff safety are symbiotic.

The theory of new generation jails is promising, but what do they look like in practice? Christine Tartaro conducted a national survey of jails and found that the implementation of the new generation jail philosophy has not yet been achieved. Many jail facilities identified themselves as new with direct supervision modules; however, only 40 percent of jail facilities actually implemented these new designs. Moreover, few jails were providing inmate services in the new modules. Another interesting finding was that jail administrators were hesitant to shift inmates from cells to modules because of concern that inmates would destroy the normative amenities and living supplies of those units.[75] Despite the partial implementation, Tartaro found that inmates in new generation designs behaved as if they had something to lose by failing to follow institutional rules. Consequently, new generation jails experienced lower rates of assaults, suicides, and vandalism compared to traditional jails with linear supervision.[76]

Other evaluations of new generation jails have also been favorable. Jeffrey Senese compared inmate infractions among offenders in new generation versus traditional jails and found that there is a reduction in every type of inmate rule violations in new generation jails with the exception of threats, property theft, and inmate order problems. For these offenses, correctional staff responded more severely, were less likely to give warnings, and were more likely to issue misconduct tickets to inmates. For misconduct, such as contraband, assault, destruction of property, insolence, suicide, and escape, the new generation jail experienced 33 percent fewer incidents.[77] James Williams and his colleagues compared inmate behavior in a new generation jail to those serving time in a traditional jail and an indirect supervision barracks. They found that inmates and staff were more satisfied with the physical environment and facilities of the new generation jail and perceived it as more secure. Violence and disciplinary problems were lower in the new generation jail.[78] The benefits of new generation jails can also be seen after inmates are released. Brandon Applegate and his colleagues studied the recidivism patterns of former jail inmates and

CORRECTIONS BRIEF

Confinement Facilities in Indian Country

The governing authority on Indian land is vested in tribal government. According to the Bureau of Justice Statistics, Indian land is defined as all lands within an Indian reservation, dependent Indian communities, and Indian trust allotments. The Native American system of corrections includes jails, confinement facilities, detention centers, and community supervision programs that are operated under the authority of tribal law. These facilities are responsible for confining roughly 2,200 prisoners each year.

Just over a third of Indian prisoners are arrested and convicted for having committed violent criminal offenses—primarily acts of violence against family members. Approximately 11 percent of prisoners in Indian country jails are serving sentences as a result of convictions for operating a motor vehicle while under the influence of drugs or alcohol. Tribal law enforcement is responsible for responding to all misdemeanors and felony crimes that fall within specific boundaries, but it is not uncommon for state and federal jurisdictions to overlap tribal jurisdiction. Federal and state agencies are also charged with providing law enforcement for felony crimes committed by American Indians.

The jurisdiction over crimes on Indian lands depends on several factors. First, jurisdiction depends on the identity of the victim and the offender. It also depends on severity of the crime as well as the location of the offense. Tribal jurisdiction extends only to crimes in which the defendant can receive a sentence of no more than 1 year in prison and/or a fine of $5,000; crimes whose legislated sanctions are greater fall outside the scope of the tribe's jurisdiction and are tried in either state or federal courts.

Just over 53,000 American Indian prisoners are housed in state, federal, and local facilities. Most of these prisoners have been placed on community supervision programs by the courts. The vast majority of remaining Indian prisoners have been remanded to state correctional facilities for their crimes. There are nearly 3 million Native Americans in the United States. American Indians comprise less than 1 percent of the U.S. population, and they account for less than 1 percent of the prison population as well—but their rate of incarceration is 24 percent higher than the overall population rate. However, 93 percent of American Indians under indictment by the courts are being held on misdemeanor charges.

Source: Minton, T. D. (2008). *Jails in Indian Country, 2007*. Washington, DC: U.S. Department of Justice, Office of Justice Programs, Bureau of Justice Statistics.

found that offenders who served time in new generation settings were not more likely to recidivate and actually had reduced postrelease offending rates in some cases.[79]

Despite advances in the design and philosophy of American jails, some criminologists continue to assert that jails are a glaring example of injustice and impediment to due process. For example, John Irwin argues that the function and purpose of jails is to confine disreputable persons not because they have committed crimes but because they are offensive and disreputable. Irwin's thesis is that **rabble**, defined as various marginalized groups such as transients, drug abusers, alcoholics, and the like, must be controlled by the criminal justice system to justify and perpetuate the stratification system of American society.[80] Irwin's thesis is radical and sparked subsequent research that largely disconfirmed his hypothesis. For instance, John Backstrand and his colleagues found no evidence that persons are arrested for their offensiveness or degree of disrepute; instead their actual criminal behavior and the seriousness of their charges influenced their status as jail inmates.[81]

CORRECTIONS FOCUS

Female Offenders Exiting an Offending Trajectory

Most of the research on crime desistance and recidivism has focused on gender-specific issues that apply almost exclusively to men. Traditionally, men have been influenced to desist from criminal activity with the help of several types of formal and informal social control, family/marital relationships, the military, and/or a good job. But caution should be taken before applying what we know about crime desistance by male offenders when attempting to explain desistance by female offenders.

It is widely felt that crime trajectories are dependent upon an offender's interest in persistent and intermittent responses to criminal opportunities and the lack of social controls in his or her life. Some research suggests that desistance is dependent upon the acceptance of adult realities, the quality of an intimate partnership, and the willing acceptance of the responsibilities associated with an adult relationship that produce strong ties to conventional others and accepted forms of social control. Others have found that a marital relationship, regardless of the quality, does not contribute to desistance. There is also evidence that suggests female offenders who marry experience an assortative mating effect and as a result are more likely to continue their criminal trajectory in conjunction with a criminally deviant partner.

Recent research also has found that social controls closely linked with various forms of social capital have stronger effects on female than male desistance. Other findings suggest that women who desist from crime do so because they have invested in a personal commitment that will change their lifestyle. These cognitive beliefs are sometimes referred to as personal agency or the ability to direct one's actions to achieve intended goals and desired outcomes. Combining personal agency with a willingness to commit to conventional social norms and a female offender's chances at ending her crime trajectory are very good. But there's more. Female offenders who report having children also report opting out of crime. This decision also tends to have a lasting effect on the decision to desist from crime. But evidence strongly suggests parenthood is a gender-specific variable that does not have the same impact on the crime trajectory of male offenders.

Source: Broidy, L. M., & Cauffman, E. E. (2006). *Understanding the female offender.* Washington, DC: U.S. Department of Justice, Office of Justice Programs, National Institute of Justice.

Unquestionably, jail confinement is laden with implicit and explicit types of punishment that affect the social and legal standing of jail inmates.[82] Pure jail confinement is reserved primarily for the most serious criminal offenders with the most extensive criminal records. For the remaining majority of criminal defendants, the contemporary jail offers a variety of programs, treatments, and nonincarceration penalties that aim to serve the interests of community safety, defendants' rights, and a more human pretrial period. Chapter 6 contains an exhaustive overview of diversion and treatment programs that are used to divert criminal offenders from the correctional process while providing needed treatments to reduce their criminal behavior. A glimpse at some programming efforts currently under way in American jails is explored next to show that more than ever, the pretrial period is invested in providing treatment and appropriate supervision to criminal offenders.

Due to the prevalence of substance abuse, mental illness, and the co-occurrence of these problems among the jail population, some jurisdictions have devised programs to divert drug-using, mentally ill offenders from jails to more appropriate treatment facilities. Some jurisdictions divert clients prior to booking; others place defendants with appropriate agencies after they have been booked into a county jail. A variety of positive outcomes have emerged. For example, persons who participate in mental health or substance abuse diversion programs tend to gain independent living skills, reduce substance use, and have lower recidivism rates than persons who do not participate in such programs and are simply jailed. Moreover, this saves significant jail space and provides appropriate, problem-specific treatment.[83–85]

To illustrate, Henry Steadman and Michelle Naples evaluated jail diversion programs (both prebooking and postbooking) in Memphis, Tennessee; Montgomery County, Pennsylvania; Multnomah County, Oregon; Phoenix/Tucson, Arizona; Hartford, New Haven, and Bridgeport, Connecticut; and Lane County, Oregon. Defendants who participated in the diversion programs were primarily female offenders with mental health problems, such as schizophrenia or mood disorders with psychotic traits. Across these sites, diverted offenders experienced lower recidivism, 2 months more time spent in the community (and thus not in jail), greater participation in mental health treatment and counseling, and taking prescribed medication. Diverted individuals did incur higher treatment costs, but these were offset by cost savings in criminal justice, such as jail. Overall, Steadman and Naples concluded that jail diversion programs that reached out to offenders with mental health needs produced positive outcomes for individuals, criminal justice systems, and communities.[86]

Treatment is not exclusively reserved for diverted offenders as jail facilities are increasingly providing substance abuse and psychiatric services to jail inmates. Treatment is important because it not only serves the often substantial psychiatric and social problems of jail inmates, but also significantly reduces inmate involvement in misconduct.[87] In fact, it has been suggested that as jail inmate populations increase, correctional administrators feel the need to furnish more treatment opportunities as a way to compensate for crowding. Ironically, research suggests that increasing the density of the jail population actually reduces jail violence—perhaps because the crowding is offset by other amenities.[88–89]

A nationwide survey conducted by Faye Taxman and her colleagues reported that:

- Sixty-one percent of jails nationally provide some type of substance abuse treatment for inmates.
- These programs serve more than 47,000 jail inmates.
- Nearly 60 percent of jails provide up to 4 hours of substance abuse group counseling each week.
- Twenty-six percent have therapeutic communities.
- Fifty-one percent have relapse prevention groups.
- Twenty-three percent have case managers of substance abuse treatment.[90]

Another programming option is to outsource the jail function to community corrections or intermediate sanctions (see Chapter 7). For example, **home incarceration programs**, also known as house arrest, home detention, or home detention with electronic monitoring, allow criminal defendants to remain in the community so that they can continue working, fulfilling family responsibilities, and participating in treatment. However, court officials limit the movements and freedom of criminal defendants so that defendants can leave their house only for work, treatment, or other court-approved reasons. All other freedoms are restricted. Offenders are monitored by electronic devices (e.g., ankle bracelets), daily reporting to jail authorities, and other methods. Home incarceration programs are used during both pretrial and postconviction periods and have met with modest success.[91–95] For instance, Robert Stanz and Richard Tewksbury examined the programs' compliance and subsequent recidivism of nearly 2,500 defendants who participated in a house arrest program. They found that 85 percent of clients successfully completed the program, and that older defendants from good neighborhoods who were charged with DUI-related charges were the most likely to successfully complete the program. Home incarceration costs were *13 times* less expensive than jail costs. On the other hand, Stanz and Tewksbury also found that recidivism rates were high with nearly 70 percent of clients rearrested within 5 years. More than half of the study group was rearrested within 1 year, and the most common crime was another DUI.[96] Still, the dramatically reduced costs mean that jail programs that include nondetention components will continue to define the modern jail.

WRAP UP

CASE STUDY CONCLUSION

Pretrial service personnel utilize a range of characteristics when determining which type of bond a defendant receives and what the bail amount will be. Primarily, pretrial release is a function of the arrest charge and the defendant's prior criminal history. Unless a defendant is facing capital charges or has a no bond warrant in which he or she must serve a jail sentence (known as a mittimus), all defendants are assigned bail. In fact, 62 percent of felons are released on bond during the pretrial period.

Chapter Summary

- Recognizance, secured, and other types of bond are used to release offenders from jail custody and into the community during the pretrial period.
- The Vera Institute of Justice's Manhattan Bail Project showed that using community ties and not relying on ability to pay was useful to guarantee a defendant's appearance in court.
- Danger risk, recidivism risk, and flight risk are the primary determinants of pretrial release and detention.
- Pretrial detention has negative effects on legal outcomes net the effects of other legally relevant variables.
- Jails are local correctional facilities that house persons accused of crimes and convicted offenders serving brief periods of confinement.
- Jails hold a diverse mix of offenders including juveniles, criminal aliens, persons wanted by other governmental agencies, fugitives, and persons awaiting placement in psychiatric facilities.
- Although jail inmates have varying criminal backgrounds, a significant number are chronic offenders with extensive arrest and prison histories.
- Suicide is a leading cause of death of jail inmates.
- New generation jails have podular designs where inmates and staff coexist.
- Innovations and reforms in jail design and function have resulted in lower recidivism rates of jail offenders and reduced misconduct while detained.

Key Terms

abscond To violate the conditions of a sentence of escaping or failing to report.

bail A form of pretrial release in which a defendant enters a legal agreement or promise that requires his or her appearance in court.

Bail Reform Act of 1966 Legislation that authorized the use of releasing defendants on their own recognizance in noncapital federal cases when appearance in court can be shown to be likely.

Bail Reform Act of 1984 Legislation that reinforced the community ties clause of the Bail Reform Act of 1966 but also provided for the preventive detention of defendants deemed dangerous or likely to abscond.

bail revocation If a defendant does not comply with the conditions of bail, the court can withdraw the defendant's previously granted release.

bond A pledge of money or some other assets offered as bail by an accused person or his or her surety (bail bondsman) to secure temporary release from custody.

bondsperson A social service professional who is contractually responsible for a criminal defendant once the defendant is released from custody.

bounty hunter A person hired by bondspersons to enforce the conditions of bail and recover the investment asset of the bondsperson.

cash-only bonds Bond in which the defendant must post 100 percent of the bond in cash to be released.

cosigned recognizance bond A bond on which a family member, close friend, or business associate signs his or her name to guarantee the defendant's appearance in court.

danger risk The level of danger that the defendant poses toward himself or herself, the specific victim in the current case, or society at large.

deposit bail system System in which the court acts as bondsperson and the defendant posts a percentage of the total bond.

direct supervision Supervision design where inmates mix in a central common room and are continuously supervised by staff.

Federal Pretrial Services Act of 1982 Legislation that established pretrial services for defendants in the United States district courts.

flight risk Likelihood that a released offender will abscond or miss a court appearance.

home incarceration programs Programs that allow criminal defendants to remain in the community so that they can continue working, fulfilling family responsibilities, and participating in treatment.

hostageship Situation in which a person volunteers to be prosecuted and punished in the place of the actual suspect in the event that the suspect fails to appear for court proceedings.

jail A local correctional facility usually operated by a county sheriff's department and used for the short-term cofinement of petty offenders, misdemeanants, persons convicted of low-level felonies, and persons awaiting transport to some other criminal justice or social service agency.

linear supervision Traditional jail design with long rows of individual cells.

Manhattan Bail Project Project that used community ties rather than ability to pay to determine pretrial release.

National Pretrial Reporting Program A national initiative sponsored by the Bureau of Justice Statistics, which collects detailed information about the criminal history, pretrial processing, adjudication, and sentencing of felony defendants in state courts in the 75 largest counties in the United States.

new generation jails Jails with podular design and direct supervision whereby inmates were housed in single-occupancy cells that adjoined a larger communal area.

presumption of innocence Guideline that ensures that defendants are considered innocent until proven guilty.

pretrial service officers Staff who interview criminal defendants and gather information about the offenders' social and criminal histories.

property bonds Houses, real estate, or vehicles that may be cosigned to the court as collateral against pretrial flight.

rabble Term used to describe marginalized groups found in American jails.

rated capacity The number of beds or inmates assigned by rating officials to institutions within a jurisdiction.

recidivism risk Likelihood that a released offender will continue to commit crime.

recognizance bond A written promise to appear in court in which the criminal defendant is released from jail custody without paying or posting cash or property.

Reese v. United States Supreme Court case that established that bounty hunters were proxy pretrial officers who had complete control of returning absconders to the court.

secured bonds Bonds that require the payment of cash or other assets to the courts in exchange for release from custody.

summons and release System also known as book and release in which defendants are taken to jail, interviewed by police, booked and processed by sheriff's deputies, and issued a summons or ticket with a court date.

surety A guarantor who assures criminal justice officials that defendants will appear in court.

Taylor v. Taintor Supreme Court case that clarified that bounty hunter behavior must conform to law, but was not bound by Fourth Amendment as is police behavior.

wergeld The assessed value of a person's life and considered their bail value in medieval England and Germany.

Critical Thinking Questions

1. During the pretrial period, are criminal defendants taken advantage of by the correctional system? What is apparently unfair about pretrial detention? Why is there not more uproar about this?
2. Are jails used too much or too little as a one stop shop for the social services in a city? How has this changed over time?
3. Why is suicide a greater problem in jails than prisons despite the great differences in time served in these two types of facilities? What does this suggest about the criminality of jail versus prison inmates?
4. How do organizations such as the Vera Institute of Justice improve the correctional process via their research? Should researchers have a greater role in attempting to improve correctional policy?

Notes

1. Garofalo, J., & Clark, R. D. (1985). The inmate subculture in jails. *Criminal Justice and Behavior, 12,* 415–434.
2. Demuth, S., & Steffensmeier, D. (2004). The impact of gender and race-ethnicity in the pretrial release process. *Social Problems, 51,* 222–242.
3. Beeley, A. L. (1927). *The bail system in Chicago*. Chicago: University of Chicago Press. Quotation cited in J. S. Goldkamp, M. R. Gottfredson, P. R. Jones, & D. Weiland. (1995). *Personal liberty and community safety: Pretrial release in the criminal court.* New York: Plenum Press.
4. Klofas, J. M. (1990). The jail and the community. *Justice Quarterly, 7,* 69–102.
5. Ruddell, R., & Mays, G. L. (2007). Rural jails: Problematic inmates, overcrowded cells, and cash-strapped counties. *Journal of Criminal Justice, 35,* 251–260.
6. DeLisi, M. (2006). *Criminal justice: Balancing crime control and due process.* Dubuque, IA: Kendall/Hunt.
7. Conklin, J. E., & Meagher, D. (1973). The percentage deposit bail system: An alternative to the professional bondsman. *Journal of Criminal Justice, 1,* 299–317.
8. Johnson, B. R., & Warchol, G. L. (2003). Bail agents and bounty hunters: Adversaries or allies of the justice system. *American Journal of Criminal Justice, 27,* 145–165.
9. Goldfarb, R. L. (1965). *Ransom: A critique of the American bail system.* New York: Harper & Row.
10. *Nicolls v. Ingersoll,* 7 Johns. 145, 154 (N.Y. 1810).
11. *Reese v. United States,* 76 U.S. 13 (1869).
12. *Taylor v. Taintor,* 83 U.S. (16 Wall.) 366 (1873).
13. Vera Institute of Justice. (2003). *A short history of Vera's work on the judicial process.* New York: Vera Institute of Justice.
14. Goldfarb, pp. 37–42.
15. Goldfarb, p. 5.
16. Goldfarb, p. 3.
17. Riker, A., & Castellano, U. (2001). The homeless pretrial release program: An innovative pretrial release option. *Federal Probation, 65,* 9–13.
18. Johnson & Warchol.
19. Burns, R., Kinkade, P., & Leone, M. C. (2005). Bounty hunters: A look behind the hype. *Policing: An International Journal of Police Strategies and Management, 28,* 118–138.
20. Clark, J., & Henry, D. A. (2003). *Pretrial services programming at the start of the 21st Century.* Washington, DC: U.S. Department of Justice, Office of Justice Programs, Bureau of Justice Assistance.
21. Clark & Henry.
22. Reaves, B. A., & Perez, J. (1994). *Pretrial release of felony defendants, 1992.* Washington, DC: U.S. Department of Justice, Office of Justice Program, Bureau of Justice Statistics.
23. Cohen, T. H., & Reaves, B. A. (2008). *Pretrial release of felony defendants in state courts.* Washington, DC: U.S. Department of Justice, Office of Justice Program, Bureau of Justice Statistics.
24. Wolf, T. J. (1997). What United States pretrial services officers do. *Federal Probation, 61,* 19–24.
25. Scalia, J. (1999). *Federal pretrial release and detention, 1996.* Washington, DC: U.S. Department of Justice, Office of Justice Programs, Bureau of Justice Statistics.

26. 18 U.S.C. §§ 3141–3150.

27. Goldkamp, J. S. (1993). Judicial responsibility for pretrial release decision-making and the information role of pretrial services. *Federal Probation, 57,* 28–35.

28. Gottfredson, M. R. (1974). An empirical analysis of pretrial release decisions. *Journal of Criminal Justice, 2,* 287–303.

29. Goldkamp, J. S. (1979). Bail decision-making and pretrial detention: Surfacing judicial policy. *Law and Human Behavior, 3,* 227–249.

30. Gottfredson, M. R., & Gottfredson, D. M. (1980). *Decision-making in criminal justice: Toward the rational exercise of discretion*. Cambridge, MA: Ballinger Publishing Company.

31. Goldkamp, J. S. (1983). Questioning the practice of pretrial detention: Some empirical evidence from Philadelphia. *Journal of Criminal Law and Criminology, 74,* 1556–1588.

32. Holmes, M. D., Hosch, H. M., Daudistel, H. C., Perez, D. A., & Graves, J. B. (1996). Ethnicity, legal resources, and felony dispositions in two southwestern jurisdictions. *Justice Quarterly, 13,* 11–30.

33. Petersilia, J., Turner, S., & Fain, T. (2000). *Profiling inmates in the Los Angeles County jails: Risks, recidivism, and release options*. Santa Monica, CA: Rand Corporation.

34. Maxwell, S. R. (1999). Examining the congruence between predictors or ROR and failures to appear. *Journal of Criminal Justice, 27,* 127–141.

35. Albonetti, C. A., Hauser, R. M., Hagan, J., & Nagel, I. H. (1989). Criminal justice decision-making as a stratification process: The role of race and stratification resources in pretrial release. *Journal of Quantitative Criminology, 5,* 57–82.

36. Demuth, S. (2003). Racial and ethnic differences in pretrial release decisions and outcomes: A comparison of Hispanic, Black, and White felony arrestees. *Criminology, 41,* 873–908.

37. Demuth & Steffensmeier.

38. Katz, C. M., & Spohn, C. C. (1995). The effect of race and gender on bail outcomes: A test of the interactive model. *American Journal of Criminal Justice, 19,* 161–184.

39. Demuth, p. 894.

40. Demuth & Steffensmeier, p. 232.

41. Goldkamp, J. S., & Jones, P. R. (1992). Pretrial drug-testing experiments in Milwaukee and Prince George's County: The context of implementation. *Journal of Research in Crime and Delinquency, 29,* 430–465.

42. Jones, P. R., & Goldkamp, J. S. (1993). Implementing pretrial drug-testing programs in two experimental sites: Some deterrence and jail bed implications. *Prison Journal, 73,* 199–219.

43. Goldkamp, J. S., Gottfredson, M. R., & Weiland, D. (1990). Pretrial drug testing and defendant risk. *Journal of Criminal Law and Criminology, 81,* 585–652.

44. Britt, C. L., Gottfredson, M. R., & Goldkamp, J. S. (1992). Drug testing and pretrial misconduct: An experiment on the specific deterrent effects of drug monitoring defendants on pretrial release. *Journal of Research in Crime and Delinquency, 29,* 62–78.

45. Goldkamp, J. S., Gottfredson, M. R., Jones, P. R., & Weiland, D. (1995). *Personal liberty and community safety: Pretrial release in the criminal court.* New York: Plenum (pp. 307–308).

46. Feeley, M. M. (1992). *The process is the punishment: Handling cases in a lower criminal court* (Rev. ed.). New York: Russell Sage Foundation.

47. For example, see Ares, C., Rankin, A., & Sturz, H. (1963). The Manhattan Bail Project: An interim report on the use of pretrial parole. *New York University Law Review, 38,* 67–92; Eisenstein, J., & Jacob, H.

(1977). *Felony justice: An organizational analysis of criminal courts.* Boston: Little, Brown; Goldfarb, R. L. (1965); Goldfarb, R. (1976). *Jails: The ultimate ghetto of the criminal justice system.* New York: Doubleday; Holmes, M., Daudistel, H., & Farrell, R. (1987). Determinants of charge reductions and final dispositions in cases of burglary and robbery. *Journal of Research in Crime and Delinquency, 24,* 233–254.

48. Williams, M. R. (2003). The effect of pretrial detention on imprisonment decisions. *Criminal Justice Review, 28,* 299–316.

49. Stinchcomb, J. B., & McCampbell, S. W. (2007). *Jail leaders speak: Current and future challenges to jail administration and operations.* Washington, DC: U.S. Department of Justice, Office of Justice Programs, Bureau of Justice Assistance.

50. Pekins, C. A., Stephan, J. J., & Beck, A. J. (1995). *Jails and jail inmates, 1993–1994.* Washington, DC: U.S. Department of Justice, Office of Justice Programs, Bureau of Justice Statistics.

51. Sabol, W. J., Minton, T. D., & Harrison, P. M. (2007). *Prison and jail inmates at midyear 2006.* Washington, DC: U.S. Department of Justice, Office of Justice Programs, Bureau of Justice Statistics.

52. DeLisi.

53. James, D. J. (2004). *Profile of jail inmates, 2002.* Washington, DC: U.S. Department of Justice, Office of Justice Programs, Bureau of Justice Statistics.

54. Surette, R., Applegate, B., McCarthy, B., & Jablonski, P. (2006). Self-destructing prophecies: Long-term forecasting of municipal correctional bed need. *Journal of Criminal Justice, 34,* 57–72.

55. Sabol et al., p. 7.

56. D'Alessio, S. J., & Stolzenberg, L. (1997). The effect of available capacity on jail incarceration: An empirical test of Parkinson's law. *Journal of Criminal Justice, 25,* 279–288.

57. Baumer, T. L., & Adams, K. (2006). Controlling a jail population by partially closing the front door: An evaluation of a 'summons in lieu of arrest' policy. *Prison Journal, 86,* 386–402.

58. Ruddell, R., Decker, S. H., & Egley, A. (2006). Gang interventions in jails: A national analysis. *Criminal Justice Review, 31,* 33–46.

59. Garofalo & Clark.

60. Backstrand, J. A., Gibbons, D. C., & Jones, J. F. (1992). Who is in jail? An examination of the rabble hypothesis. *Crime and Delinquency, 38,* 219–229.

61. DeLisi, M. (2000). Who is more dangerous? Comparing the criminality of homeless and domiciled jail inmates. *International Journal of Offender Therapy and Comparative Criminology, 44,* 59–69.

62. James, p. 1.

63. James, p. 1.

64. Karberg, J. C., & James, D. J. (2005). *Substance dependence, abuse, and treatment of jail inmates, 2002.* Washington, DC: U.S. Department of Justice, Office of Justice Programs, Bureau of Justice Statistics.

65. Maruschak, L. M. (2006). *Medical problems of jail inmates.* Washington, DC: U.S. Department of Justice, Office of Justice Programs, Bureau of Justice Statistics.

66. Mumola, C. J. (2005). *Suicide and homicide in state prisons and local jails.* Washington, DC: U.S. Department of Justice, Office of Justice Programs, Bureau of Justice Statistics.

67. Goldfarb.

68. Adler, F. (1986). Jails as a repository for former mental patients. *International Journal of Offender Therapy and Comparative Criminology, 30,* 225–236.

69. Irwin, J. (1985). *The jail: Managing the underclass in American society.* Berkeley: University of California Press.

70. Mattick, H., & Aikman, A. (1969). The cloacal region of American corrections: Prospects for jail reform. *Annals of the American Academy of Political and Social Science, 381,* 109–118.

71. Mays, G. L., & Thompson, J. A. (1988). Mayberry revisited: The characteristics and operations of America's small jails. *Justice Quarterly, 5,* 421–440.

72. Ruddell & Mays.

73. Zupan, L. L. (1991). *Jails: Reform and the new generation philosophy.* Cincinnati, OH: Anderson.

74. Nelson, W. R., O'Toole, M., Krauth, B., & Whitemore, C. G. (1983). *New generation jails.* Longmont, CO: U.S. Department of Justice, National Institute of Corrections, Jails Division.

75. Tartaro, C. (2006). Watered down: Partial implementation of the new generation jail philosophy. *Prison Journal, 86,* 284–300.

76. Tartaro, C. (2002). Examining implementation issues with new generation jails. *Criminal Justice Policy Review, 13,* 219–237.

77. Senese, J. D. (1997). Evaluating jail reform: A comparative analysis of podular/direct and linear jail inmate infractions. *Journal of Criminal Justice, 25,* 61–73.

78. Williams, J. L., Rodeheaver, D. G., & Huggins, D. W. (1999). A comparative evaluation of a new generation jail. *American Journal of Criminal Justice, 23,* 223–246.

79. Applegate, B. K., Surette, R., & McCarthy, B. J. (1999). Detention and desistance from crime: Evaluating the influence of a new generation jail on recidivism. *Journal of Criminal Justice, 27,* 539–548.

80. Irwin.

81. Backstrand, Gibbons, & Jones.

82. Pogrebin, M., Dodge, M., & Katsampes, P. (2001). The collateral costs of short-term jail incarceration: The long-term social and economic disruptions. *Corrections Management Quarterly, 5,* 64–69.

83. Hoff, R., Baranosky, M. V., Buchanan, J., Zonana, H., & Rosenheck, R. A. (1999). The effects of a jail diversion program on incarceration: A retrospective cohort study. *Journal of the American Academy of Psychiatry and the Law, 27,* 377–386.

84. Lamb, H., Shaner, R., Elliott, D., DeCuir, W. J., & Foltz, J. T. (1995). Outcomes for psychiatric emergency patients seen by an outreach police–mental health team. *Psychiatric Services, 46,* 1267–1271.

85. Steadman, H. J., Cocozza, J. J., & Veysey, B. M. (1999). Comparing outcomes for diverted and nondiverted jail detainees with mental illness. *Law and Human Behavior, 23,* 615–627.

86. Steadman, H. J., & Naples, M. (2005). Assessing the effectiveness of jail diversion programs for persons with serious mental illness and co-occurring substance use disorders. *Behavioral Sciences and the Law, 23,* 163–170.

87. Armstrong, T. A. (2002). The effect of environment on the behavior of youthful offenders: A randomized experiment. *Journal of Criminal Justice, 30,* 19–28.

88. Walters, G. D. (1998). Time series and correlational analyses of inmate-initiated incidents in a large correctional system. *International Journal of Offender Therapy and Comparative Criminology, 42,* 124–132.

89. Tartaro, C. (2002). The impact of density on jail violence. *Journal of Criminal Justice, 30,* 499–510.

90. Taxman, F. S., Perdoni, M. L., & Harrison, L. D. (2007). Drug treatment services for adult offenders: The state of the state. *Journal of Substance Abuse Treatment, 32,* 239–254.

91. Baumer, T. L., Maxfield, M. G., & Mendelsohn, R. I. (1993). A comparative analysis of three electronically monitored home detention programs. *Justice Quarterly, 10,* 121–142.

92. Courtright, K. E., Berg, B. L., & Mutchnick, R. J. (1997). The cost effectiveness of using house arrest with electronic monitoring for drunk drivers. *Federal Probation, 61,* 19–22.

93. Lilly, J. R., Ball, R. A., Curry, G. D., & McMullen, J. (1993). Electronic monitoring of the drunk driver: A seven-year study of the home confinement alternative. *Crime & Delinquency, 39*, 462–484.

94. Maxfield, M. G., & Baumer, T. L. (1990). Home detention with electronic monitoring: Comparing pretrial and postconviction programs. *Crime & Delinquency, 36*, 521–536.

95. Maxfield, M. G., & Baumer, T. L. (1992). Pretrial home detention with electronic monitoring: A non-experimental salvage evaluation. *Evaluation Review, 16*, 315–332.

96. Stanz, R., & Tewksbury, R. (2000). Predictors of success and recidivism in a home incarceration program. *Prison Journal, 80*, 326–344.

CHAPTER

6

Diversion, Pretrial Treatment, and Prevention

"Where pretrial diversion in the federal court system is offered, it generally works well."[1, p. 35]

OBJECTIVES

- Explore diversion as a means to provide treatment and alleviate crowding in the correctional system.
- Learn the various types of diversion programs.
- Understand the effectiveness, strengths, and weaknesses of diversion programs.
- Identify major programs and policy initiatives devoted to the treatment and diversion of offenders with psychiatric problems.
- Recognize what works in the diversion of criminal offenders.
- Explore prevention as an approach to criminal justice treatment.
- Identify promising prevention programs.

CASE STUDY

In 1986, New York City police investigated 1,592 murders, including that of Jennifer Dawn Levin. In August 1986, a cyclist out for a morning ride through Central Park came across a partially clad, lifeless body. The only suspect in the case proclaimed his innocence, claiming to have been attacked by the young woman who was bent on having sex with him—her desires so intent he had to kill her to escape her advances. The murder victim, Levin, was a 5-foot, 4-inch, 18-year-old female, who weighed 130 pounds. The suspect in the case was Robert Chambers, later dubbed the Preppie Killer, a 6-foot-4, 200-pound man.

Police reports indicated Levin had been sexually assaulted. Items found on or near her body included jewelry, credit cards, photographs, and her wallet. As police continued to process the crime scene, the man later identified as Jennifer's killer was standing in the crowd talking with another woman who had just finished her run along the same path. The woman later described Robert Chambers' demeanor as he watched the crime scene investigation as being oddly unattached and indifferent.

The coroner estimated the time of death to have been 4 hours prior to the discovery of the body. The coroner also noted that the victim's eyelids had pinpoint bleeding. When a body exhibits this type of injury, it is usually an indication that the blood supply to the brain has been cut off. This finding suggests that death was brought on by strangulation; so did the bruise marks on Jennifer's neck, and further investigation revealed no other signs of violent trauma.

The identification in the wallet led police to Jennifer's father. After being told of his daughter's death, Steven Levin contacted a close friend of Jennifer's, who gave police information on her whereabouts and the people she had been with early the previous evening. This information led police to the home of Phyllis Chambers, Robert's mother. When officers approached Robert they noticed fresh scratches on his face and hands. As all experienced investigators know, scratches on the face and arms generally signal defense wounds placed there by the victim in a struggle to escape an assailant. When questioned about the scratch wounds on his face, Robert stated his cat had scratched him. He provided a plausible explanation for the injuries to his hand as well. Robert told police he had been sanding floors for a woman in the building and the machine he had been using jumped and cut his fingers.

But detectives had information that placed Robert at a bar and in the company of Jennifer the night of her murder. Robert offered several explanations but eventually confessed to the crime. Robert had had a fight with his girlfriend prior to leaving with Jennifer. According to Robert, Jennifer had convinced him to leave the bar even after he had told her he didn't want to see her any more and that she had also persuaded him to walk with her to the park. Chambers described Jennifer as being very sexually aggressive and said that he had been forced to push her away several times to ward off her advances. He even claimed she had tied his hands behind his back with her panties and then began to remove his clothing. According to Chambers, he managed to get his hands free, grab Jennifer, and flip her over, causing her to land on a tree, killing her.

Chambers also indicated to police that Jennifer was having her way with him, that it was against his will, and this happened in spite of his protests to stop. Detectives didn't buy his explanation. There was simply too much evidence to the contrary, and Chambers was placed under arrest for the murder of Levin shortly after providing detectives with his account of the incident. Before being booked on the charge, Robert reportedly said, "That fucking bitch, why didn't she leave me alone?"

1. Why did the media fixate on this story and why has it had lasting public interest?
2. What ultimately happened to Robert Chambers?

"People have gone from being tax users to being taxpayers. It's an incredible turnaround, and the numbers are going to keep increasing."[2, p. 17]

Diversion

An innovative way that the correctional system controls the number of clients that it supervises is by refusing to admit many customers. Certain potential correctional clients, particularly persons who pose the littlest risk, are not entered into the correctional process; they are diverted. **Diversion** broadly refers to any procedure that prevents official entry into the criminal justice process. In some circumstances, diversion is the suspension of criminal or juvenile proceedings. In other cases, diversion refers to (1) lesser supervision, (2) referral to a noncriminal justice agency, usually a social service provider, or (3) any nonconfinement status when confinement would otherwise be used. In criminal justice usage, diversion is the official suspension of proceedings against an alleged offender at any point after a police contact or official justice system intake (e.g., booking into jail), but before the entering of a judgment and a decision whether to refer the person to a treatment or care program administered by a nonjustice or private agency.[6]

"A clear need exists, however, for more program development and evaluation related to the mechanisms by which systems agents and individuals alter their behavior as a result of diversion and treatment."[3, p. 574]

Diversion is a multifaceted technique for law enforcement, the courts, and correctional entities to prudently deflect criminal defendants whose criminal transgressions are minor and do not need the full attention of the criminal justice system. There are five major goals of diversion:

1. Avoidance of negative labeling of first-time or minor offenders.
2. Reduction of unnecessary social control.
3. Reduction of recidivism.
4. Reduction of justice system costs.
5. Provision of service and treatment.[7]

The latter point is extremely important. Diversion is also critical at providing appropriate treatment and other social services for subpopulations of offenders who need them. In other words, diversion is a humanistic and sensible way that the criminal justice system generally and the correctional domain specifically processes and serves persons accused of crimes. This chapter reviews the history and characteristics of diversion, the many types of programs and policies that serve to divert defendants from the justice system, and the effectiveness of these programs and policies.

History

Diversion is one of the clearest examples of the criminal justice system borrowing a development that was first employed by the juvenile justice system. Throughout its history, the juvenile justice system has operated with the philosophy that persons charged with delinquent offenses should be treated as clients under the care of the system rather than criminals to be punished by the state. Since the founding of the juvenile court in 1899, "the focus of the new juvenile courts was on youth rather than their offenses, on less formal processing and rehabilitation rather than punishment. Since the juvenile court

Labeling theory asserts that once a person is processed as a criminal offender, it is difficult to overcome the stigma and can lead to future criminal behavior. For this reason, diversion has been used throughout the history of the correctional system.

"In drug-court areas without an existing TASC program, judges and probation officials should consider developing one as a proven offender management structure."[4, p. 193]

was seeking rehabilitation and personalized justice for juveniles akin to a benevolent parent, it was believed that the formal, adversarial processes and sanctions employed in the criminal justice system were inappropriate for juvenile offenders."[8, p. 133]

Diversion is rooted in the theoretical tradition of **labeling theory**, a school of thought that asserts that defining people as delinquent or criminal leads to social ostracism, solidifies a delinquent self-image, and leads to increased antisocial behavior. In this way, the juvenile and criminal justice systems can actually make worse what they were designed to reduce: crime. By diverting nonserious offenders from the system, the damaging, self-fulfilling effects of labeling are avoided, people do not develop an antisocial self-image, and offending is reduced. The ideas generated by labeling theory gained broad acceptance in the 1950s and 1960s and ultimately informed policy. For instance, President Johnson's **Commission on Law Enforcement and the Administration of Justice**, established in 1965, declared war on crime, and one of the policy initiatives to emerge from the commission was the creation of youth bureaus to divert juvenile offenders from confinement to community organizations.

The use of diversion in juvenile justice became more pronounced after the enactment of the **Juvenile Justice and Delinquency Prevention Act of 1974** and its subsequent updates in 1977 and 1980. The act provides federal funding to states and communities for prevention and treatment programs especially diversion programs that deinstitutionalize adolescents convicted of **status offenses** or behaviors that are criminalized because of the age of the offender. Status offenses include behaviors such as running away, idleness, underage drinking, truancy, curfew violations, incorrigibility, and the like. In addition, the spirit of the Juvenile Justice and Delinquency Prevention Act of 1974 established that low-level offenders who are contacted for mostly trivial offenses should not be formally processed by the criminal justice system. This spirit continues today in both the juvenile and criminal justice systems. In fact, separate courts have been created to address the specialized treatment needs of groups of offenders who are perceived as less deserving of traditional sentencing procedures (see Chapter 4).

Although diversion is viewed as a positive development in the criminal justice system, it has not been without controversy. One of the main concerns about diversion where juvenile and criminal justice agents have wide latitude whether to formally select persons for entry into the system centers on the procedural rights of defendants. Arnold Binder and Virginia Binder noted that it is unlikely that the same constitutional protections of due process that occur in formal interactions with police and court personnel will apply in more informal diversion decisions. Moreover, do juveniles have the same likelihood to be selected for diversion? If not, does this suggest that procedurally speaking, the use of diversion is unequal?[9] A related concern is whether discrimination influences the decision to divert defendants by race. On this, the research is mixed but studies overwhelmingly show that legally relevant factors, such as prior criminal record and situational factors, such as suspect demeanor, are stronger determinants of diversion than race or ethnicity.[10] Duran Bell and Kevin Lang found that minority youths are more likely than White youths to receive both harsh and lenient treatment as it relates to diversion.[11] Michael Leiber and Jayne Stairs also found conflicting and at times counterintuitive race effects in the application of diversion in three Iowa juvenile courts.[12]

Another concern about diversion programs relates to **net widening**, which is the growing of the correctional population by supervising increasing number of offenders in the community. Since offenders were either detained or outright released before the implementation of a diversion program, it could be viewed as a way for the state to control more of its citizens while stabilizing the confinement population. Edwin Lemert suggested that diversion programs will result in broader social control as long as law enforcement agencies play a role in the process.[13] Herbert Covey and Scott Menard evaluated whether net widening was occurring among adult offenders in Colorado and found that it was, but only in some counties. In others, diversion was working precisely as designed by providing treatment instead of punishment and preventing many adults from

"An ounce of prevention is worth a pound of cure."[5]

CORRECTIONS BRIEF

From Drug Use Forecasting to Arrestee Drug Abuse Monitoring

In 1988 the National Institute of Justice (NIJ) developed a program designed to determine drug use among arrestees housed in America's jail system. The Drug Use Forecasting (DUF) program was instrumental in determining the validity of self-reported drug use among individuals arrested for various crimes. Until its inception, no other objective measure had been used to validate this self-reported data. As a result, DUF is credited with providing lawmakers needed information from which to develop policies governing court-ordered treatment, diversion, and incarceration options of at-risk populations.

DUF was good, but only to a point. Researchers interested in the data on arrestees' drug use felt more scientific scrutiny was required if policy makers and practitioners were to continue to rely on findings from this program. As a result, the National Institute of Justice set new requirements for the program. First, steps were taken to improve sampling procedures. A probability-based sampling technique was employed. Second, efforts at standardizing data collection were taken. Third, the instrument used in the interview process was enhanced to solicit information on new areas of drug use. Fourth, information on behaviors related to drug use by arrestees was also obtained. Fifth, the size of the sample was increased. Sixth, the interview instrument now includes questions concerning alcohol use. Eventually, the Arrestee Drug Abuse Monitoring (ADAM) program was developed.

Not surprisingly, drug use is common among adult male arrestees. Results from urinalysis involving 35 ADAM-reporting sites reveals 64 percent or more of the adult male arrestees had used a variety of controlled substances. The list of illegal substances includes: cocaine, marijuana, opiates, methamphetamine, or PCP. Overall, data indicates that between 25 and 50 percent of those adult males interviewed at ADAM sites are at-risk drug users. Newly collected information on alcohol use and related behaviors was informative, but not surprising. Data from ADAM reveals that 35 percent to 70 percent of adult male arrestees consumed five or more alcoholic drinks on at least one occasion within 30 days of their most recent arrest. Those admitting to five or more drinks within 13 days of their most recent arrest ranged from 10 percent to nearly 25 percent of adult male arrestees.

One of the most interesting features about ADAM is in its design to capture information on drug markets. However, participation in this segment of the interview seems to be related to the type of drug used by the adult male arrestee. For example, in 23 of the 35 sites analyzed, marijuana is the drug of choice. Those admitting to using other drugs such as crack cocaine, powder cocaine, heroin, and methamphetamine were less willing to share this information during the interview. ADAM data also reveals that, when measured in dollars, in high-volume sites such as Miami, Phoenix, Seattle, and Tucson, the crack cocaine market can range from 2 to 10 times larger than the market for powder cocaine and marijuana.

Interestingly, data from ADAM shows that even though the number of at-risk population arrestees is a significant portion of all adult male arrestees, very few of those deemed at risk for chemical dependency sought or received treatment for their chemical substance use problem. Data reveals that between 4 and 17 percent had received inpatient treatment 1 year prior to their arrest. The figure drops to between 2 percent and 15 percent for those who received outpatient treatment for drug use the year prior to their arrest.

Source: National Institute of Justice. (2003). *Arrestee Drug Abuse Monitoring program (ADAM)*. Washington, DC: U.S. Department of Justice, Office of Justice Programs, National Institute of Justice.

Criminologists have found mixed evidence of whether diversion results in net widening—or more persons under correctional control than is necessary.

having a possibly stigmatizing correctional status.[14] Scott Decker examined the effects of a diversion program in Missouri over an 8-year period and found significant evidence of net widening, suggesting that diversion programs may not only achieve their intended objectives but also unnecessarily burden the criminal justice system instead of providing relief.[15] Diversion programs that employ sanction-oriented threats to enforce compliance have also been shown to widen the net of persons under correctional authority.[16]

Of course, it is possible that diversion programs achieve exactly what was intended, which is divert offenders, provide services, and avoid widening the net of correctional control. Mark Pogrebin and his colleagues evaluated the Adams County (Colorado) Juvenile Diversion Project and found that it was a model program because it had adequate community and justice system resources to operate the program and established coordination between these agencies. By focusing on more serious offenders and not drawing low-risk candidates into the program, Pogrebin and his associates found that the appropriate clients received services while avoiding net widening by drawing trivial offenders into the system. Over an 18-month follow-up of nearly 900 offenders, youths who received diversionary programs had significantly lower recidivism rates than a control group of adolescents.[17]

Types

As shown in FIGURE 6-1, diversion is used at several points in the juvenile justice system, including by law enforcement, nonlaw enforcement referrals, such as parents and schools, prosecutors, and juvenile court judges. For adult offenders, diversion is also employed by several criminal justice practitioners. For instance, **police diversion** involves the use of officer discretion to use a variety of tactics, resources, and community agencies to address the criminal behavior of defendants. Often, police diversion is extremely informal and part of the day-to-day use of discretion that officers exercise while on duty. There are many examples of police diversion. For example, upon contacting a juvenile for a delinquent violation, officers can refer the youth to his or her parents and a community agency,

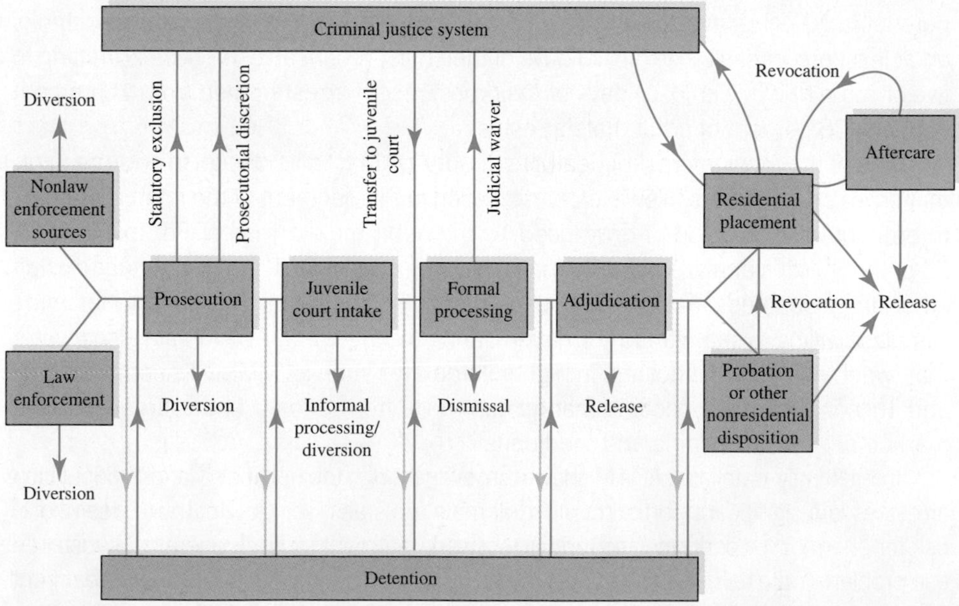

FIGURE 6-1 The Prominence of Diversion to Juvenile Justice. *Source*: Snyder, H., & Sickmund, M. (2006). *Juvenile offenders and victims: 2006 national report.* Washington, DC: U.S. Department of Justice, Office of Juvenile Justice and Delinquency Prevention, National Center for Juvenile Justice.

such as a Boys and Girls Club that provides structured activities for youths. If the child is delinquent because of unstructured time, then getting connected to an organization that provides prosocial opportunities is likely to reduce delinquency. This is a preferable situation than officially entering the youth into the system.

There are also a host of diversion options available to prosecutors specifically and the courts generally. Three of the most common are **deferred prosecution**, **deferred judgment**, and **deferred sentences** (see Chapter 1). These types of diversionary outcomes are often used interchangeably and are a widely used and cost-effective way to control the correctional population by diverting first-time offenders or persons who have never been contacted for violent crimes. An early prosecutorial diversion program was the Night Prosecutor's Program in Columbus, Ohio, which was identified by the Law Enforcement Assistance Administration (which is today known as the National Institute of Justice) as an exemplary program. In the night court, criminal complaints involving interpersonal disputes were heard 1 week after the alleged crime, and all parties, such as the alleged offender, victim, witnesses, and other interested parties, participated in a formal hearing overseen by a city attorney. The hearings used mediation as a way to resolve the disputes, and it usually worked. Only 2 percent of complaints ultimately resulted in formal filing of charges and in about 3 percent of cases did the complainant actually return to the night court to continue the charge from the original dispute.[18]

In another example, prosecutors in the Kings County (Brooklyn) District Attorney's Office developed a program called Drug Treatment Alternative-to-Prison (DTAP) which offers an 18- to 24-month treatment program for repeat drug offenders as a way to explore treatment and save prison space.[19] In most jurisdictions, chronic offenders are generally excluded from deferred prosecution efforts because of their multiple arrests, convictions, and prior incidents of noncompliance.[20]

Here is how it works. Suppose a defendant, with minimal criminal history, is arrested for theft. He or she pleads guilty to the crime in exchange for a deferred judgment period, usually ranging from 6 months to 2 years. Unlike probation, deferred sentences entail no conditions and do not require the defendant to check in with correctional personnel. Instead, clients who received a deferred sentence must simply not get arrested during the specified time period and theoretically abstain from committing crime. If the defendant remains crime free for the specified period, the guilty plea is voided and the entire event expunged from the defendant's record. The use of deferred prosecution as a means to divert nonserious offenders from the justice system was devised in 1936 by a juvenile probation officer named Conrad Printzlien. In the intervening years, thousands of youths were spared the social, emotional, and economic disruptions that can occur with having a justice system status, and the justice system benefited from enormous savings.[21]

In some jurisdictions, the criminal charge is held in **abeyance**, or suspended, until the person successfully completes the treatment protocol that was originally ordered. For example, in Iowa, deferred prosecutions were formerly used for persons arrested for domestic assault. If the person completed a batterer education program, the original charge would be dismissed. Deferred prosecution, judgments, and sentences are used for both misdemeanor and felony crimes. Deferred judgments, sentences, or suspended sentences are not an option if the crime involves a sexual assault of a child 12 years of age or younger, if the defendant has a previous felony conviction, or if the defendant has previously received a deferred judgment or similar court-ordered sanction. Jurisdictions vary as to whether the offense is expunged from the permanent record, whether the underlying arrest charge remains on the permanent record, and whether the entering of a deferred prosecution, judgment, or sentence appears as a disposition. Because of the possibility of **expungement** in some jurisdictions, which is the complete removal of a criminal record from existence, deferred sentences offer one of the best incentives for offenders to reform their criminal ways. If defendants are rearrested during the deferred

TABLE 6-1 Adjudication Outcome for Felony Defendants in the Nation's 75 Largest Counties

			Percent of Felony Defendants in the 75 Largest Counties									
			Convicted						Not Convicted			
				Felony			Misdemeanor					
Most Serious Arrest Charge	Number of Defendants	Total Convicted	Total	Plea	Trial	Total	Plea	Trial	Total	Dismissed	Acquitted	Other Outcome*
All offenses	49,349	68	57	54	3	11	11	—	25	24	1	7
Violent offenses	11,535	60	48	43	5	11	11	1	35	33	2	5
Murder	385	81	80	41	39	1	0	1	17	13	4	2
Rape	760	67	59	53	6	8	8	0	26	24	2	6
Robbery	2,628	66	58	53	6	8	8	—	32	31	1	2
Assault	6,097	55	41	38	3	14	13	1	38	36	2	6
Other violent	1,664	57	47	42	5	10	10	—	35	34	1	7
Property offenses	15,328	72	59	56	3	13	12	—	22	22	—	6
Burglary	4,165	75	66	63	3	9	9	—	21	20	1	4
Larceny/theft	4,460	69	54	50	4	15	14	1	24	24	—	7
Motor vehicle theft	1,767	74	68	65	3	5	5	0	20	19	1	7
Forgery	1,558	76	57	55	3	19	19	0	18	17	1	6
Fraud	1,516	70	59	56	3	11	11	1	18	18	0	11
Other property	1,862	67	50	49	1	17	17	—	29	28	1	4
Drug offenses	17,749	69	60	57	3	8	8	—	21	20	1	11
Trafficking	8,239	76	64	60	4	12	11	—	20	19	1	5
Other drug	9,510	63	57	55	2	6	6	—	22	21	—	16
Public-order offenses	4,737	73	59	56	3	14	14	—	22	21	1	5
Weapons	1,310	67	56	53	4	11	10	1	28	25	3	5
Driving-related	1,581	87	73	71	2	14	13	—	10	10	0	3
Other public-order	1,847	65	49	46	3	17	17	0	28	28	1	6

Note: *Other outcome includes diversion and deferred prosecution/adjudication.

Source: Cohen, T.H., & Reaves, B. A. (2006). *Felony defendants in large urban counties, 2002.* Washington, DC: U.S. Department of Justice, Office of Justice Programs, Bureau of Justice Statistics.

sentence, two courses of action are pursued. First, the deferred period is extended, for example from 6 months to 1 year, and the defendant is provided another opportunity on the deferred sentence. Second, the deferred sentence is revoked and the client is placed on probation. Importantly, a guilty plea that results in probation will not be dismissed and expunged regardless of how well the client complies while under supervision.

How Common Is Diversion?

The use of diversion or deferred prosecution is relatively common as a means to divert criminal defendants from the correctional system. As shown in TABLE 6-1, about 7 percent (about 3,500 felony cases each year) of cases adjudicated in the 75 largest counties in the United States are disposed of via diversion or deferred prosecution. Nationally, about 5 percent of cases involving serious violent crimes are disposed of by diversion. For instance, 2 percent of murder cases are adjudicated using diversion of deferred prosecution. The types of crimes that are most likely to be diverted are drug offenses. Eleven percent of drug offenses, including 16 percent of nontrafficking drug crimes, are diverted or receive deferred prosecution. Six percent of property and 5 percent of public-order offenses are diverted annually. Overall, diversion and deferred prosecution are used to dispose of more cases each month than criminal trials (see FIGURE 6-2).[22]

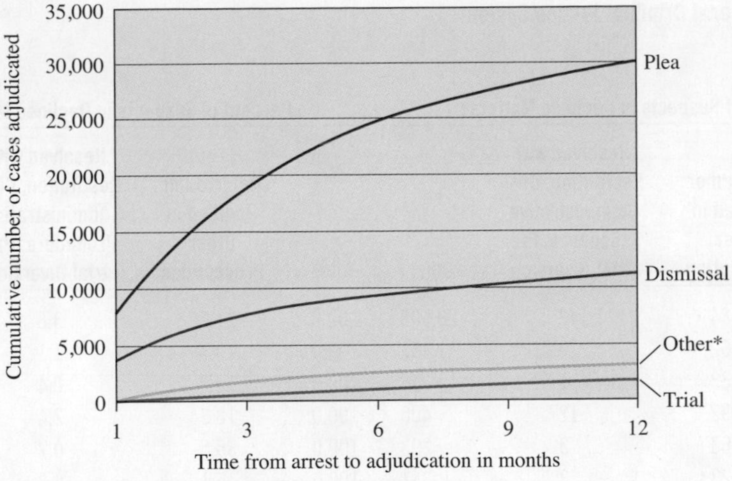

FIGURE 6–2 Method of Adjudication. *Source*: Cohen, T. H., & Reaves, B. A. (2006). *Felony defendants in large urban counties, 2002*. Washington, DC: U.S. Department of Justice, Office of Justice Programs, Bureau of Justice Statistics.

Nearly 4 percent of federal crimes are diverted each year. In the federal system, pretrial diversion is an agreement between the defendant and the United States attorney to defer and possibly drop prosecution conditioned on the defendant's good behavior and/or participation in programs (e.g., job training, counseling, education) during the specified period. As shown in **TABLE 6–2**, federal crimes, such as embezzlement, forgery, violations of postal laws and other regulatory offenses, production or possession of obscene materials, and wildlife violations are commonly resolved with diversion.[23]

Diversion is also used by local and state officials. Of more than 222,000 juvenile arrests, 87 percent are referred by police to probation and 13 percent are released. The released juveniles could have been let go for legal reasons, such as insufficient evidence, or other subjective reasons, such as the officer did not feel that a police referral was warranted. In this sense, many of these cases were unofficially diverted. Among the 87 percent of cases that are referred, nearly half are adjudicated in juvenile court and half receive other dispositions. Seven percent of the latter cases involve cases where juveniles are sent to alternative diversion programs. For the 45 percent of cases that are heard in juvenile court, 7 percent result in alternative diversion programs or receive deferred judgments. In other words, cases are routinely diverted (officially or unofficially) from the juvenile justice system in California.

Major Diversion Initiatives

As indicated earlier, the use of diversion or deferred sentences dates at least to the early decades of the 20th century. Programs that divert first-time, low-level, or generally nonserious offenders can save the justice system tremendous costs relating to prosecution, defense attorneys, judicial services, court personnel, filing fees, and detention. In addition, diversion and deferred sentences promote a sense of justice by addressing the social, medical, and personal factors associated with crime and recidivism and provide services that reduce the person's likelihood to reoffend. Some major diversion programs and policies are explored next.

TABLE 6-2 The Use of Diversion in the Federal Criminal Justice System

	Number of Suspects in Declined Matters				Percent of Suspects in Declined Matters			
Most Serious Offense Investigated	Total	Referred or Handled in Other Prosecution	Resolved with Restitution, Civil/ Administrative Procedure, Pre-trial Diversion	Other	Total	Referred or Handled in Other Prosecution	Resolved with Restitution, Civil/ Administrative Procedure, Pre-trial Diversion	Other
All offenses	31,866	6,584	1,142	23,608	100.0	21.0	3.6	75.3
Violent offenses	1,865	362	20	1,456	100.0	19.7	1.1	79.2
Murder	271	33	1	236	100.0	12.2	0.4	87.4
Assault	510	92	12	400	100.0	18.3	2.4	79.4
Robbery	476	163	3	293	100.0	35.5	0.7	63.8
Sexual abuse	380	23	3	351	100.0	6.1	0.8	93.1
Kidnapping	112	38	1	73	100.0	33.9	0.9	65.2
Threats against the President	116	13	0	103	100.0	11.2	0.0	89.8
Property offenses	10,472	1,475	635	8,208	100.0	14.3	6.2	79.6
Fraudulent	9,437	1,294	596	7,407	100.0	13.9	6.4	79.7
Embezzlement	1,160	78	216	851	100.0	6.8	18.9	74.3
Fraud	7,703	1,079	347	6,161	100.0	14.2	4.6	81.2
Forgery	376	81	31	261	100.0	21.7	8.3	70.0
Counterfeiting	198	56	2	134	100.0	29.2	1.0	69.8
Other	1,035	181	39	801	100.0	17.7	3.8	78.5
Burglary	13	6	0	6	100.0	50.0	0.0	50.0
Larceny	396	76	25	291	100.0	19.4	6.4	74.2
Motor vehicle theft	154	33	3	113	100.0	22.1	2.0	75.8
Arson and explosives	365	42	4	315	100.0	11.6	1.1	87.3
Transportation of stolen property	32	5	0	27	100.0	15.6	0.0	84.4
Other property offenses	75	19	7	49	100.0	25.3	9.3	65.3
Drug offenses	6,215	1,874	40	4,184	100.0	30.7	0.7	68.6
Public-order offenses	8,617	1,588	307	6,582	100.0	18.7	3.6	77.6
Regulatory	3,122	258	165	2,655	100.0	8.4	5.4	86.3
Agriculture	3	0	0	3	^	^	^	^
Antitrust	2	0	0	2	^	^	^	^
Food and drug	83	6	4	71	100.0	7.4	4.9	87.7

(continued)

Treatment Alternatives to Street Crime

The **Treatment Alternatives to Street Crime** (TASC) program was created in 1970 by President Richard Nixon's Special Action Office for Drug Abuse Prevention. TASC was an attempt to find a way to break the relationship between drug use and crime. The idea for the initial TASC programs came from analysis of recidivism among drug-using offenders who had been released from jail on bond. Although there were provisions for drug treatment and supervision after conviction, there were few programs in place to assist drug-dependent offenders while awaiting trial. The first TASC programs were implemented in Wilmington, Delaware; Cleveland, Ohio; and Philadelphia, Pennsylvania.

The original TASC programs focused on three main goals: (1) reducing the drug use and crime among drug-using offenders, (2) shifting the emphasis from punishment to the treatment and rehabilitation of offenders, and (3) diverting offenders to community agencies that can provide needed services. Not all offenders were eligible for TASC programs. After arrest, offenders are screened for program eligibility with an assessment of

TABLE 6-2 *(Continued)*

Most Serious Offense Investigated	Number of Suspects in Declined Matters: Total	Referred or Handled in Other Prosecution	Resolved with Restitution, Civil/Administrative Procedure, Pre-trial Diversion	Other	Percent of Suspects in Declined Matters: Total	Referred or Handled in Other Prosecution	Resolved with Restitution, Civil/Administrative Procedure, Pre-trial Diversion	Other
Public-order offenses *(continued)*								
Transportation	144	14	11	117	100.0	9.9	7.7	82.4
Civil rights	1,375	52	28	1,285	100.0	3.8	2.1	94.1
Communications	74	5	0	68	100.0	6.8	0.0	93.2
Custom laws	122	22	8	86	100.0	19.0	6.9	74.1
Postal laws	43	6	9	28	100.0	14.0	20.9	65.1
Other regulatory offenses	1,276	153	105	995	100.0	12.2	8.4	79.4
Other	5,495	1,330	142	3,927	100.0	24.6	2.6	72.7
Tax law violations	341	34	9	286	100.0	10.3	2.7	86.9
Bribery	146	19	5	122	100.0	13.0	3.4	83.6
Perjury, contempt, and intimidation	252	25	4	222	100.0	10.0	1.6	88.4
National defense	351	23	15	305	100.0	6.7	4.4	88.9
Escape	587	308	2	234	100.0	54.2	4.6	41.2
Racketeering and extortion	1,711	225	19	1,442	100.0	13.3	1.1	85.5
Gambling	92	13	1	78	100.0	14.1	1.1	84.8
Liquor offenses	7	0	0	7	^	^	^	^
Nonviolent sex offenses	1,098	223	12	843	100.0	20.7	1.1	78.2
Obscene material	17	2	3	12	100.0	11.8	17.6	70.6
Traffic	1	0	0	1	^	^	^	^
Wildlife	132	37	20	74	100.0	26.6	15.6	57.8
Environmental	6	0	1	5	^	^	^	^
Conspiracy, aiding and abetting, and jurisdictional offenses	179	35	10	132	100.0	19.8	5.6	74.6
All other offenses	575	389	17	164	100.0	68.2	3.0	28.8
Weapon offenses	3,713	1,158	22	2,489	100.0	31.6	0.6	67.8
Immigration offenses	545	63	22	419	100.0	12.5	4.4	83.1

Source: Smith, S. K., & Motivans, M. (2006). *Compendium of federal justice statistics, 2004*. Washington, DC: U.S. Department of Justice, Office of Justice Programs, Bureau of Justice Statistics.

their risk to public safety, severity of drug dependence, and appropriateness or amenability to treatment. After an individual is referred to treatment, they sign a TASC contract or treatment agreement and a TASC case manager monitors the person's compliance. Clients who fail to follow the terms of their treatment contract are referred to court and potentially processed in the traditional fashion.

The Bureau of Justice Assistance identified 10 organizational and operational standards that are critical elements of TASC programs. These are:

1. A broad base of support from the criminal justice system with a formal system for effective communication.
2. A broad base of support from the treatment system with a formal system for effective communication.
3. An independent TASC unit with a designated administrator.
4. Required staff training according to TASC policies.

5. A system of data collection for program management and evaluation.
6. Explicit eligibility criteria for TASC participants.
7. Screening procedures for the early identification of eligible offenders.
8. Documented procedures for assessment and referral.
9. Documented policies, procedures, and technology for drug testing.
10. Procedures for offender monitoring with established success/failure criteria and constant reporting to criminal justice referral sources.[24]

Today, TASC is known as Treatment Alternatives for Safe Communities and includes programs than span the criminal justice system. For example, TASC programs in Illinois include:

- Adult criminal justice services: These services are the original TASC model to divert substance-using offenders to treatment as an alternative to incarceration.
- Domestic Violence Diversion Program: This is a deferred prosecution program where persons charged with domestic battery go through a 12-month batterer education program and substance abuse treatment if needed.
- Drug courts: Sentencing alternative for nonviolent drug offenders (see Chapter 4).
- IMPACT (Integrated Multiphase Program of Assessment and Comprehensive Treatment): Delivers comprehensive treatment to offenders in Cook County Department of Corrections (Chicago).
- State Attorneys Drug Abuse Program: Places eligible drug offenders in treatment.[25]

Federal Pretrial Diversion

Federal pretrial diversion is a voluntary program that provides an alternative to prosecution for persons selected for placement in a supervised program administered by a pretrial services or probation office. Federal diversion was first used in 1947 (and was then known as deferred prosecution) as a way to remove nonserious offenders from the correctional system. Throughout its history, federal diversion used the possibility of suspended prosecution to serve as an incentive to defendants to change their antisocial behavior and habits. If they did not, prosecution would occur.

Eligibility requirements for federal diversion appear in the *U.S. Attorney's Manual*. A person is ineligible for pretrial diversion if he or she has two or more prior felony convictions, is an addict, is a current or former public official accused of violating a public trust, is accused of an offense relating to national security or foreign affairs, or has been charged with a crime that should be transferred to state courts for prosecution.

When federal diversion is used, a written agreement is made between the defendant, U.S. attorney, and chief pretrial services or probation officer. Defendants have the right to consult with counsel before agreeing to the voluntary program. The median duration of federal diversion is 12 months. Some defendants receive just 1 month and others receive as long as 5 years, depending on crime severity and other relevant risk factors. Usually, clients must also pay restitution and perform community service. Nearly 4 percent of federal crimes are adjudicated with diversion mostly for crimes such as fraud, larceny, embezzlement, and violation of regulatory offenses. Thomas Ulrich studied the outcomes of federal diversion cases over a 5-year period and found that 88 percent of cases were successfully completed and the case never resulted in prosecution.[26] In sum, diversion in the federal criminal justice system is a useful way to provide rehabilitation opportunities, reduce recidivism, and preserve court resources.

CORRECTIONS IN THE NEWS

Prison as a Last Resort: The Global Goal of Diversion, Treatment, and Reintegration Programs

Criminal justice and prison reform activists don't think crime rates decrease as a direct result of an increase in prison populations. Justice Action, an Australian-based group comprised of prisoners, former prisoners, attorneys, victims of crimes, community members, and academics believes the public has been purposely misled by political hopefuls touting get tough on crime slogans as a means of capturing votes. Consider for a moment that in Australia the prison population increased nearly 21 percent between 1995 and 2001. Also take into consideration that prison occupancy is currently at 98.9 percent of capacity. The crime rate, however, has remained constant, and 62 percent of prison inmates are repeat offenders.

Would a system less reliant on prison as the primary option for controlling convicted offenders better serve the community? Justice Action Australia suggests the opportunity for decreasing crime rates exists in the alternatives to prison, not in mandatory sentencing. Prison sentences have been linked to the intergenerational propensity toward crime, homelessness, poverty, alienation, health and mental health problems, substance use, and physical violence.

But there are barriers to alternative programs that essentially replace prison as a method of formal social control. From a political perspective, support for alternative programs gives voters the impression the candidate is soft on crime. Community members in support of such action appear to place the community in danger. But just as prison is not the answer for every convicted felon, alternative programs are not suited for every prisoner. The key is in the selection process. With a variety of programs and selection criteria, the likelihood of selecting inmates who will benefit from alternative programs increases.

Criminal justice systems all over the world use home detention as a confinement strategy for low-risk offenders with short sentences. Courts using this sanction exclude offenders who have been convicted of violent crimes or sex offenses. Offenders on home detention are limited to the confines of their homes but are allowed to leave the premises for work, school, counseling, medical appointments, and religious services or events. One restriction of home detention programs is that for convicted offenders to qualify for the program they must live within the calling district. Another restriction is that all offenders must comply with electronic monitoring, and because of this they must have a landline phone. All participants are assessed a fee that is based on their ability to pay.

For the offender with an alcohol use problem, there's Secure Continuous Remote Alcohol Monitoring (SCRAM). SCRAM relies on a monitoring devise worn around the ankle that samples perspiration to determine the presence of alcohol in a person's system. Courts generally require abstinence from alcoholic beverages for defendants awaiting trial on alcohol-related charges or for those convicted on offenses that involved alcohol. One problem, of course, is how to monitor compliance. Maybe a more significant problem is the uncertain accuracy of these devices. Even the manufacturer admits that transdermal alcohol measurement only estimates the subject's blood alcohol level and is not as accurate as a blood alcohol or Breathalyzer test. Another potentially damaging effect is that the monitoring device cannot distinguish between alcohol that is consumed and then emitted through perspiration and that which is applied externally.

Sources: *Beyond bars—Alternatives to custody justice action Australia.* (2007). Retrieved September 15, 2008, from http://www.beyondbars.org.au/BBA%20FINAL%20FACTS/Alternativesfinal.doc; Barone, P. T. (2007). *Alcohol monitoring ankle bracelets: Junk science or important scientific breakthrough?* Retrieved October 24, 2007, from http://www.1800duilaws.com/article/alcohol_monitoring_ankle_bracelets.asp.

Bazelon Center for Mental Health Law

The **Bazelon Center for Mental Health Law** was founded in 1972 and is the nation's leading advocate for children, adolescents, and adults with mental disabilities. The Bazelon Center has promoted litigation that outlawed institutional abuse and won protections against arbitrary confinement for persons with mental and developmental disabilities.

The Bazelon Center for Mental Health Law uses a coordinated approach of litigation, policy analysis, coalition building, public information, and technical support for local advocates in the following four broad areas:

1. *Advancing community membership*: The center enables people with mental disabilities to participate equally with others and utilize social, political, educational, and cultural services.
2. *Promoting self-determination*: The center supports the right to be independent, free from coercion, and protect against invasion of privacy from the state.
3. *Ending the punishment of people with mental illnesses*: The staff at the center believe that jailing people with mental illnesses is a poor substitute for adequate mental health care. This goal most directly addresses diversion.
4. *Preserving rights*: The center continues to defend the legal rights of people with mental disabilities.[27]

The Bazelon Center for Mental Health Law, named for famous federal appeals judge **David Bazelon** whose rulings pioneered the field of mental health law, has made a wide impact in several areas of law affecting people who meet the profile of those who are often detained in jail because of mental health problems (see Chapter 5). The litigation efforts of the Bazelon Center for Mental Health Law include (1) the right to treatment; (2) the right to services in the most integrated, less-restrictive setting; (3) the right to live in the community and access to housing; (4) the right to education, which culminated in what is today the Individuals with Disabilities Education Act; (5) the right to access federal entitlements; (6) the right to be protected against discrimination; (7) due process protections in civil commitment; (8) access to advocacy; and (9) rights of self-determination and privacy.

Proposition 36

Arguably the most important diversion-related criminal justice policy in recent years is **Proposition 36 (Prop 36)**. Formally known as the Substance Abuse and Crime Prevention Act of 2000, Prop 36 was approved by California voters on November 7, 2000, and resulted in a change in the way the criminal justice system responds to drug-using offenders. Inspired by Arizona's Proposition 200, which was passed in 1996, Prop 36 proposed treating drug abuse as a public health issue rather than a criminal justice concern; as such there was a shift in mandated treatment as opposed to incarceration for nonviolent drug possession offenders. Unlike many court-supervised treatment programs, Prop 36 prioritizes quality, licensed treatment and makes compassion a cornerstone of the state's rehabilitative approach. As shown in TABLE 6–3, Prop 36 is also able to serve many more drug-dependent clients than specialized drug courts.

In this way, Prop 36 is consistent with the juvenile justice system tradition of viewing offenders as persons in need of help, not persons to be punished. For instance, Prop 36 prohibits the courts from incarcerating offenders that relapse once or twice during their treatment period. Overall, the intent of Prop 36 is threefold:

Under programs that stem from Prop 36, drug-abusing, nonviolent offenders are diverted to treatment instead of clogging jail and prison space.

1. To divert from incarceration into community-based substance abuse treatment programs nonviolent defendants, probationers, and parolees charged with simple drug possession or drug use offenses.
2. To halt the wasteful expenditure of hundreds of millions of dollars on the incarceration and reincarceration of nonviolent drug users who would be better served by community-based treatment.
3. To enhance public safety by reducing drug-related crime and preserving jails and prison cells for serious and violent offenders, and to improve public health by reducing drug abuse and drug dependence through proven and effective drug treatment strategies.[28]

TABLE 6-3 Comparison of Proposition 36 to California Drug Courts

	Proposition 36	Drug Courts
Eligibility	All nonviolent drug possession offenders	Decision of courts
Parole violators	Eligible if nonviolent	Not eligible
Total participants over 4 years	140,000	Approximately 3,500
Response to problems	Treatment intensification	Jail
Benefits	Dismissal of charges/possible Expungement of record	Dismissal of charges

Source: Modified from Drug Policy Alliance. (2006). *Proposition 36: Improving lives, delivering results.* Los Angeles: Drug Policy Alliance, p. 19.

Substance Abuse and Mental Health Services Administration

The **Substance Abuse and Mental Health Services Administration** (SAMHSA) is a public health agency within the Department of Health and Human Services. The agency is responsible for improving the accountability, capacity, and effectiveness of the nation's substance abuse prevention, addictions treatment, and mental health services delivery system. With an annual budget of nearly $3.5 billion, SAMHSA seeks to help the 22 million Americans age 12 or older who have substance abuse problems and 25 million adults who live with a serious psychiatric condition. SAMHSA has three centers and a supporting office that carry out its prevention, treatment, recovery, and resilience mission (see FIGURE 6-3). They include the following:

1. The Center for Mental Health Services (CMHS) provides national leadership to ensure the application of scientifically established findings and practice-based knowledge in the treatment and prevention of mental disorders. The CMHS improves access, reduces barriers, and promotes high-quality effective programs and services for persons affected by mental health disorders, and overall promotes the rehabilitation of people with mental disorders.
2. The Center for Substance Abuser Prevention (CSAP) builds resiliency and facilitates recovery by providing national leadership in the development of programs and policies that prevent the onset of illegal drug, underage alcohol, and tobacco use. CSAP disseminates effective prevention practices and builds the capacity of criminal justice systems and social service providers to apply prevention knowledge effectively.
3. The Center for Substance Abuse Treatment (CSAT) aims to bring effective alcohol and drug treatment to every community by expanding the availability of effective treatment and recovery services for alcohol and drug problems. The CSAT also improves access, reduces barriers, and promotes high-quality effective treatment and recovery services for those affected by alcoholism and substance dependency.
4. The Office of Applied Studies (OAS) collects, analyzes, and distributes national data on behavioral health issues and publishes the *National Survey on Drug Use and Health,* the *Drug Abuse Warning Network,* and the *Drug and Alcohol Services Information System.*[29]

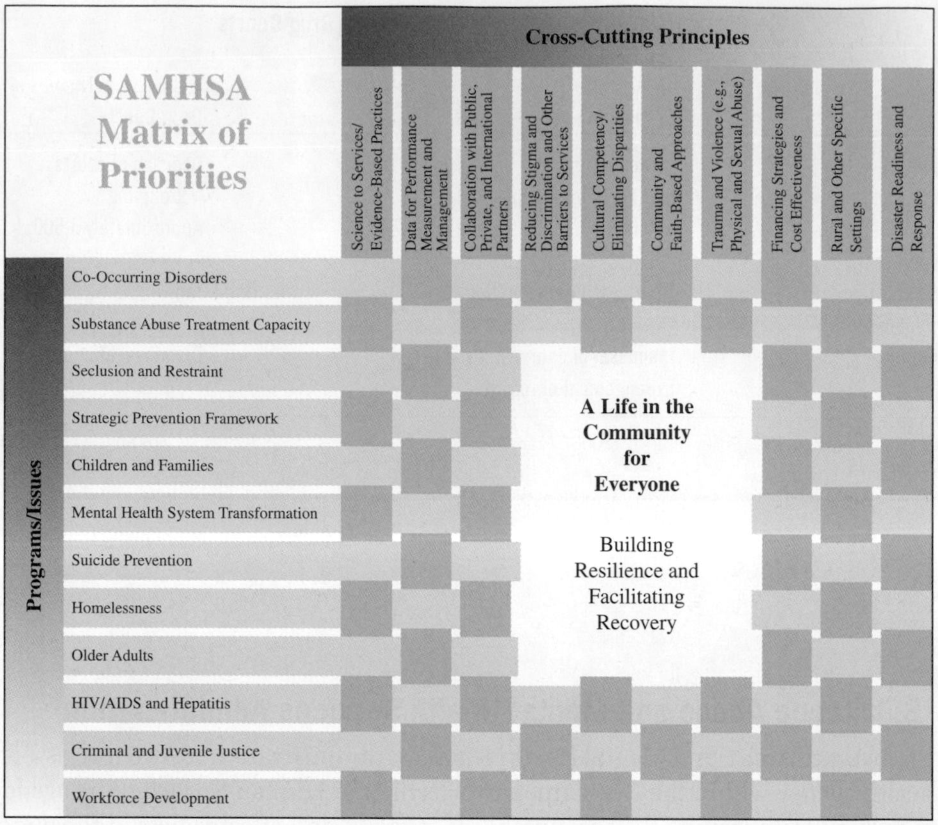

FIGURE 6–3 SAMSHA Matrix of Priorities. *Source*: Building resilience, facilitating recovery, a life in the community for everyone. U.S. Department of Health and Human Services. Retrieved December 10, 2008, from http://www.samhsa.gov/About/SAMHSA_Brochure_060607.pdf.

Evaluations of Diversion Programs

Diversion is a broad attempt to preclude the entry of low-level criminal offenders, drug abusers, and persons with mental illness into the correctional system. As this chapter has shown, there are many types of diversion programs and policies, and evaluations usually focus on a specific type of diversion program. This section examines scholarly evaluations of diversion programs to determine their effectiveness at providing services for vulnerable groups and populations in need, reducing recidivism, and reducing criminal justice system costs.

Juvenile Diversion Programs

As a criminal justice policy, diversion owes a debt of gratitude to the juvenile justice system, which almost by definition is committed to blocking offenders' entry to the justice system and instead providing needed treatment and services. Early evaluations of juvenile diversion programs tended to focus on whether the programs were able to adequately control the offender population or whether they widened the net and resulted in too much correctional control. The major determinant of their effectiveness related to how well they were implemented. Programs that were equipped to provide treatment in social service agencies outside of the justice system were effective at meeting the goals of diversion. Treatment programs that were heavy handed and coercive and basically extensions of the justice system were found to widen the net. For instance, a study by Wayne Osgood and Hart Weichselbaum indicated that adolescents perceived that diversion programs were coercive and based more on social control than treatment.[30] Early evaluations of juvenile diversion programs were also characterized by what appeared to be ideological disputes among some criminologists. For example, Arnold Binder and Gilbert Geis accused criminologists who were critical of diversion programs of being ideologically opposed to the rehabilitative, liberal ideals that diversion attempted to achieve. Unfortunately, Binder and Geis's criticism was rhetorical.[31] In response, Kenneth Polk suggested that criticisms of juvenile diversion had nothing to do with ideological axes to grind and everything to do with the actual record of program evaluations, which indicate weak effectiveness or net widening.[32] More recently, Daniel Curran suggested that a two-tiered system of juvenile diversion has developed where juvenile justice systems provide services that are evidence of greater social control, and private, social service agencies provide treatment programs that likely meet the original goals of diversion.[33]

Many contemporary evaluations of juvenile diversion programs have also been conducted. Christopher Sullivan and his colleagues recently evaluated the Mental Health Juvenile Justice Diversion Project, which is a major initiative to address the needs of juvenile delinquents in New York state. The Mental Health Juvenile Justice Diversion Project uses a knowledge-based understanding of delinquency and operates to address three problems that many delinquent youths have. First, many adolescent offenders have overlapping problems with not only delinquency, but also substance abuse, school difficulties, and abuse histories. They are known as **multiple-problem youth**.[34] Second, there is recognition that removing these children from the community via incarceration would only serve to worsen their problems. Third, delinquent youths often come from families and neighborhoods that are characterized by risk factors that increase delinquency. The program sought to address these three areas of need by diverting youths to the most appropriate agency for services. Overall, the program has shown positive results. Diverted youths were less likely to be contacted by police and less likely to be confined to an out-of-community facility as a result of their programming. However, certain characteristics of youths continued to predict recidivism, such as those with extensive prior records, prior placements in confinement, and significant mental health problems.[35]

Many states have developed comprehensive diversionary programs as a major part of their juvenile justice systems. For example, Florida has an array of options in its diversion programs. These include:

- **Restitution** or repayment to the victim in the form of community service, direct restitution to the victim, and a personal apology letter.
- Psychoeducational programs, such as teen court jury duty; Program YES, a shoplifting impact video; SHOCK, a 6-week program about risky behaviors; Urban League, a 12-week program on decision making, peer pressure, anger management, and conflict resolution; and Girls Can!, a program that addresses self-esteem, problem solving, and anger management among females.
- Substance use/abuse education and classes.
- Violence prevention and reduction including Peace in Action, a 23-week program on alternatives to violence and EVE (End Violence Early), a program specifically for youths contacted for domestic violence charges.[36]

Evaluations of Florida programs have been mixed. Richard Dembo and his colleagues evaluated the effectiveness of an intensive case management program that served youths with **psychopathic personalities** (a personality disorder characterized by severe behavioral and interpersonal traits) and followed over a 1-year period. The program had zero positive effect on recidivism as more psychopathic youths, receiving special diversion treatment or traditional services, were more likely to continue to commit crime.[37] This does not necessarily mean that the programs are generally ineffective, however. It is probable that psychopathic youths are simply so severe in their antisocial tendencies that programs are hard pressed to reduce their commitment to delinquency. Fortunately, the majority of offenders are not psychopathic, and in turn they are more amenable to treatment. Dembo and his colleagues found that nonpsychopathic youths did benefit from diversion programs in terms of their social functioning and were more likely to complete programs than their psychopathic peers.[38–39]

Other jurisdictions have developed specialized diversion programs to target specific groups. For example, the Hamilton County (Cincinnati, Ohio) Juvenile Court developed an Afrocentric diversion program designed to address the presumed specific needs of African American youths. The program paired youths with African American staff who imparted prosocial and culturally specific lessons to Black youth based on the idea that youths would be more receptive to racially matched diversion officers. Unfortunately, the program was found not to be effective. William King and his colleagues indicated that in 11 of 15 measures of adolescent and adult offending, youths who participated in the Afrocentric diversion program performed no better than ordinary probationers who did not participate in the diversion program.[40] Overall, juvenile diversion is a worldwide phenomenon as Australia, China, Hong Kong, New Zealand, and Singapore have also developed programs to divert youths from the justice system in favor of a commitment to treatment and rehabilitation.[41]

■ Diversion for Mentally Ill Persons

Despite the now decades old commitment to deinstitutionalizing mentally ill offenders, surveys indicate that only a small number of U.S. jails have diversion programs for mentally ill detainees. In 1994, Henry Steadman and his colleagues published the results of a national survey that indicated that only 34 percent of jails had a formal diversion program for jail inmates with mental illnesses. In follow-up investigation by phone interviews, it was discovered that just 18 percent of jail facilities actually had a specific diversion program in place that met the guidelines of protocol for mentally ill persons. In other words, 82 percent of jail facilities did not have a formal diversion program in place for mentally ill defendants.

Among jails that did have programs, Steadman and colleagues found that all served misdemeanant offenders, about 60 percent served felons, and slightly more than 50 percent served mentally ill persons accused of violent felonies. Most programs were funded by the state and country mental health department. Program directors' ratings of the diversion programs suggest mixed effectiveness. About 30 percent of programs were rated as somewhat effective, 35 percent were rated as moderately effective, and 35 percent were rated as very effective. The two main reasons for reduced effectiveness were high recidivism rates among clients and difficulties in creating a diversion strategy within the jail. Interestingly, telephone interviews with program directors produced polarized opinions of the program's effectiveness. Nearly 37 percent of directors reported that their diversion program was not at all effective and 40 percent of directors described their program as very effective.[42]

Beginning in 2002, the SAMHSA's Center for Mental Health Services funded 20 jail diversion programs while the Bureau of Justice Assistance funded 37 mental health courts, which are conceptually similar to the philosophy of diversion (see Chapter 4). As part of these initiatives, Henry Steadman and Michelle Naples compared diversion programs selected from Memphis, Tennessee; Montgomery County, Pennsylvania; Multnomah County, Oregon; Phoenix, Arizona; Hartford, Connecticut; and Lane County, Oregon. They discovered four key findings: (1) jail diversion works at reducing time spent in jail as persons with psychiatric problems spent on average 2 more months in the community as opposed to confinement, (2) jail diversion does not jeopardize public safety based on recidivism data, (3) jail diversion links clients to appropriate community-based service organizations, and (4) in general, jail diversion results in lower criminal justice system costs and higher treatment costs.[43]

CORRECTIONS RESEARCH

Treatment for Sex Offenders—Safeguards to Measuring Effectiveness

Not all sex offender treatment programs are created equal. Since 1980, more than 20 scientific studies have attempted to determine the effectiveness of treatment programs for sexual predators. Many of the studies indicate that the treatment programs are effective in lowering recidivism when compared to sex offenders who did not participate in the programs. Methodological problems, however, weaken the usefulness of these findings.

The findings on whether treatment programs for sexual offenders really work are mixed. A 1989 study by Furby, Weinrott, and Blackshaw found no evidence that sexual offenders were less likely to recidivate as a result of a treatment program. In 1995, Hall conducted a meta-analysis of 12 programs and reported that an overall positive impact of treatment programs does exist for decreases in future offending by sex crime perpetrators completing treatment programs. However, Hall's work has been criticized as having included preliminary findings from several studies and data from other studies that proved less than reliable.

In 1997, the Collaborative Outcome Data Committee (CODC) began reviewing sex offender treatment programs. In its first report, the CODC conducted an extensive review of 43 studies and found a small positive effect for treatment programs. The studies in this meta-analysis and the results presented by the CODC were criticized after close review of the studies that determined a potential bias in subject placement within treatment and control groups.

Good studies minimize bias and in so doing, increase the accuracy of the findings. Effectiveness in studies with minimal bias is attributed to the actual treatment. Good studies with minimal bias are also based on random sampling. Random sampling lessens the likelihood that placement in treatment and comparison groups can be influenced by the researcher. However, random sampling proves problematic in that offenders in need of the treatment may very easily be excluded from the treatment group. As a consequence of the need to randomize sample populations, researchers must consider the potential harm to society random sampling can produce.

Sexual offender treatment outcomes are difficult to assess in that programs and offenders vary across a continuum. As a result, one study, and for that matter one method, cannot determine program effectiveness. Consequently, researchers sacrifice a certain level of control over the research design since sex offenders who are court ordered to treatment programs are not randomly assigned; thus the need for a multitude of research studies and methods to access effectiveness. A certain amount of useful data is already generated by administrators of each program. Researchers have the option of measuring effectiveness using program evaluation studies. Although it is not a scientific study, a program evaluation does generate information that can be used to assess effectiveness if properly interpreted. If researchers are interested in questions not covered by the program evaluation studies, the CODC recommends studies designed to gather this data do so while maintaining the integrity of the inquiry.

Source: Beech, A., Bourgon, G., Hanson, R. K., Harris, A. J. R., Langton, C., & Marques, J. et al. (2007). *Sexual offender treatment outcome research: CODC guidelines for evaluation Part 1: Introduction and overview.* Retrieved September 15, 2008, from http://www.publicsafety.gc.ca/res/cor/rep/_fl/CODC_07_e.pdf.

A recent review of the literature similarly produced mixed and somewhat disappointing outcomes among diversion programs that target defendants with serious mental illnesses. David Loveland and Michael Boyle studied 35 programs and found that 19 programs rarely led to reductions in jail or arrest rates over time. Eight programs showed modest but statistically insignificant reductions in recidivism and 8 programs showed significant reductions.[44]

A SAMHSA-funded initiative found that two core elements of successful programs are aggressive linkage to an array of community services especially for clients who have co-occuring mental health and substance abuse disorders and nontraditional case managers who are interested in rehabilitation and treatment as opposed to punishment-oriented supervision.[45] Similarly, Kathleen Hartford and her colleagues identified three additional practices that improve diversion programs for mentally ill defendants: (1) having formal case procedures in place is important for early identification of those most in need of services, (2) having stable housing to help diverted offenders comply with treatment, and (3) having active case managers to improve compliance and reduce the likelihood of recidivism.[46]

A reason for the disparate findings in the diversion literature stems from the stark differences in offender groups within various programs. For instance, Jeffrey Draine and his colleagues contrasted the populations that received jail diversion and those who received intensive psychiatric and substance abuse treatment as part of an in-jail program. Persons in the in-jail program were predictably more likely to have probation or parole clients while most recently contacted by the criminal justice system. Clients who were diverted had significantly worse profiles in terms of their mental health diagnoses. For example, the prevalence of schizophrenia was twice as high among the diversion group. The prevalence of psychosis was nearly *20 times* higher among the diversion group. In fact, a diagnosis of psychosis increased the odds of being diverted by more than 13. This is promising in the sense that persons with severe psychiatric needs are not being jailed and can instead seek mental health treatment. On the other hand, these data show how severely disturbed the diversion population is.[47] Ultimately, diversion of mentally ill persons from the criminal courts will necessitate a greater integration of the criminal justice and mental health service systems.[48]

Prop 36

Because it is such a large-scale criminal justice policy, Prop 36 has received considerable research attention as to its effectiveness and cost savings. The Drug Policy Alliance's assessment of Prop 36 was overwhelmingly positive. In the first 4 years after the implementation of Prop 36:

- More than 140,000 people were diverted to treatment—approximately 10 times the number of people served each year in California's drug courts.
- More than 700 new drug treatment programs were licensed in California, an increase of 66 percent.
- Nearly 48,000 people completed their treatment program.
- Among persons who completed Prop 36 programs, there was a 71 percent drop in drug use.
- Employment among Prop 36 clients doubled after completing treatment.
- There was a 32 percent reduction in the number of California prisoners serving time for simple drug possession between 2000 and 2005.

- Overall, the 140,000 people diverted from prison saved taxpayers approximately $31,000 in treatment-to-incarceration costs.[49]
- Annual net savings from Prop 36 have been estimated at $140 to $190 million.[50]

Other evaluations produced results that were mixed. Yihing Hser and her colleagues reported that treatment admissions increased in several California counties after the implementation of Prop 36. For instance, treatment admissions increased 27 percent in Kern County, 21 percent in Riverside County, 17 percent in Sacramento County, and 16 percent in San Diego County mostly in outpatient drug-free programs. The typical profile of Prop 36 patients was male, employed full time, first-time offender, and user of methamphetamine or marijuana. Prop 36 patients were significantly more likely to use these drugs but less likely to use heroin.[51] The treatment demand created by Prop 36 patients displaced treatment opportunities for people who voluntary attempted to enter drug treatment. In fact, voluntary clients decreased by 8,000 each year after Prop 36 went into effect.[52]

David Farabee and his associates compared the recidivism rates of three treatment groups: 688 Prop 36 patients, 1,178 patients who were not part of Prop 36 but were referred by the criminal justice system, and 1,882 clients who entered drug treatment without any criminal justice status or referral. These groups were studied across 43 treatment programs in 13 California counties. The findings were not supportive of Prop 36 goals. Prop 36 patients with severe drug problems were significantly less likely to be treated in a residential facility than persons with similar addiction problems in the voluntary treatment group. Moreover, Prop 36 patients were significantly *more likely* than either of the control groups to be arrested for a drug crime in the 12 months after treatment admission.[53]

James Inciardi suggests that although the spirit of diversion programs like Prop 36 is good, the infrastructure of drug treatment is not up to the challenge of meeting the increased demands that such policies create. Citing information from a national sample of treatment programs, Inciardi noted that: (1) 15 percent of facilities had either closed or stopped addiction treatment; (2) 29 percent of facilities had reorganized under a different agency; (3) there was a 53 percent turnover rate among program directors and counselors; (4) only 50 percent of programs had even a part-time physician on staff; (5) less than 15 percent of programs had a nurse; and (6) very few programs had a social worker. Instead, most treatment programs across the country relied on abstinence-oriented group counseling as the predominant form of treatment.[54]

General Criminal Justice Programs

Due to its longstanding commitment to diversion, the Bazelon Center for Mental Health Law has taken a leading role at disseminating information about the effectiveness of diversion programs in place in criminal justice systems across the country. Indeed, there are a host of quality diversion programs that successfully preclude offenders from entering the correctional system while providing appropriate resources and saving taxpayer expenses. Some diversion programs that have demonstrable positive outcomes include:

- *Thresholds Jail Program:* This psychiatric rehabilitation program in the Cook County (Chicago) jail for offenders with a history of arrests, serious mental illness, and drug problems provides an array of intensive case management services. For the 30 clients who completed a 1-year program, there was an 82 percent reduction in days spent in jail and a 52 percent reduction in arrests; these reductions resulted in criminal justice savings of nearly $158,000. There was also an

86 percent reduction in days spent in the hospital, 83 percent reduction in number of hospitalizations; these reductions produced saving of nearly $917,000.[55]

- *Bernalillo County Jail Diversion Program:* This program in New Mexico uses **pre-booking diversion** in which law enforcement transports offenders to mental health agencies for evaluation and treatment and **postbooking diversion** in which defendants are connected with appropriate services in lieu of prosecution. Many of the clients of the Bernalillo County program have overlapping drug and psychiatric problems, and nearly half were contacted for felony offenses. A 1-year evaluation of the program found that 67 percent of diversion clients had not returned to jail, resulting in nearly 5,000 fewer jail bed days and a facility savings of $355,500.[56]
- *Project Link:* This university-led program features a psychiatric team that provides around-the-clock services and information for offenders with a range of social and behavioral problems, including helping them secure viable housing. Project Link has produced a significant reduction in the number of incarcerations, and average days spent in jail declined from 107 to 46 per year. Hospitalizations and number of days spent in hospital care also declined, resulting in more than $150,000 in mental health service cost savings and nearly $500 per client jail cost savings.[57]
- *Multnomah County STOP Drug Diversion Program:* This program in Oregon aimed to reduce substance abuse by improving treatment and increasing accessibility to treatment among first-time offenders. STOP contains court oversight and active judicial case management, immediate access to dedicated treatment resources, drug testing, and a range of sanctions if diverted clients are not compliant. Evaluations found that clients who participated, completed, and graduated from STOP fared significantly better than offenders who did not participate in the program. In a 2-year follow-up study, STOP graduates had 76 percent fewer arrests, 80 percent fewer felony arrests, 74 percent fewer convictions, 85 percent fewer drug arrests, 76 percent fewer property arrests, 100 percent fewer violent arrests, and 80 percent fewer parole violation arrests than a control group. The STOP program saved the Multnomah County criminal justice system nearly $2.5 million and diverted more than $10 million in collateral social costs.[58]
- *Cerro Gordo County ALERT Program:* This Iowa program uses a multidisciplinary, early-response team to reduce drug use among adolescent offenders by providing outpatient treatment. Clients receive after-school drug treatment, individual counseling, family services, and participate in motivational enhancement groups. Of 189 clients, only 12 required out-of-home placements after completing the program, 80 percent reduced or eliminated their drug use, and fewer than 17 percent reentered the juvenile justice system.[59]

Although select individual programs suggest that diversion is working, the overall record of diversion programming indicates mixed effectiveness. The national Treatment Alternatives to Street Crime (now known as Treatment Alternatives for Safe Communities) initiatives have received considerable research attention. Some of the concern for TASC programs centers on the substantial costs of substance abuse treatment, which can rival the costs posed by criminal justice interventions.

Douglas Anglin and his colleagues conducted a national evaluation of more than 2,000 offenders participating in TASC programs in Birmingham, Alabama; Canton, Ohio; Chicago, Illinois; Orlando, Florida; and Portland, Oregon. They found that (1) TASC participants received significantly more treatment services including drug counseling, urinalysis to detect drug use, and AIDS education; (2) TASC participants had lower rates of drug use after entering the program; however this occurred in only three of the five sites, suggesting an effectiveness that was modestly better than 50 percent; and (3) TASC

CORRECTIONS FOCUS

Mother–Child Programs

It's a fact; women who are arrested are much more likely to be primary caregivers for minor children than are men. In a typical year, over 3 million women are involved in a criminal activity that results in them being arrested for the crime. Female offenders with children pose a significant social problem. Society's response has been to divert as many moms from incarceration as possible. This is accomplished through the use of mother–child community corrections programs (MCCC programs). MCCC programs serve nearly a million female criminal offenders and their children. Each of these programs is community specific in that they have been designed to work with community resources; they do, however, share similar goals. Designed for moms who have committed various criminal offenses, MCCC programs operate in much the same manner as halfway houses providing mothers with aftercare, drug and/or mental health treatment, general health care, education, job placement, and social services.

In 1999, according to the Bureau of Justice Statistics, there were nearly 1.5 million children whose parents were criminal offenders. In the United States, more than 330,000 households with minor children have a parent serving time in a jail or prison. The number of households with a parent under the supervision of the criminal justice system would number closer to 1 million if the figure included parents on probation or parole.

Women under 21 are the fastest growing segment of the female offender population—and by Bureau of Justice Statistics estimates, 11 out of every 1,000 U.S. females will spend time in jail or prison during their lifetime. African American women are three times more likely to be sentenced to prison than are Caucasian females, and Hispanic women have a 15 in a 1,000 chance of being sentenced to prison for crimes they commit during their life course.

As a result of incarceration, the mother-child bond is broken or at least adversely affected, and the mother's interest in rehabilitation reflects the emotional strain of the separation. Another consequence of incarceration is the lack of support afforded a child with an intact parent–child relationship. Studies have also found that children lacking this parental bond are more likely to have greater difficulties developing meaningful interpersonal relationships as well as having problems in school.

As a result of diversion programs like MCCC, and the courts' willingness to divert mothers from a stay in a correctional facility, more than 85 percent of those women under court supervision will remain in the community for the duration of their sentence. The idea began as an extension of prison nursery programs. Typically, women in this program have been diverted from serving a sentence of 1 year or less in a county or state facility and are court ordered to the program as a condition of their probation or parole. Programs that focus on women with substance use problems are operated in conjunction with the office of the local prosecutor, drug courts, community-based substance use treatment centers, and social services. Depending on the focus of the program, community corrections programs are sometimes affiliated with churches and religious organizations in a faith-based effort to assist female offenders with children.

Sources: Shilton, M.K. (2000). *Resources for mother–child community corrections: The Mother–Child Community Corrections Project International Community Corrections Association.* Retrieved September 15, 2008, from http://www.ncjrs.gov/pdffiles1/bja/190352.pdf; Travis, J., McBride, E. C., & Solomon, A. L. (2005). *Families left behind: The hidden costs of incarceration and reentry.* Retrieved October 7, 2007, from http://www.urban.org/UploadedPDF/310882_families_left_behind.pdf.

participants had *higher* recidivism rates in three of the five cities. Interestingly, TASC programs appeared to be most effective among the most serious, drug-addicted offenders, which is precisely the group that should be targeted for intensive treatment.[60] Evaluations of TASC programs in Wisconsin, however, showed that the costs of drug treatment are worth the investment as diverted offenders had significantly lower recidivism rates than nondiverted offenders over an 18-month period.[61–62]

Despite evaluations that indicated positive aspects of TASC programs, a recent review of what works in corrections typified TASC programs as ineffective. Doris Layton MacKenzie suggested that programs that offer referrals of offenders to community agencies coupled with increased monitoring and management are ultimately not effective at reducing recidivism.[63, p. 466] Instead, Douglas Young indicated that TASC programs that stress the conditions of program participation and the risks of noncompliance are more effective forms of legal pressure than tight monitoring and use of heavy penalties for failure at treatment.[64] Similarly, Sheila Royo Maxwell found that diversion clients who *perceive* greater legal pressure or threats to complete the terms of their program are in fact more likely to comply with court orders, stay in treatment, and complete their treatment program.[65]

A major reason for the perceived ineffectiveness of diversion programs centers on whether offenders genuinely volunteered for participation in the program or felt some degree of legal pressure to enter treatment. The argument is that offenders who truly volunteer and want to stop using drugs and desist from crime have a better chance at completing treatment programs than offenders who were essentially ordered into treatment or selected diversion programs because they were better options than jail. For instance, Nahama Broner and her colleagues studied 175 mentally ill, substance-using adult jail detainees in New York City to assess the effect of diversion, treatment, and individual characteristics on criminal justice, mental health, substance use, and life satisfaction outcomes. The intervention group included nonmandated and mandated diversion tracks. The comparison participants met diversion acceptance criteria but underwent standard criminal justice processes. They found that mandated diversion clients were less likely to spend as much time in prison and more likely to spend time in the community. They also had greater linkages to residential and outpatient treatment, received more treatment, and decreased their drug use. Interestingly, those who did not perceive themselves as coerced and had insight into their mental illness received more treatment regardless of their diversion status.[66]

In sum, the overall record of diversion programs is mixed with some programs showing dramatically positive results, others showing that unexpectedly negative results, and still others showing that diversion is no more or less effective than normal criminal justice intervention. At the very least, diversion offers two big advantages over other correctional sanctions: (1) It provides the opportunity for offenders to get needed treatment and avoid the pitfalls of being a correctional client; and (2) it provides the correctional system with a release valve to control the number of clients who enter and in turn manage the costs of the administration of justice. The final section of this chapter focuses on prevention programs that attempt to provide services so early in the lives of at-risk persons and delinquents that involvement in the correctional system is bypassed.

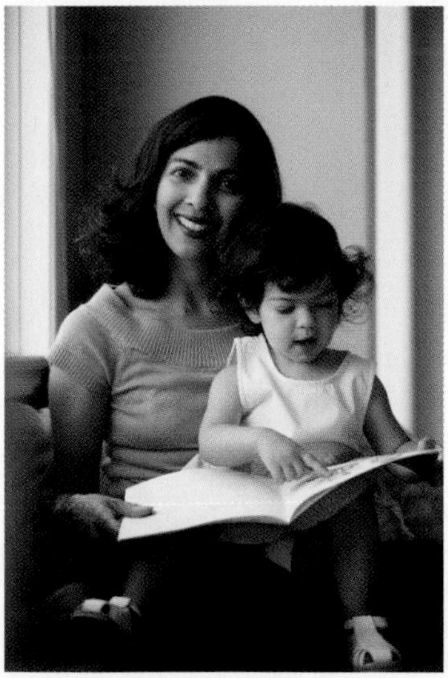

Criminologists are increasingly advocating prevention programs to forestall problem behaviors and criminal lifestyles from developing. If the United States invests heavily in prevention, there would be less reliance on the correctional system.

Prevention

Prevention is the provision of social resources to at-risk groups early in life to enhance their prosocial development while buffering their risk factors for crime. Prevention is an area that is receiving increasing amounts of scholarly and justice system attention although it is funded at significantly lower levels than law enforcement and corrections

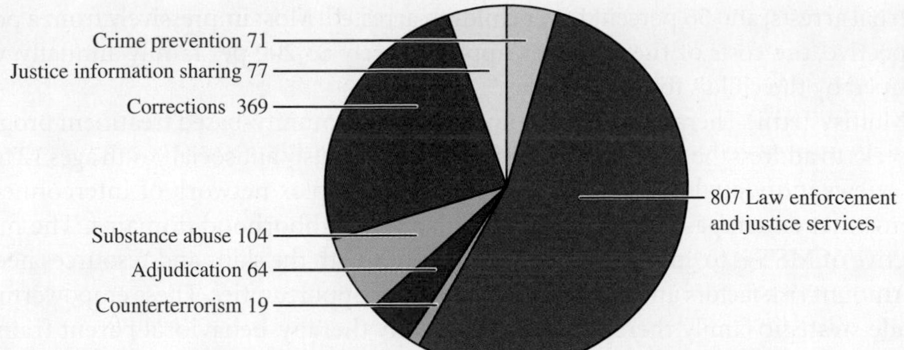

FIGURE 6–4 Criminal Justice Appropriations from the Bureau of Justice Assistance, 2005 (In Millions of Dollars). *Source*: Retrieved September 26, 2007, from http://www.ncjrs.gov/pdffiles1/bja/215665.pdf.

(see **FIGURE 6–4**). As correctional policy, prevention is still in its early stages, and much of the knowledge base on prevention programs comes from the fields of pediatrics and human development.

The most famous prevention study that demonstrated the long-term effects of early life interventions on a high-risk sample is the *Nurse–Family Partnership* program supervised by David Olds and his colleagues using a sample of 400 women and 315 infants born in upstate New York between April 1978 and September 1980. The women in the sample posed a variety of risk factors for their children adopting delinquency. All were unmarried, 48 percent were less than 15 years of age, and 59 percent of the mothers lived in poverty. Using random assignment to four groups receiving various social services, the comprehensive experimental group received nine home visits during pregnancy and 23 home visits from nurses from birth until the child's second birthday. Control subjects received standard, but less comprehensive prenatal care. All groups were followed up 15 years later and showed impressive reductions of a variety of problem behaviors associated with chronic delinquency and correctional involvement. For instance, compared to control groups, boys in the treatment groups had:

- Lower incidence of running away.
- Accumulated significantly fewer arrests and convictions.
- Accrued fewer probationary sentences and subsequent violations.
- Had fewer lifetime sexual partners.
- Had a lower prevalence of smoking, alcoholism, and casual alcohol use.

In short, the experiment offered compelling evidence that early life interventions that teach parents the skills they need to raise healthy children were achievable.

The Nurse Family Partnership program is one of the model prevention programs in the country and is part of the Blueprints for Violence Prevention program at the Center for the Study and Prevention of Violence at the University of Colorado at Boulder. The **Blueprints for Violence Prevention Program** is a national violence prevention initiative that identifies programs that meet the most scientifically rigorous standards of program effectiveness. The Blueprints program found that the nurse visits in the Olds study resulted in 79 percent fewer verified reports of child abuse and neglect; 31 percent fewer subsequent births and increased interval between births; a 30-month reduction in the receipt of Aid to Families with Dependent Children, a social welfare subsidy; 44 percent fewer maternal behavioral problems due to substance abuse; 69 percent fewer maternal arrests; and 56 percent fewer children arrested. Most impressively from a policy perspective, the costs of the program, approximately $3,200 per family annually, were recouped by the child's fourth birthday.[67]

Multisystemic Therapy (MST) is a family and community-based treatment program that seeks to address the multiple-problem needs of seriously antisocial youth ages 12 to 17. MST views individuals as being nested within a complex network of interconnected systems that encompass family, peer, school, and neighborhood domains. The major objective of MST is to empower parents and youth with the skills and resources needed to surmount risk factors and capitalize on protective opportunities. These empowerments include strategic family therapy, structural family therapy, behavioral parent training, and cognitive behavior therapies over a 4-month period. Despite the difficulties inherent in treating seriously antisocial people, preliminary evaluations of MST have shown 25 percent to 70 percent reductions in rearrest and 47 percent to 64 percent reductions in out-of-home placements. Additionally, serious juvenile offenders often experience fewer mental health problems, which contribute to substance abuse problems, and their families increase their functioning. At a cost of a mere $4,500 per youth, MST has been ranked as the most cost-effective program in the country that targets serious juvenile offenders.[68]

The Behavioral Monitoring and Reinforcement Program (BMRP), formerly called Preventive Intervention, is a school-based intervention that helps prevent juvenile delinquency, substance use, and school failure for high-risk adolescents who fit the profile of incarcerated youth. It targets juvenile cynicism about the world and the accompanying lack of efficacy to deal with problems. BMRP provides a school environment that allows students to realize that their actions can bring about desired consequences, and it reinforces this belief by eliciting participation from teachers, parents, and individuals.

The 2-year intervention begins when participants are in seventh grade and includes monitoring student actions, rewarding appropriate behavior, and increasing communication between teachers, students, and parents. School records are checked for participants' daily attendance, tardiness, and official disciplinary actions, and parents are informed of their children's progress. Teachers submit weekly reports assessing students' punctuality, preparedness, and behavior in the classroom, and students are rewarded for good evaluations. Each week, three to five students meet with a staff member to discuss their recent behaviors, learn the relationship between actions and their consequences, and role-play prosocial alternatives to problem behaviors. They are also rewarded for refraining from disruptive behavior during these meetings.

Evaluations of BMRP have demonstrated short- and long-term positive effects. At the end of the program, program students showed higher grades and better attendance compared to control students. A 1-year follow-up study showed that intervention students, compared to control students, had less self-reported delinquency; drug abuse, fewer school-based problems, such as suspension, absenteeism, tardiness, and academic failure; and lower unemployment rates. BMRP clients also were less likely to be referred to juvenile court for delinquency.[69]

Multidimensional Treatment Foster Care (MTFC) is a cost-effective alternative to residential treatment, incarceration, and hospitalization for adolescents who have problems with chronic antisocial behavior, emotional disturbance, and delinquency. Community families are recruited, trained, and closely supervised to provide MTFC-placed adolescents with treatment and intensive supervision at home, in school, and in the community. Youths are instructed with clear and consistent limits with follow-through on consequences, positive reinforcement for appropriate behavior, a relationship with a mentoring adult, and separation from delinquent peers. MTFC targets adolescents with histories of chronic and severe criminal behavior that are likely to be incarcerated as well as those with severe mental health problems at risk for psychiatric hospitalization.

In other words, prevention programs like MTFC target essentially the same population as diversion programs. Evaluations of MTFC have demonstrated that program youth compared to control group youth:

- Spend 60 percent fewer days incarcerated at 1-year follow-up.
- Had significantly fewer subsequent arrests.
- Ran away from their programs, on average, three time less often.
- Had significantly less hard drug use in the follow-up period.
- Had quicker community placement from more restrictive settings.
- Had better school attendance and homework completion at 2-year follow-up.[70–71]

Finally, the correctional system is increasingly using prevention principles to prevent offenders from relapsing into substance abuse and crime. Relapse prevention programs are centered on the following nine principles: (1) offense or cognitive behavioral chain to recognize warning signs of drug use; (2) relapse rehearsal to deal with potential relapse situations; (3) advanced relapse rehearsal; (4) identifying high-risk situations; (5) dealing with failure situations; (6) self-efficacy; (7) coping skills; (8) external support systems; and (9) program aftercare. Craig Dowden and his colleagues conducted a meta-analysis of 40 tests of relapse prevention programs and found that they were modestly successful at preventing relapse.[72]

WRAP UP

CASE STUDY CONCLUSION

Robert Chambers was described as a handsome Romeo whose future was promising and bright. He was exactly the type of defendant who is diverted from the criminal justice system. Moreover, Jennifer was portrayed in a more unflattering light and was described as "sexy" and "worldly," and her history with men was exploited. Robert Chambers's past behavior and contact with the law was ignored. It took months before the media addressed Robert's previous arrests for burglary, his drug use, and his reputation with his peers.

One defense in criminal cases is that when all else fails, blame the victim and make every attempt to publicly destroy the victim's reputation. And that's what happened. The legal community at the time condoned such efforts on the part of the defense to free their client as ethical practices. The defense, learning that Jennifer kept a diary, requested to review the manuscript, claiming it would contain information that might assist in their efforts to win an acquittal. Word leaked to the press, and the diary was quickly referred to in the media as the "sex diary." It was eventually determined by the judge, after reviewing the diary, that it contained no evidence that would further the cause of the defense or support any claim of the defendant. But the damage was done and the reference continued in the press. Interestingly, at the time, newly enacted rape shield laws in the state of New York that prohibited the defense from introducing evidence of the sexual history of the victim of a sexual assault did not apply to murder cases.

Faced with the possibility of being convicted on a pending burglary charges and a conviction on a manslaughter charge, Robert Chambers decided to cop a plea as the jury in his murder trial deliberated his fate. The court accepted Chambers's plea of guilty to first-degree manslaughter and one count of burglary. Chambers had essentially pleaded guilty to two felony charges in a state that punishes a third felony conviction with life in prison. Robert Chambers served 15 years for killing Jennifer. Sentenced in 1986, he was released on Valentine's Day in 2003. As fate would have it in October, 2007, Chambers was arrested for the sale of cocaine to an undercover police officer. During the course of the investigation, undercover officers allege that Chambers sold approximately $20,000 in cocaine in multiple transactions that took place during a 3-month period. In September 2008, Robert Chambers entered a guilty plea and was sentenced to 19 years and 4 months in prison.

Sources: Associated Press. (2007). 'Preppie Killer' held after undercover drug sting. Retrieved October 23, 2007, from http://www.msnbc.msn.com/id/21431102/; Gado, M. (n.d.). *A killing in Central Park.* Retrieved October 23, 2007, from http://www.crimelibrary.com/notorious_murders/not_guilty/park/1.html; Eligon, J. (2008). 'Preppy killer' pleads guilty to selling cocaine. Retrieved September 15, 2008, from http://www.nytimes.com/2008/08/12/nyregion/12chambers.html.

Chapter Summary

- Diversion is a way that the correctional system controls its numbers while providing treatment in lieu of punishment.
- The goals of diversion are avoidance of negative labels for first-time offenders, reduction of social control and recidivism, reduction of justice system costs, and provision of service and treatment.
- Diversion is done by police, prosecutors, and legislative policies, such as Proposition 36.

- The overall effectiveness of diversionary programs is mixed and ranges from great successes to counterproductive effects such as net widening.
- Diversion programs were borrowed form the juvenile justice system and generally target drug-using offenders and persons with mental illnesses.
- Prevention attempts to preclude antisocial behavior by providing social services at early ages to enhance prosocial development.
- A variety of effective prevention programs have shown demonstrable positive outcomes.

Key Terms

abeyance Suspended charges until the defendant successfully completes the treatment protocol that was originally ordered.

Bazelon Center for Mental Health Law The nation's leading advocate for children, adolescents, and adults with mental disabilities.

Bazelon, David Federal appeals judge whose rulings pioneered the field of mental health law.

Blueprints for Violence Prevention program A national violence prevention initiative that identifies programs that meet the most scientifically rigorous standards of program effectiveness.

Commission on Law Enforcement and the Administration of Justice Part of President Johnson's 1965 war on crime, which created youth bureaus to divert juvenile offenders from confinement to community organizations.

deferred judgment *See* deferred prosecution.

deferred prosecution Widely used and cost-effective ways for the courts to control the correctional population by diverting first-time offenders or persons who have never been contacted for violent crimes.

deferred sentences *See* deferred prosecution.

diversion Any procedure that prevents official entry into the criminal justice process.

expungement The complete removal of a criminal record from existence.

Juvenile Justice and Delinquency Prevention Act of 1974 Act that provides federal funding to states and communities for prevention and treatment programs especially diversion programs that deinstitutionalize adolescents convicted of status offenses.

labeling theory A school of thought that asserts that defining people as delinquent or criminal leads to social ostracism, solidifies a delinquent self-image, and leads to increased antisocial behavior.

multiple-problem youth Offenders with overlapping problems relating to crime, substance use, and mental illness.

net widening The growing of the correctional population by supervising increasing number of offenders in the community.

police diversion Officer discretion to use a variety of tactics, resources, and community agencies to address the criminal behavior of defendants.

postbooking diversion Program in which defendants are connected with appropriate services in lieu of prosecution.

prebooking diversion Program in which law enforcement transports offenders to mental health agencies for evaluation and treatment.

prevention The provision of social resources to at-risk groups early in life to enhance their prosocial development while buffering their risk factors for crime.

Proposition 36 (Prop 36) California policy that diverted drug offenders by framing drug use as a public health rather than criminal justice issue.

psychopathic personality A personality disorder characterized by severe behavioral and interpersonal traits.

restitution Money paid to the crime victim to recoup some of the harm caused by the offender's wrongful acts.

status offenses Violations of criminal law that only apply to children and adolescents.

Substance Abuse and Mental Health Services Administration (SAMHSA) A public health agency within the Department of Health and Human Services responsible for improving the accountability, capacity, and effectiveness of the nation's substance abuse prevention, addictions treatment, and mental health services delivery system.

Treatment Alternatives to Street Crime (TASC) A national diversion program devoted to providing substance abuse treatment for offenders.

Critical Thinking Questions

1. Are drug offenders victims of the correctional system? Why does the media minimize the criminal activity of drug offenders?
2. Given the potentially devastating labeling implications of arrest, should only persons charged with violent crimes be formally entered into the system? Should everyone else be given one or more chances on diversion?
3. Prevention can preclude criminal careers while saving much money in victimization and correctional costs. Is there any downside to prevention? Is it ethical to identify at-risk people to target for prevention services?
4. Is the correctional system ambivalent about offenders with mental illnesses? In which ways are such offenders treated better? In which ways is their treatment worse?

Notes

1. Ulrich, T. E. (2002). Pretrial diversion in the federal court system. *Federal Probation, 66,* 30–37.
2. Drug Policy Alliance. (2006). *Proposition 36: Improving lives, delivering results.* Los Angeles: Drug Policy Alliance.
3. Sullivan, C. J., Veysey, B. M., Hamilton, Z. K., & Grillo, M. (2007). Reducing out-of-community placement and recidivism: Diversion of delinquent youth with mental health and substance use problems from the justice system. *International Journal of Offender Therapy and Comparative Criminology, 51,* 555–577.
4. Anglin, M. D., Longshore, D., & Turner, S. (1999). Treatment alternatives to street crime: An evaluation of five programs. *Criminal Justice and Behavior, 26,* 168–195.
5. Quotation attributed to Benjamin Franklin and Proverbs 24:3.

6. Rush, G. E. (2000). *The dictionary of criminal justice* (5th ed.). New York: McGraw-Hill/Dushkin, p. 111.

7. Palmer, T. B., & Lewis, R. V. (1980). A differentiated approach to juvenile diversion. *Journal of Research in Crime and Delinquency, 17,* 209–229.

8. Patenaud, A. (2003). Diversion programs. In M. D. McShane & F. P. Williams, III (Eds.), *Encyclopedia of Juvenile Justice* (pp. 132–140). Thousand Oaks, CA: Sage.

9. Binder, A., & Binder, V. L. (1982). Juvenile diversion and the constitution. *Journal of Criminal Justice, 10,* 1–24.

10. Tracy, P. E. (2002). *Decision making and juvenile justice: An analysis of bias in case processing.* Westport, CT: Praeger.

11. Bell, D., & Lang, K. (1985). The intake dispositions of juvenile offenders. *Journal of Research in Crime and Delinquency, 22,* 309–328.

12. Leiber, M. J., & Stairs, J. M. (1999). Race, contexts, and the use of intake diversion. *Journal of Research in Crime and Delinquency, 36,* 56–86.

13. Lemert, E. M. (1981). Diversion in juvenile justice: What hath been wrought. *Journal of Research in Crime and Delinquency, 18,* 34–46.

14. Covey, H. C., & Menard, S. (1984). Community corrections diversion in Colorado. *Journal of Criminal Justice,* 12, 1–10.

15. Decker, S. H. (1985). A systematic analysis of diversion: Net widening and beyond. *Journal of Criminal Justice, 13,* 207–216; Binder, A. (1987). A systematic analysis of Decker's "A systematic analysis of diversion: Net widening and beyond." *Journal of Criminal Justice, 15,* 255–260; Decker, S. H. (1987). Blind faith and the juvenile justice system: A response to Binder. *Journal of Criminal Justice, 15,* 261–263.

16. Ezell, M. (1989). Juvenile arbitration: Net widening and other unintended consequences. *Journal of Research in Crime and Delinquency, 26,* 358–377.

17. Pogrebin, M. R., Poole, E. D., & Regoli, R. M. (1984). Constructing and implementing a model juvenile diversion program. *Youth and Society, 15,* 305–324.

18. Palmer, J. W. (1975). Pre-arrest diversion: The night prosecutor's program in Columbus, Ohio. *Crime & Delinquency, 21,* 100–108.

19. Sung, H., & Belenko, S. (2006). From diversion experiment to policy movement: A case study of prosecutorial innovation. *Journal of Contemporary Criminal Justice, 22,* 220–240.

20. Friday, P. C., Malzahn-Bass, & Harrington, D. K. (1981). Referral and selection criteria in deferred prosecution: The impact on the criminal justice system. *British Journal of Criminology, 21,* 166–172.

21. Rackmill, S. J. (1996). Printzlien's legacy, the "Brooklyn plan," aka deferred prosecution. *Federal Probation, 60,* 8–15.

22. Cohen, T. H., & Reaves, B. A. (2006). *Felony defendants in large urban counties, 2002.* Washington, DC: U.S. Department of Justice, Office of Justice Programs, Bureau of Justice Statistics.

23. Smith, S. K., & Motivans, M. (2006). *Compendium of federal justice statistics, 2004.* Washington, DC: U.S. Department of Justice, Office of Justice Programs, Bureau of Justice Statistics.

24. Bureau of Justice Assistance. (1992). *Treatment alternatives to street crime (TASC): Program brief.* Washington, DC: U. S. Department of Justice, Office of Justice Programs, Bureau of Justice Assistance.

25. *Adult Court and Probation Services.* (n.d.). Retrieved September 25, 2007, from http://www.tasc.org/preview/adultcourtandprobation.html.

26. Ulrich.

27. *About the Bazelon Center for Mental Health Law.* (n.d.). Retrieved September 26, 2007, from http://www.bazelon.org/about/index.htm.

28. Drug Policy Alliance.

29. SAMHSA. (n.d.). *Building resilience . . . facilitating recovery . . . a life in the community for everyone.* Retrieved September 26, 2007, from http://www.samhsa.gov/About/SAMHSA_Brochure_060607.pdf.

30. Osgood, D. W., & Weichselbaum, H. F. (1984). Juvenile diversion: When practice matches theory. *Journal of Research in Crime and Delinquency, 21,* 33–56.

31. Binder, A., & Geis, G. (1984). Ad populum argumentation in criminology: Juvenile diversion as rhetoric. *Crime & Delinquency, 30,* 624–647.

32. Polk, K. (1984). Juvenile diversion: A look at the record. *Crime & Delinquency, 30,* 648–659.

33. Curran, D. J. (1988). Destructuring, privatization, and the promise of juvenile diversion: Compromising community-based corrections. *Crime & Delinquency, 34,* 363–378.

34. Elliott, D. S., Huizinga, D., & Menard, S. (1989). *Multiple problem youth: Delinquency, substance use, and mental health problems.* New York: Springer-Verlag.

35. Sullivan et al.

36. Poythress, N. G., Dembo, R., Dudell, G., & Wareham, J. (2006). Arbitration intervention worker (AIW) services: Case management overlay in a juvenile diversion program. *Journal of Offender Rehabilitation, 43,* 7–26.

37. Dembo, R., Wareham, J., Poythress, N. G., Cook, B., & Schmeidler, J. (2006). The impact of arbitration intervention services on youth recidivism: One-year follow-up. *Journal of Offender Rehabilitation, 43,* 95–131.

38. Dembo, R., Wareham, J., Poythress, N. G., Cook, B., & Schmeidler, J. (2006). The impact of arbitration intervention services on arbitration program completion. *Journal of Offender Rehabilitation, 43,* 27–59.

39. Dembo, R., Wareham, J., Poythress, N. G., Cook, B., & Schmeidler, J. (2006). The impact of arbitration intervention services on psychosocial functioning: A follow-up study. *Journal of Offender Rehabilitation, 43,* 61–94.

40. King, W. R., Holmes, S. T., Henderson, M. L., & Latessa, E. J. (2001). The community corrections partnership: Examining the long-term effects of youth participating in an Afrocentric diversion program. *Crime & Delinquency, 47,* 558–572.

41. Lo, T. W., Maxwell, G. M., & Wong, D. S. W. (2006). Diversion from youth courts in five Asia Pacific jurisdictions: Welfare of restorative solutions. *International Journal of Offender Therapy and Comparative Criminology, 50,* 5–20.

42. Steadman, H. J., Barbera, S. S., & Dennis, D. L. (1994). A national survey of jail diversion programs for mentally ill detainees. *Hospital and Community Psychiatry, 45,* 1109–1113.

43. Steadman, H. J., & Naples, M. (2005). Assessing the effectiveness of jail diversion programs for persons with serious mental illness and co-occurring substance use disorders. *Behavioral Sciences and the Law, 23,* 163–170.

44. Loveland, D., & Boyle, M. (2007). Intensive case management as a jail diversion program for people with a serious mental illness: A review of the literature. *International Journal of Offender Therapy and Comparative Criminology, 51,* 130–150.

45. Steadman, H. J., Williams Deane, M., Morrissey, J. P., Westcott, M. L., Salasin, S., & Shapiro, S. (1999). A SAMHSA research initiative assessing the effectiveness of jail diversion programs for mentally ill persons. *Psychiatric Services, 50,* 1620–1623.

46. Hartford, K., Carey, R., & Mendonca, J. (2007). Pretrial court diversion of people with mental illness. *Journal of Behavioral Health Services & Research, 34,* 198–205.

47. Draine, J., Blank, A., Kottsieper, P., & Solomon, P. (2005). Contrasting jail diversion and in-jail services for mental illness and substance abuse: Do they serve the same clients? *Behavioral Sciences and the Law, 23,* 171–181.

48. Grudzinskas, A. J., Clayfield, J. C., Roy-Bujnowski, K., Fisher, W. H., & Richardson, M. H. (2005). Integrating the criminal justice system into mental health service delivery: The Worcester diversion experience. *Behavioral Sciences and the Law, 23,* 277–293.

49. Drug Policy Alliance.

50. Appel, J., Backes, G., & Robbins, J. (2004). California's Proposition 3: A success ripe for refinement and replication. *Criminology and Public Policy, 3,* 585–592.

51. Hser, Y., Teruya, C., Evans, E. A., Longshore, D., Grella, C., & Farabee, D. (2003). Treating drug-abusing offenders: Initial findings from a five-county study on the impact of California's Proposition 36 on the treatment system and patient outcomes. *Evaluation Review, 27,* 479–505.

52. Hser, Y., Teruya, C., Brown, A. H., Huang, D., Evans, E., & Anglin, M. D. (2006). Impact of California's Proposition 36 on the drug treatment system: Treatment capacity and displacement. *American Journal of Public Health, 97,* 104–109.

53. Farabee, D., Hser, Y., Anglin, M. D., & Huang, D. (2004). Recidivism among an early cohort of California's Prop 36 offenders. *Criminology and Public Policy, 3,* 563–584.

54. Inciardi, J. A. (2004). Proposition 36: What did you really expect? *Criminology and Public Policy, 3,* 593–598.

55. Dincin, J., Lurigio, A., Fallon, J. R., & Clay, R. (2008). *Preventing rearrests of mentally ill persons released from jail.* Retrieved September 15, 2008, from http://www.thresholds.org/jailtables.asp.

56. Judge David L. Bazelon Center for Mental Health Law. (n.d.). *Fact sheet #7: Bost-booking diversion jail-based diversion programs.* Retrieved October 3, 2007, from http://www.bazelon.org/issues/criminalization/factsheets/criminal7.htm.

57. Weisman, R. (2003). *Consensus Project.* Retrieved October 3, 2007, from http://consensusproject.org/programs/one?program_id=148.

58. Finigan, M. (2000). *Oregon: The Multnomah County STOP drug diversion program.* Washington, DC: U.S. Department of Justice, Office of Justice Programs, Bureau of Justice Assistance.

59. Bureau of Justice Assistance. (2006). *FY 2005 Annual Report.* Washington, DC: U.S. Department of Justice, Office of Justice Programs, Bureau of Justice Assistance.

60. Anglin et al.

61. Mauser, E., Van Stelle, K. R., & Moberg, D. P. (1994). The economic impact of diverting substance-abusing offenders into treatment. *Crime & Delinquency, 40,* 568–588.

62. Van Stelle, K. R., Mauser, E., & Moberg, D. P. (1994). Recidivism to the criminal justice system of substance-abusing offenders diverted into treatment. *Crime & Delinquency, 40,* 175–196.

63. MacKenzie, D. L. (2000). Evidence-based corrections: Identifying what works. *Crime & Delinquency, 46,* 457–471.

64. Young, D. (2002). Impacts of perceived legal pressure on retention in drug treatment. *Criminal Justice and Behavior, 29,* 27–55.

65. Maxwell, S. R. (2000). Sanction threats in court-ordered programs: Examining their effects on offenders mandated into drug treatment. *Crime & Delinquency, 46,* 542–563.

66. Broner, N., Mayrl, D. W., & Landsberg, G. (2005). Outcomes of mandated and nonmandated New York City jail diversion for offenders with alcohol, drug, and mental disorders. *Prison Journal, 85,* 18–49.

67. Olds, D., Hill, P., Mihalic, S., & O'Brien, R. (1998). *Blueprints for violence prevention, book seven: Prenatal and infancy home visitation by nurses.* Boulder, CO: Center for the Study and Prevention of Violence.

68. Henggeler, S. W., Mihalic, S. F., Rone, L., Thomas, C., & Timmons-Mitchell, J. (1998). *Blueprints for violence prevention, book six: Multisystemic therapy.* Boulder, CO: Center for the Study and Prevention of Violence.

69. Blueprints for Violence Prevention. (2006). *Behavioral monitoring and reinforcement program fact sheet.* Boulder, CO: Center for the Study and Prevention of Violence.

70. Chamberlain, P., & Mihalic, S. F. (2007). *Multidimensional treatment foster care fact sheet.* Boulder, CO: Center for the Study and Prevention of Violence.

71. Chamberlain, P., Leve, L., & DeGarmo, D. (2007). Multidimensional treatment foster care for girls in the juvenile justice system: Two year follow-up of a randomized clinical trial. *Journal of Consulting and Clinical Psychology, 75,* 187–193.

72. Dowden, C., Antonowicz, D., & Andrews, D. A. (2003). The effectiveness of relapse prevention with offenders: A meta-analysis. *International Journal of Offender Therapy and Comparative Criminology, 47,* 516–528.

CHAPTER

7

Intermediate Sanctions

"A poster child is badly needed for community corrections, a poster child that represents a non-violent criminal under close supervision, dealing with his addiction and lack of education, and repaying victim and community for the harm he has caused."[1, p. 1]

OBJECTIVES

- Understand the use and purpose of intermediate sanctions as part of the correctional system.
- Identify the function of fines, restitution, forfeiture, day reporting, community service, house arrest, electronic monitoring, halfway houses, and boot camps and the subpopulations of offenders these penalties are intended to serve.
- Explore the advantages and disadvantages of various types of intermediate sanctions.
- Identify the intermediate sanctions that are most effective at reducing recidivism among correctional clients.
- Examine the emergence of boot camps and how they have changed to increase their effectiveness.
- Learn what criminal offenders think about intermediate sanctions compared to confinement.

CASE STUDY

The charge is aggravated manslaughter of a child. The sentence is up to 30 years in prison. Seven guards and one nurse are on trial in the death of 14-year-old Martin Lee Anderson, who prosecutors say beat Anderson and then denied him medical aid. Video evidence suggests the guards struck the teen with their fists and knees as the child lay motionless. The nurse in the case was captured on video watching the incident and failing to intervene. Video evidence also indicates the guards covered the boy's mouth and placed ammonia capsules in his nasal passages.

The defense countered by saying the teen died of a rare genetic blood disorder related to sickle cell trait—thus denying the defendants' culpability in the case. This statement is supported by the first coroner's findings, which concluded the boy died of natural causes attributable to the blood disorder. The second coroner in the case felt otherwise.

The special prosecutor for the case ordered a second autopsy by another medical examiner. The findings from this autopsy indicate the teen died as a result of suffocation—the direct result of being forced to breathe ammonia while his mouth was covered. The state legislature closed all of the camps after the death of the teen and replaced them with more treatment-oriented programs—all part of the Martin Lee Anderson Act, which was signed into law on June 1, 2006.

1. In what ways is the death of Martin Lee Anderson symbolic of correctional boot camps?

"Fines are unequivocally punitive, designed to deter, a significant attraction now that the treatment/rehabilitation ideal has fallen from grace. The meaning of fines is clear. Unlike community service, probation, or even custody, it is doubtful whether sentencers, defendants, victims, and public at large disagree about what a fine represents."[2, p. 203]

As indicated in Chapter 6, the criminal justice system goes to considerable lengths to divert first-time and other low-level criminal offenders from the correctional process. Persons who have not been charged with serious crimes, who have substance abuse problems, and/or who suffer from mental illnesses are viewed as better served by the social service-providing network than by jail. However, not all offenders are appropriate for diversion. Many defendants are serious enough offenders that they must be officially adjudicated by the courts and placed on some correctional sentence. However, many offenders are not severe enough in their criminal activities that they must immediately be sentenced to prison. Instead, there is a large correctional middle ground that exists between diversion and prison. That middle ground includes intermediate sanctions characterized by community supervision and/or very brief stints of incarceration followed by community supervision.

This chapter explores intermediate sanctions that occur within the community, such as fines, restitution, forfeiture, day reporting, community service, house arrest, electronic monitoring, and those sanctions that involve brief periods of confinement, such as residential treatment, boot camps, and shock incarceration. The sanction that supervises the largest number of correctional clients, probation, is explored in Chapter 8. All of these forms of punishment could be viewed as opportunities for criminal defendants to reform their behavior before the most severe types of punishment are imposed.

Intermediate Sanctions

Intermediate sanctions refers to any form of correctional supervision that falls between the most lenient types of punishment, such as diversion and unsupervised probation, and the most severe types of punishment, such as prison confinement. In popular discourse, criminal justice practice, and criminological research, intermediate sanctions are also known as community corrections or community-based corrections. The main reason for the common usage of these words reflects the idea that offenders are given the opportunity for leniency and nonconfinement. Technically, intermediate sanctions span **community corrections**, which supervise the offender within as opposed to outside of society, and **institutional corrections**, which use confinement and separation from society as punishment. In the context of intermediate sanctions, periods of confinement are brief and are used as a deterrent or shock to the offender to provide motivation toward rehabilitation. For this reason, short periods of confinement are sometimes referred to as **shock incarceration**, which is discussed later in this chapter.

"A common complaint lodged against the American legal system is that it favors the wealthy, who are willing to purchase high-priced and usually quite effective legal services."[3, p. 1307]

Function

In many communities, intermediate sanctions are administered by correctional officials working in local jails (Chapter 5). Jail facilities offer an impressive array of correctional programs that are part of a more comprehensive philosophy of balancing punishment, supervision, and treatment within the correctional system. For instance, Faye Taxman and her colleagues studied used data from the National Criminal Justice Treatment Practices to evaluate the prevalence of intermediate sanction programs administered by local jails. Taxman and her colleagues found that within American jails, the following programs are offered:

- Twenty-six percent of jails offer a boot camp program serving nearly 5,000 offenders, of whom nearly 75 percent receive substance abuse treatment.
- Twenty-one percent of jails offer a day reporting program serving nearly 4,000 offenders.
- Nearly 85 percent of jails provide a work release program serving nearly 34,000 offenders, 35 percent of whom also receive substance abuse treatment.
- Fewer than 2 percent of jails offer transitional housing programs serving more than 800 offenders, nearly all of whom also receive substance abuse treatment.[7]

As shown in TABLE 7-1, each year between 60,000 and 70,000 offenders are supervised outside of a jail facility in some form of intermediate sanction. The most prevalent types are community service, **weekender** programs in which offenders work in the community but live in a weekender module of the jail on weekends for some specified period of time (e.g., 1 month of weekender sentences), and electronic monitoring. Each of these and other intermediate sanctions is explored in this chapter.[8]

TABLE 7-1 Intermediate Sanction Populations

Confinement Status and Type of Program	Number of Persons Under Jail Supervision		
	2000	2006	2007
Total	687,033	826,232	848,826
Held in jail	621,149	766,010	780,581
Supervised outside of a jail facility	65,884	60,222	68,245
Weekender programs	14,523	11,421	10,473
Electronic monitoring	10,782	10,999	13,121
Home detention	332	807	512
Day reporting	3,969	4,841	6,163
Community service	13,592	14,667	15,327
Other pretrial supervision	6,279	6,409	11,148
Other work programs	8,011	8,319	7,369
Treatment programs	5,714	1,486	2,276
Other	2,682	1,273	1,857

Source: Sabol, W. J., & Minton, T. D. (2008). *Prison and jail inmates at midyear 2007.* Washington, DC: U.S. Department of Justice, Office of Justice Programs, Bureau of Justice Statistics.

"Boot camp prisons represent all that is good and bad about corrections policy in the United States."[4, p. 389]

Intermediate sanctions, especially in the form of community corrections, are a lenient alternative to incarceration that accords criminal offenders the opportunity to rehabilitate themselves and become functioning, noncriminal members of society while still integrated in the society. That community correctional clients remain at large, embedded in the community, symbolically represents the opportunity that they are given. In fact, all intermediate sanctions attempt to strike a balance between protecting the community and rehabilitating the offender. This blended practice of law enforcement and social work functions can create tension because of the competing purposes of these goals. Importantly, intermediate sanctions are significantly less expensive than prison confinement in terms of the fiscal costs of administering the sanction and the punishment severity inflicted on the offender. For these reasons, criminal offenders and criminal justice practitioners alike often view any criminal punishment short of prison as a last resort or final opportunity for the criminal offender to reform his or her antisocial behavior.

Although intermediate sanctions are less severe forms of punishment than prison, they still represent the continuum of sanctions described in Chapter 1—that is, the range of intermediate sanctions should be utilized to match the range of risk posed by various criminal offenders. The least restrictive sanction should be reserved for the lowest risk offender, whereas the most restrictive sanctions should be reserved for offenders who pose the greatest risks of recidivism and potential threat to public safety. When offenders are not placed in the most appropriate correctional program, the results can be disastrous. For example, Christopher Lowenkamp and Edward Latessa conducted the largest evaluation study of community-based correctional treatment facilities ever published. Their study examined more than 13,000 offenders selected from 38 halfway houses and 15 community-corrections facilities in Ohio and followed them over a 2-year period. As shown in FIGURE 7–1, most programs were associated with increases in recidivism rates among low-risk offenders evidenced by the negative values in the figure. By a 2 to 1

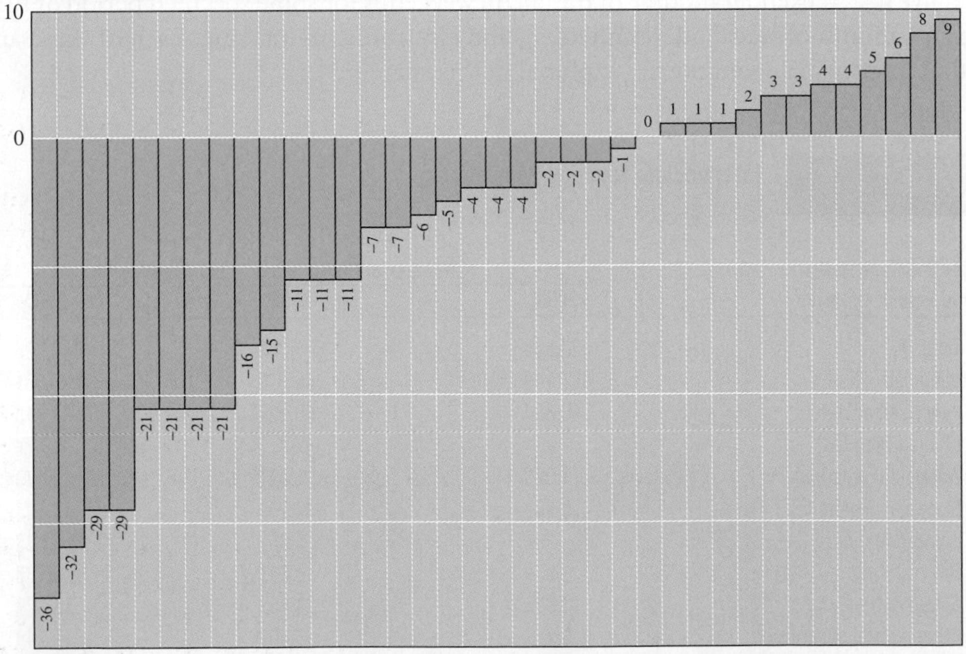

FIGURE 7–1 Recidivism Risks by Program for Low-Risk Offenders. *Source*: Lowenkamp, C. T., & Latessa, E. J. (2004). *Understanding the risk principle: How and why correctional interventions can harm low-risk offenders*. Washington, DC: U.S. Department of Justice, National Institute of Corrections, Topics in Community Corrections.

margin, correctional programs worsened offending among low-risk offenders. In fact, eight programs increased recidivism by more than 20 percent. Just 12 programs showed reductions in recidivism, and these effects tended to be very modest, ranging from 1 to 9 percent declines in reoffending.

"Intermediate sanctions . . . have become a central feature of criminal punishment in the United States."[5, p. 489]

By contrast, most programs had demonstrated effectiveness at reducing the offending patterns of high-risk offenders (see FIGURE 7–2). By almost a 3 to 1 margin, programs reduced recidivism as opposed to increasing it. Among the programs studied by Lowenkamp and Latessa, eight reduced recidivism more than 20 percent and three programs reduced it more than 30 percent.[9]

Why are intermediate sanctions more successful with high-risk offenders and **criminogenic** or crime causing among low-risk offenders? Three general arguments are generally offered. First, when low-risk offenders are placed in programs with high-risk offenders, they can learn antisocial things from more serious offenders and generally increase their criminality while being supervised. Second, and in a related fashion, low-risk offenders can be taken advantage of or exploited by more experienced offenders and be coerced into engaging in crime when they otherwise would not. Third and most importantly, highly structured intermediate sanctions by definition put many restrictions on offenders who need them. However, since low-risk offenders already lead fairly prosocial lives, the added restrictions create opportunities for noncompliance and technical violations of the supervision program. In this respect, low-risk offenders would be better off being left alone. Intermediate sanctions can be viewed as punitive because they are more intrusive and burdensome than standard probation. Because of the burdensome conditions that are a part of most intermediate sanctions, violations and noncompliance rates tend to be high.[10]

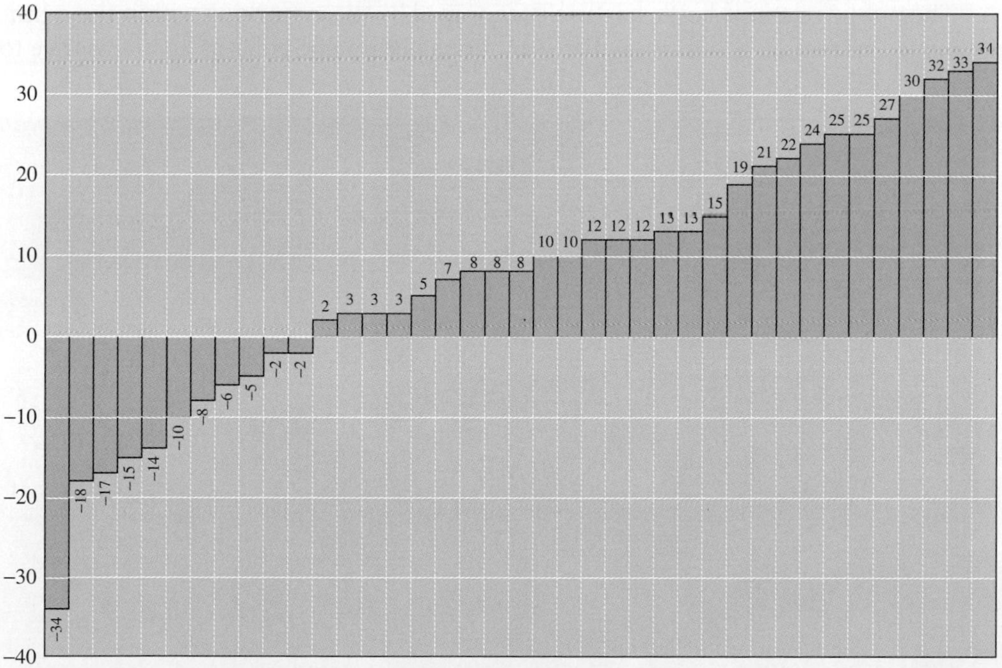

FIGURE 7–2 Recidivism Risks by Program for High-Risk Offenders. *Source*: Lowenkamp, C. T., & Latessa, E. J. (2004). *Understanding the risk principle: How and why correctional interventions can harm low-risk offenders.* Washington, DC: U.S. Department of Justice, National Institute of Corrections, Topics in Community Corrections.

"There are some offenders who feel that any agreement to participate in alternative sanctions is only prolonging the inevitability of recidivism and incarceration."[6, p. 46]

These issues concerned criminologists decades ago when the use of intermediate sanctions was still relatively new. For example, Norval Morris argued that community corrections must serve legitimate treatment and correctional needs, otherwise they will not alleviate prison crowding. Morris articulated three principles to guide the placement of offenders on community corrections. First, the sentence should be parsimonious, and the least restrictive punishment should apply. Second, offenders should receive their **just deserts**, in that no sanction should be imposed that is greater than what is deserved. In other words, the punishment and the crime need to match. Morris was apprehensive about whether policy makers could accurately make predictions of future dangerousness. Instead, sentencing should follow from observed legal characteristics like offense severity.[11] Following these principles should result in defendants being placed on the most appropriate and just intermediate sanction.

Public Image

Another important consideration about intermediate sanctions relates to the public image of supervising criminal offenders in any way other than confinement. It is believed that citizens are not naturally supportive of supervising criminals in the community and thus have to be convinced of the effectiveness and rationale of such programs. According to the Center for Community Corrections, it is the responsibility of criminal justice practitioners who oversee intermediate sanctions to build partnerships with the public and local political leaders to support supervising offenders in the community. Based on polls, the public's overriding concern is for its own safety and all other considerations come in a distant second. However, members of the public also make a clear distinction between violent and nonviolent offenders. Conventional wisdom holds that violent offenders belong behind bars, but the public is willing to entertain various community-based sanctions for other offenders, particularly if the sanctions involved drug and alcohol treatment, restitution, and work.[12]

The public relations battle has also been waged by those working within the criminal justice system. When intermediate sanctions became popular as an alternative to

Intermediate sanctions have historically faced public scorn because of their fears about leaving criminal offenders in the community.

supervising offenders behind bars, some practitioners resisted the change because of an ideological preference for traditional incarceration as *the* way to respond to criminals. For instance, a recent evaluation of practitioner opinions about boot camps indicated that sheriffs and prosecutors (the enforcement components of the justice system) preferred that boot camps have military drill and physical labor as means of protecting the public.[13] Furthermore, transitioning offenders to the community not only was viewed as weak on crime and liberal, but also meant that practitioners would need to adapt to new roles in their jobs as correctional employees.[14] There was also the concern that the increased use of intermediate sanctions would jeopardize public safety since offenders who previously would have been incarcerated were living in the community. For instance, in 1980, Kansas implemented the Community Corrections Act, which used intermediate sanctions and community supervision as a way to alleviate their overcrowded prisons. Peter Jones found that the policy did not result in more recidivism and that community-based correctional programs were effectively supervising the offender population.[15]

Still another concern is whether intermediate sanctions are too difficult for offenders to successfully complete, especially compared to the sedentary experience of serving time. Whereas offenders can simply do nothing while serving time, intermediate sanctions mandate that offenders participate in counseling, undergo drug testing and substance abuse treatment, perform community service, pay fines and restitution, and regularly interact with correctional personnel who supervise them. In other words, intermediate sanctions are laden with the standard responsibilities of adulthood, something that is not easy for many serious offenders.[16] In fact, the requirements of intermediate sanctions coupled with the behavioral deficiencies of many criminal offenders are believed by some to reduce their potential effectiveness. Thomas Blomberg and Karol Lucken suggested that by using intermediate sanctions, the criminal justice system is stacking the deck against correctional clients and likely ensuring their noncompliance and failure.[17]

In sum, intermediate sanctions must strike a balance between rehabilitative functions, such as treatment, education, counseling, job training, and reintegration and punishment functions, such as collecting restitution, custody and supervision, protecting the public, and enforcing the conditions of the offender's sentence. Across the United States, local and state correctional officials are striking a balance between these two goals. Benjamin Steiner and his colleagues surveyed community corrections agencies nationwide and found that although most agencies lean more towards punishment, there is also a strong commitment to rehabilitation. Moreover, many correctional programs prefer innovative ways to respond to the needs of offenders beyond simply punishing them.[18] Compared to confinement, intermediate sanctions are versatile criminal punishments that can fit multiple purposes needed for a diverse offender population.[19] These sanctions are explored in greater detail next.

Fines, Day Fines, and Restitution

Fines are monetary payments imposed on criminal offenders as a way to repay society for violations of the law. Fines are the oldest form of intermediate sanction, and arguably the oldest form of criminal punishment along with death. Before the formalization of criminal justice systems, fines were paid to the specific victim, his or her family, and the community. In colonial America, fines were commonly imposed in conjunction with a range of **corporal punishments** that inflicted physical pain on the offender.[20] Today, fines are the universal penalty because virtually all state and federal statutes denote some financial penalty often to supplement another sanction.

Despite the tradition and ubiquity of fines as a criminal sanction, they are poorly understood as an intermediate sanction. According to Sally Hillsman, one of the foremost experts on fines, there are several reasons why fines are poorly understood as an intermediate sanction:

- Fines are often a composite of fines, court costs, restitution, and other noncustodial sanctions, such as probation, and as such are rarely stand-alone penalties.
- Research indicates that fines are imposed most frequently for high-volume, misdemeanor and public-order crimes, such as driving while intoxicated, traffic violations, disorderly conduct, vandalism, shoplifting, and regulatory offenses, such as fishing and gaming violations.
- Fines have little rehabilitative value, and in many jurisdictions, judges see little reason to impose fines on **indigent** or poor defendants who are unlikely to pay them. Similarly, judges view fines as ineffective at deterring more affluent offenders because the fines are not severe enough to impose harm.
- Most American judges use a limited range of fine amounts because they are constrained by informal a **tariff** or **fixed-fine system** of fine amounts. This leads to fine amounts, or going rates that are structured to the lowest socioeconomic rung of criminal defendants.
- Fines are commonly waived for defendants who serve brief jail terms as a way to satisfy their sentence. In this way, fines are ordered but later retracted by the court, which sends a message that fines are not a serious sentencing option.[21]

The American use of fines is a sharp contrast to European countries that use **day fines**, which are a method of setting variable fine amounts that are punitive but just to address the economic differences among offenders. In nations such as Australia, England, and Germany, day fines are the sentence of choice and are the major alternative to imprisonment as a form of criminal punishment. Unlike the United States, where fine amounts are set by statute and thus limit the discretion of the judge to adjust the fine amount, European judges enjoy wide latitude to tailor the fine amount to the crime and the criminal. In Europe, the fine sentence is numerical and the judge can adjust the amount and therefore its punitiveness in relation to the offender. Because of this flexibility, affluent offenders receive substantially higher fines upon conviction for the same offense as indigent offenders. In this way, both affluent and indigent defendants can feel the deterrent sting of the fine precisely because the judge can adjust it to the income of the offender.[22]

Based on the promise of European day fines, which dropped incarceration rates of sentences of 6 months or less by an astounding 90 percent, the National Institute of Justice and Vera Institute of Justice developed day fine programs in the United States known as **structured fines**. Structured fines are designed to be proportionate to the seriousness of the offense while having similar economic impact on offenders with differing financial resources. Crimes are ranked according to their severity to produce a fine unit per crime. The dollar amount of the fine is figured by multiplying the number of fine units by a portion of the defendant's daily income, which is adjusted to account for dependents and other special circumstances (see TABLE 7–2). Unlike traditional tariff fines, structured fines are an economic disincentive for crime for defendants with diverse economic resources. They also help raise revenue for criminal courts.[23]

Fines are collected in a variety of ways. Particularly for petty, traffic, and misdemeanor offenses, fines are imposed upon conviction and the defendant pays upon release from custody. More frequently, community corrections personnel monitor the payment of fines in the course of supervising their client. For example, the correctional officer interviews the defendant to ascertain his or her financial situation, income, and ability to pay to arrange the schedule for repayment. Failure to pay the fine within the time span

TABLE 7-2 Structured Fine Schedule

Net Daily Income ($)	Number of Dependents (Including Self) 1	2	3	4	5	6	≥7
3	0.72	0.60	0.48	0.36	0.24	0.18	0.12
4	0.96	0.80	0.64	0.48	0.32	0.24	0.16
5	1.20	1.00	0.80	0.60	0.40	0.30	0.20
6	1.44	1.20	0.96	0.72	0.48	0.36	0.24
7	1.68	1.40	1.12	0.84	0.56	0.42	0.28
8	1.92	1.60	1.28	0.96	0.64	0.48	0.32
9	2.16	1.80	1.44	1.08	0.72	0.54	0.36
10	2.40	2.00	1.60	1.20	0.80	0.60	0.40
11	2.64	2.20	1.76	1.32	0.88	0.66	0.44
12	2.88	2.40	1.92	1.44	0.96	0.72	0.48
13	3.12	2.60	2.08	1.56	1.04	0.78	0.52
14	3.36	2.80	2.24	1.68	1.12	0.84	0.56
15	3.60	3.00	2.40	1.80	1.20	0.90	0.60
16	3.84	3.20	2.56	1.92	1.28	0.96	0.64
17	4.08	3.40	2.72	2.04	1.36	1.02	0.68
18	4.32	3.60	2.88	2.16	1.44	1.08	0.72
19	4.56	3.80	3.04	2.28	1.52	1.14	0.76
20	4.80	4.00	3.20	2.40	1.60	1.20	0.80
21	5.04	4.20	3.36	2.52	1.68	1.26	0.84
22	5.28	4.40	3.52	2.64	1.76	1.32	0.88
23	5.52	4.60	3.68	2.76	1.84	1.38	0.92
24	5.76	4.80	3.84	2.88	1.92	1.44	0.96
25	6.00	5.00	4.00	3.00	2.00	1.50	1.00
26	6.24	5.20	4.16	3.12	2.08	1.56	1.04
27	6.48	5.40	4.32	3.24	2.16	1.62	1.08
28	6.72	5.60	4.48	3.36	2.24	1.68	1.12
29	6.96	5.80	4.64	3.48	2.32	1.74	1.16
30	7.20	6.00	4.80	3.60	2.40	1.80	1.20

Source: Bureau of Justice Assistance. (1996). *How to use structured fines (day fines) as an intermediate sanction.* Washington, DC: U.S. Department of Justice, Office of Justice Programs, Bureau of Justice Statistics.

specified by the court of administrating agency could result in a warrant for noncompliance, or technically, failure to pay (see FIGURE 7-3).

There are many civil mechanisms that criminal courts use to enforce the payment of fines and restitution. These include garnishment of wages, interception of income tax refunds, suspension of driver's licenses, denial of automobile registration renewals, use of warrants authorizing seizure and sale of personal property belonging to the nonpaying offenders, and recording of fine default orders as civil judgment liens. Since fines are virtually always imposed in conjunction with another sentence, failure to pay fines is also punished by increased use of other types of intermediate sanctions, such as community service, day reporting, or home confinement. Jail confinement is also used as punishment for nonpayment although there are limits in place. For instance, in ***Tate v. Short*** (1971), the Supreme Court held that for crimes that do not have imprisonment as an authorized penalty, an offender cannot be imprisoned for failure to pay a fine unless the failure to pay is willful.[24] For crimes that are punishable by imprisonment, judges

A PRELIMINARY COMPLAINT
HAS BEEN FILED CHARGING YOU WITH
AN INDICTABLE OFFENSE

IF CONVICTED, THE COURT *MAY* IMPOSE ONE OR MORE OF THE FOLLOWING SANCTIONS:

1. JAIL OR PRISON
2. PROBATION
3. A FINE

If a fine is imposed, the Court may *structure* the level of the fine partly according to the seriousness of the offense and partly in relation to your means or ability to pay the fine. This method of computing the amount of a "structured fine" is an effort by the Court and the Polk County Attorney's Office to *equalize* the impact of criminal sanctions and to *reduce* the number of persons who are sentenced to prison, jail or formal probation.

In order for the County Attorney's Office to consider recommending a structured fine to the Court at the time of sentencing, you or your attorney must schedule an interview with a Structured Fines Officer at 286–2259, IMMEDIATELY. If you intend to secure an attorney to represent you on this charge, please make these arrangements prior to calling the Structured Fines Program.

Your ability to pay a structuring fine, as well as the length of time needed to pay the fine, is based on the information you provide in the attached AFFIDAVIT OF FINANCIAL CONDITION. It is required that you and/or your attorney complete this form prior to meeting with a Structured Fines Officer. It is also required that you take to your meeting with the Structured Fines Officer verification of your income in the form of paycheck stubs, income tax returns, etc.

POLK COUNTY ATTORNEY'S OFFICE
STRUCTURED FINES PROGRAM
POLK COUNTY COURTHOUSE, ROOM B–40
DES MOINES, IOWA 50309
(515) 286–2259.

Appointments with a Structured Fines Officer are available
Monday through Friday, from 1:30 p.m.–4:30 p.m.

FIGURE 7–3 Fine Enforcement Letter. *Source*: Bureau of Justice Assistance. (1996). *How to use structured fines (day fines) as an intermediate sanction.* Washington, DC: U.S. Department of Justice, Office of Justice Programs, Bureau of Justice Statistics.

must first consider whether the defendant could pay fines on an installment basis or use another community-based sanction before being detained for nonpayment of fines, a decision reached in ***Bearden v. Georgia*** (1983).[25]

Requiring differential fine amounts based upon the economic characteristics of defendants raises moral and legal concerns that persons are not being treated equally under the criminal law, perhaps to the degree that Fourteenth Amendment protections are infringed. Indeed, it has been argued that affluent white-collar offenders should be forced to pay exorbitant fines that would impose the same level of hardship that confinement imposes on indigent offenders.[26] This "Robin Hood" approach to fining affluent defendants is more visible in the case of organizational defendants. Based on the United States sentencing guidelines, organizations are fined according to a formula that multiplies the seriousness of the violation and the indicators of culpability. The base fine amount is determined by the following three factors: (1) the pecuniary gain of the organization from the offense; (2) the pecuniary loss caused by the organization; and (3) the amount based on the offense level. For culpability, organizations that obstruct justice receive a 3-point penalty, those with prior history of misconduct receive a 1- or 2-point penalty, and the level of authority can result in a 3- to 5-point penalty. On the other hand, organizations that accept responsibility receive a 1-point credit, and organizations that self-report misconduct, cooperate with authorities, and accept responsibility can receive a 5-point credit. Organizational fines can be quite large. In a study of 1,725 organizational defendants convicted since 1992, Nicole Piquero and Jason Davis found that some organizations have been fined as much as $500 million and that privately held, economically solvent organizations were more likely to pay greater fines than nonprofit or governmental organizations.[27]

Should the criminal justice system take advantage of the resources of wealthy defendants via punitive fines? Is it ethical for the criminal justice system to use fines as a means of subsidizing itself?

Whatever the fiscal potential of fines, they do not generally affect recidivism. Criminologists have found that fines were not helpful in reducing recidivism among offenders who were forced to pay them primarily because fines were viewed as such an indirect, almost incidental, form of punishment.[28] In fact, a recent study by Jeffrey Bouffard and Lisa Muftic found that offenders who received fines were more likely to recidivate than persons sentenced to community service.[29] The effectiveness of fines as a deterrent also depends on whether they are imposed solely or along with another form of punishment. For instance, Margaret Gordon and Daniel Glaser found that when coupled with probation, defendants who were also fined had lower recidivism rates than offenders who did not pay fines. They also found that fines were frequently imposed on very low-risk offenders, which is precisely the group that has low recidivism rates irrespective of the sanction they receive.[30]

Whereas fines are paid to the state, **restitution** is paid to the crime victim to recoup some of the harm caused by the offender's wrongful acts. All criminal courts have the authority to order convicted offenders to pay restitution to victims as part of their sentences. In many states, courts are required to order restitution to victims in cases involving certain types of crimes, typically violent felony offenses. Restitution can cover any out-of-pocket losses directly relating to the crime, including medical expenses, therapy costs, prescription charges, counseling costs, lost wages, expenses related to participating in the criminal justice process, lost or damaged property, insurance deductibles, crime-scene cleanup, or any other expense that resulted directly from the crime.[31]

When courts order restitution, they look not only at the victim's losses, but also at the offender's ability to pay. In some states, the court may reduce the total amount of restitution ordered if the offender is unlikely to be able to pay that amount. In other states, courts will order the offender to pay for the full amount of the loss, but then set a payment schedule based on the offender's finances, which may only be a minimal amount per month. Research suggests that offenders who have greater resources, more protective factors, and minimal criminal record are most likely to pay restitution on time.[32] Unfortunately, many victims wait years before they receive any restitution because of the assorted deficits of the average criminal offender. To help ensure the payment of restitution, it is often an explicit condition of probation or parole such that failure to pay restitution will result in revocation of the sentence.

Forfeiture

Another financial-based intermediate sanction is forfeiture. **Forfeiture** is the loss of ownership for the illegal use of some property or asset. Criminal forfeiture is **in personam**, which means that the criminal defendant is the target of the forfeiture that can only occur after criminal conviction. Civil forfeiture is **in rem**, which means that it targets property, it does not require formal adversarial proceedings, and adjudication of guilt is not needed. Criminal forfeiture became part of contemporary criminal justice in 1970 with the enactment of the Racketeer Influenced and Corrupt Organization (RICO) statutes that targeted the operations of organized crime activities, such as racketeering, extortion, drug trafficking, or money laundering. The RICO statutes provided the legal justification to seize any assets associated with or produced by criminal enterprises.[33–34] Many states have similarly developed RICO statutes based on the federal model.

Although it was developed to tackle organized crime, forfeiture has increasingly been used to target drug violators. Criminal justice system agents employed both criminal and civil forfeiture as a way to cripple the resources of drug offenders (which were comparable to organized crime networks) and utilize proceeds from the seized assets. Because civil forfeiture did not depend on adversarial criminal prosecution, it was viewed as a violation of the due process rights of criminal defendants. The passage of the Civil Asset Forfeiture Reform Act (CAFRA) of 2000 rectified this by providing the procedural protections available to criminal defendants to those whose assets were seized. Moreover, the prosecutor was charged with the burden of proving that particular crimes had occurred and that the seized assets were (1) the fruits of criminal activity, (2) had facilitated criminal activity, or (3) were contraband in themselves.[35] Forfeiture is also used to prevent notorious or infamous violent criminals from profiting from their crimes. The provisions of 18 U.S.C. §§ 3681-3682 authorize criminal courts to order the forfeiture of a violent criminal's proceeds from the depiction of his or her crime in a film, book, or other medium. Under federal law, proceeds from any works produced by the offender are deposited in an escrow account in the Crime Victims Fund of the United States Treasury. The money remains available in the account for 5 years to satisfy claims brought against the defendant by the victims of his or her offenses. At the end of the 5-year period, any remaining funds are released from escrow and paid into the Crime Victims Fund.[36]

Criminologists have produced mixed findings regarding the prevalence of forfeiture and the reliance of the criminal justice system on the sanction. John Worrall surveyed 1,400 municipal and county law enforcement agencies to examine their use of civil forfeiture against drug violators. Worrall found that law enforcement agencies commonly used civil forfeiture and that 40 percent of agencies reported that forfeiture was a necessary way to supplement the departmental budget.[37] James Clingermayer and his colleagues surveyed 70 law enforcement agencies in Ohio and Kentucky and found a much different situation regarding forfeiture. Although they found that virtually all jurisdictions used forfeitures, the forfeitures were overwhelmingly of the criminal variety following a criminal prosecution. Most agencies did not ever use civil forfeiture. Moreover, agencies received a very small part of their budgets from seizures and the sanctions had little impact on police procedures and policies.[38] Nevertheless, forfeiture is a useful and potentially lucrative intermediate sanction used to cost-effectively punish criminal offenders.

Day Reporting

Day reporting is a multifaceted intermediate sanction that serves both pretrial and post-conviction criminal defendants. The sanction requires that defendants report to an official criminal justice facility, such as a jail, on a daily basis to check in and demonstrate to correctional staff that they are complying with the conditions of their current legal status. For pretrial defendants who have been released on bond, day reporting usually occurs at the county jail or a community corrections facility. Depending on the conditions of their bond, defendants might be required to submit to Breathalyzer tests or provide proof that they worked or attending counseling. Because clients must daily interact with correctional staff, they theoretically reduce the incentives to engage in criminal behavior that would violate the conditions of bond. Day reporting allows defendants to remain in the community to work toward their own rehabilitation while saving jail space and costs.

CORRECTIONS FOCUS

Arrest-Related Deaths

According to U.S. Justice Department records, just over 2,000 people died while in police custody during a 3-year period beginning in 2003. State and local police were responsible for slightly more than half of the deaths, in which law enforcement officers who were involved in arrest-related deaths caused the death as a result of the perpetrator resisting arrest or attempting to flee the scene of a crime. The remaining deaths while in custody were the result of alcohol and/or drug intoxication, suicides, accidental injury, illness, or natural causes. California, Texas, and Florida were the states registering the greatest number of arrest-related deaths. Georgia, Maryland, and Montana did not report arrest-related death data for this study.

Not surprisingly, 96 percent of those who died in arrest-related incidents were men and 77 percent of this figure involved men between the ages of 18 and 44. Of this total, 44 percent were White, 32 percent were Black, and 20 percent were Hispanic. Almost 80 percent of the arrest-related deaths involved suspects who displayed a deadly weapon or threatened to do so. Nearly a third of the deaths involved a fleeing suspect, who, in the officer's opinion, posed an immediate threat to society. State law does allow for officers to use deadly force to defend themselves, another person, or when the risk of allowing the suspect to flee poses an immediate and discernable threat to society. Deaths due to Tasers were also measured. From 2003 to 2005, Tasers were blamed for the deaths of 36 people. Twenty-four of these deaths were recorded in 2005.

During this same period, there were nearly 40 million arrests made by state and local law enforcement officers, 380 police officers were killed in the line of duty as the result of either an accident or a homicide, and 174,760 officers were physically assaulted.

Source: Fox News. (2007). *2,002 died in police custody in U.S. in 2003–05, Justice Department report says.* Retrieved October 1, 2008, from http://www.foxnews.com/printer_friendly_story/0,3566,301264,00.html.

Day reporting was established in England in 1974 and first used in the United States in Hampden County, Massachusetts, in 1986.

Often, day reporting clients are selected from rosters of other intermediate sanction programs so that only the lowest-risk offenders are included. For example, the Cook County (Chicago) Day Reporting Center is comprised of clients who have already been selected for that jurisdiction's electronic monitoring program. In this program, day reporting clients are required to report to the day reporting center from 8:45 a.m. to 8:00 p.m. Monday through Friday and are unsupervised during all remaining times. A day of programming consists of lectures, treatment, support group, and other social services including GED preparation, job placement, basic skills training, drug testing, and related services.[39] An evaluation of nearly 1,400 day-reporting clients in Illinois found that clients who utilized more services offered by the day reporting center had lower recidivism rates than clients who did not take advantage of the resources provided. In addition, younger offenders and persons with more extensive criminal histories had higher recidivism rates irrespective of day reporting services that were utilized.[40]

Day reporting is also used for postconviction groups, especially probationers and parolees. **Day reporting centers** are facilities that provide an assortment of services, such as substance abuse treatment, cognitive restructuring, anger management classes, batterer education classes, parenting skills education, mental health treatment, and others designed to reduce antisocial attitudes and behaviors that lead to crime.[41] Day reporting is an explicit condition of their supervision and provides greater supervision than traditional probation because of the frequency of contact. Day reporting centers also refer correctional clients to services in the community not provided by the center. Among postconviction correctional clients, one of the main goals of day reporting is to provide

CORRECTIONS RESEARCH

Social Costs of Prison Time Served

In a society focused on incarcerating ever-increasing numbers of felons, it is not surprising to note that the rise in prison population exceeds the increase in the number of felony convictions. Between 1992 and 2002, the prison population increased by nearly 60 percent, but the increase in felony convictions was only 18 percent. Interestingly, the likelihood of receiving a prison sentence upon conviction for a felony offense did not increase. However, there was an increase in the number of parolees who violated the conditions of their parole and as a result of the violation were returned to prison.

Three strikes laws are attributed with having increased inmate numbers in several states. As a result, nearly 8,000 inmates in California correctional facilities have been sentenced to serve terms of 25 years to life for what often amounts to a third felony offense property or drug crime. Federal mandatory sentencing guidelines have added to the population under the control of the Federal Bureau of Prisons as well. State and federal laws also require additional time when felony crimes also involve the use of a firearm. Critics respond to laws and sentencing practices that result in increases in time served as unjust, cruel, and even irrational. Consequently, the increase in time served has risen by 7 months. This represents a 32 percent overall increase in average time served.

The marked increase in time served appears even more dramatic when compared to time served in other industrialized countries. For example, if convicted of a burglary in Canada, an offender could expect to spend 5.3 months in a correctional facility. The same conviction in the United States will result in a likely sentence of 16.2 months, while in England the convicted burglar would be sentenced to serve 6.8 months. Drug crimes are considered some of the most serious criminal offenses in the United States. Conviction of selling a kilogram of heroin in the United States will earn the dealer a mandatory sentence of 10 years. The same conviction in England will result in a 6-month prison sentence.

According to Department of Justice data, two thirds of the prisoners released from prison will recidivate within 3 years of their release. This same data reveals that prisoners most likely to recidivate generally spend from 1 to 5 years in prison. Recidivism rates decrease when prisoners are incarcerated for more than 5 years; a finding more closely associated with having aged out of crime than with time served. Keeping people in prison for longer periods of time merely delays recidivism; no evidence suggests it is likely to decrease it.

The logic behind mandatory prison sentences is that it will send a message to those persons likely to commit serious criminal offenses. Research on the deterrence effect has repeatedly noted that deterrence is much more closely associated with certainty of punishment. It is not closely linked to the severity of the punishment. In other words, if you don't get caught, there's no reason to fear the punishment. And criminals generally believe they will not be caught.

Mandatory sentencing costs millions of dollars and does little to decrease recidivism rates. Room and board for the average adult prisoner in a U.S. correctional facility costs between $25,000 and $30,000 a year. Eliminate the 7-month increase in average time served and a state would save in excess of $150 million a year based on a prison population of 20,000 inmates. But there are other forms of social costs as well.

Longer prison terms mean more time away from family and community. A growing body of research concludes that there are substantial emotional and financial costs that can be attributed to time served. These problems plague inmates and their families for the duration of the prison stay resulting in strained family relations that will invariably impede the reentry process upon the inmate's release.

Advocates for prison reform suggest legislatures develop creative sentencing options to replace mandatory sentencing guidelines. Proponents feel strongly that judges should have the final word in sentencing decisions—not politicians and state legislatures.

Source: Mauer, M. (2007). The hidden problem of time served in prison. *Social Research, 74*, 701–706.

offenders with the social skills needed to adjust to community life; maintain conventional, crime-free lives; and desist from antisocial habits and patterns that lead to criminal behavior. There is evidence that day reporting centers can boost prosocial skills while reducing risk factors. For instance, David Simourd and his colleagues evaluated parolees at the Day Reporting Center in Camden, New Jersey. In a 4-month period after release from prison, day reporting clients demonstrated significant reductions in criminal risk factors based on their scores on the LSI-R, suggesting that they were learning to become more prosocial.[42]

Nationally, fewer than 5,000 correctional clients participate in day reporting programs.[43] Evaluations of day reporting indicate that the sanction is a promising way to reduce recidivism and increase the prosocial functioning of criminal offenders. For instance, a 1-year follow-up study of 92 day-reporting clients in Utah found that 67 percent had no postdischarge problems, and 78 percent of the offenders remained out of jail or prison.[44] An evaluation of the Salt Lake City Day Reporting Center, which contained 297 clients, found that subjects displayed significant reductions in alcohol and drug use, property crime offending, and total offending in a 1-year follow-up.[45] Based on data from offenders in Indiana, Sudipto Roy and Jennifer Grimes found that 69 percent of clients successfully completed the day reporting program compared to 31 percent who did not.[46] Who succeeds and fails in a day reporting program depends primarily on the criminality and risk factors that the individual offender possesses. Indeed, habitual criminals have been found to be *400 percent* more likely to violate the conditions of day reporting than first-time offenders.[47] Nevertheless, day reporting has proven to be a viable, cost-effective intermediate sanction that can serve the needs of all but the most habitual offenders.[48–49]

Day reporting provides both freedom and structure by requiring that criminal defendants check in each day with correctional officials to monitor their compliance.

Community Service

Community service is a form of restitution that involves civic participation toward the improvement of the community. Examples of community service are volunteering with social service providing agencies, such as the Boys and Girls Club, cleaning public parks or roadways, and any activity that constitutes a nonpaid donation of time to the public good. As shown in FIGURE 7–4, community service is a versatile punishment that can be imposed in conjunction with diversion, pretrial supervision, another intermediate sanction, and parole. Community service can also serve as a stand-alone sentence.[50] Depending on the timing of the sentence, community service is monitored by a probation officer or community corrections specialist. In most jurisdictions, a network of social service providers are approved by the courts and defendants select the agencies with which they want to collaborate. Sometimes, defendants are ordered to donate their time to a specific social service agency, especially if the agency is in some way related to the crime. For instance, a person convicted of domestic violence may be ordered to work with practitioners in a domestic violence shelter.

There has been very little evaluation research that examines the effectiveness of community service. Douglas McDonald conducted the first evaluation of the New York City Community Service Sentencing project, which targeted chronic property offenders in three New York boroughs in the late 1970s and early 1980s. McDonald compared nearly 500 offenders who received a community service sentence to a control group of 417 persons sentenced to jail. More than 40 percent of offenders from both groups recidivated within 6 months of their sentence, suggesting that community service is not an effective deterrent of crime. However, because recidivism rates were similar across groups, it could be argued that community service is an effective intermediate sanction in that it saves jail space and correctional costs while mandating offenders to perform some civic good.[51] A recent evaluation compared the effectiveness of community service to fines among persons convicted of drunk driving in North Dakota. In a 14-month follow-up period, they found that 34 percent of offenders sentenced to community service recidivated and that DUI offenders sentenced to community service were less likely than those who were fined to be rearrested.[52] Additional research indicated that persons with less criminal history were most likely to successfully complete a community service sentence.[53]

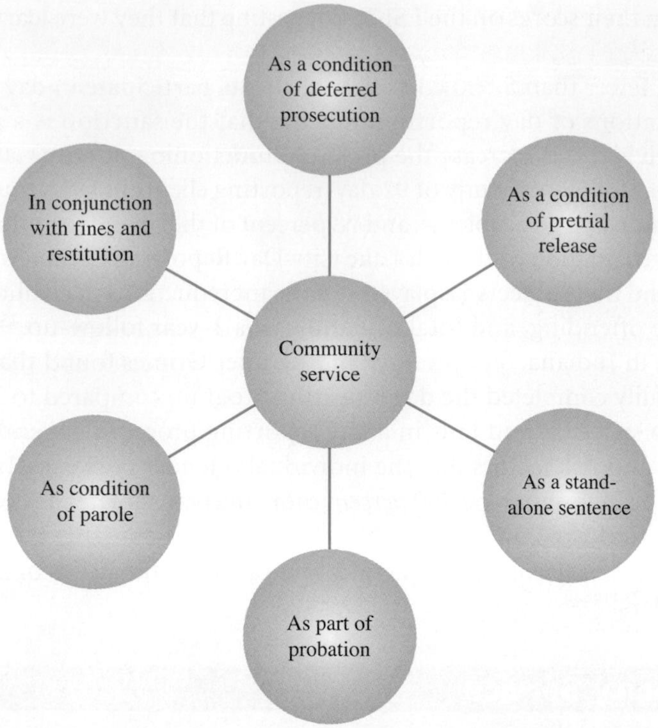

FIGURE 7–4 The Uses of Community Service in Corrections. *Source*: Modified from Harris, R. J., & Lo, T. W. (2002). Community service: Its use in criminal justice. *International Journal of Offender Therapy and Comparative Criminology, 46*, 427–444.

Unlike other intermediate sanctions, the criminal justice system does not expect significant reductions in recidivism because of community service. Because it is usually ordered in conjunction with other penalties, it is somewhat difficult to separate the potential independent effects of performing a public good on reducing crime rates. Depending on their criminal history and other social characteristics, offenders view community service as:

- An annoying, even onerous time commitment
- A welcome opportunity in lieu of jail
- An empowering experience that will likely deter future crime

Irrespective of what offenders feel about it, community service allows the criminal justice system to mandate civic activity that improves the community, and many courts permit indigent defendants to perform community service to work off fines.[54]

House Arrest and Electronic Monitoring

House arrest, variously referred to as home detention or home confinement, and **electronic monitoring** (EM) are distinct intermediate sanctions that are routinely combined for use in the same sentence. **House arrest** is a sanction where the offender must not leave his or her home with the exception of court-approved times for work and treatment. For instance, a person may be permitted to leave the house during business hours Monday through Friday. When not working or traveling to work, the client must remain in the home. Offenders can be monitored by telephone, home visits or drive-bys, work visits, or more commonly via electronic surveillance devices that are attached to the body of the offender. Introduced as an intermediate sanction in 1984, the electronic monitoring device, known in popular culture as an ankle bracelet, sends a radio transmitter signal that communicates with a programmable receiver in the offender's home, which is connected to hardwired telephone lines. These early systems were known as continuous signaling systems, which notified correctional personnel if the client left the home and therefore was in violation of his or her sentence. Unfortunately, continuous signaling systems suffered from a variety of limitations, such as removal of the monitor by the offender, breakdown and repair costs, and malfunctions that resulted in supervision errors. Over time, random calling systems, which used a locked ankle-worn band that was magnetized and connected to a telephone attachment, were developed. Today, many jurisdictions use global positioning systems (GPS), which utilize satellite signals to track the location in real time of a radio receiver that is affixed to an offender, usually via an ankle monitor.[55]

The use of electronic monitoring (EM) as an intermediate sanction is appealing for a variety of reasons, including:

- EM can be used during the pretrial phase to monitor persons on bond and ensure their appearance in court.[56]
- EM can be used postconviction to monitor offenders serving a community correctional sentence.
- EM allows offenders to remain in the community and continue to be contributing members of society.
- EM facilitates the offender's concentrated commitment to conventional behavior since their freedom is curtailed to work and treatment.
- Offenders are not permitted to go to bars or other places with criminal opportunities.
- EM allows offenders to avoid the stigma of confinement. For instance, Randy Gainey and Brian Payne interviewed offenders who had been placed on home detention with electronic monitoring and found that most viewed it as a positive experience that was certainly better than jail.[57]
- EM reduces correctional costs in a two-pronged way. First, offenders are responsible for the costs of EM supervision, thus it is self-sustaining. Second, because offenders are not being incarcerated, there are significant savings in terms of jail space, jail operating costs, and jail crowding.[58–61]

Electronic monitoring has also been criticized for a variety of reasons by criminologists and the general public. Like all intermediate sanctions, electronic monitoring is portrayed as a policy that indicates weakness in responding to criminals or gives the appearance of being soft on crime. Because of concerns about public safety, many citizens feel that incarceration in jail or prison is the most appropriate policy response to criminal defendants, and that by increasing opportunities for offenders to remain in the community, there are also increased opportunities to victimize others. To illustrate, students perceived house arrest with electronic monitoring as a weak albeit inexpensive way to manage offenders in the community; however, after learning more about the sanction, students perceived EM to be significantly more punitive and therefore tough on crime.[62]

Relating to concerns about public safety, there is another important limitation of house arrest with electronic monitoring, namely that it does not prevent criminal behaviors that occur within the home. Offenders may appear to successfully comply with their sentence by maintaining their work schedule and not going to bars while committing crimes, such as domestic violence or child abuse within their home. For example, Peter Ibarra and Edna Erez have explored how the safety and rights of domestic violence victims can be compromised when domestic batterers are placed on electronic monitoring.[63]

There is also the concern that recidivism rates among offenders placed on electronic monitoring are comparable to those sentenced to jail. As such, public safety appears to be less of a concern than keeping correctional costs down by reducing the use of incarceration. For instance, Kevin Courtright and his colleagues studied DUI offenders in Pennsylvania and found little difference in terms of rearrest and revocation between offenders placed on EM and those who were not.[64–65]

Electronic monitoring has also been criticized for net widening and unnecessarily applying correctional supervision to those who do not need it. Whereas low-level, low-risk offenders were previously diverted from the criminal justice system altogether (Chapter 6), house arrest with electronic monitoring was an opportunity to supervise offenders with relatively little costs. In their research of electronic monitoring programs in Canada, James Bonta and his colleagues found that electronic monitoring was ineffective at reducing recidivism, added little value as an intermediate sanction, and only served to widen the net of the correctional apparatus.[66] There are also those who distrust the perceived Orwellian nature of electronic monitoring, and feel that the sanction is part of a larger societal emphasis on surveillance, social control, and loss of privacy. According to Ronald Corbett and Gary Marx:

> The development of EM in the 1980s not only is a response to specific factors . . . but also reflects broader changes in surveillance. It must be viewed along with drug testing, video and audio surveillance, computer monitoring and dossiers, night vision technology, and a rich variety of other means that are changing the nature of watching. Although these extractive technologies have unique elements, they also tend to share certain characteristics that set them apart from many traditional techniques. Some of the ethos and the information-gathering techniques found in the maximum-security prison are diffusing into the broader society. We appear to be moving toward, rather than away from, becoming a "maximum-security society."[67, p. 400]

Although this viewpoint is somewhat conspiratorial, it is true that electronic monitoring represents advances in surveillance technologies that indisputably limit expectations of privacy among correctional clients assigned to house arrest.[68]

Irrespective of whether one views these sanctions as controversial, many evaluation studies have been conducted to assess the effectiveness of house arrest and electronic

Some criminologists suggest that electronic monitoring is a bad thing because it gives free society the same feel as a maximum-security prison. Are concerns about Big Brother legitimate or overblown?

CORRECTIONS FOCUS

Intermediate Sanctions, Critical Incidents, and Emotional Aftermath

Probation and parole officers have indicated when surveyed that their jobs are considerably more dangerous than in the past. Intermediate sanctions or community corrections may be the reason. One study found between 39 and 55 percent of probation and parole officers have been physically assaulted and/or threatened while performing their job responsibilities. The reason: today's probationer/parole client could be yesterday's violent offender.

When faced with a violent offender during a critical incident, some officers find themselves with little choice but to use lethal force to control the incident. Officers receive extensive training in defensive tactics and the use of lethal and nonlethal force, and as a result are well prepared for dealing with violent offenders. After all, probation and parole officers are dealing with clients who have extensive violent criminal histories who risk returning to prison if they violate the terms of their release.

Most officers will say they experienced a range of emotions before, during, and immediately after discharging their service weapon in the line of duty. It's also not uncommon for an officer who shoots an offender to have an imperfect sense of the events that transpire. Sometimes officers even fail to remember firing their weapon. Other responses to the shooting aftermath include trouble sleeping, fatigue, crying, loss of appetite, headache, and nausea. Officers may also experience recurrent thoughts, anxiety, fear of legal or administrative action, elation, or sadness. In some cases, officers experience nightmares, guilt, or fear for their safety.

Fortunately, and contrary to earlier findings, most officers cope well with the incident over time. In fact, many officers report no reaction or only a slight negative reaction during the first day and during the following week after a shooting. Most officers report no adverse negative reactions 3 months after the incident—and fewer than 20 percent of officers involved in a shooting report severe reactions 3 months after shooting an offender. Not surprisingly, officers also report feelings of elation over being alive and a sense of pride in proving their ability to handle such situations.

However, training in response tactics for violent offenses does not always involve training on how to deal with the emotional aftermath of a critical incident that results in the death of an offender. In the past, officers have been trained to expect feelings of guilt and depression regardless of the appropriateness of their actions. As often happens, agencies in anticipation of negative emotional reactions mandate psychological counseling. Officers undergoing mandatory counseling have openly admitted to guarding against disclosure of their thoughts and lying about their reactions to the incident. Evidence indicates that officers are much more comfortable talking with coworkers who also had been involved in a critical incident than with the department's psychologist.

What steps should be taken after the critical incident? At the very least, efforts should be made to:

1. Secure the crime scene.
2. Determine which officers discharged their weapons.
3. Notify supervisory personnel.
4. Contact the local prosecutor's office.
5. Assess the possibility of further retaliatory violence.

In nearly every officer-involved shooting resulting in the death of an offender, civil litigation follows. In these cases, the legal interests of the parties involved may not overlap. If the response by the officer is questionable, legal representation for that officer must be provided. Regardless of whether the shooting is justifiable, the department's legal representative should be apprised of the incident and the status of the investigation as it progresses. In some situations, family and/or friends of the offender may seek retaliatory justice, and therefore, plans must be made to protect the officer, the officer's family, and any witnesses to the event. In all cases, a thorough debriefing of the officers involved in the case should be completed as soon after the incident as possible. Under no circumstances should the officer or officers involved in the shooting process the crime scene.

Sources: Finn, P. & Kuck, S. (2003). *Addressing parole and probation officer stress.* Washington, DC: U.S. Department of Justice, Office of Justice Programs, National Institute of Justice; Linke, L. (1996). *After a critical incident: A Colorado case study.* Retrieved October 1, 2008, from http://www.nicic.org/pubs/1996/period130.pdf; Klinger, D. (2006). *Police responses to officer-involved shootings.* Washington, DC: U.S. Department of Justice, Office of Justice Programs, National Institute of Justice.

monitoring. The evidence is mixed, but mostly positive. Evaluation studies from several states, including California, Georgia, and Virginia, found evidence that offenders on house arrest and electronic monitoring have lower recidivism rates than comparable offenders on probation.[69–70] Mary Finn and Suzanne Muirhead-Steves examined the effectiveness of electronic monitoring among 128 parolees who were supervised with EM and 158 parolees who were not. Electronic monitoring had no effect on whether the parolee was recommitted to prison for a violation or on the amount of time before recommitment to prison. They also found that EM had different effects depending on the type of offenders. For example, parolees who had been convicted of sex offenses and were placed on EM were less likely to be returned to prison and remained crime-free in the community for longer periods than offenders not sentenced to electronic monitoring.[71]

Darren Gowen evaluated the outcomes of more than 17,000 federal offenders placed on home confinement between 1988 and 1996. Among six offender groups, the majority of offenders successfully completed their sentence, including probationers (94 percent), supervised releasees (90 percent), parolees (88 percent), prerelease inmates (95 percent), supervision violators (75 percent), and pretrial releasees (77 percent), respectively.[72]

One of the most recent evaluations of electronic monitoring is also the most methodologically impressive. Kathy Padgett and her colleagues explored the effectiveness of EM among 75,661 offenders placed on home confinement in Florida from 1998 to 2002 and produced several important findings. First, offenders in Florida who are placed on home confinement with EM are more likely than those not on EM to have been convicted of a violent offense. In this way, EM provides constant surveillance of offenders who are likely of the greatest concern to the public in terms of risk for violent offending. Second, since violent offenders are placed on home confinement with EM, there is little credence to the idea that the sanction is guilty of net widening. Violent offenders are under correctional supervision regardless of EM status. Third, offenders on EM were less likely to have their sentence revoked for a technical violation, which contradicts the idea of a **surveillance effect**, namely that increased correctional surveillance will result in greater noncompliance and technical violations. Fourth, offenders serving a home confinement with EM sentence were not only less likely to reoffend but also less likely to abscond. Padgett and her colleagues conclude, "EM works for serious offenders—Much of the previous research has looked at less serious offenders whereas we find an effect of EM on technical violations, reoffending, and absconding for a cohort of offender judged too serious to be placed on regular probation. This overall finding bodes well for EM's anticipated use for sex offenders and other, more serious, offenders."[73, p. 83]

Other studies are less supportive of electronic monitoring. Marc Renzema and Evan Mayo-Wilson examined studies of EM conducted between 1986 and 2002 and reported that the sanction is not an effective way to supervise correctional clients. Most of their criticism of prior evaluations of EM programs related to methodological limitations of those studies. Furthermore, Renzema and Mayo-Wilson reported that electronic monitoring is a waste of governmental resources and that the sanction is used for ideological reasons.[74] Despite these concerns, as long as EM provides significant cost savings to the correctional system while not jeopardizing public safety, it will continue to be used in the United States.

Halfway Houses/Residential Treatment

The term **halfway house** describes the residence of a criminal defendant who is partially confined and partially integrated into the community. Traditionally, halfway houses served postconviction offenders as they transitioned from prison confinement to a period of aftercare or parole. However, for a variety of reasons, such as alcohol or drug treatment, mental health counseling, or some other risk factor, halfway house clients were viewed as too risky to be entirely released to the community. Unlike prisons, which are absolutely secured, halfway houses are correctional facilities from which residents are regularly permitted to leave the facility, unaccompanied by a correctional official, to attend treatment, use community resources (pertaining to their rehabilitation), attend school or some educational program, work, or seek employment. Halfway house residents generally sleep at the facility and are free to participate in their structured activities during specified times, usually normal business hours.

Today, halfway houses are often referred to as residential communities, residential community corrections, or most commonly **residential treatment facilities.** Halfway houses are advantageous as an intermediate sanction for two reasons. They are more cost-effective than prison, and many jurisdictions utilize private halfway houses that offer even greater cost savings. Travis Pratt and Melissa Winston analyzed a nationwide census of public and private correctional facilities and found that private halfway houses were among the most cost-efficient forms of community supervision.[75]

In the federal criminal justice system, the Bureau of Prisons operates halfway houses known as **residential reentry centers (RRCs)**, which provide assistance to federal inmates nearing release. RRCs provide a safe, structured, supervised environment in addition to employment counseling, job placement, financial management assistance, and other programs that help inmates gradually rebuild their ties to the community and facilitate supervising offenders' activities during their reintegration to society. Offenders who completed drug treatment while confined in a BOP institution also participate in transitional drug treatment while in an RRC. There are five principles to RRC placement:

1. *Accountability*: RRC staff members monitor offenders 24 hours per day, and defendants are permitted to leave the facility through sign-out procedures for specific reasons relating to their treatment and supervision.
2. *Employment*: Offenders are expected to be employed full time within 15 days of their arrival at the RRC. Inmates are assisted in obtaining employment through job fairs, a network of local employers, and training classes.
3. *Housing*: Offenders are required to pay a subsistence fee to help defray the costs of their confinement, which equates to 25 percent of their gross income not to exceed the average daily cost of their RRC placement. Offenders who find suitable housing can be released from the RRC.
4. *Substance Abuse Treatment*: All RRCs offer drug testing and counseling as needed by the offender. Some offenders participate in the BOP's Transitional Drug Abuse Treatment program.
5. *Medical/Mental Health Treatment*: Offenders are expected to be responsible for their own medical expenses while residing in an RRC, although the BOP provides a 30-day supply of medication to cover the first 30 days of an inmate's stay at an RRC.[76]

As an intermediate sanction, many facets of halfway houses have been shown to be effective at reducing recidivism among correctional clients and helping them reintegrate to society. For example, in her review of evidence-based corrections, which identifies programs and policies that are effective at rehabilitating correctional clients, noted correctional researcher Doris Layton MacKenzie identified residential-based drug treatment, cognitive behavioral therapy, residential-based vocational programs, and community employment programs—all part of most halfway house curricula—as programs that are most effective at reducing crime.[77] Similar to most intermediate sanctions, halfway houses now serve both pretrial and postconviction offenders. Depending on the jurisdiction, parolees or probationers may reside in halfway houses. In some places, high-risk defendants on bond reside in halfway houses or even county jails in special **work release** or work-ender units in which offenders reside in the facility when not working or attending treatment.

CORRECTIONS IN THE NEWS

Sex Offenders Go Homeless

Stricter laws don't always mean stricter control. States across the nation have passed legislation prohibiting registered sex offenders from residing within a specified distance from a school or day care facility. The reasoning behind this restriction was obvious. The outcome was not.

Twenty-two state legislatures have passed laws prohibiting registered sex offenders from residing within 500 to 2,000 feet of a school, day care, or community park where children are likely to play. Sex offenders who violate the statute face criminal prosecution. In fact, in some states, a second violation of this restriction is a felony offense. But registered sex offenders are having difficulty finding lodging that does not conflict with state and local regulations governing their proximity to locations where children gather. With limited options and a sincere interest in avoiding arrest, sex offenders have opted to go homeless.

Homeless sex offenders are everywhere. They live in homeless shelters, under highway bridges, in low rent hotels, in downtown alleys, on public benches, in their cars, and at rest stops along the interstate highway system. States such as California, Florida, and Iowa with cities that have passed more restrictive local ordinances are experiencing the fastest increase in homeless sex offenders. It is simply impossible for sex offenders to comply with distance restrictions in several major cities. In San Francisco, all housing is within 2,000 feet of a school or park. California law also requires parolees to find housing in the county of their last legal residence. This is not possible if the sex offender had resided in San Francisco prior to his conviction.

As a result of the distance restrictions, the number of homeless in California has increased by 27 percent since 2006. Registered sex offenders now account for 2,662 of those known to be homeless in the state. Even so, homeless sex offenders are still bound by the living restrictions outlined in the state statute. The problem now faced by law enforcement and corrections is how to enforce these restrictions on a transient population. Initial attempts by authorities at tagging registered sex offenders with GPS devices have proven promising. But the program is costly and the whereabouts of many sex offenders is already unknown.

Source: Fox News. (2007). *California sex offenders declare themselves homeless to get around Jessica's law*. Retrieved October 1, 2008, from http://www.foxnews.com/story/0,2933,307080,00.html?sPage=fnc.national/crime.

Research indicates that correctional clients in residential treatment facilities report greater levels of satisfaction especially compared to when they were incarcerated. In a study of drug-abusing offenders in Idaho, Mary Stohr and her colleagues found that offenders view residential treatment in favorable terms especially because the programs are designed to facilitate the offender's rehabilitation.[78] In a study of sex offenders living in a halfway house, D. J. Williams similarly found that offenders perceived greater quality of life in residential treatment compared to prison or jail, particularly in the areas of feelings of freedom, interpersonal family relationships, and positive emotions.[79] These positive aspects are important because they can serve as healthy, prosocial circumstances to aid their transition from inmate to citizen. For instance, Christa Gillis and Nicole Crutcher examined community employment centers in Canada that are equivalent to American halfway houses and found that the job search assistance, resume preparation, and computer classes helped former offenders to secure viable employment and improved their perceptions that they could survive in conventional society.[80]

Using various data sources and types of offenders, evaluation studies found residential treatment is modestly effective at reducing recidivism and violence among criminal offenders.[81] For example, a study of halfway house clients in Colorado found that more than 40 percent of offenders fail to successfully complete their program and 50 percent were rearrested within 2 years.[82] More recent research suggests that much of the effectiveness of halfway houses centers on how explicitly the programs target the risk factors of correctional clients. For instance, an evaluation of 38 residential programs in Ohio found that on average the programs result in a modest 4 percent reduction in offenders being returned to prison; however, the programs that followed risk-based principles produced a 22 percent reduction in returns to prison.[83] Even more importantly from an administrative perspective, halfway houses provide another inexpensive opportunity to supervise criminal offenders for whom prison would be too expensive and perhaps too severe a sanction.[84]

Boot Camps/Shock Incarceration

Boot camps, sometimes referred to as shock incarceration or intensive incarceration, are short-term incarceration programs that incorporate the strict discipline, hard labor, and physical training of military basic training followed by an aftercare program, parole, or probation depending on the state and the legal classification of the offender that contains conditions and treatment. Major advantages of boot camps are that they are significantly less expensive than placing felons in traditional prison and they provide opportunities for reducing prison crowding.[85] Boot camp participants are usually young convicted felons without extensive criminal histories for whom boot camp is an opportunity for rehabilitation in lieu of prison confinement. In some jurisdictions, offenders are first sentenced briefly to traditional prison, an experience that is intended to shock the offenders and motivate them to reform their behavior; hence the term *shock incarceration*. In many juvenile justice systems, the shock incarceration is also balanced with a follow-up aftercare program, which can provide supervision and support for delinquent youths after release from custody.[86]

Boot camps were first introduced in 1983 in Georgia and Oklahoma to tremendous public and political fanfare. Of all the intermediate sanctions, boot camps are the most controversial. Citizens appreciate the harsh discipline, physical coercion, and tough love approach to simultaneously treating and punishing youthful criminals. Some academic criminologists detest boot camps for these same reasons, even suggesting that the physical coercion and verbal abuse used in boot camp facilities was cruel and unusual punishment and therefore in violation of the Eighth Amendment.[87–88] Occasionally, boot camps become national news. For instance, in 2006, Martin Lee Anderson, a 14-year-old boot camp inmate, died allegedly at the hands of eight correctional staff members who were later charged with manslaughter. According to reports, Anderson collapsed while running laps, an action that staff viewed as being noncompliant with the exercise program. Prosecutors alleged that boot camp staff suffocated Anderson by covering his mouth and forcing him to inhale ammonia fumes. Defense counsel countered that the guards were following camp procedures and restrained Anderson because he was being uncooperative. In 2007, a jury acquitted the boot camp staff of any criminal wrongdoing in Anderson's death, although Anderson's family was later awarded $2.4 million in damages in a settlement with the county.[89]

Martin Lee Anderson died while in a boot camp in 2006. Eight correctional staff members were charged with manslaughter but acquitted.

Boot camps have evolved, according to the findings from evaluation studies and fluctuations in public opinion. Three generations of boot camps exist. **First-generation boot camps** stressed military discipline, physical training, and hard work. **Second-generation** boot camps emphasized rehabilitation by adding substance abuse treatment and prosocial skills training. **Third-generation boot camps** have replaced the military components with educational and vocational skills training and often include a follow-up component in the community known as **aftercare**. According to Dale Parent, many of the changes in boot camps over time have also resulted from their perceived inability to reduce recidivism among participants. Three problems with early boot camp programs have been identified: (1) there is a low "dosage" effect, which means that the short duration of the 90- to 120-day program is too brief to result in significant behavioral change; (2) there is insufficient preparation of boot camp inmates for release back to the community; and

(3) there is an absence of a strong underlying treatment component to most programs, which appeared to inflict punishment as their sole purpose.[90]

Evaluations of boot camps in many states have produced conflicting findings about their overall effectiveness. Most of this variation depended on the study outcome, such as subsequent arrest, conviction, or reincarceration. Faith Lutze found that boot camps were successful in providing an environment of safety and discipline, which offenders felt was more conducive to rehabilitation than what a minimum-security prison could offer.[91] Even if boot camps offer an environment that seems conducive to rehabilitation, offenders do not always take advantage. For instance, a variety of criminologists have found that offenders who attended boot camp were no better than traditional prisoners in terms of reducing their antisocial attitudes, delinquent cognitions, or recidivism.[92–94]

Boot camps that incorporate an aftercare phase defined as a period of community evaluation subsequent to release from boot camp tend to produce better results. In the criminological literature, boot camps are described as moving from a concept rooted in militarism to an ethic of care.[95] Megan Kurlychek and Cynthia Kempinen evaluated a boot camp in Pennsylvania in which 383 offenders who were sentenced to traditional boot camp were compared to 337 offenders who also received a mandatory 90-day aftercare component in addition to the boot camp. Controlling for relevant background characteristics of offenders, they found that offenders who received the aftercare component had significantly lower recidivism rates than control subjects, and these effects persisted at 6 months, 12 months, and 24 months after release from boot camp.[96] Grant Duwe and Deborah Kerschner evaluated Minnesota's Challenge Incarceration Program (CIP), which is a boot camp with aftercare option, and compared recidivism rates to offenders who did not participate in the program. Offenders who were sentenced to boot camps with community follow-up remained crime free for longer periods of time than other offenders. When boot camp graduates were resentenced to prison, it was usually for technical violations that resulted in shorter prison terms. For these reasons, the CIP program saved about $6.2 million in correctional costs—directly attributable to boot camps.[97]

The effectiveness of boot camps is also contingent on the legal classification and even criminality of the participants. Boot camps were designed for offenders with little to no criminal history and tend to be most effective for such clients. When offenders with more extensive criminal records are placed in boot camp, the results are less impressive.[98] Similarly, Brent Benda and his colleagues have consistently found that boot camp graduates who have low self-control, deficits in social skills, and frequent associations with criminal peers are significantly more likely to recidivate when followed for 5 years. Boot camp alumni with gang, drug, and weapons histories were also more problematic than clients who did not have this criminal baggage.[99–101]

To summarize, the overall effects of boot camps on recidivism and related outcomes are modestly positive. Doris Layton MacKenzie, David Wilson, and their colleagues conducted an exhaustive meta-analysis of 29 studies that used 44 samples of boot camp offenders. In 9 studies, boot camp participants had lower recidivism than comparison groups who either did not participate in the boot camp or were simply sentenced to prison. In 8 studies, boot camp clients were worse than their counterparts. In 12 studies, no significant differences emerged.[102] Second- and third-generation boot camps that were most effective offered more rehabilitation components, such as drug treatment and education programs, and targeted prison-bound offenders.[103–104]

A more recent meta-analysis suggests that boot camps are generally effective at reducing recidivism among participants compared to offenders who did not serve a boot camp sentence. Evaluations favor boot camps over comparison groups for any recidivism, conviction recidivism, reincarceration, and a summary all crime outcome. In fact, the only outcome where boot camp participants fare less well than control subjects is for rearrest.[105] It is important to note, however, that even if boot camps only modestly affect recidivism, they are important because they cost significantly less money than sending the same offender to prison. These short-term costs savings will likely continue to justify the use of boot camps especially now that they are perceived as more treatment and less punishment oriented.

Criminal Offenders' Views of Intermediate Sanctions

The intermediate sanctions explored in this chapter are theoretically a win-win situation for both criminal offenders and the criminal justice system. From the offenders' perspective, intermediate sanctions allow them to remain in the community and maintain their work, family, and other responsibilities. They also avoid the risks and stigma associated with jail or prison confinement. In the event that the defendant's criminal transgression was an isolated incident, penalties such as fines, community service, and the like allow them to make amends with society while not necessarily looking and feeling like a criminal. From the justice system's perspective, intermediate sanctions alleviate jail and prison crowding, reduce associated correctional costs, deflect benign offenders from supervision case loads, contribute to society via community service, fines, and restitution, and facilitate the rehabilitation of criminal defendants. There is also the fear factor. Many criminal defendants, particularly those with minimal criminal history, can be appropriately supervised with intermediate sanctions because the looming threat of confinement serves as a powerful incentive for them to not only comply with the conditions of their sentence, but also never again run afoul of the law. For most citizens, *deterrence*, or the mere threat of criminal punishment, is sufficient to discourage crime.

Unfortunately, the same cannot be said of more serious offenders with lengthy criminal histories. For this group, intermediate sanctions are viewed as invasive, difficult, threatening, and more challenging than simply serving a period of time behind bars. For this group, there is willful noncompliance and refusal to obey the conditions of intermediate sanctions to such a degree that the justice system has little recourse but to sentence them to prison. The final section of this chapter explores this relatively new but growing area of research that explores offenders' willingness to serve intermediate sanctions versus traditional confinement.

Criminologists conducting research on offender opinions about various correctional sentences are realizing that the criminal justice system is interpreted very differently depending on the criminal history of the offender.[106] Specifically, serious offenders view prison as a relatively nonthreatening punishment that at times is preferable to intermediate sanctions. For example, Alex Piquero and Greg Pogarsky examined the relationships between offending, personality traits, and personal and vicarious experiences with criminal punishment. They found that chronic offenders were emboldened by punishment experiences; that is, involvement in the criminal justice system encouraged rather than deterred future criminal conduct.[107] Similarly, the most impulsive and incorrigible individuals were oblivious to threats of punishment for criminal behavior and *preferred* prison to punishment alternatives.[108] David May and Peter Wood conducted an interesting study in which they interviewed male and female prison inmates and examined how much probation, community service, and boot camp supervision they were willing to serve to avoid 1 year of actual imprisonment. They found that 25 percent of inmates refused to participate in any amount of boot camp to avoid 12 months in prison and in some cases, offenders would rather do prison time than either probation or community service. In this way, some of the most lenient types of intermediate sanctions are viewed in more negative terms than a year of prison confinement![109]

Based on interviews with 1,000 Texas prisoners, Ben Crouch found that older inmates with more extensive criminal histories including multiple commitments to prison preferred going to prison to serving community sentences, such as probation. According to

Research has found that both criminals and correctional practitioners have serious doubts about the likelihood of serious offenders successfully complying with intermediate sanctions.

Crouch, "prison is also preferred by those who already are largely committed to a deviant lifestyle with its attendant trips to jail and prison. For persons deeply involved 'in the life,' prison carried only the inconvenience of the sentence, not the added loss of reputation . . . going to prison may even be a badge of honor for some offenders."[110, p. 84] Rather than face the responsibilities inherent in conventional adult behavior, frequent offenders opted for the sedentary experience of prison where they could do their time with few strings attached. Indeed, Christopher Flory and his colleagues reported that many offenders feel the probability that they will violate the conditions of any form of intermediate sanction is so high that they would simply rather go to prison immediately.[111]

Research has also discovered racial differences in viewpoints about the severity of intermediate sanctions compared to prison. Peter Wood and David May studied probationers in Indiana and found that African American probationers were more likely than White offenders to refuse to participate in intermediate sanctions and instead choose imprisonment. Significant racial differences were also found for the amount of time an offender would serve in the community with Whites indicated that they would serve long stretches in the community to avoid prison. Part of the rationale given by African American correctional clients for their preference for prison was concern that they would be unable to successfully complete the terms of their intermediate sanction.[112] This matches the assessment of earlier research that found that many correctional personnel view the conditions of intermediate sanctions as too difficult for many offenders to handle.[113]

That serious offenders view intermediate sanctions as something to be avoided in favor of prison is a lose-lose situation for the criminal justice system and society. Despite attempts to reduce the confinement population, correctional officials face a difficult situation if clients prefer prison or purposely sabotage their own community corrections sentence to guarantee a prison term. There is also evidence that offenders who serve time in prison become more, rather than less, antisocial as a result of their confinement. For instance, recent research of inmates in Maryland found that prisoners become more antisocial, develop lower levels of self-control, become worse at anger management, and report more criminal tendencies by the end of their time in prison.[114] The next chapter covers probation, the sanction that supervises the greatest number of correctional clients, and which serves as the final opportunity before felons are sentenced to prison.

WRAP UP

CASE STUDY CONCLUSION

Of all the intermediate sanctions, boot camps are the most controversial. The case of Martin Lee Anderson highlights this controversy especially regarding the allegations of abuse and physical coercion by boot camp staff directed toward boot camp participants. Yet the general public and the media expressed a fondness for boot camps because of their appearance of getting tough on criminal offenders while instilling some tough love that will get the young offenders back on track to conventional society. Overall, criminologists have found little support for boot camps, which, as evidenced by the Martin Lee Anderson Act, have evolved from militaristic to a more treatment orientation.

Chapter Summary

- Intermediate sanctions are the middle ground of punishment between diversion and unsupervised penalties and jail or prison confinement.
- Intermediate sanctions allow criminal defendants to serve their sentence while remaining in the community and working toward their rehabilitation.
- A major advantage of intermediate sanctions is that they are inexpensive compared to confinement and allow offenders to avoid the stigma of prisoner status.
- Sanctions that provide comprehensive treatment to address the multiple risk factors and incorporate follow-up supervision are most effective at reducing recidivism.
- Intermediate sanctions, especially electronic monitoring, have been criticized for net widening and needlessly exercising social control of low-level offenders.
- Boot camps are the most controversial of intermediate sanctions and have evolved over time to become more treatment oriented and less militaristic/punitive oriented.
- Paradoxically, chronic and serious offenders view intermediate sanctions as annoying and difficult to successfully complete, and they actually prefer prison to more lenient community alternatives.

Key Terms

aftercare Community follow-up component of treatment in third-generation boot camps (aftercare is also used to describe parole in the juvenile justice system).

Bearden v. Georgia Supreme Court decision that held that for crimes that are punishable by imprisonment, judges must first consider whether the defendant could pay fines on an installment basis or use another community-based sanction before being detained for nonpayment of fines.

boot camps Short-term incarceration programs that incorporate the strict discipline, hard labor, and physical training of military basic training followed by an aftercare program that contains conditions and treatment.

community corrections Sanctions that allow criminal offenders to remain in the community as long as they abide by certain conditions, such as maintaining employment, participating in drug treatment, or undergoing psychological treatment.

community service A form of restitution that involves civic participation toward the improvement of the community.

corporal punishment Sanctions that inflict physical pain on the offender.

criminogenic Something that is correlated to crime or contributes to criminal behavior.

day fines Used in Europe, a method of setting variable fine amounts that are punitive and address the economic differences among offenders.

day reporting Sanction that requires defendants to report to an official criminal justice facility, such as a jail, on a daily basis to check in and demonstrate to correctional staff that they are complying with the conditions of their current legal status.

day reporting centers Facilities that provide an assortment of services, such as substance abuse treatment, cognitive restructuring, anger management classes, batterer education classes, parenting skills education, mental health treatment, and others designed to reduce antisocial attitudes and behaviors that lead to crime.

electronic monitoring (EM) The use of surveillance technology to monitor offenders in the community. *Also see* home detention and house arrest.

fines Monetary payments imposed on criminal offenders as a way to repay society for the offenders' violations of the law.

first-generation boot camps Boot camps that stressed military discipline, physical training, and hard work.

fixed-fine system *See* tariff system.

forfeiture The loss of ownership of some property or asset for its illegal use.

halfway house/residential treatment Describes the confinement status of a criminal defendant who is partially confined and partially integrated into the community.

house arrest A sanction where the offender must not leave his or her home with the exception of court-approved times for work and treatment. *Also see* home detention and electronic monitoring.

in personam Forfeiture in which the criminal defendant whose property is the target of the forfeiture can only occur after criminal conviction.

in rem Civil forfeiture that targets property; it does not require formal adversarial proceedings and adjudication of guilt.

indigent Poor defendants.

institutional corrections Confinement or the physical removal from society as a means of supervision.

intermediate sanctions Any form of correctional supervision that falls between the most lenient types of punishment, such as diversion and unsupervised probation, and the most severe types of punishment, such as prison confinement.

just deserts The philosophy of justice that assumes that individuals freely choose to violate criminal laws and therefore the state or criminal justice system has the legal or moral right and duty to punish them according to the nature of their act.

residential reentry centers (RRCs) Federal halfway houses that provide assistance to federal inmates nearing release.

residential treatment facilities Contemporary term for halfway house.

restitution Money paid to the crime victim to recoup some of the harm caused by the offender's wrongful acts.

second-generation boot camps Boot camps that emphasized rehabilitation by adding substance abuse treatment and prosocial skills training.

shock incarceration *See* boot camps/shock incarceration.

structured fines Used in the United States, fines designed to be proportionate to the seriousness of the offense while having similar economic impact on offenders with differing financial resources.

surveillance effect The idea that increased correctional surveillance will result in greater noncompliance and technical violations.

tariff system Narrow fine amounts set by statute.

Tate v. Short Supreme Court decision that held that for crimes that do not have imprisonment as an authorized penalty, an offender cannot be imprisoned for failure to pay a fine unless the failure to pay is willful.

third-generation boot camps Boot camps that have replaced the military components with educational and vocational skills training and often include a follow-up component in the community known as *aftercare*.

weekender Programs in which offenders work in the community but live in a weekender module of the jail on weekends for some specified period of time.

work release Programs that allow inmates to leave prison to work in the community during business hours and then return to prison for nights and weekends.

Critical Thinking Questions

1. Is net widening really a problem? Why are criminologists the only group that appears concerned about the growth of the correctional population in the community? Does the public mind?
2. Based on the public support of boot camps, should other tough forms of correctional punishment, such as the pillory and stocks, be reintroduced?
3. That chronic and serious offenders dislike intermediate sanctions is strong evidence of their criminality. Does this suggest that many correctional clients are simply unwilling to stop offending? What should be done with this group?
4. A recurrent issue is the importance of work at helping offenders stay crime free. Does this suggest that simply keeping people busy keeps them out of trouble? How might different theories of crime debate this?

Notes

1. Lindsay, M. C. (2000). *Demystifying community corrections: Educating the public.* Washington, DC: The Center for Community Corrections.
2. Morgan, R., & Bowles, R. (1981, April). Fines: The case for review. *Criminal Law Review,* 203–214.
3. Lott, J. R. (1987). Should the wealthy be able to "buy justice?" *Journal of Political Economy, 95,* 1307–1316.
4. Lutze, F. E. (2006). Boot camp prisons and corrections policy: Moving from militarism to an ethic of care. *Criminology & Public Policy, 5,* 389–400.
5. Gainey, R. R., Steen, S., & Engen, R. L. (2005). Exercising options: An assessment of the use of alternative sanctions for drug offenders. *Justice Quarterly, 22,* 488–520.
6. Flory, C. M., May, D. C., Minor, K. I., & Wood, P. B. (2006). A comparison of punishment exchange rates between offenders under supervision and their supervising officers. *Journal of Criminal Justice, 34,* 39–50.
7. Taxman, F. S., Perdoni, M. L., & Harrison, L. D. (2007). Drug treatment services for adult offenders: The state of the state. *Journal of Substance Abuse Treatment, 32,* 239–254.
8. Sabol, W. J., Minton, T. D., & Harrison, P. M. (2007). *Prison and jail inmates at midyear 2006.* Washington, DC: U.S. Department of Justice, Office of Justice Programs, Bureau of Justice Statistics.
9. Lowenkamp, C. T., & Latessa, E. J. (2004). *Understanding the risk principle: How and why correctional interventions can harm low-risk offenders.* Washington, DC: U.S. Department of Justice, National Institute of Corrections, Topics in Community Corrections.
10. Tonry, M. (1998). Intermediate sanctions in sentencing guidelines. *Crime & Justice, 23,* 199–254.
11. Morris, N. (1974). *The future of imprisonment.* Chicago: University of Chicago Press.
12. Lindsay.
13. Bourns, W., Veneziano, C., & Veneziano, L. (2005). A study of criminal justice policymakers' perspectives: The forgotten component in boot camp programs and goals. *Journal of Criminal Justice, 33,* 113–118.
14. Selke, W. L. (1984). An empirical analysis of the ideological barrier in community corrections. *Journal of Criminal Justice, 12,* 541–549.
15. Jones, P. R. (1991). The risk of recidivism: Evaluating the public-safety implications of a community corrections program. *Journal of Criminal Justice, 19,* 49–66.
16. DeLisi, M., & Berg, M. T. (2006). Exploring theoretical linkages between self-control theory and criminal justice system processing. *Journal of Criminal Justice, 34,* 153–163.
17. Blomberg, T. G., & Lucken, K. (1994). Stacking the deck by piling up sanctions: Is intermediate punishment destined to fail? *Howard Journal of Criminal Justice, 33,* 62–80; also see Blomberg, T. G., Bales, W. D., & Reed, K. (1993). Intermediate punishment: Redistributing or extending social control? *Law and Human Behavior, 17,* 187–201.
18. Steiner, B., Wada, J., Hemmens, C., & Burton, V. S. (2005). Correctional orientation of community corrections: Legislative changes in the legally prescribed functions of community corrections, 1992–2002. *American Journal of Criminal Justice, 29,* 141–159.
19. Byrne, J. M., & Taxman, F. S. (2006). Crime control strategies and community change: Reframing the surveillance vs. treatment debate. *Federal Probation, 70,* 3–12.
20. Rothman, D. J. (1998). Perfecting the prison: United States, 1789–1865. In N. Morris & D. J. Rothman (Eds.), *The Oxford history of the prison: The practice of punishment in western society* (pp. 100–116). New York: Oxford University Press.

21. Hillsman, S. T. (1990). Fines and day fines. In M. Tonry (Ed.), *Crime & justice: A review of research Vol. 12* (pp. 49–98). Chicago: University of Chicago Press.

22. Hillsman.

23. Bureau of Justice Assistance. (1996). *How to use structured fines (day fines) as an intermediate sanction.* Washington, DC: U.S. Department of Justice, Office of Justice Programs, Bureau of Justice Statistics.

24. *Tate v. Short,* 401 U.S. 395 (1971).

25. *Bearden v. Georgia*, 461 U.S. 660 (1983).

26. See Posner, R. A. (1980). Optimal sentences for white-collar criminals. *American Criminal Law Review, 17,* 409–418, Lott.

27. Piquero, N. L., & David, J. L. (2004). Extralegal factors and the sentencing of organizational defendants: An examination of the federal sentencing guidelines. *Journal of Criminal Justice, 32,* 643–654.

28. Critelli, J. W., & Crawford, R. F. (1980). The effectiveness of court-ordered punishment: Fines versus no punishment. *Criminal Justice & Behavior, 7,* 465–470.

29. Bouffard, J. A., & Muftic, L. R. (2007). The effectiveness of community service sentences compared to traditional fines for low-level offenders. *Prison Journal, 87,* 171–194.

30. Gordon, M. A., & Glaser, D. (1991). The use and effects of financial penalties in municipal courts. *Criminology, 29,* 651–676.

31. Gillis, J. W. (2002). *Ordering restitution to the crime victim.* Washington, DC: U.S. Department of Justice, Office of Justice Programs, Office for Victims of Crime.

32. Outlaw, M. C., & Ruback, R. B. (1999). Predictors and outcomes of victim restitution orders. *Justice Quarterly, 16,* 847–869.

33. 18 U.S.C. § 3554.

34. 18 U.S.C. § 1962.

35. Clingermayer, J. C., Hecker, J., & Madsen, S. (2005). Asset forfeiture and police priorities: The impact of program design on law enforcement activities. *Criminal Justice Policy Review, 16,* 319–335.

36. 18 U.S.C. §§ 3681-3682.

37. Worrall, J. L. (2001). Addicted to the drug war: The role of civil asset forfeiture as a budgetary necessity in contemporary law enforcement. *Journal of Criminal Justice, 29,* 171–187.

38. Clingermayer, J. C., Hecker, J., & Madsen, S. (2005). Asset forfeiture and police priorities: The impact of program design on law enforcement activities. *Criminal Justice Policy Review, 16,* 319–335.

39. Martin, C. (2001). Cook County day reporting center serves as an alternative to incarceration. *On Good Authority, 5,* 1–4.

40. Martin, C., Lurigio, A. J., & Olson, D. E. (2003). An examination of re-arrests and re-incarcerations among discharged day reporting center clients. *Federal Probation, 67,* 24–30.

41. See Gordon, J. A., Barnes, C. M., & VanBenschoten, S. W. (2006). The dual treatment track program: A descriptive assessment of a new "in-house" jail diversion program. *Federal Probation, 70,* 9–18.

42. Simourd, D. J., Lombardo, D. L., & McKernan, P. (2006). Changing criminogenic risk/need factors: A prelude to recidivism reduction. *Corrections Compendium, 31,* 6–11.

43. Sabol et al.

44. Williams, D. J., & Turnage, T. A. (2001). The success of a day reporting center program. *Corrections Compendium, 26,* 1–3, 26.

45. Bureau of Justice Assistance. (2000). *The Utah day reporting center: Success with alternative incarceration.* Washington, DC: U.S. Department of Justice, Office of Justice Programs, Bureau of Justice Assistance.

46. Roy, S., & Grimes, J. N. (2002). Adult offenders in a day reporting center: A preliminary study. *Federal Probation, 66,* 44–50.

47. Roy & Grimes.

48. Craddock, A. (2004). Estimating criminal justice system costs and cost-saving benefits of day reporting centers. *Journal of Offender Rehabilitation, 39,* 69–98.

49. Craddock, A., & Graham, L. A. (2001). Recidivism as a function of day reporting center participation. *Journal of Offender Rehabilitation, 34,* 81–97.

50. Harris, R. J., & Lo, T. W. (2002). Community service: Its use in criminal justice. *International Journal of Offender Therapy and Comparative Criminology, 46,* 427–444.

51. McDonald, D. C. (1986). *Punishment without walls: Community service sentences in New York City.* New Brunswick, NJ: Rutgers University Press.

52. Bouffard & Muftic.

53. Bouffard, J. A., & Muftic, L. R. (2006). Program completion and recidivism outcomes among adult offenders ordered to complete a community service sentence. *Journal of Offender Rehabilitation, 43,* 1–33.

54. Caputo, G. A. (1999). Why not community service? *Criminal Justice Policy Review, 10,* 503–519.

55. Reza, J. D. (2004). Do you know where your offenders are? *Law Enforcement Technology, 31,* 118–123.

56. Cooprider, K. W., & Kerby, J. (1990). A practical application of electronic monitoring at the pretrial stage. *Federal Probation, 54,* 28–35.

57. Gainey, R. R., & Payne, B. K. (2000). Understanding the experience of house arrest with electronic monitoring: An analysis of quantitative and qualitative data. *International Journal of Offender Therapy and Comparative Criminology, 44,* 84–96.

58. Vollum, S., & Hale, C. (2002). Electronic monitoring: A research review. *Corrections Compendium, 27,* 1-4, 23–27.

59. Glaser, D., & Watts, R. (1993). The electronic monitoring of drug offenders on probation. *Journal of Offender Monitoring, 6,* 1–10, 14.

60. Courtright, K. E., Berg, B. L., & Mutchnick, R. J. (1997). The cost effectiveness of using house arrest with electronic monitoring. *Federal Probation, 61,* 19–22.

61. Papy, J., & Nimer, R. (1991). Electronic monitoring in Florida. *Federal Probation, 55,* 31–33.

62. Gainey, R. R., Payne, B. K. (2003). Changing attitudes toward house arrest with electronic monitoring: The impact of a single presentation? *International Journal of Offender Therapy and Comparative Criminology, 47,* 196–209.

63. Ibarra, P. R., & Erez, E. (2005). Victim-centric diversion? The electronic monitoring of domestic violence cases. *Behavioral Sciences and the Law, 23,* 259–276.

64. Courtright, K. E., Berg, B. L., & Mutchnick, R. J. (1997). The effects of house arrest with electronic monitoring on DUI offenders. *Journal of Offender Rehabilitation, 24,* 35–51.

65. Courtright, K. E., Berg, B. L., & Mutchnick, R. J. (2000). Rehabilitation in the new machine? Exploring drug and alcohol use and variables related to success among DUI offenders under electronic monitoring: Some preliminary outcome results. *International Journal of Offender Therapy and Comparative Criminology, 44,* 293–311.

66. Bonta, J., Wallace-Capretta, S., & Rooney, J. (2000). Can electronic monitoring make a difference? An evaluation of three Canadian programs. *Crime & Delinquency, 46,* 61–75. For more criticisms of this sanction, see Schmidt, A. (1991). Electronic monitors: Realistically, what can be expected? *Federal Probation, 55,* 49–57.

67. Corbett, R. & Marx, G. T. (1991). No soul in the new machine: Technofallacies in the electronic monitoring movement. *Justice Quarterly, 8,* 399–414.

68. Lilly, J. R., & Ball, R. (1987). A brief history of house arrest. *Northern Kentucky Law Review, 20,* 505–530.

69. Glaser, D., & Watts, R. (1993). The electronic monitoring of drug offenders on probation. *Journal of Offender Monitoring, 6,* 1–10, 14.

70. Gainey, R. R., Payne, B. K., & O'Toole, M. (2000). The relationships between time in jail, time on electronic monitoring, and recidivism: An event history analysis of a jail-based program. *Justice Quarterly, 17,* 733–752.

71. Finn, M. A., & Muirhead-Steves, S. (2002). The effectiveness of electronic monitoring with violent male parolees. *Justice Quarterly, 19,* 293–312.

72. Gowen, D. (2000). Overview of the federal home confinement program 1988–1996. *Federal Probation, 64,* 11–18.

73. Padgett, K. G., Bales, W. D., & Blomberg, T. G. (2006). Under surveillance: An empirical test of the effectiveness and consequences of electronic monitoring. *Criminology & Public Policy, 5,* 61–92.

74. Renzema, M., & Mayo-Wilson, E. (2005). Can electronic monitoring reduce crime for moderate to high-risk offenders? *Journal of Experimental Criminology, 1,* 215–237.

75. Pratt, T. C., & Winston, M. R. (1999). The search for the frugal grail: An empirical assessment of the cost-effectiveness of public versus private correctional facilities. *Criminal Justice Policy Review, 10,* 447–471.

76. Federal Bureau of Prisons. (n.d.). *Community corrections.* Retrieved October 22, 2007, from http://www.bop.gov/locations/cc/index.jsp.

77. MacKenzie, D. L. (2000). Evidence-based corrections: Identifying what works. *Crime & Delinquency, 46,* 457–471.

78. Stohr, M. K., Hemmens, C., Shapiro, B., Chambers, B., & Kelley, L. (2002). Comparing inmate perceptions of two residential substance abuse treatment programs. *International Journal of Offender Therapy and Comparative Criminology, 46,* 699–714.

79. Williams, D. J. (2003). Quality of life as perceived by sex offenders on early release in a halfway house: Implications for treatment. *Journal of Offender Rehabilitation, 38,* 77–93.

80. Gillis, C. A., & Crutcher, N. (2005). Community employment centers for offenders: A preliminary exploration. *Forum on Corrections Research, 17,* 29–32.

81. See Hartman, D. J., Friday, P. C., & Minor, K. I. (1994). Residential probation: A seven-year follow-up study of halfway house discharges. *Journal of Criminal Justice, 22,* 503–515; Dowell, D. A., Klein, C., & Krichmar, C. (1985). Evaluation of a halfway house for women. *Journal of Criminal Justice, 13,* 217–226.

82. Dowdy, E. R., Lacy, M. G., & Unnithan, N. P. (2002). Correctional prediction and the level of supervision inventory. *Journal of Criminal Justice, 30,* 29–39; also see Latessa, E. J., & Travis III, L. F. (1991). Halfway house or probation: A comparison of alternative dispositions. *Journal of Crime and Justice, 14,* 53–75.

83. Lowenkamp, C. T., Latessa, E. J., & Smith, P. (2006). Does correctional program quality really matter? The impact of adhering to the principles of effective intervention. *Criminology & Public Policy, 5,* 575–594.

84. On the overuse of prison to serve minimum- and medium-risk felons, see Bonta, J., & Motiuk, L. L. (1990). Classification to halfway houses: A quasi-experimental evaluation. *Criminology, 28,* 497–506.

85. MacKenzie, D. L., & Piquero, A. (1994). The impact of shock incarceration programs on prison crowding. *Crime & Delinquency, 40,* 222–249.

86. Wells, J. B., Minor, K. I., Angel, E., & Stearman, K. D. (2006). A quasi-experimental evaluation of a shock incarceration and aftercare program for juvenile offenders. *Youth Violence and Juvenile Justice, 4,* 219–233.

87. Lutze, F. E., & Brody, D. C. (1999). Mental abuse as cruel and unusual punishment: Do boot camp prisons violate the 8th Amendment? *Crime & Delinquency, 45,* 242–255.

88. Welch, M. (1997). A critical interpretation of correctional boot camps as normalizing institutions. *Journal of Contemporary Criminal Justice, 13,* 184–205.

89. Associated Press. (2007). *Supervisor testifies in boot camp death: Guards would have stopped hitting teen if he kept exercising, director says.* Retrieved October 10, 2007, from http://www.msnbc.msn.com/id/21210732/.

90. Parent, D. G. (2003). *Correctional boot camps: Lessons from a decade of research.* Washington, DC: U.S. Department of Justice, Office of Justice Programs, National Institute of Justice.

91. Lutze, F. E. (1998). Are shock incarceration programs more rehabilitative than traditional prisons? A survey of inmates. *Justice Quarterly, 15,* 547–563.

92. MacKenzie, D. L. (1991). The parole performance of offender released from shock incarceration (boot camp prisons): A survival time analysis. *Journal of Quantitative Criminology, 7,* 213–236.

93. MacKenzie, D. L., & Brame, R. (1995). Shock incarceration and positive adjustment during community supervision. *Journal of Quantitative Criminology, 11,* 111–142.

94. Mitchell, O., MacKenzie, D. L., & Perez, D. M. (2005). A randomized evaluation of the Maryland correctional boot camp for adults: Effects on offender antisocial attitudes and cognitions. *Journal of Offender Rehabilitation, 40,* 3–4, 71–86.

95. Lutze.

96. Kurlycheck, M., & Kempinen, C. (2006). Beyond boot camp: The impact of aftercare on offender reentry. *Criminology & Public Policy, 5,* 363–388.

97. Duwe, G., & Kerschner, D. (2007). Removing a nail from the boot camp coffin: An outcome evaluation of Minnesota's Challenge Incarceration Program. *Crime & Delinquency, 54,* 614–643.

98. Stinchcomb, J. B., & Terry III, W. C. (2001). Predicting the likelihood of re-arrest among shock incarceration graduates: Moving beyond another nail in the boot camp coffin. *Crime & Delinquency, 47,* 221–242.

99. Benda, B. B. (2003). Survival analysis of criminal recidivism of boot camp graduates using elements from general and developmental explanatory models. *International Journal of Offender Therapy and Comparative Criminology, 47,* 89–110.

100. Benda, B. B., Toombs, N. J., & Peacock, M. (2003). Discriminators of types of recidivism among boot camp graduates in a five-year follow-up study. *Journal of Criminal Justice, 31,* 539–551.

101. Benda, B. B., Toombs, N. J., & Peacock, M. (2006). Distinguishing graduates from dropouts and dismissals: Who fails boot camp? *Journal of Criminal Justice, 34,* 27–38.

102. MacKenzie, D. L., Wilson, D. B., & Kider, S. B. (2001). Effects of correctional boot camps on offending. *Annals of the American Academy of Political and Social Science, 578,* 126–143.

103. MacKenzie, D. L., Brame, R., McDowall, D., & Souryal, C. (1995). Boot camp prisons and recidivism in eight states. *Criminology, 33,* 327–357.

104. MacKenzie, D. L., Wilson, D. B., & Kider, S. B. (2001). Effects of correctional boot camps on offending. *Annals of the American Academy of Political and Social Science, 578,* 126–143.

105. Wilson, D. B., MacKenzie, D. L, & Mitchell, F. N. (2005). *Effects of correctional boot camps on offending.* Longmont, CO: U. S. Department of Justice, National Institute of Corrections.

106. Payne, B. K., & Gainey, R. R. (2004). The electronic monitoring of offenders released from jail or prison: Safety, control, and comparisons to the incarceration experience. *Prison Journal, 84,* 413–435.

107. Piquero, A., & Pogarsky, G. (2002). Beyond Stafford and Warr's reconceptualization of deterrence: Personal and vicarious experiences, impulsivity, and offending behavior. *Journal of Research in Crime and Delinquency, 39,* 153–186.

108. Pogarsky, G. (2002). Identifying "deterrable" offenders: Implications for research on deterrence. *Justice Quarterly, 19,* 431–452.

109. May, D. C., & Wood, P. B. (2005). What influences offenders' willingness to serve alternative sanctions? *Prison Journal, 85,* 145–167.

110. Crouch, B. M. (1993). Is incarceration really worse? Analysis of offenders' preferences for prison over probation. *Justice Quarterly, 10,* 67–88.

111. Flory et al.

112. Wood, P. B., & May, D. C. (2003). Racial differences in perceptions of the severity of sanctions: A comparison of prison with alternatives. *Justice Quarterly, 20,* 605–631.

113. Petersilia, J., & Deschenes, E. P. (1994). Perceptions of punishment: Inmates and staff rank the severity of prison versus intermediate sanctions. *Prison Journal, 74,* 306–328.

114. MacKenzie, D. L., Bierie, D., & Mitchell, O. (2007). An experimental study of a therapeutic boot camp: Impact on impulses, attitudes, and recidivism. *Journal of Experimental Criminology, 3,* 221–246.

CHAPTER

8

Probation

"Probation is among the most important components of the criminal justice system. More offenders are sentenced to probation than to any other sanction."[1, p. 238]

OBJECTIVES

- Identify the various types of probation and the kinds of offenders who are supervised by these programs.
- Understand the magnitude of probation, trends in the size of the probation population, and its role in the correctional system.
- Learn the role and functions of probation as it relates to other components of the criminal justice system.
- Explore the historical developments of probation and the ways that it has evolved to the present.
- Conceptualize recidivism rates of probationers and the ways that offending contributes to violations and ultimately probation revocation.
- Explore evaluation studies of probation programs by understanding what works for juvenile and adult probationers.

CASE STUDY

Consider the following five defendants who you must sentence (today you are a judge):

Defendant 1: African American male, 34, pleads guilty to driving while intoxicated (third offense). He has no other criminal history. He is employed, owns a home, and has a daughter.

Defendant 2: Hispanic female, 52, pleads guilty to felony forgery, felony fraud, and felony theft. She has six prior convictions for larceny. She is employed, has been married for 36 years, and has seven children.

Defendant 3: White male, 19, pleads guilty to felony assault, possession of an illegal weapon, and possession of methamphetamine. He is on probation for drug possession stemming from an incident when he was a juvenile. He is currently receiving substance abuse and psychiatric counseling, works part time, and lives with his parents.

Defendant 4: White male, 61, pleads guilty to robbery and assault. He is a chronic transient, and the victim in the case was another transient (who also pleads guilty to assault). He has been arrested approximately 65 times, mostly for municipal violations and failure-to-appear warrants.

Defendant 5: Hispanic male, 25, was found guilty at trial of aggravated robbery, assault with intent a deadly weapon, and menacing with a deadly weapon. This is his first arrest since being released from prison 4 years ago, when he finished served time for drug and weapons convictions. He is married, employed, has two children, and has links to a local street gang.

1. While these cases may seem different, the real judge in the case sentenced all five defendants to probation with different terms and conditions. Why?

"Providing correctional personnel with a flexible means of dealing with problems in the field not only enables them to adjust terms of supervision to meet an offender's needs, but also provides a means for enhanced public protection."[2, p. 41]

When one thinks of the criminal justice system, it is usually the most dramatic penalties that immediately come to mind. Jail, prison, and capital punishment are the most severe forms of criminal punishment; as such they receive considerable research attention and tend to grab most of the headlines in the news media. It is unlikely that people first think of probation when considering the criminal justice; yet, in terms of size, number of correctional clients supervised, and involvement in the criminal justice process, probation is the biggest and arguably most important component of the correctional system. Of the more than 7 million people under correctional supervision in the United States, more than 4.2 million are on probation. The probation population is nearly six times the size of the jail inmate population and nearly three times the size of the state and federal prisoner population.[7] This chapter explores the history of probation, the various types of probation that have been developed, the social and behavioral history of probationers, and various administrative issues related to probation.

Probation

Probation is a sanction for criminal offenders who have been sentenced to a period of correctional supervision in the community in lieu of incarceration. Probation offers conditional freedom to offenders, known as **probationers**, who must abide by a variety of conditions that are imposed to facilitate their rehabilitation. Common probation conditions are substance abuse counseling and urinalysis, no contact with victims in the case, psychiatric counseling, restitution, community service, employment, and regular communication with one's probation officer. **Standard conditions** refer to universal mandates that apply to all probationers. Standard probation conditions in the federal justice system include:

- Avoid commission of any new offenses.
- Notify the supervising agency prior to leaving the district of supervision.

> "[Probation is for] those who were indicted for their first offense, and whose hearts were not wholly depraved, but gave promise of better things."[3, p. 155–156]

- Notify the supervising agency of any change in residence.
- Maintain stable employment.
- Report any new arrests without delay to the supervising agency.
- Refrain from excessive use of alcohol and any use of controlled substances.
- Avoid any place where controlled substances are used or sold.
- No association with any persons engaged in criminal activity or any person convicted of a felony unless granted permission to do so.
- Report regularly to the supervising agency.
- Comply with any directives or instructions from the supervising corrections agent.[8]

Treatment conditions address a problem or issue that, if resolved, will help the offender remain crime free, such as participation in drug treatment. **Punitive conditions** are burdens placed on probationers convicted of the most serious crimes, such as residency limitations for offenders convicted of sexual offenses.

The conditions of probation are enforced by a probation officer. A **probation officer** is the practitioner who oversees and monitors a probationer's case to determine that the defendant is complying with all conditions of probation. When probationers do not comply with their sentence, their probation officer can pursue two general courses of action. Unless there is a grievous violation, such as an arrest for a new violent felony, the probation officer will warn the probationer and potentially seek to impose new conditions or extend the period of probation. Both of these actions must be court approved before the probation department may act. Other times, the probation officer arrests the probationer for violating the terms of his or her sentence, a legal action known as a **probation violation**. When the defendant appears in court, the probation sentence can be terminated, a process known as **revocation**, which usually results in a prison sentence, or the probation sentence can be made more restrictive. Violations of probation that are based on relatively minor conditional violations are oftentimes referred to as **technical violations**. Importantly, probationers who are performing exceptionally well can also have their probation terminated early.

The Supreme Court has addressed the legal standing of probation departments to limit the due process rights of probationers. In *Mathews v. Eldridge* (1976), the Court held that there are three points on which correctional conditions must pass constitutional muster: (1) limitations on the probationer are appropriate if they temporarily meet the needs of control and supervision; (2) conditions must fit the various risks that the offender poses to community, public safety, etc.; and (3) agencies should revisit probation conditions to meet the interests of public safety and the offender.[9]

Typologies

The type of probation depends on a variety of factors, including jurisdiction, age of the offender, and the level of risk, criminality, and treatment needs of the probationer. General types of probation include:

- **Summary probation**—a sentencing option where the judge accepts a plea or verdict of guilt for a misdemeanant, suspends execution of the sentence, and summarily (without the use of a presentence investigation) imposes a period of unsupervised probation. In effect, summary probation is similar to a deferred sentence and can be viewed as the forerunner of unsupervised probation.[10]
- **Unsupervised probation**—reserved for first-time or low-level offenders with little to no probation conditions. Unsupervised probation is also comparable to a deferred sentence in that probationers do not need to meet with a probation

CORRECTIONS RESEARCH

The Challenge of Chronic Juvenile Offending in a Growing Urban Setting—The 8 Percent Problem

From 1980 to 1990, the population of Orange County, California, increased by 26 percent. Five new cities were added; 10 of the total 31 cities expanded to a population of over 100,000. Approximately 7,400 undocumented workers were added each year, and by 1990, the population of undocumented workers had reached 166,000.

Rapid population growth is generally accompanied by increases in overall crime rates—especially crimes involving juvenile offenders. During this period, juvenile crime rates skyrocketed. Increases in juvenile arrests for murder rose by 130 percent, for forcible rape by 70 percent, for robbery by 65 percent, and for felonies involving a firearm by 48 percent. Orange County Juvenile Court dispositions increased by 43 percent, juveniles sentenced to confinement in a California correctional facility increased by 40 percent to local facilities and by 169 percent to the California Youth Authority.

Crime costs money. According to records, in 1990 the average confinement in a local facility or program for a juvenile offender was 74 days. Seventy-four days of confinement at this level of intervention cost taxpayers approximately $5,500. The average length of stay for juvenile offenders committed to the California Youth Authority was 2 years, and the cost to the community was nearly $55,000.

Controlling the cost of crime means something has to be done to limit recidivism. Repeat offenders just happen to be the system's biggest problem. Research has clearly shown that fewer than 10 percent of offenders commit 50 percent or more of the serious crimes. Law enforcement officers assert that if it takes longer than 10 minutes to print an offender's criminal history, the offender is a career criminal. The general conclusion was that efforts must be made to decrease recidivism; the system needed to prevent chronic juvenile offenders from continuing to commit crimes.

With that in mind, the Orange County Probation Department combined two instruments to assess the risk potential of juvenile offenders. The first instrument was recommended by the National Institute of Corrections for use with repeat offenders. Information on predictors of recidivism was also gathered from field supervisors and was used to develop the second risk assessment tool. Using these indicators, three factor sets were found to identify high, medium, and low risk of recidivism by juvenile probationers. They included prior offense history or what is sometimes called criminal history, multiple problems that involve factors such as parental supervision, school attendance, and substance use, and age at initial assessment—a factor set that was divided into two groupings, one 15 or younger and the other 16 and older.

What followed was a 3-year longitudinal study that involved two cohorts with more than 3,000 juvenile offenders; one from 1985 and the other from 1987. The initial purpose of the investigation was to identify juvenile repeat offenders within each 3-year period. Each cohort was broken into three subgroups. The first subgroup was labeled the nonrecidivist group and consisted of juveniles with only one referral during the tracking period. The second subgroup was comprised of juveniles with two or three referrals, while the third group consisted of minors with four or more referrals during the tracking period. Only 8 percent of the juveniles in this study qualified for the third study group, but not surprisingly, they were responsible for 55 percent of all subsequent referrals during the study period.

Two questions surfaced: (1) How are these offenders different from the rest? (2) Are there any cost-effective solutions to the problem? Findings from the study revealed potential chronic offenders could be identified and targeted for early intervention at their first referral by combining the age at initial assessment factor with the multiple problem factor set. Researchers found that the majority of chronic offenders were in the 15 or younger group when first referred to the juvenile court system. During their initial contact with the system, nearly 50 percent of the chronic offenders had also been made wards of the court. This group also suffered from drug use, poor school performance, and the problems commonly associated with dysfunctional families.

The 6-year follow-up found that the group of chronic offenders spent approximately 20 months in jail at a cost of $44,000 for each offender. Because Orange County, California, experiences an increase of nearly 500 new chronic juvenile offenders per year, the cost to control each new 8 percent group could conceivably reach $22 million.

In an effort to curtail the cost to control chronic offenders, the authors of this study recommend focusing on younger minors with multiple problems who are first-time wards of the court. They found that in youth under age 15 these indicators accurately predicted 77 percent of the chronic offender cases. The degree of accuracy fell to 64 percent with youth 16 and over. Intervention should also include the youth's family. Dysfunctional family factors such as the inability to properly supervise or support their children contribute significantly to long-term chronic recidivism.

Sources: DeLisi, M. (2005). *Career criminals in society*. Thousand Oaks, CA: Sage; Kurz, G. A., & Moore, L. E. (1994). *County of Orange probation department: 8% problem study methodology*. Retrieved October 1, 2008, from http://www.ocgov.com/Probation/solution/ProblemStudyMethodology.asp; Kurz, G. A., & Moore, L. E. (1994). *County of Orange probation department: 8% problem study findings*. Retrieved October 1, 2008, from http://www.ocgov.com/Probation/solution/ProblemStudyFindings.asp.

officer; instead they must simply abstain from crime and avoid rearrest during the specified period of supervision. However, a conviction and probation sentence will remain on one's permanent criminal record and cannot be expunged. In some jurisdictions, unsupervised probation can be used for persons convicted of low-level felonies.

- **Automated probation**—a form of unsupervised probation that entails no supervision, services, or personal contacts; in some places it is known as **banked probation.** Automated probation is used primarily in large urban centers with massive probation caseloads. For example, about 70 percent of probationers in Los Angeles County (nearly 100,000 clients) received automated probation; this included 5,000 offenders convicted of violent index crimes.[11]
- **Intensive supervised probation** (ISP)—the most highly restrictive form of punishment that is designed to supervise criminal offenders who embody the most risk factors for continued involvement in crime. For instance, Joan Petersilia and Susan Turner found that about 25 percent of California offenders who received ISP were indistinguishable from prisoners in terms of their criminal backgrounds and risk to the community.[12] Clients on ISP must abide by a multitude of conditions and are subject to the most intense supervision and surveillance by probation officers. Usually, probation officers who supervise ISP clients have reduced caseloads because of the added supervision needed for their clients. Intensive supervised probation is viewed as the last resort form of community corrections before an offender is sentenced to prison.
- **Community probation**—an extension of the community policing approach to crime control where community residents and organizations work with criminal justice officials to address neighborhood disorder and related problems. In community probation, the department of probation places probation officers in community field offices where their entire caseload is devoted to residents living in specific neighborhoods. Community probation officers work with law enforcement and residents toward crime prevention, conflict resolution, problem solving, and enforcement. Although community probation may result in positive outcomes for some of its goals, a recent evaluation of a Maryland program found that recidivism rates were comparable to offenders placed on traditional probation supervision.[13]
- **Sex offender probation**—a specialized unit within a probation office in which practitioners exclusively supervise offenders convicted of sexually based offenses. Typically, probation officers who supervise sex offenders receive specialized training, have smaller and more intensive caseloads, and utilize more **field** or **home visits,** which are searches of probation clients' place of work or homes to determine their compliance with supervision. Correctional clients serving a probation sentence that is supervised by a specialized sex offender probation officer usually have more conditions than other high-risk offenders. These might include more home visits, more intensive counseling, daily arrest checks, polygraphs, and prohibited use of pornography (e.g., illicit web sites or 900 sex talk telephone numbers). Evaluations of sex offender probation indicate that probationers are subjected to very strict supervision and revoked for even the most technical violations.[14]
- **Federal probation**—supervised by the **U.S. Probation and Pretrial Services System,** which is the community corrections arm of the federal judiciary charged with supervising criminal defendants during the pretrial and postadjudication phases. In 1984, the Comprehensive Crime Control Act made probation an independent sentence.[15] Federal probation officers are located in the 94 U.S. district courts.

"Probation finds itself in an awkward position in the United States. It was originally advanced by progressive reformers who sought to help offenders overcome their problems and mitigate the perceived harshness of jails and prisons. The public is now less concerned with helping offenders than with public safety and deserved punishment."[4, p. 185]

"It is well known that courts place many on probation who do not require the kind of rehabilitative and reformative treatment which probation signifies."[5, p. 555]

Like their local and state counterparts, federal probation officers work with all facets of the justice system including judges, U.S. attorneys, defense counsel, the Federal Bureau of Prisons, the U.S. Parole Commission, local law enforcement, treatment providers, community leaders, and, of course, probationers.

- **Juvenile probation**—the oldest and most widely used way to provide court-ordered services in the juvenile justice system. In the juvenile justice system, probation can be a front end or preadjudication period of supervision or a back end, postadjudication or sentencing outcome. Nearly two thirds of all delinquency cases result in a probationary sentence (see TABLE 8–1). Given how important probation is to the treatment of delinquency, it has been referred to as the workhorse of the juvenile justice system.[16]
- **School-based probation**—a variation of juvenile probation in which a juvenile probation officer is housed in a school to provide direct supervision of students on probation. This allows the officer to spend more time on the client and provide more involvement in the student's life as well as observe his or her peer groups and school behavior. The first school-based probation was created in Lehigh County, Pennsylvania, in 1990, and programs seek to reduce disciplinary referrals in school, reduce detentions, improve attendance and grades, decrease dropout rates, and reduce recidivism. Evaluations of school-based probation indicate that the program is significantly less expensive than traditional juvenile probation and that clients engage in less serious forms of delinquency in terms of recidivism.[17]
- **Reparative probation**—a restorative justice concept that focuses on communication and problem solving among offenders, victims, and community residents rather than enforcement and punishment as a way to address crime. Reparative probation invites dialogue between key stakeholders to negotiate agreements that serve all parties. It is most commonly used for victimless crimes, such as drunk driving. There are many goals of reparative probation, including:
  - Address the needs of victims.
  - Repair harm to the community caused by the crime.
  - Ensure that offenders understand the impact of their crime.
  - Ensure that offenders acknowledge responsibility and make amends.
  - Ensure that offenders build social ties with community residents.
  - Ensure that offenders remain law abiding.[18]

Probation is the jack-of-all-trades sanction because it touches virtually all aspects of criminal justice. Upon an arrest, it is usually the department of probation that conducts a presentence investigation (PSI) (Chapter 4) that is the primary source of information that the court uses to determine which cases will be deferred from formal prosecution. The criminal and social history information in the PSI can affect bond and pretrial release, adjudication, sentencing, correctional placement, and supervision. As described by Joan Petersilia, "No other justice agency is as extensively involved with the offender and his case as is the probation department."[19, p. 159]

Probation also plays a major part in deflecting or diverting crimes from the criminal justice system and thus provides great savings on court and correctional expenditures. Aside from nominal criminal offenders, recidivism rates are relatively high. This means that offenders already on probation commit many new crimes. Once this happens, the courts have a decision to make. They can either initiate prosecution for the new crimes or simply use the new arrest as the basis for a violation or revocation of probation. Prosecutors favor the latter approach. For instance, Rodney Kingsnorth and his colleagues found that prosecutors believed that case disposition by means of a probation violation hearing

TABLE 8-1 Juvenile Probation in the United States

	Adjudicated Cases			
Most Serious Offense	Number Ordered to Placement	Percent Ordered to Placement	Number Ordered to Probation	Percent Ordered to Probation
Total delinquency	**144,000**	**23**	**385,400**	**62**
Person offense	**37,200**	**25**	**92,000**	**63**
Violent Crime Index	12,500	34	20,900	56
Criminal homicide	400	50	300	43
Forcible rape	1,000	39	1,100	44
Robbery	5,000	42	6,000	50
Aggravated assault	6,100	28	13,400	62
Simple assault	20,000	22	59,200	65
Other violent sex offense	2,700	30	5,800	64
Other person offense	1,900	21	6,200	68
Property offense	**52,700**	**23**	**147,300**	**63**
Property Crime Index	39,600	24	106,200	64
Burglary	15,500	27	37,400	64
Larceny-theft	15,900	19	54,100	65
Motor vehicle theft	7,400	35	12,400	58
Arson	700	21	2,200	64
Vandalism	5,400	17	20,800	65
Trespassing	2,300	17	8,600	63
Stolen property offense	3,100	30	5,500	54
Other property offense	2,200	19	6,100	54
Drug law violation	**14,400**	**18**	**50,900**	**64**
Public order offense	39,800	24	95,200	57
Obstruction of justice	28,400	31	52,500	57
Disorderly conduct	3,900	13	17,600	59
Weapons offense	3,200	22	9,600	65
Liquor law violation	600	10	3,500	59
Nonviolent sex offense	1,700	28	3,800	62
Other public order offense	1,900	12	8,200	50

Source: Snyder, H. S., & Sickmund, M. (2006). *Juvenile offenders and victims: 2006 national report.* Washington, DC: U.S. Department of Justice, Office of Justice Programs, Office of Juvenile Justice and Delinquency Prevention, National Center for Juvenile Justice.

"Intensive supervised probation (ISP) is a mechanism by which reality can be brought to all intermediate punishments. Allied to house arrest, treatment orders, residential conditions up to house arrest, buttressed by electronic monitoring where appropriate, and paid for by fees for service by the offenders where that is realistic, ISP has the capacity both to control offenders in the community and to facilitate their growth to crime-free lives."[6, p. 11]

and revocation was preferable to filing new charges. Because probation violations could readily result in jail or prison sentences, new charges were often rejected or dismissed to streamline the case against the offender.[20] In this way, probation and its violation can serve a quasi-judicial function.

Statistics and Trends

More criminal offenders are on probation than any other form of criminal punishment. With a population of more than 4.2 million, probation accounts for nearly 60 percent of the entire correctional population and is significantly larger than the parole, jail, and prisoner populations (see TABLE 8-2). As shown in FIGURE 8-1, the growth in probation has far outpaced other forms of criminal punishment and resulted in tremendous increases in expenditures over the past 2 decades. Since 1980, the probation population has increased *fourfold* and the rate of growth in the probation population has increased more sharply

TABLE 8-2 Adult Correctional Populations, 1995–2006

Year	Total Estimated Correctional Population	Community Supervision: Probation	Community Supervision: Parole	Incarceration: Jail	Incarceration: Prison
1995	5,342,900	3,077,861	679,421	507,044	1,078,542
2000	6,445,100	3,826,209	723,898	621,149	1,316,333
2001	6,581,700	3,931,731	732,333	631,240	1,330,007
2002	6,758,800	4,024,067	750,934	665,475	1,367,547
2003	6,883,200	4,073,987	774,588	691,301	1,390,279
2003 (revised)	6,924,500	4,120,012	769,925	691,301	1,390,279
2004	6,995,100	4,143,792	771,852	713,990	1,421,345
2005	7,051,900	4,166,757	780,616	747,529	1,448,344
2006	7,211,400	4,237,023	798,202	766,010	1,492,973
Percent change, 2005–2006	2.3	1.7	2.3	2.5	3.1
Average annual percent change, 1995–2006	2.5	2.4	1.5	3.8	3.0

Source: Glaze, L. E., & Bonczar, T. P. (2007). *Probation and parole in the United States, 2006*. Washington, DC: U.S. Department of Justice, Office of Justice Programs, Bureau of Justice Statistics.

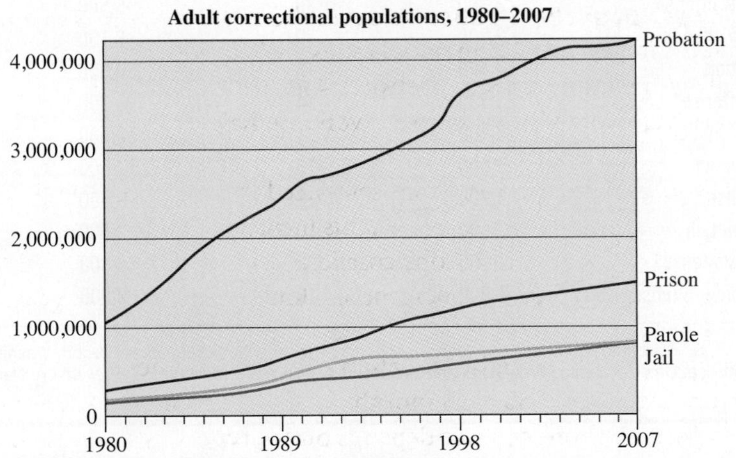

FIGURE 8–1 Correctional Population Growth. *Source*: Bureau of Justice Statistics Correctional Surveys. (2007). *The number of adults in the correctional population has been increasing.* Retrieved December 12, 2008, from http://www.ojp.usdoj.gov/bjs/glance/corr2.htm.

than the prison, parole, and jail populations. For example, between 1995 and 2006, the correctional population grew by 31 percent. Of this increase, probation accounted for 57 percent of the growth. Since 1995, between 20,000 and 120,000 probationers are added to the probation population with more modest growth in recent years (see **FIGURE 8–2**). From 1995 to 2005, the adult probation population increased at a rate of nearly 3 percent per year. Half of all probationers are serving a sentence upon conviction for a felony, 49 percent for a misdemeanor, and 1 percent for other infractions. Drug violators and persons convicted of drunk driving comprised 43 percent of the probation population.[21]

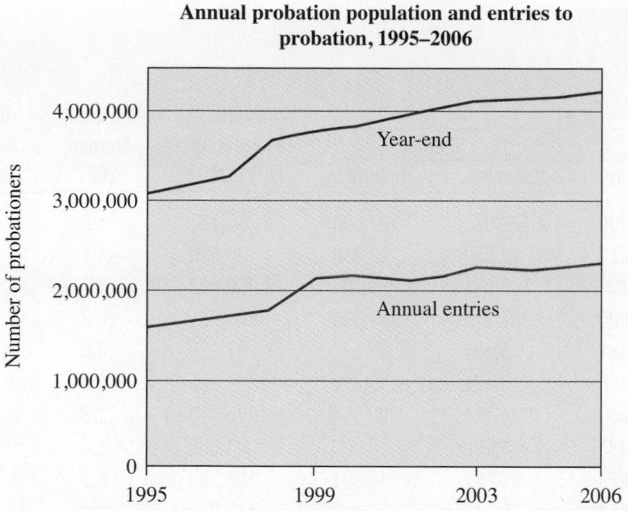

FIGURE 8–2 Annual Increases in Probation. *Source*: Glaze, L. E., & Bonczar, T. P. (2007). *Probation and parole in the United States, 2006*. Washington, DC: U.S. Department of Justice, Office of Justice Programs, Bureau of Justice Statistics.

There is great variation across the United States in terms of probation population (**TABLE 8–3**). Fewer than 25,000 offenders are serving federal probationary sentences with more than 99 percent of all probationers supervised by states. As shown in Table 8–3, the states with the largest probation populations are Texas, Georgia, California, Florida, and Ohio, with populations ranging between 430,301 and 240,706. Other states, such as New Hampshire, North Dakota, and Wyoming, have fewer than 5,000 people on probation.[22]

Among the total population of felons sentenced in state courts, 28 percent are sentenced to probation. As shown in **TABLE 8–4**, this includes 20 percent of felons convicted of violent offenses, 30 percent of felons convicted of property offenses, 30 percent of felons convicted of drug offenses, 27 percent of felons convicted of weapon offenses, and 29 percent of felons convicted of other offenses.

The average length of a straight probation sentence (not including jail time) among felons sentenced in state courts is 38 months or slightly more than 3 years (**TABLE 8–5**). The length of the probation sentence depends on the type of crime for which the felon was convicted. For instance, the average probation sentence for violent offenses was 44 months or nearly 4 years. The average sentence length for property offenses, drug offenses, and other offenses was 38 months. Probationers convicted of weapon offenses received on average a sentence of 34 months.[23]

About 57 percent of the probation population was directly sentenced to probation without any other correctional sanction. Ten percent of offenders received a **split sentence**, which included incarceration and probation, and 31 percent of probationers received a suspended probation sentence. Approximately 70 percent of probationers are serving an active sentence, 9 percent are inactive, and 10 percent have absconded; however, just 6 percent of the probation population has an active warrant for his or her arrest (for absconding or some other criminal complaint). Among offenders leaving probation, the success rate is fairly modest with 59 percent of probationers successfully completing their sentence, but 16 percent are incarcerated for new violations, 3 percent abscond, 1 percent of probationers die while serving their sentence, and the remaining 20 percent are unsuccessful for unspecified reasons.[24]

TABLE 8-3 American Probation Population

Region and Jurisdiction	Probation Population, 1/1/2007	2007				Probation Population 12/31/2007	Percent Change, 2007	Number on Probation per 100,000 Adult Residents, 12/31/2007
		Entries		Exits				
		Reported	Imputed	Reported	Imputed			
U.S. total	4,215,361	2,183,333	2,373,900	2,122,681	2,282,500	4,293,163	1.8	1,873
Federal	24,465	11,815	11,815	12,830	12,830	23,450	–4.1	10
State	4,190,896	2,171,518	2,362,100	2,109,851	2,269,700	4,269,713	1.9	1,863
Northeast	700,556	219,222	285,900	222,276	284,500	701,951	0.2	1,657
Connecticut	54,314	28,681	28,681	25,502	25,502	57,493	5.9	2,136
Maine	7,919	3,625	3,625	3,691	3,691	7,853	–0.8	754
Massachusetts	172,383	94,000	94,000	90,964	90,964	175,419	1.8	3,484
New Hampshire	4,590	3,080	3,080	3,020	3,020	4,650	1.3	454
New Jersey	133,158	40,223	40,223	46,991	46,991	126,390	–5.1	1,901
New York	122,359	36,952	36,952	39,348	39,348	119,963	–2.0	804
Pennsylvania	172,184	2,534	69,300	2,180	64,500	176,987	2.8	1,829
Rhode Island	26,017	5,747	5,747	5,627	5,627	26,137	0.5	3,167
Vermont	7,632	4,380	4,380	4,953	4,953	7,059	–7.5	1,436
Midwest	998,775	564,966	636,600	551,617	622,200	1,012,378	1.4	2,008
Illinois	141,000	59,734	59,734	57,944	57,944	142,790	1.3	1,471
Indiana	128,655	96,049	96,049	98,142	98,142	126,562	–1.6	2,646
Iowa	22,622	15,924	15,924	15,770	15,770	22,276	0.7	996
Kansas	15,518	20,084	20,084	19,471	19,471	16,131	4.0	771
Michigan	181,024	81,022	132,300	80,140	129,900	182,706	0.9	2,392
Minnesota	126,616	79,731	79,731	78,550	78,550	127,797	0.9	3,226
Missouri	55,098	25,933	25,933	24,791	24,791	56,240	2.1	1,256
Nebraska	18,731	14,896	14,896	14,717	14,717	18,910	1.0	1,417
North Dakota	4,320	2,995	2,995	2,847	2,847	4,468	3.4	896
Ohio	244,512	139,794	160,100	128,862	149,700	254,898	4.2	2,917
South Dakota	5,661	3,698	3,698	3,489	3,489	5,870	3.7	972
Wisconsin	55,018	25,106	25,106	26,894	26,894	53,230	–3.2	1,237
South	1,719,489	960,812	997,100	936,524	953,400	1,750,300	1.8	2,091
Alabama	46,367	20,101	20,101	14,723	14,723	51,745	11.6	1,468
Arkansas	31,166	9,368	9,368	8,858	8,858	31,676	1.6	1,476
Delaware	16,958	15,334	15,334	15,596	15,596	16,696	–1.5	2,513
District of Columbia	6,670	5,004	5,004	5,189	5,189	6,485	–2.8	1,362

(*continued*)

History

In the earliest forms of English criminal justice, probation was nowhere to be found. The common law tradition was very harsh, including the widespread application of corporal punishments, such as branding, flogging, and mutilation; and capital punishment for more than 100 offenses, many of them trivial. Over time, the citizenry grew uneasy over the brutality and perceived ineffectiveness of this type of justice, and eventually more progressive policies were developed. For instance, the practice of **binding over for good behavior** was an early form of community release that sometimes took the form of a pardon and other times of a suspended sentence. The person recognized as the founder of probation is **Matthew Davenport Hill**, an English attorney and judicial officer. Hill noticed a distinction within the criminal population. Whereas many offenders appeared to be committed to a life of crime and vice, others appeared amenable to rehabilitation. For offenders for whom there was a sense of hope and optimism that they could recover,

TABLE 8-3 *(Continued)*

Region and Jurisdiction	Probation Population, 1/1/2007	2007 Entries Reported	2007 Entries Imputed	2007 Exits Reported	2007 Exits Imputed	Probation Population 12/31/2007	Percent Change, 2007	Number on Probation per 100,000 Adult Residents, 12/31/2007
South *(continued)*								
Florida	272,242	236,182	243,000	233,891	239,700	274,079	0.7	1,917
Georgia	432,436	281,252	281,252	278,327	278,327	435,361	0.7	6,144
Kentucky	36,396	12,210	12,200	9,596	9,600	42,510	16.8	1,306
Louisiana	38,145	14,887	14,887	14,026	14,026	39,006	2.3	1,208
Maryland	94,100	36,786	55,200	32,416	32,400	98,470	4.6	2,301
Mississippi	24,107	9,773	9,773	12,257	12,257	21,623	−10.3	1,001
North Carolina	110,419	66,432	66,432	65,405	65,405	111,446	0.9	1,612
Oklahoma	**	**	13,800	**	13,000	**		
South Carolina	43,284	13,968	13,968	14,531	14,531	42,721	−1.3	1,264
Tennessee	52,057	23,686	23,686	23,024	23,024	56,179	7.9	1,190
Texas	431,967	182,948	182,948	180,606	180,606	434,309	0.5	2,485
Virginia	48,144	28,439	28,439	24,629	24,629	51,954	7.9	877
West Virginia	7,668	1,627	1,700	1,452	1,500	7,890	2.9	533
West	772,076	426,518	422,500	399,434	409,500	805,084	4.3	1,528
Alaska	6,111	1,215	1,215	910	910	6,416	5.0	1,269
Arizona	73,265	29,352	29,352	25,787	25,787	76,830	4.9	1,627
California	346,495	195,554	195,554	188,080	188,080	353,969	2.2	1,295
Colorado	63,032	47,993	48,500	33,351	33,900	77,635	23.2	2,094
Hawaii	18,598	6,522	6,522	5,694	5,694	19,426	4.5	1,934
Idaho	48,609	39,657	39,657	39,603	39,603	48,663	0.1	4,405
Montana	8,763	4,125	4,125	3,782	3,782	9,106	3.9	1,223
Nevada	13,208	7,549	7,549	7,296	7,296	13,461	1.9	697
New Mexico	17,878	3,484	7,600	3,042	4,700	20,774	16.2	1,400
Oregon	43,988	16,968	16,968	17,224	17,224	43,732	−0.6	1,504
Utah	10,417	5,542	5,542	5,130	5,130	10,829	4.0	584
Washington	116,487	66,041	77,400	67,152	75,000	118,885	2.1	2,390
Wyoming	5,225	2,516	2,516	2,383	2,383	5,358	2.5	1,334

Source: Glaze, L. E., & Bonczar, T. P. (2008). *Probation and parole in the United States, 2007*. Washington, DC: U.S. Department of Justice, Office of Justice Programs, Bureau of Justice Statistics.

TABLE 8-4 **Felony Sentences in State Courts**

Most Serious Conviction Offense	Total	Incarceration: Prison	Incarceration: Jail	Nonincarceration: Probation	Nonincarceration: Other
All offenses	100%	40	30	28	2
Violent offenses	100%	54	24	20	2
Property offenses	100%	37	31	30	2
Drug offenses	100%	37	30	30	3
Weapon offenses	100%	44	28	27	1
Other offenses	100%	34	35	29	2

Source: Durose, M. R., & Langan, P. A. (2007). *Felony sentences in state courts, 2004*. Washington, DC: U.S. Department of Justice, Office of Justice Programs, Bureau of Justice Statistics.

TABLE 8-5 Length of Sentences for Felony Convictions in State Courts

Most Serious Conviction Offense	Incarceration Total	Incarceration Prison	Incarceration Jail	Straight Probation
All offenses	37 mo	57 mo	6 mo	38 mo
Violent offenses	68	92	7	44
Property offenses	29	45	6	38
Drug offenses	31	51	6	38
Weapon offenses	32	47	7	34
Other offenses	24	41	6	38

Note: Means exclude life and death sentences.

Source: Durose, M. R., & Langan, P. A. (2007). *Felony sentences in state courts, 2004.* Washington, DC: U.S. Department of Justice, Office of Justice Programs, Bureau of Justice Statistics.

Hill released them to family members or guardians who vouched for the offender. In addition, police officers would periodically visit the offender to ensure he or she was making progress.

In the United States, probation, Latin for a period of proving or trial, began in 1841 and is credited as the invention of **John Augustus**. Augustus was a Boston shoemaker of financial means who secured the release of a confirmed alcoholic arrested for being a common drunk by acting as surety for him. At sentencing, Augustus asked the judge to defer sentencing for 3 weeks and to release the defendant to his custody. After 3 weeks, the offender convinced the judge of his rehabilitation and received a fine. The period of community correction alleviated the need for jail and probation was born. Until his death in 1859, Augustus supervised approximately 1,800 persons and incurred liability of nearly $250,000.

Augustus was selective as to who he would supervise. The ideal candidate was a first-time offender facing a nonserious charge who had moral character and demonstrated potential for reforming his or her criminal behavior. Augustus also developed the basic operating procedure of the modern probation system, including the following:

1. Conducting a presentence investigation
2. Mandating probation conditions
3. Developing a caseload, reporting to the court
4. Revoking the sentence[25]

In the same way that English criminal justice softened over time, reformers in the United States increasingly preferred community-based programs as opposed to confinement. During the Progressive Era, from circa 1890 to 1920, probation became widely used by criminal justice practitioners supervising juvenile offenders.[26] In 1878, Massachusetts became the first state to formally adopt probation for juveniles. All other states followed between 1878 and 1938, and by 1956 all states and the federal system had adult probation.[27] The following time line contains some of the highlights in the history of probation:

- 1841 John Augustus developed probation in the United States.
- 1878 Massachusetts introduced probation for juveniles.
- 1916 In *Ex parte United States*, the Supreme Court held that federal courts had no power to suspend criminal sentences and suggested probation legislation as a remedy.[28]

- 1925 President Calvin Coolidge signed the **Probation Act**, which established probation as a sentence in the federal courts and authorized the appointment of probation officers.
- 1940 Oversight of federal probation transferred from the Bureau of Prisons to the Administrative Office of the U.S. Courts based on the rationale that officers are appointed by the court and subject to its direction.
- 1954 All states had juvenile probation.
- 1956 All states had adult probation.
- 1973 In ***Gagnon v. Scarpelli***, the Supreme Court held that probationers are entitled to due process for preliminary and final hearings before probation can be revoked.[29]
- 1986 The Bureau of Justice Assistance funded a large-scale (14 sites in nine states) implementation and study of ISP.[30]
- 1987 In ***Griffin v. Wisconsin***, the Supreme Court held that warrantless searches of probationers' homes by probation officers is reasonable under the Fourth Amendment.[31]
- 1989 All states had ISP.
- 1994 The Violent Crime Control and Law Enforcement Act required a drug testing program for federal offenders on probation and toughened laws on address change/notification for certain criminal offenders on probation.

Throughout its history, probation has been at the center of controversy between crime control enthusiasts who favor stricter, more punitive supervision of offenders, such as prison, and progressives who favor the use of community-based corrections to inexpensively allow offenders to work toward their rehabilitation. Interestingly, probation has been criticized as an ineffective correctional sanction from both the political left and right. For instance, juvenile detention and probation came under fire in the 1970s based on the results of two correctional experiments. The **Provo Experiment** was an intermediate sanction conducted from 1959 to 1965 in Utah that provided community-based, nonresidential, unstructured, group-oriented treatment unlike the traditional methods of probation. Because the Provo Experiment was largely unstructured, youths had to rely on themselves to participate in activities that would serve to rehabilitate them. Follow-up

CORRECTIONS IN THE NEWS

Probation for First-Time Offender Who Mailed Bloody Cow's Head to Wife's Lover

Jason Michael Fife, upset over his wife's love affair, sent a bloody cow's head to the object of his wife's affection—her lover. Fife obtained the frozen cow's head from a local butcher shop under the pretense that he was going to use the skull for decoration. Fife mailed the head before it thawed so as not to alert the carrier. The box containing the frozen cow's head was delivered and left on the victim's doorstep. As the temperature that day climbed, the head began to thaw. The victim returned home, found the blood-soaked box and called police. Police then traced the delivery. And according to court records, the police were also able to trace threatening e-mails sent to the victim by Fife. Fife faces 2 years of probation and 50 hours of community service. If he successfully completes both court-ordered sanctions, his record will be expunged. Fife and his wife have since reconciled.

Source: Associated Press. (2008). *Even though it seemed the perfect gift.* Retrieved October 1, 2008, from http://www.msnbc.msn.com/id/22560285/.

was conducted 4 years after release, and youths who participated in the Provo Experiment fared the same as youths placed on probation in terms of reoffending.[32]

A second project known as the **Silverlake Experiment** was conducted between 1964 and 1968 in Los Angeles. Again, youths who received community treatment did not pose any added risk to public safety compared to those who received traditional sentences such as probation and detention.[33] Based on these experiments, it could be argued that at least for juveniles, probation is an overly harsh punishment that provides no advantage over community treatment in terms of public safety.

In 1979, a far different valuation of probation was made by Charles Murray and Louis Cox in their book, *Beyond Probation: Juvenile Corrections and the Chronic Delinquent*.[34] In their study, Murray and Cox compared the recidivism rates of 317 juvenile delinquents sentenced to institutions to 266 offenders placed in community-based programs under the Unified Delinquency Intervention Services program, which included probation, nonresidential services, residential services, wilderness programs, out-of-town camps, and intensive inpatient psychiatric counseling. Standard probation created a **suppression effect** or reduction in annual arrests of about 37 percent, whereas the reformatory created a suppression effect of more than 68 percent. All of the other programs also suppressed delinquency with the greatest reductions (82 percent) shown among the 11 youths placed in intensive treatment. In terms of crime control, *Beyond Probation* showed that the justice system should rely chiefly on incarceration for reductions in crime, not probation. Their conclusion generated considerable controversy.[35]

In the early 1980s, probation underwent a change with the advent of a new form of probation, known as intensive supervised probation, or ISP. First used in Georgia, ISP is a way to alleviate prison crowding and the need for prison expansion by supervising high-rate, serious offenders in the community. Because ISP is characterized by more intensive and frequent supervision, greater monitoring, increased surveillance and substance abuse monitoring, and overall more stringent conditions, ISP was hailed as an improvement on traditional probation, which was often viewed as little more than a slap on the wrist. Unfortunately, early evaluations of ISP were mostly negative. The programs did not decrease the frequency or seriousness of new arrests, but because of the increased monitoring, resulted in more technical and rule violations, revocations, and prison terms. Depending on the jurisdiction, ISP programs made the probation problem even worse.[36]

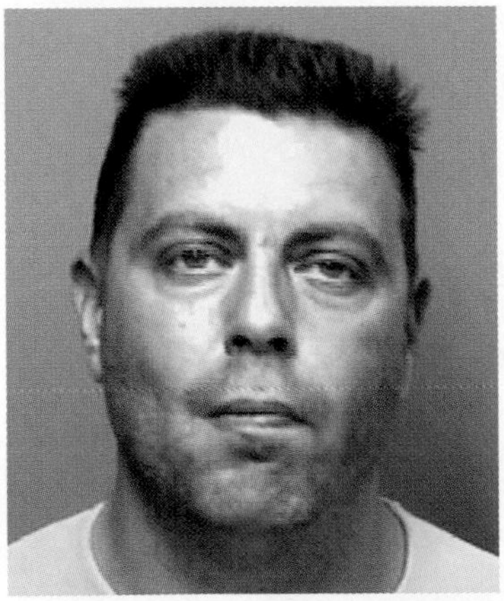

Probationer Joseph Smith was convicted of abducting, raping, and murdering 11-year-old Carlie Brucia and was sentenced to death in 2007. The case highlights the rare but atrocious situation where probationers commit heinous crimes while on supervision.

Whether probation represents an overly stringent and counterproductive sanction or a weak, liberal response to crime is open to debate. Usually that debate is between academic criminologists. However, when a probationer commits a heinous crime, the usefulness of probation becomes a national policy issue. For example, in 2004, a shocking crime gained worldwide attention and cast probation in a very negative light. Carlie Brucia, an 11-year-old Florida girl, was abducted, raped, and murdered. More shocking, the abduction was memorialized by a security camera that filmed the kidnapping, and Joseph Smith was arrested and convicted. For his crimes, Smith was sentenced in 2007 to death plus two life terms without the possibility of parole. He also had an extensive criminal history for drug possession, weapons violations, assault, and kidnapping charges and had prior sentences to prison and probation. Moreover, Smith was on felony probation for cocaine possession at the time of his capital crimes. For that reason, probation came under attack as an example of a community-based sanction that jeopardizes public safety.[37–38]

Administration and Caseloads

Unlike parole, which is always a state function administered by a single agency, probation is a local or state activity and is administered by 2,000 separate probationary agencies in the United States. Mark Cunniff and Ilene Bergsmann of the Bureau of Justice Statistics conducted a national assessment of probation in the United States and reported that more than 30 percent of probation agencies provide both pretrial and postadjudication services for both juvenile and adult offenders. Half of probation agencies are conjoined with parole services.[39] In the juvenile justice system, probation has a complex organizational structure. In some states, juvenile probation is administered at the state level, in other states it is locally administered, and in still other states both levels of administration are used. There is also variation in whether juvenile probation is a component of the judicial or the executive branch.[40]

Many correctional systems divert the least serious probationers to private probation agencies in order to save on state resources and reduce state probation caseloads.

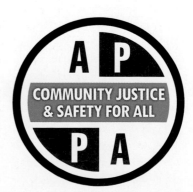

Like many areas of corrections, probation is also at times supervised by private as opposed to public or governmental entities. **Private probation** was first used in Florida in 1975 with the Salvation Army Misdemeanor Probation program, which supervised offenders convicted of low-level, misdemeanor crimes. Today, at least 10 states, including Colorado, Florida, Iowa, Missouri, Tennessee, and Utah employ private probation services to supplement probation services provided by local and state governments. In most cases, private probation is used to facilitate the lowest risk offenders. In this way, private probation provides services and oversight for clients whose criminality is not severe enough to warrant traditional probation supervision. In turn, traditional probation departments can focus almost exclusively on higher risk offenders. Phyllis Berry and Ralph Anderson evaluated a private probation agency that served 475 clients and found that upwards of 90 percent of them demonstrated positive behaviors, and the overwhelming majority of clients, especially those with stable employment, successfully completed the program.[41]

Not all private probation services supervise just misdemeanants, however. Due to the sheer size of the probation population, courts are increasingly relying on privatized probation services to also supervise felony offenders. For example, the Center for Creative Justice in Ames, Iowa, is a restorative justice organization whose mission is to help community members achieve peaceful resolution of conflicts through individualized probation services, dispute resolution strategies, and community education. It receives funding from local tax revenue, charitable donations, and user fees. The center works closely with the criminal courts to supervise probationers and connect them with necessary service providers. In part because of the low risk of their clients, the Center for Creative Justice has very low recidivism rates and most clients successfully complete their sentences.[42]

There are also problems with private probation. A recent examination of private probation guidelines in Missouri showed several administrative concerns. For instance, they found that Missouri had (1) no statewide standardized guidelines for private agency approval, (2) no requirements to provide any verification of fee collection, (3) no educational and training requirements for staff, and (4) no requirements to carry insurance. The lack of consistent guidelines leaves the opportunity for wide discretion, inconsistencies in supervision, and possible conflicts of interest with other agencies.[43]

Probation is a labor-intensive function. The preponderance of a probation officer's time is spent conducting a PSI and writing a report for the courts. Supervision of clients is also a central responsibility. Most probationers receive conditions of their sentence and nearly 50 percent of probationers receive five or more conditions.[44] Usually, probationers report to the probation or other social service agency that is providing a service. Another important component of probation is the home visit, in which the probation officer visits the domicile of the offender to ensure that the client is leading a crime-free life. According to a survey conducted by the **American Probation and Parole Association**, the official professional organization for probation and parole officers, probation officers in 38 states or territories carry firearms primarily when conducting home visits.

A P
COMMUNITY JUSTICE & SAFETY FOR ALL
P A

The American Probation and Parole Association is the official professional organization for probation officers in the United States.

The ways that probation services are administered varies greatly, especially considering the caseload of probation officers. A **caseload** is the roster of probationary clients whom a single probation officer supervises. Douglas Thomas conducted a nationally

TABLE 8-6 Suggested Probation Caseloads

Adult Probationers	Client-to-Staff Ratio
Risk level	
Intensive	20:1
Moderate to high risk	50:1
Low risk	200:1
Administrative	No limit
Juvenile probationers	
Risk level	
Intensive	15:1
Moderate to high risk	30:1
Low risk	100:1
Administrative	No limit

Source: Modified from Burrell, B. (2006). *Caseload standards for probation and parole.* Lexington, KY: American Probation and Parole Association.

representative survey of 1,197 probation administrators and found that caseloads ranged from fewer than 10 cases to more than 400. The median caseload was 41, and the national average ranged from 100 to 175.[45] To put this into perspective, the Los Angeles County Probation Department has 900 line officers who supervise more than 90,000 adult and juvenile clients (it is the largest probation department in the world). The only way that probation officers can supervise such a large population is to place many offenders, even felony offenders, on automated or banked probation. In other words, they are not supervised at all.

The American Probation and Parole Association struggles with finding the ideal caseload size for probation clients. The recommended guidelines depend on whether adults or juveniles are being supervised and on the risk level of the offender (see TABLE 8-6). For adult intensive clients, a 20:1 case to staff ratio is recommended. For moderate to high risk, the ratio is 50:1. For low-risk clients, the ratio is 200:1 and for administrative or unsupervised clients, there is no limit. For juvenile intensive clients, a 15:1 case to staff ratio is recommended. The ratios for moderate, low, and administrative risks are 30:1, 100:1, and no limit, respectively.[46]

High caseloads are problematic in the sense that probation officers simply do not have the resources to adequately supervise, monitor, and provide treatment to their clients. Nationally, probation is woefully funded. For instance, although community corrections such as probation service more than 70 percent of correctional clients, the services receive just 15 percent of state budgetary allocations.[47]

If probationer officers are ill equipped to handle the vast number of clients on their caseload, the negative consequences exist for society and the probationer officer alike. Like all state officials, probation officers are generally protected from personal liability for injuries caused from acts performed within the scope of their public office. This means that, generally speaking, probationer officers are not legally liable for the criminal behavior of their clients. However, there are exceptions. Kathryn Morgan and her colleagues reviewed case law relevant to probation supervision and found that probation officers have been held legally liable for the crimes of their clients if they conducted their duties in a negligent manner, especially if the officer was aware of threats made against specific victims.[48]

CORRECTIONS RESEARCH

Psychological Inventory of Criminal Thinking Styles

Research has found that traditional psychotherapy programs are threatening and, when dealing with inmates who have substance use problems, often confrontational. It is widely known that both factors contribute to attrition rates of nearly 50 percent for inmates participating in traditional psychotherapy intervention programs, but dropout rates are lower in psychoeducational programs. Walters explains that the focus in a psychoeducational program is on self-management, and evidence seems to suggest that programs based on self-management principles are more readily accepted by inmates who would otherwise be considered at high risk for leaving a psychotherapy program. Many of the psychoeducational programs are also peer based, thus avoiding or minimizing the stigma commonly associated with clinicians' conducting group counseling sessions.

In a study published by Glenn Walters in 2004, federal inmates were assessed on the likelihood they would complete a psychoeducational program using a PICTS assessment. PICTS is the Psychological Inventory of Criminal Thinking Styles designed by Walters that measures eight criminal thinking styles. It is an 80-item, self-report survey designed to measure eight thinking styles believed to support a lifestyle characterized by consistent criminal offending. This instrument was administered to 207 male federal inmates enrolled in a 10-week psychoeducational program. Walters found that those inmates who dropped out of the psychoeducational program scored high on seven of the eight criminal thinking styles measured by the PICTS assessment instrument. This finding was also significant when controlling for demographics such as age, race, ethnicity, and marital status.

Walter concludes that findings from his study may explain why inmates who volunteer for prison programs elect not to complete them. Interestingly, Walters learned that of the thinking styles measured, attitudes of self-importance and the desire to control one's environment did not adversely impact the likelihood an inmate would complete the course. However, according to Walters, the tendency to blame consequences of one's actions on others, impulsivity, irresponsibility, and being easily sidetracked in the pursuit of one's goals were likely indicators that an inmate participating in this study would not complete the program.

Source: Walters, G. D. (2004). Predictors of early termination in a prison-based program of psychoeducation. *Prison Journal, 84,* 171–183.

Interestingly, the research community has produced mixed findings about the effects of probation officer caseload on probationer recidivism. Robert Carter and Leslie Wilkins conducted the seminal San Francisco Project that compared the recidivism of four groups of probationers who were supervised by officers with caseloads ranging from 20 to several hundred. After 2 years, all four groups had violation rates of about 25 percent; however, offenders for officers with the highest caseload had dramatically higher violation rates. In other words, increased supervision increased the likelihood of detecting violations.[49] Subsequent research has been mixed, but most studies find that as probation caseloads increased, so did the crime rates of probationers. John Worrall and his colleagues even found a relationship between high probation caseloads and the property crime rate in California.[50]

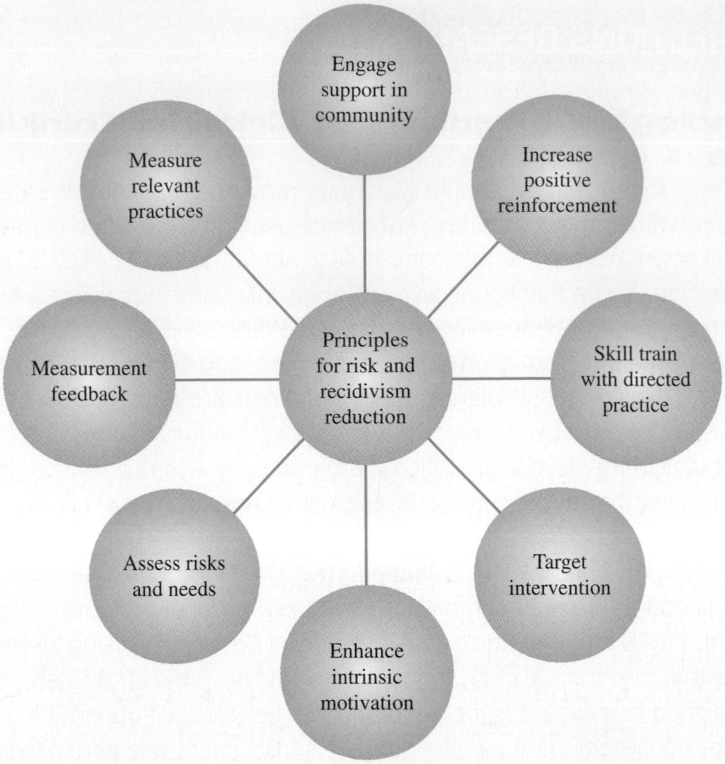

FIGURE 8–3 Eight Guiding Principles for Risk/Recidivism Reduction. *Source*: Modified from Justice System Assessment & Training. (2006). *About EBP in community corrections.* Retrieved June 2, 2008, from http://www.j-sat.com/TrainingServices/EvidenceBasedPractices.aspx.

The Criminality of Probationers

Recall that there are many types of probation to provide supervision for the range of criminality of probationers. Many probationers are so low risk in terms of their criminal history and threat to public safety that they are effectively not supervised. Instead, they are placed on unsupervised, automated, or banked probation. Low-level offenders, such as those on misdemeanor probation, tend to perform well, and upwards of 80 percent successfully complete their sentence. Of course, the same cannot be said of all probationers, especially persons on felony probation. Using the criminal records of 1,672 felony probationers in southern California, Joan Petersilia and her colleagues found that 65 percent were rearrested, 51 percent were reconvicted, and 34 were reincarcerated within a 3-year follow-up period.[51] This section explores the criminal offending and other relevant characteristics of probationers as well as factors that contribute to probation violations and ultimate revocation (see FIGURE 8–3).

Crime and Recidivism

By almost any measure, felony probationers are a group with pronounced criminal history, continued criminal involvement, and several overlapping problems that limit the likelihood of successful social adjustment. For instance, Kathleen Auerhahn's study of the California felony probationer population reported that 50 percent have at least one prior felony conviction and 22 percent have at least one prior *violent* felony conviction.[52]

Doris Layton MacKenzie and her colleagues interviewed 107 probationers from three areas of northern Virginia and measured their self-reported rates of offending in the year before being placed on probation and their current offending. The results were startling. In the year before their current probation, the 107 offenders *averaged*:

- 67 burglaries
- 43 thefts
- 251 forgeries
- 14 robberies
- 17 assaults
- 1,003 drug deals
- 642 other crimes

One offender reported 2,800 drug deals per month or 33,600 drug deals in 1 year. After these offenders were placed on probation, most of their criminal activity dropped precipitously. However, their criminal behavior did not disappear. The average annual offending rates while on probation were 3 burglaries, 11 thefts, 8 forgeries, 15 robberies, 3 assaults, 408 drug deals, and 200 annual crimes. MacKenzie and her colleagues' conclusion about the criminal activities of probationers is grim:

> Probation reduces the number of offenders who commit crimes and the rate of offending for those who continue to offend. Disappointingly, we found no evidence that what occurs during probation has any further impact on offenders . . . neither the addition of more intrusive conditions, nor the agent's knowledge of misbehavior, nor how the agent responds to misbehavior had any effect on the criminal activities or other misbehaviors of these probationers . . . although it appears that agents do respond when they receive information about misbehavior, there is little evidence that the response has any effect on changing the behavior of the offender.[53, p. 448]

Unfortunately, the high-rate criminality described in the above study is not limited to that small sample. National assessments of probationers similarly indicate a group with sustained criminal involvement. Robyn Cohen of the Bureau of Justice Statistics surveyed 13,986 inmates in 277 state correctional facilities nationwide to examine probation and parole violators serving time in prison in 1991. In that year, 162,000 probation violators were sentenced to prison. Nationally, the 162,000 probation violators committed:

- 6,400 murders (more than half of the victims were strangers)
- 7,400 rapes
- 10,400 aggravated assaults
- 17,000 robberies

Nearly half were using drugs on a daily basis. About 20 percent were convicted of new firearms charges even though felons are proscribed from possessing weapons. About 74 percent of probation violators were convicted of new criminal offenses and the remaining 26 percent had violated conditions of their probation.[54]

Patrick Langan and Mark Cunniff analyzed the offending patterns of 79,000 probationers from 17 states. They found that within 3 years, 62 percent of probationers were either rearrested for another felony or had a disciplinary hearing for violating the terms of their probation. Moreover, 46 percent were returned to jail or prison or absconded. They found that the average felony probationer had multiple conditions to address his or her substance abuse and mental health needs, and was responsible for restitution, supervision fees, and court costs. Fewer than half of probationers actually met these financial responsibilities.[55–56]

Probation Violation and Revocation

Based on the extensive criminal activity of many probationers, it is often a matter of time before probationers are in violation of their sentence and eligible for revocation. Many criminologists have studied the factors that contribute to probation violation and revocation. For instance, based on data from nearly 700 Texas offenders, Patricia Harris and her colleagues compared probation violators and probationers who were arrested for new offenses. They found that 60 percent violated the conditions of their probation and 40 percent were rearrested (one third of which were for a felony offense). Perhaps more troubling was the behavioral history of these probationers; for example, 41 percent had a history of armed or assaultive crimes, 63 percent had criminal companions, 63 percent had employment problems, 74 percent had educational deficits, and nearly 40 percent had previously been confined or placed on community supervision.[57]

In her review of the probation literature, Kathryn Morgan identified nine factors that predicted probationary outcomes, such as violation and revocation.[58] These are:

- *Criminal history*: Unquestionably the strongest indicator of whether a probationer will succeed is his or her criminal past. Offenders with multiple prior arrests, convictions, and sentences are more likely than first-time offenders to recidivate. For example, Michelle Meloy studied nearly 1,000 sex offenders on probation sampled from 17 states and found that variables such as number of prior felonies, prior jail sentences, and drug use history were significantly related to probation failure, sexual recidivism, or nonsexual recidivism.[59]
- *Property offending*: Property offenders are often embedded in a criminal lifestyle in which property crimes, such as burglary and theft, are means to obtain money for narcotics. Property offenders, who are also usually drug offenders, tend to commit crimes at higher rates, which often results in poor performance on probation.[60]
- *Employment and marital status*: Persons who are employed and have a greater **stake in conformity**, or commitment to conventional, prosocial behaviors and responsibilities, are likely to succeed on probation. Unemployed offenders, particularly chronically unemployed offenders, frequently violate probation. Married probationers fare better on probation than nonmarried clients. In their study of nearly 3,000 North Carolina offenders on felony probation, Barbara Sims and Mark Jones found that married offenders with stable employment were among the most likely offenders to successfully complete probation without incident.[61]
- *Gender*: Women tend to perform better on probation than men, particularly when women have stable living situations and conventional peers in their lives.[62] Also, probationers who have been convicted of the most serious crimes, such as predatory sex offenses, overwhelmingly tend to be men. Thus, the risks of violation for men are higher.[63]
- *Age*: Younger offenders are more likely to violate the terms of their probation, whereas older probationers, such as those over age 35, are likely to successfully comply with probation. Older offenders perform better on probation because of natural declines in their criminal activity, greater perspective on the consequences of continued criminal behavior, and being better equipped than adolescent offenders to handle the rigors of their sentence.[64]
- *Education*: Generally, the more educated a probationer is, the more likely he or she will successfully complete the terms of his or her sentence. Using data on probationers from Michigan, Roni Mayzer and her colleagues found probation absconders and violators were noteworthy for their low educational attainment.[65–66]
- *Race*: While the evidence is mixed, most studies show that African Americans are more likely than Whites to recidivate while on probation, and their probation is

more likely to be revoked. Competing explanations for this have been offered. Michael Tapia and Patricia Harris examined the odds that White, Black, and Hispanic males would have their probation revoked. African Americans were twice as likely as Whites to have their probation revoked, and Hispanic revocation rates were comparable to those of Whites. Moreover, employed Blacks were twice as likely as unemployed Whites to have probation revoked, suggesting a penalty for African Americans.[67] There is also evidence that African Americans choose to terminate their probation. Mark Jones found that 8 percent of probationers **elect to serve** prison time instead of probation, and Blacks were significantly more likely than Whites to choose prison over probation.[68]

- *Sentence length*: Lengthier probation terms are associated with greater likelihood of violations because offenders have a longer period in the community in which they must abide by probation conditions.

Probation success stories include those of offenders who reintegrate and reattach, or commit for the first time, to conventional social institutions, such as employment, marriage and family, and sobriety. For those who fail on probation, there is little to no attachment to these conventional institutions, and those who fail instead revert to habitual criminal behavior.[69] Of course, whether a probationer violates and has his or her probation revoked is ultimately the decision of his or her probation officer. Due to the high-risk backgrounds of many probationers, probation departments have developed a fairly high tolerance for certain types of misconduct, noncompliance, and even criminal activity among their clients. For instance, Mark Jones and John Kerbs surveyed federal probation officers and reported that 11 percent of respondents indicated that they worked in districts where there were formal administrative policies that limited punitive actions for certain technical violations. In other words, the discretion an officer has whether to cite probationers for violations is determined by departmental policy, not necessarily by the offender misconduct.[70]

Evaluations of Probation

Does probation work? This question is the central concern of criminal justice officials who rely on community corrections to balance the goals of public safety, rehabilitation, and cost-effectively managing government. The primary measure of success for probation is recidivism, or the rate that probationers reoffend within some specific time period, such as during their probationary sentence or 1 year after discharge. It is important to note that the success of probation is largely contingent on the criminality of the study group. For example, between 75 and 80 percent of offenders placed on probation successfully complete their sentence. This seems remarkable; however, the overwhelming majority of these successes are those who were convicted of misdemeanor offenses. Generally, misdemeanant probationers are persons for whom an isolated conviction for drunk driving constitutes their criminal record, and as such it is relatively easy for them to complete a probationary sentence.[71] For felony probationers and/or offenders with extensive criminal history, the results are far less impressive. The final section of this chapter reviews prior evaluation studies of various types of probation sentences with special attention paid to *what works* for effective probation supervision that produces the most favorable outcomes for offenders.

There have been many evaluations of probation programs; unfortunately, it is often difficult to draw conclusions about the effectiveness of probation because the programs often encompass different populations of offenders. Probation can pertain to adolescents who have been diverted, adolescents who have been convicted and are serving a community-based sentence, juveniles and adults who have served a brief period of confinement and are then supervised in the community, adults who have been convicted of federal crimes, and persons convicted of a range of crimes—from drunk driving to sex offenses, drug offenses to property offenses, nuisance to violent crimes.

Some probation programs oversee clients who are so low risk that they are not even formally supervised, whereas other programs are intensive, restrictive, last-ditch efforts for serious offenders who are likely heading to prison. Some probationers are persons with no criminal history and stable community ties, whereas other probationers are career criminals who have decades-long involvement with the justice system. In his classic review of 100 evaluations of correctional programs, Walter Bailey indicated that about 50 percent of programs were effective for some offenders, but that 25 percent had either no effect or actually increased recidivism. Much of this variation depended on the characteristics of the study group and the correctional program, prompting Bailey to conclude that evidence supporting the efficacy of correctional treatment is slight, inconsistent, and of questionable reliability.[72, p. 157]

What Works with Juvenile Probationers?

The area of probation that has historically received the most research attention is juvenile probation. Ted Palmer and Robert Wedge studied the effectiveness of juvenile probation camps, which were alternatives to confinement in the California juvenile justice system among nearly 3,000 juvenile offenders. In a 2-year follow-up, 65 percent of the former juvenile probationers were recontacted for a delinquent offense, and nearly 30 percent were committed to a state correctional institution. Palmer and Wedge reported that probation camps that provided more services, such as counseling/casework, vocational training, work details, academic training, religious activities, recreation, off-facility activities, and outside contacts tended to produce better outcomes.[73] Matthew Giblin evaluated the Anchorage, Alaska, Coordinated Agency Network (CAN) program, which included enhanced services and supervision for juvenile probationers. The CAN program consisted of intensified surveillance and monitoring compared to traditional juvenile probation. Giblin found that although there were no differences in recidivism between the groups, about 30 percent of youths serving a CAN sentence were cited for technical violations compared to 17 percent on traditional probation. The greater monitoring resulted in more accountability among juvenile probationers, thus providing a more rigorous probation experience that also kept recidivism low.[74]

The increased monitoring of probationers often leads to increased collaboration between agencies within the juvenile and criminal justice systems. An example is **police–probation partnerships**, in which juvenile probation officers go on patrol with law enforcement officers to conduct home visits of probationers; explain the terms of the sentence to the probationer; conduct searches of probationers for drugs, weapons, and other contraband; and provide basic services. One example is Operation Nightlight in San Bernardino, California, where police and probation officers searched juvenile probationers' homes, conducted return home visits, enforced curfew, conducted school contacts, and generally monitored clients. John Worrall and Larry Gaines evaluated Operation Nightlight and found that the police–probation partnership resulted in reduced juvenile arrests for serious crimes including assault, burglary, and theft.[75]

The need for multiple services is important because youths on juvenile probation often have multiple risk factors for continued involvement in delinquency. For instance, a recent evaluation of probation supervised youths in Cuyahoga County, Ohio, including Cleveland, found that they often had multiple prior involvements in the juvenile justice system; were from family backgrounds characterized by poverty, abuse, and adoption; and suffered from an array of social and behavioral problems.[76] Backgrounds characterized by abuse and delinquency often make for challenging probation clients. Sarah Vidal and Jennifer Skeem studied the effects of abuse history and psychopathic personality among juvenile probationers on the decision making of juvenile probation officers. They found that probation officers viewed youths with abuse histories and psychopathic traits as challenging, difficult-to-reach clients. Probation officers felt compassion for youths who had been abused and often went the extra mile in terms of providing greater support, resources, and assistance. Conversely, psychopathic youths were subjected to greater supervision, were viewed as unlikely to be successfully treated, and received little pity from probation officers.[77] In other words, certain risk factors can guide the type of supervision juvenile clients receive on probation.

Because of this situation, some juvenile probation programs began to focus on the strengths of the adolescent rather than concentrate just on risk factors. For example, Riley County, Kansas, initiated the Juvenile Intake and Assessment Case Management approach, which utilizes the client's assets and talents to help achieve program goals, increase involvement in prosocial activities, formalize family networks, and identify school and work opportunities. The program takes a can-do, proactive philosophy so that the adolescent can observe ways to effect prosocial change in his or her life. Don Kurtz and Travis Linnemann evaluated the strengths approach and found that youths on the program performed better than those on traditional probation and significantly better than youths on intensive probation.[78]

Some research studies found little to no difference in recidivism outcomes between various types of probation and probation versus confinement. Preston Elrod and Kevin Minor evaluated Project Explore, which is a juvenile probation program that consists of outdoor adventures, social skills training, and parent skills training and compared it to standard probation. They found that youths in Project Explore performed about the same as youths on standard probation, suggesting that the specialized and unique treatment protocols did little to reduce delinquency.[79]

Jodi Lane and her colleagues assessed probation outcomes among youths in the South Oxnard Challenge Project (SOCP), which was an experimental probation study with more than a 2-year follow-up. Unlike routine probation services, the SOCP approach used an interagency service team, focused interventions on the family, had a graduated period of intervention, and used more than 10 social service providers, victim services, and other community resources. Overall, youths on SOCP had *14 times* as many monthly contacts than youths on routine juvenile probation. Yet for both SOCP and routine probation groups, slightly more than 50 percent were referred or arrested during the intervention period and nearly 60 percent were rearrested 18 months later. Other behavioral outcomes, such as drug use, completion of community service, payment of restitution, and compliance were also similar. This suggests that despite greater efforts by the juvenile justice system to provide services, the ultimate outcomes were the same as status quo probation.[80]

Noted researchers Mark Lipsey and David Wilson conducted a **meta-analysis**, which is a quantitative study of research findings, of 200 studies of correctional interventions for serious and violent juvenile offenders within institutions and serving noninstitutional sentences, such as probation. Their study reflects the state of the art of what is known about correctional interventions among the most delinquent youth. Among noninstitutionalized offenders including probationers:

- Individual counseling, interpersonal skills counseling, and behavioral programs produced the most consistently positive treatment effects. Probation programs that incorporate these modalities are likely to produce the best outcomes with adolescents on juvenile probation.
- Probation programs that utilize multiple services and require payment of restitution have positive effects, although the evidence is less consistent.
- Work and education programs, advocacy/casework, and family and group counseling produced inconsistent but generally positive effects among adolescent probationers.

- Probation programs that focus on reduced caseloads for probation officers are at best weakly related to probation outcomes. Overall, there appears to be no significant relationship between caseload size and probationer performance.
- Probation programs that use wilderness components, early release, deterrence, and vocational programs have no effect on probationer success.[81]

What Works with Adult Probationers?

For important reasons, the criminal justice system invests in probation. The costs of supervising a felon on probation are *10 to 15 times* less expensive than prison. For the highest risk felons who are placed on ISP, the costs are approximately 150 percent higher than standard probation, but still dramatically cheaper than prison. For no other reason than these sheer differences in costs, probation will continue to grow the correctional population.[82] In addition to fiscal constraints, there are other administrative concerns as well as ethical concerns as to whether probation achieves or cheapens justice. For instance, Michael Geerken and Hennessey Hayes note that because probation is such a break compared to incarceration, many defendants willingly accept plea bargains for probationary sentences. Without the availability of probation, more offenders would opt for trials, which would secure far fewer convictions than pleas. Consequently, probation is a vital cog in the criminal justice system because it is a middle-ground sanction that serves the interests of most offenders.[83]

For adult probationers, much of the evaluation research has focused on ISP programs that address the highest risk, felonious offenders. In her review of the ISP literature, Joan Petersilia arrived at four major conclusions:

1. Most ISP programs have been probation-enhancement programs that sought to toughen the sanction with stricter enforcement, more technical violations, and greater revocation. As a result, most ISP programs have not been cost-effective since reduced costs of community supervision were offset by higher revocation and reincarceration costs.
2. Well-implemented ISP programs restore credibility to the justice system with their use of mandatory work and drug-testing requirements to target the range of serious offenders.
3. ISP programs have been effective at coercing offenders into drug treatment and continuing with that treatment.
4. ISP programs that deliver doses of both treatment and surveillance are most effective. For instance, offenders who received drug counseling, held jobs, paid restitution, and did community service were arrested at rates 10 to 20 percent lower than offenders who did not meet these responsibilities.[84]

In another overview of these programs, Edward Latessa and his colleagues acknowledged that although ISP has neither greatly alleviated prison crowding nor greatly reduced recidivism, it is a more effective form of punishment than prison in the sense that it delivers more treatment and reduces system costs.[85]

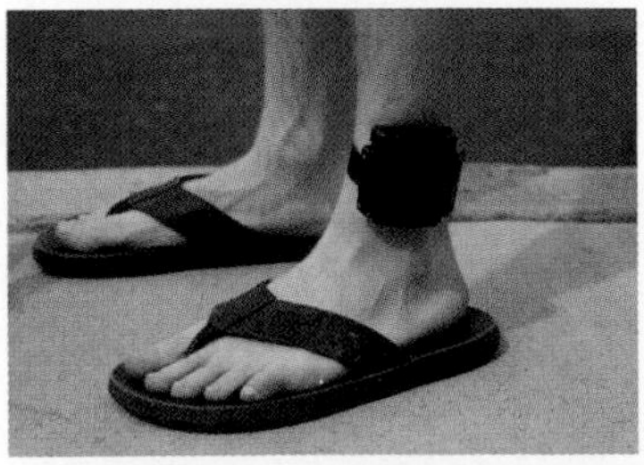

ISP uses increased surveillance and monitoring to ensure compliance of felony probationers who have the greatest correctional needs.

As this chapter has shown, probation is commonly viewed as a failure especially when judged by the recidivism rates of probationers, the problem behaviors that felony probationers demonstrate, or the isolated but significant heinous crimes occasionally committed by persons on probation. However, probation *does* work for some adult offenders—even high-risk felons with multiple problems. For instance, a recurrent theme in the criminological literature is that probationary systems that combine a law enforcement and treatment function tend to work better than probation policies that simply supervise clients and therefore serve as a proxy for the police. Paul Gendreau and his colleagues argued that the next generation of probation and intermediate sanctions generally could be described as intensive rehabilitation supervision, since the blending of treatment/social work and punishment yields the most fruit when supervising offenders in the community.[86]

There are several examples of promising probation programs that blend treatment with punishment, including:

- *Therapeutic community probation (TCP):* Therapeutic community probation integrates treatment and supervision within a controlled residential setting. The programs allow probationers to address the underlying addictions that often accompany antisocial behavior. A recent evaluation of a TCP program in Dallas, Texas, found that a mere 4 percent of TCP graduates were arrested over a 1-year follow-up, which is more than four times lower than the arrest rate of offenders receiving traditional probation.[87]
- *Probation case management (PCM):* Under the PCM model, probation officers act as case managers supervised by outside consultants with special emphasis on therapy and client advocacy, uniform client screening and assessment, and referrals to health and human services. A recent evaluation of a PCM program in San Francisco found the approach was helpful at directing clients toward the appropriate agency to provide needed psychiatric and other services.[88]
- *Cognitive therapy:* Many problem behaviors that probationers have are underscored by antisocial thinking styles or lifestyle patterns that contribute to criminal involvement. The National Institute of Corrections has a program called Thinking for a Change, which uses role-playing, instruction, group therapy, and even homework to instill prosocial interpersonal and problem-solving skills among probationers. A recent evaluation showed a 33 percent reduction in new offense crimes among probationers who completed the Thinking for a Change program.[89]
- *Strategic antiviolence units (SAV-U)*: Strategic antiviolence units were developed by University of Pennsylvania criminologists who worked in collaboration with criminal justice practitioners in Philadelphia. SAV-U teams include a probation officer with a caseload of 15 clients rated to be at high risk for homicide victimization (felony probationers in Philadelphia were murdered at a rate that was *20 times* the national homicide victimization rate). Probation clients received intensive treatment, counseling, therapy, and other individualized attention to address their specific criminogenic needs. It is believed that intensive, individualized attention will be effective at reducing homicide offending and victimization among serious felony probationers.[90]
- *Local life circumstances:* In addition to formal programs, probation officers recognize that the day-to-day life circumstances of offenders and the people they associate with are powerful predictors of whether they desist from crime. Probation officers encourage association with family members and friends who are employed, sober, and committed to clean living. On the other hand, social bonds with persons who are active offenders, substance abusers, gun carriers, and gang members are discouraged. Overall, positive role models can serve as an effective deterrent to crime among probationers.[91]

Probation is a massive part of the correctional and indeed the entire criminal justice system. More offenders are on probation than any other correctional sentence. Probation comes in a variety of forms that address the disparate risk factors, needs, and criminality of criminal offenders. The most serious and intensive types of probation are often a final chance in the community before felons are sentenced to prison. In a way, failing to take advantage of probation is a symbolic sign of an offender's break from conventional society and entrée into another society: prison. Section 3 of this text is devoted to prisons, the various forces that occur behind bars, and the ways that prisoners are ultimately released from custody and returned to the community.

WRAP UP

CASE STUDY CONCLUSION

Like all community corrections, probation is a punishment with several attractive features, for instance:

- Provides more individualized treatment or counseling than prison.
- Allows offenders greater opportunities to deal with their problems.
- Avoids subjecting offenders to the negative effects of prison, such as inmate victimization, exposure to more serious criminal role models, loss of self-esteem, and inability to support a family.
- Is no more likely to lead to recidivism than is incarceration.
- Is less expensive than incarceration.

It is likely that the five defendants would receive five different types of probation sentences. For example, the fifth defendant would likely receive intensive supervised probation (ISP) due to the seriousness of the charges and his prior record. The third and fourth defendants would likely receive probationary sentences with many conditions to facilitate the defendant's remaining in treatment and connected to conventional activities, such as work. The first two defendants would likely receive probation with minimal conditions or even unsupervised probation. The key to community corrections is that the courts can tailor the punishment and treatment conditions of the sentence to the needs of the offender while reasonably ensuring public safety. Finally, the criminal justice system is reliant on community corrections like probation for another reason: cost savings compared to prison.

Chapter Summary

- Probation varies by security level, jurisdiction, and criminality of the offender and includes summary, automated, unsupervised, federal, juvenile, reparative, community, and intensive supervised probation.
- With more than 4 million offenders, probation is the largest correctional sentence in the United States and accounts for more supervision than jail, prison, and all other intermediate sanctions.
- Probation is a versatile sanction that is utilized pretrial and postadjudication, applied to adolescents and adults, organized as a component of an executive or judicial branch, and used for first-time and repeat felony offenders.
- Law enforcement, jail detention, bond, court operations, and corrections are impacted by probation.
- Probation was developed in England and the United States as an extension of suspended sentencing and was viewed as a way to provide treatment and supervision for offenders for whom there was hope for rehabilitation.
- Although a diverse group, probationers demonstrate an array of serious risk factors for continued involvement in crime.

- Violations of probation for new crimes and noncompliance or technical reasons are common. For these reasons, probation is sometimes viewed as a failure.
- Programs that blend treatment and punishment tend to produce the most favorable outcomes for probationers.

Key Terms

American Probation and Parole Association The official professional organization for probation and parole officers.

Augustus, John Founder of probation in the United States.

automated probation A form of unsupervised probation that entails no supervision, services, or personal contacts.

banked probation A form of unsupervised probation that entails no supervision, services, or personal contacts.

binding over for good behavior An early form of community release that sometimes took the form of a pardon and other times that of a suspended sentence.

caseload The roster of probationary clients that a single probation officer supervises.

community probation An extension of the community policing approach to crime control where community residents and organizations work with criminal justice officials to address neighborhood disorder and related problems.

elect to serve Option to choose prison over a probation sentence.

Ex parte United States Supreme Court case that held that federal courts had no power to suspend criminal sentences and suggested probation legislation as a remedy.

federal probation Probation for offenders convicted of federal crimes.

field or home visits Searches of probation clients' place of work or homes to determine their compliance with supervision.

Gagnon v. Scarpelli Supreme Court case that held that probationers are entitled to due process for preliminary and final hearings before probation can be revoked.

Griffin v. Wisconsin Supreme Court case that held that warrantless searches of probationer's home by probation officers is reasonable under the Fourth Amendment.

Hill, Matthew Davenport Founder of probation in England.

intensive supervised probation (ISP) The most highly restrictive form of punishment that is designed to supervise criminal offenders who embody the most risk factors for continued involvement in crime.

juvenile probation The oldest and most widely used way to provide court-ordered services in the juvenile justice system.

Mathews v. Eldridge Supreme Court case that specified due process considerations of probation supervision.

meta-analysis Quantitative study of research findings.

police–probation partnerships Collaborative method of juvenile corrections in which juvenile probation officers go on patrol with law enforcement officers to conduct home visits of probationers, explain the terms of the sentence to the probationers, conduct searches of probationers for drugs, weapons, and other contraband, and provide basic services.

private probation Probation supervised by a private business rather than governmental agency.

probation A sanction for criminal offenders who have been sentenced to a period of correctional supervision in the community in lieu of incarceration.

Probation Act Legislation enacted in 1925 that established probation as a sentence in the federal courts and authorized the appointment of probation officers.

probation officer A practitioner who oversees and monitors a probationer's case to determine compliance.

probation violation Act by a probationer that violates the conditions of his or her probation sentence.

probationers Persons sentenced to probation.

Provo Experiment An intermediate sanction conducted from 1959 to 1965 in Utah that provided community-based, nonresidential, unstructured, group-oriented treatment unlike the traditional methods of probation.

punitive conditions Burdens placed on probationers convicted of the most serious crimes, such as residency limitations for offenders convicted of sexual offenses.

reparative probation A restorative justice concept that focuses on communication and problem solving among offenders, victims, and community residents rather than enforcement and punishment as a way to address crime.

revocation The termination of a probation sentence for noncompliance.

school-based probation A variation of juvenile probation in which a juvenile probation officer is housed in a school to provide direct supervision of students on probation.

sex offender probation A specialized unit within a probation office in which practitioners exclusively supervise offenders convicted of sexually based offenses.

Silverlake Experiment Experiment conducted between 1964 and 1968 in Los Angeles, which found youths who received community treatment did not pose any added risk to public safety compared to traditional sentences such as probation and detention.

split sentence Sentence that includes both incarceration and probation.

stake in conformity An offender's commitment to conventional, prosocial behaviors and responsibilities.

standard conditions Universal mandates that apply to all probationers.

summary probation A sentencing option where the judge accepts a plea or verdict of guilty for a misdemeanant, suspends execution of the sentence, and summarily (without the use of a presentence investigation) imposes a period of unsupervised probation.

suppression effect Reduction in arrests following a criminal justice intervention.

technical violations Probation violations that indicate noncompliance rather than new criminal behavior.

treatment conditions Conditions that address a problem or issue that, if resolved, will help the offender remain crime free, such as participation in drug treatment.

unsupervised probation A sentence that is similar to a deferred sentence reserved for first-time or low-level offenders with little to no probation conditions.

U.S. Probation and Pretrial Services System The community corrections arm of the federal judiciary charged with supervising criminal defendants during the pretrial and postadjudication phases.

Critical Thinking Questions

1. Probation has both the largest population and is the most versatile correctional sanction, yet it does not receive the attention of prisons, jails, and capital punishment. Why?
2. Should community probation be expanded? Would the involvement of citizens make it more difficult for offenders to victimize others?
3. Based on the number of probationers who receive automated or banked probation, are the recidivism rates of probationers that surprising?
4. Many probationers receive scant attention from their probation officers, but heinous crimes by probationers are relatively infrequent. Does this suggest that less is more when it comes to probation supervision?

Notes

1. Worrall, J. L., Schram, P., Hays, E., & Newman, M. (2004). An analysis of the relationship between probation caseloads and property crime rates in California counties. *Journal of Criminal Justice, 32,* 231–241.
2. Barklage, H., Miller, D., & Bonham, G. (2006). Probation conditions versus probation officer directives: Where the twain shall meet. *Federal Probation, 70,* 37–41.
3. Augustus, J. (1939). *A report of the labors of John Augustus, for the last ten years, in aid of the unfortunate.* Boston: Wright & Hasty, quoted in Petersilia, J. (1997). Probation in the United States. *Crime & Justice, 22,* 149–200.
4. Petersilia, J. (1997). Probation in the United States. *Crime & Justice, 22,* 149–200.
5. Sellin, T. (1959). Adult probation and the conditional sentence. *Journal of Criminal Law, Criminology, and Police Science, 49,* 553–556.
6. Morris, N., & Tonry, M. (1990). *Between prison and probation: Intermediate punishments in a rational sentencing system.* New York: Oxford University Press.
7. Glaze, L. E., & Bonczar, T. P. (2008). *Probation and parole in the United States, 2007.* Washington, DC: U. S. Department of Justice, Office of Justice Programs, Bureau of Justice Statistics.
8. 18 U.S.C. §§ 3553-3563.
9. *Mathews v. Eldridge,* 424 U.S. 319 (1976).
10. Wallace, G. (1960). Summary probation: A way to provide more probation service for misdemeanants. *Crime & Delinquency, 6,* 391–395.
11. Petersilia, J. (2002). Community corrections. In J. Q. Wilson & J. Petersilia (Eds.), *Crime: Public policies for crime control* (pp. 483–508). Oakland, CA: Institute for Contemporary Studies Press.
12. Petersilia, J., & Turner, S. (1986). *Prison versus probation in California: Implications for crime and offender recidivism.* Santa Monica, CA: RAND.
13. Piquero, N. L. (2003). A recidivism analysis of Maryland's community probation program. *Journal of Criminal Justice, 31,* 295–307.
14. Stalans, L. J., Juergens, R., Seng, M., & Lavery, T. (2004). Probation officers' and judges' discretionary sanctioning decisions about sex offenders: Differences between specialized and standard probation units. *Criminal Justice Review, 29,* 23–45.
15. 18 U.S.C. § 3561.

16. Torbet, P. M. (1996). *Juvenile probation: The workhorse of the juvenile justice system.* Washington, DC: U.S. Department of Justice, Office of Justice Programs, Office of Juvenile Justice and Delinquency Prevention.

17. Metzger, D. S., & Tobin-Fiore, D. (2000). *Pennsylvania: School-based probation.* Washington, DC: U.S. Department of Justice, Office of Justice Programs, Bureau of Justice Assistance.

18. Karp, D. R., & Drakulich, K. M. (2004). Minor crime in a quaint setting: Practices, outcomes, and limits of Vermont reparative probation boards. *Criminology & Public Policy, 3,* 655–686.

19. Petersilia (1997).

20. Kingsnorth, R. F., MacIntosh, R. C., & Sutherland, S. (2002). Criminal charge or probation violation? Prosecutorial discretion and implications for research in criminal court processing. *Criminology, 40,* 553–578.

21. Glaze & Bonczar.

22. Glaze & Bonczar.

23. Durose, M. R., & Langan, P. A. (2007). *Felony sentences in state courts, 2004.* Washington, DC: U. S. Department of Justice, Office of Justice Programs, Bureau of Justice Statistics.

24. Glaze & Bonczar.

25. Petersilia (1997).

26. Davis, L. (2003). Juvenile probation. In M. D. McShane & F. P. Williams III (Eds.), *Encyclopedia of juvenile justice* (pp. 303–303). Thousand Oaks, CA: Sage.

27. Petersilia (1997).

28. *Ex parte United States*, 242 U.S. 27 (1916).

29. *Gagnon v. Scarpelli*, 411 U.S. 778 (1973).

30. Petersilia, J., & Turner, S. (1993). Intensive probation and parole. *Crime & Justice, 17,* 281–335.

31. *Griffin v. Wisconsin,* 483 U.S. 868 (1987).

32. Empey, L. T., & Erickson, M. L. (1972). *The Provo experiment: Evaluating community control of delinquency.* Lexington, MA: Lexington Books.

33. Empey, L. T., & Lubeck, S. G. (1971). *The Silverlake experiment: Testing delinquency theory and community intervention.* Chicago: Aldine.

34. Murray, C. A., & Cox, Jr., L. A. (1979). *Beyond probation: Juvenile corrections and the chronic delinquent.* Beverly Hills, CA: Sage.

35. See Lundman, R. J. (1986). *Beyond probation*: Assessing the generalizability of the delinquency suppression effect measures reported by Murray and Cox. *Crime & Delinquency, 32,* 134–147.

36. Petersilia & Turner (1993).

37. Cable News Network. (2007). *Child's killer sentenced to die.* Retrieved November 6, 2007, from http://www.cnn.com/2006/LAW/03/15/taped.abduction/index.html.

38. Florida Department of Corrections. (n.d.). Inmate population information detail. Retrieved October 1, 2008, from http://www.dc.state.fl.us/ActiveInmates/detail.asp?Bookmark=5&From=list&SessionID=1070267870.

39. Cunniff, M. A., & Bergsmann, I. R. (1990). *Managing felons in the community: An administrative profile of probation.* Washington, DC: U. S. Department of Justice, Office of Justice Programs, Bureau of Justice Statistics.

40. Torbet.

41. Berry, P. E., & Anderson, R. (2001). An evaluation of a private alternative probation and counseling program: Predicting program outcomes from client characteristics. *American Journal of Criminal Justice, 26,* 121–130.

42. Center for Creative Justice. (n.d.). *Who we are*. Retrieved October 1, 2008, from http://www.creativejustice.org/.

43. Schloss, C. S., & Alarid, L. F. (2007). Standards in the privatization of probation services: A statutory analysis. *Criminal Justice Review, 32*, 233–245.

44. Petersilia (1997).

45. Thomas, D. W. (1993). *The state of juvenile probation, 1992: Results of a nationwide survey.* Washington, DC: U.S. Department of Justice, Office of Justice Programs, Bureau of Justice Statistics.

46. Burrell, B. (2006). *Caseload standards for probation and parole.* Lexington, KY: American Probation and Parole Association.

47. Petersilia (1997).

48. Morgan, K. D., Belbot, B. A., & Clark, J. (1997). Liability issues affecting probation and parole supervision. *Journal of Criminal Justice, 25*, 211–222.

49. Carter, R. M., & Wilkins, L. T. (Eds.). (1970). *Probation and parole: Selected readings.* New York: John Wiley & Sons.

50. Worrall et al.

51. Petersilia, J., Turner, S., Kahan, J., & Peterson, J. (1985). *Granting felons probation: Public risks and alternatives.* Santa Monica, CA: RAND.

52. Auerhahn, K. (2007). Do you know who your probationers are? Using simulation modeling to estimate the composition of California's felony probation population, 1980–2000. *Justice Quarterly, 24*, 28–47.

53. MacKenzie, D. L., Browning, K., Skroban, S. B., & Smith, D. A. (1999). The impact of probation on the criminal activities of offenders. *Journal of Research in Crime and Delinquency, 36*, 423–453.

54. Cohen, R. L. (1995). *Probation and parole violators in state prison, 1991.* Washington, DC: U.S. Department of Justice, Office of Justice Programs, Bureau of Justice Statistics.

55. Langan, P. A., & Cunniff, M. A. (1992). *Recidivism of felons on probation, 1986–1989.* Washington, DC: U.S. Department of Justice, Office of Justice Programs, Bureau of Justice Statistics.

56. Cunniff, M. A., & Shilton, M. K. (1991). *Variations on felony probation: Persons under supervision in 32 urban and suburban counties.* Washington, DC: U.S. Department of Justice, Office of Justice Programs, Bureau of Justice Statistics.

57. Harris, P. M., Petersen, R. D., & Rapoza, S. (2001). Between probation and revocation: A study of intermediate sanctions decision-making. *Journal of Criminal Justice, 29*, 307–318.

58. Morgan, K. D. (1994). Factors associated with probation outcome. *Journal of Criminal Justice, 22*, 341–353.

59. Meloy, M. L. (2005). The sex offender next door: An analysis of recidivism, risk factors, and deterrence of sex offenders on probation. *Criminal Justice Policy Review, 16*, 211–236.

60. Rodriguez, N., & Webb, V. J. (2007). Probation violations, revocations, and imprisonment: The decisions of probation officers, prosecutors, and judges pre- and post-mandatory drug treatment. *Criminal Justice Policy Review, 18*, 3–30.

61. Sims, B., & Jones, M. (1997). Predicting success or failure on probation: Factors associated with felony probation outcomes. *Crime & Delinquency, 43*, 314–327.

62. See Griffin, M. L., & Armstrong, G. S. (2003). The effect of local life circumstances on female probationers' offending. *Justice Quarterly, 20*, 213–239; Armstrong, G. S., & Griffin, M. L. (2007). The effect of local life circumstances on victimization of drug-involved women. *Justice Quarterly, 24*, 80–105.

63. Freeman, N. J. (2007). Predictors of re-arrest for rapists and child molesters on probation. *Criminal Justice and Behavior, 34*, 752–768.

64. Carmichael, S., Gover, A. R., Koons-Witt, B., & Inabnit, B. (2005). Successful completion of probation and parole among female offenders. *Women & Criminal Justice, 17*, 75–97.

65. Mayzer, R., Gray, M. K., & Maxwell, S. R. (2004). Probation absconders: A unique risk group? *Journal of Criminal Justice, 32,* 137–150.

66. Gray, M. K., Fields, M., & Maxwell, S. R. (2001). Examining probation violations: Who, what, and when. *Crime & Delinquency, 47,* 537–557.

67. Tapia, M., & Harris, P. M. (2006). Race and revocation: Is there a penalty for young, minority males? *Journal of Ethnicity in Criminal Justice, 4,* 1–25.

68. Jones, M. (1996).Voluntary revocations and the "elect-to-serve" option in North Carolina probation. *Crime & Delinquency, 42,* 36–49.

69. See Benedict, W. R., Huff-Corzine, L., & Corzine, J. (1998). Clean up and go straight: Effects of drug treatment on recidivism among felony probationers. *American Journal of Criminal Justice, 22,* 169–187; MacKenzie, D. L., & De Li, S. (2002). The impact of formal and informal social controls on the criminal activities of probationers. *Journal of Research in Crime and Delinquency, 39,* 243–276; Minor, K. I., & Elrod, P. (1994). The effects of a probation intervention on juvenile offenders' self-concepts, loci of control, and perceptions of juvenile justice. *Youth & Society, 25,* 490–511.

70. Jones, M., & Kerbs, J. J. (2007). Probation and parole officers and discretionary decision-making: Responses to technical and criminal violations. *Federal Probation, 71,* 9–15.

71. DeLisi, M. (2008). *Criminal justice: Balancing crime control and due process,* second edition. Dubuque, IA: Kendall/Hunt.

72. Bailey, W. C. (1966). Correctional outcome: An evaluation of 100 reports. *Journal of Criminal Law, Criminology, and Police Science, 57,* 153–160.

73. Palmer, T., & Wedge, R. (1989). California's juvenile probation camps: Findings and implications. *Crime & Delinquency, 35,* 234–253.

74. Giblin, M. J. (2002). Using police officers to enhance the supervision of juvenile probationers: An evaluation of the Anchorage CAN program. *Crime & Delinquency, 48,* 116–137.

75. Worrall, J. L., & Gaines, L. K. (2006). The effect of police-probation partnerships on juvenile arrests. *Journal of Criminal Justice, 34,* 579–589.

76. Mallett, C. A. (2006). Juvenile court probation supervised youths: At risk in Cuyahoga County, Ohio. *Corrections Compendium, 31,* 1–5, 27–33.

77. Vidal, S., & Skeem, J. L. (2007). Effect of psychopathy, abuse, and ethnicity on juvenile probation officers' decision-making and supervision strategies. *Law and Human Behavior, 31,* 479–498.

78. Kurtz, D., & Linnemann, T. (2006). Improving probation through client strengths: Evaluating strength based treatments for at risk youth. *Western Criminology Review, 7,* 9–19.

79. Elrod, H. P., & Minor, K. I. (1992). Second wave evaluation of a multi-faceted intervention for juvenile court probationers. *International Journal of Offender Therapy and Comparative Criminology, 36,* 247–262.

80. Lane, J., Turner, S., Fain, T., & Sehgal, A. (2005). Evaluating an experimental intensive juvenile probation program: Supervision and official outcomes. *Crime & Delinquency, 51,* 26–52.

81. Lipsey, M. W., & Wilson, D. B. (1998). Effective intervention for serious juvenile offenders: A synthesis of research. In R. Loeber & D. P. Farrington (Eds.), *Serious & violent juvenile offenders: Risk factors and successful interventions* (pp. 313–345). Thousand Oaks, CA: Sage.

82. Turner, S., Petersilia, J., & Deschenes, E. P. (1992). Evaluating ISP for drug offenders. *Crime & Delinquency, 38,* 539–556.

83. Geerken, M. R., & Hayes, H. D. (1993). Probation and parole: Public risk and the future of incarceration. *Criminology, 31,* 549–564.

84. Petersilia (2002).

85. Fulton, B., Latessa, E. J., Stichman, & Travis, L. F. (1997). The state of ISP: Research and policy implications. *Federal Probation, 61,* 65–75.

86. Gendreau, P., Cullen, F. T., & Bonta, J. (1994). Intensive rehabilitation supervision: The next generation in community corrections? *Federal Probation, 58,* 72–78; also see Clear, T. R., & Latessa, E. J. (1993). Probation officers' roles in intensive supervision: Surveillance versus treatment. *Justice Quarterly, 10,* 441–462.

87. Hiller, M. L., Knight, K., & Simpson, D. D. (2006). Recidivism following mandated residential substance abuse treatment for felony probationers. *Prison Journal, 86,* 230–241.

88. Chan, M., Guydish, J., Prem, R., Jessup, M. A., Cervantes, A., & Bostrom, A. (2005). An evaluation of probation case management (PCM) for drug-involved women offenders. *Crime & Delinquency, 51,* 447–469.

89. Golden, L. S., Gatchel, R. J., & Cahill, M. A. (2006). Evaluating the effectiveness of the National Institute of Corrections' "Thinking for a Change" program among probationers. *Journal of Offender Rehabilitation, 43,* 55–73.

90. Sherman, L. W. (2007). Use probation to prevent murder. *Criminology & Public Policy, 6,* 843–850.

91. MacKenzie, D. L., & De Li, S. (2002). The impact of formal and informal social controls on the criminal activities of probationers. *Journal of Research in Crime and Delinquency, 39,* 243–276.

PART

III

Prison and Offender Reentry

CHAPTER

9

Prisoners and Inmate Behavior

"While society in the United States gives the example of the most extended liberty, the prisons of the same country offer the spectacle of the most complete despotism."[1, p. 374]

OBJECTIVES

- Examine the ways that prisons bear on public policy from both crime control and due process perspectives.
- Recognize the size, growth, trends, costs, and demographic composition of the correctional population.
- Assess which types of offenders reside in prisons and the types that are most responsible for increases in the prisoner population.
- Learn the social, behavioral, and health characteristics of prisoners and the health risks that incarceration creates for offenders.
- Identify various models of inmate behavior and how these theories explain inmate adjustment to prison, misconduct, and violence.
- Understand the prevalence of various forms of prison violence.
- Assess the role of prison gangs in American prisons and the specific groups that pose the most significant threat to institutional safety.

CASE STUDY

The case of Nathan Leopold and Richard Loeb, which involved the kidnapping and murder of a young boy named Bobby Franks in Chicago in 1924, is viewed as the crime of the century by many crime historians. Although prosecutors sought the death penalty, Leopold and Loeb were sentenced to life sentences plus 99 years thanks to the defense of famous attorney Clarence Darrow. Both boys were affluent and exceedingly accomplished. After their confinement began, Leopold and Loeb took different paths. Loeb was murdered by another inmate in 1936, and Leopold was paroled in 1958 after serving 33 years in confinement. During his time behind bars, Leopold studied and became fluent in up to 27 languages, completed university courses, reclassified the prison library, helped criminologists study parole prediction, helped found the Stateville Correspondence School, became an X-ray technician, registered inmates for the World War II draft, wrote books and pamphlets, and volunteered to be infected with malaria for a prison medical project designed to find a cure for malaria.

1. How do models of inmate behavior variously predict Leopold and Loeb's conduct?

"With few and isolated exceptions, the rehabilitative efforts that have been reported so far have had no appreciable effect on recidivism."[2, p. 25]

In Part II, the many ways that the correctional system provides opportunities for offenders to remain in the community were explored. For the majority of criminals whose antisocial behavior is generally unserious, the form of correctional punishment is proportionately unserious. In this way, many offenders must perform community service, pay fines and restitution, or simply agree to obey the law while serving an unsupervised sentence of probation or some deferred sentence. More serious offenders, or at least more recidivistic offenders, serve incrementally more severe punishments, such as house arrest with electronic monitoring, boot camp, or probation. There comes a point, however, where intermediate sanctions are not appropriate either because of the level of risk posed by the offender or because of his or her recurrent noncompliance with the criminal justice system. Failing to take advantage of community-based forms of punishment is a symbolic sign of an offender's break from conventional society and entrée into another society: prison.

The current chapter examines the prisoner population in the United States, including recent trends in its size and composition by racial and gender groups. The social and behavioral profile of prisoners is also provided, which provides compelling evidence of the risk factors that inmates pose and must overcome to successfully reintegrate into conventional society. Finally, the chapter describes the various models of inmate behavior that criminologists have developed particularly as they relate to inmate violence, misconduct, and prison gang activity.

Prisoners and Public Policy

With the possible exception of the police, no other area of the criminal justice system has inspired as much public interest, political wrangling, and especially academic study as prisons. **Prisons** are correctional facilities that house convicted felons for lengthy periods of time, usually more than 1 year. Unlike the intermediate sanctions explored in Part II of this text, prisons are confinement facilities that exercise complete custodial control of convicted felons known as **prisoners, inmates**, or **convicts**. Although popular culture often describes prisons as jails (Chapter 5), they are in fact quite different. Prisons are usually located in remote areas of the state, whereas jails are local facilities. Prisons are run by a state entity, usually called the department of corrections, department of correctional services, department of correction and rehabilitation, or related terms, whereas jails are run by municipal police departments or county sheriffs. Prisons house offenders convicted of the most serious crimes, whereas jails house misdemeanants and persons convicted of low-level felonies. Finally, prisons contain the most extreme and highest risk types of offenders, such as persons sentenced to death and life imprisonment. Jails never house these offenders with the exception of temporarily detaining them while they await trial or prior to transporting them to prison after they have been sentenced.

"There is perhaps no social institution that is both so pervasive and so damaging to the lives of individuals who come into contact with it as the penal system."[3, p. 23]

Prisons and the state of the prisoner population have meaningful implications for all parts of the political spectrum. To those who advocate tough crime control policies, prisons are good because the most serious criminal offenders, or at least persons convicted of the most serious criminal offenses, are removed from conventional society. As such, prisons incapacitate the most serious criminals' opportunity to victimize others (unless the offender escapes). Prisons also impose hardship on criminals. In the words of Craig Hemmens and James Marquart, "The prison experience has historically meant to be unpleasant, and prisoners have been expected to suffer to some degree."[7, p. 297]

Roughly 30 percent of prisoners desist from criminal behavior and do not **recidivate** or reoffend after release from custody. Prisoners who are able to reform their behavior tend to reattach and recommit themselves to conventional social institutions, such as family, work, church, or military. Many former prisoners receive substantive counseling and treatment for substance abuse problems, mental illness, and other personal problems. Prison treatment programs facilitate their rehabilitation. An interesting example of assistance for former prisoners' turning their lives around is **Homeboy Industries**, whose mission is to provide former gang members, offenders, and prisoners with services and skills to help them become contributing members of society. Homeboy Industries provides a range of free services to former offenders, including employment services, tattoo removal, counseling, case management, curriculum and training, and community service. Homeboy Industries also operates several for-profit businesses including bakeries and restaurants and those that are involved in merchandising, silkscreening, and maintenance.[8]

On the other hand, crime control proponents also have at least three reasons to be dissatisfied with prisons. First and foremost, the recidivism rates among ex-prisoners are approximately 70 percent. Although prisons effectively incapacitate offenders, most do not commit themselves to rehabilitation and in this sense, the crime control capacity of prison confinement is short lived. Second, prison is the most expensive form of social control and yet seems to do little to reduce offending patterns among most prisoners. As Richard Seiter and Karen Kadela noted, "The nation has invested billions of dollars into locking up offenders. The policies around reentry have become increasingly an avoidance of risk. As a result, we have created a revolving door of offenders who will be committed to prison time and again as they fail in the community."[9, p. 381]

Third, there is evidence that incarceration and mere exposure to incarceration actually worsens inmates' antisocial attitudes and behaviors, which results in higher rates of recidivism after release. Consider the example of **Scared Straight** programs. Created in 1979 at the Rahway State Prison in New Jersey, Scared Straight programs feature an aggressive presentation of prison life by inmates serving life sentences to at-risk and adjudicated juvenile delinquents. The inmates harangue the youthful offenders, use shocking street language and profanity, and intimidate the youths in hopes that the deterrence program will literally scare the youths into renouncing their delinquency and leading productive lives. Scared Straight programs remain very popular among the general public.

HOMEBOY INDUSTRIES

"Nothing Stops A Bullet Like A Job"

Programs like Homeboy Industries are evidence that former prisoners can and often do turn their lives around and become contributing members to society.

Unfortunately, the programs do not work. In fact, instead of controlling crime, they tend to increase it. Anthony Petrosino and his colleagues conducted a systematic review of Scared Straight programs and found that youths who went through the program had *higher* rates of offenses than youths who did not. In their words, "on average these

"The general public has begun to realize that many adult offenders lack the social skills necessary to become successful, contributing members of their communities."[4, p. 2]

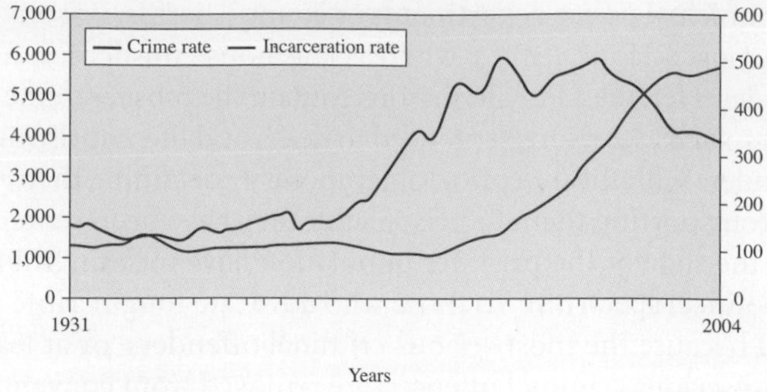

FIGURE 9–1 Crime and Incarceration Rate Trends, 1931–2004. *Source*: Modified from the JFA Institute. (2007). *Unlocking America: Why and how to reduce American's prison population.* Washington, DC: The JFA Institute.

Scared Straight was designed to motivate—with graphic and disturbing depictions of prison life—juvenile delinquents to desist from crime. Subsequent evaluations found that the program was actually counterproductive.

programs result in an increase in criminality in the experimental group when compared to a no-treatment control. According to these experiments, doing nothing would have been better than exposing juveniles to the program."[10, p. 53]

Those with more due process–oriented or progressive perspectives are even more alarmed by the state of America's prisons and the prisoner population. However, the majority of this concern does not necessarily deal with fundamental due process rights. Instead, the concern is more an overtly liberal concern about the salience of prisons in American life, particularly as prisons have impacted the poor and racial minorities and reflected on social inequality.

As shown in **FIGURE 9–1**, there has been a nearly 500 percent increase in the incarceration rate since 1980, while crime rates have stabilized and declined over the past 15 years. From this perspective, the overuse or reliance on prison in the face of declining crime is deeply troubling because it not only wastes the resources of government but also wastes the lives of prisoners. The costs of prison are enormous, especially if one considers the average victimization costs per offense. For instance, the average victim loss for a robbery is $1,258 (**TABLE 9–1**). The average costs to incarcerate a robber are $113,000. For burglary, the average victim cost is $1,545 and the average incarceration costs for a burglar are $64,000. The average victim loss for theft is $730, whereas the incarceration costs for a thief are $47,000. Finally, the victim cost for auto theft is $6,646, while the corresponding incarceration costs are $41,000. Put this way, prison is too expensive based on the costs to society.

TABLE 9–1 Victimization and Incarceration Costs for Four Common Crimes

Type of Crime	Average Victim Loss	Prison Sentence (in mos)	Pretrial Time (in mos)	Prison Time Served (in mos)	Total Time (in mos)	Incarceration Costs
Robbery	$1,258	94	5	55	60	$113,000
Burglary	$1,545	52	5	29	34	$ 64,000
Larceny theft	$ 730	34	5	20	25	$ 47,000
Auto theft	$6,646	27	5	17	22	$ 41,000

Source: Modified from the JFA Institute. (2007). *Unlocking America: Why and how to reduce America's prison population.* Washington, DC: The JFA Institute.

Prisoner Population and Trends

According to the most recent data, correctional facilities in the United States held an estimated more than 2.3 million inmates in a variety of facilities, including federal and state prisons, territorial prisons, local jails, ICE facilities, military facilities, jails in Indian country, and juvenile facilities (TABLE 9-2). Slightly more than 1.5 million inmates are state and federal prisoners, with state prisons housing about 88 percent and federal facilities housing the remaining 12 percent of inmates. According to data collected in 2007, the prison population grew at a faster rate than in the previous 5 years. As shown in FIGURE 9-2, the 2.8 percent increase in the number of prisoners was larger than the average annual growth rate of less than 2 percent between 2000 and 2005. However, the most recent growth rate was less than during the 1990s, when the prisoner population increased between 3 and 9 percent each year.[11]

"It may be more useful and more accurate to see the culture and organization of prison and street life as inextricably intertwined, with lines of influence flowing in both directions."[5, p. 407]

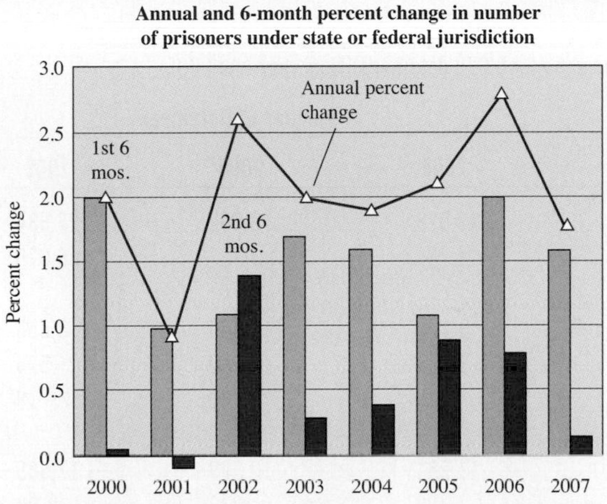

FIGURE 9-2 Annual Prison Growth. *Source*: West, H. C., & Sabol, W. J. (2008). *Prisoners in 2007.* Washington, DC: U.S. Department of Justice, Office of Justice Programs, Bureau of Justice Statistics.

TABLE 9-2 Total Incarcerated Population

	Number of Inmates 2000	2006	2007	Percent Average Annual Change, 2000–2006	Percent Change, 2006–2007
Total inmates in custody	1,937,482	2,258,983	2,293,157	2.6	1.5
Federal prisons					
Total	140,064	190,844	197,285	5.3	3.4
Prisons	133,921	183,381	189,154	5.4	3.1
Federal facilities	124,540	163,118	165,975	4.6	1.8
Privately operated facilities	9,381	20,263	23,179	13.7	14.4
Community corrections centers	6,143	7,463	8,131	3.3	9.0
State prisoners	1,176,269	1,302,129	1,315,291	1.7	1.0
Inmates held in local jails	621,149	766,010	780,581	3.6	1.9
Incarceration rate	684	751	756		

Source: West, H. C., & Sabol, W. J. (2008). *Prisoners in 2007.* Washington, DC: U.S. Department of Justice, Office of Justice Programs, Bureau of Justice Statistics.

"The prison has neither exterior nor gap; it cannot be interrupted . . . it gives almost total power over the prisoners; it has its internal mechanisms of repression and punishment; a despotic discipline."[6, p. 23]

The majority of the upsurge in the prisoner population can be attributed to more rigorous policies by the **United States Immigration and Customs Enforcement (ICE)**. Indeed, as shown in TABLE 9–3, ICE facilities reported a 43 percent increase in the number of inmates, which was nearly *14 times* greater than the increase in state and federal prison inmates. Nearly 30,000 persons are detained under the jurisdiction of ICE. Most of these prisoners are in states along the Mexican border, such as Arizona, California, New Mexico, and Texas. Over 50 percent of ICE detainees are held on immigration law violations with the remaining inmates held on criminal offenses or pending charges. These immigration offenders are held in a variety of institutions, including ICE-operated facilities, private facilities that contract with ICE, the Federal Bureau of Prisons, and most commonly, in local jails (see Table 9–3).

TABLE 9–3 ICE and the Prisoner Population

At year-end 2006, 27,634 detainees were under the jurisdiction of U.S. Immigration and Customs Enforcement (ICE). This represented a 41% increase (or 8,072 detainees) from year-end 2005.

Facility Type	Number of Detainees 2000	2005	2006	Percent Change, 2005–2006
Total	19,528	19,562	27,634	41.3
ICE-operated facilities	4,785	3,782	6,079	60.7
Private facilities under exclusive contract to ICE	1,829	2,365	3,358	42.0
Federal Bureau of Prisons	1,444	860	574	–33.3
Other federal facilities	178	46	18	–60.9
Intergovernmental agreements	11,281	12,509	17,605	40.7
State prisons	369	276	96	–65.2
Local jails	8,886	8,322	12,482	50.0
Other facilities	2,026	3,911	5,027	28.5

Four border states (Arizona, California, New Mexico, and Texas) contributed to 67.2% of this growth. The largest growth occurred in New Mexico and Texas. New Mexico nearly doubled the number of detainees, increasing from 429 in 2005 to 1,035 in 2006. The detainee population in Texas increased 76% (or 3,261 detainees). California and Arizona had similar growth rates (32% and 31%, respectively) and ranked third and fourth in detainee growth.
Of ICE detainees, 3,881 said their country of origin was in Central America, specifically El Salvador, Guatemala, and Honduras. Another 2,643 individuals said they had Mexican citizenship. These groups collectively contributed to 81% of the growth from year-end 2005 to 2006.

Over half (50.7% or 14,015) of the detainees were held on immigration law violations, 40% were held for criminal offenses, and the remaining 9.3% were pending charges or disposition. From year-end 2005 to 2006, the percentage of detainees held for immigration law violations increased by 79%. Comparatively, the number of detainees held for pending charges increased 62% and the number of detainees held for criminal offenses increased 8.9%.

Reason Held	2005	2006	Change, 2005–2006 Number of Detainees	Percent Change
Total	19,562	27,634	8,072	100
Immigration law violation	7,826	14,015	6,189	79.1
Criminal offense	10,153	11,052	899	8.9
Pending charge/disposition	1,583	2,567	984	62.2

Source: Sabol, W. J., Couture, H., & Harrison, P. M. (2007). *Prisoners in 2006*. Washington, DC: U.S. Department of Justice, Office of Justice Programs, Bureau of Justice Statistics.

In recent years, Immigration and Customs Enforcement (ICE) facilities have experienced an explosion in their inmate population.

More than 52 percent of state prisoners are serving time for violent crimes including murder, manslaughter, rape and other sexual assault, robbery, assault, kidnapping, and other violent offenses. About 21 percent of state prisoners are serving time for convictions for property offenses, such as burglary, larceny, motor vehicle theft, arson, fraud, and others. Nearly 20 percent of state prisoners are serving time for drug violations. The remaining 7 percent of state prisoners are incarcerated for public-order convictions, including weapons offenses, drunk driving, commercialized vice, morals and decency offenses, and others.[12]

Of all felony convictions in state courts, just 40 percent result in a prison sentence. Thirty percent of convicted felons are sentenced to jail, and 30 percent are sentenced to intermediate sanctions, usually probation. A surprisingly small percentage of serious felony convictions result in prison sentences. For instance, just 54 percent of violent offenses, 37 percent of property offenses, 37 percent of drug offenses, 44 percent of weapons offenses, and 34 percent of other offenses result in a state prison sentence. The length of sentence to state prison is also relatively short, with an average of 57 months. Of course, there is variation between sentence length and conviction offense. Violent offenses result in an average state prison sentence of 92 months. The average sentences for nonviolent offenses were property (45 months), drug (51 months), weapon (47 months), and other (41 months) offenses, respectively.[13]

In recent years, judicial and correctional systems have gotten tougher on offenders by mandating that prisoners convicted of serious felonies serve a greater proportion of their original sentence (i.e., *truth in sentencing*) and targeting habitual offenders with lengthy or life sentences (i.e., *three strikes*) (see Chapter 4). For these reasons, offenders are serving longer periods of time behind bars, which partially explains why imprisonment rates have increased in the face of declining crime rates. It is also important to note that truth-in-sentencing and three-strikes legislation have helped to reduce crime rates. For instance, Joanna Shepherd found that truth-in-sentencing laws result in 16 percent reductions in murder, 24 percent reductions in robbery, and 12 percent reductions in rape.[14] This results in nearly 10,000 less serious violent crimes annually.[15]

There is wide variation across states regarding the size of the prisoner population (TABLE 9–4). For example, California and Texas each house more than 172,000 inmates and are nearly the size of the federal prisoner population. The remaining states in the top 10 for prisoner population are Florida, New York, Michigan, Ohio, Illinois, Georgia, Pennsylvania, and Louisiana. By comparison, five states, New Hampshire, Vermont, Wyoming, Maine, and North Dakota have fewer than 3,000 inmates. State population and crime rates are two factors that explain the sheer differences across states in terms of inmate population.

In the federal prison system known as the **Bureau of Prisons** (**BOP**), the prisoner population is different in composition from the states. For instance, more than half of the BOP prisoners were convicted of drug offenses and fewer than 10 percent of them were convicted of violent offenses. As shown in TABLE 9–5, the offenses of federal prisoners have changed somewhat dramatically since 2000. For instance, the number of federal offenders serving time for homicide has more than doubled. Increases for other violent offenders surged nearly 50 percent between 2000 and 2006. Federal prisoners serving time for weapons offenses increased 125 percent.[16]

As of December 2008, the BOP supervised more than 202,000 prisoners who had been convicted of federal felonies. Nearly 170,000 federal inmates are supervised in BOP facilities, such as United States penitentiaries, federal correctional institutions, metropolitan detention centers, and other facilities that are explored in Chapter 10. Nearly 22,000 BOP offenders are supervised in privately managed secure facilities that in the BOP are called correctional institutions. Nationwide, there are 14 correctional institutions or private federal prisons. Nearly 12,000 federal prisoners reside in community corrections management facilities or offices.[17]

TABLE 9-4 **Prisoners by State**

Region and Jurisdiction	Number of Prisoners 2000	2006	2007	Percent Average Annual Change, 2000–2006	Percent Change, 2006–2007
U.S. total	1,331,278	1,504,660	1,532,817	2.1	1.9
Federal	125,044	173,533	179,204	5.6	3.3
State	1,206,234	1,331,127	1,353,613	1.7	1.7
Northeast	166,632	166,078	167,667	–0.1	1.0
Connecticut	13,155	13,746	14,397	0.7	4.7
Maine	1,635	1,997	2,093	3.4	4.8
Massachusetts	9,479	9,472	9,699	0.0	2.4
New Hampshire	2,257	2,737	2,930	3.3	7.1
New Jersey	29,784	27,371	26,827	–1.4	–2.0
New York	70,199	62,974	62,177	–1.8	–1.3
Pennsylvania	36,844	43,998	45,446	3.0	3.3
Rhode Island	1,966	2,149	2,481	1.5	15.4
Vermont	1,313	1,634	1,617	3.7	–1.0
Midwest	236,458	260,347	261,391	1.6	0.4
Illinois	45,281	45,106	45,215	–0.1	0.2
Indiana	19,811	26,055	27,114	4.7	4.1
Iowa	7,955	8,838	8,732	1.8	–1.2
Kansas	8,344	8,816	8,696	0.9	–1.4
Michigan	47,718	51,577	50,233	1.3	–2.6
Minnesota	6,238	9,108	9,468	6.5	4.0
Missouri	27,519	30,146	29,844	1.5	–1.0
Nebraska	3,816	4,204	4,329	1.6	3.0
North Dakota	994	1,363	1,416	5.4	3.9
Ohio	45,833	49,166	50,731	1.2	3.2
South Dakota	2,613	3,350	3,306	4.2	–1.3
Wisconsin	20,336	22,618	22,307	1.8	–1.4
South	538,997	597,828	615,535	1.7	3.0
Alabama	26,034	27,526	28,605	0.9	3.9
Arkansas	11,851	13,713	14,310	2.5	4.4
Delaware	3,937	4,195	4,201	1.1	0.1
District of Columbia	5,008	—	—	—	—
Florida	71,318	92,874	98,219	4.5	5.8
Georgia	44,141	52,781	54,232	3.0	2.7
Kentucky	14,919	19,514	21,823	4.6	11.8
Louisiana	35,207	36,376	37,341	0.5	2.7
Maryland	22,490	22,316	22,780	–0.1	2.1
Mississippi	19,239	19,219	21,502	0.0	11.9
North Carolina	27,043	32,219	33,016	3.0	2.5
Oklahoma	23,181	23,889	24,197	0.5	1.3
South Carolina	21,017	22,861	23,314	1.4	2.0
Tennessee	22,166	25,745	26,267	2.5	2.0
Texas	158,008	162,193	161,695	0.4	–0.3
Virginia	29,643	36,688	37,984	3.6	3.5
West Virginia	3,795	5,719	6,049	7.1	5.8
West	264,147	306,874	309,020	2.5	0.7
Alaska	2,128	3,116	3,072	6.6	–1.4
Arizona	25,412	33,557	35,490	4.7	5.8
California	160,412	173,942	172,856	1.4	–0.6
Colorado	16,833	22,481	22,841	4.9	1.6
Hawaii	3,553	4,373	4,367	3.5	–0.1
Idaho	5,535	7,124	7,319	4.3	2.7
Montana	3,105	3,563	3,431	2.3	–3.7
Nevada	10,063	12,753	13,245	4.0	3.9
New Mexico	4,666	6,361	6,225	5.3	–2.1
Oregon	10,533	13,667	13,918	4.4	1.8
Utah	5,541	6,340	6,415	2.3	1.2
Washington	14,666	17,483	17,757	3.0	1.6
Wyoming	1,680	2,114	2,084	3.9	–1.4

Source: West, H. C., & Sabol, W. J. (2008). *Prisoners in 2007.* Washington, DC: U.S. Department of Justice, Office of Justice Programs, Bureau of Justice Statistics.

TABLE 9-5 Federal Prisoners by Offense

Offense	2000	2006	2007	Percent Average Annual Change, 2000–2006	Percent Change, 2006–2007
Total	131,739	176,268	179,204	5.0	1.7
Violent offenses	13,740	16,507	15,647	3.1	–5.2
Homicide	1,363	2,923	2,915	13.6	–0.3
Robbery	9,712	9,645	8,966	–0.1	–7.0
Other violent	2,665	3,939	3,767	6.7	–4.4
Property offenses	10,135	10,015	10,345	–0.2	3.3
Burglary	462	519	504	2.0	–2.9
Fraud	7,506	6,437	7,834	–2.5	21.7
Other property	2,167	3,059	2,006	5.9	–34.4
Drug offenses	74,276	93,751	95,443	4.0	1.8
Public-order offenses	32,325	54,336	56,273	9.0	3.6
Immigration	13,676	19,496	19,528	6.1	0.2
Weapons	10,822	24,298	25,435	14.4	4.7
Other	7,827	10,542	11,311	5.1	7.3
Other/unspecified	1,263	1,659	1,492	4.7	–10.0

Source: West, H. C., & Sabol, W. J. (2008). *Prisoners in 2007.* Washington, DC: U.S. Department of Justice, Office of Justice Programs, Bureau of Justice Statistics.

Gender, Race, and Ethnic Differences

As mentioned at the beginning of this chapter, a hot button political issue centers on the effects of imprisonment on various social groups, especially African Americans and Hispanics. Interestingly, the variable that is most disproportionately related to imprisonment receives the least publicity. As shown in TABLE 9-6, more than 93 percent of the American prisoner population is male, with just under 7 percent female. To put this in perspective, nearly 32 percent of the prisoner population is comprised of White males, but just 3 percent of the prisoner population is comprised of African American and Hispanic women combined. In other words, the prison population is dramatic evidence of the sheer differences in crime and punishment as they relate to gender.

Demographic differences in incarceration are more apparent when rates are used because they adjust for population differences. As shown in TABLE 9-7, the incarceration rate per 100,000 residents varies by group. In 2006:

- The national incarceration rate was 506 per 100,000 U.S. residents.
- For males, the incarceration rate was 955 per 100,000 U.S. residents.
- For females, the incarceration rate was 69 per 100,000 U.S. residents.
- For White males, the incarceration rate was 481 per 100,000 U.S. residents.
- For White females, the incarceration rate was 50 per 100,000 U.S. residents.
- For African American males, the incarceration rate was 3,138 per 100,000 U.S. residents.
- For African American females, the incarceration rate was 150 per 100,000 U.S. residents.
- For Hispanic males, the incarceration rate was 1,259 per 100,000 U.S. residents.
- For Hispanic females, the incarceration rate was 79 per 100,000 U.S. residents.

TABLE 9-6 Prisoners Characteristics

	Number of Prisoners			Percent Average Annual Change,	Percent Change,
	2000	2006	2007	2000–2006	2006–2007
Total	1,331,300	1,504,700	1,532,800	2.1	1.9
Male	1,247,000	1,401,400	1,427,300	2.0	1.8
White	401,900	478,800	471,400	3.0	−1.5
Black	532,400	535,100	556,900	0.1	4.1
Hispanic or Latino	242,600	291,000	301,200	3.1	3.5
Female	84,300	103,300	105,500	3.4	2.1
White	33,600	49,200	50,500	6.6	2.6
Black	32,200	28,600	29,300	−2.0	2.4
Hispanic or Latino	13,100	17,500	17,600	4.9	0.6

Source: West, H. C., & Sabol, W. J. (2008). *Prisoners in 2007*. Washington, DC: U.S. Department of Justice, Office of Justice Programs, Bureau of Justice Statistics.

TABLE 9-7 Incarceration Rates by Race and Gender

	Imprisonment Rate per 100,000 U.S. Residents			Change,
	2000	2006	2007	2000–2007
Total	478	501	506	28
Male	915	943	955	40
White	410	487	481	71
Black	3,188	3,042	3,138	–50
Hispanic or Latino	1,419	1,261	1,259	–160
Female	59	68	69	10
White	33	48	50	17
Black	172	148	150	–25
Hispanic or Latino	78	81	79	1

Source: West, H. C., & Sabol, W. J. (2008). *Prisoners in 2007*. Washington, DC: U.S. Department of Justice, Office of Justice Programs, Bureau of Justice Statistics.

Put another way, among males, the African American to White incarceration rate ratio was nearly 8:1. The corresponding Hispanic to White ratio was nearly 3:1. For females, the African American to White ratio was 3:1 while the Hispanic to White ratio was nearly 2:1.

In addition, African Americans and Hispanics are significantly more likely to ever be incarcerated than Whites. For example, about 1 in 3 African American males, 1 in 6 Hispanic males, and 1 in 17 White males are expected to go to prison during their lifetime based on recent incarceration rates.[18] As noted by Becky Pettit, Bruce Western, and Beth Huebner, for African American and Hispanic men, prison is becoming a more likely life achievement than graduating from college or honorably serving in the military.[19–20]

Why are minorities, especially minority males, so overrepresented in prisoner populations? Two general viewpoints have been advanced to answer this question. One perspective suggests that racial disparities in prison rates (and any criminal justice system status) generally reflect biased or discriminatory treatment of racial minorities such that disparity is simply viewed as discrimination. In the words of Michael Tonry, prisons are disproportionately comprised of Blacks and Hispanics because correctional policies are unjust and "Americans have a remarkable ability to endure suffering by others."[21, p. 113]

Contrasted with the theory of widespread criminal justice discrimination is the argument that racial differences in imprisonment reflect actual differences in criminal offending by various racial groups.[22–23] Criminologists have produced compelling evidence to support this view using methodologically rigorous methods and nationally representative data. For instance, Alfred Blumstein found that 80 percent of the prison racial gap was directly explained by the greater Black involvement in crimes such as murder and robbery. More importantly, Blumstein found zero evidence of discrimination. Similarly, Patrick Langan found that 85 percent of the prison racial gap was accounted for by higher offending levels among Blacks. Robert Crutchfield and his colleagues found that 90 percent of the prison racial gap was accounted for by higher crimes rates by Blacks.[24–26] Scholars at the Vera Institute of Justice found that violent crime by Blacks explained 110 percent of murder, 84 percent of rape, and 88 percent of robbery prison admissions. Indeed, Jon Sorensen and his colleagues concluded that, "Most of the racial disproportionality in prison admissions results from differential involvement in crimes by Blacks and Whites."[27, p. 82]

The drastic racial differences in incarceration rates point to dramatic differences in offending by race and are enduring signs of social inequality to many observers.

Social and Health Characteristics

Prisoners have several serious risk factors that negatively affect their health and contribute to inmate mortality. Indeed, the criminal lifestyles of many prisoners, characterized by alcoholism and substance abuse, prostitution and high-risk sexual behaviors, smoking, and other health risks, is so severe that many offenders pose a greater public health risk as opposed to public safety risk once released into the community.[28] Persons with a history of incarceration are consistently more likely to be afflicted with infectious disease and other illnesses associated with stress. In addition, the negative health consequences of imprisonment can be seen many years later into middle adulthood.[29] According to Michael Massoglia, "the impact of incarceration on a range of health outcomes is striking. Given the detrimental impact of incarceration on health and the high number of inmates released yearly, the penal system may have a transformative effect on aggregate health and the healthcare system.[30, p. 23]

More than 3,100 prisoners died in custody each year—an average of about 60 prisoners per day. Nearly 90 percent of inmate deaths were attributed to medical conditions, and the four leading causes of death were heart disease, cancer (especially lung cancer caused by cigarette smoking), liver diseases (often caused by alcoholism), and AIDS. Suicide accounted for 6 percent of all inmate deaths but for inmates under age 35 is the leading cause of death. Homicide accounted for 2 percent of prisoner deaths. In 2006, for example, 55 prisoners were murdered by other inmates, which equates to more than one inmate-on-inmate murder per week.[31]

Medical care in American prisons is a fundamental right (see Chapter 3). According to the Bureau of Prisons, inmates have the right to health care, which includes nutritious meals, proper bedding and clothing, and a laundry schedule for cleanliness of the same, an opportunity to shower regularly, proper ventilation for warmth and fresh air, a regular exercise period, toilet articles, and medical and dental treatment.[32] The **American Correctional Association** (ACA), the oldest professional association developed by and devoted to the correctional profession, mandates that correctional systems provide

CORRECTIONS IN THE NEWS

Strike Three . . . You're Out!

But is the game over? Well, it is if you're playing in California! Since the passage of California's three-strikes law, well over 40,000 inmates are currently serving 25 years to life as guests of the California Department of Corrections. That's nearly 25 percent of the inmate prison population for the state. Compared to Georgia, with just under 6,000 inmates serving time under this same type of statute and Washington state with fewer than 300 three-strikes violators under the supervision of the department of corrections, is California's version of the law working or merely an exceptional burden on California taxpayers?

Three-strikes laws were conceptualized as a means of controlling violent career criminals. These laws were not initially intended to any great extent as a sanction for the nonviolent offender. Since three-strikes laws that are applied by the states are not mutually exclusive provisions, overlap does exist; however, no two laws read the same. But the real question is do three-strikes laws work? In other words, do these types of sanctions decrease crime rates?

In California, the number of inmates serving time under the three-strikes law has risen from 4,408 in 1994 to 42,445 in 2003. This population is comprised of both violent and nonviolent offenders. However, predictions of the increase in prison population as a result of this law have not been reached in large part due to the foresight and common sense practicality of California voters and criminal justice officials. California voters passed legislation that requires repeat offenders arrested for drug offenses who have been out of prison for 5 years to be eligible for drug treatment programs instead of being sentenced to prison even if they are three-strikes eligible. Judges and prosecutors, to their credit, have also seen fit to waive prior convictions when considering prison sentences for three-strikes offenders.

Crime data indicate that 57 percent of the offenders serving 25 years to life under California's three-strikes law are doing so for nonviolent felonies. Interestingly, more inmates are serving life sentences for drug offenses than are currently serving life for murder—10 times more! In fact, only 35 percent of the inmates serving time for three-strikes laws violations committed a crime against another person. So, the big question is do they work? Do three-strikes laws decrease crime rates?

The potential to limit recidivism is great. Keep career criminals in prison for longer periods of time and those individuals will not commit additional crimes. This makes sense. If the bad guy is locked up, his behavior is in check for the length of his prison term. But is there a deterrent effect? Not according to research. In fact, it has even been suggested that if three-strikes laws are strictly applied to all eligible offenders, there would be less than an 11 percent drop in felony crimes.

Source: Ehlers, S., Schiraldi, V., & Ziedenberg, J. (2004). *Still striking out: 10 years of California's three strikes.* Washington, DC: The Justice Policy Institute.

medical care that is consistent with community healthcare standards and delineated 22 policy guidelines that prisons are to follow in providing medical and mental health treatment.[33] Prisons follow these guidelines in order to comply with ACA standards and maintain their accreditation.

Prison medical services are superior to the often nonexistent medical care that indigent offenders receive in the community.[34] For example, mortality rates in American prisons are *19 percent lower* than mortality rates for comparable demographic groups living in society. The medical care benefit works differently by race and ethnicity. For example, White and Hispanic prisoners had death rates that were higher than their counterparts in the resident population, but African American prisoners had death rates nearly *60 percent lower* than their counterparts in the resident population.[35] More than 22,480 prisoners are infected with the human immunodeficiency virus (HIV) or have confirmed AIDS, which equates to less than 2 percent of all inmates. In 2005, 203 inmates

CORRECTIONS FOCUS

Color Me Gray—The Aging Prison Population

Not only is our prison population growing, it's aging. With the advent of the get tough on crime political philosophy and the ensuing legislation, the chances of spending time, and much more of it, in prison upon conviction has dramatically increased. During the 1980s and 1990s, truth-in-sentencing laws, three-strikes laws, abolition of parole for offenders committing certain violent crimes, and the federal Violent Crime Control Act of 1994 put offenders behind bars—far away from the remainder of society and for extended portions of their lives. As a result, the prison population is starting to gray. Aging populations, in or out of prison, require more considerations, different accommodations, and more medical attention—especially for women who typically need more medical services as they age than do men.

Prison population figures reveal three types of elderly offenders. The first is the elderly inmate convicted on their first felony offense. This group comprises 45 percent of what can be classified as elderly offenders. The second category of elderly offender is the recidivists or career criminals who are in prison after being convicted for their second or subsequent offense. And finally, there are the long-term offenders who entered prison at an early age and spend their remaining life course in prison. As they age, this group of felons simply cost more to house. Some states report spending as much as $30,000 a year to house an average inmate. The National Council on Crime and Delinquency estimates that a life sentence of 50 years will cost more than $2 million. In addition, aging leads to overcrowding and overcrowding sometimes lends itself to violence and victimization. One solution would be to provide alternative housing for elderly offenders. Because elderly offenders make suitable targets, alternative housing also would limit the likelihood an elderly inmate would be victimized by younger prisoners as well.

Source: Williams, J. L. (2006). *The aging inmate population: Southern states outlook.* Retrieved May 12, 2007, from http://www.slcatlanta.org/Publications/HSPS/aging inmates 2006 lo.pdf.

died from AIDS-related causes. The prevalence of AIDS among prisoners is nearly three times higher than the prevalence in the general population.[36]

As shown in TABLE 9–8, state and federal prisoners experience generally high levels of mental health symptoms for major depressive, mania, and psychotic disorders. More than 70 percent of state prisoners and 62 percent of federal prisoners reported one or more symptoms of a major depressive disorder. More than 72 percent of state prisoners and 65 percent of federal prisoners reported one or more symptoms of a mania disorder. More than 15 percent of state prisoners and 11 percent of federal prisoners reported one or more symptoms of a psychotic disorder. To put these in perspective, in the general population, about 8 percent have one or more symptoms of major depression, less than 2 percent have one or more symptoms of mania disorders, and 3 percent present symptoms of a psychotic disorder. In other words, in terms of mental health, prisoners are a severe risk group.

As a whole, prisoners are characterized by mental health problems; however, looking within the subpopulation of prisoners with mental health problems reveals a host of other social risk factors. For example, among state prisoners with mental health problems:

- Sixty-one percent had a current or past violent offense on their record
- Twenty-five percent had three or more prior incarcerations
- Seventy-four percent were substance dependent upon arrest

TABLE 9-8 Psychiatric Problems Among Prisoners

Symptoms in Past 12 Months or Since Admission	Percent of Inmates in State Prison	Percent of Inmates in Federal Prison
Major depressive or mania symptoms		
Persistent sad, numb, or empty mood	32.9	23.7
Loss of interest or pleasure in activities	35.4	30.8
Increased or decreased appetite	32.4	25.1
Insomnia or hypersomnia	39.8	32.8
Psychomotor agitation or retardation	39.6	31.4
Feelings of worthlessness or excessive guilt	35.0	25.3
Diminished ability to concentrate or think	28.4	21.3
Ever attempted suicide	13.0	6.0
Persistent anger or irritability	37.8	30.5
Increased/decreased interest in sexual activities	34.4	29.0
Psychotic disorder symptoms		
Delusions	11.8	7.8
Hallucinations	7.9	4.8

Source: James, D. J., & Glaze, L. E. (2006). *Mental health problems of prison and jail inmates.* Washington, DC: U.S. Department of Justice, Office of Justice Programs, Bureau of Justice Statistics.

- Thirteen percent were homeless in the year before arrest
- Twenty-seven percent had been physically or sexually abused
- Thirty percent were unemployed upon arrest
- Forty-three percent had ever received public assistance
- Nineteen percent had lived in a foster home, agency, or institution
- Fifty-two percent had an immediate family member ever imprisoned

Based on the severity of this profile, it is clear that extensive treatment and counseling is needed among the prisoner population. Unfortunately, the demand for mental health services exceeds the capacity of prison systems to provide it. For instance, 34 percent of state prisoners and 24 percent of federal prisoners who had a mental health problem received treatment after admission. The proportion of state and federal prisoners that used prescribed medications was 27 and 20 percent, respectively. The proportion of state and federal prisoners who received professional mental health therapy was 23 and 15 percent, respectively. A greater discussion of the variety of prison treatment programs appears in Chapter 10.[37]

Models of Inmate Behavior

Prisons served as a major research interest of sociologists because prisons are small, isolated societies physically set apart from conventional society and the general population. Yet within every prison, there is the same general infrastructure and set of institutions that enable the society to operate. There is organization, leadership, and population; work, economy, and commerce; and social interaction, social stratification, and social problems. In this way, prisons have been viewed as microcosms of society. For instance, cell phones are currently the hottest piece of **contraband**, or forbidden items in prison, that inmates

CORRECTIONS RESEARCH

Don't Call It Inmate Suicide, Call It Prison Suicide

A study conducted by Meredith Huey and Thomas McNulty examines the association between institutional conditions and prison suicide. According to the authors, attempting to explain suicide by an inmate from an individual perspective is limited and provides little or no real understanding of the act. In contrast to previous research on inmate suicide, Huey and McNulty focus on the effects of deprivation, overcrowding, and the interaction between these two factors on the likelihood that an inmate will commit or attempt to commit suicide.

The authors hypothesize that overcrowding is an important factor that can influence the effects of deprivation on prison suicide. Deprivation theory holds that the greater the restrictions on inmate life and the fewer rehabilitation programs available to prisoners, the greater the incidence of suicide. From an overcrowding theory perspective, crowding produces a harmful effect in that it inhibits a gradual and sustainable adaptation to prison life, which ultimately has a negative impact on socialization and the development of coping skills within the total institution.

Research from a deprivation perspective has noted that adaptation to prison life is more complete when prisoners are allowed some level of control over their environment. Prison systems are typically designed to control prisoners. This is accomplished by strict security measures accompanied by even stricter enforcement policies and practices. As a result, prisons using this approach experience less violence. However, stricter social controls also produce a negative effect. Near total deprivation dehumanizes the target—the inmate. As a result, inmates sentenced to maximum-security facilities tend to adapt slowly to their new environment and are more likely to attempt or complete the act of suicide. Deprivation also involves social isolation. Other research has found that isolation from family members is the primary reason inmates attempt suicide. Social isolation within the facility also increases the likelihood of a prisoner taking his or her own life. Research has also found that informal inmate networks that work to provide a support system can and do serve to lessen the impact of deprivation. However, these networks are generally not available in maximum-security settings.

Overcrowding causes stress and contributes to an inmate's struggle to adapt to prison life. As a result, this practice is also attributed to increasing the likelihood of prisoner suicide. Overcrowding decreases service provision, increases idleness, limits access to rehabilitation programs, and decreases personal autonomy. Limited research on overcrowding has documented that increases in prison population are generally accompanied by increases in inmate suicide.

A critical contributing factor to the likelihood of an inmate committing suicide is the element of overcrowding. Specifically, when comparing medium- to maximum-security facilities with minimum-security institutions, similar patterns of prison suicide exist only at lower levels of overcrowding. Consequently, at high levels of overcrowding, minimum-security facilities are as likely to experience similar rates of suicides as are medium- and high-security prisons. Also noted was that increases in levels of deprivation are directly associated with overcrowding, and this factor is also likely to contribute to an increase in prison suicide as the prison population expands beyond its limits.

Source: Huey, M. P., & McNulty, T. L. (2005). Institutional conditions and prison suicide: Conditional effects of deprivation and overcrowding. *Prison Journal, 85,* 490–514.

will pay hundreds of dollars to obtain. In addition to the convenience of communication, cell phones also pose security risks for prison officials because the camera, Internet, and GPS technology available on phones can help inmates orchestrate prison escape plots, drug trafficking, and other misconduct.[38] **Penologists**, criminologists who study prisons, have developed several models to understand inmate behavior and the ways that prisons operate. These models are explored in the following sections.

Deprivation Model

According to the **deprivation model**, inmate behavior is primarily a function of the oppressive structural features posed by the prison facility itself. From this perspective, the reason that prisoners have difficulty complying with prison rules and regulations is that the prison environment is overly controlling and coercive. Rigid prisons do not lend themselves to rehabilitation. As Norman Hayner and Ellis Ash observed, "A clear realization of the degenerating influence of our present prison system should encourage more experiments aiming to devise a community for offenders that will actually rehabilitate."[39, p. 583]

A concept that stems from the deprivation model is **prisonization**, the process by which inmates become socialized into the inmate subculture. According to Donald Clemmer, prisonization occurs among all inmates; however, there are specific characteristics that determine whether an offender is weakly or strongly prisonized. In cases where there is weak prisonization, the following factors are found:

- The inmate is serving a short sentence.
- The inmate has a stable personality characterized by a healthy upbringing.
- The inmate maintains relationships with positive figures outside the prison.
- The inmate refuses to partake in peer relationships with other inmates.
- The inmate refuses to accept the inmate code.
- The inmate happens to be housed in a cell with an inmate who also refuses the inmate code.
- The inmate abstains from antisocial and deviant behaviors while imprisoned.

On the other hand, in cases where there is strong prisonization, the following factors are found:

- The inmate is serving a long sentence.
- The inmate has an unstable personality and was poorly socialized.
- The inmate has few, if any, relationships with positive figures on the outside.
- The inmate shows a readiness for integration into inmate peer groups.
- The inmate blindly accepts the inmate code.
- The inmate happens to be housed in a cell with an inmate who also embraces the inmate code.
- The inmate participates in antisocial and deviant behaviors behind bars.[40]

Another important concept related to the deprivation model is the **pains of imprisonment**. Developed by Gresham Sykes, the pains of imprisonment refer to five deprivations that prison imposes on inmates. These are (1) deprivation of liberty, (2) deprivation of autonomy, (3) deprivation of security, (4) deprivation of goods and services, and (5) deprivation of heterosexual relationships.[41] These hardships, which are directly imposed by the prison structure, lead to adaptations among inmates and influence their behavior.

CORRECTIONS HISTORY

Prison Break

Prisoners always have and probably always will escape from prison. Interestingly, official records on prisoner breaks are not standardized limiting the availability, accuracy, and consistency of information on the actual number of escapes from prison. Instead, researchers interested in this topic area are forced to work with regional approximations and a variety of sources in order to determine the number of escapes, data that is primarily generated from state and/or local departments of corrections.

Information on the number of escaped prisoners captured, characteristics of escaped prisoners, the methods used to achieve the escape, how many escapees are involved in criminal activities after successfully escaping from prison, and whether overcrowding has resulted in more escapes is also limited and not easily determined. Even the U.S. Department of Justice, Bureau of Justice Statistics cannot provide this information.

But there is one data source, the National Corrections Reporting Program (NCRP), that records prisoner status once each year. The information contained in this report is obtained from all 50 states, and the California Youth Authority and has been reporting annually since 1983. In his study of prisoner escapes, Richard Culp, using data from the NCRP, determined that on average, 1.3 inmates were involved in each escape. Using this figure and the total number of prisoners in U.S. correctional facilities, Culp estimated the total number of prisoner escapes in 1997 was approximately 3,427. However, information from the Corrections Compendium survey and the *Directory of Juvenile and Adult Correctional Departments, Institutions, Agencies, and Paroling Authorities*, both published by the American Correctional Association, indicated that in 1997 there were approximately 5,743 and 9,482 escapes, respectively. A fourth source, *Corrections Yearbook*, listed the number of prisoners who had escaped or walked away from prison in 1997 at 8,496. Culp suggests that part of the discrepancy in these figures might be attributed to the lack of consistency in defining what constitutes a prison escape.

What did the author find? Reported figures representing prison escapes should be characterized only as best estimates. The available data on prison breaks is incomplete and lacks standardization. However, the author did determine, using data from three sources, that over a period of 11 years, approximately 3 percent of all inmates escape from prison sometime during their sentence. Eighty-five percent of prisoners who escape do so from low-security prisons. Of the remaining 11.5 percent of escapees who managed to escape from high-security prisons, 92 percent are recaptured within a year of their escape. Few of the escapes involved violence and in even fewer of the escapes did the inmate commit additional crimes to accomplish his escape; although the likelihood of a violent crime being committed by an escapee in recent years has increased and may be attributable to the characteristics of the inmate and the increased level of prison security. Interestingly, prison escape rates have dropped even as the prison population and the rate of incarceration has increased. The author attributes this to an increase in prison security and a gradual aging of the prison population.

Source: Culp, R. F. (2005). Frequency and characteristics of prison escapes in the United States: An analysis of national data. *Prison Journal, 85,* 270–291.

Over the years, penologists have identified many features of prisons that influence inmate behavior. These include the security level of the facility, crowding, conditions of housing, and the overall effectiveness of prison management. Richard McCorkle and his colleagues examined 371 American prisons and explored whether deprivation factors influenced prison safety as measured by assaults against inmates and staff. They found that occupancy rates, ratio of guards to inmates, and size of the institution were associated with violence, but that the racial composition of prison guards and security level of the institution most correlated with violence.[42] Recently, Glenn Walters studied prisonization between novice or first-time inmates and experienced inmates with longer sentences and more extensive criminal histories. Using measures of criminal thinking styles and social identification with criminals, Walters found that novice inmates experienced increases in criminal thinking styles after exposure to the prison environment. Chronic offenders continued to display antisocial thinking and criminal identification[43]—precisely as Clemmer theorized more than 60 years earlier.

Importation Model

As scholars travelled the country and studied various prisons, they noted consistencies in terms of the **inmate code**, the subculture that governs inmate behavior and social systems that exist in various prison facilities. The inmate code was complete with its own language or **argot** and set of principles for inmates to obey. These principles included the following:

1. Don't interfere with inmate interests, or never rat on a con.
2. Don't lose your head. Play it cool and do your own time.
3. Don't exploit other inmates or be right [meaning, do the right thing].
4. Don't weaken. Be tough and be a man.
5. Don't be a sucker and don't associate with guards who are known as "hacks" or "screws."

From the deprivation perspective, it was believed that prison facilities molded inmate responses and behaviors in a relatively consistent way.[44–48] This is a very sociological interpretation of prisons and the behavior of inmates that develops within prisons.

What if consistencies in inmate culture and behavior were created by the criminals who reside in prison, not the facility itself?[49] As noted by James Jacobs, "the view of the prison as a primitive society, governed by its own norms and inhabited by its own distinctive social types, has always been somewhat exaggerated."[50, p. 24] Over time, criminologists acknowledged that inmate characteristics had much to do with the ways that prison societies developed.

This very idea led to the importation model of inmate behavior. The **importation model** argues that inmate behavior is best explained by offender characteristics that are imported into the institution. Developed by John Irwin (a criminology professor who is a former prisoner) and his mentor Donald Cressey, the importation model suggests prisoners' individual values, beliefs, and behaviors external to the institution remain important while they adjust or adapt to the prison environment. Theoretically, variables that are risk factors for offending in society at large should correspond to risk factors for prison misconduct.[51] According to the importation model, inmates with more extensive arrest and incarceration histories, prior involvement with gangs, serious substance abuse problems, or previous use of violence should be the most difficult-to-manage offenders behind bars as well.

Several decades of research strongly support the importation model of behavior. In his research of Washington prisons in the 1940s to the 1950s, Clarence Schrag found that offenders who emerged as inmate leaders had served multiple prior terms in prison, were often incarcerated for the most serious forms of crime, had been diagnosed as psychopathic, and had been adjudicated as habitual criminals. In this way, inmate leadership tended to be an extension of antisocial behavior outside the facility. Most importantly, career criminals/inmate leaders committed significantly more major rule violations, including escape and assaulting other inmates and staff.[52] Six decades later, David Allender and Frank Marcell identified four aspects of habitual criminals that contribute to problems for correctional staff. These are:

1. A disdain for authority, particularly legal authority, that when coupled with a propensity for violence can lead to sudden and unpredictable acts of aggression.
2. An acute awareness of their environment that can be used to take advantage of less-savvy inmates.
3. Criminal versatility that allows habitual offenders to engage in assorted acts of misconduct while confined.
4. An inflated sense of self that can contribute to attempts to intimidate, coerce, and prey upon other inmates.[53]

A host of studies indicate that Irwin and Cressey were correct and that much of the antisocial conduct that occurs behind bars is reflective of the antisocial traits and behaviors that inmates imported into the facility upon admission to prison. In fact, at times, prison officials utilize the criminal expertise of prisoners as a means to clear unsolved cases. For example, the Florida Department of Corrections provided two decks of cards to its prisoner population of nearly 100,000 inmates that contained case information on 104 of the state's most troubling unsolved murder and missing person cases. Soon after the program was initiated, authorities charged two offenders with the murder of a cold case that appeared on one of the cards.[54]

In practice, contemporary inmate classification systems are largely based on importation variables, such as criminal, confinement, gang, violence, weapons, and disciplinary histories. For example, the California Department of Corrections, among the largest correctional organizations in the world, recently revised its classification system according to criminal history-based factors and found that importation variables enhanced the ability to anticipate or predict serious misconduct.[55] Recent research based on these data provided even greater support for the importance of individual-level inmate characteristics in explaining institutional misconduct. Scott Camp and Gerald Gaes tested whether different security levels made inmates more prone to institutional misconduct using 561 male inmates with equivalent classification scores. Using an experimental design, 50 percent of the inmates were placed in the lowest security prisons in California (Level I) and 50 percent were placed in the second highest security prisons (Level III). They found that inmates were equally likely to engage in misconduct, which suggests that prison misconduct was a function of inmate, not facility, characteristics.[56]

Integrated/Multilevel Model

Although the deprivation and importation models were developed as rival explanations, it has long been recognized that prisoner behavior is a reflection of both institutional and individual characteristics—known as the **integrated/multilevel model**. For instance, even in institutions characterized by considerable deprivation, individual-level traits of inmates are strong predictors of the inmate's risk of offending and victimization.[57] While environments might explain aggregate differences in violence between institutions, individual factors are at work in determining the likelihood that any prisoner will participate in disruptive or violent behavior. Penologists generally agree that individuals import characteristics from the street that make them more or less likely to engage in violence and misconduct in prison, but, the form of institutional life and how the individual chooses to do time also contribute to their behavior behind bars.

For example, Eric Poole and Robert Regoli showed that inmate characteristics were used to select individuals into types of facilities. In turn, certain facilities fostered the development of inmate codes that mediated or influenced the direct effects of inmate characteristics.[58] John Wooldredge found that individual characteristics existing before prison affected personal perceptions of crowding in the same institution. The implication was that structural factors, such as crowding, did not have universal impact on inmates in part because they were experienced differently.[59] Andy Hochstetler and Matt DeLisi found that although inmate and prison characteristics were important determinants of inmate behavior, the most important determinant was the inmate's involvement in the illicit prison economy.[60] Inmates also adapt to prison by utilizing different strategies of dealing with confinement, such as withdrawal and acting tough. These adaptations depend on the prison environment, the inmate's personal characteristics, and what an inmate thinks will protect him or her from victimization and make imprisonment most comfortable.[61–63]

Administrative Control Model

Unlike the importation and deprivation models with their emphasis on inmates, the **administrative control model** approach points to prison officials, administrators, and governance generally as the most important determinants of inmate behavior. According to administrative control theorists, such as John DiIulio, prisons characterized by the following are likely to experience less misconduct and violence than facilities that are poorly administered, managed, and controlled[64–65]:

- decisive, strong leadership
- formalized rules and organization
- effective management
- custodial culture
- proactive staff interaction with inmates
- programming opportunities

Poorly administered facilities characterized by disorganization and ineffective management have been linked to the most severe forms of inmate violence, including inmate homicides and rioting.[66–68]

Within the administrative control model, DiIulio outlined three general approaches to prison administration that bear on inmate behavior. The **control model** asserts that highly rigid control of every aspect of inmate life and staff routines is required to ensure safe prison environments. The **responsibility model** is a more liberal, flexible approach where staff and inmates enjoy relative autonomy intended to facilitate self-governance. The **consensual model** is a mix of the prior two characterized by relaxed control of staff routines but fairly rigid control of inmate routines.[69] Perhaps not unexpectedly, researchers have found that prison personnel who work in more rigidly controlled, formalized institutions report less job satisfaction and more stress than those who work in more flexible facilities.[70]

Perhaps because of the stressors of a tough, control-oriented prison management, inmates can revolt. Based on data from diverse samples, scholars have found that control-oriented, strongly administrated prisons can create stifling conditions that exacerbate inmate misconduct and violence. Instead of effectively controlling inmate behavior, the rigidity of an overly administrative regime can increase prisonization among inmates and lead to disorder.[71–75] Beth Huebner recently conducted a study of inmate violence using data from 185 state correctional facilities that encompassed nearly 4,200 inmates. She compared the coercive, control approach to remunerative controls that function as incentives to foster commitment in prison rules and goals. Overall, Huebner found that remunerative controls were able to reduce inmate violence whereas coercive controls were not effective management tools.[76]

Inmate Violence and Misconduct

The overriding goal of prison administration and staff is to create an environment with minimal inmate **misconduct**, or inmate violations of prison rules and regulations, and violence. Within each state prison system there is a codified set of violations that are comparable to criminal statutes or laws that exist in conventional society. For example, the Arizona Department of Corrections organizes disciplinary violations into three broad categories. Group A violations include inciting or participating in a riot, disturbance, demonstration, or work stoppage; taking a hostage or kidnapping; intentionally causing the death or great bodily injury of another person; sexual assault; assault or battery with a deadly weapon or any assault on staff; escape, aiding escape, or preventing the discovery of an escape; arson; negligence or carelessness causing death or great bodily injury; possession or manufacture of dangerous contraband including weapons, explosives, escape paraphernalia, official documents, prison uniforms, or other items deemed a threat to institutional security; and conspiracy to commit any Group A violation. Group B violations include 27 less-serious violations ranging from fighting, gambling, tattooing, engaging in sexual behavior, refusing to work, etc. Group C violations include 12 more trivial acts of noncompliance including horseplay, bartering, feigning illness, littering, and failure to maintain a clean living area. Violation of these rules can result in a variety of punishments, including reprimand, restrictions, extra duties, loss of privileges, restitutions, increased parole risk, recommendation to lose time served, and additional detention.[77] These punishments are in place to facilitate inmate compliance and institutional safety.

Of course, this is a tall order considering the risk factors, criminal propensity, and criminal careers that typify many American prisoners. Occasionally, inmates misbehave for the most trivial of reasons, such as in 2007, when more than 33 prisoners in New Mexico set fires, flooded their cells, and damaged prison property when they were informed that their dinner menu would be modified to include only one dinner sausage.[78] By and large, however, prisons are dangerous places because of the antisocial tendencies of prisoners. For instance, Nancy Wolff and her colleagues explored inmate violence among a large sample of nearly 8,000 inmates selected from 14 prisons. They found that the rate of assault among male inmates was over *18 times* higher than the assault victimization rate of males in the general population. For female prisoners, the rate of assault was a staggering *27 times* higher than the assault victimization rate among women in the general population. For both male and female inmates, 20 percent reported that they have been physically victimized in the prior 6 months. Male inmates were significantly more likely than female inmates to be assaulted with a weapon and to have physical force used against them by prison staff.[79]

Sexual violence is one of the most important safety issues in American corrections. In 2003, the **Prison Rape Elimination Act**, which required the Bureau of Justice Statistics to conduct a comprehensive statistical review and analysis of the incidence and effects

CORRECTIONS IN THE NEWS

Violence in Prisons

Violence in prison is not as random as you might think. Research reveals the use of force by inmates in a prison setting is generally not mindless; one or both of the parties involved ordinarily has a reason for participating in the violence. Very seldom were the parties or combatants strangers. Interestingly, most claim their actions were in self-defense and that they had had no interest in initiating the altercation.

Several reasonably easy-to-accept explanations exist for violence in prisons. Evidence from various sources indicates that the average inmate is by and large a poor communicator. Inmates also have little or no experience in initiating and/or managing a peaceful conflict resolution process and are seldom known for their willingness to compromise. Often times their attempts to communicate only exacerbate the situation.

Inmates involved in physical altercations report the incidences stem from power struggles; attempts at achieving or maintaining meaningful levels of respect; out of a sense of fairness, loyalty, or honor to other inmates and/or associations; and in the case of material reasons, over such items as cigarettes, drugs, telephone calling cards, and other items of contraband. Race was also a factor. In nearly 17 percent of the cases reviewed, racial animosity was the primary indicator for violence.

But there are other factors involved in this scenario. The prison system itself is partially to blame. Prisons are considered, and for very good reasons, dangerous places in which to reside. And in order to survive the prison culture, which parallels the culture of the inner-city street, inmates must be willing and capable of defending themselves through the use of force if they expect to maintain a well regarded level of respect and dignity as perceived by other inmates.

Studies indicate that one in five adult inmates is likely to be assaulted during his or her time in prison. In order to survive, an inmate must prepare her- or himself for the likelihood of being physically attacked. This requires that an inmate prepare both physically and psychologically in order to limit his or her chances of being victimized by another inmate. After all, it's been said that the best defense is a strong offense. This philosophy in turn develops in the inmate in the form of a defensive, hostile, and at times confrontational demeanor.

By the necessity of its own design, prison systems generate a sense of competition. The prison system's social structure requires inmates to interact with other prisoners whose behavior they cannot accurately predict. Also, by the nature of inmate culture, seeking assistance from prison officials is strongly condemned and is generally viewed as a weakness—and this impression of being weak is not an image any inmate wishes to portray. What serves as the impetus for these violent acts? All in all, the stimuli for these incidents seem rather primal. Research posits inmate-on-inmate violence is the result of verbal challenges, invasions of space and/or privacy, insults, a hostile gesture, and occasionally an invitation to engage in physical combat.

Source: Edgar, K., O'Donnell, I., & Martin, C. (2003). *Prison violence: The dynamics of conflict, fear, and power.* Portland, OR: Willan.

of prison rape and sexual abuse, was passed. In 2007, the Bureau of Justice Statistics surveyed inmates from 146 state and federal prisons and found that more than 60,500 inmates or 4.5 percent of the inmate population reported sexual victimization. Of these victimizations, more than 38,600 involved staff–inmate sexual misconduct and 27,500 involved inmate–inmate victimization.[80]

It is difficult to estimate the prevalence of sexual misconduct in prisons because of feelings of shame and embarrassment that victims might feel that would discourage reporting, the illegality of sexual contact between staff and prisoners, and the clandestine nature of the offense itself. Nancy Wolff and her colleagues concluded that prevalence estimates of sexual violence in prisons range between 1 and 41 percent with an average of about 2 percent.[81] In their review of the literature on sexual violence occurring in prisons, Tonisha Jones and Travis Pratt concluded that studies typically report prison

CORRECTIONS BRIEF

Prison Rape: Is This a Crime that Can Be Prevented?

Victims and prison officials differ in their opinions as to whether prison rape can be prevented. Proving a charge of sexual assault is difficult at best when working with a victim on the outside. But imagine how difficult it would be to pursue a case of rape that involves a victim who is an inmate and a perpetrator who is also a convicted felon.

In prisons, where far too often control is shared by the guards and the convicts, sex is a commodity that is sometimes traded for protection. But is the protection worth the cost? Inmates who agree to sexual transactions are generally thought of as punks—property to be used and traded. Generally, what begins as a sexual relationship between two inmates ends in prostitution.

To what extent does this problem of prison rape exist? A study published by the Bureau of Justice Statistics reported 8,210 allegations of sexual violence reported nationwide. Forty-two percent of these allegations of sexual assault involved prison staff and 37 percent involved inmate-on inmate nonconsensual sexual acts. Of these 8,210 allegations of sexual misconduct, authorities were able to substantiate nearly 2,100 incidents of sexual violence. Males were the reported victim in nearly 90 percent of the inmate-on-inmate rape cases brought to the attention of correctional authorities.

It is impossible to determine accurately the number of actual rapes that occur either in or out of prison. Official crime data represents only those offenses reported to law enforcement. At present there are no reliable estimates of the extent of unreported sexual victimization among prison and jail inmates and youth held in residential facilities. And since the victim of rape in a men's correctional institution is male, underreporting is the norm and not the exception.

Some studies report over 20 percent of prisoners are victims of sexual assault ranging from coerced sexual contact to rape. Correctional authorities estimate the number of rape victims at approximately 12,000 victims per year. Even so, the crime of rape involving an inmate is rarely prosecuted. As with most crimes committed in correctional facilities, local prosecutors rely on department of corrections officials to handle the investigation, the case, and the punishment.

From a prosecution perspective, the problem lies in substantiating the evidence. First, witness credibility is a major obstacle. Second, corroborating testimony is difficult to obtain at best. Third, indifference is yet another, and possibly the most insurmountable obstacle.

Maybe the answer is to stop the problem before it becomes an issue for the courts. Routine activities theory would label the intended victim of a prison rape as a suitable target. According to research, the suitable target in this scenario is the prison inmate who also happens to be gay. Studies have found gay men in prison are much more likely to be targets of sexual aggression than they are to be sexual predators. Should gay inmates be housed in a separate facility? Or maybe it is just an issue of deliberate indifference that needs to be corrected.

Source: Beck, A. J., & Hughes, T. A. (2005). *Sexual violence reported by correctional authorities, 2004*. Washington, DC: U.S. Department of Justice, Office of Justice Programs, Bureau of Justice Statistics.

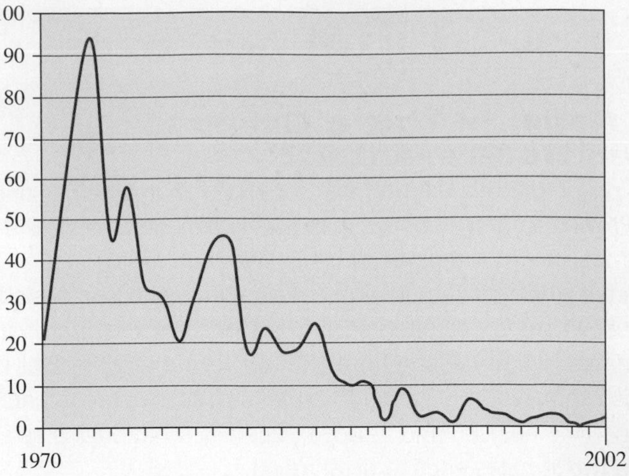

FIGURE 9–3 Riots in American Prisons per 1 Million Inmates, 1970–2002. *Source*: Modified from Retrieved January 11, 2008, from http://www.asca.net/documents/FACTSHEET.pdf.

sexual victimization rates ranging between 1 and 20 percent.[82] Certain inmates, such as younger inmates; inmates who most recently arrived in prison; inmates with mental, physical, or developmental disabilities; and homosexual inmates are significantly at risk for sexual victimization in American prisons.[83]

Although prisons are inarguably dangerous places, it is important to note that advances in inmate classification, improved technology and surveillance of inmates, and overall advances in staff training, professionalization, and knowledge make today's prisons safer than they were in previous eras. As shown in FIGURE 9–3, despite an explosion in the prison population of more than 500 percent, the number of **riots**—disturbances of prison order involving multiple inmates and usually resulting in property damage and violence—in correctional facilities had declined dramatically in recent decades. In fact, since the early 1970s, prison riots have declined nearly twentyfold.

The declining prevalence of riots is illustrative of the improvements in correctional management, design, and operations in recent decades when considering the circumstances that led to the deadliest prison riot in American history at the Penitentiary of New Mexico in Santa Fe in 1980. Between 1975 and 1980, the **Penitentiary of New Mexico** transitioned from a facility that offered employment opportunities, recreational programs, and other amenities to one with few productive services for inmates. There were five wardens during this tenure, and this disruptive leadership trend precluded any effective continuity in prison management. Moreover, the facility increasingly relied on inmate informants or **snitches** as the primary method of social control. In fact, the inmate informant system was so widespread that a large subpopulation of informants was segregated from the general population. During the riot, the inmate informants in protective custody were the primary targets of the violence that resulted in 33 inmate murders, more than 400 assaults and other injuries, and $200 million in damages.[84–86]

The 1980 prison riot at the Penitentiary of New Mexico in Santa Fe was the deadliest in American history and involved 33 inmate murders.

Similar reductions occur for inmate murders of correctional staff and prison escapes. In the early 1980s, the rate of correctional staff murdered by inmates ranged between 20 and 25 staff per 1 million inmates. Today, that rate ranges between 0 and 1 staff murders per 1 million inmates. Also in the early 1980s, prison escapes were fairly common, about 10–12 per 1,000 inmates. Today, the rate of prison escapes is 1 per 1,000 inmates.[87] Cece Hill recently conducted a survey of 43 American and Canadian prison systems and found that only 287 known escapes were attempted in the previous year. Interestingly, there were more than 2,000 walkaways from custody. Walkaways are technically escapes, but do not involve physically breaking out of the prison facility. Instead, walkaways consist of an offender with access to the community simply failing to return to prison. About 80 percent of these offenders are apprehended.[88]

Keep in mind that aggregate statistics about prison violence and misconduct obscure the tremendous variation between inmates in terms of their institutional behavior. Just as early penologists noted the wide ranging ways that inmates adjusted to prison life, it is also important to remember the sheer differences in propensity for violence that exist in the inmate population. In fact, most prisoners in American prisons are well behaved while incarcerated and have zero involvement in serious acts of violence, such as rape, assault, and murder. For most inmates, institutional misconduct is generally limited to relatively unserious acts of noncompliance with prison rules, such as disobeying an officer, being in an unauthorized area, failing to clean their cell, refusal to work, and related violations.

To illustrate, Matt DeLisi studied the criminal careers behind bars of more than 1,000 inmates serving time in Arizona prisons and found that more than 33 percent never received a ticket for a violation of prison rules and nearly 10 percent received only one misconduct ticket. On the other hand, 33 percent of inmates received between 5 and 29 violations and a small cohort of inmates, about 8 percent, had more than 30 violations on their prison record. In fact, a small cohort of violent offenders was responsible for 100 percent of the murders, 75 percent of the rapes, 80 percent of the arsons, and 50 percent of the aggravated assaults.[89]

Using a large sample of nearly 25,000 inmates in the Florida Department of Corrections, Mark Cunningham and Jon Sorensen found that several inmate characteristics predict violent prison misconduct. Younger offenders, those serving shorter sentences, gang members, those with histories of violence, and offenders with prior prison terms were most likely to commit violence. Conversely, older offenders, those serving longer sentences and those with minimal criminal and violence histories were less likely to commit violent acts behind bars.[90] The effect of youth is especially important, for instance, even among a sample of incarcerated murderers, young age was a strong predictor of prison violence.[91]

Prison Gangs

Prison gangs are organizations that operate within prison systems as criminal organizations consisting of a select group of inmates who have established an organized chain of command and are governed by an established code of conduct that centers on criminal activity and other forms of intimidation.[92] Prison gangs, also known as **security threat groups (STGs)**, are the greatest threat to prison safety in the United States.

According to the National Alliance of Gang Investigators Associations:

- More than 1,600 STGs and 113,627 gang members operate in American prisons.
- The most frequently identified STGs by race are Aryan Brotherhood and Nazi Lowriders (White), Blood, Crip, Gangster Disciples, and Black Guerilla Family (African American), and Mexican Mafia, Latin Kings, La Nuestra Familia, and Texas Syndicate (Hispanic).
- Many STG inmates have ties to terrorist groups or may be susceptible to recruitment by terrorists. For example, there are at least 27 members of al Qaeda at the Administrative Maximum Security Prison in Florence, Colorado.[93]

It has been reported that prison gang members are 30 to 75 percent more likely than nongang inmates to commit serious violations of prison rules.[94] Gerald Gaes and his colleagues conducted one of the most impressive studies of prison gang behavior using the

CORRECTIONS RESEARCH

Why Are Prison Gangs Considered a Security Threat Group?

Nearly 75 percent of correctional institutions in the United States have policies prohibiting inmates from recruiting other gang members. But when asked, an overwhelming percentage of inmates indicated new inmates are often recruited by established prison gangs. And from what has been learned about prison gang operations, inmate affiliation with a prison gang also benefits the gang when the inmate is released from prison. But what does this mean for the street gang member or gang leader who is convicted of a crime and sentenced to prison? Are you familiar with the phrase "a home away from home?" The single biggest difference in the life of a street gang member sentenced to prison is the territory in which he or she will be operating.

Gang domination of the economic activities within a correctional institution is well documented. Gangs have been linked to a variety of illegal operations such as the distribution of illegal drugs, prostitution, loan sharking, gambling, extortion, and the newest racket—the cellular phone call. The distribution of illegal substances is generally the number one money maker for prison gangs. Simply put, gangs make money off of other inmates. Some of this money is exchanged between inmates, but big money transactions occur on the outside; often the money is exchanged between family members of the inmates involved in the illegal activity.

Various sources suggest that prison gangs control from 30 to nearly 40 percent of the total drug trade that takes place in correctional institutions. Therefore, it should come as no surprise that drug deals gone bad are the largest source of violent conflict and have been linked to crimes ranging from prison riots to killings. Very little scientific research has been conducted on prison gangs; what is known about violence attributable to prison gangs comes from research targeting street gangs. This research has revealed that gang members, especially those members who comprise the core element of the gang, commit more crimes. Being embedded within a gang increases the likelihood of involvement in criminal acts. This finding likely transcends prison walls and results in a sustainable gang subculture.

Sources: Knox, G. W. (2006). The problem of gangs and security threat groups (STG's) in American prisons today: Recent research findings from the 2004 Prison Gang survey. Retrieved October 1, 2008, from http://www.ngcrc.com/corr2006.html; Gaes, G. G., Wallace, S., Gilman, E., Klein-Saffran, J., & Suppa, S. (2002). The influence of prison gang affiliation on violence and other prison misconduct. *Prison Journal, 82,* 359–385.

entire population of male inmates within the Bureau of Prisons, which included more than 82,500 inmates. Nearly 7,500 of these BOP inmates were gang members. In addition, their study contained information on 27 known prison gangs. Their analyses showed that gang affiliation increases the likelihood of violent and other forms of misconduct, even after controlling for individual characteristics of inmates that prior research has established are associated with a violent predisposition.[95] In addition, core gang members were significantly more violent and prone to misconduct than peripheral gang members.

Prison gangs are so troublesome that they can cripple an entire state prison system under certain conditions. For example, Paige Ralph and James Marquart found that a loosening of social control in Texas prisons unleashed a gang problem that produced a *tenfold* increase in the rate of murders, weapon assaults, and sex assaults. The change in social control within Texas prisons was a direct outgrowth of the *Ruiz v. Estelle* appellate court decision in which several aspects of Texas correctional policies, such as overcrowding, frequent and excessive use of guard–inmate force, inadequate medical care, arbitrary disciplinary practices, and denial of access to legal resources were in violation of the Eighth Amendment.[96] While the decision made prisons more humane, it also undeniably relaxed the degree of social control, and during a 2-year span, prison gang members committed more homicides than in the previous 20 years.

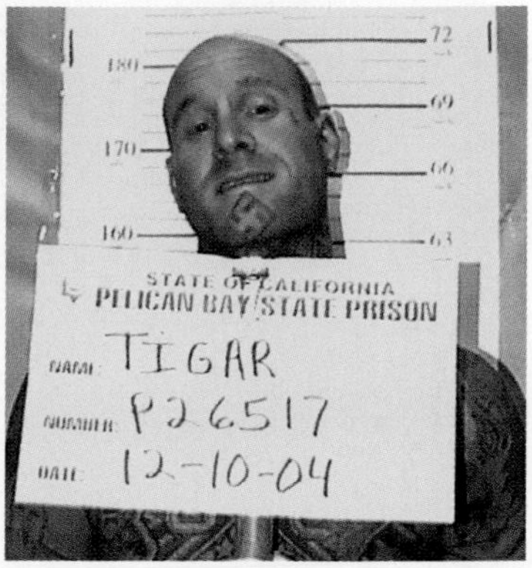

White supremacists gangs are among the most serious threats to institutional safety in the United States.

James Byrne and Don Hummer identified criteria that correctional systems use to identify and classify inmates as members of prison gangs or security threat groups. These include (1) an inmate admits to criminal street gang membership; (2) an inmate is identified as a gang member by a parent or guardian; (3) an inmate is identified as a gang member by a documented reliable informant; (4) an inmate resides or frequents a gang's area, adopts its style of dress, hand signs, or tattoos, and associates with known gang members; (5) an inmate was arrested more than once in the company of identified gang members for offenses that are consistent with usual criminal street gang activity; (6) an inmate is identified as a gang member by physical evidence such as photographs; or (7) an inmate was stopped in the company of known gang members four or more times.[97]

Although there are hundreds of known prison gangs, a handful of groups have a national presence in correctional facilities; these groups are profiled next.

Aryan Brotherhood

The **Aryan Brotherhood**, also known as AB or the Brand, is arguably the most notorious prison gang operating in American prisons. The Aryan Brotherhood was founded on Neo-Nazi, White supremacist principles as a means of protection against Black and Hispanic prison gangs in California's San Quentin State Prison. Today, the AB has moved away from supremacist philosophy (currently the Nazi Low Riders are the most explicitly White supremacist prison gang) and favors Irish and Viking imagery. Its primary allies are the Mexican Mafia and Hells Angels, and its principal enemies are La Nuestra Familia and the Black Guerilla Family.

The Aryan Brotherhood is noteworthy for its organizational skills, extreme use of violence, and effect on correctional policies. For instance, the AB was responsible for the stabbing of four correctional staff at the United States Penitentiary in Marion, Illinois, on October 22, 1983, that resulted in the death of two guards. Throughout the 1980s and 1990s, AB leaders were isolated in administrative-segregation or supermax facilities, which are explored at length in Chapter 10.[98] Today, leaders of the AB are being prosecuted by the Department of Justice for hundreds of criminal acts, including murder, extortion, narcotics trafficking, and other crimes conducted behind bars.[99]

Mexican Mafia

The **Mexican Mafia**, also known as MM, EME, or Emeros, is an STG that was formed during the 1950s by Los Angeles street gang members serving time in the California prison system. The Mexican Mafia is a Hispanic gang that is primarily active in the federal and California prison systems that uses an organizational structure similar to the Italian Mafia, with each facility governed by a general with subordinate captains, lieutenants, and soldiers. The Mexican Mafia has a complex system of alliances with other prison gangs. For example, they are allied with the Mexikanemi prison gang, which is active in Texas prisons, but have an antagonistic relationship with the Texas Syndicate, another Hispanic STGs operating in Texas prisons. The Mexican Mafia has prior working relationships with White prison gangs, but is antagonistic to African American prison gangs.[100]

La Nuestra Familia

La Nuestra Familia is an STG that was formed in the 1960s by Mexican-American prisoners in the California prison system, particularly Soledad Prison. La Nuestra Familia, which has a constitution and paramilitary organizational structure, primarily operates in West Coast prisons but has a national presence. Hispanic prisoners also make a distinction between those from northern California, known as *nortenos,* or northerners, and those from southern California, known as *surenos*, or southerners. They have loose associations with the Black Guerilla Family and are antagonistic to other Hispanic gangs, such as the Texas Syndicate, Mexican Mafia, and Mexikanemi, and White gangs, such as the Aryan Brotherhood.[101]

Black Guerilla Family

The **Black Guerilla Family**, or **BGF**, was founded in 1966 by former Black Panther George Jackson and is the most politically oriented prison gang based on its Marxists leanings and goal of overthrowing the American government, which it views as racist and unjust. The BGF is an African American prison gang with a paramilitary organizational structure consisting of a central committee, supreme leader, and other military ranks. They have a nationwide presence but exist primarily in prisons on the East and West Coasts. They are loosely partnered with other Black STGs and La Nuestra Familia, but are antagonistic to the Aryan Brotherhood, Texas Syndicate, and Mexican Mafia.[102]

Responding to Prison Gangs

Although most prisoners are not involved in security threat groups, the reality is that the bulk of violence, drug trafficking, and other misconduct occurring within prisons is perpetrated by prison gang members. Many states developed security threat group assessments as part of the initial diagnostic and classification process that offenders experience upon entry to the prison system. Gang intelligence units gather objective and validated information that supports the placement of prisoners into the most appropriate institutional setting.[103] Specialized correctional gang units also give prison gang members the opportunity to repudiate their gang membership and provide correctional officials with gang intelligence in exchange for assignment in protective custody and at times access to more privileges. During these debriefings, prison gang members are officially decertified from the gang from the perspective of prison officials. Of course, the **decertification process** does not apply from the perspective of active gangs members, since some security threat groups, such as the Aryan Brotherhood, offer only one option out of the gang: death.

To help inmates get into the frame of mind to possibly decertify, awareness programs are in place. For instance, the Connecticut Gang Awareness Program (GAP) is a mandatory 2-month program for inmates in security threat groups to help them reevaluate their current status. Inmates are kept in a close monitoring unit, which is highly restrictive, until they pass the GAP program. For gang members who maintain their gang involvement, other programs are used. For example, Pennsylvania officials developed the Long-Term Segregation Unit, which houses STG inmates in a highly restrictive environment with very few privileges, which are limited to treatment, religious services, and academic study.[104] Correctional systems also use more informal means to alleviate the prison gang threat. For instance, prison gang members are often frequently moved within facilities or transferred to other institutions as a way to dilute the gang presence within a particular housing unit or facility.[105]

Despite their involvement in violence and misconduct, not all penologists support efforts of prison systems to crack down on prison gang members. Hans Toch likened the classification of gang-affiliated inmates to a "tribunal of inquisition." According to Toch:

> Prison administrators unquestionably have their problems with gangs and have found some gangs difficult to deal with, but they are not thereby entitled to translate their sense of helplessness and frustration into an indiscriminate practice of scapegoating and railroading affiliated youths. To abrogate the basic rights of irritating or annoying people as a matter of institutional policy appears to be a primitive response.[106, p. 286]

The primitive response that Toch refers to is witch burning. Despite complaints such as these, the Supreme Court, in the case ***Wilkinson v. Austin*** (2005), affirmed the due process rights of inmates are preserved by classification into high-security or supermax settings.[107]

It is clear that prisoners are a high-risk group in terms of their social, behavioral, and psychiatric histories, their sustained involvement in crime and criminal justice system involvements, and their correctional needs. While most prisoners are relatively compliant with prison rules, some inmates, especially those active in security threat groups, continue to recidivate behind bars and commit severe acts of violence, such as murder, rape, and rioting. In the next chapter, the ways that prison systems classify, manage, supervise, and treat prisoners is explored. The importance of this is twofold. First, effective management and treatment serves the goal of rehabilitation and facilitates prison order and safety. Second, treatment programs serve to provide prisoners the skills they will need upon release on parole or upon termination of their prison sentence.

WRAP UP

CASE STUDY CONCLUSION

Leopold and Loeb used their intellectual gifts to accomplish a great deal during their time in confinement in Illinois prisons. Their intellectual pursuits are clear evidence of the importation model of inmate behavior—they acted in prison as they had before prison. That Loeb was fatally stabbed by another inmate points to the dangers and deprivations that the prison structure and inmate society present, which supports an integrated and deprivation model of inmate behavior. For instance, if Loeb was targeted because of his involvement in a child murder—coupled with rumors of his homosexual relationship with Leopold—then the inmate subculture is further implicated. The accomplishments of Leopold also show that even murderers can and often do lead productive lives while serving their lengthy prison terms.

Source: Higdon, H. (1999). *Leopold & Loeb: The crime of the century.* Chicago: University of Illinois Press.

Chapter Summary

- Prisons are a controversial topic because they are expensive, seemingly ineffective based on offender recidivism data, and contribute to social inequality among racial and gender groups.
- The prison population has increased more than 500 percent in recent decades and today contains nearly 2.4 million persons behind bars.
- The prisoner population is 93 percent male and 7 percent female.
- About 1 in 3 African American males, 1 in 6 Hispanic males, and 1 in 17 White males will serve some time in prison. Virtually all of these racial and ethnic differences are explained by racial differences in criminal offending.
- More than 3,100 prisoners die annually primarily from heart disease, cancer, liver disease, AIDS, and suicide.
- Prisoners have a variety of serious needs based on their social histories of victimization, substance use, psychiatric problems, and public assistance.
- Several models of inmate behavior have been developed, which attribute the cause of inmate behavior to prisons (deprivation), inmates (importation), and administration (administrative control) and offer both person and facility explanations (integrated/multilevel).
- Inmates commit diverse forms of misconduct, ranging from noncompliance with prison rules to violent crimes including murder, rape, and rioting.
- Contemporary American prisons are significantly safer than during prior eras in terms of rioting, murders of staff, and escapes.
- Prison gangs, or security threat groups, are the most formidable threat to institutional safety.
- Organized primarily by race and ethnicity, groups such as the Mexican Mafia, La Nuestra Familia, Black Guerilla Family, and Aryan Brotherhood are dangerous prison gangs.

Key Terms

administrative control model Inmate behavior approach that points to prison officials, administrators, and governance generally as the most important determinants of inmate behavior.

American Correctional Association (ACA) The oldest professional association developed by and devoted to the correctional profession.

argot The prisoner language.

Aryan Brotherhood A White prison gang.

Black Guerilla Family (BGF) An African American prison gang.

Bureau of Prisons (BOP) The federal prison system.

consensual model A mix of the control and responsibility models characterized by relaxed control of staff routines but fairly rigid control of inmate routines.

contraband Materials prohibited in correctional facilities, such as weapons, drugs, and cell phones.

control model Inmate behavior model that asserts that highly rigid control of every aspect of inmate life and staff routines is required to ensure safe prison environments.

convicts Offenders sentenced to prison.

decertification process The official process where a prison gang member repudiates his or her membership and provides intelligence to correctional officials.

deprivation model Inmate behavior model that proposes that inmate behavior is primarily a function of the oppressive structural features posed by the prison facility itself.

Homeboy Industries Organization that provides free services and work opportunities for former offenders.

importation model Argued that prisoner behavior and the conditions of prisons were mostly a function of the characteristics, values, beliefs, and behaviors that criminals employed on the outside of prison.

inmate code The subculture that governs inmate behavior and social systems that exist in various prison facilities.

inmate (or prisoner) A defendant who has been sentenced to jail or prison.

integrated/multilevel model Explanation of inmate behavior that uses both inmate and facility variables.

La Nuestra Familia A Hispanic prison gang.

Mexican Mafia A Hispanic prison gang.

misconduct Inmate violations of prison rules and regulations.

pains of imprisonment Deprivations of liberty, autonomy, security, goods and services, and heterosexual relationships.

Penitentiary of New Mexico Prison that experienced the deadliest prison riot in U.S. history, which resulted in 33 inmate murders.

penologists Criminologists who study prisons.

prison gangs Organizations that operate within prison systems as criminal organizations consisting of a select group of inmates who have established an organized chain of command and are governed by an established code of conduct that centers on criminal activity and other forms of intimidation.

Prison Rape Elimination Act Legislation that required the Bureau of Justice Statistics to conduct a comprehensive statistical review and analysis of the incidence and effects of prison rape and sexual abuse.

prisoners Offenders sentenced to prison. *Also see* inmate.

prisonization The socialization process whereby inmates embrace the oppositional and antisocial culture of the prisoner population.

prisons Correctional facilities that house convicted felons for lengthy periods of time, usually more than 1 year.

recidivate (recidivism) To reoffend after release from correctional supervision.

responsibility model A more liberal, flexible inmate behavior approach where staff and inmates enjoy relative autonomy intended to facilitate self-governance.

riots Disturbances of prison order involving multiple inmates and usually resulting in property damage and violence.

Scared Straight Ineffective program designed to deter juvenile delinquents from a life of crime.

security threat groups (STGs) An organized inmate gang that engages in predatory, criminal behavior behind bars.

snitches Inmate informants.

United States Immigration and Customs Enforcement (ICE) Agency responsible for enforcement of immigration laws.

Wilkinson v. Austin Supreme Court case that held that supermax classification does not violate due process (Fourteenth Amendment) rights of prisoners.

Critical Thinking Questions

1. Which model of inmate behavior seems the most accurate? Is the deprivation model simply an attempt to ignore the serious risks of prisoners?
2. Are prisons poorly or well run? What evidence can you provide to support both positions? Do contemporary prisons seem safer than they were in previous eras?
3. Should state prisoners simply be segregated by race and gang? What are some pros and cons of such an approach to control inmate misconduct and violence?
4. Is prison rape seen as a more terrifying ordeal than rape in society? If so, is this sexist?
5. Many people view prisons as schools of crime. Does the idea of prisonization capture this public sentiment? What other social and cultural forces contribute to prisonization?

Notes

1. De Beaumont, G., & de Tocqueville, A. (1994). On the penitentiary system in the United States and its application in France. In J. E. Jacoby (Ed.), *Classics of criminology* (pp. 372–386). Prospect Heights, IL: Waveland Press.
2. Martinson, R. (1974). What works? Questions and answers about prison reform. *The Public Interest, 35*, 22–54.

3. Massoglia, M. (2008). Incarceration as exposure: The prison, infectious disease, and other stress related illnesses. *Journal of Health and Social Behavior, 49,* 56–71.

4. Allender, D. M. (2004). Offender reentry: A returning or reformed criminal? *FBI Law Enforcement Bulletin, 73,* 1–13.

5. Hunt, G., Riegel, S., Morales, T., & Waldorf, D. (1993). Changes in prison culture: Prison gangs and the case of the "Pepsi generation." *Social Problems, 40,* 398–409.

6. Foucault, M. (1998). Complete and austere institutions. In T. J. Flanagan, J. W. Marquart, & K. G. Adams (Eds.), *Incarcerating criminals: Prisons and jails in social and organizational context* (pp. 23–30). New York: Oxford University Press.

7. Hemmens, C., & Marquart, J. W. (2000). Friend or foe? Race, age, and inmate perceptions of inmate-staff relations. *Journal of Criminal Justice, 28,* 297–312.

8. Homeboy Industries. (2008). Homeboy Industries homepage. Retrieved October 1, 2008, from http://www.homeboy-industries.org/index.php.

9. Seiter, R. P., & Kadela, K. R. (2003). Prisoner reentry: What works, what does not, and what is promising. *Crime & Delinquency, 49,* 360–388.

10. Petrosino, A., Turpin-Petrosino, C., & Buehler, J. (2003). Scared Straight and other juvenile awareness programs for preventing juvenile delinquency: A systematic review of the randomized experimental evidence. *Annals of the American Academy of Political and Social Science, 589,* 41–62.

11. West, H. C., & Sabol, W. J. (2008). *Prisoners in 2007.* Washington, DC: U.S. Department of Justice, Office of Justice Programs, Bureau of Justice Statistics.

12. West & Sabol.

13. Durose, M. R., & Langan, P. A. (2007). *Felony sentences in state courts, 2004.* Washington, DC: U.S. Department of Justice, Office of Justice Programs, Bureau of Justice Statistics.

14. Shepherd, J. M. (2002). Police, prosecutors, criminals, and determinate sentencing: The truth about truth-in-sentencing laws. *Journal of Law and Economics, 45,* 509–534.

15. Shepherd, J. M. (2002). Fear of the first strike: The full deterrent effect of California's two- and three-strikes legislation. *Journal of Legal Studies, 31,* 159–201.

16. West & Sabol.

17. Federal Bureau of Prisons. (2008). *Weekly population report.* Retrieved October 1, 2008, from http://www.bop.gov/locations/weekly_report.jsp#.

18. Bonczar, T. P. (2003). *Prevalence of imprisonment in the U.S. population, 1974–2001.* Washington, DC: U.S. Department of Justice, Office of Justice Programs, Bureau of Justice Statistics.

19. Pettit, B., & Western, B. (2004). Mass imprisonment and the life course: Race and class inequality in United States incarceration. *American Sociological Review, 69,* 151–169.

20. Huebner, B. M. (2005). The effect of incarceration on marriage and work over the life course. *Justice Quarterly, 22,* 281–303.

21. Tonry, M. (1994). Racial disproportion in U.S. prisons. *British Journal of Criminology, 34,* 97–115.

22. Pratt, T. C. (1998). Race and sentencing: A meta-analysis of conflicting empirical research results. *Journal of Criminal Justice, 26,* 513–523.

23. DeLisi, M., & Regoli, B. (1999). Race, conventional crime, and criminal justice: The declining importance of skin color. *Journal of Criminal Justice, 27,* 549–558.

24. Blumstein, A. (1982). On the racial disproportionality of United States' prison populations. *Journal of Criminal Law & Criminology, 73,* 1259–1281.

25. Langan, P. A. (1985). Racism on trial: New evidence to explain the racial composition of prisons in the United States. *Journal of Criminal Law & Criminology, 76,* 666–683.

26. Crutchfield, R. D., Bridges, G. S., & Pitchford, S. R. (1994). Analytical and aggregation biases in analyses of imprisonment: Reconciling discrepancies in studies of racial disparity. *Journal of Research in Crime and Delinquency, 31,* 166–182.

27. Sorensen, J., Hope, R., & Stemen, D. (2003). Racial disproportionality in state prison admissions: Can regional variation be explained by differential arrest rates? *Journal of Criminal Justice, 31,* 73–84.

28. Marquart, J. W., Brewer, V. E., Mullings, J. L., & Crouch, B. M. (1999). Health risk as an emerging field within the new penology. *Journal of Criminal Justice, 27,* 143–154.

29. Massoglia, M. (2008). Incarceration, health, and racial health disparities. *Law and Society Review, 42,* 275–306.

30. Massoglia.

31. Bureau of Justice Statistics. (n.d.). *Deaths of prisoners in state correctional facilities.* Retrieved October 1, 2008, from http://www.albany.edu/sourcebook/pdf/t600102006.pdf.

32. Cripe, C. A., & Pearlman, M. G. (2005). *Legal aspects of corrections management*. Boston, MA: Jones & Bartlett, p. 226.

33. American Correctional Association. (2001). *Record detail.* Retrieved January 16, 2008, from http://www.aca.org/government/policyresolution/view.asp?ID=9.

34. Marquart et al.

35. Mumola, C. J. (2007). *Medical causes of death in state prisons, 2001–2004.* Washington, DC: U.S. Department of Justice, Office of Justice Programs, Bureau of Justice Statistics.

36. Maruschak, L. M. (2007). *HIV in prisons, 2005.* Washington, DC: U.S. Department of Justice, Office of Justice Programs, Bureau of Justice Statistics.

37. James, D. J., & Glaze, L. E. (2006). *Mental health problems of prison and jail inmates.* Washington, DC: U.S. Department of Justice, Office of Justice Programs, Bureau of Justice Statistics.

38. Associated Press. (2006). *Cell phones becoming new prison "cash."* Retrieved October 1, 2008, from http://www.msnbc.msn.com/id/12498707/.

39. Hayner, N. S., & Ash, E. (1940). The prison as a community. *American Sociological Review, 5,* 577–583.

40. Clemmer, D. (1940). *The prison community.* New York: Holt, Rinehart, and Winston.

41. Sykes, G. M. (1958). *The society of captives: A study of a maximum security prison.* Princeton, NJ: Princeton University Press.

42. McCorkle, R. C., Miethe, T. D., & Drass, K. A. (1995). The roots of prison violence: A test of deprivation, management, and "not-so-total" institution models. *Crime and Delinquency, 41,* 317–331.

43. Walters, G. D. (2003). Changes in criminal thinking and identity in novice and experienced inmates: Prisonization revisited. *Criminal Justice and Behavior, 30,* 399–421.

44. Clemmer, D. (1950). Observations on imprisonment as a source of criminality. *Journal of Criminal Law and Criminology, 41,* 311–319.

45. Fox, V. (1954). The effect of counseling on adjustment in prison. *Social Forces, 32,* 285–289.

46. McCorkle, L. W., & Korn, R. (1954). Resocialization within walls. *Annals of the American Academy of Political and Social Science, 293,* 88–98.

47. Sykes, G. M. (1956). Men, merchants, and toughs: A study of reactions to imprisonment. *Social Problems, 3,* 130–138.

48. Sykes, G. M., & Messinger, S. L. (1960). *Theoretical studies in the social organization of the prison.* New York: Social Science Research Council.

49. See Jacobs, J. B. (1977). *Stateville: The penitentiary in mass society.* Chicago: University of Chicago Press.

50. Jacobs, J. B. (1979). Race relations and the prison subculture. *Crime and justice: An annual review of research, volume 1,* 1–28.

51. Irwin J., & Cressey, D. R. (1962). Thieves, convicts and the inmate culture. *Social Problems, 10*, 142–155.

52. Schrag, C. (1954). Leadership among prison inmates. *American Sociological Review, 19*, 37–42.

53. Allender, D. M., & Marcell, F. (2003). Career criminals, security threat groups, and prison gangs: An interrelated threat. *FBI Law Enforcement Bulletin, 72*, 8–12.

54. Associated Press. (2007). *Inmates dealt cards to crack cold cases.* Retrieved July 24, 2007, from http://www.msnbc.msn.com/id/19937180/.

55. Berk, R. A., Ladd, H., Graziano, H., & Baek, J. (2003). A randomized experiment testing inmate classification systems. *Criminology & Public Policy, 2*, 215–242.

56. Camp, S. D., & Gaes, G. G. (2005). Criminogenic effects of the prison environment on inmate behavior: Some experimental evidence. *Crime & Delinquency, 51*, 425–442.

57. Bonta, J., & Gendreau, P. (1990). Re-examining the cruel and unusual punishment of prison life. *Law and Human Behavior, 14*, 347–366.

58. Poole, E. D., & Regoli, R. M. (1983). Violence in juvenile institutions: A comparative study. *Criminology, 21*, 213–232.

59. Wooldredge, J. D. (1997). Explaining variation in perceptions of inmate crowding. *Prison Journal, 77*, 27–40.

60. Hochstetler, A., & DeLisi, M. (2005) Importation, deprivation, and varieties of serving time: An integrated lifestyle-exposure model of prison offending. *Journal of Criminal Justice, 33*, 257–266.

61. McCorkle, R. C. (1992). Personal precautions to violence in prison. *Criminal Justice and Behavior, 19*, 160–173.

62. Toch, H. (1977). *Living in prison: The ecology of survival.* New York: Free Press.

63. Toch, H., & Adams, K. (1989). *Coping: Maladaptation in prisons.* New Brunswick, NJ: Transaction.

64. DiIulio, J. J. (1987) *Governing prisons: A comparative study of correctional management.* New York: Free Press.

65. DiIulio, J. (1991). *No escape: The future of American corrections.* New York: Basic Books, pp. 33–59.

66. Reisig, M. D. (2002). Administrative control and inmate homicide. *Homicide Studies, 6*, 84–103.

67. Useem, B., & Kimball, P. A. (1989) *States of siege: U. S. prison riots, 1971–1996.* New York: Oxford University Press.

68. Useem, B., & Reisig, M. D. (1999) Collective action in prisons: protests, disturbances, and riots. *Criminology, 37*, 735–760.

69. DiIulio.

70. Reisig, M. D., & Lovrich, N. P. (1998). Job attitudes among higher-custody state prison management personnel: A cross-sectional comparative assessment. *Journal of Criminal Justice, 26*, 213–226.

71. Berk, B. B. (1966). Organizational goals and inmate organization. *American Journal of Sociology, 71*, 522–534.

72. Poole, E. D., & Regoli, R. M. (1980). Roles stress, custody orientation, and disciplinary actions: A study of prison guards. *Criminology, 18*, 215–226.

73. Reisig, M. D. (1998). Rates of disorder in higher-custody state prisons: A comparative analysis of managerial practices. *Crime & Delinquency, 44*, 229–244.

74. Reisig, M. D., & Lee, Y. (2000). Prisonization in the Republic of Korea. *Journal of Criminal Justice, 28*, 23–31.

75. Winfree, L. T., Mays, G. L., Crowley, J. E., & Peat, B. J. (1994). Drug history and prisonization: Toward understanding variations in inmate institutional adaptations. *International Journal of Offender Therapy & Comparative Criminology, 38*, 281–296.

76. Huebner, B. M. (2003). Administrative determinants of inmate violence: A multilevel analysis. *Journal of Criminal Justice, 31,* 107–117.

77. Stewart, T. L. (1996). *Director's instruction #6, inmate discipline system* [Memo]. Retrieved January 15, 2008, from http://www.azcorrections.gov/adc/policy_inclusion.asp?menuName=/all_includes/custom-menus/di.htm&fileName=/Policies/DI006.htm#ATTACHMENT%20C.

78. Associated Press. (2007). *Inmates have sausage temper tantrum*. Retrieved September 14, 2007, from http://www.msnbc.msn.com/id/20772719/.

79. Wolff, N., Blitz, C. L., Shi, J., Siegel, J., & Bachman, R. (2007). Physical violence inside prisons: Rates of victimization. *Criminal Justice and Behavior, 34,* 588–599.

80. Beck, A. J., & Harrison, P. M. (2007). *Sexual victimization in state and federal prisons reported by inmates, 2007*. Washington, DC: U.S. Department of Justice, Office of Justice Programs, Bureau of Justice Statistics.

81. Wolff, N., Shi, J., Blitz, C. L., & Siegel, J. (2007). Understanding sexual victimization inside prisons: Factors that predict risk. *Criminology & Public Policy, 6,* 535–564.

82. Jones, T. R., & Pratt, T. C. (2008). The prevalence of sexual violence in prison: The state of the knowledge base and implications for evidence-based correctional policy making. *International Journal of Offender Therapy and Comparative Criminology, 52,* 280–295.

83. Dumond, R. W., & Dumond, D. A. (2007). Correctional health care since the passage of PREA. *Corrections Today, 69,* 76–79.

84. Useem, B. (1985). Disorganization and the New Mexico prison riot of 1980. *American Sociological Review, 50,* 677–688.

85. Colvin, M. (1992). The penitentiary in crisis: From accommodation to riot in New Mexico. Albany: SUNY Albany Press.

86. Colvin, M. (2007). Applying differential coercion and social support theory to prison organizations: The case of the Penitentiary of New Mexico. *Prison Journal, 87,* 367–387.

87. *Fact sheet: Corrections safety*. (n.d.). Retrieved January 11, 2008, from http://www.asca.net/documents/FACTSHEET.pdf.

88. Hill, C. (2006). Prison violence and escapes. *Corrections Compendium, 31,* 11–17.

89. DeLisi, M. (2003). Criminal careers behind bars. *Behavioral Sciences and the Law, 21,* 653–669.

90. Cunningham, M. D., & Sorensen, J. R. (2007). Predictive factors for violent misconduct in close custody. *Prison Journal, 87,* 241–253.

91. Sorensen, J. R., & Cunningham, M. D. (2007). Operationalizing risk: The influence of measurement choice on the prevalence and correlates of prison violence among incarcerated murderers. *Journal of Criminal Justice, 35,* 546–555.

92. Lynam, M. (1989). *Gangland*. Springfield, IL: Charles C. Thomas, p. 48.

93. National Alliance of Gang Investigators Associations. (2007). *2005 national gang threat assessment*. Washington, DC: U.S. Department of Justice, Office of Justice Programs, Bureau of Justice Assistance.

94. DeLisi, M., Berg, M. T., & Hochstetler, A. (2004). Gang members, career criminals, and prison violence: Further specification of the importation model of inmate behavior. *Criminal Justice Studies, 17,* 369–383.

95. Gaes, G. G., Wallace, S., Gilman, E., Klein-Saffran, J., & Suppa, S. (2002). The influence of prison gang affiliation on violence and other prison misconduct. *Prison Journal, 82,* 359–385, p. 381.

96. Marquart, J. W., & Crouch, B. M. (1985). Judicial reform and prisoner control: The impact of *Ruiz v. Estelle* on a Texas penitentiary. *Law and Society Review, 19,* 557–586.

97. Byrne, J., & Hummer, D. (2007). In search of the "tossed salad man" (and others involved in prison violence): New strategies for predicting and controlling violence in prison. *Aggression and Violent Behavior, 12,* 531–541.

98. Walker, R. (2008). Robert Walker's Gangs OR Us: *Aryan Brotherhood*. Retrieved October 1, 2008, from http://www.gangsorus.com/aryan.htm.

99. For example, see Federal Indictment, retrieved October 1, 2008, from http://fl1.findlaw.com/news.findlaw.com/hdocs/docs/crim/usmills101702ind.pdf.

100. Walker, R. (2008). *Robert Walker's Gangs OR Us: Mexican Mafia*. Retrieved October 1, 2008, from http://www.gangsorus.com/mexican-mafia.htm.

101. Walker, R. (2008). *Robert Walker's Gangs OR Us: La Nuestra Familia*. Retrieved October 1, 2008, from http://www.gangsorus.com/nuestra-familia-gang.htm.

102. Walker, R. (2008). *Robert Walker's Gangs OR Us: Black Guerilla Family*. Retrieved October 1, 2008, from http://www.gangsorus.com/BGF.htm.

103. Vigil, D. A. (2006). Classification and security threat group management. *Corrections Today, 68,* 32–34.

104. Austin, J., & McGinnis, K. (2004). *Classification of high-risk and special management prisoners: A national assessment of current practices*. Washington, DC: National Institute of Corrections.

105. Trulson, C. R., Marquart, J. W., & Kawucha, S. K. (2006). Gang suppression and institutional control. *Corrections Today, 68,* 26–28, 30–31.

106. Toch, H. (2007). Sequestering gang members, burning witches, and subverting due process. *Criminal Justice and Behavior, 32,* 274–288.

107. *Wilkinson v. Austin,* 544 U.S. 74 (2005).

CHAPTER

10

Prison Organization, Management, and Programs

"There is nothing inherent in the nature of prisons or their clientele that makes better prisons impossible." [1, p. 235]

OBJECTIVES

- Examine the different types of prison facilities that exist in the federal and state correctional systems.
- Assess the number of prisons and expenditures relating to prisons.
- Explore medical and mental health services that prisons provide.
- Learn the legal rights of prisoners that relate to classification, management, transfer, and daily living.
- Explore institutional and classification factors that contribute to prison misconduct and violence.
- Understand the various educational, vocational, religious, and substance abuse treatment programs that exist in American prisons.
- Examine treatment programs devoted to sex offenders.
- Objectively assess what works in correctional treatment.

CASE STUDY

After their incarceration, some inmates elect to change their religious identification; most common is a switch from traditional Christianity to one of several non-Judeo–Christian religions including Native American, Islam, Black Hebrew Israelism, Buddhism, Hinduism, Christian Identity, Odinsim, Wicca, and secular humanism. Recent research has found religious conversions are associated with personal crisis where the primary motivator is spiritual searching. Inmates who eventually convert from one religion to another are generally those who are looking for a system of beliefs that gives meaning to their own personal misfortunes as well as a process by which this discontent can be resolved. Not surprisingly, inmates seeking a new spiritual foundation accept and discard religious role guidelines until they find a suitable match.

Persons attempting to deal with their personal discontent often are inspired by the search for such remedies and according to the author, find answers and guidance in books, music, the media, friends, and family. Research suggests this is evident among those groups considered to be radicalized Western Muslims. This could be a problem because individuals with limited religious experience and knowledge may be easily persuaded by those touting a radical religious philosophy. Criminologist Mark Hamm suggests that the best manner in which to deal with such a problem is by providing religious mentors—individuals who can discuss and interpret teaching that may otherwise be adopted without question.

Correctional intelligence officers indicated that prisoners were likely targets for religious conversions to radical religious movements due to their high degree of vulnerability. Intelligence officials indicated that recruitment of inmates by terrorist groups is extremely rare. These officials also indicated that terrorist recruitment efforts focus on small numbers of dedicated followers and have little or no ambition in recruiting large groups. Interestingly, recruitment is a more significant problem in high-security facilities than in low- to medium-security institutions. High-level security operations have fewer options for prisoners. These institutions are overcrowded. They have more serious gang problems. They have a political climate that demands some type of affiliation to meet the need for personal protection. In short, during their confinement, some inmates transform from prisoner to fledgling terrorist.

1. How do prison environments contribute to radicalism among inmates?
2. Are the effects of religious change among inmates always negative?

"The reason that some offenders are kept in supermax right up to the day of their release is that they are more combative, antisocial, or impulsive than others; it is not surprising that such men would show higher recidivism."[2, p. 650]

As explored in Chapter 9, there is great variation in the risk factors, criminality, and behaviors of American prisoners. Because of this, prison facilities are designed and prison programs are devised to supervise the range of prisoners. The current chapter examines prison organization and classification procedures, their effects on institutional safety, and programs designed to rehabilitate inmates.

Prison Organization and Classification

Security Level

The Bureau of Prisons operates institutions at five different security levels to supervise federal prisoners at the most appropriate level according to the offenders' classification and assorted risks. BOP security levels are based on features such as the presence of external control towers, security barriers, or detection services; the type of housing within the institution; internal security features; and the staff-to-inmate ratio.

- **Minimum-security institutions**, also known as **federal prison camps**, have dormitory housing, low staff-to-inmate ratios, and little to no perimeter fencing. Minimum-security institutions are oriented toward work and treatment programs. Many federal prison camps are located adjacent to larger correctional facilities or military bases and are used to serve labor needs of the larger facilities. There are also smaller satellite BOP camps that serve a similar purpose as federal prison camps.

- **Low-security institutions**, also known as **federal correctional institutions**, have double-fenced perimeters, mostly dormitory or cubicle housing, and strong work and program components. The staff-to-inmate ratio is higher in these institutions compared to minimum-security facilities.
- **Medium-security institutions** have strengthened perimeters, usually double fences with electronic detection systems, mostly cell-type housing, a wide variety of work and treatment programs, higher staff-to-inmate ratios, and overall greater internal controls.
- **High-security institutions**, also known as **United States penitentiaries**, have highly secured perimeters featuring walls or reinforced fences, multiple- and single-occupancy cell housing, the highest staff-to-inmate ratio, and close control of inmate movements.
- **Administrative institutions** are facilities with special missions, such as the detention of pretrial offenders, the treatment of inmates with serious medical problems, or the containment of extremely dangerous and violent inmates. Administrative institutions are equipped to supervise inmates of all classification backgrounds. Examples of administrative institutions are metropolitan detention centers, federal detention centers, metropolitan correctional centers, federal transfer centers, and the medical center for federal prisoners. The most famous administrative BOP facility is the **Administrative-Maximum United States Penitentiary** in Florence, Colorado, which houses the most dangerous and notorious prisoners in the federal system. This facility is explored later in this chapter in the supermax section.
- **Federal correctional complexes** are clusters of BOP facilities located within close proximity to each other. Federal correctional complexes increase efficiency through the sharing of services and help with emergency preparedness and related administrative concerns.[7]

"Few problems in modern criminology are more perplexing than the role of imprisonment in reforming the adult criminal."[3, p. 257]

At the state level, there is not a uniform approach to establishing security levels for prisons as there is in the federal system. However, state governments employ the same general logic when classifying inmates to the most appropriate custody level within the most appropriate prison facility.[8] As shown in FIGURE 10-1, offenders are admitted to prison and initially classified according to their social and criminal histories (Chapter 4). Based on the offender's sentence, psychiatric and medical needs, prior criminal record, prior adjustment to confinement, security threat group history, and other considerations, offenders are transferred to the appropriate facility where they are again internally classified and receive housing, program, and work assignments.

At any point during an inmate's confinement, he or she can be transferred to another facility and reclassified if necessary. An inmate's behavior while in custody is an important determinant of whether he or she will be transferred to a different facility or placed into a more restrictive setting. For instance, prisoners who recurrently commit misconduct or engage in prison violence (Chapter 9) can be placed into more restrictive housing units or higher security institutions. State prison systems use some version of the following security level for their institutions:

- **Minimum-security state prisons** house the lowest security inmates in terms of their sentence, institutional adjustment, criminal history, and other factors. Housing in minimum-security prisons is usually dormitory style with bunk beds in a large room, such as a gymnasium. Minimum-security prisons are secured by a

"A clear realization of the degenerating influence of our present prison system should encourage more experiments aiming to devise a community for offenders that will actually rehabilitate."[4, p. 583]

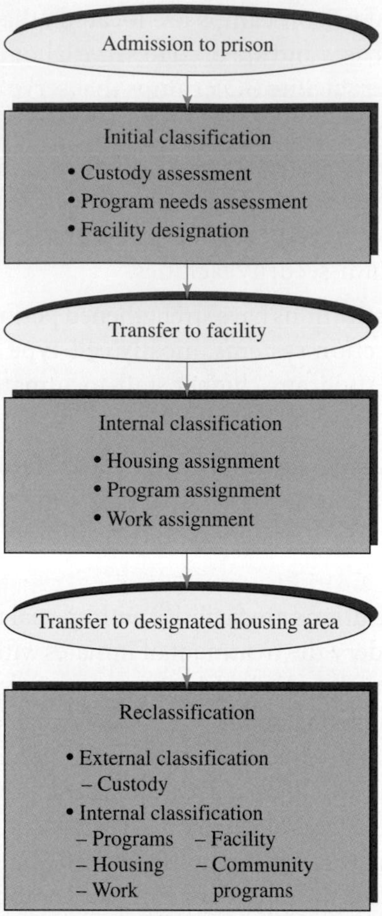

FIGURE 10–1 Inmate Classification and Institutional Assignment. *Source*: Hardyman, P. L., Austin, J., Alexander, J., Johnson, K. D., & Tulloch, O. C. (2002). *Internal prison classification systems: Case studies in their development and implementation*. Washington, DC: National Institute of Corrections.

fence but usually do not have armed towers or roving security details. Generally, there is less supervision and control over inmates in minimum-security prisons because their criminality and risk do not warrant much supervision and control. Many minimum-security prisons have *work release programs* where prisoners leave the facility during business hours for employment in the community. Other transitional programs are offered to prepare prisoners for their ultimate release to the community (Chapter 12).

- **Medium-security state prisons** house medium- or moderate-security inmates in terms of their sentence, institutional adjustment, criminal history, and other factors. Housing in medium-security prisons is similar to minimum security in that dormitory-style bunk beds are used. However, medium-security housing involves routine patrol from correctional staff where inmates are checked on; this is known as **direct supervision**. Medium-security prisons also contain individual cells for higher security inmates who violate prison rules. Fencing, armed towers, and armed security patrols serve to secure these facilities. Although medium-security prisons provide an assortment of treatment and rehabilitation programs, offenders occasionally leave the facility, such as to work on prison farms. In the community, medium-security prisoners are supervised by armed guards.
- **Maximum-security state prisons** house the highest risk prisoners in terms of their sentence, institutional adjustment, criminal history, and other factors. Some

states refer to these as **close-security prisons.** Because inmates in these institutions pose high risks to institutional safety, they cannot be housed in dormitory units. Instead, close security involves rows and tiers of individual cells in a design known as linear supervision. All inmate movements are restricted and supervised by correctional staff. Inmates only leave their cells for work, for recreation (if available), and for programming or treatment needs. Maximum-security prisons are surrounded by double, reinforced fences and monitored with armed towers and armed officer patrols.

- **Supermaximum-security (supermax) state prisons** are special prisons used to house inmates who pose extraordinary risks to institutional safety because of their involvement in prison misconduct and violence. Leaders of prison gangs and inmates who have assaulted, raped, or murdered other inmates or correctional workers are housed in supermax prisons. In recent years, state correctional systems have used the term *state penitentiary* to describe that state's most secure facility. For example, the Iowa State Penitentiary houses Iowa's most severe prisoners and the Ohio State Penitentiary houses violent inmates who are ineligible for parole. Perhaps the most infamous supermax state facility is the Pelican Bay State Prison in California, which houses more than 3,000 gang members and other high-risk inmates. Within supermax prisons, there are special or security housing units (SHU, pronounced *shoe*), which isolate inmates in their cell for 23–24 hours daily. Because of the sheer isolation and deprivation of this approach, supermax is controversial and the subject of prisoner litigation.

"Conventional wisdom in criminology is that rehabilitation has been found to be ineffective. In fact, the lack of demonstrated effectiveness is agreed upon by criminologists of nearly every persuasion and theoretical orientation."[5, p. 39]

Facilities and Expenditures

The Bureau of Justice Statistics has conducted a census of correctional facilities every 5 years since 1974 to produce a national snapshot of prison systems in the United States. Based on data from the most recent available census, James Stephan found that there were 1,821 correctional facilities including 102 at the federal level and 1,719 at the state level. In addition, there are 415 private correctional facilities most of which are at the federal level. About 71 percent are confinement facilities and the remaining 29 percent are community-based facilities. About 54 percent of all facilities were rated as mini-

In many states, the most violent and noncompliant prisoners are housed in supermax prisons—an environment that criminologists found can worsen their antisocial tendencies.

"That life in one prison is much more disagreeable than in another does not in itself signify that a Fourteenth Amendment liberty interest is implicated when a prisoner is transferred to the institution with the more severe rules."[6]

CORRECTIONS RESEARCH

The Impact of Supermax Prisons on Recidivism

Life in a supermax facility is exceedingly simple and isolated. Prisoners are housed in single cells the entire sentence. Supermax prisoners are allowed out of their cells to shower three times each week and five times during the week to exercise. Surveillance is continual and commissary privileges are limited. On the rare occasion when they are allowed to meet with another person or a review committee, they are placed in a cage or in some other manner heavily restrained.

There has been significant criticism by various groups as to the effectiveness of supermax prisons. Some critics present evidence that supermax prisoners disproportionately represent a subgroup of inmates with mental health issues who need treatment. Other researchers have found supermax prisoners become hardened or embedded in isolation and find dealing with others difficult once released from confinement or returned to the general prison population.

The literature on supermax prisoner demographic and personal characteristics that does exist seems to indicate that supermax prisoners are a diverse group—both in their history of offending and in their patterns of behavior. The available information also suggests that a sizable proportion of inmates who serve a portion of their sentence in a supermax facility exhibit significant patterns of psychological impairment as well.

In their study on recidivate offending and supermax prisoners, Lovell et al. tested three hypotheses. The first hypothesis focused on the likely behavior of prisoners and recidivism if they had spent any of their sentences in a supermax facility. The authors were also curious to learn whether offenders released directly from supermax confinement to the community were more likely to recidivate than those who were released later. Finally, Lovell et al. asked whether supermax offenders were more likely to reoffend than their counterparts.

Overall, the rate of recidivism after release from prison for supermax prisoners was higher than for general prison population inmates, but the difference in recidivism rates for an inmate having served time in a supermax lockup also varied by the temporal proximity of their eventual release from the correctional facility. From this study, it was learned that direct release supermax inmates had much higher recidivism rates than did former inmates who did not serve time in a supermax setting.

Interestingly, supermax inmates who served their time in supermax lockup until their sentence had expired and were then directly released typically were younger, had a greater number of past offenses, and also had a greater number of administrative rule violations. Lovell et al. also found that when both direct-release and later-release prisoners (those inmates spending greater than 90 days in the general population prior to being released after a supermax sentence) were compared based on age at first offense and criminal history, that 69 percent of the direct-release group committed new felonies, while only 53 percent of the later-release prisoners recidivated. As a result, the authors feel that a supermax sentence is significantly associated with higher recidivism rates for inmates released directly from a supermax setting to the community.

Source: Lovell, D., Johnson, L. C., & Cain, K. C. (2007). Recidivism of supermax prisoners in Washington State. *Crime & Delinquency, 53,* 633–656; King, K., Steiner, B., & Breach, S. R. (2008). Violence in the supermax: A self-fulfilling prophecy. *Prison Journal, 88,* 144–168.

mum security, 26 percent as medium security, and 20 percent as maximum security. Since the last census of correctional facilities, the number of maximum-security facilities increased 12 percent while the number of minimum-security facilities increased 19 percent. Medium-security facilities decreased 8 percent. At the inmate level, 22 percent of inmates were classified as minimum security, 42 percent as medium security, and 36 percent as maximum security.[9]

Private prisons, private, for-profit businesses hired by the government to supervise lower risk inmates, house slightly more than 7 percent of the total prisoner population.[10] The premise behind private prisons is that businesses could supervise low-risk prisoners more cost-effectively than governments while freeing prison space for higher risk offenders. Interestingly, Travis Pratt and Jeff Maahs conducted a meta-analysis of studies that evaluated the costs of private prisons. Overall, they discovered that private prisons are generally no more cost-effective than public prisons.[11] Additionally, private prisons appear to be equally rehabilitative as public prisons in that they produce equivalent recidivism outcomes.[12]

Prisons serve a variety of functions to address the punishment and treatment needs of inmates. The primary purpose is general confinement evidenced that about 90 percent of correctional purposes are simply geared toward general confinement or incapacitation. Correctional facilities are also used for boot camp/shock incarceration; reception, diagnosis, and classification; medical treatment or hospitalization; substance abuse treatment; youthful offender placement; and work-release programs. The second most common facility type is described as *other*. These facilities house very specific subpopulations of offenders, such as geriatric inmates, sex offenders, inmates in protective custody, inmates with profound psychiatric problems, and condemned offenders.

As a rule, prisons are crowded places with limited capacity to house inmates. The **rated capacity** is the number of beds or inmates assigned by a rating official to institutions within a jurisdiction. The **operational capacity** is the number of inmates that can be accommodated based on the facility's staff, programs, and services. The **design capacity** is the number of inmates that planners intended for the facility. According to the newest census of state and federal correctional facilities, one in eight correctional facilities operated under a court order or **consent decree** to limit its population including 18 state prison systems and the District of Columbia.[13]

As shown in FIGURE 10–2, direct expenditures for corrections increased dramatically in recent decades. Between 1982 and 2005, the correctional system increased an astonishing 619 percent, and annual spending on corrections exceeded $60 billion. In terms of

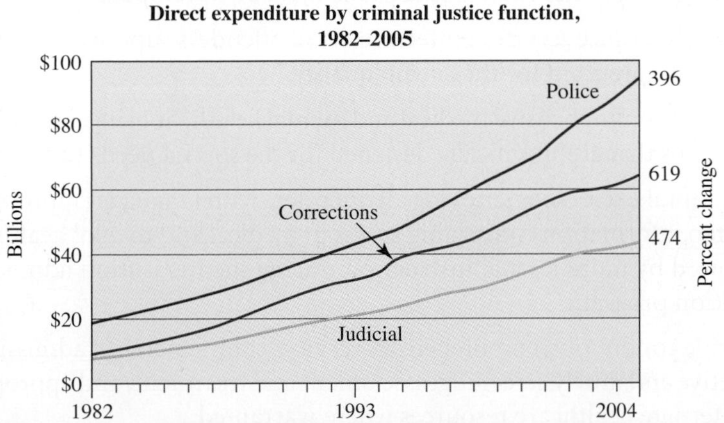

FIGURE 10–2 Correctional Expenditures Up 619 Percent. *Source*: Hughes, K. A. (2006). *Justice expenditure and employment in the United States, 2003*. Washington, DC: U.S. Department of Justice, Office of Justice Programs, Bureau of Justice Statistics.

per capita spending, corrections expenditures increased 423 percent from $40 per U.S. resident in 1982 to $209 per U.S. resident today. Less than 3 percent of local and state expenditures are devoted to corrections. By comparison, local and state governments spend 29 percent on education, 14 percent on public welfare, and 7 percent on health care and hospitals.[14]

Within these correctional costs, prisons account for the bulk of all spending. At the state level, prison expenditures account for nearly 80 percent of all correctional spending. Salary, wages, and benefits for correctional staff account for about 67 percent of all prison expenditures, with operating costs accounting for most of the remaining 33 percent. More than $3 billion is spent annually on medical care, more than $1 billion on food services, and nearly $1 billion on utilities for inmates.[15]

Medical Services

Persons under correctional supervision have a constitutional right to adequate health care. Correctional systems must use a comprehensive, holistic approach to providing medical and mental health services, which are sensitive to the cultural, subcultural, age, and gender needs of the diverse prisoner population. All prison health care services must be consistent with community healthcare standards. According to the American Correctional Association, prisons systems should:

- Be delivered by qualified and appropriately credentialed healthcare professionals.
- Include a comprehensive health promotion and disease prevention program designed to meet the specific health maintenance needs of the specific residential population.
- Employ a stratified system of service delivery to maximize the efficient use of medical and mental healthcare resources.
- Include corrections officers who work in medical and mental healthcare units as active participants in the multidisciplinary treatment team.
- Create community linkages, which will facilitate the continuation of the treatment plan by community health and mental healthcare agencies for persons being released from incarceration.
- Establish appropriate classification, program, and housing assignments for juvenile and elderly offenders with mental illnesses, chronic illnesses, or terminal illnesses. Medical health, mental health, and substance abuse programs that address the unique needs of these populations must be developed.
- Establish hospice services for terminally ill offenders supported by a compassionate release program for those who qualify.
- Establish comprehensive medical and mental health, housing, and substance abuse programs that are specifically designed for the special needs of female offenders.
- Upon intake screening, provide all offenders with language-appropriate oral and written information concerning access to medical and mental healthcare services, followed by more formal instruction during the institution admission and orientation program.
- Provide continuous, comprehensive services commencing at admission, including effective and timely screening, assessment and treatment, and appropriate referral to alternate healthcare resources where warranted.
- Establish a system to provide access to emergency treatment 24 hours per day.
- Establish a formal process to screen for, identify, treat, and manage inmates with infectious diseases.

- Provide appropriate healthcare training programs that are cognizant of cultural, subcultural, age, and gender issues for all correctional and healthcare staff, and allow for continuing professional and medical education programs.
- Provide a medical records system to document diagnosis and treatment programs to facilitate treatment continuity and cooperation between healthcare professionals, consistent with privacy, confidentiality, and security requirements.
- Provide a pharmaceutical distribution system that conforms to applicable state and federal laws and established formularies.
- Provide a continuing quality improvement program, including risk management programs and peer review activities to monitor and evaluate healthcare services.
- Establish a patient bill of rights.
- Provide a system for medical and administrative review of grievances relating to health care.
- Provide screening for dual-diagnosis and substance abuse.
- Provide (preferably by pharmacist) all inmates who are given new prescriptions with oral counseling or written information about their medication.
- Provide a sufficient supply of prescription medication upon release.
- Provide the opportunity to establish a living will and/or advanced directive.[16]

Although adequate health care is a fundamental right of prisoners (discussed later in the chapter), medical and mental health services within prisons vary across the country. Medical care is provided as the exclusive function of 6 percent of prisons, such as Federal Medical Centers, but in the remaining 94 percent of institutions, the prison hospital is one area of the facility. During initial classification, inmates are assessed for medical and psychiatric problems including medications and other services. It is important to recognize that service availability does not necessarily mean that prisons are providing substandard

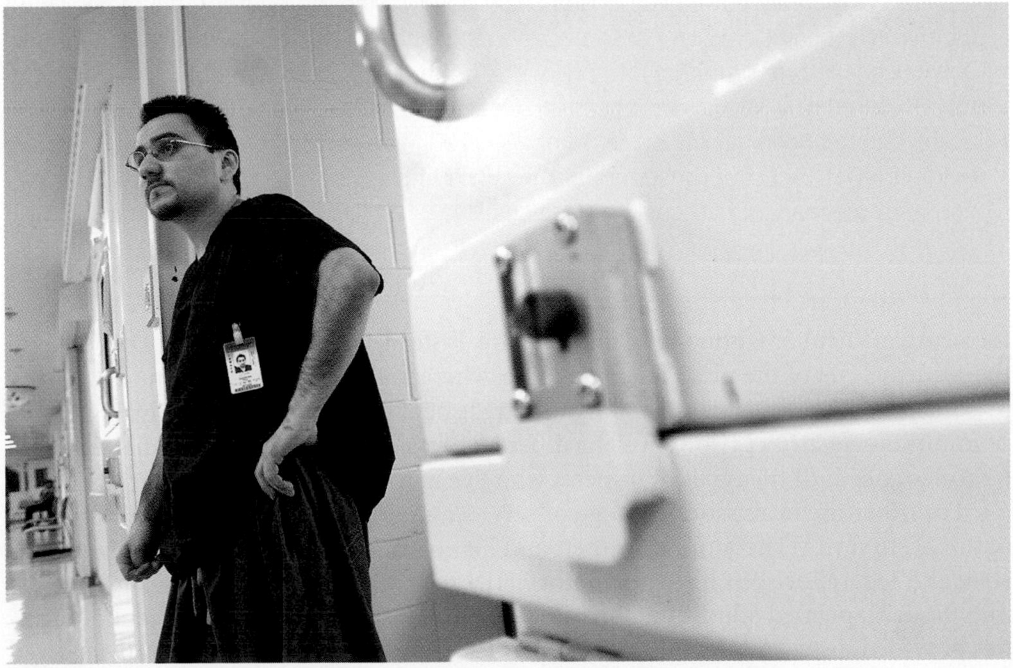

Despite their status of prisoner, inmates in the United States have fundamental rights to medical and mental health care, and more than $3 billion is spent annually to provide these services.

CORRECTIONS BRIEF

Differences Between Prisons in the West and Prisons in China

China's prison law holds that "a prison shall, with regard to prisoners, implement the principle of combining punishment with reform and combining education with labour, in order to transform them [convicted prisoners] into law-abiding citizens" (p. 93). In 2000, China had nearly 700 correctional facilities and an inmate population of approximately 1.5 million convicted prisoners. There are distinct differences between Western and Chinese philosophies toward corrections, but there are many similarities as well.

Western prisons, those correctional facilities in Europe, Canada, and the United States, are dominated by the ideology of deterrence and retribution. This is especially the case with the U.S. prison system. In the Chinese prison system, the dominant ideology is rehabilitation and treatment—a policy that has been in place since 1949, one that is similar, although with distinct differences as to how prisoners are viewed, to the Western medical model. In China, the medical model means prisoners are treated as patients because most Chinese prisoners are considered sick people, even though they could easily be classified as normal people.

In addition, Western philosophy towards correctional models focuses on containment, while the Chinese philosophy on corrections is based on the perspective that people can be changed. It is strongly felt that prisoners can be reformed and that they can also be educated. In support of this perspective, China points to the successful rehabilitation of war criminals, many of whom became law-abiding citizens after their release. China's correctional officials believe that successfully rehabilitating a convicted person is a long process, so their system is not structured to support a 1-year or even a 10-year prison rehabilitation program. Correctional officials in China support a gradual and extended program of rehabilitation as opposed to most Western treatment programs, which expect results much sooner.

China is less concerned with the numbers of prisoners housed in each institution. In fact, the majority of Chinese prisons hold nearly twice the number of inmates as do their Western counterparts. For example, in the United States, the current standard for new prisons is a maximum of 500 prisoners. In Germany, prisons typically hold no more than 325 inmates. The largest prison in Sweden holds fewer than 300 prisoners and the average correctional facility holds fewer than 100 inmates. By contrast, China's prisons holding fewer than 500 prisoners are few in number, and the typical Chinese prison houses more than 1,000 convicted persons.

medical treatment or withholding medical care. Instead, the range of services depends on the security level of the prison. For example, whereas 99 percent of maximum-security prisons provide psychiatric screening and treatment of their inmates, only 87 percent of minimum-security prisons do. The difference reflects the different criminal risks and treatment needs of the types of inmates who live in these distinct prison settings.[17]

For other medical issues, a range of services are provided in American prisons. A national survey by Theodore Hammett and his colleagues indicated that 33 percent of state and federal prisons have mandatory HIV testing of inmates. All prisons provide inmates with printed educational materials on HIV and AIDS and 82 percent of facilities provided instructor-led educational services. About 76 percent of prisons surveyed test inmates for syphilis. About 70 percent of state and federal prisons contract out for health services to community hospitals.[18] For example, all prisoners incarcerated under

Chinese prisons also differ in general appearance. Whereas the architectural structure of Western prisons varies by level of security, Chinese prisons look very similar regardless of security level. Housing of prisoners differs as well. In Western prisons, inmates are housed in one- or two-person cells. Cells contain a bed, a toilet, a sink, and possibly a table and chair and are approximately 10 meters by 10 meters in size. Chinese prisons provide dormitory-style housing for inmates. Each prisoner has approximately 5 square meters of living space. The few single or double occupancy cells are reserved for foreign prisoners. Prison officials feel dorm living lessens tension and promotes communication and that it can reduce the frequency of inmate suicide.

Chinese prisons are located far from populated areas. Western prisons are located within 50 miles of a metropolitan area with a population of at least 10,000 persons. The primary reason for locating Western prisons close to or within a community is the availability of emergency services as well as workforce recruitment. This idea is taking hold in China, where correctional officials now feel that in order to recruit highly qualified employees, provide training opportunities, and make visitation by family members possible, correctional facilities must be located near larger communities. Because of this, all new and proposed prisons in China have been or will be built near medium-sized cities.

Both Chinese and Western prisons offer inmates the opportunity to earn an education and/or a vocational trade. But in Western prisons, teachers who conduct courses for inmates in an institutional setting have the same credentials as those teaching in an area high school or college—and the teacher–student ratio is low: 1 teacher to 10 students. Not so in China. Chinese prisons can be easily characterized as lacking qualified teaching personnel and having a high teacher–student ratio of 1:30. As for the vocational programs, convicted persons in Chinese prisons participate only in those vocational programs that can produce profit for the prison. This is attributed to the lack of financial resources available to China's prison system.

In Western prisons, inmates have the right to file lawsuits and legal petitions, and this action is common. In China, inmates are not afforded the right to petition the courts for legal regress when the claims involve prisoner rights or prison conditions. China also lacks community corrections programs, but does allow visitation, and more than 60 percent of Chinese prisons allow for conjugal visitation.

Source: Zongxian, W. (2003). Western prisons and Chinese prisons: Focusing on differences. *European Journal of Crime, Criminal Law & Criminal Justice, 11,* 93–113.

the jurisdiction of the Texas Department of Criminal Justice receive medical, dental, and psychiatric care from the University of Texas Medical Branch and Texas Tech University Health Sciences Center. Each prison within the state provides ambulatory care clinics, 16 prisons contain infirmaries, and there is a state prison hospital.[19] In this way, prisoners have access to all types of medical care; however, that care is sometimes provided inside prisons and other times in the community.

Legal Rights of Prisoners

The organization, management, and daily operations of American prisons are not exclusively the domain of correctional administrators; they also receive significant oversight from the courts.[20] As explored in Chapter 3, although prisons are by definition uncomfortable, punitive, and depriving, they must be humane. When prison conditions are so oppressive, they are at risk of violating the Eighth Amendment prohibition against cruel and unusual punishment. The standard that is used to evaluate the overall quality of a prison environment is the totality-of-conditions test established in *Pugh v. Locke* (1976), which found that Alabama prisons were so appalling and debilitating that they worked to deteriorate the health and spirit of inmates and thus reduce the likelihood of successful rehabilitation. The totality-of-conditions test relates to the aggregate characteristics of the facility that are used to show an Eighth Amendment violation.[21]

In recent decades, appellate courts, especially the United States Supreme Court, have ruled on a variety of issues that pertain to the ways that correctional officials organize, manage, and provide fundamental day-to-day services to prisoners. Some of the major areas of prisoner rights are:

- *Deliberate indifference and health care*: An important test of prison conditions centers on the healthcare services that prisons provide to inmates. In *Estelle v. Gamble* (1976), the Court held that deliberate indifference to a prisoner's serious medical needs constituted cruel and unusual punishment. According to the Court, "Deliberate indifference to serious medical needs of prisoners constitutes the unnecessary and wanton infliction of pain proscribed by the Eighth Amendment. This is true whether the indifference is manifested by prison doctors in their response to the prisoner's needs or by prison guards in intentionally denying or delaying access to medical care or intentionally interfering with the treatment once prescribed."[22]
- *Deliberate indifference and quality of life*: The concept of deliberate indifference was modified in *Wilson v. Seiter* (1991) with the establishment of the deliberate indifference standard, which is that the conditions at a prison are not unconstitutional unless it can be shown that prison administrators show deliberate indifference to the quality of life in prisons and inmates' most basic needs.[23]
- *Deliberate indifference and protection against violent inmates*: In 1994, the deliberate indifference doctrine was broadened in the case of *Farmer v. Brennan* where the Court held that a prison official may be liable under the Eighth Amendment for denying humane conditions of confinement if he or she knows that inmates face a substantial risk of serious harm, for example, because of gang animosity, and disregards that risk by failing to take reasonable measures to abate it.[24] In other words, administrators must protect inmates. Michael Vaughn reviewed 35 cases that led to the *Farmer* decision and concluded that correctional officials are potentially liable in cases of inmate-on-inmate assault in four broad circumstances, which are when (1) they fail to segregate vulnerable inmates from aggressors, (2) they fail to provide protection promised to a specific inmate, (3) they fail to provide protection to an inmate on an enemy hit list, and (4) they fail to enforce court orders and consent decrees mandating protection for vulnerable inmates.[25]
- *Classification and transfer*: Upon classification, inmates are placed within the most appropriate module and institution for their treatment and security needs. Although offenders can express preferences about which prison facility they want to live, there is no fundamental right. In *Meachum v. Fano* and *Montayne v. Haymes*, the Court held that state correctional agencies can assign inmates to any facility within the state, meaning that inmates can go from good to bad prisons without any due process violations.[26–27] If inmates become serious threats to institutional safety, they can be transferred to prisons in a different state (*Olim v. Wakinekona*, 1983) or the federal system (*Howe v. Smith*, 1981) without any infringements on due process.[28–29] An exception to these decisions was reached in *Vitek v. Jones* (1980), in which the Court held that transfer to a mental hospital

CORRECTIONS HISTORY

An Annotated History of Religion Behind Bars

The issue of religious rights of Native American prisoners in U.S. correctional facilities is address by both the First and Fourteenth Amendments. Clearly stated in the First Amendment free exercise clause is the individual's right to practice his or her chosen religion. The Fourteenth Amendment makes this clause applicable to the states through the equal protection clause.

In *Sherbert v. Verner* (1963) and later in *Wisconsin v. Yoder* (1972), limitations on when government institutions are allowed to restrict or prohibit religious customs and practices were established. Two elements must be established for the decision by prison officials to be considered constitutional. The first is that correctional authorities must identify a compelling interest that supports the restriction. Second, authorities must also show that no other less-restrictive measure is available.

In *Turner v. Safley* (1987) and *O'Lone v. Shabazz* (1987), the U.S. Supreme Court relaxed restrictions on the compelling argument and allowed prison officials to ban religious customs if doing so was in the best interest of the institution. This meant that the sacred ceremonial sweat lodges could be banned without a compelling reason. As a result, based on the new reasonable standard, discretion was once again afforded prison authorities.

In 1993, the U.S. Congress passed the Religious Freedom Restoration Act (RFRA). This act restored the compelling interest and least-restrictive means test for the issue of religious freedoms for prison inmates. In *Werner v. McCorter* (1995, p. 1480) the Court addressed when the RFRA could be invoked. In the Court's opinion, the need for the RFRA originates when prison rules "significantly inhibit or constrain conduct or expression that manifests some central tenet of a prisoner's individual beliefs." Other bills written to protect Native American religious practices for inmates have been introduced, but the controversy over which party to the bill should be responsible for the final decisions over Native American religious claims, the government or Native American tribespeople, tabled each of the measures. And in 1997, the Court ruled in *City of Boerne v. Flores* that the compelling interest test was the most demanding test known to constitutional law and once again returned discretion in matters of religious freedoms for Native Americans to the government.

Enter the Religious Land Use and Institutionalized Person Act of 2000. This act restored the compelling interest and less-restrictive means tests for decisions involving sacred religious ceremonies within the confines of U.S. correctional facilities. However, states have ruled in favor of correctional authorities in several cases brought under the Religious Land Use and Institutionalized Person Act. A court in Florida ruled that denying Native Americans "holy ground was not a substantial burden on their faith because it did not bar prisoners from engaging in other religious practices" (*Wilson v. Moore*, 2003, p. 1350). However, in 2002, the Massachusetts Appeals Court recommended their department of corrections settle the state's disagreement with Native American prisoners over a ban on sweat lodges. The appeals court did so, informing the department that if the case came before the court, their finding would be in favor of the inmates. A settlement was reached, and within months purification ceremonies were permitted inside three Massachusetts correctional facilities. But the controversy over Native American rights to religious freedoms is far from settled. The First and Fourteenth Amendments' free exercise and equal protection clauses continue to be interpreted and applied on a case-by-case basis.

Source: Vezzola, M. A. (2007). Harmony behind bars. *Prison Journal, 87,* 195–210; *City of Boerne v. Flores* 521 U.S. 507 (1997); *Wilson v. Moore* 270 F. Supp 2d 1328, 1353 (N.D. Fla 2003).

required protected liberty interests, which required a separate and formal hearing complete with due process protections.[30]

- *Solitary confinement and supermax classification*: Arguably the most punitive (and from an inmate's perspective, most difficult) classification is solitary confinement, also known as administrative segregation. As described earlier, administrative segregation is used by correctional officials to punish inmates who commit serious acts of institutional misconduct. In *Hewitt v. Helms* (1983), the Court held that inmates can be transferred to solitary confinement after an informal, nonadversarial review of their alleged misconduct by staff and that this informal proceeding does not violate due process rights. In *Wilkinson v. Austin* (2005), the Court held that as long as states have procedures that provide sufficient protections of due process (e.g., conviction for organized crime, leadership of inmate gang, etc.), states may assign prisoners to supermax prisons.[31–32]

Prison Organization, Management, and Institutional Safety

The correctional system responds primarily to the criminal propensity or risk profile of offenders in determining the most appropriate sentence, placement on an intermediate sanction, inmate classification, and placement in prison. Minimum-risk offenders receive minimum-security punishments and maximum or supermax prisoners receive commensurate punishments. There are dramatic differences in prison safety across security levels. For example, the rate of inmate assaults on correctional employees is 8 times higher in maximum-security prisons than minimum-security prisons. In the BOP, the differences in assault rates are more than *60 times* higher in maximum-security prisons than in minimum-security prisons. In state prisons, the assault rate difference is 4 times higher in maximum-security prisons, and in private prisons the difference is 5 times higher in maximum-security prisons than in minimum-security prisons.[33]

Despite the logical matching of offender risk with punishment severity, penologists have historically disagreed with the organization and management of maximum-security prisons and even suggested that these facilities, and not the various risks or criminal propensities of prisoners that reside in these facilities, were primarily responsible for the inability of prisons to effectively rehabilitate prisoners. More than 50 years ago, Gresham Sykes noted:

> It seems likely, therefore, that a major barrier to the rehabilitation of the adult criminal in a maximum security prison, is to be attributed not only to the "unnaturalness" of his social environment and the lack of scientifically tested therapeutic devices but also to the corruption of the guard's authority in maintaining custody and discipline. Since these functions have long been held to be opposed to the aim of reformation, it would appear that a profound re-evaluation of the importance of these functions for the rehabilitation of the adult criminal is needed.[34, p. 262]

Some penologists theorize that control-oriented prison organizations, such as those commonly found in the highest security facilities, make the rehabilitation of prisoners almost impossible. According to Susan Clark Craig, rehabilitation emphasizes inmate responsibility, autonomy, and a socially cohesive inmate community. However, more restrictive settings control almost every aspect of an inmate's daily life, thus there is little chance for the conditions that make rehabilitation possible to emerge. Since control-oriented facilities must house more severe inmates, many administrators simply emphasize institutional safety over inmate autonomy and opportunity for rehabilitation.[35]

CORRECTIONS BRIEF

K-9s as an Option to Traditional Use-of-Force Alternatives

Administrative policy and practical experience strongly support the practice of quick and immediate intervention when attempting to control inmate behavior. But is it possible to maintain compliance without using traditional use-of-force options? If an institution lacks resources to ensure inmate safety, inmates will strike preemptively whenever necessary to guarantee their personal safety. Younger inmates soon learn that the only way to stay safe and create a don't-mess-with-me reputation is to strike first. What this means is that one of the factors associated with the frequency and intensity of violence attributable to inmates is the level of security provided by the staff.

Safety and security are also issues of concern for prison guards as well. Research has shown that nearly 90 percent of prison guards report being assaulted or threatened with physical harm while performing their duties. What options do correctional officers have for maintaining control and ensuring their personal safety? There are stun guns, rubber projectiles, chemical agents, and riot batons. But weapons are generally not an option when working directly with inmates. There are also liability issues when using force or weapons to contain an incident. In *Hudson v. McMillion* (1992), the Court ruled that liability in use-of-force situations depends on whether the force employed to contain a situation was used in good faith. Using force in good faith simply means the force was used appropriately to maintain or restore order. It also means the amount of force used cannot be construed as if it were done maliciously or purposefully to cause harm. Even so, the use of force must be considered the minimum force needed to contain the incident.

Dogs are intimidating, and they project fear that can be a useful and functional deterrent to inmates' aberrant behavior and/or noncompliance. Research by Robert Bodnar has determined that inmates have a primal fear of K-9s, which provides correctional officers with a viable alternative to other forms of physical force. K-9 units also serve as an immediate response protocol. Bodnar notes that the mere presence of a K-9 unit can restore order even without direct contact with combative inmates; these units are also capable of maintaining a level of security based solely on inmate perception.

Source: Bodnar, R. J. (2006). Staff and inmate perceptions of using K-9 patrol dogs in a direct supervision jail. *American Jails, 20*, 77–87.

Indeed, in their review of the evidence of prison violence, James Byrne and Don Hummer concluded that some combination of **informal social control** mechanisms, such as the ways that inmates and correctional staff tacitly coexist to maintain institutional safety and **formal social control** mechanisms, such as strict administrative control, is the best approach to ensuring prison safety. Unfortunately, Byrne and Hummer acknowledge that the precise tipping point or threshold of informal and formal social controls has yet to be determined.[36]

CORRECTIONS FOCUS

Pets and Prisoner Rehabilitation: Prison-Based Animal Programs

How common are prison-based animal programs? In a study by Gennifer Furst, the frequency of prison-based animal programs (PAP) and their potential for beneficial effects was assessed. Anecdotal evidence seems to support such programs, but independent assessments are lacking. Intuitively, a program designed around the potentially therapeutic bond between humans and animals seems logical. After all, doctors and psychologists have recommended such unions for a variety of medical issues including recuperation from surgery, chemical addictions, and aging disorders. Formally known for noninmate populations, animal-assisted therapy (AAT) has also proven uniquely beneficial for patients who are victims of abuse and for people with mental health issues.

Animals can and do have a calming effect. They are also credited with helping develop a sense of empathy. Prisoners typically report a reduction in feelings of isolation and frustration when involved with animal-based treatment programs. But prison-based animal programs are different than animal-assisted therapy programs. The primary difference is that PAP is not part of the prison's counseling program; PAP animals are not provided solely for their therapeutic potential. But PAP animals do provide a vocational outlet for inmates. Prisoners involved in PAP are required to interact with their assigned animal; they are also required to help train the animal. There are certain safeguards in place for the sake of the animal volunteer, however. Since animal abuse has been associated with various levels of domestic assault and other forms of violent crimes, before being granted access to a PAP animal, prisoners undergo a screening process that takes into account past crimes, behaviors, and conduct while in prison.

Inmates appreciate pets. Pets have no interest in an inmate's criminal past and are unequivocally nonjudgmental. Pennsylvania inmate James Paluch used to violate prison rules, sneaking food from the dining hall to his cell just to feed his "babies," his "bird friends." Robert Stroud, known as the Birdman of Alcatraz, was considered a violent inmate, except when tending to his flock. He eventually raised hundreds of birds while in federal prison, selling them to other prisoners and using the money to support his mother. Stroud also spent his time writing and publishing two books on birds.

In a yearlong study of criminally insane patients at the Oakwood Forensic Center in Ohio, researchers found patients who were allowed access to and the opportunity to care for small animals required half the medication of their control group counterpart. One finding from this experiment of considerable interest was that during the yearlong study, the treatment group experienced no suicide attempts. The control group, the group without the treatment, experienced eight such attempts.

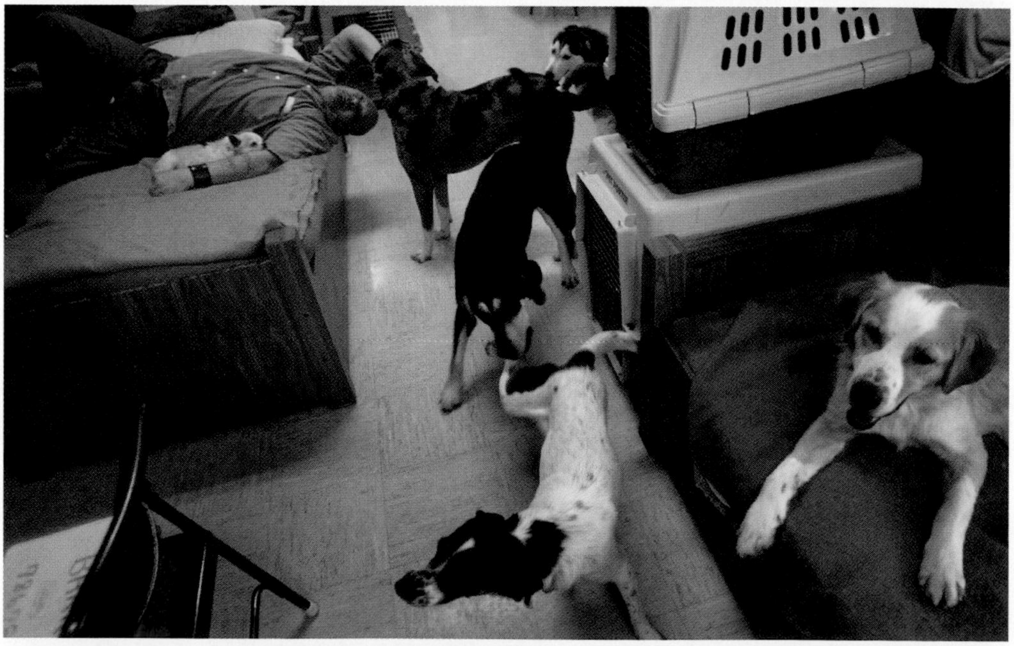

A variety of innovative programs are designed to enhance the ability of inmates to demonstrate empathy for others, which is an important deterrent to victimizing others.

The Bureau of Land Management for the state of New Mexico operated a project called the Wild Mustang Program from 1988 until 1992. Inmates involved in the Wild Mustang Program became caregivers as their charge was to capture, tame, and rehabilitate wild mustangs. The program afforded inmate participants an opportunity to act as their own boss and an opportunity to meet new challenges. Some of the participants reported increases in levels of self-esteem and the ability to deal with stressful situations. This program was also credited with a reduction in both frequency and severity of actions requiring disciplinary actions.

In her study, Gennifer Furst determined 36 states have prison-based animal programs. These programs are implemented at 159 different sites. They involve a variety of different types of animals including farm animals housed on prison farms, wild animals, dogs, and cats. The oldest program, a working farm, was established in Wisconsin in 1885. Thirty-four PAPs have been added since 2000. Furst also found that 16 programs allow inmates an opportunity to participate in their PAP regardless of their crimes; 42 PAPs exclude inmates based on a list of specific types of crimes—ranking high on that list are crimes against animals and crimes involving children; only 5 programs rely on psychological evaluations to determine eligibility; 12 programs require a certain level of education before an inmate is eligible to participate in the program.

The benefit most often cited by prison administrators was the sense of responsibility instilled in the inmate from the responsibility of caring for their animal. Equally important was the lack of negative consequences associated with this type of program with one exception: the resistance to the program by correctional staff directly in charge of its operation. It is possible that a portion of this resistance is associated with the lack of space and resources needed to effectively meet the demands of PAP. These programs also provide adequate care and safe refuge for abandoned or soon-to-be destroyed animals. According to one source, as many as 91,000 horses annually have been killed in the United States for various reasons.

Research has found that handling animals reduces stress. It also lowers blood pressure. People generally talk to their pets in a softer, slightly higher pitched, but calmer voice and tend to focus specifically on the animal, excluding all other environmental stimuli. And since the likelihood of developing a positive and meaningful relationship with another inmate is slim and the opportunity to develop a relationship with a noninmate is almost nonexistent, animals may very well be the only source of companionship that serve both inmate and institution.

Sources: Frust, G. (2006). Prison-based animal programs: A national survey. *Prison Journal, 86,* 407–430.

An array of studies examined the ways that a prison's security classification, organizational structure, managerial philosophy, and other factors influence the safety of the institution. The factors include:

- *Custody/security level*: Historically, penologists asserted that coercive, rigid, tightly controlled prisons result in more misconduct and contribute to less safe, humane facilities. Empirically, the link between facility custody/security level and how well the prison operates is equivocal. Eric Poole and Robert Regoli surveyed 144 prison guards from a maximum-security prison and found that more rigid, control-oriented facilities increase stress among guards. In turn, guards adapt to this stress by becoming even more vigilant at controlling inmate behavior, which leads to higher levels of inmate misconduct.[37] On the other hand, facilities governed by a strict, administrative-control philosophy where conflicts between administrators and correctional staff were resolved tended to be safer. Michael Reisig found that well-managed, control-oriented prisons were less likely to have inmate homicides than poorer managed prisons.[38]
- *Sentence/security level*: A major variable used to classify inmates is sentencing severity. Persons convicted of the most serious crime, such as murder, receive the most serious sentences, such as life imprisonment without the possibility of parole or death are housed in maximum-security prisons. However, sentencing severity has a counterintuitive relationship to inmate behavior. Inmates

serving shorter sentences tend to be less compliant than persons sentenced to life imprisonment without parole or death. According to Mark Cunningham, "despite the severity of their offenses and the bleakness of their institutional futures, the majority of these offenders do not continue on a trajectory of serious violence following their admission to prison."[39, p. 250] Cunningham and Jon Sorensen compared the disciplinary records of more than 9,000 Florida prisoners serving time in high-security, close-custody facilities and found that life imprisonment without parole inmates were a stabilizing force among inmates. In fact, parole-eligible inmates serving 10- to 19-year sentences were the most disruptive.[40] Contrary to the notion that those serving the most severe sentences have nothing to lose and thus engage in misconduct, research suggests that short-time inmates actually feel empowered to misbehave because their sentence is so brief.[41]

- *Solitary confinement/supermax classification*: As noted in Chapter 2, American prisons were founded on the use of **solitary confinement**, isolation in one's cell for the purpose of contemplation, prayer, and penitence, to reform prisoners. Over time, solitary confinement came under attack from prison reformers who suggested that the sheer isolation and deprivation of solitary confinement can result in psychiatric damage to inmates and is ineffective as a correctional management technique. In fact, a psychopathological condition known as SHU (security housing unit) syndrome has been developed. **SHU syndrome** is characterized by inmate thought disturbances, perceptual changes, thought, concentration, and memory difficulties, extreme anxiety, and other symptoms of mental illness that appear to be produced by the sensory deprivations of solitary confinement in SHU or supermax units. Most importantly, many inmates who present with SHU syndrome have no preexisting history of mental illness.[42–44]

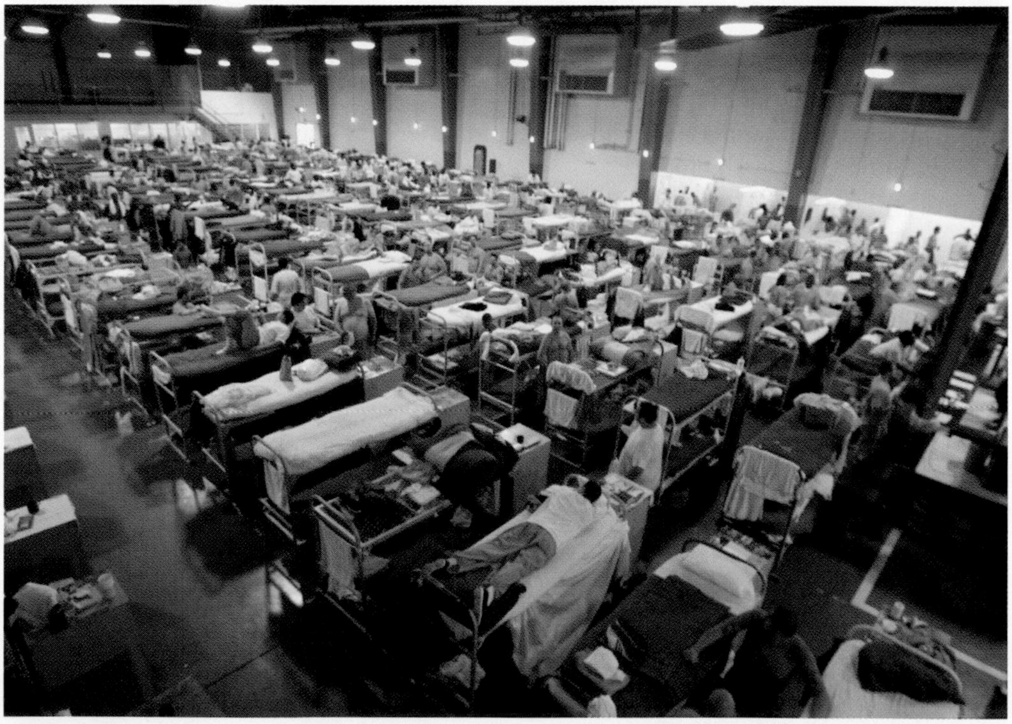

Overall, research indicates that crowding is not a significant cause of inmate misconduct and threats to institutional safety.

Although much has been written about supermax prisons[45–46], actual research on the topic has been described as almost nonexistent.[47] Overall, research on the effectiveness of supermax prisons is mixed. Chad Briggs and his colleagues studied 24 states that developed supermax prisons and found that in some states, the supermax reduced assaults against staff, in other states supermax increased assaults against staff, and in other states there were no significant effects.[48] David Lovell and his colleagues compared recidivism outcomes of supermax and control prisoners in Washington state and found supermax prisoners had more extensive and violent criminal histories and higher levels of misconduct. Those released directly from supermax housing to the community had recidivism rates nearly five times the rate of nonsupermax prisoners and more than twice the rates of supermax prisoners who were placed in less-restricted housing prior to release.[49] This suggests that going directly from supermax confinement to free society is a recipe for recidivism.

- *Crowding*: According to the deprivation model (Chapter 9), uncomfortable prison conditions can increase inmate misconduct. A common area of research on this examined the effects of prison crowding or inmate density on misconduct. Steven Levitt studied the effects of overcrowding, which is characteristic of higher security prisons, on crime rates. Levitt used data on prison overcrowding litigation by inmates in 12 states from 1971 to 1993. Overall, he found that a one-inmate reduction in prison overcrowding was associated with an increase of 16 serious crimes per year.[50] Based on these findings, more densely packed prisons result in greater public safety. Shanhe Jiang analyzed data from a national survey of inmates in state prisons and found that crowded facilities experienced more drug abuse among inmates and higher levels of nondrug misconduct. Interestingly, Jiang found that medium-security facilities experienced the most misconduct.[51] A recent meta-analysis of 16 studies of the relationship between prison crowding and inmate misconduct found crowding has little to no effect on inmate behavior.[52]

Prison Programming and Treatment

From the beginning, the general public has held an ambivalent view of prisons and their ability (or inability) to effectively correct prisoners' antisocial behaviors. That prisons evolved from the Pennsylvania and Auburn approaches (Chapter 2) to today, policy makers and correctional administrators responded to popular perceptions of whether prisons were meeting their intended goal: to rehabilitate criminals. Irrespective of the correctional era, American society faced the reality that crime seemed to thrive regardless of the size of the correctional population or the methods of correctional treatment.

Also from the beginning, progressives and professional elites greatly disliked prisons because they viewed them as barbaric and contrary to the rehabilitative needs of prisoners. This idea was made famous by de Beaumont and de Tocqueville's assessment, "While society in the United States gives the example of the most extended liberty, the prisons of the same country offer the spectacle of the most complete despotism."[53, p. 380] Within academic criminology, there was also considerable distaste for prisons and the ways that correctional administrators managed them. In the most influential criminology textbook ever produced, Edwin Sutherland and Donald Cressey noted that "restriction of freedom within walls, like the general restriction of freedom stemming from incarceration itself, is imposed because it is painful to the recipient. The pain may or may not be viewed as having a reformative effect; it is desired as retribution and as a general deterrent."[54, p. 518]

CORRECTIONS IN THE NEWS

International Treaty Obligations: Detention of Foreign Nationals

Here's an interesting fact. U.S. corrections agencies have treaty obligations under the Vienna Convention on Consular Relations that outline procedures to be taken when an arrest or detention involves a foreign national. Why is this important? The stipulations in this treaty agreement allow for similar treatment of U.S. citizens in arrest and detention situations in foreign countries who have agreed to the treaty.

In all cases, foreign nationals who have been arrested and detained must be asked if they would like to contact their consular. If they elect not to make contact, there are some cases that carry with it the mandatory notification of the consular. This notification must be made without delay.

Whenever a mandatory notification is made and the foreign national has elected not to contact his or her consular, the agency has the obligation of informing the foreign national the notification was made. Regardless of the circumstances for the detainment of a foreign national, under no circumstances should it be made known to the consular officer if the foreign national has applied for asylum in this country.

Included in this procedure is the requirement that the consular be allowed to communicate with the detainee. But communicating with the prisoner is not limited to a phone call. It also includes the right to visit the inmate in jail or prison and to arrange for legal representation, but consular officers may not act as attorneys for detainees. The word *consul* does not mean *counsel*.

What makes this treaty agreement complicated is that aliens, including those with resident alien registration cards, also referred to as *green cards*, retain their foreign nationality. This means that foreign nationals, regardless of their visa or immigration status, have the right to have their consular notified.

In the case of an arrest, the responsibility of making the notification lies with the arresting officer and not the prosecutor or the court. This responsibility does not extend to foreign nationals stopped for traffic offenses or when the detention is brief and routine. The purpose behind this treaty agreement is to allow foreign nationals the opportunity to contact consular offices. When the foreign national is simply cited and released, their access to the consular is not seriously threatened. This stipulation primarily applies to lesser offenses and investigations. However, if the investigation results in a detention, regardless of the length of the detention, judged by the restriction on the freedom of the foreign national to leave, appropriate steps should be taken to address the need to notify consular officers.

Source: National Institute of Corrections. (n.d.). *Consular notification regarding detention of foreign nationals*. Longmont, CO: U.S. Department of Justice, National institute of Corrections.

Why do prisons seem so unable to rehabilitate criminal offenders? Interesting answers come from offenders themselves. For example, prior research investigated prisoner assessments of why imprisonment is ineffective at reducing criminal behavior among inmates after they are released. Several interesting findings were produced:

- Forty-four percent of prisoners indicated they developed more hostile or critical views of society as a result of their confinement.
- Prisoners were nearly twice as likely to report that prisons had no deterrent effect as opposed to a strong deterrent effect on criminal behavior.
- Ninety-two percent of prisoners believed that prisons are simply universities of crime where offenders acquire additional skills, attitudes, and behaviors that lend themselves to continued criminal behavior.
- Fifty-eight percent of prisoners felt that their rehabilitation would result from personal change, not any policy that society would provide for them.[55]

During the 1970s, a variety of events led to the decline of rehabilitation as the guiding force of correctional policy and the ascendance of incapacitation. First and foremost, there was an explosion of crime beginning in the 1960s that did not peak until the early 1990s. Thus during the 1970s, violent crime in the United States was at unprecedentedly high levels and crime was viewed as the number one social problem according to public opinion polls. In 1975, James Q. Wilson published *Thinking About Crime*, which showcased the increase of crime and disorder that occurred at the same time that domestic spending on public welfare programs associated with President Lyndon Johnson's Great Society increased. According to Wilson, the general liberalization of public policy seemed to enable the increase in crime, vice, and disorder.[56] The importance of this for correctional policy is that the public was angry about crime and viewed criminals as a group deserving of punishment, not treatment.

Also during the 1970s, academic criminologists began to suggest that correctional treatment does not work based on evaluations of treatment programs. The most famous example of this approach was Robert Martinson's conclusion that, "With few and isolated exceptions, the rehabilitative efforts that have been reported so far have had no appreciable effect on recidivism."[57, p. 25] Martinson's conclusion was based on a systematic review of 231 correctional evaluation studies conducted between 1945 and 1967, which showed that about 48 percent of programs have some rehabilitative value whereas 52 percent do not. From this, the **nothing works** philosophy was born, which argues that for all intents and purposes, correctional treatment is ineffective. The nothing works idea spread and became the conventional wisdom that dominated correctional management. In addition, the nothing works doctrine justified a de-emphasis on rehabilitation and an emphasis on incapacitation within corrections.

Although the nothing works doctrine was influential, it required a somewhat pessimistic viewpoint to be believed. If only slightly less than half of correctional programs work, that means that nearly half of correctional programs *do work*. Over time, more rehabilitation-oriented criminologists conducted sophisticated quantitative analyses not only of whether correctional programs worked but also the ways that successful programs worked. From these studies, three important principles of effective correctional intervention were developed: (1) programs should target the highest risk offenders for treatment; (2) programs should be behavioral in nature and target antisocial factors/behaviors that are most strongly correlated with criminal offending; and (3) programs should be tailored to the individual offender's needs and learning styles (see TABLE 10–1).[58–63]

Today, both criminology and correctional systems invest heavily and believe in programming to rehabilitate prisoners. The nothing works doctrine is gone and in its place is the **what works** doctrine, which uses evidence-based information to inform and design correctional treatment programs and is described later in this chapter.

Educational and Vocational Programs

As described in Chapter 9, prisoners have a variety of risk factors that make their transition to mainstream society more difficult. For example, 40 percent of state prisoners and 27 percent of federal prisoners have neither a high school diploma nor GED. By comparison, just 18 percent of the general population failed to obtain a GED or high school diploma. Even educational attainment is often impacted by the antisocial tendencies of prisoners. For instance, nearly 35 percent of jail inmates in a national survey reported that behavioral problems were the main reason for dropping out of high school. Nearly 16 percent reported that incarceration status during adolescence or involvement in illegal activities prompted them to drop out of high school.[64]

All federal prisons and 92 percent of state prisons have an education program for inmates. Most of these services are devoted to basic adult education and secondary education so that prisoners can earn a GED. More than 80 percent of federal prisons and 27 percent of state prisons offer college courses. Nearly 94 percent of federal prisons provided vocational training as do 56 percent of state prisons. Other educational services provided in American prisons include special education for prisoners with developmental and learning disabilities and study release programs (fewer than 10 percent of state and federal prisons provide these services).[65]

TABLE 10-1 Inmate Risks and Treatment Needs

Factor	Risk	Dynamic Need
History of antisocial behavior	Early and continuing involvement in a number and variety of antisocial acts in a variety of settings	Build noncriminal alternative behavior in risky situations
Antisocial personality pattern	Adventurous pleasure seeking, weak self-control, restlessly aggressive	Build problem-solving skills, self-management skills, anger management and coping skills
Antisocial cognition	Attitudes, values, beliefs, and rationalizations supportive of crime; cognitive emotional states of anger, resentment, and defiance; criminal versus reformed identity; criminal versus anticriminal identity	Reduce antisocial cognition, recognize risky thinking and feeling, build up alternative less risky thinking and feeling, adopt a reform and/or anticriminal identity
Antisocial associates	Close association with criminal others and relative isolation from anticriminal others; immediate social support for crime	Reduce association with criminal others, enhance association with anticriminal others
Family and/or marital	Two key elements are nurturance and/or caring and monitoring and/or supervision	Reduce conflict, build positive relationship, enhance monitoring and supervision
School and/or work	Low levels of performance and satisfactions in school and/or work	Enhance performance, rewards, and satisfactions
Leisure and/or recreation	Low levels of involvement and satisfactions in anticriminal leisure pursuits	Enhance involvement, rewards, and satisfactions
Substance abuse	Abuse of alcohol and/or other drugs	Reduce substance abuse, reduce the personal and interpersonal supports for substance-oriented behavior, enhance alternatives to drug abuse

Source: Adapted from Andrews, D. A., Bonta, J., & Wormith, J. S. (2006). The recent past and near future of risk and/or need assessment. *Crime & Delinquency, 52,* 7–27, p. 11.

Nationwide, there are more than 140,000 prisoners participating in educational programs. Nearly 110,000 inmates are in vocational training and an additional 5,000 prisoners participate in a work release program. Nearly 7,000 prisoners are in transitional housing to prepare for their release to the community.[66] Research suggests that educational programs provide immediate and long-term benefits among former prisoners. Mary Ellen Batiuk and her colleagues studied 10-year recidivism levels among more than 300 males released from a medium-security prison in Ohio. Inmates who completed at least 2 years of a college education program had greater employment success and lower recidivism levels than inmates who did not complete 2 years of college while confined.[67]

A variety of work and vocational programs exist in American prisons, and inmate work has been a defining feature of prison history since the Auburn system. As examined in Chapter 2, the following five types of inmate labor systems have been used:

1. *Contract labor system,* where private contractors provide prisons with machinery and raw materials in exchange for the inmate labor to produce finished products.
2. *Piece-price system,* where contractors give raw materials to prisons, which use convict labor to produce finished products. Once the goods are manufactured, they are sold by the piece to the contractor, who resells them on the open market.
3. *Lease system,* where contractors bid against each other to own the rights to inmate labor. Inmates work outside the prison facility, under the supervision of a private contractor, who is responsible for the inmates' food, shelter, and clothing.

4. *Public account system*, where the state retains control of inmate labor and provides convicts with the machinery and raw materials to produce finished products. The state sells the products on the open market and uses the profits to defray the cost of prison operations.
5. *State-use system*, where prison labor is used to produce goods for state-supported institutions, such as schools and hospitals.

Perhaps the greatest innovation in inmate work was the creation of **Federal Prison Industries** (also known as **UNICOR**). Founded in 1934, UNICOR has operated factories and employed inmates in the BOP and produced a wide array of products for use by the U.S. government. UNICOR has also provided tens of thousands of inmates with the vocational training and work experience they needed to become gainfully employed, law-abiding citizens after release.

Federal Prison Industries (FPI) is one of the most successful and cost-effective enterprises of the federal government and is based on the following four principles:

1. Safe prison management and better prison discipline through the reduction of idleness.
2. Cost efficiency. Investments in prison industries can lower expenditures on day-to-day prison operations and enable inmates to produce items of value for the government, such as furniture, electronics, signs, and military gear. Sale of these products generates revenue that can be used to offset expenses that would otherwise have to be met through appropriated funds. FPI staff salaries are funded out of such earnings, and, for many years, FPI revenues were also used to subsidize educational and other programs for inmates.
3. Job training and rehabilitation.
4. Inmate financial responsibility. UNICOR mandates that the wages inmates earn through employment in prison labor programs help them meet those obligations. In 1987, the BOP initiated the Inmate Financial Responsibility Program (IFRP), which mandated that all inmates with court-recognized financial obligations must use at least 50 percent of their FPI earnings to pay their debts. To date, more than $80 million has been collected.[68]

Another major prison vocational program is the **Prison Industry Enhancement Certification Program (PIECP)**, which allows inmates to work for a private employer in the community and earn the same wage as nonimprisoned workers. PIECP was created in 1979 and serves as a way for state prisons to form partnerships with private companies to facilitate offender reintegration. Nearly 7,000 prisoners are currently employed in PIECP jobs and the program has served more than 70,000 inmates since its inception. Compared to other prison work programs, offenders who participated in PIECP found jobs more quickly and remained employed for longer periods. PIECP prisoners also had lower recidivism rates than those in other work programs. In addition, as shown in FIGURE 10-3, PIECP provides direct and indirect economic benefits including tax revenue, payment of family support, payment to a federal victims' fund, and others.[69]

Religious Programs

Education and work are two of the most important social institutions in American society; however, another important institution is religion. Evidenced by their very names, such as penitentiaries, houses of correction, or reformatories, prisons have been used as the vehicle to rehabilitate prisoners, and historically this transformation was explicitly religious in nature. In recent years, religion has been brought back to prison and a variety of religious or **faith-based programs** have been developed.[70–71] In 2002, the BOP started the Life Connections Program, which is an 18-month, residential program that offers a

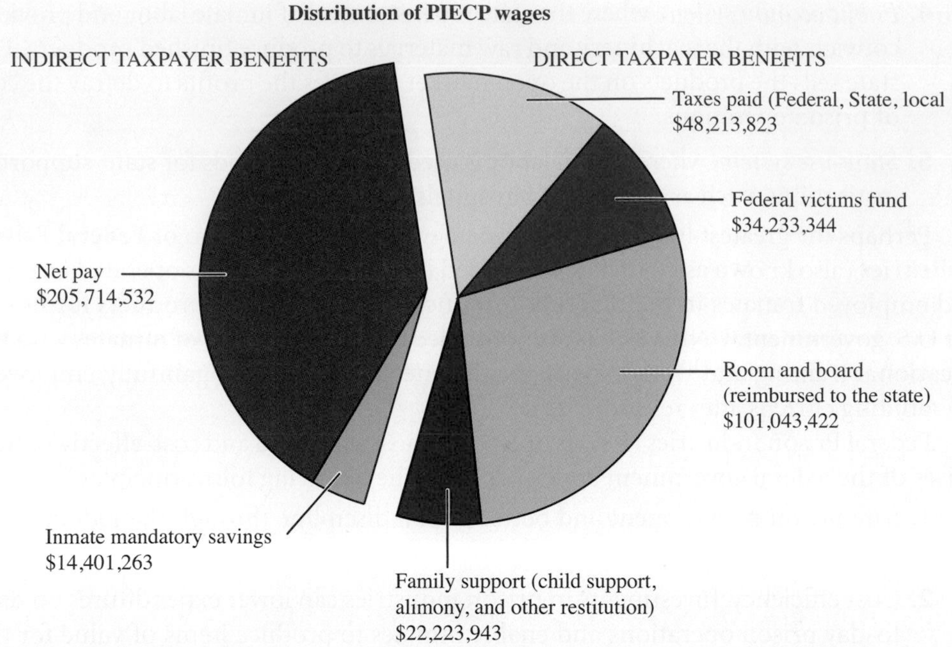

FIGURE 10–3 Prison Industry Enhancement Certification Program. *Source*: Moses, M. C., & Smith, C. J. (2007). Factories behind fences: Do prison "real work" programs work? *National Institute of Justice Journal, 257*, 32–35.

multifaith curriculum taught by clergy hired from the community. Inmates work, study, pray, and work with religious mentors, both during confinement and during an aftercare component. A recent evaluation of the Life Connections Program found that prisoners who are extremely motivated to make changes in their lives (e.g., repudiate antisocial ways for prosocial living) were more likely to participate in the Life Connections Program. In this way, the faith-based program serves as a mechanism by which prisoners who have already undergone a cognitive-behavioral change attempt to go straight.[72]

It is unclear whether religious programming in prison significantly reduces institutional misconduct and postrelease recidivism. Byron Johnson and his colleagues compared inmates who completed the Prison Fellowship program to inmates who did not participate in the program in four New York prisons. They found no differences between these groups in their involvement in general and serious prison infractions; however, inmates who were more intensively involved in the Prison Fellowship program were significantly less likely to be rearrested after release.[73] In a subsequent study, Johnson followed the prisoners over an 8-year period and generally found few differences in recidivism between those who participated in the Prison Fellowship program and those who did not. Again, offenders with more extensive involvement in the program had better adjustment and were less likely to be rearrested or reincarcerated.[74]

Kent Kerley and his colleagues evaluated Operation Starting Line, which is a faith-based program in Mississippi prisons, and examined its effects on negative emotions and aggressive behaviors among inmates. The program involved entertainment and faith-based messages from musicians, athletes, and other public figures, after which inmates met in smaller groups to pray and engage in religious study. A survey of nearly 300 inmates indicated that prisoners reported healthier emotions and affective states after the program and reduced anger and bitterness. In addition, program participants got into fewer arguments and fights with staff and other inmates.[75] Although these are promising findings, to date there is insufficient research to evaluate the overall effectiveness of faith-based programs. For example, a recent meta-analysis indicated that faith-based programs reduce recidivism in sex offenders by more than 31 percent, but this estimate is based on just one study.[76]

Substance Abuse Treatment

There is tremendous need for drug and alcohol treatment among the prisoner population, and prison systems devote a considerable amount of resources to treat inmates' substance abuse problems. Faye Taxman and her colleagues studied 74 prisons and 24 special drug treatment prison facilities based on data from the National Criminal Justice Treatment Practices survey, which is a nationwide survey of treatment practices in correctional settings. Overall, they found:

- Seventy-four percent of prisons provide drug and alcohol education programs.
- Fifty-five percent of prisons provide up to 4 hours of substance abuse group counseling per week.
- Forty-six percent of prisons provide between 5 and 25 hours of substance abuse group counseling per week.
- Eleven percent of prisons provide more than 26 hours of substance abuse group counseling per week.
- Twenty percent of prisons provide a segregated **therapeutic community** unit, which is a treatment-intensive institutional program for inmates with substance abuse problems.
- Nearly 10 percent of prisons have a nonsegregated therapeutic community.
- Forty-five percent of prisons provide **relapse prevention groups**, which are treatment programs designed to educate offenders about signs, precursors, and situations that can lead to relapses in drug abuse.
- Seven percent of prisons provide case management for prisoners.[77]

An extensive literature review has looked at the effects of substance abuse treatment on a range of behavioral outcomes among prisoners. Generally, researchers have found that substance abuse treatment in prison produces positive behavioral outcomes after offenders are released to the community. The effects are strongest for shorter follow-up periods, such as 1 year. When ex-offenders are followed for longer periods of time the treatment effect declines. Another important factor is the type of substance abuse treatment that was provided. Inmates in work release therapeutic communities tend to perform better than those who receive treatment in the main prison facility. Clifford Butzin and his colleagues studied the effects of drug treatment during work release among 1,300 Delaware prisoners followed up to 5 years after release. Former prisoners who had received treatment were twice as likely as nontreated offenders to remain crime free and remained in the community for twice as long before subsequent arrest. More importantly, habitual offenders who completed work release therapeutic community drug treatment showed the largest positive treatment effect.[78]

Another important dimension of prison-based substance abuse treatment is aftercare, or a period of community follow-up to help offenders transition their treatment from prison to the community setting. Evaluations of drug treatment programs with aftercare in California found that treatment offenders had better employment records, lower recidivism, and lengthier stays in the community before reincarceration than former prisoners who did not participate in drug treatment.[79–80] An evaluation of a similar program in Texas showed that 25 percent of prisoners who participated in drug treatment with aftercare were reincarcerated compared to 42 percent of untreated control subjects and 64 percent who dropped out of treatment.[81] Of course, prison drug treatment does not always achieve its intended goal. Wayne Welsh and his colleagues studied the misconduct rates of more than 1,000 inmates, including some who participated in a therapeutic community, others who received traditional drug treatment, and untreated offenders. Over time, there were no differences in their misconduct—in other words, drug treatment did not help make inmates more compliant with prison rules. Instead, traditional risk factors, such as young age and prior violence, were linked to misconduct.[82]

Sex Offender Treatment

No type of criminal poses greater challenges for the correctional system than **sex offenders**, persons who commit sexually based offenses, such as rape, child molestation, incest, and related offenses. When correctional systems fail to monitor, supervise, treat, or punish sex offenders, the results can be disastrous. The case of Dean Schwartzmiller is illustrative. In 2007, Schwartzmiller was sentenced to 152 years in prison upon convictions for multiple counts of sexual offenses against children. His criminal history spanned nearly 40 years and included arrests in multiple states and other countries. Police found detailed written records containing more than 36,000 children's names, which authorities believe were potential victims. Schwartzmiller is considered the most prolific sex offender in recent history (his roommate, also a sex offender, was sentenced to 800 years in prison for similar crimes).[83] The case outraged the American public because of the seeming inability of the criminal justice system to control such a violent, recidivistic offender.

Nearly 20 percent of prisons offer sex offender therapy, which provides services to approximately 30,000 inmates nationwide.[84] The effective treatment and supervision of sex offenders begins with a comprehensive assessment of factors that relate to the offender's criminal behavior. These include many of the same factors used in the assessment of all offenders (Chapter 4), such as criminal history, school, work, and family history, psychiatric needs and cognitive development, and prior involvements with the criminal justice system.[85]

In addition to the usual background factors, there are several other constructs that are risk factors for committing sexually based offenses. Correctional staff members screen sex offenders for the following characteristics:

- Deviant sexual arousal, interests, or preferences
- Obsessive sexual preoccupation
- Pervasive anger or hostility
- Emotional management difficulties
- Self-regulation difficulties
- Impulsivity
- Antisocial orientation and pro-offending attitudes
- Cognitive distortions
- Social isolation and poor social skills
- Emotional callousness and absence of empathy[86]

As shown in FIGURE 10-4, these traits are what correctional programs nationwide focus on when treating sex offenders.

The overall and long-term recidivism rates of criminal offenders are not promising. When violent offenders, especially those who commit sexually based offenses are considered, the recidivism numbers are not promising. Karl Hanson and Monique Bussiere conducted a meta-analysis of 61 studies encompassing nearly 29,000 sex offenders. More than 13 percent of sex offenders committed an additional sex offense after release from prison. The recidivism rate for nonsex offenses was 12 percent. Within sex offenders,

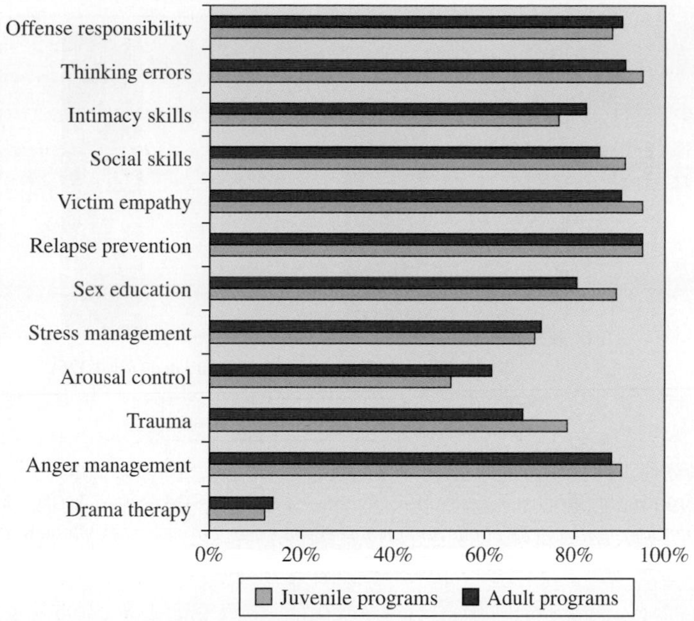

FIGURE 10–4 Components of Sex Offender Treatment Programs. *Source*: Center for Sex Offender Management. (2006). *Understanding treatment for adults and juveniles who have committed sex offenses.* Washington, DC: U.S. Department of Justice, Office of Justice Programs, Center for Effective Public Policy.

there were important group differences—rapists had the highest sex offense recidivism (19 percent) and nonsex offense recidivism (22 percent). When recidivism was defined as any type of reoffense, the rates were much higher; the overall recidivism level was 36 percent with 37 percent of child molesters and 46 percent of rapists reoffending in some way.[87]

Recently, Friedrich Losel and Martin Schmucker meta-analyzed 69 studies of more than 22,000 treated and untreated sex offenders. Among treated sex offenders, the recidivism levels were 11 percent for sexual recidivism, nearly 7 percent for violent recidivism, and more than 22 percent for any recidivism. For untreated offenders, the respective levels were 18 percent, 12 percent, and nearly 33 percent. When adjustments for base rates of offending are considered, prison treatment of sex offenders produces 37 percent reductions in sexual reoffending and 31 percent reductions in general recidivism.[88]

Nevertheless, it is clear that correctional treatment for sex offenders is preferable to not providing treatment for incarcerated sex offenders. As shown in FIGURE 10–5, the sexual and general recidivism patterns of sex offenders are unfortunately high; however, the reoffending is greater among untreated sex offenders among a study of approximately 9,400 sex offenders. The treatment effect is especially important among juvenile sex offenders (FIGURE 10–6) where a study of 3,000 adolescent sex offenders showed that those who receive treatment reoffend at more than 50 percent lower rates than untreated adolescent sex offenders.

What Works in Correctional Treatment?

At one point in recent correctional history, there existed a great deal of skepticism about the fruitfulness of correctional treatment. Since treatment programs were about equally likely to succeed or fail and because so many prisoners resorted to crime after release from prison, rehabilitation fell out of favor among the general public, politicians, and correctional administrators. Still, it was not disputed that half of correctional programs yielded

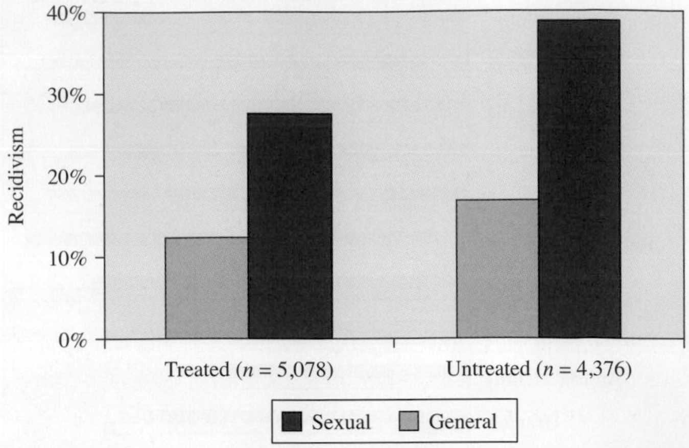

FIGURE 10–5 Treatment Effectiveness for Sex Offenders. *Source*: Center for Sex Offender Management. (2006). *Understanding treatment for adults and juveniles who have committed sex offenses.* Washington, DC: U.S. Department of Justice, Office of Justice Programs, Center for Effective Public Policy.

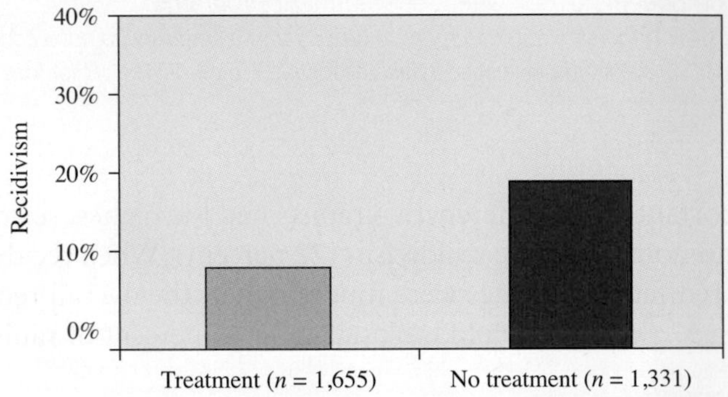

FIGURE 10–6 Treatment Effectiveness for Juvenile Sex Offenders. *Source*: Center for Sex Offender Management. (2006). *Understanding treatment for adults and juveniles who have committed sex offenses.* Washington, DC: U.S. Department of Justice, Office of Justice Programs, Center for Effective Public Policy.

some positive outcome. Over time, a more optimistic opinion of rehabilitation gained momentum and the phrase "nothing works" was discarded in favor of "what works?" In recent years, criminologists used comprehensive reviews of evaluation studies and sophisticated quantitative meta-analyses of these studies to determine the overall effectiveness of various types of correctional interventions. The advantage of this approach is that it provides an overall, across-study understanding of how well treatment programs reduce offending among prisoners.

Steve Aos and his colleagues systematically reviewed the evidence from 291 program evaluations of the treatment of prisoners conducted over a 35-year span. They produced several important findings:

- Correctional industries programs in prison reduce recidivism nearly 8 percent.
- Vocational education programs in prison reduce recidivism nearly 13 percent.
- Basic adult education programs in prison reduce recidivism 5 percent.

- Employment assistance/job training of prisoners in the community reduces recidivism nearly 5 percent.
- Prison therapeutic communities with aftercare reduce recidivism 7 percent; without aftercare reduces recidivism 5 percent.
- Cognitive-behavioral drug treatment in prison reduces recidivism 7 percent.
- General and specific cognitive-behavioral programs for the general prisoner population reduce recidivism more than 8 percent.
- Among sex offenders, these programs reduce recidivism 15 percent.[89]

Essentially, the main goal of correctional treatment programs is to motivate offenders to desist from antisocial thought and behavioral patterns in favor of prosocial thought and behavior patterns. For example, a rehabilitated offender would view a new job as the means to get his or her life back on track. An unrehabilitated offender would view a new job as an opportunity to embezzle. In corrections, **moral reconation therapy** is a cognitive-behavioral treatment that attempts to instill moral, prosocial thinking and decision-making strategies. Gregory Little conducted a meta-analysis of moral reconation therapy and found that it significantly reduces recidivism among nearly 2,500 former prisoners and probationers.[90] Similarly, Joy Tong and David Farrington reviewed 26 studies of another cognitive-behavioral program called Reasoning and Rehabilitation. Among prisoners in Canada, the United States, and the United Kingdom, prisoners who completed the Reasoning and Rehabilitation program showed a 14 percent decline in recidivism compared to control subjects.[91]

Getting prisoners to think and act differently has served as the overriding purpose of American prisons since their inception. The reason for this is simple: more than 90 percent of prisoners will ultimately be released from prison and return to the community. The ability of prisons to transform offenders from antisocial to prosocial directly bears on their ability to comply with parole (Chapter 11) and reintegrate to society (Chapter 12). These topics are explored next.

WRAP UP

CASE STUDY CONCLUSION

There is evidence that religious conversions produce both positive and negative impacts on prison security. From the positive perspective, religious affiliation teaches self-discipline, which ultimately aids in rehabilitation. Studies have revealed that conversion to nontraditional religions reduces predatory violence in correctional institutions. But there is also the slight chance that radical religious indoctrination will inspire ideologically inspired criminality. Extremist groups have long felt prisons are fertile grounds for recruitment and that some of the nation's most dangerous terrorists are currently serving time in American prisons; the likelihood that a subculture of religious extremists will develop is not beyond reason. This increases the probability that small groups of like-minded extremists will conduct terrorist operations once released from prison.

Source: Hamm, M. S. (2007). *Terrorist recruitment in American correctional institutions: An exploratory study of nontraditional faith groups.* Washington, DC: U.S. Department of Justice, Office of Justice Programs, National Institute of Justice.

Chapter Summary

- Prisons are broadly organized into three main security levels: minimum, medium, and maximum.
- Both state correctional systems and the BOP have supermaximum prisons that use solitary confinement and other punitive restrictions to supervise the most violent prisoners.
- Adequate medical and mental health services are a constitutional right and prisons provide an array of services to meet inmate needs.
- The Supreme Court has ruled on a variety of issues pertaining to the daily life of prisoners and the ways that prisons are operated and managed, such as access to health care, protection against violent inmates, quality of life, classification, and transfer.
- Research has indicated that the ways that prisons are managed and organized affects inmate adjustment and misconduct.
- A host of educational, vocational, and religious programs exist within prisons to prepare inmates for life in conventional society.
- Considerable resources are devoted to treating the substance abuse problems of prisoners.
- Specialized programs target the unique risk factors posed by sex offenders.
- Although it was once believed that nothing works in terms of correctional treatment, meta-analyses show that many correctional programs are effective at reducing recidivism.

Key Terms

administrative institutions Federal prison facilities with special missions.

Administrative-Maximum United States Penitentiary Prison in Florence, Colorado, that houses the most dangerous and notorious prisoners in the federal system.

close-security prisons Another name for maximum-security state prisons.

consent decree Court order for correctional officials to improve prison conditions.

design capacity The number of inmates that planners intended for the facility.

direct supervision Supervision design where inmates mix in a central common room and are continuously supervised by staff.

faith-based programs Programs that use religious instruction and prayer to reduce problem behaviors.

federal correctional complexes Clusters of BOP facilities located within close proximity to each other.

federal correctional institutions Another name for low-security institutions.

federal prison camps Another name for minimum-security institutions.

Federal Prison Industries Federal prison labor program founded in 1934.

formal social control Official, administrative control policies.

high-security institutions Federal prisons with highly secured perimeters featuring walls or reinforced fences, multiple and single occupancy cell housing, the highest staff-to-inmate ratio, and close control of inmate movements.

informal social control Ways that inmates and correctional staff tacitly coexist to maintain institutional safety.

low-security institutions Federal prisons with double-fenced perimeters, mostly dormitory or cubicle housing, and strong work and program components. The staff-to-inmate ratio is higher in these institutions compared to minimum-security facilities.

maximum-security state prisons Prisons that house the highest risk prisoners in terms of their sentence, institutional adjustment, criminal history, and other factors.

medium-security institutions Federal prisons with strengthened perimeters, usually double fences with electronic detection systems, mostly cell-type housing, a wide variety of work and treatment programs, higher staff-to-inmate ratios, and overall greater internal controls.

medium-security state prisons Prisons that house medium- or moderate-security inmates in terms of their sentence, institutional adjustment, criminal history, and other factors.

minimum-security institutions Federal prisons that have dormitory housing, low staff-to-inmate ratios, and little to no perimeter fencing.

minimum-security state prisons Prisons that house the lowest security inmates in terms of their sentence, institutional adjustment, criminal history, and other factors.

moral reconation therapy A cognitive-behavioral treatment that attempts to instill moral, prosocial thinking and decision-making strategies.

nothing works Philosophy that argues that for all intents and purposes, correctional treatment is ineffective.

operational capacity The number of inmates that can be accommodated based on the facility's staff, programs, and services.

Prison Industry Enhancement Certification Program (PIECP) Program that allows inmates to work for a private employer in the community and earn the same wage as nonimprisoned workers.

private prisons Private, for-profit businesses hired by the government to supervise lower risk inmates.

rated capacity The number of beds or inmates assigned by a rating official to institutions within a jurisdiction.

relapse prevention groups Treatment programs designed to educate offenders about signs, precursors, and situations that can lead to relapses in drug abuse.

sex offenders Persons who commit sexually based offenses, such as rape, child molestation, incest, and related offenses.

SHU syndrome Condition characterized by inmate thought disturbances, perceptual changes, thought, concentration, and memory difficulties, extreme anxiety, and other symptoms of mental illness that appear to be produced by the sensory deprivations of solitary confinement in SHU or supermax units.

solitary confinement Isolation in one's cell for the purpose of contemplation, prayer, and penitence to reform prisoners.

supermaximum-security (supermax) state prisons Special prisons used to house inmates who pose extraordinary risks to institutional safety because of their involvement in prison misconduct and violence.

therapeutic community A prison programming technique where treatment offenders are removed from the general population and are placed in settings devoted to treatment.

UNICOR Another name for Federal Prison Industries.

United States Penitentiaries Another name for high-security institutions.

what works Doctrine that uses evidence-based information to inform and design effective correctional treatment programs.

Critical Thinking Questions

1. The isolation of supermax prisons has come full circle since the founding of prisons. Does this suggest that it is needed to control noncompliant prisoners? If so, why is this controversial?
2. Do prisoners receive too much criticism because of their inability to desist from crime? Is a life of crime similar to a life of smoking or a life of exercise—habits that are very difficult to break?

3. Ultimately, is cognitive-behavioral change up to each individual prisoner? To reduce recidivism, must minds be changed before behavior will follow?
4. Are any prisons really country clubs as often described by the media? What features of prisons contribute to such an image?
5. Given the devastation caused by sexually based offenses and the difficulty in treating sex offenders, should sex offending receive an automatic life sentence? What do you think about making sex offenses eligible for capital punishment?

Notes

1. DiIulio, J. J. (1987). *Governing prisons: A comparative study of correctional management*. New York: The Free Press.
2. Lovell, D., Johnson, L. C., & Cain, K. C. (2007). Recidivism of supermax prisoners in Washington State. *Crime & Delinquency, 53*, 633–656.
3. Sykes, G. M. (1956). The corruption of authority and rehabilitation. *Social Forces, 34*, 257–262.
4. Hayner, N. S., & Ash, E. (1940). The prison as a community. *American Sociological Review, 5*, 577–583.
5. Gottfredson, M. R. (1979). Treatment destruction techniques. *Journal of Research in Crime and Delinquency, 16*, 39–54.
6. *Meachum v. Fano*, 427 U.S. 215 (1976).
7. Federal Bureau of Prisons (2008). *Prison types & general information*. Retrieved October 7, 2008, from http://www.bop.gov/locations/institutions/index.jsp.
8. Byrne, J. M., & Roberts, A. R. (2007). New directions in offender typology design, development, and implementation: Can we balance risk, treatment, and control? *Aggression and Violent Behavior, 12*, 483–492.
9. Stephan, J. J. (2008). *Census of state and federal correctional facilities, 2005*. Washington, DC: U.S. Department of Justice, Office of Justice Programs, Bureau of Justice Statistics.
10. Camp, S. D., & Gaes, G. G. (2002). Growth and quality of U.S. private prisons: Evidence from a national survey. *Criminology & Public Policy, 1*, 427–450.
11. Pratt, T. C., & Maahs, J. (1999). Are private prisons more cost-effective than public prisons? A meta-analysis of evaluation research studies. *Crime & Delinquency, 45*, 358–371.
12. Bales, W. D., Bedard, L. E., Quinn, S. T., Ensley, D. T., & Holley, G. P. (2005). Recidivism of public and private state prison inmates in Florida. *Criminology & Public Policy, 4*, 57–82.
13. Stephan.
14. Hughes, K. A. (2006). *Justice expenditure and employment in the United States, 2003*. Washington, DC: U.S. Department of Justice, Office of Justice Programs, Bureau of Justice Statistics.
15. Stephan, J. J. (2004). *State prison expenditures, 2001*. Washington, DC: U.S. Department of Justice, Office of Justice Programs, Bureau of Justice Statistics.
16. American Correctional Association. (2001). *Public correctional policy on correctional health care*. Retrieved January 24, 2008, from http://www.aca.org/government/policyresolution/view.asp?ID=9.

17. Beck, A. J., & Maruschak, L. M. (2001). *Mental health treatment in state prisons, 2000.* Washington, DC: U.S. Department of Justice, Office of Justice Programs, Bureau of Justice Statistics.

18. Hammett, T. M., Kennedy, S., & Kuck, S. (2007). *National survey of infectious diseases in correctional facilities: HIV and sexually transmitted diseases.* Washington, DC: U.S. Department of Justice, Office of Justice Programs, National Institute of Justice.

19. Raimer, B. G., & Stobo, J. D. (2004). Health care delivery in the Texas prison system. *Journal of the American Medical Association, 292,* 485–489.

20. For an examination, see Smith, C. E. (2007). Prisoners' rights and the Rehnquist Court era. *Prison Journal, 87,* 457–476.

21. *Pugh v. Locke,* 406 F.2d 318 (1976).

22. *Estelle v. Gamble,* 429 U.S. 97 (1976).

23. *Wilson v. Seiter,* 501 U.S. 294 (1991).

24. *Farmer v. Brennan,* 511 U.S. 825 (1994).

25. Vaughn, M. S. (1996). Prison civil liability for inmate-against-inmate assault and breakdown/disorganization theory. *Journal of Criminal Justice, 24,* 139–152.

26. *Meachum v. Fano,* 427 U.S. 215 (1976).

27. *Montayne v. Haymes,* 427 U.S. 236 (1976).

28. *Olim v. Wakinekona,* 461 U.S. 238 (1983).

29. *Howe v. Smith,* 452 U.S. 473 (1981).

30. *Vitek v. Jones,* 445 U.S. 480 (1980).

31. *Hewitt v. Helms,* 459 U.S. 460 (1983).

32. *Wilkinson v. Austin,* 544 U.S. 74 (2005).

33. Stephan.

34. Sykes, p. 262.

35. Craig, S. C. (2004). Rehabilitation versus control: An organizational theory of prison management. *Prison Journal, 84* (Suppl), 92S–114S.

36. Byrne, J. M., & Hummer, D. (2007). Myths and realities of prison violence: A review of the evidence. *Victims and Offenders, 2,* 77–90.

37. Poole, E. D., & Regoli, R. M. (1980). Role stress, custody orientation, and disciplinary actions: A study of prison guards. *Criminology, 18,* 215–226.

38. Reisig, M. D. (2002). Administrative control and inmate homicide. *Homicide Studies, 6,* 84–103.

39. Cunningham, M. D. (2008). Institutional misconduct among capital murderers. In M. DeLisi & P. J. Conis (Eds.), *Violent offenders: Theory, research, public policy, and practice* (pp. 237–254). Boston: Jones & Bartlett.

40. Cunningham, M. D., & Sorensen, J. R. (2006). Nothing to lose? A comparative examination of prison misconduct rates among life-without-parole and other long-term high-security inmates. *Criminal Justice and Behavior, 33,* 683–705.

41. Flanagan, T. J. (1980). Time served and institutional misconduct: Patterns of involvement in disciplinary infractions among long-term and short-term inmates. *Journal of Criminal Justice, 8,* 357–367.

42. Grassian, S. (1983). Psychopathological effects of solitary confinement. *American Journal of Psychiatry, 140,* 1450–1454.

43. Grassian, S., & Friedman, N. (1986). Effects of sensory deprivation in psychiatric seclusion and solitary confinement. *International Journal of Law and Psychiatry, 8,* 49–65.

44. Arrigo, B. A., & Bullock, J. L. (2008). The psychological effects of solitary confinement on prisoners in supermax units: Reviewing what we know and recommending what should change. *International Journal of Offender Therapy and Comparative Criminology, 52,* 622–640.

45. Pizarro, J., & Stenius, V. M. K. (2004). Supermax prisons: Their rise, current practices, and effect on inmates. *Prison Journal, 84,* 248–264.

46. Pizarro, J. M., Steniu, V. M. K., & Pratt, T. C. (2006). Supermax prisons: Myths, realities, and the politics of punishment in American society. *Criminal Justice Policy Review, 17,* 6–21.

47. Mears, D. P., & Reisig, M. D. (2006). The theory and practice of supermax prisons. *Punishment & Society, 8,* 33–57.

48. Briggs, C. S., Sundt, J. L., & Castellano, T. C. (2003). The effect of supermaximum security prisons on aggregate levels of institutional violence. *Criminology, 41,* 1341–1376.

49. Lovell et al.

50. Levitt, S. D. (1996). The effect of prison population size on crime rates: Evidence from prison overcrowding litigation. *Quarterly Journal of Economics, 111,* 319–351.

51. Jiang, S. (2005). Impact of drug use on inmate misconduct: A multilevel analysis. *Journal of Criminal Justice, 33,* 153–163.

52. Franklin, T. W., Franklin, C. A., & Pratt, T. C. (2006). Examining the empirical relationship between prison crowding and inmate misconduct: A meta-analysis of conflicting research results. *Journal of Criminal Justice, 34,* 401–412.

53. de Beaumont, G., & de Tocqueville, A.(1994). On the penitentiary system in the United States and its application in France. In J. E. Jacoby (Ed.), *Classics of criminology* (pp. 372–386). Prospect Heights, IL: Waveland Press.

54. Sutherland, E., & Cressey, D. (1978). *Criminology.* Philadelphia: J.B. Lippincott.

55. Kolstad, A. (1996). Imprisonment as rehabilitation: Offenders' assessment of why it does not work. *Journal of Criminal Justice, 24,* 323–335.

56. Wilson, J. Q. (1975). *Thinking about crime.* New York: Basic Books.

57. Martinson, R. (1974). What works? Questions and answers about prison reform. *The Public Interest, 35,* 22–54.

58. Andrews, D. A., Zinger, I., Hoge, R. D., Bonta, J., Gendreau, P., & Cullen, F. T. (1990). Does correctional treatment work? A clinically relevant and psychologically informed meta-analysis. *Criminology, 28,* 369–404.

59. Cullen, F. T., & Gendreau, P. (2001). From nothing works to what works: Changing professional ideology in the 21st century. *Prison Journal, 81,* 313–338.

60. Gendreau, P., & Ross, R. R. (1979). Effective correctional treatment: Bibliotherapy for cynics. *Crime & Delinquency, 25,* 463–489.

61. Gendreau, P., & Ross, R. R. (1987). Revivification of rehabilitation: Evidence from the 1980s. *Justice Quarterly, 4,* 349–407.

62. Palmer, T. (1975). Martinson revisited. *Journal of Research in Crime and Delinquency, 12,* 133–152.

63. Cullen, F. T. (2005). The twelve people who saved rehabilitation: How the science of criminology made a difference—The American Society of Criminology 2004 presidential address. *Criminology, 43,* 1–42.

64. Harlow, C. W. (2003). *Education and correctional population.* Washington, DC: U.S. Department of Justice, Office of Justice Programs, Bureau of Justice Statistics.

65. Harlow.

66. Taxman, F. S., Perdoni, M. L., & Harrison, L. D. (2007). Drug treatment services for adult offenders: The state of the state. *Journal of Substance Abuse Treatment, 32,* 239–254.

67. Batiuk, M. E., Moke, P., & Rountree, P. W. (1997). Change and rehabilitation: Correctional education as an agent of change—A research note. *Justice Quarterly, 14,* 167–180.

68. Roberts, J. W. (2008). *Work, education, and public safety: A brief history of Federal Prison Industries.* Retrieved October 7, 2008, from http://www.unicor.gov/about/organization/history/overview_of_fpi.cfm.

69. Moses, M. C., & Smith, C. J. (2007). Factories behind fences: Do prison "real work" programs work? *National Institute of Justice Journal, 257,* 32–35.

70. Hewitt, J. D. (2006). Having faith in faith-based prison programs. *Criminology & Public Policy, 5,* 551–558.

71. O'Connor, T. P., Duncan, J., & Quillard, F. (2006). Criminology and religion: The shape of an authentic dialogue. *Criminology & Public Policy, 5,* 559–570.

72. Camp, S. D., Klein-Saffran, J., Kwon, O., Daggett, D. M., & Joseph, V. (2006). An exploration into participation in a faith-based prison program. *Criminology & Public Policy, 5,* 529–550.

73. Johnson, B. R., Larson, D. B., & Pitts, T. C. (1997). Religious programs, institutional adjustment, and recidivism among former inmates in prison fellowship programs. *Justice Quarterly, 14,* 145–166.

74. Johnson, B. R. (2004). Religious programs and recidivism among former inmates in prison fellowship programs: A long-term follow-up study. *Justice Quarterly, 21,* 329–354.

75. Kerley, K. R., Matthews, T. L., & Schultz, J. T. (2005). Participation in Operation Starting Line, experience of negative emotions, and incidence of negative behavior. *International Journal of Offender Therapy and Comparative Criminology, 49,* 410–426.

76. Aos, S., Miller, M., & Drake, E. (2006). *Evidence-based adult corrections programs: What works and what does not.* Olympia: Washington State Institute for Public Policy.

77. Taxman et al.

78. Butzin, C. A., O'Connell, D. J., Martin, S. S., & Inciardi, J. A. (2006). Effect of drug treatment during work release on new arrests and incarcerations. *Journal of Criminal Justice, 34,* 557–565.

79. Wexler, H. K., DeLeon, G., Thomas, G., Kressel, D., & Peters, J. (1999). The Amity prison TC evaluation. *Criminal Justice and Behavior, 26,* 147–167.

80. Prendergast, M. L., Hall, E. A., Wexler, H. K., Melnick, G., & Cao, Y. (2004). Amity prison-based therapeutic community: 5-year outcomes. *Prison Journal, 84,* 36–60.

81. Knight, K., Simpson, D. D., & Hiller, M. L. (1999). Three-year reincarceration outcomes for in-prison therapeutic community treatment in Texas. *Prison Journal, 79,* 337–351.

82. Welsh, W. N., McGrain, P., Salamatin, N., & Zajac, G. (2007). Effects of prison drug treatment on inmate misconduct: A repeated measures analysis. *Criminal Justice and Behavior 34,* 600–615.

83. Robertson, J. (2007, February 10). *Molester gets 800 years in prison.* Retrieved January 28, 2008, from http://www.paloaltodailynews.com/article/2007-2-10-02-10-07-bc-serial-molest.

84. Taxman et al.

85. Center for Sex Offender Management. (2007). *The importance of assessment in sex offender management: An overview of key principles and practices.* Washington, DC: U.S. Department of Justice, Office of Justice Programs, Center for Effective Public Policy.

86. Center for Sex Offender Management. (2006). *Understanding treatment for adults and juveniles who have committed sex offenses.* Washington, DC: U.S. Department of Justice, Office of Justice Programs, Center for Effective Public Policy.

87. Hanson, R. K., & Bussiere, M. T. (1998). Predicting relapse: A meta-analysis of sexual offender recidivism studies. *Journal of Consulting and Clinical Psychology, 66,* 348–362.

88. Losel, F., & Schmucker, M. (2005). The effectiveness of treatment for sexual offenders: A comprehensive meta-analysis. *Journal of Experimental Criminology, 1,* 117–146.

89. Aos et al.

90. Little, G. L. (2005). Meta-analysis of moral reconation therapy: Recidivism results from probation and parole implementations. *Cognitive-Behavioral Treatment Review, 14,* 14–16.

91. Tong, L. S. J., & Farrington, D. P. (2006). How effective is the "Reasoning and Rehabilitation" program in reducing reoffending? A meta-analysis of evaluations in four countries. *Psychology, Crime & Law, 12,* 3–24.

CHAPTER

11

Parole

"Dangerous men are seldom distinguishable from run-of-the-mill parolees."[1, pp. 1–2]

OBJECTIVES

- Assess the size of the parole population and historical trends in its use.
- Learn the history and current status of federal parole.
- Understand the profile of paroled offenders in terms of social and criminal history and likelihood of recidivism.
- Explore legal aspects of parole, rights of parolees, and liability issues related to parole.
- Recognize the predictors of parole release and other factors that contribute to parole decision making.
- Explore the correlates of parole violation and revocation.
- Identify promising parole programs that have increased its effectiveness.

CASE STUDY

It could be said that when parole is successful, it is invisible. Prisoners who participate in educational, work, or religious programs and/or who achieve sobriety due to treatment received in prison and in the community are most likely to successfully adjust to freedom. Even though they are on parole, they have desisted from crime and decided to be conventional, contributing members of society. In short, when parole is successful, former offenders have gone straight or made good. They quietly go about their lives.

It could also be said that when parole is or even if it appears to be unsuccessful, it is front page news. In 2007, two career criminals who were on parole in Connecticut committed a crime that horrified the country. Steve Hayes, 44, and Joshua Komisarjevsky, 26, are believed to have burglarized the home of a prominent physician, critically injuring him and murdering his wife and two daughters. The pair were arrested and charged with a variety of serious crimes including aggravated sexual assault, arson, burglary, robbery, larceny, and others. They are being held on $15 million bail and face the death penalty because of six counts of capital felony offenses. Despite having 18 prior burglaries and 26 prior arrests over a 27-year period, the defendants did not have violent crimes on their record and were deemed as good risks for parole release and had been regularly meeting with their parole officers.

1. How can infamous crimes result in reforms to correctional sentences like parole?

"At the border between prisons and the community, parole is a unique enterprise which of necessity manifests in its practice the latent concepts of danger and security, normality and pathology, and social order and disorder."[2, p. 11]

High-profile cases such as those in our case study are thankfully rare, yet they illustrate the serious criminal pasts of many parolees in the United States. To many, parole is the most serious form of community corrections because of the criminality of the population. Unlike probationers, half of whom were simply convicted of misdemeanors, parolees are all convicted felons and virtually all have served time in prison. For these reasons, parolees are the most high-risk group of correctional clients. Because of this, the parole board must be mindful of the assorted risks that parolees pose when deciding which inmates to grant another opportunity for redemption. This chapter explores parole, the policies that determine parole release, background and recidivism patterns of parolees, and innovative ways that correctional officials attempt to improve the effectiveness of parole.

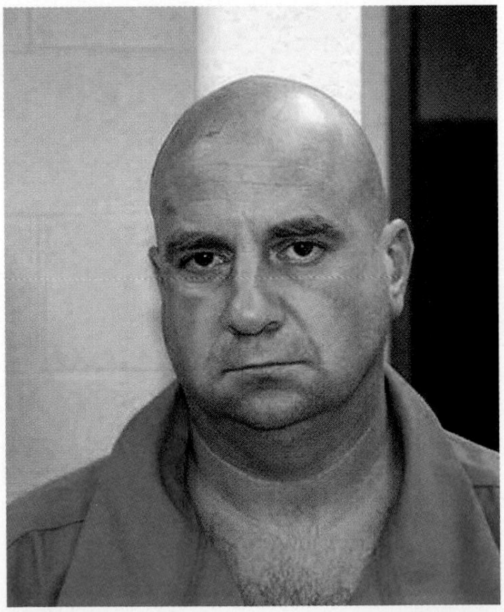

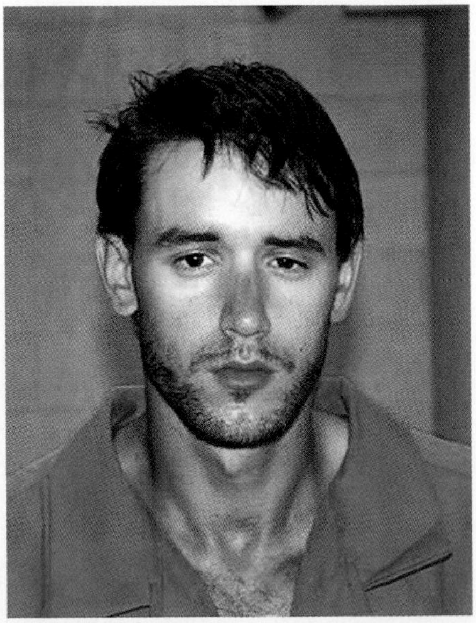

Notorious cases such as the Connecticut home invasion make parole one of the most controversial sentences in corrections and one of the most susceptible to public opinion.

CORRECTIONS FOCUS

Life After Imprisonment: Elderly Inmates' Perspective on Release Anxieties

Given the already troublesome nature of coping with prison life as an elderly inmate, what expectations do elderly inmates have of life after imprisonment? In a study conducted by Elaine Crawley and Richard Sparks, elderly male prisoners—inmates between the ages of 65 and 84—reported a sobering realization that time in prison diminishes one's contact with family as well as a man's role as protectorate, but more disturbingly increases an inmate's preoccupation with dying in prison.

It may come as a surprise, but elderly men with determinate sentences express serious concern about the time when they will once again experience life outside of prison. Older prisoners sentenced later in life are generally overwhelmed by the prison culture and strict routine. Often, these elderly inmates purposefully detach themselves from friends and family; this slightly less than selfless act serves best to relieve the elderly prisoner of his own feelings of guilt and despair while in prison. Many elderly inmates report that coping with prison life is easier if contact to family members has been eliminated. But as a result of severing attachments to loved ones early in their prison stay, elderly prisoners unknowingly detach themselves from those who could relieve reentry anxiety the most.

But there are other problems. Prison, as a total institution, contributes to feelings of habituation or institutionalization. Prison regimens are not unlike lifestyle restrictions in the military, with certain obvious exceptions. As a result, elderly inmates generally lack interest or the will to survive in a world without structure. While in prison, elderly inmates depend on both formal and informal networks of caregiving. It's not uncommon for elderly inmates to assist other inmates suffering from the infirmities of age with simple everyday tasks such as those associated with grooming, personal hygiene, cleaning of prison cells, or with their meals. Prisoners also indicate that while being institutionalized, medical assistance can be summoned day or night at no cost to the inmate.

There is also the concern of housing upon release. For many soon-to-be released elderly inmates, the fear of being homeless is a real and imminent threat. Sex offenders have unique concerns about their pending release from prison as well. In addition to the anxieties expressed by other elderly inmates, the threat of physical assault and continued public embarrassment ranked high on the lists of fears for this classification of prisoners.

Source: Crawley, E., & Sparks, R. (2006). Is there life after imprisonment? *Criminology & Criminal Justice, 6*, 63–82.

Parole

"Parole selection and release procedures take place within both a formal system of rules, regulations, statutes, and norms and an informal system of attitudes of parole board members, public sentiment, custom, and values."[3, p. 173]

Parole is a conditional sentence of completing a prison sentence in the community rather than in confinement. A paroled offender can legally be recalled to prison to serve the remainder of the sentence if he or she does not comply with the conditions of parole that are specified in a signed **parole contract**. **Parole conditions** are mandated conditions that are intended to serve the treatment and supervision needs of the person on parole, known as a **parolee**. Parole conditions are comparable to probation conditions and include seeking or maintaining employment, attending mental health counseling or therapy, participating in substance abuse treatment, taking drug tests, avoiding contact with victims in their case, and abstaining from contact with other negative influences such as felons or fellow gang members (if applicable). More than 80 percent of parolees have various conditions by which they must abide. Parolees are supervised by a **parole officer** who works for a state **parole agency**. Parole officers supervise parolees, monitor them for parole violations, and have the authority to arrest parolees for failing to comply with their sentence, a process known as **parole violation**. Parole officers also have authority to arrest parolees and make a recommendation to the court to terminate the parole sentence and resentence the offender to prison. This process is known as **parole**

"It is a naïve sort of self-importance that makes a judge or criminologist believe he can detect the minutest details of difference that distinguish one offender from another."[4, p. 74]

revocation. Unlike probation, which is supervised by county-level agencies, parole is a state function that is administered by one executive department per state.

Two types of parole exist. **Discretionary parole** occurs when parole boards release prisoners. **Parole boards** are administrative entities that are legally charged with the discretionary authority to conditionally release prisoners based on a statutory or administrative determination of eligibility. **Mandatory parole** occurs in jurisdictions using determinate sentencing statutes (Chapter 4) where inmates are conditionally released from prison after serving a portion of their original sentences minus any **good time** or time spent in prison without major disciplinary incidents.[7] Some states use both types of parole.

Parole plays four critical roles in the criminal justice system.

1. Parole boards determine the actual length of prison sentences once an offender has served the minimum term of his or her sentence. On a case-by-case basis, the parole board determines whether a prisoner is ready to be released into the community. In this sense, the parole board, an executive branch agency, has considerable oversight on the judiciary.
2. Parole agencies supervise parolees and therefore oversee the reintegration of returning prisoners.
3. Parole boards and parole officers are authorized to revoke parolee sentences if they are not in compliance. In this sense, parole serves an important crime-control function by removing high-risk criminal offenders from the community once it is clear that they are recidivistic and noncompliant.
4. Parole boards serve as a safety valve to reduce prison crowding.[8]

The major distinction between parole and all of the other forms of community corrections is that parolees are placed in the community *after* serving time in prison. Conversely, other intermediate sanctions place offenders in the community in lieu of prison. There is a technical exception to this rule. Once offenders are sentenced to state prison, they are first sent to a diagnostic and classification facility within the state department of corrections that will determine the most appropriate facility placement for each inmate as discussed in Chapter 10. Some inmates are classified as so low risk that they are immediately granted parole even though they were sentenced to prison by the courts. This process is known as a **direct sentence** or **automatic parole.** Offenders who receive a direct sentence truly never serve time in prison even though they are granted parole. For most offenders, however, parole is granted after serving some portion of a sentence behind bars.

Statistical Profile and Data Trends

According to the most recently available data, there are nearly 825,000 persons on parole in the United States or a rate of 360 parole clients per 100,000 adult residents in the United States. About 710,000 of these are on state parole and nearly 90,000 offenders are on federal parole. In turn, the parole rate in the general population is nearly 10 times higher among state (319 per 100,000 adult residents) than federal (40 per 100,000 adult residents) parole. As shown in TABLE 11–1, there is great variation across states in the parole population. Some states, such as California and Texas, have more than 100,000 offenders on parole while other states, such as Maine, have fewer than 40 offenders on parole. Nationally, 1 in every 360 adults is under parole supervision.

Like all correctional populations, parole is disproportionately comprised of males (88 percent) with relatively few females (12 percent). In terms of race and ethnicity, the parole population is comprised 42 percent by Whites, 37 percent by African Americans, 19 percent by Hispanics, 1 percent by American Indians, and 1 percent by Asian Americans. About 96 percent of parole sentences exceed 1 year, and the remaining 4 percent

TABLE 11-1 **Parole Population**

Region and Jurisdiction	Parole Population, 1/1/2007	2007 Entries Reported	2007 Entries Imputed	2007 Exits Reported	2007 Exits Imputed	Parole Population, 12/31/2007	Percent Change, 2007	Number on Parole per 100,000 Adult Residents, 12/31/2007
U.S. total	799,058	505,965	555,900	482,180	531,400	824,365	3.2	360
Federal	88,993	43,077	43,077	39,397	39,397	92,673	4.1	40
State	710,065	462,888	512,800	442,783	492,000	731,692	3.0	319
Northeast	152,744	55,405	70,000	54,210	67,500	155,288	1.7	367
Connecticut	2,567	2,319	2,319	2,709	2,709	2,177	–15.2	81
Maine	31	2	2	1	1	32	3.2	3
Massachusetts	3,435	4,952	4,952	5,178	5,178	3,209	–6.6	64
New Hampshire	1,621	709	709	677	677	1,653	2.0	162
New Jersey	14,405	9,505	9,505	8,867	8,867	15,043	4.4	226
New York	53,001	25,467	25,467	24,799	24,799	53,669	1.3	360
Pennsylvania	76,386	11,432	26,000	11,060	24,300	78,107	2.3	807
Rhode Island	332	515	515	385	385	462	39.2	56
Vermont	966	504	504	534	534	936	–3.1	190
Midwest	130,821	71,105	105,400	64,837	98,800	136,343	4.2	270
Illinois	/	/	34,300	/	35,000	33,354	:	344
Indiana	8,205	9,217	9,217	7,060	7,060	10,362	26.3	217
Iowa	3,578	2,500	2,500	2,532	2,532	3,546	–0.9	155
Kansas	4,886	5,278	5,278	5,322	5,322	4,842	–0.9	232
Michigan	18,486	13,173	13,173	10,528	10,528	21,131	14.3	277
Minnesota	4,445	5,715	5,715	5,416	5,416	4,744	6.7	120
Missouri	18,815	14,114	14,114	13,080	13,080	19,849	5.5	443
Nebraska	797	1,015	1,015	1,012	1,012	800	0.4	60
North Dakota	372	784	784	814	814	342	–8.1	69
Ohio	17,603	10,007	10,007	10,035	10,035	17,575	–0.2	201
South Dakota	2,767	1,845	1,845	1,800	1,800	2,812	1.6	466
Wisconsin	16,767	7,457	7,457	7,238	7,238	16,986	1.3	395
South	238,484	106,989	108,000	101,793	102,800	243,512	2.1	291
Alabama	7,508	2,464	2,464	2,182	2,182	7,790	3.8	221
Arkansas	18,057	9,082	9,082	7,751	7,751	19,388	7.4	904
Delaware	544	366	366	375	375	535	–1.7	81
District of Columbia	5,341	2,468	2,468	2,240	2,240	5,569	4.3	1,169
Florida	4,790	7,036	7,036	7,172	7,172	4,654	–2.8	33
Georgia	22,958	11,935	11,935	11,782	11,782	23,111	0.7	326
Kentucky	11,755	5,945	5,945	4,959	4,959	12,741	8.4	392
Louisiana	23,832	13,652	13,652	13,399	13,399	24,085	1.1	746
Maryland	14,351	7,122	7,122	7,617	7,617	13,856	–3.4	324
Mississippi	1,899	1,021	1,021	905	905	2,015	6.1	93
North Carolina	3,236	3,552	3,552	3,477	3,477	3,311	2.3	48
Oklahoma	/	/	1,000	/	1,000	/	:	:
South Carolina	2,766	599	599	932	932	2,433	–12.0	72
Tennessee	9,570	4,568	4,568	3,474	3,474	10,496	9.7	222
Texas	100,053	33,897	33,897	32,202	32,202	101,748	1.7	582
Virginia	7,201	1,845	1,845	2,196	2,196	6,850	–4.9	116
West Virginia	1,523	1,437	1,437	1,130	1,130	1,830	20.2	128
West	175,387	215,958	215,958	204,653	204,653	187,343	6.8	361
Alaska	973	705	705	634	634	1,044	7.3	212
Arizona	6,213	12,256	12,256	12,006	12,006	6,463	4.0	140
California	111,744	169,625	169,625	163,428	163,428	118,592	6.1	439
Colorado	8,196	7,927	7,927	6,572	6,572	9,551	16.5	264
Hawaii	2,119	798	798	601	601	2,316	9.3	233
Idaho	2,482	1,527	1,527	1,277	1,277	2,732	10.1	252
Montana	703	680	680	539	539	844	20.1	116
Nevada	3,518	2,638	2,636	2,332	2,332	3,824	8.7	202
New Mexico	2,831	1,650	1,650	1,559	1,559	2,922	3.2	200
Oregon	21,189	9,231	9,231	8,024	8,024	22,396	5.7	782
Utah	3,242	2,617	2,617	2,485	2,485	3,374	4.1	190
Washington	11,568	5,923	5,923	4,880	4,880	12,611	9.0	257
Wyoming	609	381	381	316	316	674	10.7	170

Source: Glaze, L. E., & Bonczar, T. P. (2008). *Probation and parole in the United States, 2007*. Washington, DC: U.S. Department of Justice, Office of Justice Programs, Bureau of Justice Statistics.

"Success and low self-control are therefore antithetical, thus it is likely that low self-control, the anti-matter of rehabilitation and compliance, is related to criminal justice."[5, p. 160]

TABLE 11-2 Offenders on Parole by Parole Type

	Percent of Adults Entering Parole	
Type of Entry	**2000**	**2006**
Discretionary parole	37	35
Mandatory parole	54	52
Reinstatement	6	9
Other	2	3
Total estimated entries*	470,400	536,200

*Includes offenders on state parole and federal postcustody release.

Source: Glaze, L. E., & Bonczar, T. P. (2007). *Probation and parole in the United States, 2006*. Washington, DC: U.S. Department of Justice, Office of Justice Programs, Bureau of Justice Statistics.

of parole sentences are under 1 year. Thirty-seven percent of parole sentences are for drug crimes, 26 percent for violent crimes, 24 percent for property crimes, 7 percent for public order crimes, and 6 percent for other types of crimes.[9]

The parole population has grown between 1 and 3 percent each year over the past decade. In 2006, nearly 540,000 offenders were placed on parole. As shown in TABLE 11-2, 52 percent of these were placed on mandatory parole and 35 percent were placed on discretionary parole. Nine percent of paroles were reinstated, and 3 percent used some other combination of parole sentence.

Perhaps more than any other form of criminal punishment, parole has been the most susceptible to fluctuations in public opinion. From its inception, parole was hailed as a mechanism to both permit criminal offenders an opportunity for reform and cost-effectively reduce the prison population. Over time, however, the public and policy makers grew tired of parole because the sanction was neither providing the necessary treatment or correction to reform criminals nor were criminals serving meaningful terms behind bars. Due to indeterminate sentencing and parole, there was little truth-in-sentencing. The controversy surrounding parole was aptly described by Ernest Burgess more than 70 years ago: "Why should the police go to all the trouble to arrest a criminal, the state's attorney to prosecute, the judge and jury to convict and sentence him and then have the parole board turn him loose on the streets to resume his criminal activities?"[10, p. 491]

Recent changes in how parole is administered demonstrate how susceptible it is to political pressure. For instance, as shown in FIGURE 11-1, between 1980 and 2000, the discretionary parole release rate plunged by about 50 percent. During the same period, mandatory parole releases doubled. Also, the percentage of prisoners who served the entire prison term (and thus precluded a parole sentence) nearly doubled between 1990 and 2000.[11] A snapshot comparison of parole procedures in 1976 and 1999 also shows this trend (FIGURE 11-2). In 1976, 65 percent of parole releases were made by parole boards; by 1999 that share dropped to 24 percent. In contrast, mandatory parole releases increased from 35 percent of the total share in 1976 to 76 percent of the total share in 1999.

This means that the discretionary freedom of parole boards has been severely curtailed, evidenced by a pronounced shift in state parole policies away from discretionary release by parole boards in favor of determinate sentences and mandatory supervised release. Timothy Hughes and his colleagues at the Bureau of Justice Statistics reported that by 2000, 16 states (Arizona, California, Delaware, Florida, Illinois, Indiana, Kansas, Maine, Minnesota, Mississippi, North Carolina, Ohio, Oregon, Virginia, Washington, and Wisconsin) had abolished discretionary parole for all offenders. Certain violent offenders were denied discretionary parole in Alaska, Louisiana, New York, and Tennessee. Also by

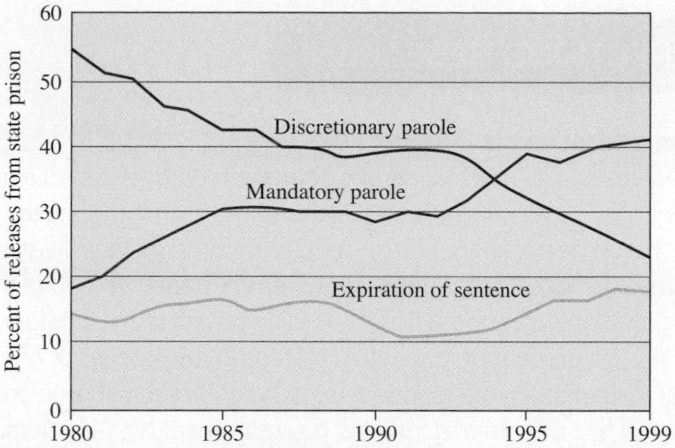

"*Prison and parole systems are gradually being given back to the community and becoming more responsive to public pressures.*"[6, p. 366]

FIGURE 11–1 Trends in State Parole, 1980–1999. *Source*: Hughes, T. A., Wilson, D. J., & Beck, A. J. (2001). *Trends in state parole, 1990–2000*. Washington, DC: U.S. Department of Justice, Office of Justice Programs, Bureau of Justice Statistics.

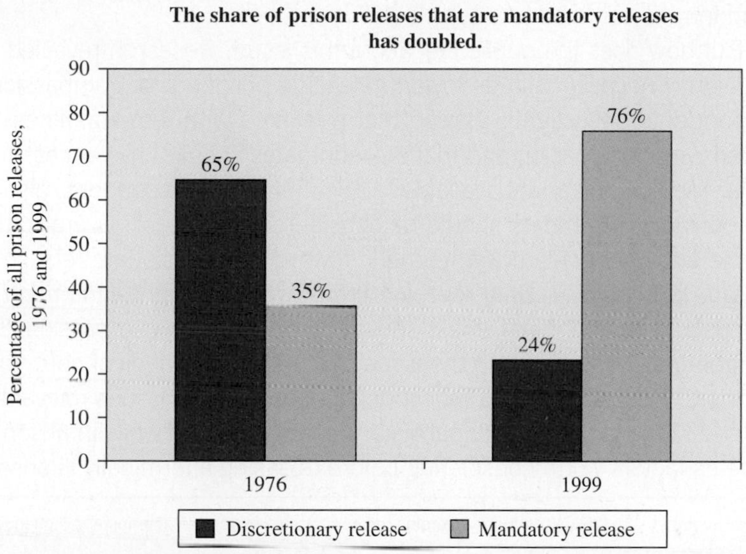

FIGURE 11–2 The Shift from Discretionary to Mandatory Parole Release. *Source*: Travis, J., & Lawrence, S. (2002). *Beyond the prison gates: The state of parole in America*. Washington, DC: The Urban Institute.

2000, 35 states and the District of Columbia had adopted the federal truth-in-sentencing standard that requires Part I violent offenders to serve at least 85 percent of their sentence before they are eligible for parole. By adopting this standard, states received federal funds under the Violent Offender Incarceration and Truth-in-Sentencing (VOITIS) incentive grant program established by the 1994 Crime Act.[12]

An unintended consequence in the shift from discretionary to mandatory parole release is that it may result in overall poorer performance of offenders on parole. If parole release was dependent on the discretion of the parole board, then there existed tremendous incentive for prisoners to work toward their rehabilitation and desist from crime. Discretionary parole required earnest attempts by prisoners to turn their lives around. On the other hand, if parole release is mandatory, there is less incentive to be compliant other than being good enough in prison to secure good time credits. Research by Connie Ireland and JoAnn Prause suggests that those released on discretionary parole have lower recidivism rates than parolees released via mandatory parole.[13]

CORRECTIONS RESEARCH

Compassionate Release

Otherwise referred to as medical parole, compassionate release is a process by which offenders with terminal illnesses are released from prison prior to completing their sentence to allow them to spend the remaining time in their lives with friends and family. Estimates suggest the percentage of inmates aged 55 or older in the American correctional system will approach nearly 20 percent of the total inmate population by 2010. Over 40 percent of inmates in state and 48 percent of offenders in federal correctional institutions have reported some type of medical problem while incarcerated. Research has determined inmates typically are at higher risk for illness than the general population, and the likelihood of terminal illnesses among prisoners is also greater. Dying in prison presents its own unique problems. Over time, visits by family members decrease in frequency and duration. A terminal illness coupled with a life sentence represents just another failure in the minds of terminally ill inmates. Death in prison is a decidedly lonely experience as grief and suffering seem more pronounced for an inmate confined to a cell block.

But how does the public feel about this issue? Research revealed the presence of a slightly negative attitude toward releasing prisoners for compassionate reasons. Respondents only slightly agreed that prisoners with terminal illnesses should be treated with compassion and that these inmates should have access to the same or similar medical treatment available to nonoffenders. Respondents also reported that only nonviolent offenders should be considered for release. Overall, students in this sample were generally unsympathetic toward compassionate release for prisoners who are terminally ill. Data revealed there was only slight agreement that inmates diagnosed with a terminal illness should be treated with compassion. Students were also generally ambivalent to the issue of comparable medical care for terminally ill prisoners. Respondents did feel strongly about certain issues relevant to a medical release. These included criminal history, conduct record while in prison, and time left to live as factors worth considering before releasing a terminally ill prisoner.

Source: Boothby, J. L. (2007). Attitudes regarding the compassionate release of terminally ill offenders. *Prison Journal, 87,* 408–415.

In 2006, nearly 520,000 parolees exited supervision. Of these:

- Forty-four percent successfully completed their full-term parole sentence or were released from parole supervision early.
- Thirty-nine percent were returned to prison for violating their parole. In this sense, they "exited" parole because they entered prison. Of these, 11 percent violated parole with a new conviction/sentence, 26 percent were revoked, and 2 percent were returned to prison for other reasons.
- Eleven percent had their parole terminated for absconding.
- Two percent of parolees had their sentences terminated for other unsatisfactory behavior.
- One percent involved transfers to other criminal justice sentences.
- One percent of the parolees died.
- One percent had their parole sentences ended for other, undisclosed reasons.[14]

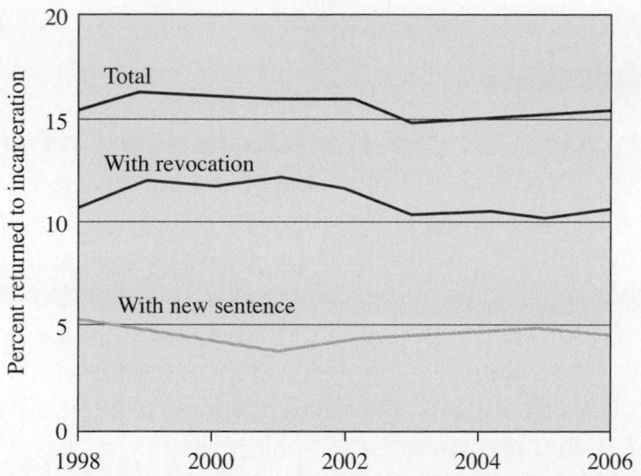

FIGURE 11–3 Parole Returns to Prison. *Source*: Glaze, L. E., & Bonczar, T. P. (2007). *Probation and parole in the United States, 2006*. Washington, DC: U.S. Department of Justice, Office of Justice Programs, Bureau of Justice Statistics.

Over the prior decade, the rate of parolee returns to prison has remained fairly stable (FIGURE 11–3). Approximately 15 percent of parolees are returned to prison each year. Of these, about 10 percent have their parole revoked for violations of conditions and 5 percent have it revoked for new charges, convictions, and sentences. Parole is also used by states as a safety valve to control prisoner population. When the prisoner population swells and places limits on existing prison capacity, there is often an increase in parole releases. As new prison space becomes available, parole release is restricted.[15]

Federal Parole

Nearly 90 percent of parolees in the United States are on state parole; however, there are nearly 90,000 persons on federal parole. Parole in the federal criminal justice system has a convoluted and somewhat confusing history. In 1867, the first statute providing for the reduction of sentences of federal prisoners because of good conduct was enacted. Although this process was not officially known as parole, it typified a practice whereby prison sentences could be reduced in exchange for compliant institutional behavior. Federal parole was officially created in 1910 with three parole boards consisting of the warden of the federal institution (three federal penitentiaries existed during this era), the physician in the institution, and the superintendent of prisons of the Department of Justice. Any prisoner sentenced to 1 year or more was eligible for parole after completion of at least 33 percent of his or her sentence. Those sentenced to life imprisonment were eligible for federal parole after serving 15 years of their sentence.[16]

A single federal board of parole known as the **United States Board of Parole** was created in 1930. In addition to the sentence and time served requirements, federal parole was awarded if it appeared to the Board of Parole "that such applicant will live and remain at liberty without violating the laws and if in the opinion of the Board such release is not incompatible with the welfare of society."[17, p. 7] Parole officers served under the Board of Parole but were actually employees of the Bureau of Prisons. In 1938, the Federal Juvenile Delinquency Act was approved. This legislation provided that juveniles could be paroled by the Board of Parole at any time after commitment, meaning that juveniles were not subject to the minimum term requirement before parole eligibility. In 1950, the Youth Corrections Act was passed by Congress and affected federal parole in four ways: (1) it mandated indeterminate sentences of 0 to 6 years for young offenders except in cases involving very serious offenses; (2) it mandated parole release for all young offenders at least 2 years prior to the expiration of their maximum sentence; (3) it authorized courts

CORRECTIONS BRIEF

Life Without Parole for Juvenile Offenders

Records indicate just over 2,200 youth offenders are serving life sentences with no chance for parole. Since there is no national database to support this figure, only records from departments of correction for individual states, the figure is at best a reasonably accurate estimate of the number of youth offenders incarcerated for life without parole (LWOP) in the United States. This figure is based on data from 40 of the 42 states that permit sentencing youth offenders to LWOP. Of these 2,225 LWOP inmates, just over 350 are serving sentences of life without parole for crimes they committed before they reached their 16th birthday.

Data from 38 state correctional departments also reveals just over 84 percent of youths serving LWOP were 16 or 17 years old at the time they were sentenced by the courts. Court records indicate they were responsible for crimes of murder, kidnapping, sexual assault, child molestation, burglary, and theft. Youth offenders who committed homicide, however, were the most likely offenders to be sentenced to LWOP. In fact, 92 percent of the LWOP sentences were handed down by the courts to youth offenders who had committed murder—and not necessarily premeditated murder. Most of the murders committed by youth offenders fall under the felony murder statute; that is, the murder occurred while the juvenile was participating in another felony—usually robbery.

Times have changed. From 1962 until 1981, on average only two youth offenders were sentenced to LWOP each year. In 1996, 152 youth offenders were sentenced to LWOP. This figure has gradually decreased, but predictions are it will never return to pre-1981 figures. Sentencing is sometimes a response by the courts to the public's perception of crime and the demand for safer communities. Curiously, more youth offenders are sentenced to LWOP than are adult offenders. From 1985 until 2001, in 11 of these 17 years, youth homicide offenders were more likely to be sentenced to death or life without parole than were adult homicide offenders.

Source: Amnesty International. (2005). *The rest of their lives: Life without parole for child offenders in the United States.* Retrieved October 7, 2008, from http://hrw.org/reports/2005/us1005/TheRestofTheirLives.pdf.

to commit offenders for a period of observation prior to sentencing; and (4) it provided that the Board of Parole could grant an early discharge from parole supervision, which suspended the conviction.

Since the early decades of the 20th century, there has been a shift from unconditionally releasing offenders from prison to conditionally releasing them on parole. As shown in FIGURE 11-4, during the 1920s, 40 percent of prisoners were unconditionally released. During the later decades of the 20th century, just 10–15 percent of parolees were released unconditionally. This change in parole policy reflects many correctional changes, especially the shift from indeterminate to determinate sentencing.

In 1976, the United States Board of Parole was officially titled as the **United States Parole Commission** after the passage of the Parole Commission and Reorganization Act. The Parole Commission and Reorganization Act ushered in a new era in parole, where explicit guidelines for decision-making processes were mandated. These explicit criteria included providing parolees with reasons for their parole denial, granting parolees access to their own case files, providing parolees with representatives at hearings if requested, allowing parolees to suggest modifications to parole conditions, terminating parole after

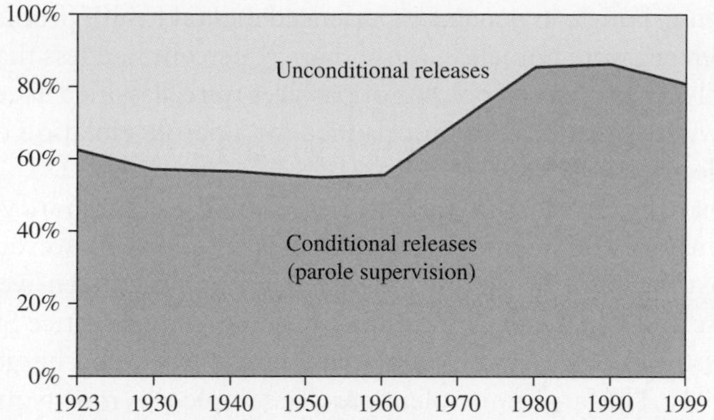

FIGURE 11-4 Historical Shifts in Parole. *Source*: Travis, J., & Lawrence, S. (2002). *Beyond the prison gates: The state of parole in America*. Washington, DC: The Urban Institute.

5 years in the community, and generally providing more due process rights to the parolee during the parole decision-making process.

In 1984, the Comprehensive Crime Control Act created the **United States Sentencing Commission** to establish sentencing guidelines for the federal courts and install a formal system of determinate sentences. These sentencing guidelines took effect on November 1, 1987; thus defendants sentenced on or after that date served determinate terms and were not eligible for parole consideration. This means that for all intents and purposes, federal parole was abolished in 1987 and federal correctional clients who were not in a Bureau of Prison facility were dubbed **supervised releases**. Technically, this means that since 1987, there has been no federal parole.

However, due to federal offenders who were sentenced prior to November 1, 1987, the United States Parole Commission has been unable to legally phase out federal parole. Federal parole was extended via the Judicial Improvements Act of 1990, the Parole Commission Phase-out Act of 1996, and the Twenty-first Century Department of Justice Appropriations Authorization Act of 2002. Only when the last federal offender sentenced before November 1, 1987, terminates his or her case will federal parole end.[18]

Criminal History of Parolees

Parolees are a high-risk group in terms of their criminal and social histories. National assessments of the parole population indicate that parolees often have extensive criminal histories. For many parolees, their criminal career consists of brief periods of being criminally active in the community, placement on lower types of intermediate sanctions, such as probation, continued criminal offending, and cycling out of jail and prison. Due to the revolving door nature of confinement and community supervision, parole has been likened to serving life imprisonment on an installment plan. Nationally, 56 percent had previously served time in prison before their most recent parole release. Among these recidivists:

- Ten percent had two prior incarcerations.
- Fifteen percent had three to five prior incarcerations.
- More than 10 percent had been imprisoned six or more times.
- About 55 percent were already being supervised by the criminal justice system, mostly by parole and probation, when they were most recently convicted and imprisoned.

In addition, parolees demonstrate additional serious risk factors for criminal activity. Nearly 85 percent of parolees had drug and alcohol involvement at the time of their

The United States Sentencing Commission established sentencing guidelines by installing a system of determinate sentences that effectively abolished federal parole.

One in 10 parolees in the United States has been incarcerated six or more times in his or her criminal career.

most recent offense. Fourteen percent experienced mental health problems upon arrest and nearly 12 percent were homeless. More than 51 percent had less than a high school education. Finally, more than 45 percent of parolees were classified as **rereleases**, which means that they were most recently imprisoned for a parole violation or a new offense committed while on parole.[19]

If parolees have extensive criminal histories, it could be that more violent offenders account for the majority of the prior arrests and incarcerations. However, recent research indicates that parolees as a whole are a high-risk group with extensive criminal pasts. Matthew Durose and Christopher Mumola of the Bureau of Justice Statistics studied the offending histories of nearly 211,000 nonviolent parolees discharged from prisons in 15 states in 1994. The large nonviolent parolee sample was mostly male (90 percent; 10 percent female), young (66 percent were 34 or younger), minority (49 percent non-White), and undereducated (40 percent had less than a high school diploma).

The average prison sentence for this group was nearly 52 months, and the median time served was just 39 months. The actual amount of time served was significantly shorter in duration. The average time served was 16 months and the median time served was 11 months. Among this large sample of nonviolent parolees, the average percent of sentence served before release was just 33 percent.

As shown in TABLE 11-3, even nonviolent parolees are extensively involved in crime prior to their most recent imprisonment and release. Nearly 95 percent had at least one prior arrest, and more than 31 percent had at least one prior violent arrest. Decades of criminological research assert that offenders with five or more arrests are habitual or career criminals.[20–21] To put this in perspective, the average number of prior arrests among nonviolent parolees was 9.3 arrests. More than 46 percent had previously been imprisoned and the average number of prior criminal convictions was 4.1.

More recent cohorts of nonviolent parolees are even more extensively involved in crime. As shown in TABLE 11-4, more than 22 percent of nonviolent parolees released in 1997 had at least one prior violent felony conviction, which would encompass crimes such as murder, rape, armed robbery, assault, child abuse, kidnapping, and others. More than 15 percent of nonviolent parolees had two prior sentences to prison or probation and more than 27 percent had three or more prior sentences. Nearly 23 percent had been imprisoned or placed on probation four or more times prior to their most recent release.[22]

TABLE 11-3 Criminal History of Nonviolent Parolees, 1994 Cohort

Prior arrest	
Percent with at least one prior arrest for—	
Any crime	94.5
Any violent crime	31.4
Mean number of prior arrests	9.3
Median number	7.0
Prior conviction	
Percent with at least one prior conviction for—	
Any crime	84.3
Any violent crime	10.2
Mean number of prior convictions	4.1
Median number	3.0
Percent with at least one prior prison sentence	46.2

Source: Durose, M. R., & Mumola, C. J. (2004). *Profile of nonviolent offenders exiting state prisons.* Washington, DC: U.S. Department of Justice, Office of Justice Programs, Bureau of Justice Statistics.

TABLE 11-4 Criminal History of Nonviolent Parolees, 1997 Cohort

Criminal history	Percent
Prior convictions	
At least one violent	22.2
None violent	59.0
No prior convictions	18.8
Number of prior sentences to incarceration or probation	
0	18.9
1	15.7
2	15.3
3	27.4
4	14.4
5 or more	8.3

Source: Durose, M. R., & Mumola, C. J. (2004). *Profile of nonviolent offenders exiting state prisons.* Washington, DC: U.S. Department of Justice, Office of Justice Programs, Bureau of Justice Statistics.

Finally, even nonviolent parolees demonstrate a set of risk factors that suggest that continued criminal activity is likely. For instance, among the 1997 national cohort of nearly 211,000 nonviolent parolees:

- More than 8 percent had used a weapon in their most recent offense, including nearly 20 percent of those convicted of public-order offenses.
- More than 22 percent had a prior violent conviction.
- Nearly 64 percent were on probation, parole, or escape status at time of offense.
- More than 65 percent had multiple prior sentences.
- More than 88 percent had any serious offender indicator on their criminal record.[23]

Recidivism

Parole is successful for an offender who manages to abide by the conditions of his or her sentence for the specified parole period and does not get rearrested. As described earlier in this section, only 44 percent of parolees successfully complete their sentence.[24] Success rates are largely contingent on the type and method of release. Among inmates facing their first release on parole, 64 percent succeed, whereas among inmates facing rerelease on parole, just 21 percent succeed. Inmates who received discretionary release by parole boards had a success rate of 54 percent, and those released via mandatory parole had a 33 percent success rate. The lowest success rate, 17 percent, was found among offenders who had received mandatory rerelease.[25]

There appears to be a clear relationship between the number of times that a parolee has cycled through the correctional system and his or her likelihood of success on parole. FIGURE 11-5 illustrates, for example, parole successes from 1990 to 2000. Across the decade, roughly 40 percent of parolees successfully completed their sentence. Among prisoners who faced their first release on parole, the success rates were appreciably higher and hovered between 55 and 65 percent. For prisoners facing rerelease on parole, the success rates ranged between 15 and 23 percent.[26]

Based on the criminal history profile of the parolee population, it is somewhat expected that parolees would have relatively high rates of **recidivism** or reoffending after release. One of the most methodologically impressive studies of parolee recidivism is based on the records of more than 272,000 offenders released from prisons in Arizona,

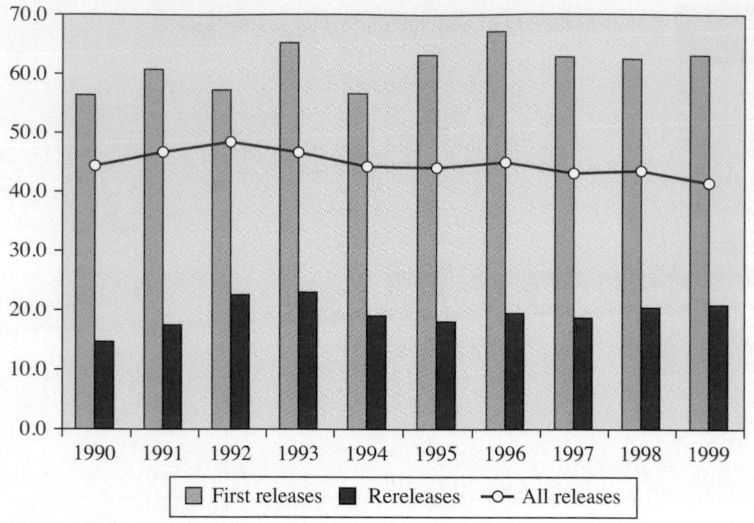

FIGURE 11-5 Parole Success 1990–1999. *Source*: Travis, J., & Lawrence, S. (2002). *Beyond the prison gates: The state of parole in America.* Washington, DC: The Urban Institute.

California, Delaware, Florida, Illinois, Maryland, Michigan, Minnesota, New Jersey, New York, North Carolina, Ohio, Oregon, Texas, and Virginia. Patrick Langan and David Levin found high rates of rearrest, reconviction, and reincarceration among former prisoners (FIGURE 11-6). Based on these national data:

- Within 6 months of release, 30 percent of offenders are rearrested, 11 percent are reconvicted, and 5 percent are sent back to prison.
- Within 1 year of release, 44 percent are rearrested, 22 percent are reconvicted, and 10 percent are sent back to prison.
- Within 2 years of release, 59 percent are rearrested, 36 percent are reconvicted, and 19 percent are sent back to prison.
- Within 3 years of release, 68 percent are rearrested, 47 percent are reconvicted, and 25 percent are sent back to prison.[27]

Again, offenders with more extensive criminal histories were more likely to continue offending after release from prison. For instance, among released prisoners with 7 to 10

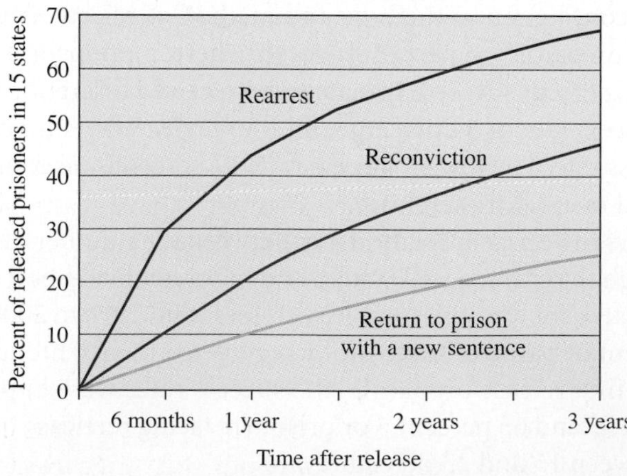

FIGURE 11-6 Recidivism Among Released Prisoners. *Source*: Langan, P. A., & Levin, D. J. (2002). *Recidivism of prisoners released in 1994.* Washington, DC: U.S. Department of Justice, Office of Justice Programs, Bureau of Justice Statistics.

career arrests, more than 70 percent were rearrested within 3 years. Among those with 11 to 15 career arrests, more than 79 percent were rearrested. Among those with 16 or more career arrests, more than 82 percent were rearrested within 3 years of prison release.[28]

Legal Aspects of Parole

There are four primary legal issues relating to parole supervision and the legal rights of parolees. These are (1) the legal standing of parole in regard to an offender's access to courts or habeas corpus; (2) the Fourth Amendment rights relating to a parolee's right against unreasonable search and seizure; (3) the Fourteenth Amendment rights to due process, particularly as due process relates to parole revocation hearings; and (4) liability issues for parole boards and parole agents stemming from the criminal behavior of paroled offenders.

Even though parolees are being conditionally supervised in the community, they are technically similar to prisoners in that there are restraints on their liberty. A seminal case addressing the basic legal standing of parole is ***Jones v. Cunningham.*** In *Jones v. Cunningham* (1963), the Supreme Court addressed the question of whether a parolee is in custody in relation to the habeas corpus statute within the United States Constitution. They ruled that parolees are considered in custody because of restraints placed on their freedom. In this regard, parolees can invoke the habeas corpus statute to challenge the conditions and constitutionality of their sentence in the same way as confined prisoners.[29]

Given the conditional nature of parole, parolees live with a variety of limits on their freedom and have restricted access to other people, alcohol, certain locations, and firearms. Because of this, it is normal for parole agents to search their clients to ensure they are not in possession of contraband or other restricted items. Indeed, a parole home visit is essentially an opportunity to search an offender's person and home.

The courts have consistently ruled that as long as parole officers have a reasonable suspicion that a client is engaging in criminal behavior or is in possession of contraband, searches are lawful.[30] Importantly, the reasonable suspicion criterion is lower than the probable cause criterion stated in the Fourth Amendment. In this sense, parolees (and probationers) have lower Fourth Amendment rights than citizens not on parole or probation. In ***Griffin v. Wisconsin*** (1987), the Supreme Court held that probation or parole agencies must be able to act based upon a lesser degree of certainty than the Fourth Amendment would otherwise require in order to intervene before an offender causes harm to her- or himself or society.[31]

The lower threshold of reasonable suspicion to conduct searches was refined in ***United States v. Knights*** (2001), in which the Supreme Court held that searches of probationers based on reasonable suspicion are permitted because there is enough likelihood that criminal conduct is occurring that an intrusion on the probationer's significantly diminished privacy interests is reasonable.[32] The notion that parolees are more likely to engage in crime and thus officials are justified to have reasonable suspicion about them was also addressed in ***Pennsylvania Board of Probation and Parole v. Scott*** (1998). In *Pennsylvania Board of Probation and Parole v. Scott* (1998), the Court held that the costs of allowing a parolee to avoid the consequences of his or her violation are compounded by the fact that parolees are more likely to commit criminal offenses than average citizens.[33]

Another legal aspect of parole centers on the due process rights inherent in the parole revocation process. As a general rule, the Supreme Court has consistently ruled that since parolees have by definition already been found guilty of their underlying crime in a court of law, the rights to due process are less salient than they are before an adjudication or finding of guilt. In this way, the due process rights of parolees are somewhat diminished compared to average citizens.[34]

CORRECTIONS IN THE NEWS

Man Accused of Killing His Parents Released

Seventeen years—that's the time Martin Tankleff spent in prison after being convicted on charges of murdering his parents. The appeals court ordered Martin's release after reviewing information that suggests Seymour and Arlene Tankleff may have been murdered by someone else. The court felt that a conviction would not be likely if the case was once again presented to a jury.

Martin Tankleff found the bodies of his parents in their home on September 7, 1988. Police investigators immediately focused on the young man, advised him of his rights, and then falsely informed him that his father, who did not die until several weeks after the attack, had woken from his unconscious state and named Martin as the assailant. Martin suggested to the police that it may have been a business partner who owed his father hundreds of thousands of dollars who actually killed his parents, but the partner denied any involvement and charges were never brought against him.

The decision to release Martin was linked in part to police procedure during Martin's interrogation. According to police records, Martin was read his Miranda warning, but decided to waive his rights. During the interview, he confessed saying he was angry about being slighted by his parents. He even commented on being forced to drive a "crummy old Lincoln." After being told his father had identified him as the killer, he commented on how he might have blacked out and committed the crime. Tankleff ultimately refused to sign the prepared confession. He was only 17 years old when he was accused of having stabbed and bludgeoned his parents to death.

In a nationally televised trial, Martin Tankleff was convicted and sentenced to 50 years to life in prison for the murder of his parents. Several years later, the case came to the attention of the Innocence Project, an organization headed by attorney Barry Scheck, whose primary purpose is to exonerate individuals believed to be wrongfully convicted. According to Scheck, "This is one of those cases that has bothered the legal community for more than a decade."

Source: Associated Press. (2007). *Man freed after parent-killing conviction tossed.* Retrieved December 28, 2007, from http://www.cnn.com/2007/CRIME/12/28/parents.killed.ap/index.html.

Of course, this does not mean that parole proceedings are void of due process. In *Morrissey v. Brewer* (1972), the Court held that due process rights expressed in the Fourteenth Amendment establish the right of a parolee to a preliminary and final hearing before his or her parole can be revoked.[35] A year later in ***Gagnon v. Scarpelli*** (1973), the Court further ruled that in special circumstances, the state is required to furnish counsel to parolees during revocation hearings.[36] More recently, in *Young v. Harper* (1997), the Court held that other early release programs that are functionally similar to parole are also subject to the due process guidelines established in *Morrissey* and *Gagnon*.[37] Interestingly, a parole board can change its mind and rescind the parole of an offender who was recently granted parole—and this rescinding of parole can occur without a hearing.[38]

In addition to the due process rights involved in parole revocation, there is also the question of whether there is a liberty interest in parole release that is protected by the Fourteenth Amendment. There is not a right to be paroled when parole is a discretionary decision. In ***Greenholtz v. Inmates*** (1979), the Court held that the decision to grant parole is a subjective, potential outcome—it is not guaranteed. Because of this, there is not a liberty interest inherent in the parole release decision, and thus there is no constitutional right to due process.[39]

The opposite logic applies in cases where parole release is mandatory and based on specified guidelines. In ***Board of Pardons v. Allen*** (1987), the Court held that any statute that mandates parole creates a presumption that the parole release will be granted. In other words, if there is a reasonable probability that releasing an offender on mandatory parole will not result in risk to the community and the offender is parole eligible, he or she should be released.[40]

CORRECTIONS IN THE NEWS

71 Felony Charges: Michael Devlin Is Sentenced to Four Life Sentences Plus 60 Years in Prison

Michael Devlin had already pleaded guilty to kidnapping, sexual assault, and attempted murder and was serving three life sentences when he entered yet another guilty plea on charges of making pornographic photos and videos and transporting a minor across state lines for purposes of committing sexual assault. These crimes involved two young men, one who had been abducted at age 11 in 2001, and the other a 13-year-old boy who had been kidnapped in January 2007.

The first victim was kidnapped at gunpoint while riding his bicycle in his neighborhood close to home. Several years later, the second victim was abducted shortly after getting off of his school bus near his rural home. A young witness to the second incident provided police with a description of Devlin's vehicle, which ultimately was responsible for authorities locating both missing boys. Devlin, a former pizzeria manager, pleaded guilty to his crimes.

Meanwhile, concern for Devlin's safety is so great that Missouri prison authorities are contemplating providing Devlin with a new identity, placing him in protective custody, and moving him to an out-of-state prison facility just to keep him alive. Michael Devlin, age 41 in 2007, will be eligible for parole shortly after his 100th birthday.

Sources: Associated Press. (2007a). *Michael Devlin sentenced to three life terms in Hornbeck kidnapping*. Retrieved December 27, 2007, from http://www.foxnews.com/story/0,2933,3004959,000.html; Associated Press. (2007b). *Kidnapper gets extra 170 years in prison*. Retrieved December 27, 2007, from http://www.msnbc.msn.com/id/22359068/.

Finally, the courts have ruled on liability issues that stem from the release and supervision of paroled offenders. The basic question is: "To what degree are parole board members or parole officers liable for the subsequent crimes of parolees that they either released or supervised?" This issue arose from a heinous California case where a convicted sex offender who had been paroled after serving just 5 years of a 20-year sentence later abducted, raped, tortured, and murdered a young girl, crimes for which he was convicted. The family of the victim sued the state alleging that the state was responsible for their daughter's death because it chose to release the violent offender on parole. In ***Martinez v. California*** (1980), the Court held that parole boards have absolute immunity from litigation stemming from third-party accusations of negligence. The logic that the Supreme Court used was this: Although parole release was a state action, the subsequent violent crimes of the offender were not state action; they were the actions of the violent offender. Consequently, parole board members are not legally or civilly responsible for her death.[41] Public officials, such as parole board members or parole officers, also have qualified immunity, which protects their actions from liability as long as they were conducting their duties in good faith. This decision was reached in *Harlow v. Fitzgerald* (1982).[42]

By and large, the courts consider four main factors when assessing the civil liability of parole officials regarding claims of negligence involving a third party, such as the victim of a paroled offender. These include:

- Whether a special relationship between parole officer and parolee existed that required the officer to exercise control over the parolee's behavior.
- Whether the parole officer's actions were ministerial (required by law) or discretionary.
- Whether the parole officer was aware of threats made by the parolee to harm the specific victims.
- Whether the parole officer failed to properly supervise the parolee or warn a potential victim of the dangerous behavior of the parolee.[43]

In sum, as long as parole agents behave in ways that do not violate clear statutory or constitutional rights, they are generally absolved from liability. They are liable, however, when their behavior, action, or inaction stems from an improper basis.

Determinants of Parole

For nearly a century, criminologists studied the characteristics, behaviors, and personalities of prisoners to inform their decision making about which offenders should be released on parole. Often, these characteristics were the same factors that seemed to lend themselves to an offender's successful rehabilitation while on parole. Over time, certain factors consistently appeared as predictors of parole release as well as correlates of parole success or failure. For instance, in an early landmark study, Clark Tibbitts examined the criminal careers of 3,000 men paroled from the Illinois State Reformatory between 1921 and 1927 and identified several factors that influenced parole performance. These included:

- Family background
- Race, ethnicity, and nationality
- Nature of the criminal offense
- Number of criminal accomplices
- Nature and length of sentence
- Length of time served before parole
- Whether the defendant accepted a plea bargain
- Trial recommendations for leniency on the defendant
- Prior criminal record
- Infraction record while in prison
- Prior employment history
- Employment status upon arrest
- Type of criminal, such as first time, occasional, or habitual
- Residency status
- Neighborhood of residency
- Neighborhood into which he was paroled
- Prison work assignments
- Intelligence
- Personality type
- Psychiatric profile
- Social type[44]

Interestingly, criminologists during this era also developed an assortment of **typologies**, categorical classification systems of offenders. At least 10 social types were commonly used in early determinations of parole release and evaluations of offender success on parole. An *erring citizen* was an older person who violated the responsibility of an entrusted position, such as committing white-collar crime. *Marginally delinquent* was a borderline classification between an erring citizen and a socially inadequate person. A *socially inadequate person* was an offender who failed to establish himself or herself in conventional society and exhibited family and work failure. A *farmer* was a rural person who led a normal life but became easily involved in situations that led to trouble. A *ne'er-do-well* was an irresponsible person who seldom worked, lived by the easiest way, and had a reputation as a thief, gambler, or drunkard. A *floater* (also known as a *hobo*) was a person who drifted about the country riding freights and committing minor offenses along the way. A *socially maladjusted* parolee was a person who could not adjust to conventional society because of criminal orientation or serious personality disturbances. A *drunkard* was an offender who was a chronic alcoholic. A *drug addict* was a person who was a chronic drug abuser. A *sex deviant* was a man who engaged in deviant sexual practices.[45]

Although typologies made intuitive sense, they were often unhelpful in determining parole eligibility or evaluating parole success. Typologies are subjective and usually not mutually exclusive; that is, offenders could fit into several different social types. Early penologists recognized these limitations. For instance, Hornell Hart determined that parole violations "could be reduced one-half through scientific utilization of data already being collected by the authorities of that institution."[46, p. 405]

Parole Prediction

Over time, attempts to predict parole readiness and parole success shifted from typological approaches to actuarial prediction instruments. **Actuarial prediction instruments** use behavioral and social indicators on an offender's record to inform decisions about correctional placement. Actuarial parole prediction is considered more scientific and less subjective than typologies based on the impressions of correctional staff or criminologists. These impressions are known as **clinical predictions.** Several criminologists worked on parole prediction instruments between the 1920s and 1960s. Prior criminal history, prior prison history, and institutional adjustment (e.g., disciplinary infractions, participation in work and treatment programs, etc.) were consistently the strongest predictors of parole readiness and parole success.[47–49]

By 1960, three interrelated factors led to a more scientifically objective approach to parole. First, as mentioned earlier in this chapter, the 1960s ushered in a new era of parole where the indeterminate sentence and unconditional release were supplanted by determinate sentences and increasing reliance on conditional parole release. As shown in Figure 11–4, a sharp increase in parole began in 1960 and did not plateau until 2 decades later. Second, the criminal law also changed to reflect changing philosophies in sentencing. For instance, by 1962, the American Law Institute listed four primary reasons for parole denial in the Model Penal Code, which serves as a guide for state legislatures for revising their criminal statutes. These were (1) there is a substantial risk that the parolee will not conform to the conditions of parole; (2) the parolee's release would depreciate the seriousness of the crime or promote disrespect for the law; (3) the parolee's release would have a substantially adverse effect on institutional discipline; and (4) continued correctional treatment, medical care, or vocational or other training in the institution will substantially enhance the capacity to lead a law-abiding life when released at a later date.[50]

Third, criminologists continued to study parole and refine the actuarial variables that could be used to produce the most objective, formalized standards for determining parole eligibility and release. For the most part, criminologists found that parole boards were objective in deciding which offenders to release and that any disparities that existed in parole outcomes were attributable to objective differences in offender risk, such as criminal history.[51–54]

A major advance in parole determination occurred in 1973 when the United States Board of Parole (today known as the United States Parole Commission) adopted the use of the salient factor score. The **salient factor score** is an actuarial risk assessment instrument used by federal parole officials to determine parole readiness.[55–57] The salient factor score contains six items:

1. Item A		Prior convictions/adjudications (adult or juvenile) None = 3; one = 2; two or three = 1; four or more = 0
2. Item B		Prior commitment(s) of more than 30 days (adult/juvenile) None = 1; one or more = 1; three or more = 0
3. Item C		Age at current offense/prior commitments
	26 years or older	Three or fewer prior commitments = 3; four prior commitments = 2; five or more prior commitments = 1
	22–25 years	Three or fewer prior commitments = 2; four prior commitments = 1; five or more prior commitments = 0
	20–21 years	Three or fewer prior commitments = 1; four or more prior commitments = 0
	19 years or younger	Any number of prior commitments = 0
4. Item D		Recent commitment-free period (3 years) No prior commitment of more than 30 days (adult or juvenile) or released to the community from last such commitment at least 3 years prior to the commencement of the current offense = 1; otherwise = 0
5. Item E		Probation/parole/confinement/escape status violator Neither on probation, parole, confinement, nor escape status at the time of the current offense; nor committed as a probation, parole, confinement, or escape status violator this time = 1; otherwise = 0
6. Item F		Older offenders If the offender was 41 years of age or more at the commencement of the current offense (and the total score from Items A–E above is 9 or less) = 1; otherwise = 0.[58]

For parolees, commitment and reattachment to conventional (noncriminal) life is the operating principle that determines whether that parolee succeeds after release from prison. In many respects, an offender's success on parole begins in prison evidenced by the significantly higher success rates among parolees who were released at the discretion of the parole board. Parole boards consider a variety of factors, such as the inmate's involvement in work, educational, and other correctional programming, infraction history, substance abuse history, gang involvement, criminal and incarceration history, social support, and the inmate's **parole plan**—the offender's plan after release from prison in terms of proposed employment, living arrangements, and other life circumstances when deciding to grant conditional release.

Decades of research indicate that inmates who appear ready to reconnect to conventional society and repudiate their criminal past are likely those who will be given the opportunity for parole. Crime victims also have their greatest effect on criminal justice decision making in determinations of parole. Parole boards find that **victim impact statements** or testimonials from crime victims about how their victimization has affected their life are compelling and make the granting of parole more unlikely. Indeed, Kathryn Morgan and Brent Smith found that victim participation in parole hearings, particularly when victims give oral testimony to parole boards, is the most influential factor in the decision to grant or deny parole.[59]

Similarly, Joel Caplan reviewed the factors that affect parole and found that institutional behavior, crime severity, criminal history, and victim input are among the strongest influences on the parole decision.[60] Beth Huebner and Timothy Bynum studied more than 500 sex offenders and found that criminal history and specific details about the victims in prior cases were particularly relevant in decisions whether to parole felons convicted of sexually based offenses.[61] On the other hand, the predictors of parole failure are largely the opposite of the predictors of success. Offenders who recidivate are those who have no stake in conformity, meaning they are unemployed, do not participate in treatment, have no social support, and, of course, continue to run afoul of the law.[62]

Victim impact statements are an example of crime victims' affecting the correctional process.

Parole Violation and Revocation

Parole is a conditional sentence where an offender is permitted to live and work in the community in lieu of serving his or her entire sentence in prison confinement. Because of this legal structure, parole is a very tenuous status where an offender's opportunity to remain on parole is a function of the offender's ability to comply with parole conditions, the offender's parole prognosis or assessment of risk, and any subsequent antisocial behavior. When a parolee fails to abide by the conditions of the parole sentence, he or she has committed a parole violation. Two general types of parole violations exist. **Technical parole violations** are violations of the specific conditions of the sentence. Also known as administrative violations, technical violations include failing to report to the parole officer or missing a scheduled drug test. **Criminal parole violations** are new criminal offenses committed while the offender is on parole.

In the course of their duties, parole officers strike a balance between being a social worker and a law enforcement officer. Angela West and Richard Seiter described this balance as a blend of the **casework style**, which refers to counseling, advising, and assisting parolees with their problems, and the **surveillance style**, which involves offender monitoring and enforcement of the conditions of parole. Although the surveillance or enforcement aspects of correctional supervision get all the headlines, most parole officer activity is spent in the casework style, where they work with the parolee in hopes of his or her complying with the sentence.[63] Other research also shows that parole officers place great value in the treatment and casework aspects of their work, even if resource limitations and other constraints of their job push them towards surveillance duties.[64–65]

In practice, parolees are much more likely to commit technical rather than criminal parole violations, and when criminal parole violations occur, they tend to involve low-level or even trivial offenses. For example, the United States Parole Commission employs eight categories of offense seriousness for parole violations (see TABLE 11–5). Category one involves the least serious offenses including all administrative parole violations, misdemeanor offenses except assault, theft of less than $2,000, and possession of a controlled substance. This means that parole systems are designed to tolerate some amount of low-level criminal activity among parolees. Consequently, parole officers must utilize great discretion in determining which violations are serious enough to result in the issuance of a warrant for parole violation and ultimate parole revocation. In some jurisdictions, parole officers do not even have the authorization to employ discretion on technical violations. Some jurisdictions have administrative orders in place where specified low-level criminal offenses are exempt from determining violation of a parolee's sentence.[66]

In many cases, the meeting between a parole officer and a parolee to discuss an alleged violation of parole is perfunctory. Parole officers often either take no action and simply lecture the parolee for their technical violation or make conditions more stringent to help assure compliance. In turn, parolees often admit to their parole violations particularly

TABLE 11-5 United States Parole Commission Guidelines for Parole Violation/Revocation

Offense Characteristics: Severity of Offense Behavior	Offender Characteristics: Parole Prognosis (Salient Factor Score 1998) Very Good (10–8)	Good (7–6)	Fair (5–4)	Poor (3–0)
	Guideline range			
Category One	≤4 months	≤8 months	8–12 months	12–16 months
	Guideline range			
Category Two	≤6 months	≤10 months	12–16 months	16–22 months
	Guideline range			
Category Three	≤10 months	12–16 months	18–24 months	24–32 months
	Guideline range			
Category Four	12–18 months	20–26 months	26–34 months	34–44 months
	Guideline range			
Category Five	24–36 months	36–48 months	48–60 months	60–72 months
	Guideline range			
Category Six	40–52 months	52–64 months	64–78 months	78–100 months
	Guideline range			
Category Seven	52–80 months	64–92 months	78–110 months	100–148 months
	Guideline range			
Category Eight	100+ months	120+ months	150+ months	180+ months

Source: United States Parole Commission. (2003). *U.S. Parole Commission rules and procedures manual.* Washington, DC: U.S. Department of Justice, United States Parole Commission.

when the violation is technical in nature. Peter Hoffman and James Beck described this scenario in this way:

> Most alleged parole violators charged with administrative violations or misdemeanor offenses admit the charges against them at the revocation hearing. Those who initially deny the charged violation often make a plea of mitigating circumstances at the revocation hearing rather than actually contest the facts of the violation. Thus, although some revocation hearings involved contested factual issues with examination and cross-examination of witnesses, the sole question in most revocation hearings involving administrative or misdemeanor charges is the appropriate sanction for the violation.[67, p. 451]

In 1996, the United States Parole Commission began a pilot project designed to expedite the processing of parole violations involving technical, misdemeanor, and even low-level felony offenses. **Revocation by consent** occurred when a parolee (1) waived his or her right to a formal revocation hearing; (2) acknowledged responsibility for the alleged violation; and (3) accepted a specified revocation penalty determined by the parole commission based on the specifics of his or her case.

The revocation by consent policy served two beneficial purposes in that it preserved due process rights of the parolee while conserving resources that would normally be needed for standard parole revocation hearings. Among more than 800 federal parolees involved in the pilot program, more than 85 percent accepted the terms of revocation by consent and more than 80 percent of these were simply reparoled. Revocation by consent became official policy in 1998 and today revocations by consent account for 40 percent of all revocation actions made by the United States Parole Commission.[68]

Of course, parolees do not always cooperate with parole officers and consent to a revocation of their sentence. Many criminologists have studied the factors that influence parole revocation. As is the case in virtually every area of criminal justice discretion, legal characteristics such as criminal history are the most important predictor of legal outcome, in this case revocation. Sara Steen and Tara Opsal examined parole revocation among offenders in Kentucky, Michigan, New York, and Utah and found that parolees who had previously been imprisoned before their most recent sentence were 121 percent more likely than parolees without preexisting prison history to commit a criminal violation and 80 percent more likely to incur a technical violation.[69] For many parolees, criminal history is often very difficult to surmount. For instance, Kate Hanrahan and her colleagues interviewed young offenders who had their parole revoked to explore offender assessments of revocation. Offenders acknowledged the difficult, uphill battle of complying with parole sentences and also reported that many of their families were tired and burdened by the parolees' criminal pasts. In this way, some families lacked the financial and emotional resources to help paroled offenders toward their rehabilitation.[70]

Lynn Langton studied parole outcomes among more than 4,000 offenders paroled from the California Youth Authority and found that low self-control was consistently related to parole violation and revocation.[71] In this way, the very interpersonal and personality features that contribute to delinquency in the first place are also formidable barriers to rehabilitation after release from confinement.

Ultimately, parole violation and parole revocation are dependent on the risk profile of parolees themselves. Many parole officers are apprehensive about the risks posed by parolees and officers vary in terms of their tolerance for noncompliance. Richard Seiter explained "the emphasis on surveillance of community offenders results in a trend to violate parolees for minor technical violations, as administrators and parole boards do not want to risk keeping offenders in the community. If these minor violators later commit a serious crime, those deciding to allow them to continue in the community despite technical violations could face criticism or even legal action."[72, p. 51] Indeed, because of their criminal history and various antisocial risk factors, parole is a difficult sentence for many felony offenders to successfully complete. Some offenders consider parole to be so difficult that a sizable proportion of correctional clients simply prefer to serve their entire sentence in confinement so they can be fully and unconditionally released.[73]

Parole failure also takes its toll on the correctional system. As shown in **FIGURE 11–7**, the number of parole violators returned to prison has increased *sevenfold* from 1977 to

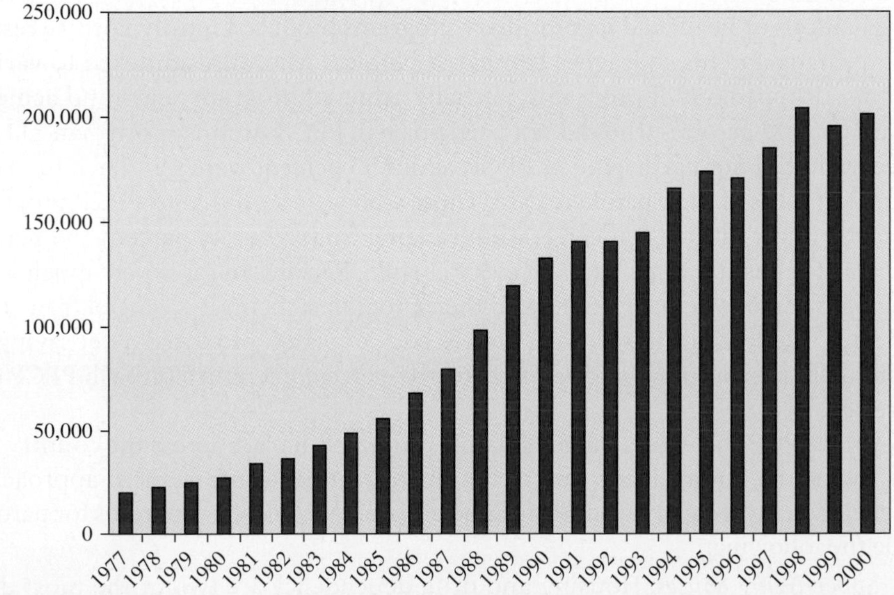

FIGURE 11–7 Parole Violators to Prison Increases Sevenfold. *Source*: Travis, J., & Lawrence, S. (2002). *Beyond the prison gates: The state of parole in America.* Washington, DC: The Urban Institute.

2000.[74] Based on these data, it is easy to conclude that parole is an abject failure. Fortunately, this is not the case. There is a wide range of innovative programs and correctional policies in place that have shown promising signs of parole success. This chapter concludes with coverage of parole programs and criminal justice initiatives designed to increase the effectiveness of parole.

Parole Programs and Policies

As mentioned at the beginning of this chapter, when parole is successful it is often invisible. Parolees quietly comply with the conditions of their sentence, go to work, participate in treatment and counseling, reconnect with family and friends, and, most importantly from the correctional system's perspective, desist from criminal offending. According to a 2007 report by researchers with the Bureau of Justice Statistics, 44 percent of all parolees in the United States successfully completed their sentences. This means that for hundreds of thousands of parolees each year, the transition from prison to community is a successful one.[75]

Correctional systems devote tremendous resources toward making parole more effective and reducing the volume of parole violators and revocations that cycle back to prison. One of the foremost parole initiatives is the Preventing Parole Failure Program developed by the California Department of Corrections. The Preventing Parole Failure Program is a network of service providers that offer drug treatment, literacy training, employment readiness training, job placement assistance, and other services to paroled offenders. Most of the services are community based and provided on an outpatient basis; however, more intensive treatment is provided in residential settings, such as halfway houses. After serving as a pilot program in 1996–1997, the program was renamed the **Preventing Parole Crime Program (PPCP)** and greatly expanded to also include programs geared toward substance abuse education, math and literary skills development, and housing assistance. Parolees participated in an array of service programs such as Jobs Plus, Offenders Employment Continuum, Residential Multi-Service Center, Computerized Literacy Learning Center, Substance Abuse Treatment and Recovery, and Parolee Services Network. More than 80 percent of California parole departments have access to PPCP units.[76]

Evaluations of PPCP and its subsidiary programs produced mostly positive results. Sheldon Zhang and his colleagues compared parolees who were admitted to various programs, dropped out of programs, partially achieved program goals, and achieved program goals to parolees who did not participate in PPCP. Among more than 211,000 parolees who did not participate in PPCP, about 53 percent were sent back to prison within 12 months of their parole release. Those who were admitted to PPCP programs had mostly lower rates of reincarceration ranging from 39 to 44 percent (56 percent for substance abuse treatment and recovery clients). Recidivism rates were much lower among parolees who actually completed their programs; their rates ranged from 15 to 40 percent.[77] Reductions in sending parolees back to prison produced a net savings of $21 million in prison costs, which equates to a 47 percent net return on each PPCP dollar invested.[78]

Beyond PPCP, there are a range of parole programs in place across the country that utilize treatment, enforcement, and a combined treatment-enforcement approach to more effective parole supervision. Some innovative and promising programs for parolees include the following:

- *Sober-living houses*: Housing and drug dependency are two of the most difficult challenges that paroled offenders face. A solution that addresses both needs is **sober living houses**, which are drug- and alcohol-free residences for paroled offenders who want to maintain their sobriety. Sober living houses also provide a safe environment that supports parolee compliance with other aspects of their sentence, such as medical care, mental health treatment, and job training. A recent evaluation of 19 sober living houses in California found that nearly half of parolees placed in sober living houses remained there 6 months after release and 51 percent of offenders remained completely substance free.[79]

- *Faith-based programs*: In recent years, there has been a resurgence in the use of religion as a social institution to correct criminal behavior. Clergy and other religious officials often volunteer in prisons and assist parolees during the transition process. The New Jersey State Parole Board created a community partnership unit, which has developed a variety of programs—many of which provide group counseling to parolees specifically targeting chemical dependency needs. In 3 years, the community partnership unit has secured jobs for more than 800 parolees and produced more than $7 million in services through religious programs.[80]
- *Parole diversion*: Another innovation of the New Jersey State Parole Board's community programs unit is the diversion of nonviolent drug-dependent parolees to drug treatment facilities. Since many technical parole violations are related to drug use, the program removes low-risk offenders from the parole revocation process (and thus from reconfinement) and diverts them to one of four diversion programs in the state where they receive intensive substance abuse and life-skills counseling. After diverted offenders successfully complete the program, they are again released on parole with an aftercare component to continue their drug treatment. Parole diversion is useful because it reduces parole revocations, reduces prison crowding, and increases treatment exposure for parolees.[81]
- *Gang reduction aggressive supervision parole (GRASP):* GRASP, another innovation of the New Jersey State Parole Board, involves the specific targeting of parolees who are known to be active in security threat groups while in prison. Gang members receive the most intensive parole supervision and are subject to laws that target gangs, such as civil injunctions against gangs and loitering. Programs like GRASP attempt to disrupt the linkages between prison and street gangs.[82]
- *Relapse prevention therapy*: Relapse prevention therapy is used at multiple points in the correctional process, including pretrial supervision, probation, jail, prison, and parole. Essentially, relapse prevention therapy educates offenders about the precursors and circumstances that often contribute to substance use so that offenders can avoid these situations. The educational program targets offenders and their family and friends and often includes relapse rehearsal, coping skills, and positive thinking training. Since many parolees have substance abuse histories, relapse prevention therapy is a useful complement to other drug treatment and counseling programs that parolees use.[83]
- *Proactive gang resistance enforcement, suppression, and supervision (PROGRESS)*: The Wausau, Wisconsin, Division of Community Corrections developed the PROGRESS program to target high-risk parolees. It allowed parole officers and law enforcement officers to conduct home visits of high-risk parolees during unexpected times (the programs are also known as *police–parole partnerships*). In 2 years of operation, PROGRESS found 200 offenders in violation of their parole mostly by curfew violation, drug use, and contact with unauthorized persons. Because of the random nature of the home searches, the program also increased rule compliance and resulted in overall lower arrests rates among parolees.[84]
- *Random drug testing*: Drug testing is a standard component of most parole sentences; however, its effectiveness is reduced if offenders manipulate drug tests because they are regularly scheduled. A recent evaluation of randomized drug

testing of parolees indicated that offenders are about 11 percent more likely to be employed and enrolled in school than parolees assigned to a no-drug-testing control group. In this way, the threat of drug testing can help ensure parolee compliance at least in the short term.[85]

Criminologists are also busily brainstorming ways to improve the effectiveness of parole while saving correctional costs and preserving public safety. For instance, Joan Petersilia advocates the implementation of **earned discharge parole**, where parolees receive a reduction in their sentence upon completion of prosocial activities, such as completing drug treatment, work, or educational programs. According to Petersilia, an earned discharge parole sentence of 3 years would work as follows: Parolees who are arrest free in their first year of parole will receive a 1-month reduction of sentence for every month of arrest-free activity in their second year. Thus, 2 years of arrest-free activity will result in a 1-year reduction in the parole sentence. Parolees can reduce their 2-year sentence by 6 months upon completion of community service and payment of all victim restitution. Parolees can reduce their sentence an additional 6 months by maintaining full-time employment or completing an educational program. Parolees can reduce their entire sentence from 3 years to 6 months by achieving stability in housing, employment, and treatment for 6 months.[86] Given the importance of the successful transition of prisoner to citizen, a new era of criminological study known as reentry has developed from parole and is explored in Chapter 12.

WRAP UP

CASE STUDY CONCLUSION

The two defendants were viewed as good parole risks because they did not have prior violent convictions on their criminal record, and certainly no prior crimes that approached the violence of the current charges. In the wake of the crime, Connecticut lawmakers established home invasion as a new crime, increased the penalty of residential burglary, and mandated that those convicted of burglary or home invasion serve at least 85 percent of their sentence before parole eligibility. At least in Connecticut, parole has become more stringent because of this heinous incident.

Sources: Maruna, S. (2001). *Making good: How ex-convicts reform and rebuild their lives.* Washington, DC: American Psychological Association; Foxnews.com. (2007). *Prosecutor to seek death penalty in deadly Connecticut home invasion.* Retrieved October 7, 2008, from http://www.foxnews.com/story/0,2933,291018,00.html; WFSB.com. (2008). *Special session nets new home invasion law: Senate defeats 'three strikes' amendment.* Retrieved October 7, 2008, from http://www.wfsb.com/print/15120600/detail.html.

Chapter Summary

- Approximately 825,000 offenders are on parole.
- Parole has historically been the most susceptible sentence to public opinion and crime trends.
- Federal parole has a long and convoluted history such that federal parole no longer exists due to changes in sentencing policy.
- Parolees are a high-risk group with often extensive criminal histories and are likely to be rearrested and reincarcerated.
- Parolees have the same access to the courts as prisoners, are entitled to due process rights during revocation proceedings, are not entitled to discretionary parole, and have reduced Fourth Amendment rights regarding search and seizure.
- Criminal history and other antisocial behavioral measures are the strongest predictors of parole violation and revocation.
- States have developed an array of innovative programs that address the overlapping substance abuse, mental health, and social deficiencies that parolees have.

Key Terms

actuarial prediction instruments Method that uses behavioral and social indicators on an offender's record to inform decisions about correctional placement.

automatic parole The immediate granting of parole to low-risk offenders even though they were sentenced to prison by the courts.

Board of Pardons v. Allen Supreme Court case that held that any statute that mandates parole creates a presumption that the parole release will be granted.

casework style Parole officer style that refers to counseling, advising, and assisting parolees with their problems.

clinical predictions Correctional assessments based on expert opinion.

criminal parole violations New criminal offenses committed while an offender is on parole.

direct sentence *See* automatic parole.

discretionary parole Release that occurs when parole boards have the discretionary authority to conditionally release prisoners based on a statutory or administrative determination of eligibility.

earned discharge parole Type of parole in which parolees receive a reduction in their sentence upon completion of prosocial activities, such as completing drug treatment, work, or educational programs.

Gagnon v. Scarpelli Supreme Court case that held that probationers are entitled to due process for preliminary and final hearings before probation can be revoked.

good time Time spent in prison without major disciplinary incidents.

Greenholtz v. Inmates Supreme Court case that held that the decision to grant parole is a subjective, potential outcome—it is not guaranteed.

Griffin v. Wisconsin Supreme Court case that held that parolees can be searched based upon reasonable suspicion of the officer.

Jones v. Cunningham Supreme Court case that held that parolees are considered in custody and can invoke the habeas corpus statute to challenge their sentence.

mandatory parole Type of parole that occurs in jurisdictions using determinate sentencing statutes where inmates are conditionally released from prison after serving a portion of their original sentences minus any good time.

Martinez v. California Supreme Court case that held that parole boards have absolute immunity from litigation stemming from third-party accusations of negligence.

Morrissey v. Brewer Supreme Court case that held that due process rights expressed in the Fourteenth Amendment establish the right of a parolee to a preliminary and final hearing before his or her parole can be revoked.

parole Form of correction in which the convicted person completes a prison sentence in the community rather than in confinement.

parole agency State agency that administers parole.

parole boards Administrative entities that are legally charged with the discretionary authority to conditionally release prisoners based on a statutory or administrative determination of eligibility.

parole conditions Mandated conditions that are intended to serve the treatment and supervision needs of a person on parole.

parole contract A legal document containing the terms and conditions of parole.

parole officer Agent who supervises parolees, monitors them for parole violations, and has the authority to arrest parolees for failing to comply with their sentence.

parole plan The offender's plan after release from prison in terms of proposed employment, living arrangements, and other life circumstances.

parole revocation Situation that occurs when parolees have their parole sentence terminated and are resentenced to prison.

parole violation Violation of the terms of parole.

parolee A person on parole.

Pennsylvania Board of Probation and Parole v. Scott Supreme Court case that held that the costs of allowing a parolee to avoid the consequences of his or her violation are compounded by the fact that parolees are more likely to commit criminal offenses than average citizens.

Preventing Parole Crime Program (PPCP) California initiative with programs for parolees geared toward substance abuse education, math and literary skills development, housing assistance, and other services.

recidivism Reoffending after release from criminal justice custody.

rereleases Parolees recently imprisoned for parole violation or a new offense committed while on parole.

revocation by consent Situation that occurs when a parolee waives right to a formal revocation hearing, acknowledges responsibility for the alleged violation, and accepts a specified revocation penalty determined by the parole commission based on the specifics of the case.

salient factor score An actuarial risk assessment instrument used by federal parole officials to determine parole readiness.

sober living houses Drug- and alcohol-free residences for paroled offenders who want to maintain their sobriety.

supervised releases In the federal system, a term of supervision that the court imposes to follow a period of imprisonment.

surveillance style Parole officer style that involves offender monitoring and enforcement of the conditions of parole.

technical parole violations Violations of the specific conditions of the sentence.

typologies Categorical classification systems of offenders.

United States Board of Parole The federal board of parole, which was founded in 1930.

United States Parole Commission The federal parole board after its name change in 1976.

United States Sentencing Commission (U.S.S.C.) An independent commission in the judicial branch that was established by the Sentencing Reform Act provisions of the Comprehensive Crime Control Act of 1984 to establish sentencing guidelines for the federal courts and install a formal system of determinate sentences.

United States v. Knights Supreme Court case that held that searches of parolees based on reasonable suspicion are permitted because there is enough likelihood that criminal conduct is occurring.

victim impact statements Testimonials from crime victims about how their victimization has affected their life.

Critical Thinking Questions

1. Should states follow the lead of the federal justice system and abolish parole? Would this reduce crime? Would this meaningfully affect the prison population?
2. Should parole be used as a reward for inmates who demonstrate exceptional behavior and treatment accomplishments over a period of time? In cases where prisoners are doing extremely well, should parole be awarded regardless of their sentence?

3. Given the role of substance abuse among parolees and among parole treatment, should drug offending be punished more harshly?
4. Which make more sense: determinate or indeterminate sentences? How did indeterminate sentences change sentences from being viewed as progressive to punitive?

Notes

1. McCleary, R. (1978). *Dangerous men: The sociology of parole*. Monsey, NY: Willow Tree Press.
2. Simon, J. (1993). *Poor discipline: Parole and the social control of the underclass, 1890–1990*. Chicago: University of Chicago Press.
3. Thomas, P. A. (1963). An analysis of parole selection. *Crime & Delinquency, 9,* 173–179.
4. Glueck, S. (1932). Individualization and the use of prediction devices. *Journal of Criminal Law and Criminology, 23,* 67–76.
5. DeLisi, M., & Berg, M. T. (2006). Exploring theoretical linkages between self-control theory and criminal justice system processing. *Journal of Criminal Justice, 34,* 153–163.
6. Bottomley, A. K. (1990). Parole in transition: A comparative study of origins, developments, and prospects for the 1990s. In M. Tonry & M. Morris (Eds.), *Crime and justice: A review of research: Vol. 12* (pp. 319–374). Chicago: University of Chicago Press.
7. Hughes, T. A., Wilson, D. J., & Beck, A. J. (2001). *Trends in state parole, 1990–2000.* Washington, DC: U.S. Department of Justice, Office of Justice Programs, Bureau of Justice Statistics.
8. Travis, J., & Lawrence, S. (2002). *Beyond the prison gates: The state of parole in America*. Washington, DC: The Urban Institute, Justice Policy Center.
9. Glaze, L. E., & Bonczar, T. P. (2008). *Probation and parole in the United States, 2007.* Washington, DC: U.S. Department of Justice, Office of Justice Programs, Bureau of Justice Statistics.
10. Burgess, E. W. (1936). Protecting the public by parole and by parole prediction. *Journal of Criminal Law and Criminology, 27,* 491–502.
11. Hughes et al.
12. Hughes et al.
13. Ireland, C. S., & Prause, J. (2005). Discretionary parole release: Length of imprisonment, percent of sentence served, and recidivism. *Journal of Crime & Justice, 28,* 27–49.
14. Glaze & Bonczar.
15. Wilson, J. A. (2005). Bad behavior or bad policy? An examination of Tennessee release cohorts, 1993–2001. *Criminology & Public Policy, 4,* 485–518.
16. Hoffman, P. B. (2003). *History of the federal parole system*. Washington, DC: U.S. Department of Justice, United States Parole Commission.
17. Hoffman.
18. DeLisi, M. (2008). *Criminal justice: Balancing crime control and due process* (2nd ed.). Dubuque, IA: Kendall/Hunt; Hoffman.
19. Hughes et al.
20. Wolfgang, M. E., Figlio, R. M., & Sellin, T. (1972). *Delinquency in a birth cohort*. Chicago: University of Chicago Press.
21. DeLisi, M. (2005). *Career criminals in society*. Thousand Oaks, CA: Sage.
22. Durose, M. R., & Mumola, C. J. (2004). *Profile of nonviolent offenders exiting state prisons*. Washington, DC: U.S. Department of Justice, Office of Justice Programs, Bureau of Justice Statistics.

23. Durose & Mumola.

24. Glaze & Bonczar.

25. Hughes et al.

26. Travis & Lawrence.

27. Langan, P. A., & Levin, D. J. (2002). *Recidivism of prisoners released in 1994.* Washington, DC: U.S. Department of Justice, Office of Justice Programs, Bureau of Justice Statistics.

28. Langan & Levin.

29. *Jones v. Cunningham,* 371 U.S. 236 (1963).

30. Colbridge, T. D. (2003). Probationers, parolees, and the Fourth Amendment. *FBI Law Enforcement Bulletin, 72,* 22–31.

31. *Griffin v. Wisconsin,* 483 U.S. 868 (1987).

32. *United States v. Knights,* 534 U.S. 112 (2001).

33. *Pennsylvania Board of Probation and Parole v. Scott,* 524 U.S. 357 (1998).

34. Hemmens, C., & del Carmen, R. V. (1997). Exclusionary rule in probation and parole revocation proceedings: Does it apply? *Federal Probation, 61,* 32–39.

35. *Morrissey v. Brewer,* 408 U.S. 471 (1972).

36. *Gagnon v. Scarpelli,* 411 U.S. 778 (1973).

37. *Young v. Harper,* 520 U.S. 143 (1997).

38. *Jago v. Van Curen,* 454 U.S. 14 (1981).

39. *Greenholtz v. Inmates,* 442 U.S. 1 (1979).

40. *Board of Pardons v. Allen,* 482 U.S. 369 (1987).

41. *Martinez v. California,* 444 U.S. 277 (1980).

42. *Harlow v. Fitzgerald,* 457 U.S. 800 (1982).

43. Morgan, K. D., Belbot, B. A., & Clark, J. (1997). Liability issues affecting probation and parole supervision. *Journal of Criminal Justice, 25,* 212–222.

44. Tibbitts, C. (1931). Success or failure on parole can be predicted: A study of the records of 3,000 youths paroled from the Illinois State Reformatory. *Journal of Criminal Law and Criminology, 22,* 11–50.

45. Ohlin, L. E. (1951). *Selection for parole: A manual of parole prediction.* New York: Russell Sage Foundation.

46. Hart, H. (1923). Predicting parole success. *Journal of Criminal Law and Criminology, 14,* 405–413.

47. Allen, R. M. (1942). A review of parole prediction literatures. *Journal of Criminal Law and Criminology, 32,* 548–554.

48. Ohlin, L. E., & Lawrence, R. A. (1952). A comparison of alternative methods of parole prediction. *American Sociological Review, 17,* 268–274.

49. Glaser, D. (1955). The efficacy of alternative approaches to parole prediction. *American Sociological Review, 20,* 283–287.

50. Gottfredson, M. R., & Gottfredson, D. M. (1987). *Decision making in criminal justice: Toward the rational exercise of discretion* (2nd ed.). New York: Plenum Press, p. 231.

51. Gottfredson, D. M., & Ballard, K. B., Jr. (1966). Differences in parole decisions associated with decision-makers. *Journal of Research in Crime and Delinquency, 3,* 112–119.

52. Gottfredson, D. M., Ballard, K. B., Jr., & O'Leary, V. (1966). Uniform parole reports: A feasibility study. *Journal of Research in Crime and Delinquency, 3,* 97–111.

53. Gottfredson, D. M., Wilkins, L. T., & Hoffman, P. B. (1978). *Guidelines for parole and sentencing.* Lexington, MA: Lexington Books.

54. Glaser, D. (1964). *The effectiveness of a prison and parole system.* Indianapolis, IN: Bobbs-Merrill.

55. Hoffman, P. B. (1994). Twenty years of operational use of a risk prediction instrument: The United States Parole Commission's salient factor score. *Journal of Criminal Justice, 22,* 477–494.

56. Hoffman, P. B., & Beck, J. L. (1985). Recidivism among released federal prisoners: Salient factor score and five-year follow-up. *Criminal Justice and Behavior, 12,* 501–507.

57. Hoffman, P. B., & Beck, J. L. (1976). Salient factor score validation: A 1972 release cohort. *Journal of Criminal Justice, 4,* 69–76.

58. United States Parole Commission. (2003). *U.S. Parole Commission rules and procedures manual.* Washington, DC: U.S. Department of Justice, United States Parole Commission.

59. Morgan, K., & Smith, B. L. (2005). Victims, punishment, and parole: The effect of victim participation on parole hearings. *Criminology & Public Policy, 4,* 333–360.

60. Caplan, J. M. (2007). What factors affect parole? A review of empirical research. *Federal Probation, 71,* 16–19.

61. Huebner, B. M., & Bynum, T. S. (2006). An analysis of parole decision making using a sample of sex offenders: A focal concerns perspective. *Criminology, 44,* 961–992.

62. See Gottfredson, D. M., Gottfredson, M. R., & Garofalo, J. (1977). Time served in prison and parole outcomes among parolee risk categories. *Journal of Criminal Justice, 5,* 1–12; Gottfredson, M. R. (1979). Parole board decision making: A study of disparity reduction and the impact of institutional behavior. *Journal of Criminal Law and Criminology, 70,* 77–88; Carroll, J. S., Wiener, R. L., Coates, D., Galegher, J., & Alibrio, J. J. (1982). Evaluation, diagnosis, and prediction in parole decision making. *Law & Society Review, 17,* 199–228; Morgan, K. D., & Smith, B. (2005). Parole release decisions revisited: An analysis of parole release decisions for violent inmates in a southeastern state. *Journal of Criminal Justice, 33,* 277–287.

63. West, A. D., & Seiter, R. P. (2004). Social worker or cop? Measuring the supervision styles of probation and parole officers in Kentucky and Missouri. *Journal of Crime & Justice, 27,* 27–57.

64. Herie, M., Cunningham, J. A., & Martin, G. W. (2000). Attitudes toward substance abuse treatment among probation and parole officers. *Journal of Offender Rehabilitation, 32,* 181–195.

65. Quinn, J. F., & Could, L. A. (2003). Prioritization of treatment among Texas parole officers. *Prison Journal, 83,* 323–336.

66. Jones, M., & Kerbs, J. J. (2007). Probation and parole officers and discretionary decision-making: Responses to technical and criminal violations. *Federal Probation, 71,* 9–15.

67. Hoffman, P. B., & Beck, J. L. (2005). Revocation by consent: The United States Parole Commission's expedited revocation procedure. *Journal of Criminal Justice, 33,* 451–462.

68. Hoffman & Beck.

69. Steen, S., & Opsal, T. (2007). "Punishment on the installment plan": Individual-level predictors of parole revocation in four states. *Prison Journal, 87,* 344–366.

70. Hanrahan, K., Gibbs, J. J., & Zimmerman, S. E. (2005). Parole and revocation: Perspectives of young adult offenders. *Prison Journal, 85,* 251–269.

71. Langton, L. (2006). Low self-control and parole failure: An assessment of risk from a theoretical perspective. *Journal of Criminal Justice, 34,* 469–478.

72. Seiter, R. P. (2002). Prisoner reentry and the role of parole officers. *Federal Probation, 66,* 50–54.

73. Halsey, M. J. (2006). Negotiating conditional release: Juvenile narratives of repeat incarceration. *Punishment & Society, 8,* 147–181.

74. Travis & Lawrence.

75. Glaze & Bonczar.

76. Zhang, S. X., Roberts, R. E. L., & Callanan, V. J. (2005). Multiple services on a statewide scale: The impact of the California PPCP. *Corrections Compendium, 30,* 6–7, 30–35.

77. Zhang, S. X., Roberts, R. E. L., & Callanan, V. J. (2006). Preventing parolees from returning to prison through community-based reintegration. *Crime & Delinquency, 52,* 551–571.

78. Zhang, S. X., Roberts, R. E. L., & Callanan, V. J. (2006). The cost benefits of providing community-based correctional services: An evaluation of a statewide parole program in California. *Journal of Criminal Justice, 34,* 341–350.

79. Polcin, D. L. (2006). What about sober living houses for parolees? *Criminal Justice Studies, 19,* 291–300.

80. D'Amico, J. (2007). "Ask and you will receive": Creating faith-based programs for former inmates. *Corrections Today, 69,* 78–82.

81. Butler, R., & Garcia, V. (2005). Diversion of nonviolent substance abuse parolees: Putting research into practice. *Corrections Today, 67,* 112–114.

82. Butler, R., & Garcia, V (2006). Parole supervision of security threat groups: A collaborative response. *Corrections Today, 68,* 60–63.

83. Parks, G. A. (2007). New approaches to using relapse prevention therapy in the criminal justice system. *Corrections Today, 69,* 46–49.

84. Hagenbucher, G. (2003). PROGRESS: An enhanced supervision program for high-risk criminal offenders. *FBI Law Enforcement Bulletin, 72,* 20–24.

85. Kilmer, B. (2008). Does parolee drug testing influence employment and education outcomes? Evidence from a randomized experiment with noncompliance. *Journal of Quantitative Criminology, 24,* 93–123.

86. Petersilia, J. (2007). Employ behavioral contracting for "earned discharge" parole. *Criminology & Public Policy, 6,* 807–814.

CHAPTER

12

Reentry

"Incarceration imparts a social stigma on families and children, often eliciting strong feelings of shame and anger in the family and associates of inmates."[1, p. 284]

OBJECTIVES

- Assess the size of the reentry population.
- Learn the recent history and policy developments of reentry.
- Identify the major reentry initiatives employed by correctional systems.
- Explore the criminological background of reentry regarding the shaming and reintegration of former prisoners.
- Become aware of the collateral societal issues raised by offenders returning to the community from prison.
- Identify institutional barriers to offender reentry.
- Learn what works in reentry programs.

CASE STUDY

Although primarily an issue pertaining to prisons, reentry is also important to jails. Each year more than 12 million inmates are released from municipal and county jails, and many inmates have a variety of personal problems that contribute to their antisocial behavior and serve as a barrier to functional membership in society. Researchers with the Bureau of Justice Assistance developed the APIC model for jail administrators to help inmates be successful. The APIC model is:

- **A**ssess the inmate's clinical and social needs and public safety risks.
- **P**lan for the treatment and services required to address the inmate's needs.
- **I**dentify required community and correctional programs responsible for postrelease services.
- **C**oordinate the transition plan to ensure implementation and avoid gaps in care with community-based services.

1. With this model in mind, how can jail administrators help inmates prepare for reentry while they are still incarcerated in jail?

"America is the land of second chances, and when the gates of the prison open, the path ahead should lead to a better life."[2]

In Chapter 11, the many uphill challenges of paroled criminal offenders were explored. In the course of working toward their rehabilitation, it is difficult for many parolees to improve their life chances due to the multitude of problems that they have. For this reason, the parole literature has somewhat narrowly focused on recidivism—or the failings of paroled offenders as the sole area of interest. This was noted by John Irwin nearly 40 years ago, that there is little "awareness of the broader aspects of the reentry problem. This general blindness seems to be related to formal and informal societal conceptions of the ex-convict."[7, p. 109]

Unfortunately, paying attention exclusively to recidivism obscures the other important social issues that arise when large numbers of offenders circulate into the community from prison. In addition to dealing with the stigma of prison, parolees must maneuver the difficult transition from an environment characterized by violence, malaise, and disease to life on the outside. For other paroled offenders, prison and correctional statuses are badges of honor and parole release is simply another opportunity to resume habitual antisocial behavior.

For more than a decade, policy makers and criminologists have broadened their interest in paroled offenders and the issues that complicate and facilitate their reintegration. The parole or release of prisoners is known as reentry. The current chapter explores reentry as a new area of the correctional process, including the policies and programs that enable offender reentry and the various societal issues that are affected by prisoners returning to the community.

Reentry

With the exception of prisoners who serve life sentences until their death in confinement, prisoners who die or are killed while serving any type of sentence, and prisoners who are executed by the state, *all* prisoners are eventually released back to the community. In other words, the other side of the incarceration coin is reentry. **Reentry** is the process of preparing and supporting offenders incarcerated in adult prisons and juvenile correctional facilities as they complete their terms and return to society.

When the reentry process is successful, both the released prisoner and society benefit. The main public benefit of successful offender reentry is increased public safety or

CORRECTIONS IN THE NEWS

5 Years to Life

He's not a prophet. Warren Jeffs no longer claims to be a prophet, but the message he sent his congregation prior to stepping down clearly depicts a man professing his unquestionable connection with God. Jeffs was the leader of a group of religious fundamentalists who engaged in polygamous unions, a practice renounced by the mainstream Church of Jesus Christ of Latter Day Saints over a century ago. According to court transcripts, Jeffs used his authority as head of the Fundamentalist Church of Jesus Christ of Latter Day Saints to arrange marriages that, on occasion, involved an older man marrying a much younger woman.

Testimony revealed that as the leader of this fundamentalist group, Jeffs used religion to forcibly convince a female minor to enter into marriage and then engage in a sexual relationship with her 19-year-old first cousin. This, according to the victim, was against her will, but agreed to only because Jeffs convinced her that to do otherwise would jeopardize her salvation.

In Utah, persons 14 years of age or younger can only grant consent for sex under special circumstances. In this case, those circumstances did not exist. The day after Jeffs's conviction, the victim's husband was charged with rape. Jeffs will face similar charges in Arizona.

Source: CBS News. (2007). *Polygamist sect head gets 5 years to life: Warren Jeffs sentenced for his role in arranged marriage of teenage cousins*. Retrieved April 7, 2008, from http://www.cbsnews.com/stories/2007/11/20/national/main3528126.shtml.

less crime. Other benefits include increased participation in social institutions, such as the labor force, families, neighborhoods, schools, and faith communities. Due to the increased participation in conventional activities, there are social and financial benefits associated with successful reentry.[8] A review of correctional treatment programs that bear on offender reentry yielded an average cost-benefit ratio of nearly 1:35. In other words, for every dollar that is invested in correctional programs that seek to improve the prosocial behavior of ex-offenders, $35 is saved in victimization and related criminal justice system costs.[9]

"Concepts such as 'flourishing,' 'a meaningful life,' and 'offender happiness' are not consistent with the current social and political antipathy toward offenders or with the punitive-retributive model of criminal justice."[3, p. 886]

Population Profile

More than 650,000 prisoners are released from state and federal prisons each year, which equates to nearly 1,800 offenders each day. The current level of prisoner reentry has

For every dollar invested in reentry programs, $35 is saved in victim and criminal justice system costs. In addition, successful reentry means the transition from offender to ex-offender.

CORRECTIONS FOCUS

Racial and Ethnic Differences in the Prevalence of Imprisonment

According to a Bureau of Justice Statistics survey of offenders at year-end 2001, over 5.6 million adults had previously served time in state or federal prisons. The prevalence of imprisonment is not spread evenly across demographic characteristics, however. For instance, about 5 percent of male adult U.S. residents had served time in prison compared to 0.5 percent of females. This tenfold difference reflects offending differences between men and women.

Similar disparities are also seen across racial and ethnic groups. For instance, if current incarceration rates remain unchanged, about 1 in 3 African American males, 1 in 6 Hispanic males, and 1 in 17 White males are expected to be imprisoned in their lifetime. For women, the respective rates are about 1 in 19 African American females, 1 in 50 Hispanic females, and 1 in 118 White females.

These data clearly show that different social groups are not only differentially involved in crime, but differentially affected by imprisonment and ultimately, reentry.

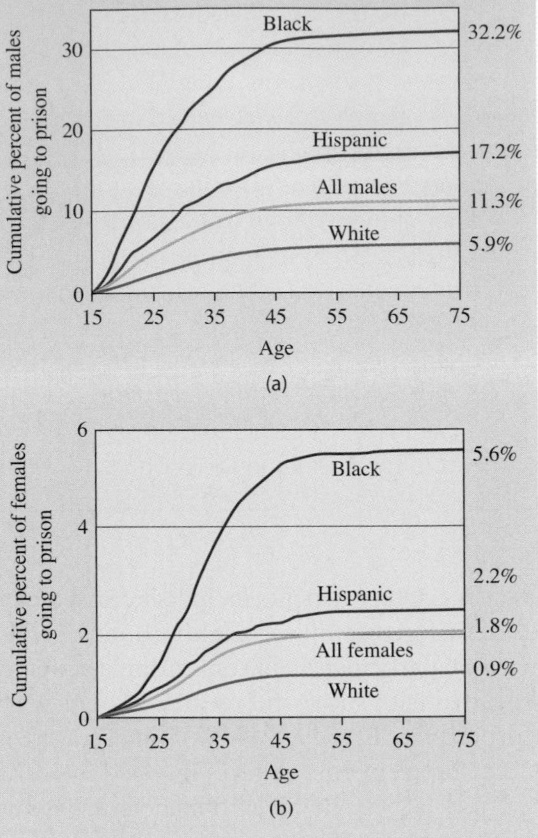

(a) Cumulative Percentage of Males Going to Prison. (b) Cumulative Percentage of Females Going to Prison.

Source: Bonczar, T. P. (2003). *Prevalence of imprisonment in the U.S. population, 1974–2001*. Washington, DC: U.S. Department of Justice, Office of Justice Programs, Bureau of Justice Statistics.

"Reentry has become the new buzzword in correctional reform."[4, p. 314]

increased sixfold since 1970.[10] There are presently 4 million former prisoners and nearly 12 million former felons who live and work in society.[11]

A portrait of the increases in the reentry population can be seen in FIGURE 12-1. In 1980, fewer than 250,000 offenders were on parole. By 2000, the population swelled to nearly 750,000 parolees. Additionally, the annual entries to parole increased steadily between 1980 and 1990 and increased moderately between 1990 and 2000. Indeed, the sheer increases in the parole population rendered reentry a more important correctional issue.

However, the growing size of the reentry population is only part of the reason that it is an important policy issue. The other important consideration is the traditionally high recidivism rates of parolees and other persons released from prison (Chapter 11). FIGURE 12-2 displays the percentages of ex-prisoners who are rearrested within 3 years of their release from confinement. The data are based on Bureau of Justice Statistics research of more than 272,000 persons released from prisons in 15 states in 1983 or 1994. Overall, about 70 percent of former prisoners are rearrested within 3 years. There is some variation in 3-year recidivism rates among the type of offender. For example, about 60 percent of ex-prisoners most recently convicted of felony crimes are rearrested within 3 years. For property offenders, between 70 and 75 percent are rearrested. For drug offenders, between 50 and 65 percent are rearrested. For offenders convicted of public-order offenses, the prevalence of arrest ranged between 55 and 60 percent.[12]

"A high level of stigmatization in the society is one of the very factors that encourages criminal subculture formation by creating populations of outcasts with no stake in conformity, no chance of self-esteem within the terms of conventional society—individuals in search of an alternative culture that allows them self-esteem."[5, p. 102]

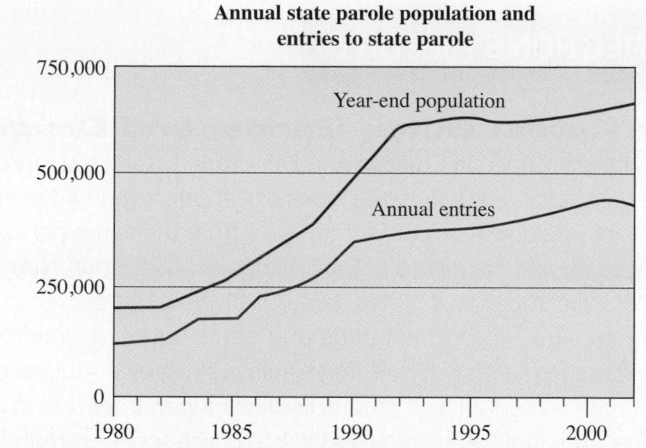

FIGURE 12–1 Prisoners Reentering Society, 1980–2002. *Source*: Bureau of Justice Statistics. (2003). *Reentry trends in the United States*. Retrieved March 1, 2008, from http://www.ojp.usdoj.gov/bjs/reentry/reentry.htm.

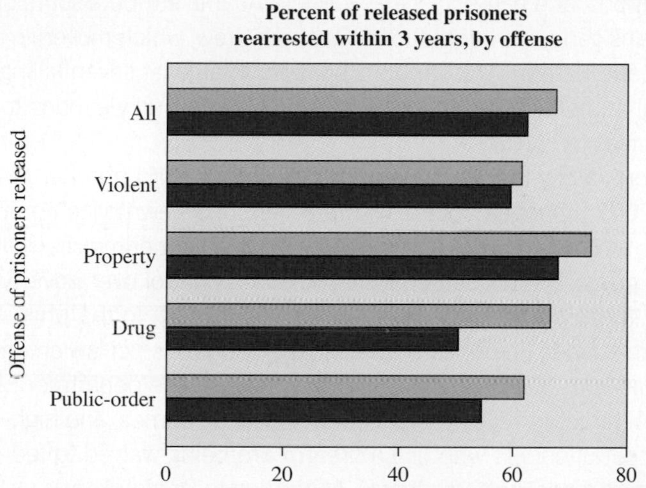

FIGURE 12–2 Recidivism Rates of Former Prisoners, 1983 and 1994. *Source*: Bureau of Justice Statistics. (2003). *Reentry trends in the United States*. Retrieved March 1, 2008, from http://www.ojp.usdoj.gov/bjs/reentry/reentry.htm.

Why is it apparently so difficult for former prisoners to desist from crime and become crime-free, contributing members of society? There are many answers that partially provide explanation, one of which is the risk profile of soon-to-be released inmates. In terms of educational and employment background, marital and family factors, associates and social interaction patterns, psychiatric and substance abuse profile, and community functioning, soon-to-be-released prisoners face many obstacles to succeeding in conventional society.[13] In a national assessment of state and federal prisoners about to be released, Joan Petersilia estimated that 84 percent of state prisoners and 65 percent of federal inmates reported problems in three or more of the aforementioned areas of need. Perhaps most distressing, fewer than 1 percent of state inmates and 3 percent of federal prisoners indicated no problems in any of the areas of need![14]

Policy Background

To address this growing and at-risk population, policy makers recently made offender reentry a priority for not only reducing crime but also collateral problems that often accompany crime. Throughout his administration and specifically in his 2004 State of

"The 'credential' of a criminal record, like educational or professional credentials, constitutes a formal and enduring classification of social status, which can be used to regulate access and opportunity across numerous social, economic, and political domains."[6, p. 4]

CORRECTIONS HISTORY

Murder Rates: Guns, Gangs, and Drugs

Murder rates have dropped in Chicago and New York. In fact, the murder rate in both of these cities has fallen below the rate experienced more than 40 years ago. Murder in New York City was down 17 percent in 2007 from the same period in 2006. The city experienced an all-time high of 2,245 killings in 1990 when New York was titled the murder capital of the United States. Experts attribute this decrease in this particular violent crime to tracking crime trends and crime-targeting practices that involve increasing enforcement efforts by placing significantly greater numbers of police officers in high-crime areas. Chicago credits its declining murder rate to a tough stance on gangs, guns, and drugs. According to Chicago police spokeswoman Monique Bond, "Those three ingredients . . . That's really what leads to random violence."

Murder rates in other large metropolitan cities have not decreased. Baltimore, Atlanta, and Miami continue to experience increases in homicide cases. The reason, according to police sources, could easily be that of gun availability, more specifically assault weapons, and gang violence. Police in Atlanta attribute some of the increase to a New Orleans gang, the International Robbing Crew, which moved in and set up shop after Hurricane Katrina. This group is suspect in at least seven killings in the Atlanta area. Miami authorities attribute the availability of assault weapons to the increase in homicide cases for 2007.

Baltimore, a city that had been on track for a record number of homicide cases as of July 2007, changed course with the help of a new police commissioner. Baltimore police attribute murder and other forms of violent crimes in their city to poverty, drugs, and guns. The police department has no control over poverty levels. But it is addressing these crime-related issues thanks, in part, to the philosophy of its new police commissioner, Frederick H. Bealefeld III, and his strict law enforcement policies. With support from Mayor Shelia Dixon, the city's police department has stepped up enforcement targeting repeat violent offenders, drug crimes, and high-crime neighborhoods. Repeat offenders who use a firearm are being waived to federal court where the sentencing guidelines are stricter. According to Daniel Webster, co-director of the Center for Gun Policy and Research at Johns Hopkins University, "They [Baltimore police] have become more focused, appropriately, on getting illegal guns off the streets and violent gun offenders off the street."

Source: Associated Press. (2008). *Chicago, NYC see lowest number of murders in more than 40 years.* Retrieved October 7, 2008, from http://www.foxnews.com/story/0,2933,318866,00.html.

the Union address, President George W. Bush addressed the importance of reentry as a policy issue and pledged substantial support of programs to support prisoner reentry through the **White House Office of Faith-Based and Community Initiatives.** Launched as the result of the first executive order of President Bush's administration, the White House Office of Faith-Based and Community Initiatives is charged with leading a comprehensive effort to enlist, equip, enable, empower, and expand the work of faith-based and other community organizations. The model has been expanded to 11 federal agencies that are called *Center for Faith-Based and Community Initiatives.*[15] Some of the federal reentry initiatives to stem from these administrative orders include:

- *Ready4Work*: **Ready4Work** is a Department of Labor program that uses faith-based and community organizations to help ex-offenders find work and escape

President Bush's Office of Faith-Based and Community Initiatives is a leader in supporting community organizations to assist in offender reentry.

cycles of recidivism. Founded in 2003, Ready4Work is a $25 million program that emphasizes employment-focused programs that incorporate mentoring, job training, job placement, case management, and other comprehensive transitional services. The program costs $4,500 per offender and serves nearly 5,000 offenders. Ready4Work placed nearly 60 percent of participants into jobs. Fewer than 3 percent of participants were reincarcerated within 6 months of release and fewer than 7 percent were returned to prison within 1 year, which is more than 52 percent lower than ex-offenders not involved in the program.[16] Ready4Work participants who also received mentoring as part of their services were twice as likely to obtain a job and stayed in the program for much longer than nonmentored participants.[17]

- *Prisoner Reentry Initiative*: The **Prisoner Reentry Initiative** is an extension of the Ready4Work program that provides services to 6,250 ex-prisoners annually. To date, more than 10,300 former offenders have enrolled in the Prisoner Reentry Initiative, and more than 6,000 have been placed in jobs. The 1-year postrelease recidivism rate of the Prisoner Reentry Initiative participants is less than half the national average recidivism rate.[18]
- *Mentoring Children of Prisoners Program*: The **Mentoring Children of Prisoners Program** is a program within the Department of Health and Human Services that awards competitive grants to eligible organizations supporting mentoring programs for children with incarcerated parents. To date, more than 70,000 children have been paired with mentors, and the program is on track to provide mentors to 100,000 children with incarcerated parents.[19]
- *Access to Recovery*: **Access to Recovery** is a program within the Substance Abuse and Mental Health Services Administration that provides people seeking drug and alcohol treatment with vouchers to pay for a range of community services. Since 2003, Access to Recovery has served more than 170,000 clients.[20]

The faith-based and community initiative approach is not exclusively a federal enterprise. To date, 35 governors and more than 100 mayors have established faith-based and community organizations to address problems relating to returning prisoners.[21]

At this writing, both houses of Congress have bills in progress to continue support of reentry initiatives. Both the Senate Recidivism Reduction and Second Chance Act of 2007 (S. 1060) and the House of Representatives Second Chance Act of 2007 (H.R. 1593) are written to reauthorize the grant program originally created by the Omnibus Crime Control and Safe Streets Act of 1968.

Serious Violent Offender Reentry Initiative

The most important criminal justice policy effort related to reentry is the **Serious Violent Offender Reentry Initiative (SVORI)**. SVORI is a collaborative federal initiative that addresses reentry outcomes in the areas of criminal justice, employment, education, health, and housing. Due to the multifaceted services involved, SVORI is funded by the United States Department of Justice, United States Department of Education, United States Department of Health and Human Services, United States Department of Housing and Urban Development, and United States Department of Labor. The goal of the SVORI is to reduce recidivism levels among former prisoners and to reduce reincarceration by providing tailored supervision and services to improve the odds for a successful transition to the community.

More than $100 million in funding was awarded to 69 local and state agencies operating 89 programs involved in the SVORI. Of the agencies involved, 45 programs were for adult offenders, 37 programs were for juvenile offenders, and 7 programs served both populations. Most programs served all offenders, but 16 programs were for males only and 1 program served exclusively female offenders.

The SVORI targets prisoners, substance abusers, and offenders with mental illnesses. Another important facet of the initiative is that it specifically targets serious and violent offenders—those who commit the disproportionate share of crimes and the very population that previous programming efforts tended to avoid because of assumptions about the futility of treating serious offenders. As shown in FIGURE 12–3, there are three stages of reentry. First, prison services include initial screening and assessment of prisoners, treatment and education, training, personal development, and reentry planning. During the prison services phase of the SVORI, the goal is to protect and prepare prisoners. Second, community supervision includes assessment and planning, case management, transitional housing, supervision and monitoring, and the service integration of treat-

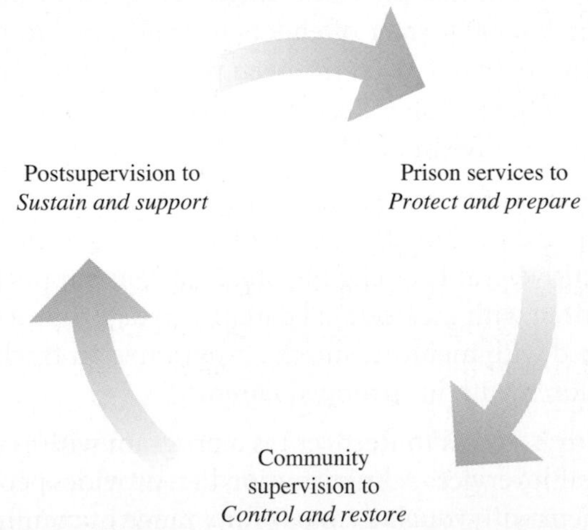

FIGURE 12–3 Stages of Reentry. *Source*: Lattimore, P. and Visher, C. Multi-site Evaluation of the Serious and Violent Offender Reentry Initiative. Modified from https://www.svori-evaluation.org/documents/reports/SVORI_TwoPage_Eval_Overview.pdf. Retrieved March 1, 2008.

ment and aftercare. During the community supervision phase of the SVORI, the goal is to control and restore offenders. Third, postsupervision includes community reintegration activities toward the goal of sustaining and supporting ex-offenders.

To evaluate the effectiveness of the SVORI, the National Institute of Justice selected the Research Triangle Institute (RTI) and Urban Institute to conduct evaluation studies. Initial evaluations indicate that nearly 75 percent of programs using SVORI funds fill service gaps to meet the needs of the ex-prisoners. Among adult programs, the most common areas of focus are employment and community integration. For juveniles, the most common areas of focus are family, community integration, and employment.[22] A major finding is that the SVORI is raising the bar in terms of providing services to prisoners during the later stages of their confinement and early stages of release. Across the board, participants in the SVORI receive more services than prisoners and ex-prisoners who do not participate in the initiative.[23]

Christy Visher, Pamela Lattimore, and their colleagues surveyed 935 men being served by various SVORI programs. They found many areas of need, as evidenced by the following:

- Thirty-six percent were unemployed during the 6 months before going to prison.
- Thirty-eight percent did not have a high school diploma or GED.
- Forty-two percent never held a job for more than 1 year.
- Sixty-nine percent perpetrated violence during the 6 months before going to prison.
- Fifty-nine percent were victims of violence in the 6 months before going to prison.
- Fifty-six percent were victims of violence during incarceration.
- Eighty-four percent reported that their friends had prison experience.
- Eighty-two percent reported that their friends had substance abuse problems.
- Seventy-eight percent reported that their family had prison experience.
- Seventy-two percent reported that their family had substance abuse problems.[24]

Based on this behavioral background, it is expected that an assortment of services are needed to assist released prisoners in the community. In terms of health services, large numbers of SVORI offenders need healthcare insurance, medical and mental health treatment, and alcohol or drug treatment. In terms of family services, more than 60 percent of SVORI participants report a need for parenting classes and nearly half report assistance with child care and child support payments. There is also a host of logistical difficulties for ex-prisoners reentering society. Between 80 and 94 percent of former prisoners indicated need for more education, general financial assistance, obtaining a driver's license, job training, and work.

Fortunately, the SVORI is providing offenders with services to address their many needs. As shown in FIGURE 12-4 and FIGURE 12-5, large percentages of offenders receive services both before being released from custody and after their release into the community. While still incarcerated, many offenders received life-skills training, dental care, and medical services. Nearly all offenders receive a needs and risk assessment and treatment plan. Once in the community, 65 percent received assistance with resume preparation and interviewing skills and 71 percent received job referrals and placement.[25]

Criminological Background

Criminologists often express concern that criminal justice policy makers do not consult their expertise when making policies that target criminal offenders. However, this does

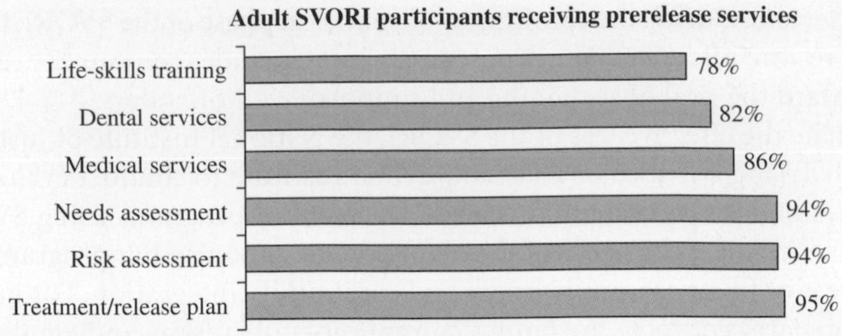

FIGURE 12-4 Prerelease Services of SVORI. *Source*: Visher, C. A., & Lattimore, P. K. (2007). Major study examines prisoners and their reentry needs. *National Institute of Justice Journal, 258*, 30–33.

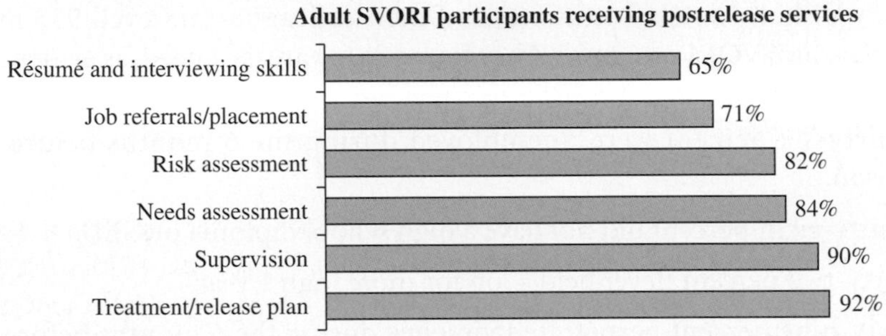

FIGURE 12-5 Postrelease Services of SVORI. *Source*: Visher, C. A., & Lattimore, P. K. (2007). Major study examines prisoners and their reentry needs. *National Institute of Justice Journal, 258*, 30–33.

not apply to reentry. In 1989, John Braithwaite published *Crime, Shame, and Reintegration*, which is a major criminological theory that not only influenced criminological research but also had an effect on policy matters related to crime. Braithwaite focused on the ways that social control policies attempt to punish wrongdoers and focused on **shaming**, which he defined as "all processes of expressing disapproval which have the intention or effect of invoking remorse in the person being shamed and or condemnation by others who become aware of the shaming."[26, p. 9] According to Braithwaite, there are two general types of shaming. **Disintegrative shaming** stigmatizes both the offender and his or her crimes and serves to ostracize criminals from society. Disintegrative shaming is theorized to isolate criminal offenders, force them into criminal subcultures, and help to perpetuate the cycle of crime and punishment. **Reintegrative shaming** punishes and stigmatizes the criminal act while acknowledging the fundamental decency and goodness of the offender. The emphasis is upon a condemnation of the act rather than the actor:

> There is a stick followed by a carrot, condemnation followed by community responses aimed at binding the offender to the social order. In this case, shaming has two faces: It makes certain that the inappropriateness of the misconduct is known to the offender and to all observers, and it presents an opportunity to restore the offender to membership in the group.[27, p. 55]

By focusing on the criminal wrongdoing instead of condemning the person, reintegrative shaming brings the offender "back into the community of law-abiding or respectable citizens through words or gestures of forgiveness or ceremonies to decertify the offender as deviant."[28, pp. 100–101]

Not all persons are equally likely to be shamed. According to the theory, **interdependency** is the extent to which individuals participate in networks where they are dependent on others and others, in turn, are dependent on them. Basically, interdependency refers

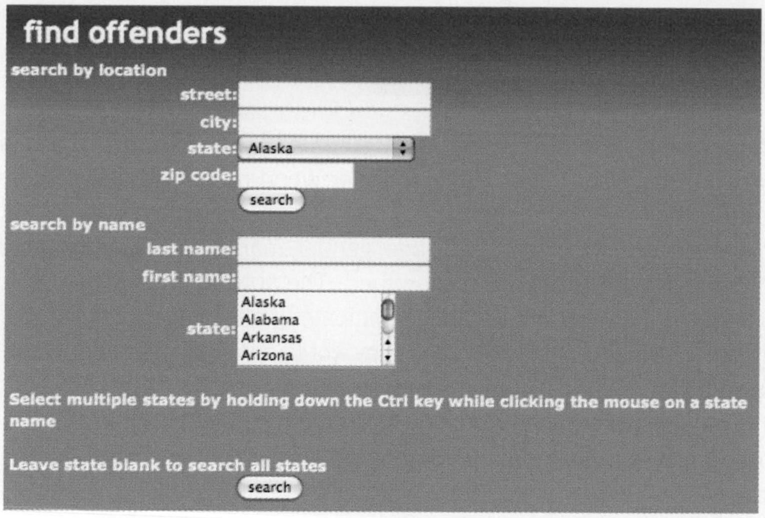

The various correctional policies that target convicted sex offenders are consistent with Braithwaite's idea of disintegrative shaming.

to the degree to which a person is successfully participating in conventional social roles and responsibilities, such as working, maintaining family and other relationships, and participating in other prosocial institutions. Those with high levels of interdependency are the easiest to shame since they are so socially embedded, responsible, and have much to lose. Conversely, people who are unemployed, have few friends or family members, and seem adrift in society are more difficult to shame and therefore more difficult to control. To put the theory in the perspective of offender reentry, ex-prisoners with no stake in conformity are prone for continued crime.

A variety of scholars have evaluated Braithwaite's theory as it relates to diverse groups of criminal offenders from various samples around the world. Kristina Murphy and Nathan Harris surveyed 652 tax violators in Australia and found that offenders who perceived that their case was handled in a reintegrative rather than stigmatizing manner were less likely to subsequently commit tax fraud. Those who stopped committing tax violations also reported fewer feelings of shame and a greater desire to abide by tax laws.[29]

Toni Makkai and John Braithwaite examined changes in compliance with regulations by nursing homes in Australia and found support for the theory.[30] Carter Hay examined the effects of perceived reintegrative shaming used in parental disciplining on self-reported delinquency among American high school students and found that reintegrative shaming in parental disciplining had only a negligible impact on future delinquency.[31] Similarly, Ekaterina Botchkovar and Charles Tittle interviewed citizens from Russia and found that contrary to the theory, both reintegrative and disintegrative forms of shaming resulted in increased antisocial behavior.[32]

Jon Vagg surveyed more than 2,000 youths from Hong Kong and found that disintegrative shaming whereby delinquents were swiftly punished and stigmatized was very effective as a method of social control. In practice, Hong Kong society preferred disintegrative rather than reintegrative shaming.[33] Similar findings on the effects of shaming on recidivism were produced from respondents in Iceland.[34] Lening Zhang and Sheldon Zhang explored the relationship between reintegrative shaming and predatory forms of delinquency using data from the National Youth Survey. Consistent with the theory, they hypothesized that parent and peer disapproval of delinquent behavior and forgiveness of the transgressor would contribute to lower delinquency. The findings were mixed. Parental forgiveness and peer shaming reduced the likelihood of predatory delinquency. However, peer forgiveness significantly increased the likelihood of predatory delinquency.[35]

CORRECTIONS RESEARCH

Willingness to Serve Alternative Sanctions

Correctional researchers David May and Peter Wood recently examined the factors that influence the decision to serve out a prison term or participate in an alternative program. Variables such as education, age, gender, marital status, length of sentence, and the alternative sanctions were examined. The authors found that as education levels increased, so did willingness to participate in alternative programs. However, prisoners with more education indicated they would agree to fewer months in alternative programs than did those inmates with less education. The authors caution that it is possible inmates with more education assessed the risk of violating program rules, and subsequently the likelihood of violating program rules, against the time spent in the program when responding to this question.

Interestingly, young inmates are more willing to participate in alternative programs than are their older counterparts. The authors' initial interpretation of this finding is that it may be an indication that older inmates are accustomed to prison life and find it a more comfortable option. The next variable, gender, had no significant impact on the inmate's decision to select an alternative sanction, but it did influence the inmates' perception of the number of months they would agree to serve if it meant avoiding a stay in prison. As a function of gender, it was learned that women were willing to serve more time in an alternative program instead of going to prison than were men. Not surprisingly, married inmates were more likely to agree to an alternative program than were those inmates who were not married. But this willingness persisted only for probation and did not include boot camp programs. Finally, findings from this study indicate inmates who have served more time in prison were less likely to opt for an alternative program.

Source: May, D. C., & Wood, P. B. (2005). What influences offenders' willingness to serve alternative sanctions? *Prison Journal, 85,* 145–167.

As described earlier, Braithwaite's theory has also found its way into criminal justice practice. Lawrence Sherman and his colleagues conducted experiments among Australian offenders that applied reintegrative shaming principles to 1,300 violent offenders, drunk drivers, adolescent property offenders, and shoplifters. The offenders were randomly assigned to traditional court or to reintegrative conferences as a formal response to their crime. The reintegrative conferences significantly reduced recidivism among violent offenders and drunk drivers but not among the other two groups.[36–37] Kenneth Jensen and Stephen Gibbons reported that shame is a powerful emotion that can help serious delinquents, even career criminals, to repudiate their criminal lifestyle, desist from crime, and rejoin conventional society.[38] Overall, the logic of reintegration theory forms the basis for many offender reentry programs that are reviewed later in this chapter.

Braithwaite's theory and the criminological response to it clearly favor reintegrative shaming as a humanistic, reasoned attempt to help former prisoners connect to conventional society. In contrast, disintegrative shaming is construed as overly punitive, stigmatizing, and probably counterproductive if it serves to isolate and alienate former prisoners and perhaps motivate them to reoffend. An interesting exception to this rule pertains to sex offenders, especially persons convicted of sexually based crimes against children. The general public is fearful of the recidivism risks that sex offenders pose and generally supports unique social control policies that target sex offenders, such as

CORRECTIONS IN THE NEWS

Would-Be Assassin Freed After Serving 30 Years

In 1977, Sara Jane Moore was found guilty and sentenced to life in prison for her unsuccessful attempt to assassinate then-President Gerald Ford in 1975. Moore, who now says she was blinded by her radical political views, was within 40 feet of the president when she made her assassination attempt. If it had not been for the actions of a disabled Marine veteran, Oliver Sipple, who observed Moore take aim with her .38-caliber revolver and reacted instantly by pushing Moore's arm upward, President Ford might have been fatally wounded.

Moore's response to the incident, "I am very glad I did not succeed. I know that it was wrong to try." According to Moore, her attempt on the president's life was based in part on her belief that the government had declared war on the left. These beliefs may have been ignited through her association with the Symbionese Liberation Army, a domestic terrorist group responsible for the kidnapping of Patty Hearst, the daughter of millionaire Randolph Hearst, in 1974. Moore eventually became involved with radical leftists, ex-convicts, and other extremists. In an interesting twist, Moore began working for the FBI as a confidential informant during her involvement with the Symbionese Liberation Army. But approximately 4 months prior to the assassination attempt, the FBI ended its working relationship with Moore. In 1977, Moore was sent to a West Virginia women's prison. Two years later, she escaped; several hours after her escape she was recaptured and returned to prison. She was released in December 2007 at age 77.

Source: Associated Press. (2008). *Would-be assassin of President Ford freed.* Retrieved October 7, 2008, from http://www.msnbc.msn.com/id/22454599/.

community notification or sex offender registries and more importantly from a reentry perspective, residency restriction laws. **Residency restrictions laws** restrict where sex offenders can live; these restrictions range from 1,000 to 2,500 feet from schools, parks, day care centers, bus stops, or other places where children congregate. To date, 22 states have residency restriction laws barring sex offenders from living in various places in the community.[39]

Whether residency restriction laws are effective depends on whether one invests more heavily in public safety or more heavily in the life chances of convicted sex offenders. Paul Zandbergen and Timothy Hart studied sex offenders in Orange County, Florida, using geographic information systems technology. They found that the laws severely curtailed where sex offenders could live, with bus stops exerting the greatest amount of

Residency restriction laws limit how close to schools, parks, and places where children congregate sex offenders can live. The laws are controversial and their effectiveness has been questioned.

restriction on sex offender access to housing. Increasing the exclusionary area from 1,000 to 2,500 feet had little effect, and the most available housing was in sparsely populated rural areas.[40]

Jill Levenson and Leo Cotter interviewed 135 sex offenders and found that 22 percent had to move out of their home because of the laws, 57 percent reported difficulty finding housing, 48 percent reported financial suffering, and 60 percent reported emotional suffering.[41] These conditions can lead to homelessness and increased social isolation among sex offenders. To the degree that residency restrictions place additional burden, stress, and isolation on sex offenders, it is possible that the laws can produce the unintended consequence of pushing offenders to reoffend out of desperation over their living situation. Another perspective is that each individual offender makes the personal choice to reoffend or not irrespective of the policies or restrictions that the law imposes. Still another perspective is that residency restriction laws are working exactly as planned and theorized by Braithwaite. They are punitive and intended to shame the offender for his or her criminal conduct. More pointedly, they are designed to ostracize and isolate ex-prisoners who society does not want to be a part of their community.

Reentry and Societal Issues

Due to relatively recent changes in sentencing guidelines and correctional policies, prisoners serve generally lengthier prison terms. As a consequence, the difficulty of reentry is likely greater than among previous cohorts of prisoners. Joan Petersilia noted:

> Returning prisoners will have served longer prison sentences than in the past, be more disconnected from family and friends, have a higher prevalence of untreated substance abuse and mental illness, and be less educated and employable than their predecessors. Legal and practical barriers facing ex-offenders have also increased, affecting their employment, housing, and welfare eligibility. Without help, many released inmates quickly return to crime.[42]

The assorted societal issues that are impacted by the incarceration and return of prisoners are known as **collateral consequences of imprisonment**. These collateral consequences of imprisonment can contribute to related social problems and make reentry difficult for society at large and offenders. Although reentry is a difficult challenge, there is evidence that the general public supports efforts to help former prisoners turn their lives around and desist from crime. Barry Krisberg and Susan Marchionna of the National Council on Crime and Delinquency reported on the results of a national public opinion poll of voter attitudes toward prisoner rehabilitation and reentry policies. They found:

- Seventy-four percent of Americans expressed concern about crime in their community.
- Seventy-nine percent of Americans were fearful about the annual release of approximately 650,000 prisoners.
- By an eight to one margin, Americans favor rehabilitation services for prisoners as opposed to a punishment-only system.
- Seventy percent of Americans favored reentry services both during confinement and after release.
- Only 14 percent of Americans thought that released prisoners were less likely to commit new crimes.
- Thirty-one percent of Americans thought that offenders were more likely to commit crime.

- Fifty-five percent of Americans thought that offenders were equally likely to reoffend.
- Seventy-eight percent of Americans supported legislation to support offender reentry.[43]

What these data mean is that Americans tend to have a balanced understanding of the challenges posed by returning prisoners. Although they overwhelmingly favor rehabilitation and providing additional opportunities for ex-offenders, the general public has a sobering assessment of the risks that offenders pose to public safety. These and other important societal issues are explored next.

Crime and Violence

Among the most obvious collateral problems of returning prisoners is their continued criminal involvement and threats to public safety. In many cases, offender reentry refers to a returning criminal rather than a reformed criminal.[44] At least, this is largely the sentiment of the American public. Nearly 80 percent of Americans are genuinely concerned or fearful about the specter of nearly 1,800 prisoners being released from prison each day.[45] Released prisoners are extremely likely to reengage in criminal activity after their release. Many ex-prisoners have extensive criminal histories, and their criminal backgrounds are often difficult to overcome. Still others do not want to desist from crime and simply see crime and incarceration as a way of life. As noted by Peter Wood, "the social and non-social reinforcements offered by doing crime and 24/7 contact with other offenders while incarcerated increase the likelihood of re-offending."[46, p. 20]

Perhaps the clearest evidence of the likelihood of continued crime and violence by ex-prisoners stems from a study of nearly 250,000 prisoners released from institutions in 13 states. Richard Rosenfeld and his colleagues produced several findings that suggest that returning prisoners constitute a major threat to public safety based on their recidivism patterns after release. For instance:

- Arrest frequencies among ex-prisoners are between *30 and 45 times higher* than those for the general population.
- The arrest ratio (released prisoners compared to the general population) for violent crime is 26:1.
- The arrest ratio (released prisoners compared to the general population) for property crime is 18:1.
- The arrest ratio (released prisoners compared to the general population) for drug crime is 23:1.
- Approximately 20 percent of all adults arrested in the United States are recently released prisoners.

Based on these analyses, Rosenfeld and his colleagues concluded that "[t]he nation faces a growing threat to public safety not simply from the escalating number of ex-prisoners reentering the community but from the growing ratio of persons exiting to those entering prison."[47, p. 102]

The Urban Institute's *Returning Home: Understanding the Challenges of Prisoner Reentry,* which is a survey of released prisoners across the United States, also sheds light on the threats to public safety posed by returning prisoners. By their own admission, released prisoners have extensive criminal histories that serve as a formidable barrier to reentry. For instance, 80 percent of those admitted to and released from the Philadelphia prison system had previously been incarcerated there. In Massachusetts, a staggering 99 percent of offenders released from the Department of Corrections in 2002 had previously been confined in a Massachusetts jail or prison.[48]

CORRECTIONS FOCUS

Reentry for High-Risk Youth Offenders: A Strategy for Success

Reentry or intensive aftercare is a significant problem that, if handled effectively, can reduce the risk of recidivism in high-risk youth offenders. Transitioning a high-risk youth offender from a supervised and sometimes highly structured correctional setting to an unstructured home/community environment without placing the offender at risk to fail must be done one small step at a time!

First, the offender's readiness and suitability for release must be determined prior to release. The most successful programs use limited, but well-calculated efforts to reacquaint offenders with their community. These programs are designed to establish initial contact with parents outside the correctional setting, school systems, and potential employers.

Then comes the formal reentry—a step prior to final community placement. High-risk youth offenders are placed in a transitional setting on a short-term basis, usually in a halfway house located close to the institution. During the offenders' stay, staff has the opportunity to work with the offenders and assist them with plans for completing the transition to independent living. It is imperative at this point that all links to community resources be verified by the staff. The greater the degree of idleness upon release, the greater the likelihood the offender will become involved in some form of criminal activity. A vital element in this step of the process is the intense monitoring relationship between staff and offender. It's not uncommon for high-risk offenders in transition to be required to abide by curfew restrictions, be electronically monitored, and to submit to scheduled and unscheduled drug and alcohol testing. These requirements are generally phased out over time and as a reward for good behavior.

Once the community placement stage is reached, the success of the program is dependent on the offender's ability to adjust to the community setting, the offender's participation in behavioral modification programs, employment, trade and vocational training programs, the offender's family, and the efforts of his or her case manager to assist and monitor the transitioning offender. The key element in this equation is far too often the structure of the offender's family. Unfortunately, in many cases, the structure of a high-risk offender's family can best be described as dysfunctional. This presents a serious but not insurmountable obstacle to success. As with every offender program, the primary goal is to reduce recidivism. What works and what doesn't all depends on a multitude of factors, not the least of which is the offender.

Source: Gies, S. V. (2003). *Aftercare services*. Washington, DC: U.S. Department of Justice, Office of Justice Programs, Office of Juvenile Justice and Delinquency Prevention.

The *Returning Home* respondents who were rearrested after they were released were those with more extensive criminal and substance use histories and were also more likely to have used drugs immediately before their most recent prison sentence. Chronic offenders were rather quickly rearrested and resentenced to prison. For example, among Illinois offenders who were part of the reentry program, 22 percent were reconvicted of a crime within 11 months of release. In Maryland, 32 percent of offenders were rearrested within 6 months of release.[49]

Somewhat more positive reentry outcomes are found among juvenile offenders. For instance, He Len Chung and his colleagues studied reentry among 413 serious juvenile delinquents released from confinement in Philadelphia, Pennsylvania, and Phoenix, Arizona. All youths were involved in an intensive aftercare component, which is the juvenile justice system equivalent of parole. During the first 3 months of release, juveniles reported approximately 13 treatment contacts from school or other treatment providers per month. Within 3 months of release, 65 percent of former delinquents had no contact with the justice system. Unfortunately, 35 percent of the offenders were back in contact with the juvenile justice system; more chronic delinquents were the most likely to have subsequent contacts. More than 70 percent reported regular school attendance and 42 percent reported working at least 21 hours per week. Overall, 80 percent of participants were engaged in school or work.[50]

Community

In addition to crime and violence, returning prisoners also have an effect on the communities to which they return. It is important to note, however, that ex-prisoners do not return to the community in either a random or equitable way. A handful of cities and a handful of neighborhoods within the nation's largest cities receive a disproportionate amount of returning prisoners. For example, more than 50 percent of all Illinois offenders released from prison return to Chicago. In Maryland, more than 50 percent of prisoners return to Baltimore. In Texas, about 25 percent of prisoners return to Houston. In New Jersey, two counties receive nearly 35 percent of all released prisoners. In Idaho, five counties receive nearly 75 percent of all returning prisoners.

At the neighborhood level, 8 percent of Chicago neighborhoods receive 34 percent of all prisoners. In Massachusetts, almost 50 percent of returning prisoners go to fewer than 10 percent of Boston's block groups or neighborhoods. A small group of neighborhoods in Richmond receive approximately 50 percent of all returning prisoners in Virginia, and in Michigan, 7 percent of zip codes in the Detroit-area receive more than 41 percent of the total returning prisoners.[51]

Neighborhoods that receive high volumes of returning prisoners are characterized by social and economic disadvantages, including high levels of unemployment, families living below the federal poverty line, vice, disorder, and crime. Dina Rose and Todd Clear devised the concept of **coercive mobility**, which includes the dual processes of mass incarceration and reentry that disrupt the social networks of disadvantaged communities and lead to increased social problems. The effects of incarceration and reentry disrupt the economic structure of the neighborhood, weaken family stability and parental capacity, and undermine conventional or prosocial beliefs within the neighborhood.[52–53]

Coercive mobility creates a host of interrelated reentry problems. Rose and Clear interviewed ex-offenders and found that rather than work in menial, low-paying jobs, some ex-prisoners opted for unemployment entitlements and relied on family members for financial assistance, which created strain for the family. In turn, financial strain reduces the level of civic participation and also can undermine the ability for successful association activities, resulting in lower social capital. Another consequence of the coerced placement of many unemployed felons into neighborhoods is an increase in men congregating on street corners or in front of local stores. This results in fewer legitimate customers and discourages outside investors from establishing businesses in places where many ex-prisoners appear to be loitering and poised to get into trouble.[54]

Coercive mobility means that the dual processes of mass incarceration and reentry disrupt social networks in disadvantaged communities and lead to additional social problems.

Perhaps most importantly from a criminological perspective, coercive mobility disrupts patterns of social interaction, weakens the social organization of communities, and erodes the stigma of criminal justice system involvement. In neighborhoods where large numbers of residents are routinely arrested, incarcerated, and then released, it is normative to have correctional involvement. These conditions lead to increased crime and violence. This means that areas characterized by **concentrated disadvantage** or neighborhoods with extreme poverty, racial segregation, and high crime rates are in an impossible situation. They have many residents leave the community via imprisonment, which after a certain point reduces community cohesiveness and increases crime. These neighborhoods then must deal with returning prisoners—many of whom have multiple risk factors for continued criminal involvement.[55–56]

Public Health

An important byproduct of criminal violence is the threat to public health. A variety of scholars have studied the public health risks that are posed by former prisoners after they return home. Often, health risks of ex-prisoners are made worse by other areas of need. For example, many ex-prisoners have little in the way of social support to provide temporary housing for them after release. In this way, some prisoners leave prison, an environment where they had shelter and medical services, for the street, where they have neither shelter nor health services. In the event that prisoners have serious medical needs, homelessness serves to make them worse.[57]

In addition, chronic offenders who are recurrently incarcerated and released are significantly likely to engage in risky, unhealthy lifestyles characterized by substance abuse, smoking, drinking, illicit sexual behavior, and unsafe driving. Persistent offenders are also more likely to develop cardiovascular diseases and psychological distress.[58] In part because of these risky lifestyles, former prisoners are disproportionately responsible for an array of infectious disease in the United States. For instance, between 20 and 26 percent of those infected with HIV, between 29 and 43 percent of those infected with Hepatitis C, and 40 percent of those with tuberculosis have recently been incarcerated.[59]

Ingrid Binswanger and her colleagues studied more than 30,000 inmates released from prisons in Washington state and found that the mortality rate of former prisoners was nearly four times higher than the general population. The disparities between former prisoners and the general public are more pronounced during the first 2 weeks after release from prison. During the first 14 days of release from custody, the risk of death among former prisoners was nearly *13 times* higher than among other state residents. The leading causes of death of former prisoners were drug overdose, cardiovascular disease, homicide, and suicide.[60] Similarly, Alex Piquero and his colleagues studied homicide victimization risk among nearly 4,000 persons released from the California Youth Authority. They found an elevated risk of being murdered among former prisoners. Among the parolee population, those with very low levels of self-control were about 170 percent more likely than offenders with greater self-control to be murdered.[61] This suggests that the interpersonal style and personality of former prisoners often lends itself to confrontation, violence, and death.

Employment

One of the foremost indicators of an individual's attachment to and investment in conventional society is work. Work provides income and benefits so that people can become financially independent, allows one to feel as if he or she is contributing to society, and keeps people busy so there is less time to get into trouble. For these reasons, obtaining a job and maintaining that job go a long way in helping ex-prisoners reconnect to society.

The importance of work to ex-prisoners is apparent in The Urban Institute's *Returning Home: Understanding the Challenges of Prisoner Reentry,* which is a survey of released prisoners in Maryland, Illinois, Ohio, and Texas. The survey indicates the following:

- Ex-prisoners felt that having a job would help them stay clean and out of prison, yet only about 20 percent of them had secured a job immediately upon release.
- Although ex-prisoners overwhelmingly report that job training is critical to their reentry, only 1–25 percent of offenders in various states actually participate in employment readiness programs while in prison.
- Ex-prisoners who worked while incarcerated were more likely to have full-time employment in the weeks immediately after release.
- Ex-prisoners who worked upon reentry were less likely to commit drug, property, and violent crimes.
- Ex-prisoners who worked upon reentry were less likely to be reincarcerated.[62]

Employer reluctance in hiring ex-prisoners may partially explain high unemployment among ex-offenders. Devah Pager recently found that 30 to 50 percent of ex-prisoners are less likely than nonoffenders to be considered for work by employers, suggesting that a prison sentence creates a major obstacle. More importantly, Pager found that African American ex-offenders are more than three times less likely than White ex-offenders to be called back by employers after an initial job interview. In fact, White ex-offenders received more favorable treatment from employers than African Americans *without* criminal records in her study.[63] Pager and Lincoln Quillian found that even if employers indicate that they are willing to hire former prisoners, in practice they do not.[64] Others argue that employer reluctance to hire ex-prisoners is not racilly discriminatory but instead reflects genuine concerns about the abilities of the at-risk offender population. For instance, Satoshi Kanazawa found that racial differences in work outcomes such as pay did not exist once cognitive abilities were considered. In addition, Kanazawa criticized Pager's work because it did not consider the baseline differences between Whites and African Americans in criminal history, which would partially explain why employers appeared discriminatory by race.[65]

Irrespective of whether employers discriminate against ex-offenders, there is no question that ex-prisoners must face stigmatizing effects of their criminal past—but there are additional work-related issues that affect their reentry. Bruce Western and his colleagues estimated that incarceration creates a 10- to 30-percent penalty on wages and earnings.[66] A comparatively low salary can motivate offenders to pursue additional funds from illegal methods, such as selling drugs. In addition, time spent in prison can erode an offender's job skills and marketability, which, based on the profile of prisoners, was likely low to begin with. Imprisonment precludes the ability of offenders to work at a specific job for an extended period of time. This means that it takes even longer to move up the ranks and achieve higher salary when offenders must start at lower-end jobs upon reentry. In sum, the combined effects of their own poor work histories, low educational attainment, reduced work skills and marketability, the stigma of being an ex-prisoner, and various concerns from employers result in dire employment prospects for many reentering offenders.[67]

Family

Of all of the unintended consequences of felony offenders cycling in and out of prison, the short- and long-term damage to their families, particularly their children, is probably the most serious. As shown in TABLE 12-1, parents are critical to the healthy social and cognitive development of their children. When parents are incarcerated, the negative effects are many. For instance, parent-child separation occurring during infancy can lead

TABLE 12-1 Negative Effects of Parental Incarceration/Release on Child Development

Developmental Stage	Negative Effects
Infancy	Impaired parent–child bonding
Early childhood	Anxiety, developmental regression, stress, trauma
Middle childhood	Trauma, stress, impaired reactive behaviors
Early adolescence	Rejection of limits on behavior, trauma-reactive behaviors
Late adolescence	Premature termination of parent–child relationship, intergenerational crime and incarceration

Source: Modified from Gabel, K., & Johnston, D. (Eds.). (1997). *Children of incarcerated parents.* Lanham, MD: Lexington Books.

to impaired bonding between parent and child. When parents are in prison, on parole, back in prison, or living with the demands of a conditional sentence, it is very difficult to effectively bond with their children. Throughout childhood and adolescence, the processes of incarceration and reentry (and the likelihood of future incarceration) wreak havoc on child development. These effects are especially pronounced when mothers are separated from their children as a result of their confinement.[68]

In fact, researchers found that children of incarcerated parents are significantly at risk for sadness and depression, aggression, withdrawn behavior, truancy and school failure, other psychiatric problems, and delinquency.[69–70] Joseph Murray and David Farrington found that children whose parents were incarcerated and sporadically reentered society were nearly four times more likely to be adult offenders themselves compared to children whose parents were not incarcerated. The long-term effects of parental incarceration, separation, and reentry have exerted negative effects on persons up to nearly age 50.[71–72]

Based on data from the National Longitudinal Survey of Youth, Beth Huebner and Regan Gustafson found that children of incarcerated mothers were at least 75 percent more likely to become involved in the criminal justice system compared to children whose mothers had not been incarcerated.[73] Interestingly, the long-term effects of parental incarceration were not observed based on data from a Swedish birth cohort of more than 15,000, which the authors attribute to more reintegration-friendly policies and cultural practices in Sweden compared to England and the United States.[74]

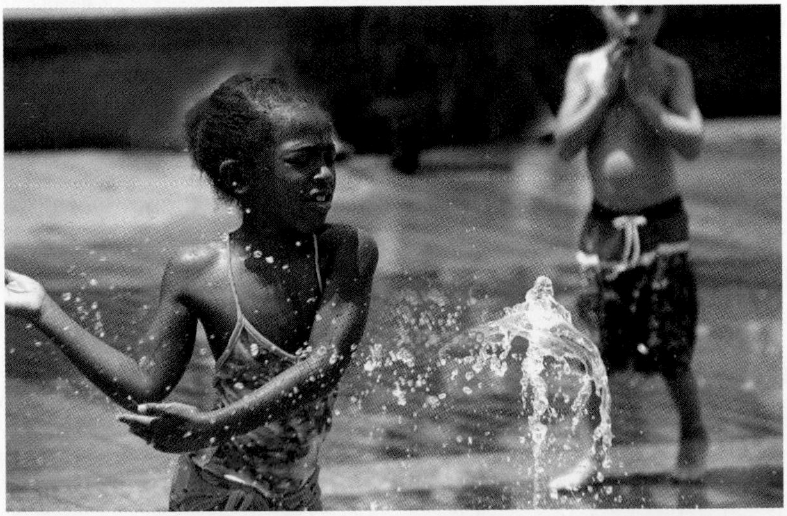

Research has found that children of incarcerated mothers are 75 percent more likely to become involved in the criminal justice system than children whose mothers were not in prison.

CORRECTIONS RESEARCH

Criminally Involved, Drug-Using Mothers

There exists a drug-consuming, transient, undereducated, and criminally involved group of women without the necessary resources to support their children. In a study of criminally involved, drug-using mothers, Bogart et al. found women with these demographics changed residences nearly every 7 months, generally to live with someone new. Researchers also found these women were undereducated and thus not likely to find gainful employment and rarely had a significant other they could depend on for financial assistance. Participants in this study also reported using some type of illegal drug on average every other day in the past 30 days—and more than half of the sample acknowledged criminal involvement in a variety of crimes during the previous 6 months.

Interestingly, researchers found an ethnic-racial difference within the cohort of criminally involved, drug-using mothers for those who do and those who do not have custody of their children. Bogart et al. learned that Hispanic, Native American, and interracial mothers were more likely than Caucasian and African American women to have custody of their biological children. This finding contradicts early research on this topic. The authors suggest one possible explanation is age. African American mothers were the oldest and Caucasian mothers were the third oldest subgroups within this cohort of five age groups.

Women who cared for their children in this sample reported using alcohol, marijuana, crack, and cocaine. Use of marijuana was nearly twice that for women with children than for women without children—but women without children report twice the use of drugs that require injection such as speedballs, a combination of cocaine and heroin—a mixture often used by women working as prostitutes.

The study also revealed that this group of women was poverty stricken, addicted to chemical substances, and likely to be rearrested for various crimes. The authors recommend as one potential solution for this problem, prison-based treatment programs that involve vocational education and parenting classes. They also suggest providing safe and secure housing as an aftercare intervention in efforts to replace punishment with more effective forms of rehabilitation.

Source: Bogart, J. G., Stevens, S. J., Hill, R. J. & Estrada, B. D. (2005). Criminally involved drug-using mothers: The need for system change. *Prison Journal, 85*, 65–82.

Susan Phillips and her colleagues studied more than 1,000 children from the Great Smoky Mountains study to explore how parental criminal justice involvements, such as arrest, incarceration, and release from confinement affected the social development of their children. The results were staggering. Among children whose parent or parental-figure cycles in and out of prison:

- Eighty-seven percent had parents with substance abuse problems, mental illness, or low educational attainment.
- Thirty-eight percent had been in foster care, single-parent homes, or homes with four or more children.
- Thirty-eight percent lived in poverty.
- Forty-five percent experienced some type of severe economic strain.
- Fourteen percent had been abused or experienced inadequate care.

- Nineteen percent had moved residences four or more times in a 5-year period.
- Twenty-six percent had a new parent figure enter the household.
- Twenty-six percent had experienced some type of family instability.[75]

Of course, children are not the only family members negatively affected by incarceration and reentry. Other family members and significant others of former prisoners are also disadvantaged by their relative's incarceration experience. Many family members avoid visiting relatives in prison because of the distance between home and prison, transportation issues, inability to get time off work, and other reasons. Family members also must face economic hardships in part caused by having the other adult confined and thus unemployed for long periods of time. Rebecca Naser and Christy Visher interviewed 247 family members of prisoners in four states and found high rates of unemployment, public assistance, and other hardships among the families. Returning prisoners also increase anxiety among family members as many former prisoners quickly resume criminal activity and drug use, which further alienates and at times endangers their families.[76]

Still another risk posed by offender reentry relates to the serious health risks that former prisoners pose to their family members. For instance, many female ex-offenders have significant histories of abuse at the hands of their significant others. For this reason, an important component of reentry among women is the development of independence to avoid patterns of victimization and exploitation.[77] In addition, the rates of HIV infection among prisoners are six times higher than rates among the general population, which means that spouses or other intimate partners of returning prisoners face health risks stemming from exposure that could have occurred behind bars.[78] Finally, offender reentry poses an obvious but often unacknowledged problem for families: the offenders themselves. Many families enjoy reprieves from the antisocial and often violent behavior of family members while they are incarcerated. Once the offenders are released, so too are the interpersonal problems, abuse, and violence that they carry with them.

Civic Participation

One of the most detrimental consequences of being a convicted felon is the loss of various legal and civic rights—a process known as **civil death**. Civil death has long historical roots. For instance, the ancient Greeks either temporarily or permanently restricted the legal rights of citizens convicted of various crimes. These persons were described as *atimia,* which roughly translates to *outlaws*. The ancient Romans imposed the punishment of *infamia* (comparable to infamy), which was disgrace and loss of civic rights upon criminal conviction.[79] There are a host of legal rights that are affected by felony conviction or prisoner status. As shown in TABLE 12–2, ex-prisoners are often barred from voting, from serving on juries or holding public office, from owning firearms, and from having access to jobs, financial aid for higher education, and public housing. Many bans on civic participation, such as employment restrictions against persons convicted of sex offenses against children, are perfectly justified in the interest of public safety. For the bulk of offenders who are not violent, however, long-term bans on civic participation could be counterproductive.[80] It is likely that these legal restrictions negatively impact ex-prisoners' ability to fully reconnect to society.

Wendy Pogorzelski and her colleagues examined the extent of legal barriers to reentry among more than 3,000 ex-prisoners in New Jersey, all of whom had some diagnosed Axis I mental disorder, such as schizophrenia, major depression, bipolar disorder, psychotic disorder, etc. Across a range of domains, ex-prisoners face an assortment of restrictions that can impede their successful reentry to society. For instance:

- Depending on the type of crime for which they were convicted, ex-prisoners in New Jersey are statutorily banned from 22 categories of employment, including

TABLE 12-2 Barriers to Civic Participation

Jury service	47 states restrict right to serve on a jury
Privacy	50 states mandate registration of sex offenders
Public assistance	17 states permanently deny benefits for certain drug offenders
Public housing	47 states permit restrictions on access to public housing
Parental rights	48 states allow for termination of parental rights for certain offenses
Marital dissolution	20 states consider criminal conviction as grounds for dissolution
Immigration status	50 states can deport resident aliens for criminal offenses
Voting	48 states deny right to vote to current prisoners
Public office	40 states restrict the right to hold public office
Financial aid	50 states restrict aid for drug offenders
Firearms	43 states have restrictions on handgun ownership

Source: Modified from Uggen, C., Manza, J., & Thompson, M. (2006). Citizenship, democracy, and the civic reintegration of criminal offenders. *Annals of the American Academy of Political and Social Science, 605,* 281–310.

public sector jobs, public schools, housing authorities, airports, banks, and places where alcohol is served or sold retail.

- Those with drug distribution convictions have lifetime restrictions on their eligibility for public assistance.
- Offenders are barred from serving on juries, and those on parole are ineligible to vote.
- There are lifetime restrictions on housing, including ineligibility for public housing if they have a history of violence.
- For any conviction, an offender's admission to college or university is at the discretion of the institution, and offenders can be temporarily or permanently barred from receiving financial aid.
- For some ex-offenders, there is a lifetime ban on adoption and foster care, and child custody rights can be terminated for felony convictions.[81]

One of the most controversial issues surrounding the civic participation of convicted felons and ex-prisoners is the right to vote. **Felon disenfranchisement** refers to the denial of voting rights of persons with various criminal justice systems statuses. The logic behind these laws is that by engaging in felonious behavior, prisoners and ex-prisoners forfeit some of the most basic rights and privileges held by adults in the United States.

The harshness and frequency of disenfranchisement laws depends on the criminal justice status of the offender. For instance, nearly all states bar prisoners from voting in part because prison is the most serious punishment regularly imposed and in part for the logistical problems posed by confinement. About 70 percent of states disenfranchise parolees and about 60 percent of states disenfranchise probationers. Approximately 30 percent of states disenfranchise former felons who are not currently supervised by the criminal justice system.[82]

Jeff Manza and Chris Uggen argue that the disenfranchisement of felons and ex-felons is a serious threat to American democracy and a symbolic barrier to reentry for former prisoners. FIGURE 12-6 also shows that today's laws are generally more lenient than they have traditionally been. Once offenders have successfully completed their sentence (prison, parole, or probation), they can vote in more than 70 percent of states. Finally, it is unclear how many ex-prisoners would vote in elections in the first place. Manza and

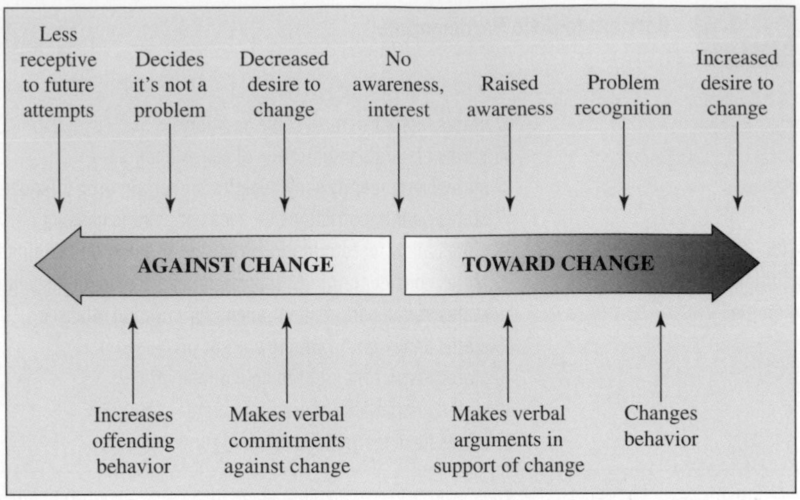

FIGURE 12–6 Offender Change and Reentry. *Source*: Walters, S. T., Clark, M. D., Gingerich, R., & Meltzer, M. L. (2007). *Motivating offenders to change: A guide for probation and parole.* Washington, DC: National Institute of Corrections.

Uggen estimated that between 20 and 25 percent of felons would vote in midterm elections and between 30 and 40 percent would vote in presidential elections. Both estimates are about 20 percent below the overall national turnout in these elections. However, these are simply estimates based upon demographic characteristics that generally match the reentry population.[83] Given all of the challenges that ex-prisoners have in terms of housing, health care, work, family responsibilities, treatment, and complying with parole, it is probable that voting is not among the most important issues in the lives of ex-offenders. For the large proportion of former prisoners who have not desisted from crime and continue to abuse substances and pursue a criminal lifestyle, voting has probably never been an issue.

It is clear that ex-prisoners contribute to a host of important social problems. In this way, an offender's decision to desist from crime or to continue his or her criminal career not only affects the individual offender, but that offender's family, community, and society. Given the criminal histories of many returning prisoners, the road to successful reentry is often a steep, uphill climb, but successful reentry is not impossible. The last section of this chapter reviews the conditions and characteristics of reentry programs that have been successful and also highlights innovative and exciting programs that help returning offenders each day.

What Works in Reentry Programs

A variety of conditions help to increase the overall effectiveness of reentry programs. For instance, because reentry is a process and not a discrete event where an offender simply decides that he or she will transform from offender to respectable citizen (recall Figure 12–3), programs work best when they extend the reentry process to include (1) an institutional component that begins at least 6 months prior to release, (2) a structured reentry phase that occurs before release and about 1 month after release, and (3) an integration phase that follows the ex-prisoner for several months. Institutionally, these conditions increase the likelihood that an offender will successfully reenter society by alerting the offender of the long-term nature of reintegrating into society. Ex-offenders are not reformed overnight. Reentry takes considerable planning, thought, time, resources, and assistance from others.

It is important to note, however, that within this institutional structure, the offender is ultimately the person most responsible for his or her reentry. Faye Taxman, James Byrne, and their colleagues describe this as the active participant model.[84–85] The **active participant model** is a situation in which the offender takes part in the decision-making process when examining the risks, needs, and community factors that affect his or her involvement in crime and then uses this information to strategically address personal criminogenic needs.

According to the active participant model, offenders engage in multiple levels of change during the course of reentry. While in prison, they engage in *precontemplation*, during which they begin to consider that a noncriminal lifestyle is possible and become motivated to change their behavior. During the *contemplation* stage, offenders more concretely identify parts of their lifestyle that need to be changed as they relate to their housing situation, support network, and work prospects. During the *preparation* stage, offenders figure out how to change by building confidence in their ability to effect change in their life. Upon release, the offenders go into the *action* phase, during which time they make changes in areas that are negative and historically have contributed to their criminal behavior. While in the community, ex-prisoners are in the *maintenance* phase, during which they establish a noncriminal network to support a prosocial lifestyle and work toward financial independence. Because many ex-prisoners do not initially succeed at reentry, there is also a *relapse* stage during which offenders acknowledge their mistakes but do not submit to shame and once again work toward their rehabilitation.[86–87] Some jurisdictions refer to the gradual, phased approach to reentry as the *continuum-of-care model* in which offenders step down from prisoner to community release to aftercare service phases. Ralph Fretz reports that ex-prisoners who successfully complete all phases of continuum-of-care reentry programs have 30 percent lower recidivism rates than ex-prisoners who do not participate.[88]

As shown in Figure 12–6, reentry ultimately begins and ends with the ex-prisoner. Those who are aware of their criminal tendencies, beliefs, and behaviors are more likely to change than those who either have no awareness of their antisocial patterns or do not wish to desist from crime. Even if a returning prisoner is highly motivated to change, he or she cannot do it without supports from the community. By definition, reentry means that ex-prisoners must have the opportunity to obtain the skills needed to function in society, must have the opportunity to work, and must have the opportunity to utilize the social services available in their community.[89] This means that communities, especially businesses, need to be flexible enough to provide opportunities so that offenders can truly become former offenders. Indeed, engaging communities has been described as an essential ingredient of the offender reentry process.[90] One solution to enhancing the reentrant–community relationship is the establishment of neighborhood centers that provide access to services for returning offenders and their families. These centers can tailor services to the specific needs of offenders and ease the transition for offenders by providing multiple services within one organization within the neighborhood. This also transfers resources and the burden of providing the services from the community at large to the specific neighborhoods most affected by reentry.[91]

Due to the increased importance of reentry to the correctional process and the criminal justice system as a whole, a variety of evaluation studies of reentry programs has been conducted in recent years.[92] These programs are reviewed by substantive areas.

Comprehensive Programs

Due to the multifaceted needs that reentering offenders have, policy makers devised programs that address multiple problems areas across domains, such as work, housing, family counseling, substance abuse, and other areas. For instance, the Maine Department of Corrections has a program called Transition, Reunification, and Reentry that provides services to female offenders leaving Maine correctional facilities. The program is founded on the principle that all people, including prisoners, are worthy of unconditional

CORRECTIONS BRIEF

Project Greenlight: Do Reentry Programs Designed with Community Reintegration Really Work?

Considering that inmates released from prison have done little more than spend time behind bars, the prospect of habilitation is highly unlikely. It's not necessarily that inmates have failed program after program after program, but possibly that the programs have failed the inmates. Simply stated, prison programs fail to deter future criminal offending and do very little to assist inmates with their efforts to return to the community. This failure to deter future criminal offending is associated with increased costs in crime reaction strategies and future costs due to increases in inmate populations. Research strongly suggests that prisoners, once released, return home having undergone minimal change and habilitation. Consequently, they have a tendency to fall into familiar patterns of behavior that often result in formal and informal barriers to reintegration.

An initiative called Project Greenlight was designed to assist inmates from prisons in upstate New York to return to the community. Inmates participated in the project during the first 8 weeks following their release. This project is an eclectic blend of various key elements previously operating without collaboration in other successful programs.

The cornerstone of Project Greenlight is the belief that crime is the result of poor socialization. The developers feel poor socialization restricts access to social institutions and inhibits the procurement of common goals. As a result, strain, frustration, and anger develop over time, and this increases the likelihood that offenders will recidivate. Thus, a successful program will decrease the likelihood of an emotional response to environmental stimuli that produce criminal behavior.

The first hurdle an inmate recently released from prison faces is finding employment. Very few employers are interested in hiring former convicts, especially those with extensive criminal histories. Project Greenlight confronts this barrier to reintegration by offering former inmates access to job counselors who assist former inmates to develop resumes and improve interview skills. Counselors then search for employment possibilities and match the jobs to inmates whose skill level makes them eligible for the position—but the project does more than offer participants the chance of obtaining employment. It also works with former inmates by providing training and guidance on practical social skills.

Project Greenlight provides instruction on everyday tasks most of us take for granted, including activities ranging from using a subway card to opening a checking account. Before leaving the institution, inmates also receive instructions on what they need to do to regain voting rights and how to obtain identification documents needed to apply for Medicaid coverage. One component of Project Greenlight is the development of individualized release plans. Some inmates are capable of functioning on the outside with nothing more than a calendar and a wristwatch, while others function more comfortably with a much more structured agenda. The release plan is also shared with the inmate's parole officer to make him or her aware of the agreement and the goals that have been set.

respect and personal support. In this way, the program clearly employs the reintegration perspective advanced by Braithwaite and described earlier in this chapter. Transition, Reunification, and Reentry begins 6 months prior to release and continues for 6 months after the women are integrated back into the community. In conjunction with the Maine Department of Corrections, the program is administered by the Volunteers of America Northern New England staff who assist female ex-prisoners with an assortment of needs, such as housing, transportation, counseling and treatment, medical care, work, nutrition education, and others.[93]

Project Greenlight involved 725 inmates. Most of the inmates were monitored for at least 1 year and some for as long as 2 years. The treatment group of 334 inmates was part of the Greenlight project and received the full intervention. A second group of 113 inmates was released directly from the institution without services. A third group of 278 inmates participated in an established program called transitional services. Both the treatment group and the group of inmates assigned to the transitional services program were from the same prison.

Data from the project revealed that for the variables of employment, family relationships, and use of homeless shelter no differences existed between the Project Greenlight group and the two other groups. The Project Greenlight group showed more favorable attitudes toward the conditions of their parole, but the number of conduct violations varied little from the number of violations for those in the two other groups.

Interestingly, the Project Greenlight group showed higher rates of recidivism. In fact, the overall recidivism rate for the treatment group was 10 percent higher than that of the traditional services program group 12 months after release. Also of interest, the treatment group had 12 percent more parole revocations than did the control group that was released directly from the institution into the community with no intervention. In short, Project Greenlight failed to match the results of either other group even though the intervention was more intensive and was touted as providing individualized treatment.

The problem is not in the concept, but rather the delivery. The individual components that comprised Project Greenlight have a history of producing positive, sometimes robust outcomes. It's been suggested that one possible explanation for the lack of a positive outcome could be the delivery of the cognitive-behavioral component. Cognitive-behavioral training has been used in the past with excellent results. However, in this project the class size was doubled and the service delivery was shortened to just 8 weeks. Typically, cognitive-behavioral training takes place in classes of 10 to 13 students over a period of 4 to 6 months. As a result, it is highly unlikely that inmates benefited from this training. Researchers also found that risk assessment tools were dropped from the program and that planners opted for a broad-based intervention—sort of a one-size-fits-all approach to treatment delivery.

Project Greenlight was far less successful than it was hoped it would be. One possible explanation is that it did not target the specific needs of the participants. It has also been suggested that the project was poorly implemented. Another reason might be that the project is not really a reentry program. An evaluation of the program found no real reentry component and no community follow-up initiative. In short, Project Greenlight is simply a prison-based program. As such, it does little to reintegrate the offender to the community and/or decrease recidivism.

Sources: Wilson, J. A. (2007). *Habilitation or harm: Project Greenlight and the potential consequences of correctional programming.* Washington, DC: U. S. Department of Justice, Office of Justice Programs, National Institute of Justice.

Unfortunately, comprehensive programs do not always produce the expected outcomes. For example, **Project Greenlight** is an intensive reentry program that is delivered during the 8 weeks immediately preceding an offender's release from custody. Project Greenlight includes cognitive-behavioral skills training, employment and housing assistance, drug education and awareness, family counseling, practical skills training, information on community-based services, information on parole, and an individualized release plan.

Although Project Greenlight participants were more knowledgeable and positive about parole and utilized more community services, they showed worse outcomes compared to inmates who were released from New York prisons without any prerelease services. Project Greenlight participants were more likely to get rearrested at 6- and 12-month follow-up periods, had higher rates of felony arrests, and had more parole revocations at 6- and 12-month follow-up periods. Project evaluators believed that the program was poorly matched to offenders receiving services and that there were implementation problems.[94–95]

Employment Programs

Across the United States, correctional systems administer vocational, work, or employment programs designed to provide the work skills that inmates will need when they reenter society. For instance, in New Jersey, the Early Intervention program targets mentally ill offenders who receive disability insurance but are still capable of work. Prior to release, offenders are referred to a Department of Labor specialist who provides information and other services that are specifically tailored to the individual offender's needs. At the very least, the information and services provide initial social supports for the offender as he or she attempts to find work upon release.[96]

A traditional way that prisons prepare inmates for reentry is work release. **Work release** allows inmates to leave prison to work in the community during business hours and then return to prison for nights and weekends. Susan Turner and Joan Petersilia studied a cohort of more than 2,400 inmates released from Washington state prisons to evaluate the effectiveness of work release programs. Of more than 1,100 inmates who finished their prison sentences in a work release program, fewer than 5 percent committed new crimes—virtually all of which were low-level property crimes such as forgery and petty theft. In addition, those who participate in work release programs were somewhat less likely to recidivate compared to those who simply served their entire sentence in traditional prison. But, to the degree that inmates acquire work skills and experience to help with the transition to society, the program was viewed as effective.[97]

William Saylor and Gerald Gaes conducted a series of evaluations of the Post Release Employment Project, which studied the effectiveness of the UNICOR program described in Chapter 11. Overall, inmates who participate in vocational, work, or employment programs tend to have lower rates of institutional misconduct, lower recidivism rates after release, and higher rates of employment upon reentry. Moreover, these positive effects can be seen even 12 years after release.[98–100]

Educational Programs

Due to the high prevalence of illiteracy and school dropout among prisoners, educational services are an important asset for offenders returning to the community. An innovative program is TEPOhio, which is a distance-learning videoconferencing program that instructs inmates in writing resumes and cover letters, using community resources, building and enhancing job search skills, and other self-help skills. TEPOhio has institutional and aftercare phases and lasts for 10 weeks. Ex-prisoners can use e-mail and toll-free telephone services to continue utilizing services after their release.[101] In addition to its practical purposes, programs such as these also provide offenders with some of the very job skills, such as using e-mail, that are common in most jobs.

It is critical for returning offenders to improve their skills and increase their education even if these new skills do not immediately translate into reduced recidivism. Richard Tewksbury and Gennaro Vito evaluated educational programming administered to jail inmates in Kentucky. They found that inmates significantly increased their reading and math skills and the increased literacy was theorized to lead to greater employment and reduced offending. Unfortunately, the recidivism rates of former inmates who participated in educational programs were comparable to reoffending among those who did not.[102–103]

WRAP UP

CASE STUDY CONCLUSION

For reentry to be successful, it must begin while offenders are still incarcerated. Using the APIC model, jail administrators get started by training staff to become involved in reentry and investing in helping inmates become productive citizens. Offenders must be screened, and personalized reentry strategies in which specific community resources (e.g., substance abuse treatment, psychiatric counseling, etc.) are identified as the support system for a particular offender after release must be developed. There must also be follow-up to ensure that offenders and the system are maintaining their commitment to successful reentry. If not, offenders often circulate back into correctional custody.

Source: Mellow, J., Mukamal, D. A., LoBuglio, S. F., Solomon, A. L., & Osborne, J. W. L. (2008). *The jail administrator's toolkit for reentry*. Washington, DC: U.S. Department of Justice, Office of Justice Programs, Bureau of Justice Assistance.

Chapter Summary

- About 650,000 offenders are released from prison annually or approximately 1,800 per day.
- Reentry reflects a shift from narrowly focusing on parole recidivism to exploring the multiple domains that affect the likelihood of an offender successfully returning to society.
- Many federal initiatives are geared toward reentry issues; most notable is the Serious Violent Offender Reentry Initiative (SVORI).
- A major basis for the emphasis on reentry stems from John Braithwaite's reintegration theory.
- Several correctional policies are designed to stigmatize and restrict the reintegration of sex offenders.
- Returning prisoners contribute to and are affected by an array of societal issues, such as crime and violence, community cohesion, public health risks, family strife, and civic participation.
- Many states have laws that deny basic legal and civic rights to ex-prisoners and convicted felons.
- Reentry programs that begin prior to release and continue for a period of aftercare in the community are more likely to result in prosocial changes for ex-prisoners.

Key Terms

Access to Recovery A program within the Substance Abuse and Mental Health Services Administration that provides people seeking drug and alcohol treatment with vouchers to pay for a range of community services.

active participant model A situation in which the offender takes part in the decision-making process when examining the risks, needs, and community factors that affect his or her involvement in crime and then uses this information to strategically address personal criminogenic needs.

civil death The loss of legal and civic rights after criminal conviction.

coercive mobility The dual processes of mass incarceration and reentry that disrupt the social networks of disadvantaged communities and lead to increased social problems.

collateral consequences of imprisonment The assorted societal issues that are impacted by the incarceration and return of prisoners.

concentrated disadvantage Neighborhoods with extreme poverty, racial segregation, and high crime rates.

disintegrative shaming Type of shaming that stigmatizes both the offender and his or her crimes and serves to ostracize criminals from society.

felon disenfranchisement The denial of voting rights of persons with various criminal justice system statuses.

interdependency The extent to which individuals participate in networks where they are dependent on others and others in turn are dependent on them.

Mentoring Children of Prisoners Program A program within the Department of Health and Human Services that awards competitive grants to eligible organizations supporting mentoring programs for children with incarcerated parents.

Prisoner Reentry Initiative An extension of the Ready4Work program that provides services to 6,250 ex-prisoners annually.

Project Greenlight An intensive reentry program that is delivered during the 8 weeks immediately proceeding an offender's release from custody.

Ready4Work A Department of Labor program that uses faith-based and community organizations to help ex-offenders find work and escape cycles of recidivism.

reentry The process of preparing and supporting offenders incarcerated in adult prisons and juvenile correctional facilities as they complete their terms and return to society.

reintegrative shaming Type of shaming that punishes and stigmatizes the criminal act while acknowledging the fundamental decency and goodness of the offender.

residency restrictions laws Laws that restrict where sex offenders can live. Restrictions range from 1,000 to 2,500 feet from places such as schools, parks, day care centers, bus stops, or other places where children congregate.

Serious Violent Offender Reentry Initiative (SVORI) A collaborative federal initiative that addresses reentry outcomes in the areas of criminal justice, employment, education, health, and housing.

shaming All processes of expressing disapproval that have the intention or effect of invoking remorse in the person being shamed and/or condemnation by others who become aware of the shaming.

White House Office of Faith-Based and Community Initiatives Executive-branch unit charged with leading a comprehensive effort to enlist, equip, enable, empower, and expand the work of faith-based and other community organizations.

work release Programs that allow inmates to leave prison to work in the community during business hours and then return to prison for nights and weekends.

Critical Thinking Questions

1. Is disintegrative shaming necessarily a bad thing? Are some offenders fully deserving of ostracism and shame? If so, which types?
2. Do the difficulties of offender reentry showcase the importance of early life prosocial steps such as school completion, healthy friendships, and work? Can these deficiencies really be overcome?
3. Should the state take a greater role in providing parenting services and mentoring programs to the children of prisoners? Would this be compassionate or overstepping the role of the state?
4. How has President George W. Bush been a savior to offender reentry? Does this facet of his presidency receive much media attention? Why or why not?

Notes

1. Huebner, B. M., & Gustafson, R. (2007). The effect of maternal incarceration on adult offspring involvement in the criminal justice system. *Journal of Criminal Justice, 35,* 283–296.
2. Bush, G. W. (2004, January 20). *State of the Union Address*, available at www.whitehouse.gov/news/releases/2004/01/20040120=7.html.
3. Wormith, J. S., Althouse, R., Simpson, M., Reitzel, L. R., Fagan, T. J., & Morgan, R. D. (2007). The rehabilitation and reintegration of offenders: The current landscape and some future directions for correctional psychology. *Criminal Justice and Behavior, 34,* 879–892.
4. Austin, J. (2001). Prisoner reentry: Current trends, practices, and issues. *Crime & Delinquency, 47,* 314–334.
5. Braithwaite, J. (1989). *Crime, shame, and reintegration*. New York: Cambridge University Press.
6. Pager, D. (2007). *Marked: Race, crime, and finding work in an era of mass incarceration*. Chicago: University of Chicago Press.
7. Irwin, J. (1970). *The felon*. Englewood Cliffs, NJ: Prentice Hall.
8. Lattimore, P. K., Brumbaugh, S., Visher, C., Lindquist, C., Winterfield, L., Salas, M., et al. (2004). *National portrait of Serious and Violent Offender Reentry Initiative (SVORI)*. Washington, DC: RTI International and Urban Institute, p. 1.
9. Welsh, B. C. (2004). Monetary costs and benefits of correctional treatment programs: Implications for offender reentry. *Federal Probation, 68,* 9–13.
10. Petersilia, J. (2004). What works in prisoner reentry? Reviewing and questioning the evidence. *Federal Probation, 68,* 4–8.
11. Uggen, C., Manza, J., & Thompson, M. (2006). Citizenship, democracy, and the civic reintegration of criminal offenders. *Annals of the American Academy of Political and Social Science, 605,* 281–310.
12. U.S. Department of Justice. Bureau of Justice Statistics. (2003). *Reentry trends in the United States*. Retrieved October 7, 2008, from http://www.ojp.usdoj.gov/bjs/reentry/reentry.htm.
13. See Visher, C. A., & Travis, J. (2003). Transitions from prison to community: Understanding individual pathways. *Annual Review of Sociology, 29,* 89–113.
14. Petersilia, J. (2005). From cell to society: Who is returning home? In J. Travis & C. Visher (Eds.), *Prisoner reentry and crime in America* (pp. 15–49). New York: Cambridge University Press.
15. *Improving prisoner reentry services through faith and community-based partnerships*. (n.d.). Retrieved October 7, 2008, from http://www.whitehouse.gov/government/fbci/pdf/improving_prisoner_reentry.pdf.

16. U.S. Department of Labor. Center for Faith-Based and Community Initiatives. (n.d.). *Prisoner reentry*. Retrieved October 7, 2008, from http://www.dol.gov/cfbci/reentry.htm.

17. U.S. Department of Labor. Center for Faith-Based and Community Initiatives. (n.d.). *Our mission*. Retrieved October 7, 2008, from http://www.dol.gov/cfbci.

18. U.S. Department of Justice. Office of Justice Programs. (n.d.). *Learn about reentry*. Retrieved October 7, 2008, from http://www.reentry.gov/learn.html.

19. U.S. Department of Health and Human Services. (n.d.). *The Center for Faith-Based & Community Initiatives*. Retrieved October 7, 2008, from http://www.hhs.gov/fbci.

20. U.S. Department of Health and Human Services. Substance Abuse and Mental Health Services Administration. (n.d.). *SAMHSA access to recovery grants*. Retrieved October 7, 2008, from http://atr.samhsa.gov.

21. Bush, G. W. (2008). *Fact sheet: The Faith-Based and Community Initiative: A quiet revolution in the way government addresses human need.* Retrieved October 7, 2008, from http://www.whitehouse.gov/news/releases/2008/01/20080129-8.html.

22. Lattimore, P. K., Visher, C. A., & Steffey, D. M. (2008). Prerelease characteristics and service receipt among adult male participants in the SVORI multi-site evaluation. Washington, DC: RTI International and The Urban Institute.

23. Winterfield, L., Lattimore, P. K., Steffey, D. M., Brumbaugh, S., & Lindquist, C. (2006). The Serious and Violent Offender Reentry Initiative: Measuring the effects on service delivery. *Western Criminology Review, 7,* 3–19.

24. Visher, C. A., & Lattimore, P. K. (2007). Major study examines prisoners and their reentry needs. *National Institute of Justice Journal, 258,* 30–33.

25. Visher & Lattimore.

26. Braithwaite, p. 9.

27. Braithwaite, p. 55.

28. Braithwaite, pp. 100–101.

29. Murphy, K., & Harris, N. (2007). Shaming, shame and recidivism: A test of reintegrative shaming theory in the white-collar crime context. *British Journal of Criminology, 47,* 900–917.

30. Makkai, T., & Braithwaite, J. (1994). Reintegrative shaming and compliance with regulatory standards. *Criminology, 32,* 361–386.

31. Hay, C. (2001). An exploratory test of Braithwaite's reintegrative shaming theory. *Journal of Research in Crime and Delinquency, 38,* 132–153.

32. Botchkovar, E. V., & Tittle, C. R. (2005). Crime, shame, and reintegration in Russia. *Theoretical Criminology, 9,* 401–422.

33. Vagg, J. (1998). Delinquency and shame: Data from Hong Kong. *British Journal of Criminology, 38,* 247–264.

34. Baumer, E., Wright, R., Kristinsdottir, K., & Gunnlaugsson, H. (2002). Crime, shame, and recidivism: The case of Iceland. *British Journal of Criminology, 42,* 40–59.

35. Zhang, L., & Zhang, S. (2004). Reintegrative shaming and predatory delinquency. *Journal of Research in Crime and Delinquency, 41,* 433–453.

36. Sherman, L., Strange, H., & Woods, D. (2000). *Recidivism patterns in the Canberra Reintegrative Shaming Experiments (RISE).* Canberra, Australia: Australian National University Press.

37. Sherman, L. (2003). Reason for emotion: Reinventing justice with theories, innovations, and research: The American Society of Criminology 2002 Presidential Address. *Criminology, 41,* 1–38.

38. Jensen, K., & Gibbons, S. (2002). Shame and religion as factors in the rehabilitation of serious offenders. *Journal of Offender Rehabilitation, 35,* 215–230.

39. Levenson, J., Zgoba, K., & Tewksbury, R. (2007). Sex offender residence restrictions: Sensible crime policy or flawed logic? *Federal Probation, 71,* 2–9.

40. Zandbergen, P. A., & Hart, T. C. (2006). Reducing housing options for convicted sex offenders: Investigating the impact of residency restriction laws using GIS. *Justice Research and Policy, 8,* 1–24.

41. Levenson, J. S., & Cotter, L. P. (2005). The impact of sex offender residence restrictions: 1,000 feet from danger or one step from absurd? *International Journal of Offender Therapy and Comparative Criminology, 49,* 168–178.

42. Petersilia, p. 4.

43. Krisberg, B., & Marchionna, S. (2006). *Attitudes of U.S. voters toward prisoner rehabilitation and reentry policies.* Washington, DC: National Council on Crime and Delinquency.

44. Allender, D. M. (2004). Offender reentry: A returning or reformed criminal? *FBI Law Enforcement Bulletin, 73,* 1–10.

45. Krisberg & Marchionna.

46. Wood, P. B. (2007). Exploring the positive punishment effect among incarcerated adult offenders. *American Journal of Criminal Justice, 31,* 8–22.

47. Rosenfeld, R., Wallman, J., & Fornango, R. (2005). The contribution of ex-prisoners to crime rates. In J. Travis & C. Visher (Eds.), *Prisoner reentry and crime in America* (pp. 80–104). New York: Cambridge University Press.

48. Justice Policy Center Reentry Researchers. (2006). *Understanding the challenges of prisoner reentry: Research findings from the Urban Institute's prisoner reentry portfolio.* Washington, DC: The Urban Institute.

49. Justice Policy Center Reentry Researchers.

50. Chung, H. L., Schubert, C. A., & Mulvey, E. P. (2007). An empirical portrait of community reentry among serious juvenile offenders in two metropolitan cities. *Criminal Justice and Behavior, 34,* 1402–1426.

51. Justice Policy Center Reentry Researchers.

52. Rose, D. R., & Clear, T. R. (1998). Incarceration, social capital, and crime: Implications for social disorganization theory. *Criminology, 36,* 441–479.

53. Clear, T. R. (2007). *Imprisoning communities: How mass incarceration makes disadvantaged neighborhoods worse.* New York: Oxford University Press.

54. Rose, D., & Clear, T. (2002). *Incarceration, reentry and social capital: Social networks in the balance.* Washington, DC: U.S. Department of Health and Human Services.

55. Clear, T. R., Rose, D. R., Waring, E., & Scully, K. (2003). Coercive mobility and crime: A preliminary examination of concentrated incarceration and social disorganization. *Justice Quarterly, 20,* 33–64.

56. Lynch, J. P., & Sabol, W. J. (2004). Assessing the effects of mass incarceration on informal social control in communities. *Criminology & Public Policy, 3,* 267–294.

57. Burgess-Allen, J., Langlois, M., & Whittaker, P. (2006). Health needs of ex-prisoners, implications for successful resettlement: A qualitative study. *International Journal of Prisoner Health, 2,* 291–301.

58. Piquero, A. R., Daigle, L. E., Gibson, C., Piquero, N. L., & Tibbetts, S. G. (2007). Are life-course-persistent offenders at risk for adverse health outcomes? *Journal of Research in Crime & Delinquency, 44,* 185–207.

59. Hammett, T. M., Harmon, M., & Rhodes, W. (1997). The burden of infectious disease among inmates or and releasees from U.S. correctional facilities. *American Journal of Public Health, 92,* 1789–1794.

60. Binswanger, I., Stern, M. F., Deyo, R. A., Heagerty, P. J., Cheadle, A., Elmore, J. G., et al. (2007). Release from prison: A high risk of death for former inmates. *New England Journal of Medicine, 356,* 157–165.

61. Piquero, A. R., MacDonald, J., Dobrin, A., Daigle, L. E., & Cullen, F. T. (2005). Self-control, violent offending, and homicide victimization: Assessing the general theory of crime. *Journal of Quantitative Criminology, 21,* 55–71.

62. Justice Policy Center Reentry Researchers.

63. Pager, D. (2003). The mark of a criminal record. *American Journal of Sociology, 108,* 937–975.

64. Pager, D., & Quillian, L. (2005). Walking the talk? What employers say versus what they do. *American Sociological Review, 70,* 355–380.

65. Kanazawa, S. (2005). The myth of racial discrimination in pay in the United States. *Managerial and Decision Economics, 26,* 285–294, p. 293.

66. Western, B., Kling, J. R., & Weiman, D. F. (2001). The labor market consequences of incarceration. *Crime & Delinquency, 47,* 410–427.

67. Stafford, C. (2006). Finding work: How to approach the intersection of prisoner reentry, employment, and recidivism. *Georgetown Journal on Poverty Law & Policy, 13,* 261–281.

68. Arditti, J. A., & Few, A. L. (2006). Mothers' reentry into family life following incarceration. *Criminal Justice Policy Review, 17,* 103–123.

69. Bernstein, N. (2005). *All alone in the world: Children of the incarcerated.* New York: The New Press.

70. Murray, J., & Farrington, D. P. (2006). Evidence-based programs for children of prisoners. *Criminology & Public Policy, 5,* 721–736.

71. Murray, J., & Farrington, D. P. (2006). Parental imprisonment: Effects on boys' antisocial behavior and delinquency through the life-course. *Journal of Child Psychology and Psychiatry, 46,* 1269–1278.

72. Murray, J., & Farrington, D. P. (2008). Parental imprisonment: Long-lasting effects on boys' internalizing problems through the life-course. *Development and Psychopathology, 20,* 273–290.

73. Huebner & Gustafson.

74. Murray, J., Janson, C., & Farrington, D. P. (2007). Crime in adult offspring of prisoners: A cross-national comparison of two longitudinal samples. *Criminal Justice and Behavior, 34,* 133–149.

75. Phillips, S. D., Erkanli, A., Keeler, G. P., Costello, E. J., & Angold, A. (2006). Disentangling the risks: Parent criminal justice involvement and children's exposure to family risks. *Criminology & Public Policy, 5,* 677–702.

76. Naser, R. L., & Visher, C. A. (2006). Family members' experiences with incarceration and reentry. *Western Criminology Review, 7,* 20–31.

77. Leverentz, A. M. (2006). Love of a good man? Romantic relationships as a source of support or hindrance for female ex-offenders. *Journal of Research in Crime and Delinquency, 43,* 459–488.

78. Harman, J. J., Smith, V. E., & Egan, L. C. (2007). The impact of incarceration on intimate relationships. *Criminal Justice and Behavior, 34,* 794–815.

79. Ewald, A. C. (2002). The ideological paradox of criminal disenfranchisement law in the United States. *University of Wisconsin Law Review, 2002,* 1045–1138.

80. Bushway, S. D., & Sweeten, G. (2007). Abolish lifetime bans for ex-felons. *Criminology & Public Policy, 6,* 697–706.

81. Pogorzelski, W., Wolff, N., Pan, K., & Blitz, C. L. (2005). Behavioral health problems, ex-offender reentry policies, and the "Second Chance Act." *American Journal of Public Health, 95,* 1718–1724.

82. Manza, J., & Uggen, C. (2004). Punishment and democracy: Disenfranchisement of nonincarcerated felons in the United States. *Perspectives on Politics, 2,* 491–505; also see Manza, J., & Uggen, C. (2006). *Locked out: Felon disenfranchisement and American democracy.* New York: Oxford University Press.

83. Manza & Uggen.

84. Taxman, F., & Bouffard, J. (2000). The importance of system issues in improving offender outcomes: Critical elements of treatment integrity. *Justice Research and Policy, 2,* 9–30.

85. Taxman, F., Young, D., & Byrne, J. (2004). Transforming offender reentry into public safety: Lessons from OJP's Reentry Partnership Initiative. *Justice Research and Policy, 5,* 101–128.

86. Taxman, F. S. (2004). The offender and reentry: Supporting active participation in reintegration. *Federal Probation, 68,* 31–35.

87. Walters, S. T., Clark, M. D., Gingerich, R., & Meltzer, M. L. (2007). *Motivating offenders to change: A guide for probation and parole.* Washington, DC: National Institute of Corrections.

88. Fretz, R. (2005). Step down programs: The missing link in successful inmate reentry. *Corrections Today, 67,* 102–107.

89. Byrne, J. M., & Hummer, D. (2005). Thinking globally, acting locally: Applying international trends to reentry partnerships in the United States. *International Journal of Comparative and Applied Criminal Justice, 29,* 79–96.

90. Wilkinson, R. A. (2005). Engaging communities: An essential ingredient to offender reentry. *Corrections Today, 67,* 86–89.

91. Clear, T. R., Rose, D. R., & Ryder, J. A. (2001). Incarceration and the community: The problem of removing and returning offenders. *Crime & Delinquency, 47,* 335–351.

92. See Seiter, R. P., & Kadela, K. R. (2003). Prisoner reentry: What works, what does not, and what is promising. *Crime & Delinquency, 49,* 360–388.

93. Fortuin, B. (2007). Maine's female offenders are reentering and succeeding. *Corrections Today, 69,* 34–37.

94. Wilson, J. A. (2007). Habilitation or harm: Project Greenlight and the potential consequences of correctional programming. *National Institute of Justice Journal, 257,* 1–47.

95. Wilson, J. A., & Davis, R. C. (2006). Good intentions meet hard realities: An evaluation of the Project Greenlight reentry program. *Criminology & Public Policy, 5,* 303–338.

96. Brucker, D. (2006). Reentry to recovery: A promising return-to-work approach for certain offenders with mental illness. *Criminal Justice Policy Review, 17,* 302–313.

97. Turner, S., & Petersilia, J. (1996). Work release in Washington: Effects on recidivism and corrections costs. *Prison Journal, 76,* 138–164.

98. Saylor, W. G., & Gaes, G. G. (2001). The differential effect of industries and vocational training on postrelease outcomes for ethnic and racial groups. *Corrections Management Quarterly, 5,* 17–24.

99. Saylor, W. G., & Gaes, G. G. (1997). Training inmates through industrial work participation and vocational and apprenticeship instruction. *Corrections Management Quarterly, 1,* 32–43.

100. Saylor, W. G., & Gaes, G. G. (1996). The effect of prison employment and vocational/apprenticeship training on long-term recidivism. *Forum on Corrections Research, 8,* 12–14.

101. Roberts, M., & McGlone, J. (2007). TEPOhio: Acting as a bridge between institutional programming and community aftercare. *Corrections Today, 69,* 26–29.

102. Tewksbury, R. A., & Vito, G. F. (1994). Improving the educational skills of jail inmates: Preliminary program findings. *Federal Probation, 58,* 55–59.

103. Vito, G. F., & Tewksbury, R. A. (1999). Improving the educational skills of inmates: The results of an impact evaluation. *Corrections Compendium, 24,* 1–17.

PART

IV

Special Topics in Corrections

CHAPTER

13

Juvenile Corrections

"Juvenile court history has again demonstrated that unbridled discretion, however benevolently motivated, is frequently a poor substitute for principle and procedure."[1]

OBJECTIVES

- Identify the structure and processes of the juvenile justice system.
- Learn the statistical profile and trends of juvenile offenders in the correctional system.
- Explore intermediate sanctions and probation as they relate to juveniles.
- Assess detention, commitment, and aftercare and the types of juveniles that receive these placements.
- Understand juvenile corrections history from the colonial era to the present.
- Recognize landmark Supreme Court cases that guided juvenile justice.
- Examine the current state of juvenile justice and juvenile corrections.
- Investigate current strategy for dealing with serious, violent, and chronic juvenile offenders.

CASE STUDY

The Beltway Snipers

In 2005, 2 years after his arrest for killing 10 people, the conviction on two counts of murder and the subsequent death sentence of John Allen Muhammad was upheld by the Virginia Supreme Court. But Jonathan Shapiro, defense counsel for John Allen Muhammad, said the fight was not over. Muhammad had appealed his conviction on two counts of murder based on claims that the antiterrorism law used to obtain evidence needed to convict him was unconstitutional. However, the Virginia Supreme Court upheld the constitutionality of the law and in a unanimous decision rejected this appeal. Muhammad also argued in his appeal that the state could not prove he had pulled the trigger. According to Virginia's triggerman rule, capital punishment cannot be considered an option unless proof can be presented to the courts that the defendant pulled the trigger. In their four-to-three decision, the Court held that the pair (Muhammad and 17-year-old Lee Boyd Malvo) was acting together and because of this conspiracy and the level of the offense, each party involved was responsible in the deaths of the victims. In essence, the court held that Muhammad and Malvo acted as a sniper team.

1. Do you agree with the U.S. Supreme Court's decision to disallow capital punishment in murders cases when the defendant charged with the crime is a juvenile?

While still a juvenile, Lee Boyd Malvo was a co-defendant in one of the nation's worst cases of spree murder.

"Violence in prison is the logical and predictable result of the commitment of a collection of individuals whose life histories have been characterized by disregard for law, order, and social convention."[2, p. 215]

Throughout this text, the correctional system has been shown to be a system that tries to provide offenders with as many opportunities as possible to reform their antisocial behavior. Unless an offender commits an extremely serious crime, such as murder, the norm of the correctional process is to receive the lowest form of punishment, and if that fails, to receive additional punishment of increasing severity. Diversion gives way to probation, which gives way to intensive supervised probation. If offenders continue to be noncompliant, an array of intermediate sanctions and short-term stints in jail are used. For persons convicted of serious felonies and/or for persons with extensive criminal histories characterized by criminal justice system failure, prison is an option of last resort. Almost all prisoners eventually reenter society on parole, and the process begins anew. Corrections works like a triage system where the most serious cases are dealt with first and the less-serious cases wait.

This characterization is taken to a new level in juvenile corrections. Since the founding of the juvenile court in 1899, the juvenile justice system has explicitly operated on the premise of treating or rehabilitating delinquent offenders. In this way, the juvenile correctional system is genuinely designed to correct a delinquent's behavior and thus is ideologically different from the adult correctional system, which invests more heavily in incapacitation and punitive measures.

"These are state delinquents. They are the most serious, violent, and chronic that the juvenile justice system has had to handle, and they come with a long list of failures."[3, p. 25]

This sentiment is portrayed by Mark Lipsey, who is a well-known juvenile justice program evaluator:

> The primary rationale for maintaining a separate juvenile justice system is that belief that juvenile offenders should be treated differently from adult offenders. . . . Juveniles by definition are immature and may warrant more latitude to make a mistake than adults and more help to recover from it. In addition, their habits and propensities may be relatively malleable so that rehabilitative intervention may be effective in changing the trajectory of their antisocial behavior. Moreover, their youth means that if the trajectory is not changed, they potentially have long and destructive criminal careers in front of them.[6, p. 143]

This chapter explores the history and structure of the juvenile justice system with emphasis on the correctional processes, such as probation, detention, and aftercare. Special attention is paid to juvenile offenders in correctional facilities and the interesting history of the use of capital punishment in the juvenile justice system.

Juvenile Corrections History

The history of juvenile justice in the United States is appalling and brutal. Justice was personal and meted out with exceptional brutality. This tradition is rooted in English Common Law, where the very ideas of crime and punishment were heavily influenced by religion. During the colonial era, criminal behavior was viewed as not only a legal violation but also a moral violation. Crimes were viewed as affronts to God and God's law and thus criminals were treated in very punitive and vengeful ways.

Colonial Era

American colonial society was similarly harsh about children and the control of children's behavior. Throughout society, there was a general notion that children were particularly susceptible to vice and moral violations. For instance, in 1641, the General Court of Massachusetts Bay Colony passed the Stubborn Child Law, which stated that children who disobeyed their parents would be put to death. The language and certainly the spirit of the Stubborn Child Law were drawn from the Book of Deuteronomy. The Stubborn Child Law descended from the Puritans' belief that unacknowledged social evils would bring the wrath of God down upon the entire colony. The Puritans believed they had no choice but to react to juvenile misbehavior in a severe and calculated manner. However, not all colonies adopted the Stubborn Child Law. Outside Massachusetts, children found guilty of a serious crime frequently were punished via corporal punishments or inflictions of physical pain such as whipping, mutilating, caning, and other methods.[7–8]

What would today be considered normal and routine adolescent behavior, such as hanging out, was in early eras considered grievous delinquent behavior: sloth and idleness. Today, the use of death or beatings for minor types of delinquency seems shocking; however, there are similarities between colonial juvenile justice and contemporary juvenile justice. In both eras, adult society held ambivalent views about children. On one hand, children and adolescents were seen as innocents who were not fully developed and required compassion, patience, and understanding. From this perspective, juvenile justice should be tempered, tolerant, and used to teach or discipline. On the other hand, children and adolescents were viewed as disrespectful, annoying, and simply different than adults. It was believed that children were born in sin and should submit to adult authority.

The Child Savers

Over time, the puritanical approach to defining, correcting, and punishing delinquency came under attack. Not only had these severe forms of juvenile justice failed to control

"Give the offender some rope, enough to yank himself out of a life of crime, or to hang himself and wind up in prison."[4, p. 262]

delinquency, but also they were portrayed as primitive and brutal. In 1825, a progressive social movement known as the **Child Savers** changed the course of juvenile justice and made corrections a primary part of it. Rather than framing delinquency as an issue of sin and morality, the Child Savers attributed delinquency to environmental factors, such as poverty, immigration, poor parenting, and urban environments. Based on the doctrine of ***parens patriae***, which means the state is the ultimate guardian of children, the Child Savers sought to remove children from the adverse environments that they felt contributed to delinquency.

The Child Savers actively pursued the passage of legislation that would permit placing children in reformatories, especially juvenile paupers. The goal of removing children from extreme poverty was admirable, but resulted in transforming children into nonpersons (or people without legal rights). Children were shunted into factories, poorhouses, orphanages, and houses of refuge, where they were poorly treated with almost no attention given to their individual needs. The first and most famous was the New York House of Refuge, which opened in 1825 and served to incarcerate thousands of children and adolescents viewed as threats to public safety and social order.[9]

Another curious method of juvenile corrections during this era was the use of transportation. Between the 1850s and the Great Depression, approximately 250,000 abandoned children from New York were placed on orphan trains and relocated to locations in the West where they were adopted by Christian farm families. The process of finding new homes for the children was haphazard. At town meetings across the country, farming families took their pick of the orphan train riders. Children who were not selected got back on board the train and continued to the next town. The children who were selected and those who adopted them had 1 year to decide whether they would stay together. If either decided not to, the child would be returned, boarded on the next train out of town, and offered to another family.[10]

Juvenile Court

Progressive reformers continued looking for new solutions to the growing problem of juvenile delinquency. Their most significant remedy was the creation of the juvenile court in Cook County (Chicago), Illinois, in July 1899 in the court of Judge Julian Mack. The juvenile court attempted to closely supervise problem children, but unlike the houses of refuge, this new form of supervision was to more often occur within the child's own home and community, not in institutions.

In the juvenile court, procedures were civil as opposed to criminal, perhaps because social workers spearheaded the court movement. They thought that children had to be *treated,* not punished, and the judge was to be a wise and kind parent. The new court segregated juveniles from adult offenders at all procedural stages. The philosophy of the juvenile court was stated by Judge Mack, "not so much to punish as to reform, not to degrade but to uplift, not to crush but to develop, not to make the delinquent an offender but a worthy citizen."[11, p. 120]

The juvenile court reaffirmed and extended the doctrine of *parens patriae.* This paternalistic philosophy meant that reformers gave more attention to the needs of children than to their rights. In their campaign to meet the needs of children, the Child Savers expanded the role of the state to include the handling of children in the judicial system. Because of its innovative approach, the juvenile court movement spread quickly. By 1910, 32 states had established juvenile courts and by 1945, all states had done so.[12]

As juvenile courts across the United States continued in operation, two concerns emerged that served as an impetus for reforms. First, the informality of juvenile proceedings was seen as good in that justice could be tailored to the needs of individual youth. However, the informality also invited disparate treatment of offenders. The second and related point was that the juvenile court needed to become more formalized to ensure

"You can change your life. With considerable effort, that message might come to inform all our work with children, even children in crisis, even tough kids in terrible places. You can change your life."[5, p. 200]

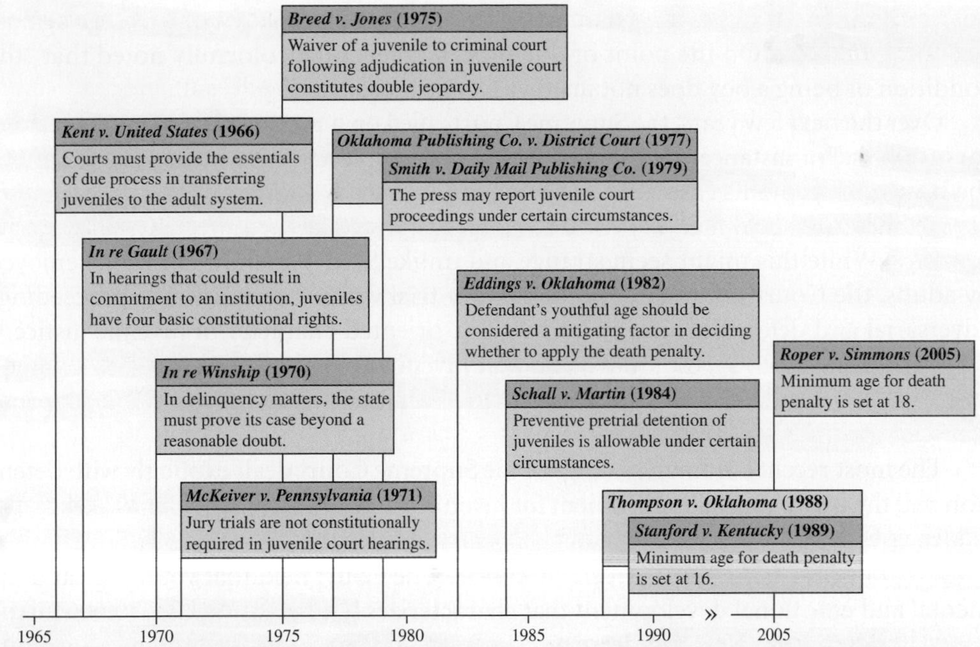

FIGURE 13–1 Landmark Juvenile Justice Cases. *Source*: Snyder, H. N., & Sickmund, M. (2006). *Juvenile offenders and victims: 2006 national report.* Washington, DC: U.S. Department of Justice, Office of Justice Programs, Office of Juvenile Justice and Delinquency Prevention.

the due process rights of delinquents that were comparable to the due process rights of adults in the criminal courts. These rights were established in a series of landmark cases during the 1960s and 1970s and are explored next (FIGURE 13–1).

The Supreme Court and Juvenile Justice

The first of the major due process cases centering on juvenile justice was *Kent v. United States* (1966). The case involved Morris Kent, who, at age 16, was charged with rape and robbery while already on probation. Kent's attorney filed a motion requesting a hearing on the issue of whether the case would be heard in District of Columbia juvenile court. The judge did not rule on this motion and allowed the case to be waived to criminal court, where Kent was found guilty on six counts of house breaking and robbery and sentenced to 30 to 90 years in prison. Kent had confessed to the police; thus his guilt was never in question.

Upon appeal, the Supreme Court ruled that the waiver was invalid and that Kent was entitled to a hearing that measured up to the essentials of due process and fair treatment. The Court also decided that Kent's attorneys should have had access to all records involved in the waiver (the original judge had simply decided to waive the case after an unspecified investigation), and that the judge should have provided a written statement of the reasons for the waiver. Interestingly, the Court acknowledged that although juvenile courts care more about defendants than adult courts do, defendants lacked the due process protections and thus received the worst of both worlds.[13]

Because Kent technically applied to Washington, DC, the case that is viewed as establishing due process for juveniles is *In re Gault* (1967). The case centered on 15-year-old Gerald Gault, who, while on probation, made crank telephone calls to a neighbor and was subsequently committed to a training school for 3 years. Upon ultimate appeal, the Supreme Court ruled that in hearings that could result in commitment to an institution, juveniles have (1) the right to notice of charges, (2) the right to counsel, (3) the right to question, confront, and cross-examine witnesses, and (4) the right of privilege against self-incrimination. On the point of due process, the Court colorfully noted that "the condition of being a boy does not justify a kangaroo court."[14, p. 387]

Over the next few years, the Supreme Court ruled on a variety of due process matters for juveniles. For instance, ***In re Winshop*** (1970) established that in delinquency matters, the state must prove its case beyond a reasonable doubt.[15] In ***McKeiver v. Pennsylvania*** (1971), the Court held that jury trials are not constitutionally required in juvenile court hearings. While this might seem strange and unlike Sixth Amendment rights enjoyed by adults, the Court's rationale was that a jury trial would make juvenile proceedings adversarial and defeat the informal, treatment-oriented character of juvenile justice.[16] In ***Breed v. Jones*** (1975), the Court held that juveniles could not be waived to criminal court following adjudication in juvenile court because it violated the double jeopardy clause of the Fifth Amendment.[17]

The most recent landmark rulings of the Supreme Court dealt explicitly with detention and the use of capital punishment for juveniles. In ***Eddings v. Oklahoma*** (1982), the Court reversed the death sentence of a 16-year-old who had been convicted in criminal court for the murder a law enforcement officer. The Court held that young age and the mental and emotional development that characterizes young age should be considered mitigating factors in capital sentencing.[18] In ***Schall v. Martin*** (1984), the Court held that preventive pretrial detention of juveniles is allowable under certain circumstances, such as the likelihood of recidivism. The case stemmed from the crimes of Gregory Martin, who, at age 14, was arrested and charged with armed robbery, assault, and possession of a weapon. The trial court found that Martin was a serious risk for continued criminal activity and should be confined pending his adjudication for the protection of the public. Upon appeal, the Supreme Court ruled that preventive detention was constitutional because enough procedures were in place to protect juveniles from wrongful deprivations of liberty. In this case, the protections were provided by notice, there was a statement of the facts and reasons for detention, and a probable cause hearing was conducted.[19]

The Supreme Court returned to the issue of capital punishment in 1988 in ***Thompson v. Oklahoma***, in which it held that imposing the death penalty on a person who was 15 years at the time of his or her crime violated the Eighth Amendment's prohibition against cruel and unusual punishment.[20] One year later in ***Stanford v. Kentucky*** (1989), the Court held that no consensus exists that forbids the sentencing to death of a person who commits capital murder at age 16 or 17.[21] That conclusion changed in the 2005 in the landmark case ***Roper v. Simmons***, which rendered capital punishment unconstitutional as applied to persons under age 18. The *Roper* decision invalidated the death penalty for juveniles, which is a far different approach than earlier eras of juvenile corrections. The *Roper* decision effectively reversed the decision reached in *Stanford v. Kentucky*. According to the Supreme Court, several factors contribute to a changing consensus about applying the death penalty to juveniles: (1) several states had abolished the juvenile death penalty in the intervening years since *Stanford*; (2) states that retained the juvenile death penalty ostensibly never used it; (3) the juvenile death penalty was not used in most parts of the westernized world; and (4) there was greater appreciation for the developmental differences between adolescents and adults in terms of decision making, emotional and behavioral control, and other neurocognitive factors that influence criminal decision making.[22]

Contemporary Juvenile Corrections

The beginning of the contemporary approach to juvenile corrections and juvenile justice occurred in 1974 with the passage of the **Juvenile Justice and Delinquency Prevention Act**. The act was the most sweeping change in juvenile justice since the creation of the juvenile court in 1899 with the passage of the Chicago Juvenile Court Act. The major points of the Juvenile Justice and Delinquency Prevention Act were:

- The decriminalization of status offenders so that they were not considered delinquent.
- The deinstitutionalization of juvenile corrections so that only the most severe delinquents would be eligible for confinement, status offenders should not be institutionalized, and juveniles in adult jails and prisons should be separated by sight and sound from adults.
- The broadened use of diversion as an alternative to formal processing in juvenile court.
- The continued application of due process constitutional rights to juveniles.
- The creation of the federal **Office of Juvenile Justice and Delinquency Prevention (OJJDP)**, which funded research to evaluate juvenile justice programs and disseminated research findings on the juvenile justice system.

The Juvenile Justice and Delinquency Prevention Act was modified in 1977, 1980, 1984, 1988, and as recently as 2002. For instance, in 1980 the act specified the jail and lockup removal requirement, which meant that juveniles could not be detained or confined in adult jails or lockups. Adult facilities had a 6-hour grace period to ascertain the age of the offender or transport the youth to a juvenile facility (rural jails had up to 48 hours). In 1988, the act specified the disproportionate minority confinement requirement, which required juvenile corrections to gather data on the racial composition of their population compared to the racial composition of the state. In 2002, this was changed to disproportionate minority contact, whereby racial data was mandated for all aspects of the juvenile justice system. Correctional systems comply with OJJDP guidelines to remain eligible for federal allocations from the Formula Grants Program.[23–25]

During this era, the nation experienced dramatic increases in juvenile homicides, other types of juvenile violence, and an increasingly visible juvenile gang problem in major U.S. cities. As a result, states enacted legislation that increasingly targeted youths involved in the most serious forms of delinquency. During the 1990s, 45 states made it easier to transfer juvenile offenders to adult criminal courts. Thirty-one states expanded the sentencing options to include **blended sentencing**. Blended sentencing provides methods for juvenile courts to combine juvenile and adult punishment that is tailored to the needs of the individual offender. For instance, juvenile courts can combine a juvenile disposition with a criminal sentence that is suspended. If the delinquent complies with the juvenile disposition, the criminal sentence is never imposed. If not, the youth is eligible to receive the adult sentence.

In 34 states, there are once an adult, always an adult provisions that specify that once a youth has been tried as an adult, any subsequent offenses must also be waived to criminal court. Laws were modified to reduce or remove traditional juvenile court confidentiality provisions and make juvenile records more open in 47 states. In 22 states, laws increased the role of victims of juvenile crimes by allowing them to be heard in the juvenile justice process.[26]

Nationwide, adolescents account for about 1 percent of new court commitments to adult state prisons. This equates to a juveniles-in-adult-prisons count of approximately 4,100—many of them for armed robbery, assault, burglary, murder, and sexual assault.[27] More punitive measures such as waivers are justified based on the serious violence and chronic delinquencies of the most serious offenders; however, some of these provisions carry unintended consequences. For example, research suggests that youths who are waived to criminal court and receive adult punishments ultimately have higher recidivism levels than youths who receive juvenile court dispositions. David Myers studied 494 violent juvenile delinquents in Pennsylvania and found that even when prior delinquency history and criminality was statistically controlled, youths who had received transfers to criminal court were more violent, frequent offenders after release.[28] A study examined 475 pairs of Florida juveniles who were matched on seven factors with one youth in each pair receiving adult punishment and the other paired youth receiving juvenile punishment. Controlling for delinquent career variables and demographic controls, youths waived to criminal court were not only more likely to recidivate but also more likely to commit a violent offense.[29] Recent research suggests that adult punishment carries certain advantages over its juvenile system approach. Aaron Kupchik interviewed 95 offenders who had served time in five adult or juvenile correctional facilities. Contrary to expectations, juveniles reported that adult facilities did a better job than juvenile facilities at providing various treatment and counseling services.[30]

It is conventional wisdom within criminology to lament the increasing toughness or punitive stance that society takes toward juvenile delinquents primarily through the process of transfer to criminal court.[31] But it should be noted that the last 40 years of juvenile justice reflect a profound commitment to due process and the legal rights of adolescents, the abolishment of the juvenile death penalty, and a general hands-off policy stance toward status and low-level delinquents. Indeed, the juvenile justice system and particularly juvenile corrections have noted the diversity of the delinquent population and focused resources disproportionately toward the most serious youths. The final section of this chapter describes that system-wide commitment to the most serious, violent, and chronic delinquents.

The Juvenile Justice System

Age is the only social characteristic that necessitates a separate justice system. There are not separate justice systems for men and women, different racial and ethnic groups, or social class or income groups. Within a jurisdiction, there are local, state, and federal laws that apply to all citizens equally, and upon alleged violation of those laws, there is a single adult criminal justice system that responds to them. But age is different. Children and adolescents receive a separate and in many ways different justice system than adults. For historical reasons that will be examined, even the terminology of these systems is different.

The **juvenile justice system** is the set of agencies that process persons under the age of 18 for violations of the law. Juveniles or minors who are ultimately found guilty of crimes are known as **delinquents or juvenile delinquents**. In the juvenile justice system, the word *crime* is not used. Instead, violations of criminal law are **delinquent offenses** and violations of criminal law that only pertain to children and adolescents are known as **status offenses**. For example, acts including murder, theft, and arson are delinquent offenses. Acts including **truancy** or nonattendance of school, running away from home, and being incorrigible or ungovernable are status offenses. Whereas police officers are empowered to contact or arrest both juveniles and adults, the **juvenile court** has original jurisdiction to proceed against minors only. Adults cannot be prosecuted in juvenile court, although juveniles can also be prosecuted in adult criminal court.

There are a variety of semantic differences between the criminal and juvenile justice systems. Whereas adults are arrested, juveniles receive police contacts. Whereas adults are booked and jailed, juveniles are taken into custody. Once in court, juvenile are proceeded against, not prosecuted; found to be delinquent or **adjudicated** as opposed to convicted; and issued a **disposition** as opposed to being sentenced. When juveniles are placed into custody awaiting adjudication, they are **detained.** When they are placed into custody after adjudication, they are **committed.** In general, juvenile detention is comparable to adult jail and juvenile commitment is comparable to adult prison. Juveniles are categorically exempt from capital punishment.

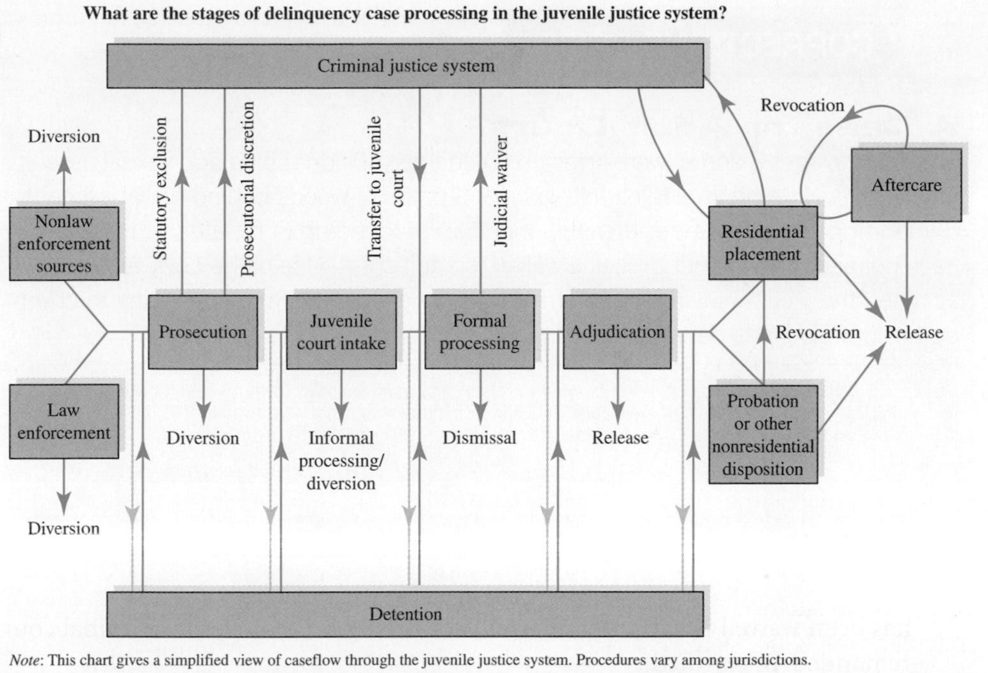

FIGURE 13–2 The Juvenile Justice System. *Source*: Snyder, H. N., & Sickmund, M. (2006). *Juvenile offenders and victims: 2006 national report.* Washington, DC: U.S. Department of Justice, Office of Justice Programs, Office of Juvenile Justice and Delinquency Prevention.

Structure and Processes

As shown in **FIGURE 13–2**, the juvenile justice system operates much like the criminal justice system in that both systems funnel cases out. There are numerous opportunities for an individual's case to be removed from the system. One important difference between the systems is that diversion is used extensively in the juvenile justice system. Once they contact youths for delinquent offenses, law enforcement officers divert about 25 percent of all delinquency cases. Diversion amounts to letting the youth off with a warning or discussion with the youth and his or her parents. Other cases are diverted to social service providers that can provide services to meet the needs of the juvenile. Diversion also exists throughout the court process.

Another defining feature of the juvenile justice system is the reliance on probation (Chapter 8), which has been referred to as the workhorse of the juvenile justice system. Once juvenile cases, which are known as petitions, enter the juvenile justice system, they follow two general pathways. Approximately 50 percent of cases are informally disposed of through informal probation that is comparable to a deferred sentence in the adult criminal justice system. As long as the adolescent stays out of trouble while on informal probation, the case is dismissed and the matter ends. If not, the case is referred to the court as a **delinquency petition** and ultimately scheduled for an **adjudicatory hearing** or juvenile trial.

In some circumstances, a juvenile's conduct is considered serious enough to warrant adult prosecution. When a juvenile is prosecuted in criminal court, the process is known as **transfer or waiver**. There are five general types of waivers:

1. A **judicial waiver** occurs when the judge decides to transfer the case to criminal court based on the severity of the charges and/or the severity of the youth's delinquent record. This is the most common, traditional form of waiver and research suggests that judges are the most discerning in terms of selecting only the most serious, violent, and chronic youths to waive to adult court.[32] A juvenile case that

CORRECTIONS BRIEF

A Case for Adult Court?

Three boys, ages 8 and 9, were arrested on charges of kidnapping and sexual assault after allegedly luring an 11-year-old girl into a patch of woods behind her apartment, demanding she expose her breasts, and then proceeding to rape her. Prosecutors have not decided whether to seek a waiver to adult court. One of the boys' fathers has accused the victim of lying. He claimed the 11-year-old victim is just trying to cover up her promiscuous behavior.

Source: CBS News. (2007). *Boys 8 and 9 charged with rape: Police in Georgia charge three boys with kidnapping and raping 11-year-old girl.* Retrieved November 20, 2008, from http://www.cbsnews.com/stories/2007/11/19/national/main3522075.shtml.

Youths who are prosecuted as adults are waived or transferred to criminal court. This process often leads to greater recidivism among transferred youths.

has been waived is variously referred to as being bound over to criminal court, remanded, or certified.

2. A **legislative waiver** occurs when certain offenses are statutorily excluded from prosecution in juvenile court and require adult prosecution.
3. A **prosecutorial waiver** occurs when the district attorney, county attorney, or prosecutor uses his or her discretion to prosecute the youth as an adult in criminal court. A prosecutorial waiver is also known as a direct file, which means that both juvenile and criminal courts hold original jurisdiction over the case or the courts have concurrent jurisdiction.
4. A **demand waiver** occurs when the delinquent chooses criminal prosecution.
5. A **reverse waiver** occurs when a transferred case that qualifies for criminal prosecution is sent back to juvenile court to be processed. The undoing of a waived case is called **decertification**. Youths with few prior referrals, youths with secondary roles in crimes, and cases involving less-serious felonies are those likely to receive a reverse waiver.[33]

After an adjudication of guilt, delinquents face similar correctional outcomes as in the adult system. The most serious delinquents are detained in secure detention facilities. Most are placed on probation and thus in the juvenile justice system, probation is used before and after the adjudication process. For youths who are placed in detention, most are ultimately released on **aftercare** or juvenile parole. These parts of the juvenile justice system are explored in greater detail later in this chapter.

Statistics and Trends

According to the National Report on Juvenile Offenders and Victims, more than 1.6 million delinquency cases arrived in juvenile court in 2006. Nearly 700,000 of these cases, or 42 percent, did not result in a petition. However, this does not mean the cases simply end. Of the nonpetitioned cases, 31 percent resulted in probation placements, 30 percent received another sanction (e.g., teen court, community service, etc.), and 39 percent were dismissed.

Nearly 935,000 cases were petitioned in juvenile court, of which 1 percent were waived to adult court, 67 percent resulted in adjudicated delinquent dispositions, and 32 percent result in not adjudicated delinquent dispositions. Among the adjudicated cases,

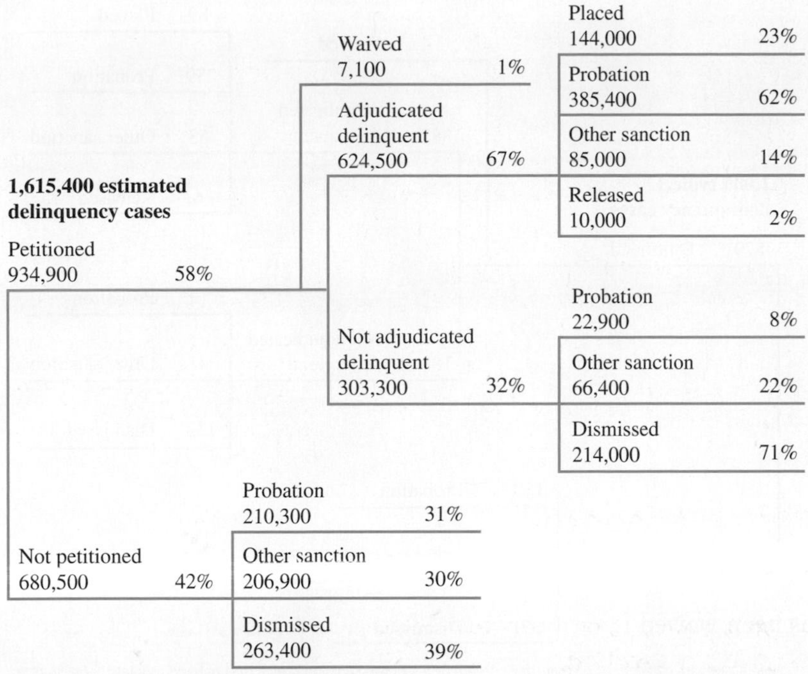

Note: Percentages might not total 100 due to rounding.

FIGURE 13-3 Processing of Juvenile Cases. *Source*: Snyder, H. N., & Sickmund, M. (2006). *Juvenile offenders and victims: 2006 national report.* Washington, DC: U.S. Department of Justice, Office of Justice Programs, Office of Juvenile Justice and Delinquency Prevention.

23 percent, or about 144,000 youths, were placed in secured facilities. Nearly 400,000 youths, or 62 percent, were placed on probation with 14 percent receiving some other sanction, and 2 percent receiving outright release. Among the more than 303,000 cases that resulted in not adjudicated findings, 71 percent were dismissed, 22 percent received other sanctions, and 8 percent received probation (see FIGURE 13-3).[34]

FIGURE 13-4 illustrates the juvenile justice system based on a scale of 1,000 cases. It is clear that probation is widely used as a placement for nonpetitioned youths, for youths who are adjudicated delinquents, and for those not adjudicated as delinquents. Only 89 cases out of 1,000 result in institutional placements in the juvenile system. The 4 cases that are waived to adult court obviously can result in adult jail or adult prison confinement.

Nearly 97,000 juvenile offenders are held in residential placement in the United States; approximately two thirds of those are in public facilities and one third in private facilities. As shown in TABLE 13-1, this includes more than 33,000 youths adjudicated for person crimes, such as homicide, sexual assault, robbery, and assault. Nearly 27,000 youths are confined for property offenses including burglary, auto theft, arson, and theft. About 8,000 adolescents are in secured custody for drug crimes, nearly 10,000 for public order crimes, and more than 14,000 for violations of juvenile justice sentences. Fewer than 5,000 youths are placed in custody for status offenses. In descending order, these placements are for ungovernability (parents indicate that they cannot control the child's behavior), running away, truancy, curfew violations, and underage drinking.[35]

As shown in FIGURE 13-5, by a ratio of about 20 to 1, youths in confinement facilities are adjudicated for delinquent as opposed to status offenses. Another important trend is that delinquent wards are likely to be serving time in publicly administered state facilities whereas less-serious status offenders are primarily housed in private facilities.

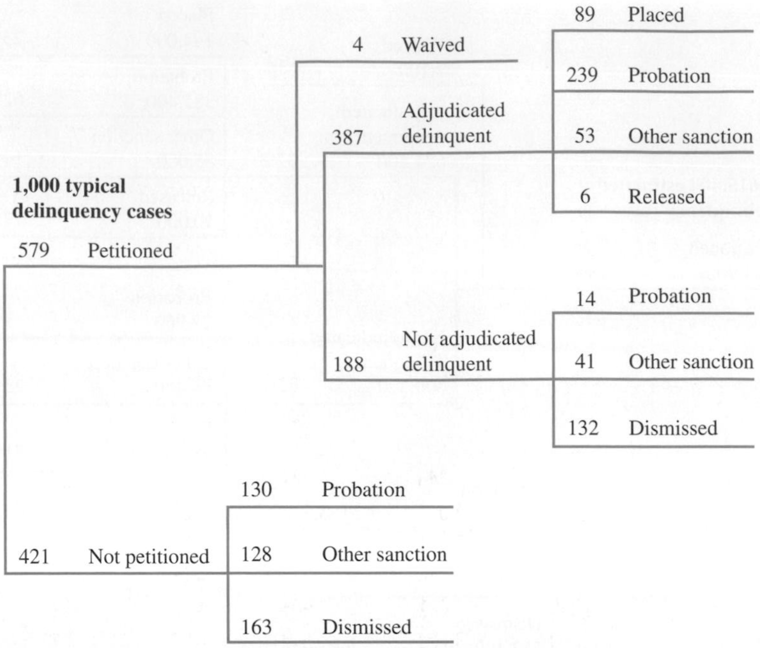

Note: Cases are categorized by their most severe or restrictive sanction. Detail may not add to totals because of rounding.

FIGURE 13–4 Typical Outcome of 1,000 Delinquency Cases. *Source*: Snyder, H. N., & Sickmund, M. (2006). *Juvenile offenders and victims: 2006 national report.* Washington, DC: U.S. Department of Justice, Office of Justice Programs, Office of Juvenile Justice and Delinquency Prevention.

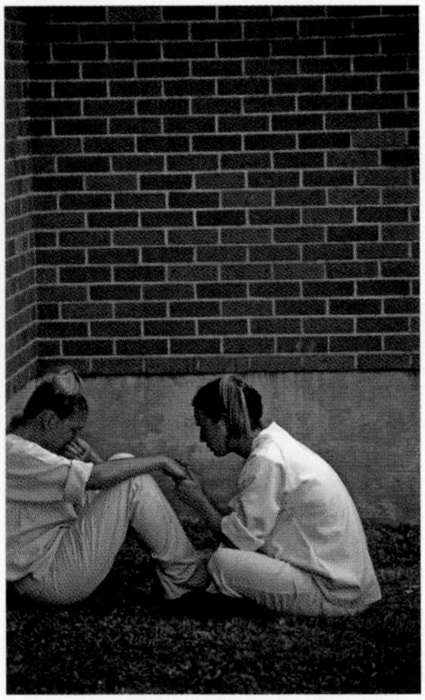

Adolescents in jail have suicide rates 19 times higher than youths in the general population. Those housed in adult jails are 36 times more likely to commit suicide than youths housed in juvenile detention.

Each day, roughly 7,500 adolescents are held in adult jails in the United States. There are many risks for adolescents who are jailed, however brief their incarceration might be. For instance, although juveniles are 1 percent of the American jail population, they are the victims of 21 percent of assaults and 16 percent of sexual assaults occurring in jails. Juveniles are 19 times more likely to commit suicide in jail compared to adolescents in the general population. Youths in adult jails are 36 times more likely to commit suicide than youths housed in juvenile detention facilities.[36] Nationwide, 26 youths died while in custody. Ten died from suicide, 6 from accidents, 6 from illness, 2 from homicide, and 2 from other causes.[37]

A major difference between the juvenile and criminal justice systems is that adolescents do not serve lengthy sentences while detained or committed to correctional facilities. Nationwide, the median time in custody for detained youth is a mere 15 days. The median time in custody for a committed delinquent to a public facility is 105 days and to a private facility 121 days. Only 13 percent of all youths committed to confinement will serve more than 1 year behind bars.[38]

Juvenile delinquency is a tremendous burden on society and the most antisocial youths impose staggering costs in terms of victimization and correctional costs. A recent study by Brandon Welsh and his colleagues is illustrative. Welsh and his collaborators estimated the victimization costs created by the self-reported delinquency of 503 boys from the Pittsburgh Youth Study and produced several important findings, which include:

- The cohort reported 12,514 crimes or about 25 crimes each.
- The victimization ranged from $89 million to $110 million stemming from victims' pain, suffering, and lost quality of life.
- Thirty-four chronic offenders averaged 142 crimes, which was nearly 10 times the criminal activity of other delinquents.
- Chronic offenders imposed five to eight times the victimization costs than nonchronic offenders.[39]

TABLE 13-1 Youths in Custody

	Juvenile Offenders in Residential Placement, 2003			Percent Change 1997–2003		
		Type of Facility			Type of Facility	
Most Serious Offense	**All**	**Public**	**Private**	**All**	**Public**	**Private**
Total offenders	**96,655**	**66,210**	**30,321**	**–8**	**–12**	**3**
Delinquency	**91,831**	**64,662**	**27,059**	**–7**	**–12**	**11**
Person	33,197	23,499	9,671	–6	–13	21
Criminal homicide	878	803	73	–54	–56	–28
Sexual assault	7,452	4,749	2,698	34	20	68
Robbery	6,230	5,157	1,073	–33	–35	–22
Aggravated assault	7,495	5,745	1,741	–21	–24	–7
Simple assault	8,106	4,984	3,113	22	21	25
Other person	3,036	2,061	973	38	22	87
Property	26,843	18,740	8,073	–16	–18	–10
Burglary	10,399	7,481	2,904	–17	–21	–7
Theft	5,650	3,793	1,848	–22	–26	–12
Auto theft	5,572	3,756	1,812	–15	–14	–16
Arson	735	514	220	–19	–25	0
Other property	4,487	3,196	1,289	–4	–4	–6
Drug	8,002	4,851	3,137	–12	–23	15
Drug trafficking	1,810	1,284	522	–37	–41	–24
Other drug	6,192	3,567	2,615	0	–14	28
Public order	9,654	6,782	2,866	0	–5	11
Weapons	3,013	2,346	665	–28	–29	–24
Other public order	6,641	4,436	2,201	20	16	29
Technical violation	14,135	10,790	3,312	14	5	56
Status offense	**4,824**	**1,548**	**3,262**	**–29**	**–11**	**–36**
Ungovernability	1,825	253	1,571	–36	–45	–34
Running away	997	417	577	–33	–14	–43
Truancy	841	207	634	–37	–49	–32
Curfew violation	203	65	138	5	–18	21
Underage drinking	405	210	186	27	86	–10
Other status offense	553	396	157	–14	98	–64

Source: Snyder, H. N., & Sickmund, M. (2006). *Juvenile offenders and victims: 2006 national report.* Washington, DC: U.S. Department of Justice, Office of Juvenile Justice and Delinquency Prevention, National Center for Juvenile Justice.

Based on these offending data, it is clear that a small proportion of youths have serious delinquency careers that will justify continued interventions from the juvenile correctional system.

Federal Juvenile Justice

Unlike states, there is no separate juvenile justice system in the federal system. Instead, adolescent offenders are prosecuted and sentenced in United States District Courts and committed to Bureau of Prisons facilities.[40] Many arrests of juveniles occur on American Indian reservations where the Federal Bureau of Investigation has responsibility of more than 200 reservations across the country.

Each year, federal authorities arrest about 400 juveniles. Federal law requires that federal authorities investigate whether the conduct was a delinquent offense under state

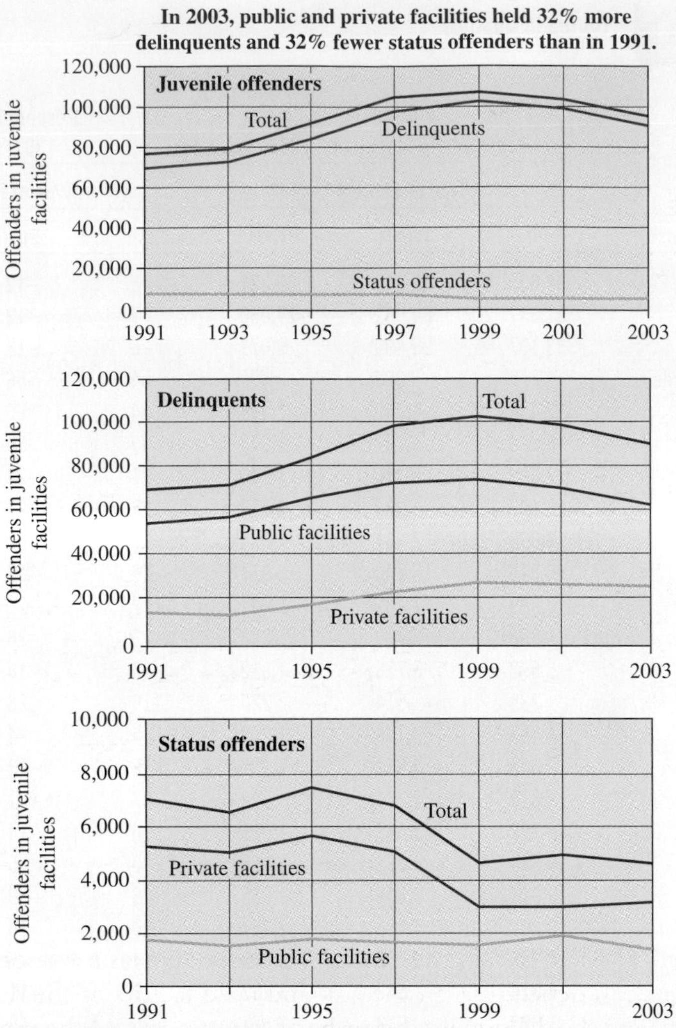

FIGURE 13–5 Delinquent and Status Offenders in Confinement. *Source*: Snyder, H. N., & Sickmund, M. (2006). *Juvenile offenders and victims: 2006 national report.* Washington, DC: U.S. Department of Justice, Office of Juvenile Justice and Delinquency Prevention, National Center for Juvenile Justice.

law and surrender the juvenile to state authorities as necessary. However, the attorney general can certify a case for federal delinquency prosecution if:

- The state does not have or refuses to take jurisdiction over the case.
- The state does not have programs or services available that are adequate to the needs of the juvenile.
- The juvenile is charged with a violent felony, drug trafficking, or firearms offense, and the case involves a substantial federal interest.

Federal delinquency prosecutions are heard by a U.S. District Court judge in a closed session without a jury. Sentencing outcomes are similar to state juvenile courts and federal probation or confinement usually ends no later than the juvenile's 21st birthday. Persons as young as age 13 can be prosecuted under federal law for murder. About 3,000 youths are confined in the BOP.[41]

Intermediate Sanctions

A range of intermediate sanctions (Chapter 7) is used in the juvenile justice system to provide supervision and control in a community setting. Intermediate sanctions allow

CORRECTIONS FOCUS

School Shooters

Evidence from the hard drive of Pekka-Eric Auvinen, an 18-year-old student who authorities in Finland say perpetrated a school shooting in November 2007 resulting in the deaths of six students, a school nurse, the principal, and himself, had chatted with a 14-year-old Philadelphia teenager, Dillon Cossey, about video games and other topics of interest, including the Columbine school shooting.

The Philadelphia teenager was taken into custody in 2007 for having allegedly prepared an attack on Plymouth Whitemarsh High School in Philadelphia. Information from another student Dillon tried to recruit provided enough probable cause for police to obtain a search warrant. Searching the residence, police found a rifle, swords, knives, a book on bomb making, and videos of the Columbine shooting. They also located violence-filled notebooks. According to reports, Dillon Cossey had told a friend that he had been bullied and was preparing an attack like the one against Columbine High School.

Police have also accused Dillon's mother of assisting her son prepare for the attack against Plymouth Whitemarsh High. She has been charged with purchasing three weapons for her underage son, including a 9-mm semiautomatic rifle equipped with a laser sighting system.

Source: Associated Press. (2007). *Police: Finland Teen Shooter Left a Suicide Note.* Retrieved November 13, 2007, from http://www.msnbc.msn.com/id/21686096/.

the juvenile justice system to use graduated sanctions to apply the proportionately most challenging sanction depending on the risk and need factors of the delinquent. The process of matching the delinquent, his or her delinquency, and the most appropriate disposition or punishment is known as graduated sanctions (FIGURE 13–6).

In recent years, many intermediate sanctions have been influenced by **restorative justice**, which is an alternative justice model that seeks to repair the harm caused by delinquency by bringing together the offender, victim, and societal members to collectively resolve the issues caused by the crime. These include:

- *Diversion:* Diversion is the replacement of formal juvenile justice system processing with informal, less punitive interventions usually from social service agencies. Diversion programs avoid the stigmatizing exposure of youth to the justice system and reduce problem behavior. Contemporary diversion programs are evidence based and attempt to serve both delinquent youth and their families.[42]
- *Community service:* For most dispositions in the juvenile justice system, community service is part of the total sentence. For instance, 92 percent of the Serious and Violent Offender Reentry Initiative (SVORI) programs that specifically target juveniles require community service to instill a sense of responsibility and reciprocity towards the delinquent's community. Some of the community services include working with Habitat for Humanity, animal care and training, and community beautification and landscaping.[43]
- *Family group conferences:* After a delinquent's admission of guilt, family group conferences are held between the offender, victim, and supporters of both parties. A trained mediator/facilitator brings the group together to discuss the crime, the harm it caused, and ways the parties can repair their relationships. The process is intended to build community and serve as a disincentive for offenders to

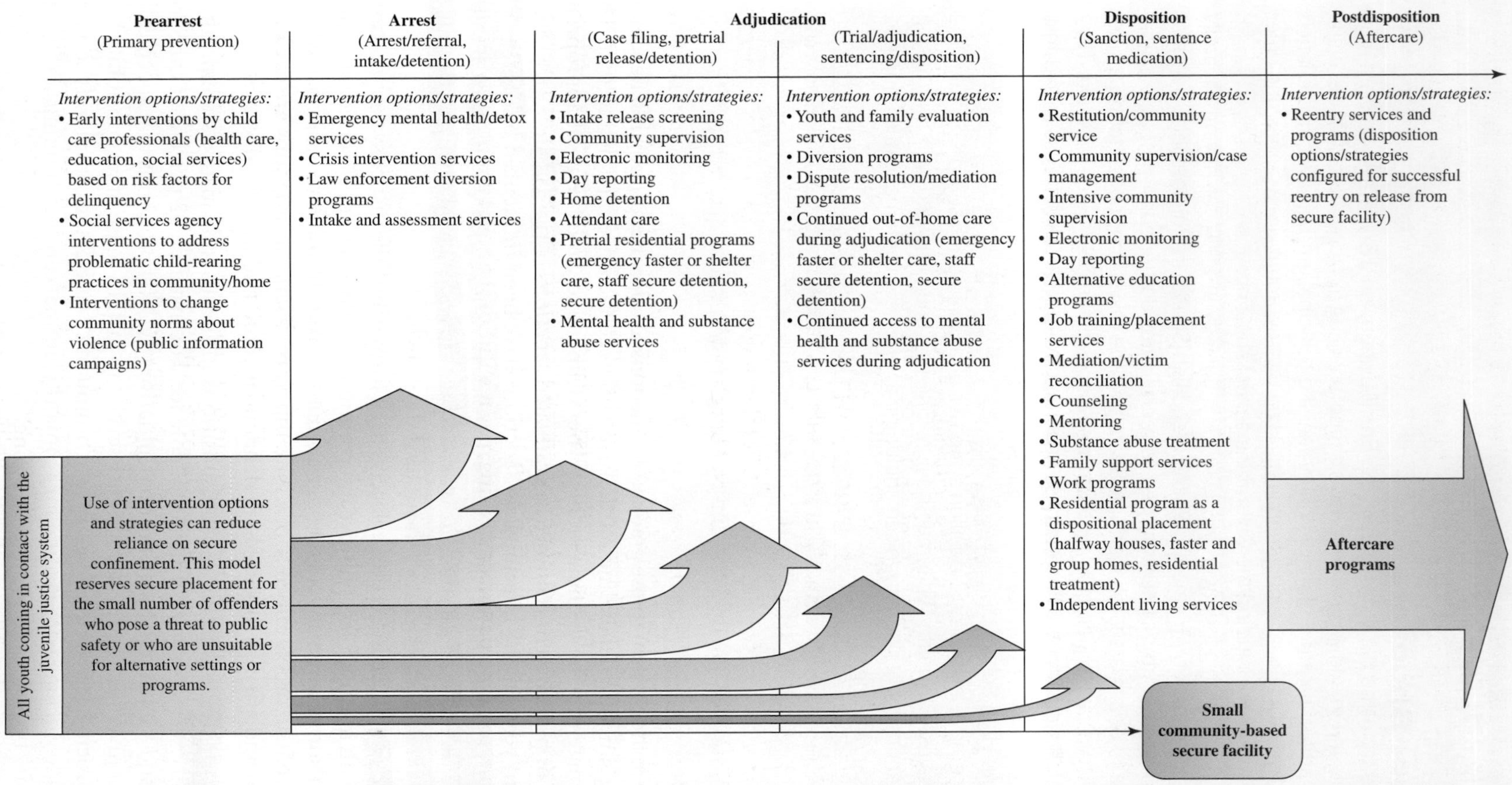

FIGURE 13–6 Graduated Sanctions. *Source*: Zavlek, S. (2005). *Planning community-based facilities for violent juvenile offenders as part of a system of graduated sanctions.* Washington, DC: U.S. Department of Justice, Office of Justice Programs, Office of Juvenile Justice and Delinquency Prevention.

recidivate. Support of family group conferences is promising.[44] For instance, a recent experiment involving 800 youths tracked for 2 years found that family group conference participants were less likely to recidivate and had lower levels of offending.[45]

- *Teen court:* A standard part of juvenile corrections is diversion in which delinquents utilize social service agencies as part of their punishment in lieu of formal processing in the juvenile court. A **teen court** is a restorative justice approach in which first-time offenders publicly admit guilt before a group of peers who, in turn, impose a sentence. The sentence involves a positive interaction with a peer group, which is supposed to provide empowerment and motivate youths to behave. Teen court cases began in 1994, and today there are nearly 1,000 teen courts nationwide. Most teen court participants complete the program, and recidivism rates tend to be low—in the range of 25 to 30 percent.[46–47] Teen court has also recently been found to be effective for repeat juvenile offenders with a prior adjudication.[48] Despite initially low recidivism among teen court graduates, there is also evidence that recidivism rates increase steadily for up to 4 years.[49]
- *Curfews:* One of the status offenses that has been targeted by juvenile justice agents is curfew, which is the specified times, such as 10:00 p.m. to 6:00 a.m., when minors are prohibited from being outdoors or in places beside their homes. **Curfew enforcement** limits the opportunities youths have to engage in delinquency. A recent evaluation of curfew enforcement in Palm Bay, Florida, indicated that parents reported improvements in their children's behaviors after curfew enforcement began. More importantly, crimes rates in Palm Bay declined 28 percent during the period of curfew enforcement. Total nonviolent crime was down 33 percent, shoplifting declined 52 percent, and burglary was reduced 20 percent.[50]
- *Juvenile conference committees:* **Juvenile conference committees** are panels of six to nine volunteers from the community who meet monthly to hear juvenile complaints referred by the family court. Generally, juvenile conference committees hear cases of youths charged with misdemeanor offenses and only those with zero or one known prior act of delinquency. Although the process is not adversarial and delinquents do not admit guilt, they receive a sentence (called a recommendation) to participate in counseling, pay restitution, conduct community service, or write a letter of apology.[51]

Probation

Juvenile probation is the oldest and most widely used vehicle through which a range of court-ordered services is rendered. Probation may be used at the front end of the juvenile justice system for first-time, low-risk offenders or at the back end as an alternative to institutional confinement for more serious offenders.[52] The increased monitoring of probationers often leads to increased collaboration between agencies within the juvenile justice system. An example is police-probation partnerships, in which juvenile probation officers go on patrol with law enforcement officers to conduct home visits of probationers; explain the terms of the sentence to the probationers; conduct searches of probationers for drugs, weapons, and other contraband; and provide basic services. One example is Operation Nightlight in San Bernardino, California, where police and probation officers searched juvenile probationers' homes, conducted return home visits, enforced curfew, conducted school contacts, and generally monitored clients. John Worrall and Larry Gaines evaluated Operation Nightlight and found that the police-probation partnership resulted in reduced juvenile arrests for serious crimes including assault, burglary, and theft.[53]

The effectiveness of juvenile probation has been studied extensively. Ted Palmer and Robert Wedge studied the effectiveness of juvenile probation camps, which were alternatives to confinement in the California juvenile justice system among nearly 3,000 juvenile offenders. In a 2-year follow-up, 65 percent of the former juvenile probationers were recontacted for a delinquent offense, and nearly 30 percent were committed to a state correctional institution. Palmer and Wedge reported that probation camps that provided more services, such as counseling/casework, vocational training, work details, academic training, religious activities, recreation, off-facility activities, and outside contacts tended to produce better outcomes.[54] Matthew Giblin evaluated the Anchorage, Alaska, Coordinated Agency Network (CAN) program, which included enhanced services and supervision for juvenile probationers. The CAN program consisted of intensified surveillance and monitoring compared to traditional juvenile probation. Giblin found that although there were no differences in recidivism between the groups, about 30 percent of youths serving a CAN sentence were cited for technical violations compared to 17 percent on traditional probation. The greater monitoring resulted in more accountability among juvenile probationers, thus providing a more rigorous probation experience that also kept recidivism low.[55]

The need for multiple services is important because youths on juvenile probation often have multiple risk factors for continued involvement in delinquency. For instance, a recent evaluation of probation supervised youths in Cuyahoga County (Cleveland), Ohio, found that they often had multiple prior involvements in the juvenile justice system; were from family backgrounds characterized by poverty, abuse, and adoption; and suffered from an array of social and behavioral problems.[56]

Backgrounds characterized by abuse and delinquency often make for challenging probation clients. Sarah Vidal and Jennifer Skeem studied the effects of abuse history and psychopathic personality among juvenile probationers on the decision making of juvenile probation officers. They found that probation officers viewed youths with abuse histories and psychopathic traits as challenging, difficult-to-reach clients. Probation officers felt compassion for youths who had been abused and often went the extra mile in terms of providing greater support, resources, and assistance. Conversely, psychopathic youths were subjected to greater supervision, were viewed as unlikely to be successfully treated, and received little pity from probation officers.[57] In other words, certain risk factors can guide the type of supervision juvenile clients receive on probation.

Because of this situation, some juvenile probation programs began to focus on the strengths of the adolescent rather than concentrate just on risk factors. For example, Riley County, Kansas, initiated the Juvenile Intake and Assessment Case Management approach, which utilizes the client's assets and talents to help achieve program goals, increase involvement in prosocial activities, formalize family networks, and identify school and work opportunities. The program takes a can-do proactive philosophy so that the adolescent can observe ways to effect prosocial change in his or her life. Don Kurtz and Travis Linnemann evaluated the strengths approach and found that youths on the program performed better than those on traditional probation and significantly better than youths on intensive probation.[58]

Some research studies found little to no difference in recidivism outcomes between various types of probation or probation versus confinement. Preston Elrod and Kevin Minor evaluated Project Explore, which is a juvenile probation program that consists of outdoor adventures, social skills training, and parent skills training and compared it to standard probation. They found that youths in Project Explore performed about the same as youths on standard probation, suggesting that the specialized and unique treatment protocols did little to reduce delinquency.[59]

Mark Lipsey and David Wilson conducted a meta-analysis of 200 studies of correctional interventions for serious and violent juvenile offenders within institutions and serving noninstitutional sentences, such as probation. Their study reflects the state of the art of what is known about correctional interventions among the most delinquent youth, which includes:

- Individual counseling, interpersonal skills counseling, and behavioral programs produce the most consistently positive treatment effects.
- Probation programs that utilize multiple services and require payment of restitution have positive effects, although the evidence is less consistent.
- Work and education programs, advocacy/casework, and family and group counseling produced inconsistent but generally positive effects among adolescent probationers.
- Probation programs that use wilderness components, early release, deterrence, and vocational programs have no effect on probationer success.[60]

Lipsey also estimated the expected recidivism levels for juvenile probation programs. Routine probation yields an expected recidivism level of 50 percent. When a minimal program is added, recidivism drops to 46 percent. When standard juvenile probation is coupled with the best intervention type, the recidivism level is 40 percent. When these conditions are present and the program implementation is good, the recidivism drops to 35 percent. Finally, when all of these conditions are met and the program lasts more than 6 months, the recidivism level is 32 percent.[61] This shows that more programming, quality implementation, and sustained application make juvenile probation better.

Detention and Commitment

The most severe form of punishment that the juvenile justice system imposes is commitment to a secured facility. As shown in TABLE 13-2, there are nearly 3,000 juvenile corrections facilities in the United States. Nearly 40 percent of juvenile correctional facilities are group homes, which are locked residential facilities with usually fewer than 50 residents.

TABLE 13-2 Juvenile Confinement Facilities in the United States

		Facility Type						
Facility Operation	Total	Detention Center	Shelter	Reception/ Diagnostic Center	Group Home	Boot Camp	Ranch/ Wilderness Camp	Long-Term Secure
Total	2,964	769	289	104	1,136	56	157	389
Facility type by operation								
	100%	100%	100%	100%	100%	100%	100%	100%
Public	40	80	28	52	18	68	39	67
State	17	18	5	42	10	25	16	56
Local	23	62	22	10	7	43	23	12
Private	60	19	72	48	82	32	61	33
Operation by facility type								
Total	100%	26%	10%	4%	38%	2%	5%	13%
Public	100	52	7	5	17	3	5	22
State	100	27	3	9	23	3	5	22
Local	100	71	10	1	12	4	5	7
Private	100	8	12	3	53	1	5	7

Source: Snyder, H. N., & Sickmund, M. (2006). *Juvenile offenders and victims: 2006 national report.* Washington, DC: U.S. Department of Justice, Office of Justice Programs, Office of Juvenile Justice and Delinquency Prevention.

These facilities are similar to halfway houses for parolees in the adult system. Other facility types include detention centers, long-term secure facilities, shelters, ranch or wilderness camps, reception/diagnostic centers, and boot camps.

A variety of characteristics differentiate juvenile correctional facilities. For example, group homes, shelters, and wilderness camps are mostly operated by private correctional entities, whereas detention centers and long-term secure facilities—commonly known as juvenile jails and prisons—are usually administered by public local or state governments. About 81 percent of juvenile facilities are locked with the remaining 19 percent maintained by staff security. Youths who are pending adjudication are technically being detained. Those who have been adjudicated are committed and reside in more restrictive settings. Juvenile correctional facilities also vary in size. Group homes and shelters service 10 to 50 residents (as mentioned previously), whereas long-term secure facilities and reception/diagnostic centers can hold nearly 1,000 residents.[62]

Arguably the most controversial approach to juvenile corrections in recent decades has been **boot camps**, which are short-term incarceration programs modeled after military basic training that use physical exercise, drill, and coercion to instill self-discipline in young offenders. From their first use in 1983, boot camps were popular among the general public for their use of harsh discipline and tough love to put wayward youth on a straight (law-abiding) path. Boot camps were unpopular among academics who disliked the populist approach and questioned whether the programs were effective.[63]

The effectiveness of boot camps is an open question, but most criminological research suggests that they are ineffective at reducing recidivism. For instance, Doris Layton MacKenzie reviewed 17 studies of 18 samples of juvenile offenders placed in boot camps and found that 10 samples experienced lower recidivism but in 8 groups the boot camp cohort fared worse after release. Overall, youths who completed boot camps usually recidivated at about the same levels as control groups of offenders.[64]

Some positive results have emerged from boot camp programs that contain an aftercare component in which treatment is provided after the youths have completed boot camp and reentered society.[65] Due to the multiple risk factors that serious delinquents have, it is probably unrealistic to expect a short-term intervention such as boot camp to resolve their complex and deep-seated problems. Brent Benda and his colleagues studied boot camp graduates over 5 years and found that more than 60 percent of males and 42 percent of females recidivated within the follow-up. The strongest predictor of failure was low self-control, which is a personality and behavioral construct that is formed early in life and is difficult to change—especially by a 30- to 60-day boot camp program.[66]

If the most serious type of delinquent is most likely to be committed to an institution, it makes sense that a portion of these offenders will continue to misbehave behind bars. Chad Trulson studied the institutional misconduct of nearly 5,000 state-committed delinquents from a large southern juvenile correctional system. Trulson found that males, racial minorities, and youths with gang and extensive delinquency histories were most likely to engage in serious forms of misconduct. Delinquent history included variables including age at first formal referral to juvenile court, age at first state commitment to detention, number of felony adjudications, whether the offender was on probation at the time of their most recent offense, gang history, and use of violence against his or her own family. Thus, by the time serious delinquents are placed in confinement, their criminal careers are well under way and not likely to abate. Trulson concluded:

> Correctional systems cannot undo the histories of the delinquents they are charged with supervising and rehabilitating. For the most part, when delinquents reach state commitment, they are considered the most serious, violent, and incorrigible delinquents in the state. Oftentimes, unrealistic expectations are placed on correctional systems to change a lifetime of behavior in a year or less and also to make sure the changes hold once a youth returns to the environment that produced them.[67, p. 29]

CORRECTIONS IN THE NEWS

DNA Identifies Three in Gang Rape Case

Three teens have been identified as being involved in the sexual assault of a woman in West Palm Beach, Florida. The suspects, aged 18, 17, and 14, are accused of raping, sodomizing, and beating the woman and her 12-year-old son. The assailants also forced the son to have sex with his mother as part of the assault.

The victim stated that as many as 10 teens assaulted her and her son. DNA evidence found on the woman's dress tied two of the suspects to the crime. DNA evidence from the youngest assailant was found on a condom left at the scene. The teens attempted to destroy evidence of the crime by dousing the victims with cleaning fluids.

Source: Associated Press. (2007). *Gang rape suspects linked by DNA*. Retrieved November 18, 2007, from http://www.foxnews.com/printer_friendly_wires/2007Nov02/0,4675,GangRapeTeens,00.html.

Using data from nearly 4,000 male wards in the California Youth Authority, John MacDonald found that institutional misconduct was often simply an extension of delinquent behavior that delinquents demonstrated in the community. For example, for each violent crime that a ward had in his delinquent history, the odds of committing a violent infraction in confinement increased nearly 20 percent. Similarly, the odds of violent misconduct increased nearly 30 percent as gang criminal history increased.[68]

Psychopathic youths are among the most violent and noncompliant wards in juvenile institutions.

One explanation for the somewhat distressing prevalence of institutional misconduct among serious juvenile offenders relates to psychopathy, a personality disorder that is strongly associated with antisocial behavior. A host of researchers have linked psychopathy to institutional misconduct and violence. For instance, Sarah Spain and her colleagues found that psychopathic adolescents accumulated more total, violent, verbal, and administrative violations while in custody and also had significantly worse treatment outcomes. Psychopathic youths took much longer to complete or achieve minimal success in treatment.[69] A study of 226 incarcerated adolescent offenders found that about 9 percent exhibited high levels of psychopathic traits; however these youths had the most violent and versatile criminal histories.[70]

Among a sample of adjudicated adolescents, Daniel Murrie and his colleagues found that the risk of prison violence increased 10 percent for each point above the mean Psychopathy Checklist-Revised score. Overall, psychopathic inmates tend to be the most aggressive and difficult-to-manage inmates. Glenn Walters conducted a meta-analysis of 41 studies and found a moderate correlation between psychopathy and institutional adjustment. The studies encompassed adult and juveniles, offenders from four countries, various follow-up periods, and inmates from prisons, forensic hospitals, and psychiatric facilities. Upon release, psychopaths were significantly likely to commit general, violent, and sexual recidivism.[71]

Given the various risks posed by detained and confined youth, some might question whether there is any hope in treating serious and violent delinquents. The answer is a resounding yes. A recent study found that for every dollar spent on intensive treatment for violent delinquents confined in state custody, more than $7 is saved.[72] Moreover, well-designed and administered interventions yield impressive savings in terms of subsequent delinquency. To illustrate, Mark Lipsey evaluated interventions for institutionalized offenders and estimated that with minimal programming, about 50 percent of youth recidivate. When the best intervention type is applied, 44 percent recidivate, and when the program has over 6 months' duration, the rate drops to 36 percent. When these conditions are present and a nonjuvenile justice provider is used, recidivism drops to 31 percent. With good implementation, recidivism drops to 26 percent and with 2 years of duration, the recidivism level is 21 percent.[73]

Aftercare

Each year approximately 100,000 juvenile offenders are released from secure correctional placements in the United States, and nationally, more than half will recidivate.[74] Juveniles who are returning to society from confinement face many of the same obstacles that adult offenders face upon reentry (Chapter 12). Given the timing of an adolescent incarceration, it disrupts a youth's school chances and many times eligibility to be in school (many incarcerated youth have been expelled). Being an adolescent ex-con is also stigmatizing, which can negatively affect job opportunities and the likelihood of other prosocial connections. Of course, juveniles on parole or aftercare also have an array of behavioral problems that require treatment and extensive intervention to overcome.

Due to the challenges posed by aftercare, some jurisdictions developed reentry courts, which provide enhanced supervision and case management to retuning juvenile parolees. The first reentry court was developed in West Virginia, and the approach has also been developed in Indiana and Pennsylvania. Reentry courts have resulted in greater integration between juvenile probation departments and the juvenile court. Reentry court typically consists of court-administered day treatment programs where youths on aftercare can attend to the conditions of their conditional release.[75]

Several studies of released juvenile wards have been conducted. Benda and his colleagues studied more than 400 17-year-old youths released from the Arkansas Division of Youth Services and followed the sample for 2 years to access recidivism rates and entry into the adult correctional system. Slightly more than 65 percent of the sample was rearrested. Prior delinquency was a powerful predictor of failure to comply with aftercare conditions and entry into the adult criminal justice system. Specifically, gang membership increased the odds of recidivism more than 330 percent and prior incarcerations increased the odds more than 350 percent.[76]

Based on their offending history, youths who are institutionalized and released could be viewed as the next generation of adult prisoners. For instance, Ashley Blackburn and her colleagues examined the self-reported offending of a sample of nearly 1,100 incarcerated youths. The group averaged six police contacts, nearly five placements in juvenile detention, and nearly two probation sentences. In the preceding year, 36 percent reported a robbery offense, 56 percent had beaten someone, 37 percent had threatened others with a gun or knife, 10 percent had stabbed someone with a knife, 20 percent had shot someone with a gun, 18 percent had participated in a drive-by shooting, and 18 percent had seriously injured or killed someone.[77]

As indicated earlier in this chapter, the Office of Juvenile Justice and Delinquency Prevention developed a comprehensive strategy for dealing with serious, violent, and chronic juvenile offenders. Based on the assorted risk factors that this group has, it is likely that serious, violent, and chronic juvenile offenders have difficulty on parole. Chad Trulson and his colleagues studied the reentry of a cohort of 2,436 delinquents paroled from state custody. During the follow-up period, fully 85 percent of the cohort was arrested at least once, and nearly 80 percent of the offenders were arrested for a felony offense. Youths most likely to recidivate were those with the earliest starting delinquency careers, those with the greatest number of felony adjudications, gang members, and males. Part of the problem with their unsuccessful aftercare phase was that many offenders continued to commit crime while institutionalized. For instance, 20 percent of the cohort was assaultive toward correctional staff, and 30 percent had force used against them for noncompliant and disruptive behavior.[78]

Despite the challenge of reentry for many formerly institutionalized youth, there are success stories in juvenile aftercare. The Intensive Aftercare Program is a phased aftercare program that begins while youths are still confined and continues after the youths have

CORRECTIONS IN THE NEWS

Teen Thrill Killers

In Michigan, mutilation of a corpse is punishable by 10 years in prison. First-degree premeditated murder is punishable by life in prison. Two teens, one aged 17 and the other 18, face counts of first degree murder and mutilation of a corpse in the stabbing and decapitation murder of Daniel Sorenson. The motive for the crime is not yet clear, although investigators have ruled out Daniel's Sorenson's criminal history as a registered sex offender and that he owed both teens a small amount of money as the reason for the murder. To dispose of the body and evidence, the teens allegedly torched the victim's hands and feet, wrapped the body in a plastic tarp, dumped the body along the roadside, doused the body in gasoline, set the body on fire, and tossed the head into the Rouge River.

Source: Associated Press. (2007). *Teens charged with blowtorching corpse: Mich. thrill-seekers accused of stabbing acquaintance, decapitating him.* Retrieved November 13, 2007, from http://www.msnbc.msn.com/id/21757239/.

been released. Within the Intensive Aftercare Program, youths receive a case manager who develops and monitors services that will be provided upon release. These services include interpersonal skills training, cognitive behavioral training, counseling, substance abuse treatment, and others.[79] The program has incorporated the strengths-based approach of wraparound programs and is part of the Targeted Reentry initiative of the Boys and Girls Clubs of America, which has been implemented in 14 states.[80]

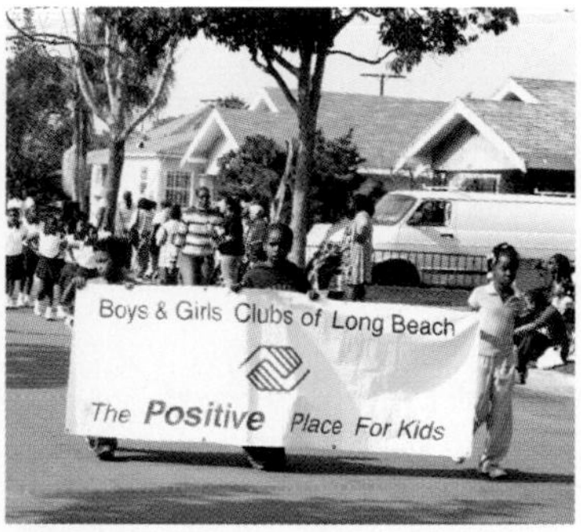

Community organizations such as the Boys and Girls Club of America provide structured, prosocial activities for young people and are an important part of delinquency prevention programs.

The California Youth Authority utilized the Lifeskills '95 interactive aftercare treatment program designed to assist chronic, high-risk juvenile offenders in dealing with day-to-day problems and adjusting to community life. The program contains 13 primary and 29 secondary treatment modules that address problem behaviors, psychiatric issues, and thinking strategies. These modules include instruction on denial and handling distorted belief systems, reality orientation, managing obsessions and compulsions, and other substantive areas that empower formerly institutionalized youths to reassess their thinking strategies before they manifest in antisocial behavior. Evaluations of this program have been positive.[81]

Comprehensive Strategy for Serious, Violent, and Chronic Juvenile Offenders

In 1993, the OJJDP published the **Comprehensive Strategy for Serious, Violent, and Chronic Juvenile Offenders**, which is a research-based framework of strategic responses to help local and state juvenile justice systems respond to delinquency. In 1995, OJJDP conducted a national training and assistance initiative to put the Comprehensive Strategy into place. The Comprehensive Strategy has two main components: prevention and graduated sanctions (FIGURE 13–7). Prevention targets youths who are at risk for delinquency involvement and attempts to bolster their prosocial development by focusing on healthy and nurturing families, safe communities, school attachment, prosocial peer relations, personal development and life skills, and healthy lifestyle choices. In other words, prevention provides education and guidance on the very factors that will insulate youths from selecting a delinquent career. Graduated sanctions, which is the second component of the Comprehensive Strategy, targets the same prosocial developmental points but for a different target population of youths who have already begun their delinquent careers.[82–84]

The Comprehensive Strategy is multidisciplinary and uses the continuum of sanctions that exist in the juvenile justice system to address the needs of the range of youthful

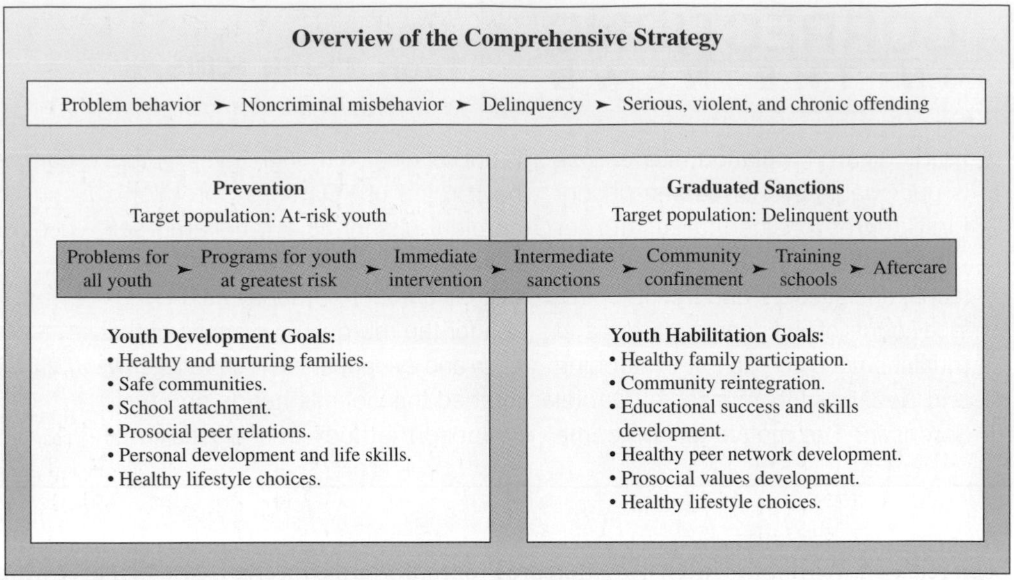

Overview of the Comprehensive Strategy
Problem behavior ➤ Noncriminal misbehavior ➤ Delinquency ➤ Serious, violent, and chronic offending
Prevention
Target population: At-risk youth
Graduated Sanctions
Target population: Delinquent youth
Problems for all youth ➤ Programs for youth at greatest risk ➤ Immediate intervention ➤ Intermediate sanctions ➤ Community confinement ➤ Training schools ➤ Aftercare
Youth Development Goals:
• Healthy and nurturing families.
• Safe communities.
• School attachment.
• Prosocial peer relations.
• Personal development and life skills.
• Healthy lifestyle choices.
Youth Habilitation Goals:
• Healthy family participation.
• Community reintegration.
• Educational success and skills development.
• Healthy peer network development.
• Prosocial values development.
• Healthy lifestyle choices.

FIGURE 13–7 Comprehensive Strategy for Serious, Violent, and Chronic Offenders. *Source*: Coolbaugh, K., & Hansel, C. J. (2000). *The comprehensive strategy: Lessons learned from the pilot sites.* Washington, DC: U.S. Department of Justice, Office of Justice Programs, Office of Juvenile Justice and Delinquency Prevention.

offenders from those first experimenting with problem behaviors to those with sustained and violent records. It is guided by the following six principles:

1. Strengthening the family in its primary responsibilities to instill moral values and provide support and guidance to children.
2. Supporting core social institutions, such as schools, churches, and community organizations to help to develop capable, mature, and responsible youth.
3. Promoting delinquency prevention as the most cost-effective approach to reducing juvenile delinquency.
4. Intervening immediately and effectively when delinquent behavior first emerges to prevent it from becoming worse.
5. Establishing a system of graduated sanctions that holds each juvenile offender accountable, protects public safety, and provides programs and services that meet treatment needs.
6. Identifying and controlling the small percent of serious, violent, and chronic juvenile offenders who commit the majority of felony offenses.

What happens if nothing is done to prevent or intervene in delinquent careers once they are under way? A study by Kimberly Kempf-Leonard and her colleagues is telling. Kempf-Leonard and her associates studied more than 27,000 delinquent careers from the 1958 Philadelphia birth cohort study and followed the members of this cohort until age 27. Among youths who had been serious delinquents, 48 percent were arrested as adults. Of violent delinquents, 53 percent were arrested as adults. Among chronic delinquents, 59 percent were arrested during adulthood. Of those who were serious and chronic juvenile offenders, 63 percent were arrested during adulthood. Among violent and chronic delinquents, over 63 percent were arrested as adults.[85] In short, the deeper a youth becomes entrenched in his or her delinquency, the more likely antisocial behavior will be a lifelong problem.

In part because of the Comprehensive Strategy, there is an emerging consensus in criminology that centers on the combined importance of multilevel prevention programs to forestall problem behaviors, multidisciplinary treatment programs to intervene and address risk factors for delinquent youth, and graduated sanctions to target the most difficult-to-reach delinquents.[86–88] At the prevention level, one of the model programs in the United States is the Promoting Alternative Thinking Strategies (PATHS) Curriculum, which is a comprehensive program for promoting emotional and social competencies and reducing aggression and behavior problems in elementary school-aged children while simultaneously enhancing the educational process in the classroom. The PATHS curriculum is ideally administered from kindergarten through fifth grade and taught three times per week for a minimum of 20 minutes per day. The PATHS lessons include instruction in identifying and labeling feelings; expressing, assessing the intensity of, understanding, and managing feelings; delaying gratification, controlling impulses, and reducing stress; interpreting social cues; and understanding the perspectives of others. Compared to control subjects, youths who have gone through the PATHS curriculum have shown improved self-control; improved understanding and recognition of emotions; increased ability to tolerate frustration; and improved thinking and planning skills in conjunction with decreased anxiety, depression, conduct problems, and symptoms of sadness.[89] In other words, prevention programs like PATHS directly address the social and behavioral disadvantages of aggressive youth and provide the very skills that will insulate them from manifesting problem behaviors later in adolescence.

At the treatment level one of the model programs in the United States is Multisystemic Therapy (MST), which is an intensive family- and community-based treatment that addresses the multiple needs of serious, violent, and chronic juvenile delinquents. Within the context of support and skill building, MST therapists help parents and teachers by placing developmentally appropriate demands on the adolescents and his or her family for responsible, prosocial behavior. For a usual duration of 60 contact hours over a 4-month span, MST interventions can include strategic family therapy, structural family therapy, behavioral parent training, and cognitive behavior therapies. Evaluations of the effectiveness of MST among seriously antisocial youths have shown 25- to 70-percent reductions in rearrest, 47- to 64-percent reductions in out-of-home placements, extensive improvements in family functioning, and decreased mental health problems.[90]

An added advantage of MST is that it has produced impressive reductions in recidivism among juvenile sex offenders. Charles Borduin and Cindy Schaeffer examined the effectiveness of MST among youths convicted of both aggressive and nonaggressive sexual offenses. Among aggressive juvenile sex offenders who received MST, the recidivism rates for sexual offenses (17 percent), nonsexual offenses (33 percent), and any offense (33 percent) were markedly lower than aggressive juvenile sex offenders who did not receive MST but instead received usual services. For those who received usual services, the recidivism rates were 58 percent for sexual offenses, 75 percent for nonsexual offenses, and 83 percent for any offense. Similar trends were found for nonaggressive juvenile sex offenders with (8 percent for sexual offenses, 25 percent for nonsexual offenses, and 25 percent for any offense) and without MST (25 percent for sexual offenses, 50 percent for nonsexual offenses, and 58 percent for any offense).[91]

In the event that prevention and treatment efforts are unsuccessful, the juvenile justice system will continue to process delinquents with an emphasis on graduated sanctions to best match the severity of offender with severity of punishment. The most serious, violent, and chronic delinquents are noteworthy for their antisocial behavior. For example, Donna Vandiver prospectively studied recidivism patterns among a cohort of 300 males who had committed sexual offenses during adolescence. During the follow-up period, 53 percent were rearrested with 10 percent of the sample accumulating four or

TABLE 13-3 The Final Persons Executed for Crime Committed During Adolescence

Executions of Under-18 Offenders: January 1, 1973–December 31, 2004

Name	Year of Execution	State	Age at Offense	Age at Execution	Race/ Ethnicity
Charles Rumbaugh	1985	TX	17	28	White
James Terry Roach	1986	SC	17	25	White
Jay Kelly Pinkerton	1986	TX	17	24	White
Delton Prejean	1990	LA	17	30	Black
Johnny Frank Garrett	1992	TX	17	28	White
Curtis Paul Harris	1993	TX	17	31	Black
Frederick Lashley	1993	MO	17	29	Black
Ruben Montoya Cantu	1993	TX	17	26	Hispanic
Christopher Burger	1993	GA	17	33	White
Joseph John Cannon	1998	TX	17	38	White
Robert Anthony Carter	1998	TX	17	34	Black
Dwayne A. Wright	1998	VA	17	26	Black
Sean R. Sellers	1999	OK	16	29	White
Douglas Christopher Thomas	2000	VA	17	26	Black
Steve E. Roach	2000	VA	17	23	White
Glen Charles McGinnis	2000	TX	17	27	Black
Gary Graham (Shaka Sankofa)	2000	TX	17	36	Black
Gerald L. Mitchell	2001	TX	17	33	black
Napoleon Beazley	2002	TX	17	25	Black
T. J. Jones	2002	TX	17	25	Black
Toronto Patterson	2002	TX	17	27	Black
Scott A. Hain	2003	OK	17	32	White

Source: Snyder, H. N., & Sickmund, M. (2006). *Juvenile offenders and victims: 2006 national report.* Washington, DC: U.S. Department of Justice, Office of Justice Programs, Office of Juvenile Justice and Delinquency Prevention.

more arrests. In other words, they were chronic delinquents *after* serving a commitment or probationary sentence for an adolescent sex offense. Nearly 10 percent of the sample were subsequently arrested for violent crimes, including capital murder, aggravated robbery, aggravated and simple assault, retaliation, and violation of a protective order.[92] These are precisely the types of juvenile delinquents who are waived to adult court and sentenced to adult time, and are among the 4,100 or so adolescent offenders serving time in adult prisons. For a look at the final juvenile executions carried out in the United States, see TABLE 13-3.

WRAP UP

CASE STUDY CONCLUSION

Lee Boyd Malvo provided testimony on behalf of the prosecution in the case against John Muhammad that described in vivid detail the plans Muhammad had to kill as many as six people a day for a month. Malvo related to the court that on one occasion, while staking out a fast food restaurant, he had been instructed by Muhammad to shoot a pregnant woman. Malvo also told the court that Muhammad was intent on training 140 homeless men; their mission would be to shut things down in America. According to Malvo, Muhammad had plans to bomb schools and kill children and he even had plans to kill a police officer and then detonate a bomb at the officer's funeral.

Shortly after his arrest, Lee Malvo was a boastful, confident young man who exhibited no remorse for the crimes he had committed. But in his testimony against Muhammad, Malvo changed his statement and his attitude. Originally, Malvo claimed to have shot all but one of the victims. He explained to the court that the two men had agreed upon this story since he was a teenager. Malvo did admit to firing the bullets that killed a Montgomery County bus driver and again in two instances where both victims survived the shooting. Malvo has been sentenced to life in prison after pleading guilty to six counts of first-degree murder.

Sources: Morello, C. (2005, April 23). Va. court upholds Muhammad sentences: Sniper could be sent to another state. *The Washington Post*, p. B01; Boorstein, M. (2004, October 27). Malvo gets two more life terms. *The Washington Post*, p. B01; Londono, E., & Rich, E. (2006, May 24). Malvo describes two-step plan phase two involved blowing up schools, children's hospitals. *The Washington Post*, p. A01.

Chapter Summary

- The juvenile justice system is a separate justice system for persons under the age of 18 that places an emphasis on rehabilitation and treatment as opposed to punishment.
- Nearly 100,000 youths are detained or committed in the United States with about 4,100 in adult prisons and 7,500 in adult jails.
- A range of intermediate sanctions are used to address the diversity of the delinquent population.
- Juvenile probation is the workhorse of the juvenile justice system and is used preadjudication, postadjudication, and as a form of diversion.
- Youths adjudicated of the most serious offenses are placed in detention or commitment for usually no more than 1 year. Afterward, they reenter society through a process of aftercare.
- Historically, juvenile justice was harsh with mundane behaviors eligible for corporal and even capital punishment.
- Attempts to develop policies in the interests of children have sometimes met with unintended consequences, such as the Child Savers' use of incarceration in houses of refuge.

- From the 1960s through 1980s, the Supreme Court ruled on several landmark cases that applied due process to adolescents.
- After years of variously defining the appropriate minimum age of capital sentencing, the juvenile death penalty was invalidated in 2005.
- Today, there is a concerted focus on the range of juvenile delinquents evidenced by the Comprehensive Strategy for Serious, Violent, and Chronic Juvenile Offenders.

Key Terms

adjudicated To be found guilty in juvenile court.

adjudicatory hearing Juvenile trial.

aftercare Juvenile parole.

blended sentencing Method by which juvenile courts combine juvenile and adult punishment that is tailored to the needs of the individual offender.

boot camps Short-term incarceration programs that incorporate the strict discipline, hard labor, and physical training of military basic training followed by an aftercare program that contains conditions and treatment.

Breed v. Jones Court case that ruled that juveniles could not be waived to criminal court following adjudication in juvenile court because it violated the double jeopardy clause of the Fifth Amendment.

Child Savers Progressive social movement that put juveniles in houses of refuge.

committed Status of a juvenile who has received a prison sentence.

Comprehensive Strategy for Serious, Violent, and Chronic Juvenile Offenders A research-based framework of strategic responses to help local and state juvenile justice systems respond to delinquency.

curfew enforcement Policies that limit the opportunities youths have to engage in delinquency.

decertification The undoing of a waived case.

delinquency petition Juvenile filing of charges.

delinquent *See* juvenile delinquent.

delinquent offenses Violations of criminal law.

demand waiver Type of waiver into criminal court that occurs when a delinquent chooses criminal prosecution.

detained Status of a juvenile in jail confinement while awaiting court proceedings.

disposition Juvenile sentence.

Eddings v. Oklahoma Court ruling that established that age is a mitigating factor in capital sentencing.

In re Gault Case that established a juvenile's right to notice of charges, right to counsel, right to question, confront, and cross-examine witnesses, and the right of privilege against self-incrimination.

In re Winshop Court case that established that in delinquency matters, the state must prove its case beyond a reasonable doubt.

judicial waiver Transfer of a case to criminal court by a judge based on the severity of the charges and/or the severity of the youth's delinquent record.

juvenile conference committee Panel of six to nine volunteers from the community who meet monthly to hear juvenile complaints referred by the family court.

juvenile court Court with original jurisdiction over minors.

juvenile delinquent Minor found guilty of a crime.

Juvenile Justice and Delinquency Prevention Act of 1974 Act that provides federal funding to states and communities for prevention and treatment programs, especially diversion programs that deinstitutionalize adolescents convicted of status offenses.

juvenile justice system The set of agencies that process persons under the age of 18 for violations of the law.

Kent v. United States Court case that established that essentials of due process must apply to waivers.

legislative waiver Type of waiver into criminal court that occurs because certain offenses are statutorily excluded from prosecution in juvenile court and require adult prosecution.

McKeiver v. Pennsylvania Court case that established that jury trials are not constitutionally required in juvenile court hearings.

Office of Juvenile Justice and Delinquency Prevention (OJJDP) Federal agency that funded research to evaluate juvenile justice programs and disseminated research findings on the juvenile justice system.

parens patriae Doctrine that asserts that the state is the ultimate guardian of children.

prosecutorial waiver Type of judicial waiver into criminal court that occurs when the district attorney, county attorney, or prosecutor uses his or her discretion to prosecute a youth as an adult in criminal court.

restorative justice An alternative justice model that seeks to repair the harm caused by delinquency by bringing together the offender, victim, and societal members to collectively resolve the issues caused by the crime.

reverse waiver Type of judicial waiver that occurs when a transferred case that qualifies for criminal prosecution is sent back to juvenile court to be processed.

Roper v. Simmons Case in which the Supreme Court ruled that it was unconstitutional to impose the death penalty on offenders younger than 18 at the time of their capital crimes.

Schall v. Martin Case that established that preventive pretrial detention of juveniles is allowable under certain circumstances, such as the likelihood of recidivism.

Stanford v. Kentucky Court case that established that juveniles age 16 or 17 are eligible for the death penalty.

status offenses Violations of criminal law that only apply to children and adolescents.

teen court A restorative justice approach where first-time offenders publicly admit guilt before a group of peers, who, in turn, impose a sentence.

Thompson v. Oklahoma Case that established that the execution of persons under 16 is unconstitutional.

transfer *See* waiver.

truancy Nonattendance of school.

waiver Prosecution of a juvenile in criminal court.

Critical Thinking Questions

1. Given the risks of suicide and victimization, is it ever appropriate to detain an adolescent in an adult jail? Why is it still done?
2. Can you envision a scenario in which *Roper v. Simmons* is overturned and the United States resumes executions of teenage murderers? What factors could lead to such an outcome?
3. Which is the best waiver in terms of selecting only the worst juvenile delinquents for adult prosecution? Is it then not sound policy to remove judicial discretion via legislative waivers?
4. Truancy can be youthful folly or a troubling early indicator of a criminal career. How can authorities differentiate between these two scenarios?

Notes

1. *In re Gault,* 387 U.S. 1 (1967).
2. Poole, E. D., & Regoli, R. M. (1983). Violence in juvenile institutions. *Criminology, 21,* 213–232.
3. Trulson, C. R., Caeti, T. J., Marquart, J. W., & Mullings, J. L. (2005). In between adolescence and adulthood: Recidivism outcomes of a cohort of state delinquents. *Youth Violence and Juvenile Justice, 3,* 1–33.
4. Smallheer, R. (1999). Sentence blending and the promise of rehabilitation: Bringing the juvenile justice system full circle. *Hofstra Law Review, 28,* 259–289.
5. Ayers, W. (1997). *A kind and just parent: The children of the juvenile court.* Boston: Beacon Books.
6. Lipsey, M. W. (1999). Can intervention rehabilitate serious delinquents? *Annals of the American Academy of Political and Social Science, 564,* 142–166.
7. Rothman, D. J. (1970). *The discovery of the asylum.* Boston: Little, Brown.
8. Regoli, R. M., Hewitt, J. D., & DeLisi, M. (2008). *Delinquency in society* (7th ed.). New York: McGraw-Hill.
9. Platt, A. (1969). *The child savers: The invention of delinquency*. Chicago: University of Chicago Press.
10. O'Connor, S. (2001). *Orphan trains.* Boston: Houghton Mifflin.
11. DeLisi, M. (2003). Delinquency. In M. D. McShane & F. P. Williams, III (Eds.), *Encyclopedia of juvenile justice* (pp. 119–122). Thousand Oaks, CA: Sage.
12. Regoli et al., note 8.
13. *Kent v. United States*, 383 U.S. 541 (1966).
14. *In re Gault,* 387 U.S. 1 (1967), p. 387.
15. *In re WInshop,* 397 U.S. 358 (1970).
16. *McKeiver v. Pennsylvania*, 403 U.S. 528 (1971).
17. *Breed v. Jones,* 421 U.S. 519 (1975).
18. *Eddings v. Oklahoma,* 455 U.S. 104 (1982).
19. *Schall v. Martin,* 467 U.S. 253 (1984).
20. *Thompson v. Oklahoma*, 487 U.S. 815 (1988).
21. *Stanford v. Kentucky*, 492 U.S. 361 (1989).
22. *Roper v. Simmons*, 543 U.S. 551 (2005).
23. Krisberg, B., & Schwartz, I. (1983). Rethinking juvenile justice. *Crime & Delinquency, 29,* 333–364.

24. Krisberg, B., Schwartz, I. M., Litsky, P., & Austin, J. (1986). The watershed of juvenile justice reform. *Crime & Delinquency, 32,* 5–38.

25. Snyder, H. N., & Sickmund, M. (2006). *Juvenile offenders and victims: 2006 national report.* Washington, DC: U.S. Department of Justice, Office of Justice Programs, Office of Juvenile Justice and Delinquency Prevention.

26. Snyder & Sickmund.

27. Snyder & Sickmund.

28. Myers, D. L. (2003). Recidivism of violent youths in juvenile and adult court: A consideration of selection bias. *Youth Violence and Juvenile Justice, 1,* 79–101; also see, Myers, D. L., & Kiehl, K. (2001). Predispositional status of violent youthful offenders: Is there a "custody gap" in adult criminal court? *Justice Research and Policy, 3,* 115–143.

29. Lanza-Kaduce, L., Lane, J., Bishop, D. M., & Frazier, C. E. (2005). Juvenile offenders and adult felony recidivism: The impact of transfer. *Journal of Crime & Justice, 28,* 59–77.

30. Kupchik, A. (2007). Correctional experiences of youth in adult and juvenile prisons. *Justice Quarterly, 24,* 247–270.

31. See Benekos, P. J., & Merlo, A. V. (2008). Juvenile justice: The legacy of punitive policy. *Youth Violence and Juvenile Justice, 6,* 28–46; Zimring, F. E. (2005). *American juvenile justice.* New York: Oxford University Press.

32. Burrow, J. (2008). Reverse waiver and the effects of legal, statutory, and secondary legal factors on sentencing outcomes for juvenile offenders. *Crime & Delinquency, 54,* 34–64.

33. Jordan, K. L., & Myers, D. L. (2007). Decertification of transferred youth: Examining the determinants of reverse waiver. *Youth Violence and Juvenile Justice, 5,* 188–206.

34. Snyder & Sickmund.

35. Snyder & Sickmund.

36. Campaign for Youth Justice. (2007). *Jailing juveniles. The dangers of incarcerating youth in adult jails in America,* accessed December 30, 2008 at www.campaignforyouthjustice.org/Downloads/NationalReportsArticles/CFYJ-Jailing_Juveniles_Report_2007-11-15.pdf.

37. Snyder & Sickmund.

38. Snyder & Sickmund.

39. Welsh, B. C., Loeber, R., Stevens, B. R., Stouthamer-Loeber, M., Cohen, M. A., & Farrington, D. P. (2008). Costs of juvenile crime in urban areas: A longitudinal perspective. *Youth Violence and Juvenile Justice, 6,* 3–27.

40. 18 U.S.C. § 5032.

41. Snyder & Sickmund.

42. See Gavazzi, S. M., Wasserman, D., Patridge, C., & Sheridan, S. (2000). The growing up FAST diversion program: An example of juvenile justice program development for outcome evaluation. *Aggression and Violent Behavior, 5,* 159–175.

43. Winterfield, L., & Brumbaugh, S. (2005). *Characteristics of prisoner reentry programs for juveniles.* Washington, DC: Urban Institute and RTI International.

44. Hayes, H., & Daly, K. (2003). Youth justice conferencing and reoffending. *Justice Quarterly, 20,* 725–764.

45. McGarrell, E. F., & Hipple, N. K. (2007). Family group conferencing and re-offending among first-time juvenile offenders: The Indianapolis experiment. *Justice Quarterly, 24,* 221–246.

46. Harrison, P., Maupin, J. R., & Mays, G. L. (2001). Teen court: An examination of the processes and outcomes. *Crime & Delinquency, 47,* 243–264.

47. Minor, K. I., Wells, J. B., Soderstrom, I. R., Bingham, R., & Williamson, D. (1999). Sentence completion and recidivism among juveniles referred to teen court. *Crime & Delinquency, 45,* 467–480.

48. Forgays, D. K., & DeMilio, L. (2005). Is teen court effective for repeat offenders? A test of the restorative justice approach. *International Journal of Offender Therapy and Comparative Criminology, 49,* 107–118.

49. Rasmussen, A. (2004). Teen court referral, sentencing, and subsequent recidivism: Two proportional hazards models and a little speculation. *Crime & Delinquency, 50,* 615–635.

50. Jones, M. A., & Sigler, R. T. (2002). Law enforcement partnership in community corrections: An evaluation of juvenile offender curfew checks. *Journal of Criminal Justice, 30,* 245–256.

51. Hassett-Walker, C. (2002). Juvenile conference committees: Issues in assessing a diversionary court program. *Journal of Criminal Justice, 30,* 107–119.

52. Torbet, P. M. (1996). *Juvenile probation: The workhorse of the juvenile justice system.* Washington, DC: U.S. Department of Justice, Office of Justice Programs, Office of Juvenile Justice and Delinquency Prevention, p. 1.

53. Worrall, J. L., & Gaines, L. K. (2006). The effect of police-probation partnerships on juvenile arrests. *Journal of Criminal Justice, 34,* 579–589.

54. Palmer, T., & Wedge, R. (1989). California's juvenile probation camps: Findings and implications. *Crime & Delinquency, 35,* 234–253.

55. Giblin, M. J. (2002). Using police officers to enhance the supervision of juvenile probationers: An evaluation of the Anchorage CAN program. *Crime & Delinquency, 48,* 116–137.

56. Mallett, C. A. (2006). Juvenile court probation supervised youths: At risk in Cuyahoga County, Ohio. *Corrections Compendium, 31,* 1–5, 27–33.

57. Vidal, S., & Skeem, J. L. (2007). Effect of psychopathy, abuse, and ethnicity on juvenile probation officers' decision-making and supervision strategies. *Law and Human Behavior, 31,* 479–498.

58. Kurtz, D., & Linnemann, T. (2006). Improving probation through client strengths: Evaluating strength based treatments for at risk youth. *Western Criminology Review, 7,* 9–19.

59. Elrod, H. P., & Minor, K. I. (1992). Second wave evaluation of a multi-faceted intervention for juvenile court probationers. *International Journal of Offender Therapy and Comparative Criminology, 36,* 247–262.

60. Lipsey, M. W., & Wilson, D. B. (1998). Effective intervention for serious juvenile offenders: A synthesis of research. In R. Loeber & D. P. Farrington (Eds.), *Serious & violent juvenile offenders: Risk factors and successful interventions* (pp. 313–345). Thousand Oaks, CA: Sage.

61. Lipsey & Wilson.

62. Snyder & Sickmund.

63. Cullen, F. T., Blevins, K. R., Trager, J. S., & Gendreau, P. (2005). The rise and fall of boot camps: A case study in common-sense corrections. *Journal of Offender Rehabilitation, 40,* 53–70.

64. MacKenzie, D. L. (2006). *What works in corrections: Reducing the criminal activities of offenders and delinquents.* New York: Cambridge University Press.

65. Wells, J. B., Minor, K. I., Angel, E., & Stearman, K. D. (2006). Quasi-experimental evaluation of a shock incarceration and aftercare program for juvenile offenders. *Youth Violence and Juvenile Justice, 4,* 219–233.

66. Benda, B. B., Toombs, N. J., & Corwyn, R. F. (2005). Self-control, gender, and age: A survival analysis of recidivism among boot camp graduates in a 5-year follow-up. *Journal of Offender Rehabilitation, 40,* 115–132.

67. Trulson, C. R. (2007). Determinants of disruption: Institutional misconduct among state-committed delinquents. *Youth Violence and Juvenile Justice, 5,* 7–34.

68. MacDonald, J. M. (1999). Violence and drug use in juvenile institutions. *Journal of Criminal Justice, 27,* 33–44.

69. Spain, S. E., Douglas, K. S., Poythress, N. G., & Epstein, M. (2004). The relationship between psychopathic features, violence, and treatment outcome: The comparison of three youth measures of psychopathic features. *Behavioral Sciences and the Law, 22,* 85–102.

70. Campbell, M. A., Porter, S., & Santor, D. (2004). Psychopathic traits in adolescent offenders: An evaluation of criminal history, clinical, and psychosocial correlates. *Behavioral Sciences and the Law, 22,* 23–47.

71. Walters, G. D. (2003). Predicting criminal justice outcomes with the psychopathy checklist and lifestyle criminality screening form: A meta-analytic comparison. *Behavioral Sciences and the Law, 21,* 89–102.

72. Caldwell, M. F., Vitacco, M., & Van Rybroek, G. J. (2006). Are violent delinquents worth treating? A cost-benefit analysis. *Journal of Research in Crime and Delinquency, 43,* 148–168.

73. Lipsey & Wilson.

74. Snyder & Sickmund.

75. National Council of Juvenile and Family Court Judges. (2004). *Three innovative court-involved reentry programs.* Washington, DC: U.S. Department of Justice, Office of Justice Programs, Office of Juvenile Justice and Delinquency Prevention.

76. Benda, B. B., Corwyn, R. F., & Toombs, N. J. (2001). Recidivism among adolescent serious offenders: Prediction of entry into the correctional system for adults. *Criminal Justice and Behavior, 28,* 588–613.

77. Blackburn, A. G., Mullings, J. L., Marquart, J. W., & Trulson, C. R. (2007). The next generation of prisoners: Toward an understanding of violent institutionalized delinquents. *Youth Violence and Juvenile Justice, 5,* 35–56.

78. Trulson et al.

79. Altschuler, D. M., & Armstrong, T. L. (2002). Juvenile corrections and continuity of care in a community context: The evidence and promising directions. *Federal Probation, 66,* 72–77.

80. Barton, W. H. (2006). Incorporating the strengths perspective into intensive juvenile aftercare. *Western Criminology Review, 7,* 48–61.

81. Josi, D. A., & Sechrest, D. K. (1999). A pragmatic approach to parole aftercare: Evaluation of a community reintegration program for high-risk youthful offenders. *Justice Quarterly, 16,* 51–80.

82. Wilson, J. J., & Howell, J. C. (1993). *The comprehensive strategy for serious, violent, and chronic juvenile offenders.* Washington, DC: U.S. Department of Justice, Office of Justice Programs, Office of Juvenile Justice and Delinquency Prevention.

83. Howell, J. C. (1998). New approach to juvenile crime: The promise of graduated sanctions in a juvenile justice system. *Corrections Compendium, 23,* 1–25.

84. Howell, J. C. (2003). Diffusing research into practice using the comprehensive strategy for serious, violent, and chronic juvenile offenders. *Youth Violence and Juvenile Justice, 1,* 219–245.

85. Kempf-Leonard, K., Tracy, P. E., & Howell, J. C. (2001). Serious, violent, and chronic juvenile offenders: The relationship of delinquency career types to adult criminality. *Justice Quarterly, 18,* 449–478.

86. DeLisi, M. (2005). *Career criminals in society.* Thousand Oaks, CA: Sage.

87. Farrington, D. P., & Coid, J. W. (2003). *Early prevention of adult antisocial behavior.* New York: Cambridge University Press.

88. Farrington, D. P., & Welsh. B. C. (2007). *Saving children from a life of crime: Early risk factors and effective interventions.* New York: Oxford University Press.

89. Greenberg, M. T., Kusche, C. A., & Mihalic, S. F. (2006). *PATHS: Blueprints for violence prevention, Book 10.* Boulder: Center for the Study and Prevention of Violence, Institute of Behavioral Sciences, University of Colorado.

90. Henggeler, S. W., Mihalic, S. F., Rone, L., Thomas, C., & Timmons-Mitchell, J. (1998). *MST: Blueprints for violence prevention, Book 6.* Boulder: Center for the Study and Prevention of Violence, Institute of Behavioral Sciences, University of Colorado.

91. Borduin, C. M., & Schaeffer, C. M. (2001). Multisystemic treatment of juvenile sex offenders: A progress report. *Journal of Psychology and Human Sexuality, 13,* 25–42.

92. Vandiver, D. M. (2006). A prospective analysis of juvenile male sex offenders: Characteristics and recidivism rates as adults. *Journal of Interpersonal Violence, 21,* 673–688.

CHAPTER

14

Women and Corrections

"The gender gap in crime—with males accounting for much more law violation than females—is virtually a truism in criminology. The relationship holds regardless of whether the data analyzed are arrest rates, victimization incidence reports on characteristics of offenders, or self-reports of criminal behavior. As far as we can tell, males have always been more criminal than females, and gender differences emerge in every society that has been studied systematically."[1, p. 248]

OBJECTIVES

- Evaluate the size of the female correctional population.
- Assess recent trends in the growth of the correctional population of women.
- Investigate the historical ways that female delinquency and crime have been conceptualized and punished.
- Explore the historical development of the ways that women have been supervised in the correctional system.
- Note the legal issues pertaining to the differential correctional supervision of offenders by gender.
- Understand gender-specific offending patterns and the role of victimization and marginality in female crime.
- Learn the status of women in terms of noncompliance and recidivism while being supervised by the criminal justice system.
- Appreciate correctional programming for women with attention to what works for female offenders.

CASE STUDY

The case of Aileen Wuornos is fascinating in that it is both extreme and unlike the case of nearly every other female offender, yet common in terms of the links between her background and criminal behavior. Wuornos was executed in Florida in 2002 stemming from six death sentences for murders committed in 1989–1990 (she also admitted committing a seventh homicide). Wuornos was a prostitute who murdered customers who she reported raped her or attempted to rape her during the course of their prostitution encounter. Although she is known as one of the few female serial killers, that depiction is technically not correct since serial murder involves some sexual element in conjunction with the homicide event usually in the form of sexual sadism. Wuornos, who was a lesbian, denied any sexual motivation or gratification for the murders and instead robbed and eliminated the victims as witnesses. There is considerable evidence that she was a psychopath and presented with antisocial personality disorder and borderline disorder. Although Wuornos was exceptional in terms of the severity of her crimes and the seriousness of her legal treatment, her story is characteristic of many female offenders who are involved in the correctional system in the United States.

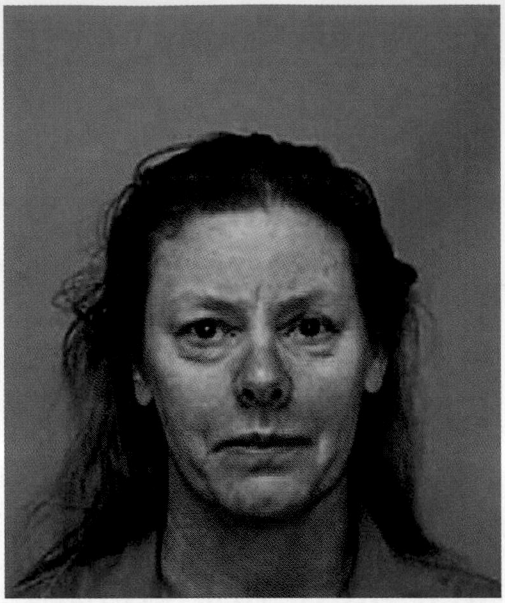

The life, crimes, and execution of female serial killer Aileen Wuornos shocked the people of the United States.

1. What events in Wuornos's life contributed to her life of crime?

"Existing classification models for women—many of them designed for male prisoners—are not relevant to the needs of women offenders."[2, p. 1]

Historically, female offenders and correctional clients have been viewed as an afterthought by the criminal justice system. This is unfortunate, because although women criminals share many features with male offenders, there are also important differences in their criminal careers, life experiences, and adjustment to the correctional system. This chapter explores the special topic of women and corrections, including the ways that women follow gender-specific pathways into crime and justice.

Women in the Correctional System

Two major points are commonly made about women in the correctional system. First, correctional populations are overwhelmingly comprised of men, reflecting the dramatic gender differences in criminal offending. Second, in recent years, women have been catching up. For most correctional populations (with the exception of death rows), the rate of increase among women is significantly higher than the rate of increase among men. As shown in TABLE 14-1, the rate of growth in probation, jail, prison, and parole is much higher among women. Between 1990 and 2000, the female probation population grew 76 percent, the female jail population grew 89 percent, the female prison population increased 106 percent, and the female parole population surged 105 percent.[6]

Another way to assess the recent surge of women as correctional clients is to assess the proportion of women who are serving various sentences. TABLE 14-2 displays the proportion of the female population involved in the criminal justice system. In 1985, 1 in

"*Women's criminal careers reflect gender differences in legitimate and illegitimate opportunity structures, in personal networks, and in family obligations.*"[3, p. 378]

TABLE 14-1 Correctional Populations by Gender, 1990 and 2000

	1990	2000	Percent Increase
Probation			
Females	480,642	844,697	76
Males	2,189,592	2,994,853	37
Jail			
Females	37,198	70,414	89
Males	365,821	543,120	48
Prison (state and federal)			
Females	44,065	91,612	108
Males	729,840	1,290,280	77
Parole			
Females	42,513	87,063	105
Males	488,894	638,464	31
Total			
Females	604,418	1,093,786	81
Males	3,774,147	5,466,699	45

Source: Bloom, B., Owen, B., Covington, S., & Raeder, M. (2003). *Gender-responsive strategies: Research, practice, and guiding principles for women offenders.* Washington, DC: U.S. Department of Justice, Office of Justice Programs, National Institute of Corrections.

TABLE 14-2 Number of Women Serving Correctional Sentences Has Increased

1 woman in ____ adult women in the United States had this correctional status:

	Any Correctional Status	Probation	Jail	Prison	Parole
1985	227	267	4,762	4,167	4,762
1990	161	202	2,632	2,326	2,273
1995	124	159	1,961	1,587	1,493
1996	120	157	1,852	1,471	1,316
1997	115	151	1,754	1,408	1,333
1998	109	144	1,628	1,230	1,262

Source: Greenfeld, L. A., & Snell, T. L. (2000). *Women offenders.* Washington, DC: U.S. Department of Justice, Office of Justice Programs, Bureau of Justice Statistics.

227 women had any correctional status. In 1998, the rate was 1 in 109. For probation, the rate increased from 1 in 267 to 1 in 144. For jail, the figures went from 1 in 4,762 to 1 in 1,628. For prison, it went from 1 in 4,167 to 1 in 1,230. For parole, the change was 1 in 4,762 to 1 in 1,262.[7]

Probation and Parole

At year-end 2008, when the most recent correctional data were available, there were fewer than 1 million women on probation, which represented 23 percent of the probation population; and there were 96,000 women on parole, which represented 12 percent of the parole population.[8] The female probation population is about 10 times the size of the female inmate population. The women parole and prisoner populations are of comparable size.

"The historical legacy of poorer prison conditions, the greater stigma applied to women who offend, and the amalgamation of female prisons, which has caused many women to be held far from home, may together go some way to explaining why women appear to have a hard time than men in coming to terms with imprisonment."[4, p. 323]

Jail and Juvenile Corrections

There are fewer than 99,000 women in American jails. By comparison, there are more than 661,000 men in American jails. As shown in FIGURE 14–1, the number of men in jail is nearly seven times the number of women.[9]

Despite the gender differences in the jail population, females have become a larger part of the jail population in recent years. As shown in TABLE 14–3, the proportion of women to men in American jails nearly doubled between 1983 and 2004.[10]

Females account for 15 percent of juveniles in custody, including 14 percent of the delinquent and 40 percent of the status offender population. Among juveniles who are detained, girls comprise 18 percent of the population. Among juveniles who are committed, girls represent 12 percent of the population.[11]

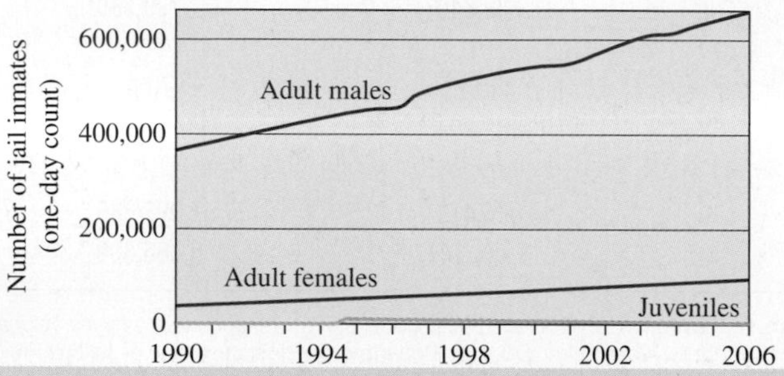

FIGURE 14–1 Jail Population by Gender and Age Status, 1990–2006. *Source*: Bureau of Justice Statistics (n.d.). *Almost nine out of every ten jail inmates were adult males.* Retrieved April 7, 2008, from http://www.ojp.usdoj.gov/bjs/glance/jailag.htm.

TABLE 14–3 Jail Population by Gender

Year	Total Inmates	Male		Female	
		Number	Percent	Number	Percent
1983	225,781	210,451	93	15,330	7
1985	274,063	254,986	93	19,077	7
1988	334,566	306,379	92	28,187	8
1989	384,954	349,180	91	35,774	9
1990	403,019	365,821	91	37,198	9
1991	424,129	384,628	91	39,501	9
1992	441,780	401,106	91	40,674	9
1993	455,600	411,500	90	44,100	10
1994	479,800	431,300	90	48,500	10
1995	499,300	448,000	90	51,300	10
1996	510,400	454,700	89	55,700	11
1997	557,974	498,678	89	59,296	11
1998	584,372	520,581	89	63,791	11
1999	596,485	528,998	89	67,487	11
2000	613,534	543,120	89	70,414	11
2001	623,628	551,007	88	72,621	12
2002	658,228	581,411	88	76,817	12
2003	684,431	602,781	88	81,650	12
2004	706,907	619,908	88	86,999	12

Source: Elias, G. (2007). *Facility planning to meet the needs of female inmates.* Washington, DC: U.S. Department of Justice, Office of Justice Programs, National Institute of Corrections.

CORRECTIONS IN THE NEWS

Nun Faces Jail Time

A 79-year-old Roman Catholic nun, Norma Giannini, faces 10 years in prison as a result of a no-contest plea to charges she sexually assaulted two male parishioners over 40 years ago, when they were both children. Her decision means the case will not be tried in court—"She didn't put the victims through a trial," her attorney said. Some would question her concern for the victims as the basis of her no contest plea since a no contest plea means court records lack testimony that could be used in a civil hearing.

When both victims were in their 50s, they were prepared to tell the court about the history of abuse they endured. According to one of the victims, the first incident of sexual abuse occurred in 1965, when Giannini told him to unbutton her habit. The child took no action, and so Giannini unbuttoned her clothing and had the victim touch her breasts. This was the first of between 60 and 80 incidents of abuse this victim could recall. The second victim recalled nearly 100 incidents of sexual abuse, beginning in the seventh grade. Both victims reported the abuse had included sexual intercourse.

The church acknowledges that since learning of these crimes during the 1990s, Giannini has received extensive counseling, is closely monitored, and has been denied access to minors.

Source: Associated Press. (2007). *Nun pleads no contest in Wis. sex abuse case.* Retrieved November 13, 2007, from http://www.msnbc.msn.com/id/21760393/.

State and Federal Prison

At year-end 2008, when the most recent correctional data were available, there were nearly 114,000 women in state and federal prisons in the United States. Nearly 101,000 of these women are confined in state prisons, with the remaining 13,000 or so in federal prison. In recent years, the rate of growth of women in prison has increased more than the same rate for men. For instance, between 2000 and 2005, the average annual growth rate of the prisoner population was less than 2 percent. For women, the growth rate was nearly 3 percent and exceeded 4 percent for federal prisoner growth. Approximately 40 percent of women in prison are limited to four jurisdictions—California, Texas, Florida, and the Bureau of Prisons.[12] A state-by-state listing of women in prison is shown in TABLE 14–4.

"Females are viewed as 'evil women'; their needs are determined largely by their deviations from gender-role expectations."[5, p.123]

Forty percent of women in prison are housed in just four correctional systems: California, Florida, Texas, and the Bureau of Prisons.

TABLE 14-4 Female Prisoner Population

Region and Jurisdiction	Number of Female Prisoners 2000	2006	2007	Average Annual Change 2000–2006	Percent Change 2006–2007
U.S. Total	93,234	112,459	114,420	3.2	1.7
Federal	10,245	12,975	13,338	4	2.8
State	82,989	99,484	101,082	3.1	1.6
Northeast	9,082	9,730	9,707	1.2	–0.2
Connecticut	1,406	1,594	1,496	2.1	–6.1
Maine	66	145	152	14	4.8
Massachusetts	663	846	790	4.1	–6.6
New Hampshire	120	172	202	6.2	17.4
New Jersey	1,650	1,428	1,410	–2.4	–1.3
New York	3,280	2,859	2,754	–2.3	–3.7
Pennsylvania	1,579	2,249	2,463	6.1	9.5
Rhode Island	238	280	282	2.7	0.7
Vermont	80	157	158	11.9	0.6
Midwest	14,598	17,670	17,832	3.2	0.9
Illinois	2,849	/	/	:	:
Indiana	1,452	2,167	2,295	6.9	5.9
Iowa	592	789	717	4.9	–9.1
Kansas	504	638	625	4	–2
Michigan	2,131	2,170	2,080	0.3	–4.1
Minnesota	368	562	602	7.3	7.1
Missouri	1,993	2,579	2,522	4.4	–2.2
Nebraska	266	413	399	7.6	–3.4
North Dakota	68	157	147	15	–6.4
Ohio	2,808	3,701	3,822	4.7	3.3
South Dakota	200	350	369	9.8	5.4
Wisconsin	1,367	1,424	1,527	0.7	7.2
South	39,652	47,086	48,503	2.9	3
Alabama	1,826	2,050	2,158	1.9	5.3
Arkansas	772	1,042	1,066	5.1	2.3
Delaware	597	571	577	–0.7	1.1
District of Columbia	356	~	~	:	:
Florida	4,105	6,489	6,854	7.9	5.6

The incarceration rate of women per 100,000 U.S. residents is 69. By comparison, the incarceration rate of men per 100,000 U.S. residents is 955. In other words, the incarceration rate of women is nearly 14 times lower than for men.[13]

In state prisons, which hold the bulk of both male and female prisoners, more than 52 percent of inmates are serving time for violent crimes, 21 percent for property crimes, nearly 20 percent for drug crimes, and 7 percent for public-order crimes. There are gender differences in terms of the composition of prisoners by crime type. For instance, the percentages of male inmates in state prisons for the following crimes are:

- More than 53 percent for violent crimes
- 20 percent for property crimes
- 19 percent for drug crimes
- 7 percent for public-order crimes

TABLE 14-4 *(Continued)*

Region and Jurisdiction	Number of Female Prisoners 2000	2006	2007	Average Annual Change 2000–2006	Percent Change 2006–2007
South *(continued)*					
Georgia	2,758	3,557	3,545	4.3	–0.3
Kentucky	1,061	2,058	2,441	11.7	18.6
Louisiana	2,219	2,389	2,458	1.2	2.9
Maryland	1,219	1,081	1,184	–2	9.5
Mississippi	1,669	1,789	1,962	1.2	9.7
North Carolina	1,903	2,686	2,626	5.9	–2.2
Oklahoma	2,394	2,547	2,607	1	2.4
South Carolina	1,420	1,603	1,604	2	0.1
Tennessee	1,369	1,958	1,923	6.1	–1.8
Texas	13,622	13,799	13,931	0.2	1
Virginia	2,059	2,893	2,933	5.8	1.4
West Virginia	303	574	634	11.2	10.5
West	19,657	24,998	25,040	4.1	0.2
Alaska	284	518	564	10.5	8.9
Arizona	1,964	3,151	3,460	8.2	9.8
California	11,161	11,977	11,628	1.2	–2.9
Colorado	1,333	2,302	2,335	9.5	1.4
Hawaii	561	734	746	4.6	1.6
Idaho	493	777	800	7.9	3
Montana	306	354	301	2.5	–15
Nevada	846	1,136	1,179	5	3.8
New Mexico	511	667	576	4.5	–13.6
Oregon	596	1,020	1,060	9.4	3.9
Utah	381	623	631	8.5	1.3
Washington	1,065	1,496	1,514	5.8	1.2
Wyoming	156	243	246	7.7	1.2

/Not reported.
:Not calculated.
~Not applicable.

Source: West, H. C. & Sabol, W. J. (2008). *Prisoners in 2007.* Washington, DC: U.S. Department of Justice, Office of Justice Programs, Bureau of Justice Statistics.

For women, the respective rates are:

- 35 percent for violent crimes
- 29 percent for property crimes
- 29 percent for drug crimes
- 6 percent for public-order crimes

In state prisons, women are disproportionately sentenced for property crimes, such as fraud, forgery, larceny, and drug violations.[14] A further breakdown of inmate composition by offense appears in TABLE 14-5.

Capital Punishment

Capital punishment is rarely used on female offenders primarily because women commit only about 10 percent of homicides. Women account for just over 2 percent of death

TABLE 14-5 Prisoners by Crime Type, Gender, and Race

	All Inmates	Male	Female	White	Black	Hispanic
Total	100%	100%	100%	100%	100%	100%
Violent offenses	53%	54.3%	35.4%	50.1%	54.6%	54.7%
Murder	12.9	13	11.2	10.5	14.3	13.4
Manslaughter	1.3	1.2	1.9	1.5	1.3	1
Rape	4.7	5	0.6	6.4	4.1	2.8
Other sexual assault	8	8.5	1.7	12.3	4.2	9
Robbery	13.7	14.1	8.6	8.2	18.9	12.8
Assault	10	10	8.8	8.6	9.5	13.3
Other violent	2.5	2.5	2.7	2.6	2.3	2.5
Property offenses	19.2%	18.5%	28.6%	24.4%	16.1%	16.2%
Burglary	9.6	9.8	6.3	11.6	8.5	8.6
Larceny	3.5	3.2	8	4.3	3.2	2.4
Motor vehicle theft	1.7	1.7	1.5	1.9	1.1	2.8
Fraud	2.5	1.9	10.4	3.8	1.9	1
Other property	1.9	1.9	2.3	2.7	1.4	1.5
Drug offenses	19.5%	18.9%	28.7%	15.4%	22.5%	21.3%
Public-order offenses	7.6%	7.7%	6.1%	9.4%	6.3%	7.3%
Other/unspecified	0.6%	0.6%	1.2%	0.8%	0.5%	0.5%

Note: Data are for inmates with a sentence of more than 1 year under the jurisdiction of state correctional authorities. Detail may not add to total due to rounding.

Source: West, H. C. & Sabol, W. J. (2008). *Prisoners in 2007*. Washington, DC: U.S. Department of Justice, Office of Justice Programs, Bureau of Justice Statistics.

sentences and constitute just 1.4 percent of persons on death row. Since 1973, of the more than 7,600 persons sentenced to death in the United States, only 157 were women. Since 1990, only 50 women have been executed, which is 0.6 percent of all executions.[15]

When this book was published, there were 54 women on death row in the United States. Condemned women were primarily in California, which had 15 women on death row; Texas, which had 10 women on death row; Pennsylvania, which had 5 women on death row; and North Carolina, which had 4 women on death row.[16]

When women are sentenced to death, the most common circumstances involve the woman murdering her husband or boyfriend and/or murdering one or more of her children. Often, condemned women who murdered their husbands or lovers were themselves the victims of physical abuse and other types of victimization.[17]

History

The antisocial behavior of females has never been viewed in the same way as the antisocial behavior of males. Two empirical truths reinforce the notion that female crime is somehow different. First, there is less crime occurring among women than among men, which supports the idea that for men, crime is a somewhat normal behavior, but for women, crime is less normal. Second, the gender gap in crime is most apparent for the most serious forms of antisocial behavior, such as murder, rape, kidnapping, and armed robbery. Thus it was widely recognized that there were real gender differences in antisocial behavior and that women appeared to be less criminal than men. This resulted in an interesting societal reaction to female crime. Women were at once viewed as better, more pure than men and in some ways held on a pedestal. However, when women did commit crime, the societal response included more outrage and condemnation because criminal women were not only violating the law, they were violating the normative role of women. This outrage was pronounced in the event that women committed sexual forms of delinquency or engaged in improper ways regarding sexual behavior. This quotation from a British prison warden captures this sentiment:

> The gentler sex, as a whole, are superior in virtue to the sterner sex; but when woman falls, she seems to possess a capacity almost beyond man, for running into all that is evil.[18, p. 298]

The history of the correctional supervision of women is deplorable. During colonial times, women were placed in detention along with men, which resulted in widespread prevalence of rape, prostitution, and other depravities. Just like today, correctional facilities contained many more men than women so to alleviate the physical and sexual abuses of female inmates, they were segregated from men. In this sense, women in early jails suffered the worst of both worlds. On one hand, if they were housed alongside male prisoners, they were preyed upon by male inmates and male correctional officials. On the other hand, when they were segregated from male prisoners, they were packed into small, crowded quarters which were justified on logistical grounds that so few women should receive few amenities. This was noted in de Beaumont and de Toqueville's classic treatise, *On the Penitentiary System in the United States and its Application in France*, which was published in 1833: "It is because they occupy little space that they have been neglected."[19, p. 72] Regardless of their criminal history or risk factors, women were placed together, which meant that first-time or novice offenders were housed alongside the most disturbed, violent, and recidivistic women.

Elizabeth Gurney Fry was a leader in the dignified and humane treatment of female prisoners, and her reforms resulted in changes still used today.

Elizabeth Gurney Fry is often credited for spearheading the humane and dignified treatment of female offenders. Fry was a Quaker who visited the Newgate jail in London in 1813 (recall that William Penn and the Pennsylvania Quakers founded the Pennsylvania model prison in the United States). She was appalled at the abusive treatment of female prisoners and the squalor in which they lived. Fry founded the Ladies Association for the Reformation of Female Prisoners in Newgate and later the British Ladies Society for the Reformation of Female Prisoners. Her progressive efforts led to increased attention to women prisoners and helped to bring reforms, such as the segregation of inmates by sex or gender, the use of female guards to supervise female offenders, and less reliance on hard labor for women.[20]

Over time, correctional reforms resulted in the establishment of separate correctional facilities for women or separate buildings to house females. For instance, in 1825, the New York House of Refuge added separate buildings to house female detainees, and in 1828, all U.S. jails were required to segregate inmates by gender.[21] In 1835, the first independent state prison for women was founded with the completion of the **New York Mount Pleasant Female Prison.** Mount Pleasant was located on a hill behind the men's prison, Sing Sing. Both facilities practiced the Auburn system (Chapter 2) characterized by congregate work conditions, solitary confinement in cells, and punitive forms of punishment including the straightjacket, gagging, and beatings.[22] Early women's prisons were designed to fit traditional gender expectations in terms of the activities in which female prisoners should engage. Many women's facilities were more like cottages and included domestic activities, such as cooking, cleaning, housekeeping, and sewing as opposed to hard labor. The federal Bureau of Prisons established its first female correctional facility in 1927 with the completion of the Federal Industrial Institution for Women in Alderson, West Virginia, a prison often known simply as **Alderson.** Today, Alderson is a federal prison camp for minimum-security offenders. A famous recent inmate at Alderson was Martha Stewart.

Media mogul Martha Stewart was a recent inmate at Alderson Federal Prison Camp, which, in 1927, became the first federal prison for women.

Another distinction in the correctional history of female offenders relates to the role of status offenses. As described in Chapter 13, juvenile justice is based on the doctrine of *parens patrie*, whereby the state acts as a parent to meet the interests of children. Throughout American history, children who misbehaved or challenged adult authority were described in a variety of ways including idle, incorrigible, and ungovernable.

Indeed, these terms are actual status offenses for which youths have been and still are sanctioned. In the case that females were out of control, the system usually defined them as immoral or wayward.

Wayward girls were those who were sexually precocious or engaged in behaviors that adults viewed as improper and conflicting with what girls should do. In this sense, although both boys and girls were controlled by status offenses, delinquent girls were especially so. For example, after the Juvenile Justice and Delinquency Prevention Act of 1974 decriminalized status offenses, the institutionalization rates for status offenses among females dropped nearly 50 percent.

The historical use of status offenses to label wayward girls has not only been done by justice officials but also the families of wayward girls. In other words, it was not just a societal response to wayward girls that led to their detention but feelings of powerlessness on the part of their parents. Recent research found that family members feel that at-risk delinquent girls are so out of control that they would be better served by living in detention.[23]

Fortunately, when wayward or delinquent girls are placed into juvenile custody, there are numerous services to help them, particularly in residential facilities. Barbara Bloom and her colleagues conducted an assessment of 62 juvenile justice facilities in California to examine how many and what types of services are provided in contemporary juvenile justice systems for females. They found that residential facilities provided virtually all programs, including:

- Counseling (family, individual, coed peer support group and single sex support group)
- Educational skills training (education training, GED, vocational)
- Life skills training (victim awareness, life skills, anger management, grief management, parenting skills, and family planning/sex education)
- Substance abuse treatment (12-step groups, group and individual counseling, sober living homes, inpatient treatment, and detoxification)
- General services (shelter, food, clothing, housing, transportation, child care, recreational activities, foster care, medical and dental care, and independent living)
- Mentoring[24]

From modest beginnings, the correctional system for women today includes more than 100 state and federal confinement facilities exclusively for women, nearly 100 facilities that house both women and men in separate housing units, and over 3,000 jails that have separate units for women. In addition, approximately 40,000 correctional professionals are employed in correctional institutions operated exclusively for women.[25]

Legal Issues

Due to the disparate treatment afforded to women in the criminal justice system and particularly corrections, the question could be asked: Are female correctional clients entitled to the same rights as men? The answer is yes. The Fourteenth Amendment guarantees that all citizens are entitled to equal protection of the laws and due process. This means that the same procedural steps that occur for men in the correctional system also pertain to women.

The landmark case on the correctional supervision of women is ***Craig v. Boren*** (1976). Curiously, *Craig v. Boren* is not even a criminal justice case per se. Instead, it reviewed an Oklahoma law that prohibited the sale of 3.2 percent beer to males under 21 and to females under 18. The rationale for the law was that since males (and intoxicated males) contribute so much more to crimes such as drunk driving there should be limits on young men's accessibility to beer. However, the Court held that the law constituted a

The landmark case *Craig v. Boren* in 1976 established that there must be parity between correctional facilities and treatment programs for men and women inmates.

denial of equal protection under the law because males 19 and 20 were held to different standards than females of the same ages. Specifically, the Court ruled that "classifications by gender must serve important governmental objectives and must be substantially related to achievement of those objectives." [26, p. 429]

The same logic has been used in a variety of cases in the federal appeals courts. The consensus in these decisions is that there must be parity of treatment for male and female inmates. This means that there must be generally equivalent facilities and treatment programs for men and women. But because of the sheer differences in the size of the correctional populations by gender, there cannot be totally equivalent facilities and treatment programs. For example, FIGURE 14–2 shows the sparseness of women-only facilities in the

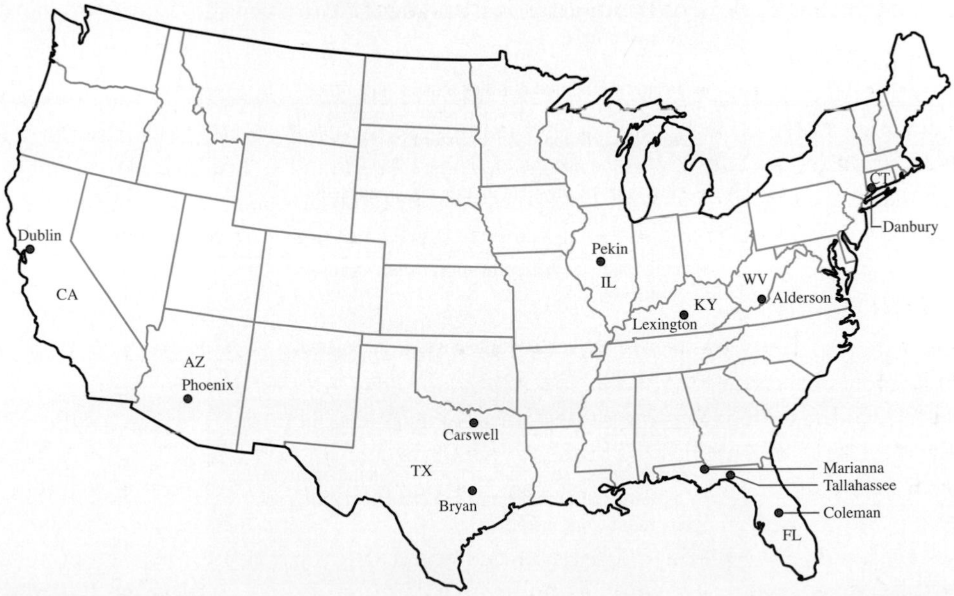

FIGURE 14–2 Women's Facilities in the Bureau of Prisons. *Source*: United States General Accounting Office. (1999). *Women in prison: Issues and challenges confronting U.S. correctional systems.* Washington, DC: USGAO.

Bureau of Prisons, which reflects the small size of that population compared to men. In other words, there is no constitutional right to identical treatment in prison.[27]

For example, in 1993, the Bureau of Prisons implemented a new classification system for female offenders to account for their reduced likelihood to be violent or attempt escape. As a result of this classification system, several facilities changed their mission to provide more low- and minimum-security bed space for female offenders. The BOP also provides programs and services that are comparable to those at facilities for male offenders. For example, in the area of job training, the agency's apprenticeship training programs have been accredited by the Women's Bureau of the U.S. Department of Labor, Bureau of Apprenticeship and Training. These programs assist in preparing women for a wide range of positions, including auto mechanic, electrician, plumber, painter, bricklayer, data processor, and secretary. The BOP offers apprenticeship programs in 40 different trades to female inmates.[28]

Gendered Pathways

As shown in FIGURE 14–3, there are many commonalities in the social and behavioral background of women compared to male offenders discussed throughout the text. Both are young, disproportionately non-White, have family problems, and are underachieving in terms of work and educational attainment. Both have overlapping problems with substance abuse and crime. Although female offenders are free agents in the sense that

National Profile of Women Offenders

A profile based on national data for women offenders reveals the following characteristics:

- Disproportionately women of color.
- In their early to mid-30s.
- Most likely to have been convicted of a drug-related offense.
- From fragmented families that include other family members who also have been involved with the criminal justice system.
- Survivors of physical and/or sexual abuse as children and adults.
- Individuals with significant substance abuse problems.
- Individuals with multiple physical and mental health problems.
- Unmarried mothers of minor children.
- Individuals with a high school or general equivalency diploma (GED) but limited vocational training and sporadic work histories.

FIGURE 14–3 National Profile of Women Offenders. *Source*: Bloom, B., Owen, B., Covington, S., & Raeder, M. (2003). *Gender-responsive strategies: Research, practice, and guiding principles for women offenders*. Washington, DC: U.S. Department of Justice, Office of Justice Programs, National Institute of Corrections.

they choose to commit crime, extensive research has found that women are more likely than men to play secondary roles in criminal offending, such as acting as a lookout, driving a getaway car, or participating in the planning but not the execution of a crime. For instance, researchers found that women play secondary roles alongside primary male offenders in general felony offending, violent felony offending, substance abuse, and theft to obtain various types of drugs, gang delinquency, public-order crimes, white-collar offenses, and theft offenses to obtain heroin.[29]

In addition to the role they play in crimes, there is also a number of variables where women are different and in fact significantly more at risk than men. Foremost is the issue of victimization. Among state inmates, women are more than three times likely than men to have ever been abused. Among federal inmates, women are more than five times as likely as men to have ever been abused. Among jail inmates, the gender abuse ratio is nearly 4 to 1, and for probationers the ratio exceeds 4 to 1. Female offenders are also more likely to have been sexually assaulted, to have been raped, and to have been abused during adolescence, adulthood, or both periods.[30] Victimization is a standard feature in the life histories of many female offenders (TABLE 14-6).

Female Criminal Careers

In recent years, female offenders have increasingly been studied from a life-course or criminal careers perspective to understand the ways that women offend similarly and dissimilarly than men. The aspects of criminal careers that are unique to women are known as **gendered pathways**, which are the gender-specific ways that offending is related to women's social and economic marginality. This new approach to studying women and crime is compatible with traditional feminist techniques. According to Joanne Belknap, "In many ways the life-course perspective is seemingly pro-feminist in nature: It purports to address significant childhood and adult experiences and to view how these, particularly social bonds, are related to delinquent, criminal, and deviant behavior."[31, p. 68]

TABLE 14-6 Prior Abuse of Correctional Clients by Gender

	State Inmates		Federal Inmates		Jail Inmates		Probationers	
Before Admission	**Male**	**Female**	**Male**	**Female**	**Male**	**Female**	**Male**	**Female**
Ever abused	16.1%	57.2%	7.2%	39.9%	12.9%	47.6%	9.3%	40.4%
Physically	13.4	46.5	6.0	32.3	10.7	37.3	7.4	33.5
Sexually	5.8	39.0	2.2	22.8	5.6	37.2	4.1	25.2
Both	3.0	28.0	1.1	15.1	3.3	26.9	2.1	18.3
Age of victim at time of abuse								
17 or younger	14.4%	36.7%	5.8%	23.0%	11.9%	36.6%	8.8%	28.2%
18 or older	4.3	45.0	2.7	31.0	2.3	26.7	1.1	24.7
Both	2.5	24.7	1.3	14.2	1.3	15.8	0.5	12.5
Age of abuser								
Adult	15.0%	55.8%	6.9%	39.0%	12.1%	46.0%	8.5%	39.2%
Juvenile only	0.9	1.0	0.2	0.2	0.8	1.3	0.6	
Rape before admission	4.0%	37.3%	1.4%	21.4%	3.9%	33.1%	—	—
Completed	3.1	32.8	1.0	17.9	3.0	26.6	—	—
Attempted	0.8	4.3	0.3	3.2	0.7	5.6	—	—

Source: Harlow, C. W. (1999). *Prior abuse reported by inmates and probationers.* Washington, DC: U.S. Department of Justice, Office of Justice Programs, Bureau of Justice Statistics.

Several studies have examined how pathways into delinquency unfold into delinquent careers among women. Marguerite Warren and Jill Rosenbaum studied 159 women who had been incarcerated in California during the 1960s. They found that women had similar criminal careers as men in the sense that there was a generalized involvement in many types of crimes, such as violence, property, and drug offenses. However, women were disproportionately likely to have arrests for prostitution, theft, forgery, fraud, and drug violations.[32]

Using self-reported offending history data from a sample of 1,000 Colorado inmates, which included nearly 200 women, Kim English found that forgery was the primary criminal offense of women, but they also dabbled in an assortment of offenses. More women reported committing assaults than men did, but women tended to commit just one assault in a year, and it was usually domestic in nature. When men were involved in assaults, they committed several annually, against both partners and strangers. Women also reported greater frequency in drug sales than men, primarily because the income from drug trafficking was lower than among male offenders. This suggests that a pay gap exists even among female and male drug dealers.[33]

In many ways, the abuses that female criminals experience reflect their sexualized and subordinated status in a patriarchal society. Using a sample of women who had been arrested a minimum of 30 times, Matt DeLisi found that ironically, it is through the status of sexual object that many female offenders survive, namely through prostitution. Along with theft, forgery, and fraud, prostitution is the primary way that women on the streets get money, and the money is often quickly used to obtain drugs to numb themselves.[34] DeLisi's study is noteworthy because it contains female offenders with extreme criminal careers in terms of number of arrests and convictions, incarcerations, and career length. It also points to the diversity of the female offender population.

This issue was recently revisited by Stephen Cernkovich and his colleagues' study of female offenders spanning the years 1982 to 1995. In 1982, they compared two groups of delinquent girls who were living in juvenile institutions. One group was minimally delinquent and one group was severely delinquent. On many measures, the severe group had more risk factors. For instance, severely delinquent girls had less family caring and trust, less communication with parents, received less parental control and supervision, experienced more parental conflict, and received less disapproval of delinquent behaviors from their parents. But both groups experienced comparable levels of physical abuse, sexual abuse, money worries, and changes in residence. In 1995, the delinquent groups—who were then criminal women—closely resembled one another on virtually all variables.

This study also illuminated the ways that early childhood abuse can result in a serious criminal career. For instance, girls who had the worst sexual abuse histories were *334 percent* more likely than others to be chronic adult offenders. Girls who were physically abused as minors were *600 percent* more likely than other girls to be habitual criminals. And those with both forms of victimization were an additional *260 percent* more likely to be serious offenders.[35]

Perhaps the most comprehensive study of female criminal careers comes from the ongoing analyses of a birth cohort of more than 1,000 persons from the Dunedin (New Zealand) Multidisciplinary Health and Development Study. The study contains data on male and female respondents collected through age 32. Analyses indicated that four general groupings of offenders emerged from the data: low offenders, childhood-only offenders, adolescence-only offenders, and the severe group called life-course–persistent offenders. Across a battery of variables relating to family, cognitive, and peer factors, women in the life-course group were much more severe. These women also experienced greater and more severe symptoms of domestic and child abuse; worse social functioning, poorer health outcomes; and higher involvement in diverse forms of crime.[36]

Victimization and Marginality

Cathy Spatz Widom chronicled the **cycle of violence** whereby physical abuse, sexual abuse, and neglect incurred during childhood dramatically increase the risks for delinquency and a host of maladaptive behaviors during adolescence and adulthood. This effect is especially strong among girls who are sexually abused.[37–38]

As described earlier, compared to male delinquents, female offenders have significantly more extensive victimization histories, including sexual, physical, and emotional abuses. Often, this abuse begins at home when girls are very young, especially if there is a nonbiological male parental or authority figure in the household. Many young female offenders run away from home and lead transient lifestyles. Eventually, the victimization, oppressive home life, and vulnerabilities of the street lead to drug use.[39]

Along with various forms of victimization, gendered pathways are also characterized by social isolation and marginality. Peggy Giordano and her colleagues found that delinquent girls are often those who had difficulty in school and were labeled as outcasts, which in turn fueled more antisocial behavior. Over time, girls with backgrounds such as this associate with other troubled youth and increase their chances for further victimization and withdrawal from conventional peers. As women cycle out of jail and prison, they become left behind in terms of their job skills and often become reliant on governmental assistance.[40–41]

There is evidence that abusive backgrounds and victimization experience manifests differently by race. For instance, Kristi Holsinger and Alexander Holsinger compared African American and White female delinquents and found racial differences. Although both groups experienced significant trauma, African American girls had more violent crimes in their delinquent histories and generally better mental health. White girls internalized their violence and had more severe mental health problems and self-injurious behaviors, such as suicide attempts.[42] There are also race differences in the relationship between self-esteem and delinquency. Among Whites, those with high self-esteem were less likely to offend, but among African Americans, those with high self-esteem were more likely to offend.[43]

The cycle of violence where physical and sexual abuse lead to antisocial behavior and continued victimization is a common profile of many female offenders in the United States.

In their review of the literature, Ronald Mullis and his colleagues describe the typical female delinquent as one who:

- Is young
- Is impoverished
- Is likely to have experienced abuse or exploitation
- Abuses drugs and alcohol
- Is likely to have unmet medical and mental health needs
- Lacks hope for the future
- Perceives life as oppressive[44]

Female offenders with extensive criminal careers also have extensive criminal justice experience. Despite the importance of victimization and marginality in the lives of women offenders, their repeated violations of the law ultimately result in serious prosecution and criminal punishment. Emily Gaardner and Joanne Belknap interviewed girls who were transferred to criminal court and ultimately sentenced to adult prison. Based on the waiver procedures described in Chapter 13, these girls' offending careers were similar to those described previously, but their involvement in more serious crimes resulted in more severe adult punishment. Several collateral problems emerge for girls who are incarcerated in adult prisons, such as feelings of isolation due to their segregation from women inmates and difficulties in maintaining their schooling while confined.[45–46] Indeed, many delinquent girls and women offenders face difficulties in the correctional system evidenced by their noncompliance and recidivism. These issues are explored next.

Noncompliance and Recidivism

It could be said that the more severe the form of correctional supervision, the more severe the risk level and supervision needs of the offender. This includes women offenders. Although less literature has specifically studied women and their degree of compliance with criminal sentences, serious offenders often have difficulty dealing with the conditions of their sentence. As a result, recidivism levels among women are high albeit lower than male recidivism levels.

Although noncompliance and recidivism among female offenders are at least comparable to male offenders, women constitute a significantly lower threat to public safety given the low offending prevalence in violent crimes, such as murder, rape, and kidnapping. There is also evidence that women are more amenable to correctional interventions than men. For instance, Peter Wood and Harold Grasmick surveyed 224 women and 181 men inmates about their assessment of intermediate sanctions. They found that women were significantly more open minded about various types of community corrections and considered them less punitive than men.[47]

Probation

As a general rule, women fare better than men on probation. Women have lower recidivism rates, and given the salience of drug use to female criminality, women probationers greatly benefit from substance abuse treatment and urinalysis tests that are standard components of most probation sentences. David Olson and his colleagues studied 3,400 adult probationers in Illinois, including nearly 700 females. They found that women had lower recidivism rates and also that fewer variables predicted probation outcomes for women.[48] This supports the rationale of gendered pathways where nontraditional variables that are often not included in risk assessment instruments predict correctional outcomes among women. In terms of traditional variables that do predict probation outcomes, White women and older women are more likely to successfully complete their sentences.[49]

Some jurisdictions developed special case management forms of probation for drug-involved women probationers. Unlike standard probation, the case management approach uses a case manager who has increased contact with clients, a lower caseload, a therapeutic and advocacy orientation, and an emphasis on referring clients to health and human service providers. Despite the special focus of case management probation for female offenders, a recent evaluation suggests that it provides no benefits over standard probation. After a 12-month follow-up, more than 49 percent of the case management and 50 percent of the standard probation women had been reincarcerated.[50]

Another innovation in probation involves the combined use of boot camp and a period of intensive probation, a sentence known as shock probation. Leanne Alarid and her colleagues studied 122 women who completed a shock probation program in Houston, Texas, and found that women who were involved in conventional activities and attached to their parents had lower recidivism than those who did not. They also found that women probationers who were married were *more* likely to recidivate in part because female felons are disproportionately likely to select drug-using, criminal males as their partners.[51]

Probationers are often similar to prisoners in their level of criminality and as a result can provide cost savings for correctional systems. Cassia Spohn and David Holleran compared felony drug offenders sentenced to felony probation to those sentenced to prison. Although the groups were similar in terms of their criminal histories, those who were sent to prison had higher recidivism rates and failed more quickly than those on probation. This suggests that felony offenders can be managed on probation with the added benefits of reduced recidivism and cost savings on prison space.[52]

Surveys of probation officers suggest that they view female probationers as more time consuming, emotionally complex, and challenging than male clients despite being less likely to violate probation.[53] Interestingly *female* probation officers were the most vocal in suggesting that women on their caseload are more difficult to supervise than men. Probation officers reported that in addition to the usual risk factors, such as drug problems and criminal history, female probationers present unique needs. Many female probationers are single parents and have difficulty with child care and often must bring their children to meetings with their probation officer. Single parenthood places financial burdens on female probationers that, coupled with poor work history, can lead to noncompliance.[54] A recent study of juvenile probation officers indicated that female clients are considered manipulative, emotional, and generally unpleasant to supervise.[55]

Prison Adjustment and Misconduct

Many female prisoners have extensive criminal histories in terms of prior arrests, convictions, and incarcerations (TABLE 14-7). Roughly 16 percent of women prisoners have both juvenile and adult criminal histories. Nearly one third of female prisoners are chronic recidivists. Eight percent of women had between 6 and 10 arrests, and 5 percent had 11 or more arrests prior to entering prison.[56] This means that thousands of female prisoners enter prison with difficult-to-overcome records of antisocial behavior.

In part because of their history of victimization, substance abuse, and the psychological problems underlying them, women offenders have difficulty adjusting to prison. Compared to women in the general population, female prisoners have significantly higher rates of major depression disorder, borderline personality disorder, and posttraumatic stress disorder, as well as increased histories of overnight psychiatric hospitalizations. A study of a cohort of 800 women entering North Carolina prisons found high prevalence

TABLE 14-7 Criminal History of Prisoners

Criminal History	Percent of State Prison Inmates	
	Female	Male
Past convictions		
None	35	23
Juvenile only	3	7
Adult only	46	39
Both adult and juvenile	16	31
Number of prior convictions		
0	35	23
1	17	17
2	16	16
3–5	19	25
6–10	8	12
11 or more	5	6
Status at arrest		
None	47	53
Probation	34	21
Parole	18	25
Escapee	1	1

Source: Greenfeld, L. A., & Snell, T. L. (2000). *Women offenders*. Washington, DC: U.S. Department of Justice, Office of Justice Programs, Bureau of Justice Statistics.

of these psychiatric symptoms and antisocial personality disorder. Many women entering prison have also experienced acute forms of trauma including rape, assault, and other victimization.[57]

Nationally, nearly 24 percent of women in state prisons and nearly 15 percent of women in federal prisons are mentally ill. Once they enter prison, female prisoners experience worsening of their mental health symptoms including anxiety, depression, and hostility.[58] The behavioral profile of women inmates with mental problems is particularly troubling. For instance:

- Forty percent have current or past violent offenses on their record.
- Thirty-six percent have three or more prior probations or incarcerations.
- Seventy-five percent are dependent on drugs or alcohol.
- Sixty-four percent used drugs in the month preceding their most recent arrest.
- Thirty-four percent used cocaine or crack in the month before their most recent arrest.
- Seventeen percent used methamphetamine in the month before their most recent arrest.
- Seventeen percent were homeless in the year before their most recent arrest.
- Nearly 70 percent had prior sexual or physical abuse.
- Forty-seven percent had parents who were drug abusers.
- More than 50 percent were charged with prison rule violations.
- More than 10 percent were injured in a fight since entering prison.[59]

CORRECTIONS BRIEF

Former Beauty Pageant Queen/ Law Student Faces Time in Prison for Kidnapping and Torture

Kumari Fulbright, age 25, was accused of falsely imprisoning and torturing her ex-boyfriend. With the assistance of accomplices, Fulbright is said to have sought to retrieve jewelry she believed had been stolen from her by her ex-boyfriend. What follows is what Tucson Police Sgt. Fabian Pacheco alleges happened.

Fulbright invited her ex-boyfriend to her apartment. After he arrived, she excused herself to take a shower. Two men entered the apartment and placed the ex-boyfriend in restraints, binding him with plastic ties and duct tape. They then questioned him about the jewelry and threatened to shoot him. Fulbright finished her shower and joined the interrogation. It was at this time Fulbright is alleged to have bitten her ex-boyfriend on the forearm, right hand, and ear and to have threatened him with a knife. The ex-boyfriend was then transported to another residence where the assault continued. Eventually, he was taken back to Fulbright's apartment where Fulbright, armed with a firearm, stood guard preventing her ex-boyfriend from leaving after the men left. The ex-boyfriend managed to free himself from the restraints, and a struggle with Ms. Fulbright began over the gun. The fight continued as the ex-boyfriend ran from the apartment screaming for help.

Two of Ms. Fulbright's accomplices are thought to have fled the country. They are facing charges of kidnapping, armed robbery, and aggravated assault. Ms. Fulbright and her other accomplice have been formally charged. Fulbright was released after posting bond.

Source: Associated Press. (2008). *Law student, pageant princess—and kidnapping suspect.* Retrieved January 3, 2008, from http://www.cnn.com/2008/CRIME/01/03/beauty.indicted.ap/index.html.

A similar portrait exists among delinquent girls. Elizabeth Cauffman and her colleagues compared mental health symptoms across gender in both a community and institutionalized juvenile sample. In both groups, girls had more mental health symptoms. Detained girls in particular had poorer mental health compared to their male peers.[60]

Caitlin Thompson and Ann Loper investigated how adjustment patterns in incarcerated women were related to length of sentence in a sample of nearly 700 female inmates. Inmates were divided into groups based on prison sentence length—long-term (10 or more years), medium-term (2–10 years), and short-term (less than 2 years) and administered psychiatric and prison adjustment questionnaires. They found that long- and medium-term inmates reported higher feelings of conflict and committed significantly more nonviolent and institutional offenses than short-term inmates. No significant relationship between sentence length and emotional adjustment was found. Women serving lengthier sentences exhibit more difficulty with conflict and institutional misconduct than short-term inmates.[61]

Adjustment to prison is hampered by the violent and chaotic environment in many facilities. Mark Pogrebin and Mary Dodge interviewed 54 women who had served time in Colorado prisons. The women reported an array of stressful and dangerous situations that from their perspective typified the women's prison. Older women and those with more extensive criminal histories harassed and preyed upon younger and first-time inmates. The women reported high levels of drug use and fighting. In addition, the woman suggested that prison medical services were inadequate to meet their needs, especially psychiatric needs, and that some staff coerced women into sexual relationships. Based on the interviews, Pogrebin and Dodge concluded that a major limitation of women's prisons compared to men's facilities was the lack of inmate classification. As a result, serious, career offenders were commonly housed with low-risk, first-time prisoners.[62]

The likelihood of continued misconduct and violence behind bars is not the same for all female offenders. The majority of women never engage in violence while incarcerated, and many manage to comply with prison regulations. Among women who do receive infraction tickets, the misconduct is usually relatively unserious. However, a handful of women who are chronic offenders commit the bulk of misconduct in a particular facility and are also responsible for the violent acts occurring in women's prisons.[63] Miles Harer and Neal Langan studied more than 200,000 inmates in the Bureau of Prisons, which included nearly 25,000 women. They found that the rate of violent misconduct was limited to less than 3 percent of federal female inmates. Women and men also had comparable rates of fighting with other inmates. However, for the most serious offenses such as murdering another inmate, attempting to murder another inmate, aggravated assault on another inmate, and possession of a dangerous weapon, the female involvement was a fraction of the male involvement.[64]

Emily Wright and her colleagues studied misconduct among nearly 300 women serving time in Missouri. They found that women who experienced childhood abuse, had unstable family relationships, and had current psychiatric problems committed more prison misconduct at two points of time.[65] Interestingly, the structure of prison mutes the effect of some risk factors on institutional misconduct. For example, Emily Salisbury and her colleagues studied the validity of an offender needs instrument that was specifically designed for female offenders. They found that histories of abuse and mental health problems were the strongest predictors of misconduct in prison. Other factors including adult abuse, parental stress, and financial well-being were not applicable to women's day-to-day prison lives and thus were unrelated to misconduct. However, these factors did influence compliance rates of women serving community-based sentences such as parole.[66]

Parole and Reentry

One of the most impressive large-scale studies of recidivism among female prisoners surveyed nearly 24,000 women released from prisons in 15 states. Elizabeth Piper Deschenes and her colleagues examined recidivism patterns and the impact of prior criminal history of postrelease success over a follow-up of 3 years. They produced several important findings, including the following:

- Sixty-three percent of women had no prior prison terms, thus many were first-time inmates.
- Women had significantly lower recidivism rates than men as measured by subsequent arrests, convictions, prison sentences, and prison terms.
- Sixty percent of women were subsequently rearrested.
- Forty percent of women had a subsequent conviction.
- About 30 percent of women returned to prison (18 percent for new sentences and 12 percent for violations of parole).
- Women who had served time for property or drug offenses were more likely to recidivate.
- Women were disproportionately involved in property crimes, but tended to engage in multiple forms of criminal behavior.
- Women with more extensive criminal histories were more likely to fail on parole and continue committing crime.

- Of the women who had additional contacts with the justice system, virtually all had previously been arrested.
- Of the 13,573 women who were rearrested after release from prison, the average number of prior arrests was more than 11 and the average number of prison convictions was nearly 5.[67]

One of the most difficult obstacles to overcome among correctional clients is housing, particularly when an offender has recently been released from state custody. The reentry phase (Chapter 12) can include periods of homelessness, which can serve to push offenders into recidivating. Kristy Holtfreter and her colleagues studied the effects of poverty and state-sponsored housing support on recidivism among 134 women serving felony probation or parole sentences in Oregon or Minnesota. Over a 6-month follow-up, Holtfreter and her colleagues found that poverty status resulted in a fivefold increase in the odds of rearrest and a thirteenfold increase in the odds of supervision violation. In addition, poor women offenders who received state-sponsored support for housing needs had reduced odds of recidivism by 83 percent.[68]

Women who have jobs or unemployment benefits are less likely to commit crimes shortly after release.[69] For instance, Pamela Schram and her colleagues studied 546 female parolees and suggested that poor assessment of offender needs among women often contributes to problems with parole compliance. Women who had stable living and work arrangements and adequate substance abuse treatment fared well on parole. Women who lacked these prosocial supports often failed. These were often the same women who were underexamined in terms of their parole needs.[70]

Nancy Harm and Susan Phillips interviewed female parolees who reported that drug relapses were often brought on by difficulties finding work and reconnecting to family members. In this sense, drug use and parole noncompliance was strongly related to adjustment difficulties and social disadvantage.[71] Brent Benda studied 300 women and 300 men who completed boot camp, were placed on parole, and followed for 5 years. He found several gender differences in terms of what predicted successful completion of parole or recidivism. Among women, childhood abuse victimization, adult abuse victimization, stress, depression, suicidal thoughts, and living with a criminal partner predicted recidivism. In contrast, women who had satisfying, prosocial relationships with family, friends, and crime-free partners were likely to desist from offending. Benda concluded that "abuse, adverse feelings and thoughts, and criminal partners play a larger role in women's recidivism than in men's."[72, p. 339] Given the gender inequality that exists for income and employment status, reentry is an especially difficult time for women offenders rendering parole and reintegration very difficult for many ex-felons to surmount.[73–74]

Correctional Programming for Women

Throughout this text there has been considerable examination of the lengths that correctional systems go to accurately classify offenders for the most appropriate placement. There is an array of diagnostic assessment tools to inform decisions about sentencing, pretrial release, appropriateness for pretrial programs, probation, inmate classification, parole, and others.

Unfortunately, the same energy has not been applied to women (FIGURE 14-4). Often, female offenders were assessed for their risk factors using the same correctional instruments that are used on male offenders. When female offenders were similar to male offenders in terms of criminal history and the usual assortment of risk factors (e.g., unemployed, gang involved, antisocial personality disorder diagnosis, etc.), then traditional assessment tools were effective. However, for women who followed gendered offending pathways, the instruments were less successful. For instance, the Level of

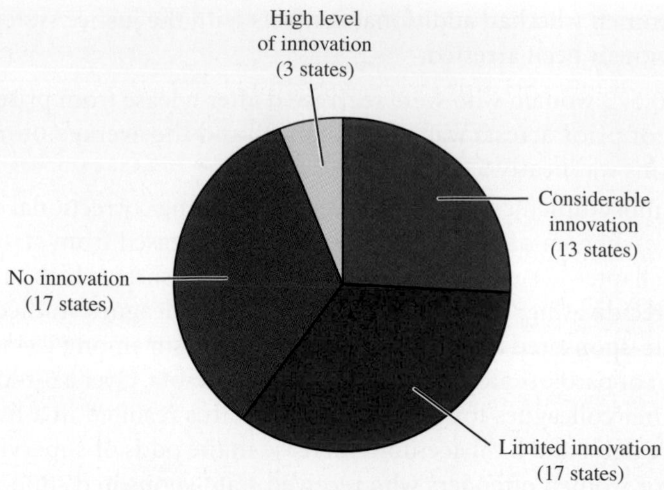

FIGURE 14–4 Level of Innovation in Women Offenders' Programming. *Source*: Morash, M., Bynum, T. S., & Koons, B. A. (1998). *Women offenders: Programming needs and promising approaches.* Washington, DC: U.S. Department of Justice, Office of Justice Programs, National Institute of Justice.

Service Inventory-Revised assessment tool, a commonly used correctional assessment tool, misclassified women who were mostly drug offenders or who had extensive victimization history.[75]

Patricia Van Voorhis and Lois Presser conducted a national assessment of current practices of women inmate classification. The study was funded by the National Institute of Corrections Classification of Women Offenders Initiative and found the following:

- Only eight states classify women using a gender-responsive instrument.
- No state uses a gender-response internal classification system.
- Only four states (Idaho, New York, Massachusetts, and Ohio) have a separate custody classification system for women.
- Only 14 states have validated their custody classification systems for a sample of women offenders.[76]

Based on increased understanding of the unique needs that women correctional clients have and the likely inability of existing correctional systems to provide them, changes have been made. In recent years, **gender-responsive strategies** that address the unique needs of female offenders have been developed. These are:

- **Guiding principle 1 (gender)**: Acknowledge that gender makes a difference.
- **Guiding principle 2 (environment)**: Create an environment based on safety, respect, and dignity.
- **Guiding principle 3 (relationships)**: Develop policies, practices, and programs that are relational and promote healthy connections to children, family, significant others, and the community.
- **Guiding principle 4 (services and supervision)**: Address substance abuse, trauma, and mental health issues through comprehensive, integrated, and culturally relevant services and appropriate supervision.
- **Guiding principle 5 (socioeconomic status)**: Provide women with opportunities to improve their socioeconomic conditions.
- **Guiding principle 6 (community)**: Establish a system of community supervision and reentry with comprehensive, collaborative services.[77]

Alameda County's Santa Rita Jail applied gender-responsive strategies to create **Maximizing Opportunities for Mothers to Succeed (MOMS)**, a gender-responsive program in the Alameda County, California, Santa Rita Jail. MOMS promotes the healthy development of children by increasing the capacity of their incarcerated mothers for self-sufficiency, increasing parenting skills with an emphasis on successful parent-child bonding, and reducing recidivism among incarcerated pregnant women and incarcerated mothers of young children.

MOMS includes intensive individual and group case management, commitment to a continuum of care, community-based postrelease services, and attention to program staffing both for officers and civilian staff. The program includes educational training for offenders and provides a bridge to community-based services, such as housing, substance abuse treatment, and mental health services. Since 1999, the MOMS program has served more than 680 women. In one year, 214 clients were served, representing 537 children, 114 of whom were under age 5. MOMS was responsible for 29 residential treatment placements, 44 placements to outpatient treatment services, 14 referrals to mental health services, and 19 reunifications of noncustodial parents with their children. In terms of recidivism, of the 214 MOMS participants in one year, 191 clients were not rearrested or returned to custody—a recidivism rate of only 10 percent![78]

The Bureau of Prisons offers a community residential program called **Mothers and Infants Nurturing Together (MINT)** for women who are pregnant at the time of commitment. The MINT program promotes bonding and parenting skills for low-risk female inmates who are pregnant. Women are eligible to enter the program if they are in their last 3 months of pregnancy, have less than 5 years remaining to serve on their sentences, and are eligible for furlough. The inmate or a guardian must assume financial responsibility for the child's medical care while residing at MINT. The mother then has 3 months to bond with the newborn child before returning to an institution to complete her sentence. In select MINT programs, the inmate may stay for an additional period of bonding with the child. Women in the MINT program participate in the following:

- Prenatal and postnatal programs such as childbirth, parenting, and coping skills classes.
- Chemical dependency treatment.
- Physical and sexual abuse counseling.
- Budgeting classes.
- Vocational and educational programs.

Prior to the birth, the mother must make arrangements for a custodian to take care of the child. Institution staff, MINT staff, and community social service agencies may aid the inmate with placement. Ultimately, it is at the discretion of the inmate's unit team to refer an inmate to the MINT program.[79]

In addition to confinement-based programs, justice systems have also devised programs to assist women upon reentering society on parole. In Delaware, officials devised the KEY **therapeutic community**, which is a prison programming technique in which treatment offenders are removed from the general population and are placed in a setting devoted to treatment. KEY uses a nonconfrontational approach and female counselors to assist women inmates in discussing very personal and difficult drug dependency and other issues. The program served high-risk offenders who had psychiatric history, had contemplated or attempted suicide, and had hostility and anger control problems. To ensure continuity in care, Delaware authorities created CREST, which is a work-release program based on the therapeutic community approach. Women who participate in the programs report that the strict rules and accountability of the programs prepare them for the environment outside of prison.[80]

At the California Institution for Women, the **Forever Free** program is a voluntary, 4-month intensive residential treatment program for drug-abusing women that includes an aftercare component. Forever Free includes relapse prevention and treatment sessions on self-esteem, anger management, assertiveness training, healthy relationships, codependency, parenting classes, and education on health and sexual behavior.

A recent evaluation compared Forever Free graduates to women who participated in a standard 2-month drug education course. Both groups were followed for 1 year. The results, which are listed here, were impressive:

- Forever Free women had a recidivism rate of 40 percent (60 percent for control subjects).
- Forever Free women had a drug reuse rate of 51 percent (77 percent for control subjects).
- Forever Free women had an employment rate of 67 percent (less than 50 percent for control subjects).
- Forever Free women had child custody rates of 48 percent (28 percent for control subjects).
- Forever Free women had better psychological functioning and less need for community services than control subjects.[81]

Each of these programs produced positive outcomes among female offenders, but what works overall in providing correctional treatment to women? Craig Dowden and Donald Andrews conducted a meta-analysis of treatment programs for women. They found that the most common treatment approach (31 percent of all programs) focused on interpersonal criminogenic targets, which are family processes and antisocial peers. These programs produce the strongest reductions in recidivism. Programs that address personal criminogenic targets that include antisocial thinking styles and deficits in self-control also result in reduced recidivism. Interestingly, they found that correctional programs that address school/work issues and substance abuse did not affect recidivism.[82] In the 21st century, correctional officials will continue to develop treatment programs that attend to the gender-responsive needs of women offenders, particularly if recent trends on increasing female crime continue.

WRAP UP

CASE STUDY CONCLUSION

The life history of Wuornos is nearly as appalling as her ultimate crimes. She was the daughter of a teenage girl and a convicted child molester who ultimately committed suicide in prison. Wuornos was abandoned by her mother and raised by grandparents who she alleges sexually and physically brutalized her. Wuornos herself became pregnant at 14 and had a child, for which she was banished. This led to a life on the streets where Wuornos was extensively involved in drugs and prostitution and accumulated a lengthy, multistate criminal history including arrests for armed robbery, assault, weapons offenses, public order crimes, and others. Eventually, Aileen would be connected to the deaths of Richard Mallory, Dick Humphreys, Troy Burress, David Spears, Walter Gino Antonio, Peter Siems, and Charles Carskaddon.

Source: Myers, W. D., Gooch, E., & Meloy, J. R. (2005). The role of psychopathy and sexuality in a female serial killer. *Journal of Forensic Sciences, 50*, 652–657.

Chapter Summary

- Women comprise 23 percent of the probation and 12 percent of the parole population.
- There are nearly 99,000 women in jail and 114,000 in state and federal prison. There are only 54 women on death row.
- In recent years, the rate of growth of women in all correctional populations except capital punishment has increased more sharply than among men.
- Female criminality has been sexualized in the sense that girls and women were harshly punished for behaviors that conflicted with traditional gender roles.
- In the correctional system, women were poorly treated and received substandard services, which were justified by their small population compared to men.
- Correctional services and treatment programs for women must be generally equivalent to those for male offenders. There must be parity in services by gender but not identical services.
- Women offenders have significantly worse victimization histories than men in addition to more acute psychiatric symptoms.
- Gendered pathways of crime are characterized by victimization and abuse, drug abuse, and criminal careers with an emphasis on property offending, drug crimes, and prostitution.
- Women perform somewhat better than men on criminal justice sanctions but female offenders still demonstrate high levels of noncompliance and recidivism.
- Gender-responsive strategies address the unique needs of female offenders and are used to guide current correctional treatment programs.
- An array of treatment programs is successful at reducing problem behaviors and recidivism among women.

Key Terms

Alderson First women's federal prison, founded in 1927.

Craig v. Boren Supreme Court case that ruled that classifications by gender must serve important governmental objectives and must be substantially related to achievement of those objectives.

cycle of violence Common profile of female offenders in which physical abuse, sexual abuse, and neglect incurred during childhood dramatically increase the risks for delinquency and a host of maladaptive behaviors during adolescence and adulthood.

Forever Free A voluntary, 4-month intensive residential treatment program for drug-abusing women that includes an aftercare component.

Fry, Elizabeth Gurney Quaker who was instrumental in spearheading the humane and dignified treatment of female offenders.

gender-responsive strategies Treatments that address the unique needs of female offenders.

gendered pathways Gender-specific ways that offending is related to women's social and economic marginality.

guiding principle 1 (gender) Gender-responsive strategy that promotes acknowledging that gender makes a difference.

guiding principle 2 (environment) Gender-responsive strategy that suggests creating an environment based on safety, respect, and dignity.

guiding principle 3 (relationships) Gender-responsive strategy that suggests developing policies, practices, and programs that are relational and promotes healthy connections to children, family, significant others, and the community.

guiding principle 4 (services and supervision) Gender-responsive strategy that promotes addressing substance abuse, trauma, and mental health issues through comprehensive, integrated, and culturally relevant services and appropriate supervision.

guiding principle 5 (socioeconomic status) Gender-responsive strategy that recommends providing women with opportunities to improve their socioeconomic conditions.

guiding principle 6 (community) Gender-responsive strategy that suggests establishing a system of community supervision and reentry with comprehensive, collaborative services.

Maximizing Opportunities for Mothers to Succeed (MOMS) A gender-responsive program that promotes the healthy development of children by increasing the capacity of their incarcerated mothers for self-sufficiency, increasing parenting skills with an emphasis on successful parent-child bonding, and reducing recidivism among incarcerated pregnant women and incarcerated mothers of young children.

Mothers and Infants Nurturing Together (MINT) BOP community residential program for women who are pregnant at the time of commitment.

New York Mount Pleasant Female Prison First independent women's prison, founded in 1835.

therapeutic community A prison programming technique where treatment offenders are removed from the general population and are placed in settings devoted to treatment.

Critical Thinking Questions

1. Why was Aileen Wuornos a cause célèbre? What does this say about continued views of female crime?
2. Should the courts make every effort to not incarcerate mothers given their disproportionate role in child rearing?
3. Has the recent imprisonment boom negatively affected children and families? What is more destructive: the removal of mothers via prison or their underlying criminal behavior?
4. In the United States, should violence against women be taken more seriously given its role in the cycle of violence among women offenders? Does American society take violence against women seriously?
5. Female prisoners pose fewer safety risks than male inmates. Should states attempt to deincarcerate the female prisoner population, and if so, would this affect the crime rate?

Notes

1. Heimer, K. (2000). Changes in the gender gap in crime and women's economic marginalization. *Criminal Justice 2000*. Washington, DC: U.S. Department of Justice.
2. VanVoorhis, P., & Presser, L. (2001). *Classification of women offenders: A national assessment of current practices*. Washington, DC: U.S. Department of Justice, Office of Justice Programs, National Institute of Corrections.
3. English, K. (1993). Self-reported crime rates of women prisoners. *Journal of Quantitative Criminology, 9*, 357–382.
4. Zedner, L. (1998). Wayward sisters: The prison for women. In N. Morris & D. J. Rothman (Eds.), *The Oxford history of the prison: The practice of punishment in Western society* (pp. 295–324). New York: Oxford University Press.
5. Erez, E. (1992). Dangerous men, evil women: Gender and parole decision making. *Justice Quarterly, 9*, 105–126.
6. Bloom, B., Owen, B., Covington, S., & Raeder, M. (2003). *Gender-responsive strategies: Research, practice, and guiding principles for women offenders*. Washington, DC: U.S. Department of Justice, Office of Justice Programs, National Institute of Corrections.
7. Greenfeld, L. A., & Snell, T. L. (2000). *Women offenders*. Washington, DC: U.S. Department of Justice, Office of Justice Programs, Bureau of Justice Statistics.
8. Glaze, L. E., & Bonczar, T. P. (2008). *Probation and parole in the United States, 2007*. Washington, DC: U.S. Department of Justice, Office of Justice Programs, Bureau of Justice Statistics.
9. U.S. Department of Justice, Office of Justice Programs. (n.d.). *Almost nine out of every ten jail inmates were adult males*. Retrieved March 18, 2008, from http://www.ojp.usdoj.gov/bjs/glance/jailag.htm.
10. Elias, G. (2007). *Facility planning to meet the needs of female inmates*. Washington, DC: U.S. Department of Justice, Office of Justice Programs, National Institute of Corrections.
11. Snyder, H. N., & Sickmund, M. (2007). *Juvenile offenders and victims: 2006 national report*. Washington, DC: U.S. Department of Justice, Office of Justice Programs, Office of Juvenile Justice and Delinquency Prevention.

12. West, H. C., & Sabol, W. J. (2008). *Prisoners in 2007*. Washington, DC: U.S. Department of Justice, Office of Justice Programs, Bureau of Justice Statistics.

13. West & Sabol.

14. West & Sabol.

15. Streib, V. L. (2006). *Death penalty for female offenders, January 1, 1973 through June 30, 2006*. Retrieved October 17, 2008, from http://www.deathpenaltyinfo.org/FemDeathDec2007.pdf.

16. U.S. Department of Justice, Office of Justice Programs. (2007). *Capital punishment, 2006—Statistical tables*. Retrieved March 22, 2008, from http://www.ojp.usdoj.gov/bjs/pub/html/cp/2006/tables/cp06st12.htm.

17. Farr, K. A. (1997). Aggravating and differentiating factors in the cases of white and minority women on death row. *Crime & Delinquency, 43*, 260–278.

18. Zedner, p. 298.

19. de Beaumont, G., & de Tocqueville, A. (1833/1964). *On the penitentiary system in the United States and its application in France*. Carbondale, IL: Southern Illinois University Press.

20. Zedner.

21. Zedner.

22. Rafter, N. H. (1998). Prisons for women, 1790–1980. In T. J. Flanagan, J. W. Marquart, & K. G. Adams (Eds.), *Incarcerating criminals: Prisons and jails in social and organizational context* (pp. 30–45). New York: Oxford University Press.

23. David, C. P. (2007). At-risk girls and delinquency: Career pathways. *Crime & Delinquency, 53*, 408–435.

24. Bloom, B., Owen, B., Deschenes, E. P., & Rosenbaum, J. (2002). Improving juvenile justice for females: A statewide assessment in California. *Crime & Delinquency, 48*, 526–552.

25. Stephan, J. J. (2008). *Census of state and federal correctional facilities, 2005*. Washington, DC: U.S. Department of Justice, Office of Justice Programs, Bureau of Justice Statistics.

26. *Craig v. Boren*, 429 U.S. 190 (1976).

27. Cripe, C. A., & Pearlman, M. G. (2005). *Legal aspects of corrections management* (2nd ed.). Boston, MA: Jones and Bartlett.

28. Federal Bureau of Prisons. (n.d.). *Female offenders*. Retrieved March 21, 2008, from http://www.bop.gov/inmate_programs/female.jsp.

29. Alarid, L. F., Marquart, J. W., Burton, V. S., Cullen, F. T., & Cuvelier, S. J. (1996). Women's roles in serious offenses: A study of adult felons. *Justice Quarterly, 13*, 431–454, 435.

30. Harlow, C. W. (1999). *Prior abuse reported by inmates and probationers*. Washington, DC: U.S. Department of Justice, Office of Justice Programs, Bureau of Justice Statistics.

31. Belknap, J. (2007). *The invisible woman: Gender, crime, and justice* (3rd ed.). Belmont, CA: Thomson/Wadsworth.

32. Warren, M., & Rosenbaum, J. (1986). Criminal careers of female offenders. *Criminal Justice and Behavior, 13*, 393–418.

33. English.

34. DeLisi, M. (2002). Not just a boy's club: An empirical assessment of female career criminals. *Women & Criminal Justice, 13*, 27–45.

35. Cernkovich, S. A., Lanctot, N., & Giordano, P. C. (2008). Predicting adolescent and adult antisocial behavior among adjudicated delinquent females. *Crime & Delinquency, 54*, 3–33.

36. Odgers, C. L., Moffitt, T. E., Broadbent, J. M., Dickson, N., Hancox, R. J., Harrington, H., et al. (2008). Female and male antisocial trajectories: From childhood origins to adult outcomes. *Development and Psychopathology, 20,* 673–716.

37. Widom, C. S. (1989). The cycle of violence. *Science, 244,* 160–166.

38. Widom, C. S. (2000). Childhood victimization: Early adversity, later psychopathology. *National Institute of Justice Journal, 1,* 2–9.

39. Sullivan, C. J. (2006). Early adolescent delinquency: Assessing the role of childhood problems, family environment, and peer pressure. *Youth Violence and Juvenile Justice, 4,* 291–313.

40. Lanctot, N., Cernkovich, S. A., & Giordano, P. C. (2007). Delinquent behavior, official delinquency, and gender: Consequences for adulthood functioning and well-being. *Criminology, 45,* 131–158.

41. Giordano, P. C., Millhollin, T. J., Cernkovich, S. A., Pugh, M. D., & Rudolph, J. L. (1999). Delinquency, identity, and involvement in relationship violence. *Criminology, 37,* 17–40.

42. Holsinger, K., & Holsinger, A. M. (2005). Differential pathways to violence and self-injurious behaviors: African American and white girls in the juvenile justice system. *Journal of Research in Crime and Delinquency, 42,* 211–242.

43. Hubbard, D. J. (2006). Should we be targeting self-esteem in treatment for offenders: Do gender and race matter in whether self-esteem matters? *Journal of Offender Rehabilitation, 44,* 39–57.

44. Mullis, R., Cornille, T., Mullis, A., & Huber, J. (2004). Female juvenile offending: A review of characteristics and contexts. *Journal of Child and Family Studies, 13,* 205–218.

45. Gaardner, E., & Belknap, J. (2002). Tenuous borders: Girls transferred to adult court. *Criminology, 40,* 481–517.

46. Gaardner, E., & Belknap, J. (2004). Little women: Girls in adult prison. *Women & Criminal Justice, 15,* 51–80.

47. Wood, P. B., & Grasmick, H. G. (1999). Toward the development of punishment equivalencies: Male and female inmates rate the severity of alternative sanctions compared to prison. *Justice Quarterly, 16,* 19–50.

48. Olson, D. E., Lurigio, A. J., & Alberden, M. (2003). Men are from Mars, women are from Venus, but what role does gender play in probation recidivism? *Justice Research and Policy, 5,* 33–54.

49. Carmichael, S., Gover, A. R., Koons-Witt, B., & Inabnit, B. (2005). Successful completion of probation and parole among female offenders. *Women & Criminal Justice, 17,* 75–97.

50. Chan, M., Guydish, J., Prem, R., Jessup, M. A., Cervantes, A., & Bostrom, A. (2005). Evaluation of probation case management (PCM) for drug-involved women offenders. *Crime & Delinquency, 51,* 447–469.

51. Alarid, L. F., Burton, V. S., & Cullen, F. T. (2000). Gender and crime among felony offenders: Assessing the generality of social control and differential association theories. *Journal of Research in Crime and Delinquency, 37,* 171–199.

52. Spohn, C., & Holleran, D. (2002). The effect of imprisonment on recidivism rates of felony offenders: A focus on drug offenders. *Criminology, 40,* 329–358.

53. Norland, S., & Mann, P. J. (1984). Being troublesome: Women on probation. *Criminal Justice and Behavior, 11,* 17–28.

54. Seng, M., & Lurigio, A. J. (2005). Probation officers' views on supervising women probationers. *Women & Criminal Justice, 16,* 65–85.

55. Gaardner, E., Rodriguez, N., & Zatz, M. S. (2004). Criers, liars, and manipulators: Probation officers' views of girls. *Justice Quarterly, 21,* 547–578.

56. Greenfeld & Snell.

57. Jordan, B. K., Schlenger, W. E., Fairbank, J. A., & Caddell, J. M. (1996). Prevalence of psychiatric disorders among incarcerated women: II. Convicted felons entering prison. *Archives of General Psychiatry, 53,* 513–519.

58. Islam-Zwart, K. A., Vik, P. W., & Rawlins, K. S. (2007). Short-term psychological adjustment of female prison inmates on a minimum security unit. *Women's Health Issues, 17,* 237–243.

59. James, D. J., & Glaze, L. E. (2006). *Mental health problems of prison and jail inmates.* Washington, DC: U.S. Department of Justice, Office of Justice Programs, Bureau of Justice Statistics.

60. Cauffman, E., Lexcen, F., J., Goldweber, A., Shulman, E. P., & Grisso, T. (2007). Gender differences in mental health symptoms among delinquent and community youth. *Youth Violence and Juvenile Justice, 5,* 287–307.

61. Thompson, C., & Loper, A. B. (2005). Adjustment patterns in incarcerated women. *Criminal Justice and Behavior, 32,* 714–732.

62. Pogrebin, M. R., & Dodge, M. (2001). Women's accounts of their prison experience: A retrospective view of their subjective realties. *Journal of Criminal Justice, 29,* 531–541.

63. Casey-Acevedo, K., & Bakken, T. (2004). Women adjusting to prison: Disciplinary behavior and the characteristics of adjustment. *Journal of Health & Social Policy, 17,* 37–60.

64. Harer, M. D., & Langan, N. P. (2001). Gender differences in predictors of prison violence: Assessing the predictive validity of a risk classification system. *Crime & Delinquency, 47,* 513–536.

65. Wright, E. M., Salisbury, E. J., & Van Voorhis, P. (2007). Predicting the prison misconducts of women offenders: The importance of gender-responsive needs. *Journal of Contemporary Criminal Justice, 23,* 310–340.

66. Salisbury, E. J., Van Voorhis, P., & Spiropoulos, G. V. (2008). The predictive validity of a gender-responsive needs assessment: An exploratory study. *Crime & Delinquency,* in press.

67. Deschenes, E. P., Owen, B., & Crow, J. (2007). *Recidivism among female prisoners: Secondary analysis of the 1994 BJS recidivism data set.* Washington, DC: U.S. Department of Justice, Office of Justice Programs, National Institute of Justice.

68. Holtfreter, K. Reisig, M. D., & Morash, M. (2004). Poverty, state capital, and recidivism among women offenders. *Criminology & Public Policy, 3,* 185–208.

69. Jurik, N. C. (1983). The economics of female recidivism: A study of TARP women ex-offenders. *Criminology, 21,* 603–622.

70. Schram, P. J., Koons-Witt, B. A., Williams, F. P., & McShane, M. D. (2006). Supervision strategies and approaches for female parolees: Examining the link between unmet needs and parolee outcome. *Crime & Delinquency, 52,* 450–471.

71. Harm, N. J., & Phillips, S. D. (2001). You can't go home again: Women and criminal recidivism. *Journal of Offender Rehabilitation, 32,* 3–21.

72. Benda, B. B. (2005). Gender differences in life-course theory of recidivism: A survival analysis. *International Journal of Offender Therapy and Comparative Criminology, 49,* 325–342.

73. Richie, B. E. (2001). Challenges incarcerated women face as they return to their communities: Findings from life history interviews. *Crime & Delinquency, 47,* 368–389.

74. Reisig, M. D., Holtfreter, K., & Morash, M. (2002). Social capital among women offenders: Examining the distribution of social networks and resources. *Journal of Contemporary Criminal Justice, 18,* 167–187.

75. Reisig, M. D., Holtfreter, K., & Morash, M. (2006). Assessing recidivism risk across female pathways to crime. *Justice Quarterly, 23,* 384–405.

76. VanVoorhis & Presser.

77. Bloom, B., Owen, B., & Covington, S. (2005). *A summary of research, practice, and guiding principles for women offenders*. Washington, DC: U.S. Department of Justice, Office of Justice Programs, National Institute of Corrections.

78. McCampbell, S. W. (2006). *Gender-responsive strategies for women offenders: Jail applications*. Washington, DC: U.S. Department of Justice, Office of Justice Programs, National Institute of Corrections.

79. Federal Bureau of Prisons. (n.d.). *Female offenders*. Retrieved March 21, 2008, from http://www.bop.gov/inmate_programs/female.jsp.

80. Garrison, A. (2002). *Process evaluation assessing the gender appropriateness of the KEY/CREST programs*. Washington, DC: U.S. Department of Justice, Office of Justice Programs, National Institute of Justice.

81. Hall, E. A., Prendergast, M. L., Wellisch, J., Patten, M., & Cao, Y. (2004). Treating drug-abusing women prisoners: An outcomes evaluation of the Forever Free program. *Prison Journal, 84,* 81–105.

82. Dowden, C., & Andrews, D. A. (1999). What works for female offenders: A meta-analytic review. *Crime & Delinquency, 45,* 438–452.

CHAPTER

15

Capital Punishment and Civil Commitment

"Only a fraction of even the most vicious killers ever get executed. Neither deterrence nor justice can possibly be achieved in this way."[1, p. 103]

OBJECTIVES

- Explore capital punishment and its place in the correctional system.
- Examine the unique and turbulent history of capital punishment, including changes in its legal status.
- Understand the deterrent effects of capital punishment.
- Assess the retributive rationale for capital punishment.
- Understand the methods by which the death sentence is administered.
- Review the appeal process involved in death sentences.
- Evaluate the role of race in the administration of capital punishment.
- Learn about civil commitment as a new way to monitor sexually violent offenders.

CASE STUDY

From 1978 through 2008, 73 condemned offenders on California's death row have died. Forty offenders died of natural causes. Fourteen condemned offenders committed suicide. Two inmates died of drug overdoses. One inmate died of a heart attack after exposure to pepper spray. One inmate was murdered by other inmates while exercising. And one inmate was shot by guards while on the exercise yard. Thus, 59 death row inmates in California died from nonexecution deaths. By comparison, California has executed only 13 offenders since 1978 (another inmate with death sentences in California was executed in Missouri). As of 2008, there were 669 inmates on death row in California. On California's death row, nonexecution is nearly five times more common than execution as the manner of death.

1. Why are there so few executions in California?
2. What accounts for the length of time on death row?

"Death rows as currently constituted are draconian, deleterious, gratuitously wasteful of limited fiscal and staff resources, and serve no legitimate penological interest."[2, p. 29]

There is nothing like **capital punishment** or the use of death as a criminal punishment in the world of criminal justice. Statistically, an execution is a rare event. By December 1, just 36 condemned offenders were executed in the United States during 2008. In 2007, only 42 persons were executed. Moreover, there are 3,220 state and federal death row inmates.[7] Put another way, the death row population is over *600 times* smaller than the non-death row prisoner population. Many states that have the death penalty either do not use it or administer it with great infrequency.

Despite the rarity of a condemned offender actually being executed, the death penalty galvanizes the general public, policy makers, news commentators, and criminologists and is among the most politicized of talking points. Outgoing governors sometimes grant reprieves to death row inmates, or in the case of the former Governor Ryan of Illinois, **commute** the sentences of the entire condemned population to life imprisonment. The timing of these reprieves is crucial. The general public is overwhelmingly supportive of the death penalty, and politicians who appear weak on crime (evidenced by nonsupport of the death penalty) face risks at the polls. Indeed, the death penalty is the clearest symbol of a society's commitment to crime control and revulsion toward the worst criminals.

Capital punishment embodies important social, moral, and legal debates. Since condemned offenders wait for prolonged periods of time, some have speculated that death row syndrome is an unconstitutional form of psychological torture in which inmates never know when they will be actually put to death.[8] The status of the death penalty itself hinges on the social, moral, and legal debates that give it life. For instance, the Supreme Court held in ***Roper v. Simmons*** (2005) that the execution of persons who were under the age of 18 when they committed their capital crimes was unconstitutional.[9] Similarly, the United States is an exception among westernized nations in that it has retained the death penalty. Furthermore, several foreign nationals, most of whom are Mexican nationals, have been sentenced to death in the United States. Thus, the international debate whether the United States can lawfully execute a foreign national, particularly if that defendant's country of origin does not use the death penalty, remains unresolved.

In short, capital punishment represents the most extreme sanction in the correctional system. It is a punishment so severe that it does not purport to correct criminal behavior, but instead vanquish a society's most severe offenders. In life and death terms, capital punishment is the end of the criminal justice process. This chapter explores the death penalty, including the ways that it is administered, its legal history and current status, the backgrounds of persons sentenced to death, legal statutes, and arguments in favor and against its use. In addition, this chapter explores a relatively new phenomenon in the correctional system, civil commitment.

CORRECTIONS FOCUS

Killer Cop?

Kathleen Savio's body was exhumed in an attempt to determine if the cause of her death was something other than an accident. Kathleen Savio, the third wife of Police Sgt. Drew Peterson, died in 2004 under what some described as questionable circumstances. At the time, the case was brought before a coroner's jury to determine if criminal charges were warranted. Evidence indicating that the victim had been found face down in an empty bathtub, hair soaked in blood, was presented to the jury. It was also known that in 2002, Kathleen had obtained a protective order against Sgt. Peterson—evidence indicating the possibility that a physically abusive relationship also existed. However, the coroner's jury ruled the death accidental and no charges were filed.

Prosecutors are convinced that the elements of the crime are consistent with efforts to stage an accidental death and persuaded the court to grant an order to exhume Kathleen's body. Forensic evidence suggests that the injury to the back of Kathleen's head, a 1-inch gash, would not have caused her to lose consciousness and therefore, does not explain how she may have accidentally drowned in the bathtub. In February 2008, the Illinois State Attorney's Office determined that Savio's death was a homicide, and the case was reopened when Sgt. Peterson's fourth wife went missing; she was last seen October 28, 2007. According to Sgt. Peterson, his wife left him for another man.

Source: Associated Press. (2007). *Body of police officer's third ex-wife exhumed: Investigation under way into disappearance of Chicago cop's fourth wife.* Retrieved November 13, 2007, from http://www.msnbc.msn.com/id/21769873; Cable News Network. (2008). Death of former cop's third wife ruled a homicide. Retrieved October 20, 2008, from http://edition.cnn.com/2008/CRIME/02/21/missing.wife/?iref=mpstoryview.

"If we execute murderers and there is in fact no deterrent effect, we have killed a bunch of murderers. If we fail to execute murderers, and doing so would in fact have deterred other murders, we have allowed the killing of a bunch of innocent victims. I would much rather risk the former. This, to me, is not a tough call."[3]

The case of convicted juvenile murderer Christopher Simmons ultimately led to the Supreme Court ruling that the application of capital punishment to juveniles is unconstitutional.

"The respect for the law is the obverse side of our hatred for the criminal transgressor."[4, pp. 585–586]

Capital Punishment

The 3,220 prisoners under sentences of death are held on death rows in 39 jurisdictions, which include 37 states, the federal criminal justice system, and the United States military. Thirteen states (Alaska, Hawaii, Iowa, Maine, Massachusetts, Michigan, Minnesota, New Jersey, North Dakota, Rhode Island, Vermont, West Virginia, and Wisconsin) and the District of Columbia do not have the death penalty. About half of the death row population is comprised of inmates from California, Texas, Florida, and Pennsylvania.

The preponderance of death penalty activity occurs at the state level. For instance, as of 2008, only 50 persons resided on federal death row, and the United States government has executed 3 persons since 1976. In 2008, 109 inmates received death sentences, and 36 persons were executed. Of those under the sentence of death in 2008, 56 percent were White, 42 percent were African American, 12 percent were Hispanic, and 2 percent were of other races. Less than 2 percent of the death row population is constituted by females, thus males comprised over 98 percent of condemned offenders.[10]

Death Penalty Statutes and Legal Processes

Only the most serious forms of criminal conduct can potentially qualify for a death sentence. Essentially, the criterion is to be convicted of a **felony murder** defined as the commission of a homicide in conjunction with some other serious felony offense, such as kidnapping, rape, armed robbery, child sexual assault, or additional homicides. Rape was excluded as a capital crime in the landmark case *Coker v. Georgia* (1977).[11] Erlich Coker was serving a lengthy prison term upon convictions for murder, rape, kidnapping, and assault when he escaped from prison in 1974 and subsequently committed burglary, rape, and auto theft. For these crimes (rape was the most serious charged), Coker was sentenced to death—a sentence that was held as grossly disproportionate for rape and thus unconstitutional. Capital offenses for the states and federal government appear in TABLE 15–1 and TABLE 15–2.

Death penalty statutes essentially describe the conditions under which a homicide is escalated into a capital crime. Two types of circumstances are considered. **Aggravating circumstances**, such as serial murder or hate/bias-motivated murder, are characteristics that make the crime seem worse in totality and thus deserving of death as the only appropriate punishment. **Mitigating circumstances**, such as youth, mental retardation, or victimization, render a crime less serious or add context that seems to reduce the overall viciousness of the behavior.

Aggravating and mitigating circumstances resuscitated the death penalty after its ban between 1972 and 1976 because they allowed states to limit discretion by providing sentencing guidelines for the judge and jury when deciding whether to impose death. These guided discretion statutes were approved by the Supreme Court in five cases (*Gregg v. Georgia*, *Jurek v. Texas*, *Roberts v. Louisiana*, *Woodson v. North Carolina*, and *Proffitt v. Florida*) collectively referred to as the *Gregg* decision. This landmark decision held that the new death penalty statutes in Florida, Georgia, and Texas were constitutional, and that the death penalty itself was constitutional under the Eighth Amendment.

The *Gregg* decision resulted in three other procedural reforms:

1. **Bifurcated trials**, in which there are separate deliberations for the guilt and penalty phases of the trial. Only after the jury has determined that the defendant is guilty of capital murder does it decide in a second trial whether the defendant should be sentenced to death or given a lesser sentence of prison time.
2. Automatic appellate review of convictions and sentence.
3. **Proportionality review**, which helps the state to identify and eliminate sentencing disparities by comparing the sentence in the case with other cases within the state.[12–16]

TABLE 15-1 **Capital Statutes by State**

Alabama. Intentional murder with 18 aggravating factors (Ala. Stat. Ann. 13A-5-40(a)(1)-(18)).
Arizona. First-degree murder accompanied by at least 1 of 14 aggravating factors (A.R.S. § 13-703(F)).
Arkansas. Capital murder (Ark. Code Ann. 5-10-101) with a finding of at least 1 of 10 aggravating circumstances; treason.
California. First-degree murder with special circumstances; train wrecking; treason; perjury causing execution.
Colorado. First-degree murder with at least 1 of 17 aggravating factors; treason.
Connecticut. Capital felony with eight forms of aggravated homicide (C.G.S. 53a-54b).
Delaware. First-degree murder with aggravating circumstance.
Florida. First-degree murder; felony murder; capital drug trafficking; capital sexual battery.
Georgia. Murder; kidnapping with bodily injury or ransom when the victim dies; aircraft hijacking; treason.
Idaho. First-degree murder with aggravating factor; aggravated kidnapping; perjury resulting in death.
Illinois. First-degree murder with 1 of 21 aggravating circumstances.
Indiana. Murder with 16 aggravating circumstances (IC 35-50-2-9).
Kansas. Capital murder with eight aggravating circumstances (KSA 21-3439).
Kentucky. Murder with aggravating factors; kidnapping with aggravating factors (KRS 32.025).
Louisiana. First-degree murder; aggravated rape of victim under age 12; treason (La. R.S. 14:30, 14:42, and 14:113).
Maryland. First-degree murder, either premeditated or during the commission of a felony, provided that certain death eligibility requirements are satisfied.
Mississippi. Capital murder (97-3-19(2) MCA); aircraft piracy (97-25-55(1)MCA).
Missouri. First-degree murder (565.020 RSMO 2000).
Montana. Capital murder with 1 of 9 aggravating circumstances (46-18-303 MCA); capital sexual assault (45-5-503 MCA).
Nebraska. First-degree murder with a finding of at least 1 statutorily defined aggravating circumstance.
Nevada. First-degree murder with at least 1 of 15 aggravating circumstances (NRS 200.030, 200.033, 200.035).
New Hampshire. Six categories of capital murder (RSA 630:1, RSA 630:5).
New Jersey. Murder by one's own conduct, by solicitation, committed in furtherance of a narcotics conspiracy, or during commission of a crime of terrorism (NJSA 2C:11-3C).
New Mexico. First-degree murder with at least one of seven statutorily defined aggravating circumstances (Section 30-2-1 A, NMSA).
New York. First-degree murder with 1 of 13 aggravating factors (NY Penal Law § 125.27).
North Carolina. First-degree murder (NCGS §14-17).
Ohio. Aggravated murder with at least 1 of 10 aggravating circumstances (O.R.C. secs. 2903.01, 2929.02, and 2929.04).
Oklahoma. First-degree murder in conjunction with a finding of at least one of eight statutorily defined aggravating circumstances.
Oregon. Aggravated murder (ORS 163.095).
Pennsylvania. First-degree murder with 18 aggravating circumstances.
South Carolina. Murder with 1 of 11 aggravating circumstances (§ 16-3-20(C)(a)).
South Dakota. First-degree murder with 1 of 10 aggravating circumstances; aggravated kidnapping.
Tennessee. First-degree murder with 1 of 15 aggravating circumstances (Tenn. Code Ann. § 39-13-204).
Texas. Criminal homicide with 1 of 9 aggravating circumstances (TX Penal Code 19.03).
Utah. Aggravated murder (76-5-202, Utah Code Annotated).
Virginia. First-degree murder with 1 of 13 aggravating circumstances (VA Code § 18.2-31).
Washington. Aggravated first-degree murder.
Wyoming. First-degree murder.

Source: Bureau of Justice Statistics: (2008). *Capital punishment, 2007—statistical tables.* Retrieved December 26, 2008, from http://www.ojp.usdoj.gov/bjs/pub/html/cp/2007/tables/cp07st01.htm.

"In executing murderers, we declare that deliberate murder is absolutely evil and absolutely intolerable. This is a painfully difficult proclamation for a self-doubting community to make. But we dare not stop trying. Communities may exist in which capital punishment is no longer the necessary response to deliberate murder. America today is not one of them."[5, p. 17]

"The righteousness of capital punishment does not depend on whatever evidence is marshaled about the future dangerousness of capital offenders."[6, p. 38]

TABLE 15-2 Federal Death Penalty Statutes

8 U.S.C. 1342—Murder related to the smuggling of aliens.
18 U.S.C. 32-34—Destruction of aircraft, motor vehicles, or related facilities resulting in death.
18 U.S.C. 36—Murder committed during a drug-related drive-by shooting.
18 U.S.C. 37—Murder committed at an airport serving international civil aviation.
18 U.S.C. 115(b)(3) [by cross-reference to 18 U.S.C. 1111]—Retaliatory murder of a member of the immediate family of law enforcement officials.
18 U.S.C. 241, 242, 245, 247—Civil rights offenses resulting in death.
18 U.S.C. 351 [by cross-reference to 18 U.S.C. 1111]—Murder of a member of Congress, an important executive official, or a Supreme Court justice.
18 U.S.C. 794—Espionage.
18 U.S.C. 844(d), (f), (i)—Death resulting from offenses involving transportation of explosives, destruction of government property, or destruction of property related to foreign or interstate commerce.
18 U.S.C. 924(i)—Murder committed by the use of a firearm during a crime of violence or a drug-trafficking crime.
18 U.S.C. 930—Murder committed in a federal government facility.
18 U.S.C. 1091—Genocide.
18 U.S.C.1111—First-degree murder.
18 U.S.C. 1114—Murder of a federal judge or law enforcement official.
18 U.S.C. 1116—Murder of a foreign official.
18 U.S.C. 1118—Murder by a federal prisoner.
18 U.S.C. 1119—Murder of a U.S. national in a foreign country.
18 U.S.C. 1120—Murder by an escaped federal prisoner already sentenced to life imprisonment.
18 U.S.C. 1121—Murder of a state or local law enforcement official or other person aiding in a federal investigation; murder of a state correctional officer.
18 U.S.C. 1201—Murder during a kidnapping.
18 U.S.C. 1203—Murder during a hostage taking.
18 U.S.C. 1503—Murder of a court officer or juror.
18 U.S.C. 1512—Murder with the intent of preventing testimony by a witness, victim, or informant.
18 U.S.C. 1513—Retaliatory murder of a witness, victim, or informant.
18 U.S.C. 1716—Mailing of injurious articles with intent to kill or resulting in death.
18 U.S.C. 1751 [by cross-reference to 18 U.S.C. 1111]—Assassination or kidnapping resulting in the death of the president or vice president.
18 U.S.C. 1958—Murder for hire.
18 U.S.C. 1959—Murder involved in a racketeering offense.
18 U.S.C. 1992—Willful wrecking of a train resulting in death.
18 U.S.C. 2113—Bank-robbery–related murder or kidnapping.
18 U.S.C. 2119—Murder related to a carjacking.
18 U.S.C. 2245—Murder related to rape or child molestation.
18 U.S.C. 2251—Murder related to sexual exploitation of children.
18 U.S.C. 2280—Murder committed during an offense against maritime navigation.
18 U.S.C. 2281—Murder committed during an offense against a maritime fixed platform.
18 U.S.C. 2332—Terrorist murder of a U.S. national in another country.
18 U.S.C. 2332a—Murder by the use of a weapon of mass destruction.
18 U.S.C. 2340—Murder involving torture.
18 U.S.C. 2381—Treason.
21 U.S.C. 848(e)—Murder related to a continuing criminal enterprise or related murder of a federal, state, or local law enforcement officer.
49 U.S.C. 1472-1473—Death resulting from aircraft hijacking.

Source: Bureau of Justice Statistics (n.d.). Retrieved December 26, 2008, from http://www.ojp.usdoj.gov/bjs/pub/html/cp/2007/tablescp07st01.htm.

CORRECTIONS BRIEF

Any Last Words?

Prisoner: Ronald Clark O'Bryan, No. 529
Date of execution: March 30, 1984
Last statement:

> What is about to transpire in a few moments is wrong! However, we as human beings do make mistakes and errors. This execution is one of those wrongs yet doesn't mean our whole system of justice is wrong. Therefore, I would forgive all who have taken part in any way in my death. Also, to anyone I have offended in any way during my 39 years, I pray and ask your forgiveness, just as I forgive anyone who offended me in any way. And I pray and ask God's forgiveness for all of us respectively as human beings. To my loved ones, I extend my undying love. To those close to me, know in your hearts I love you one and all. God bless you all and may God's best blessings be always yours.

Prisoner: Thomas Barefoot, No. 621
Date of execution: October 30, 1984
Last statement:

> I hope that one day we can look back on the evil that we're doing right now like the witches we burned at the stake. I want everybody to know that I hold nothing against them. I forgive them all. I hope everybody I've done anything to will forgive me. I've been praying all day for Carl Levin's wife to drive the bitterness from her heart because that bitterness that's in her heart will send her to Hell just as surely as any other sin. I'm sorry for everything I've ever done to anybody. I hope they'll forgive me. Sharon, tell all my friends good-bye. You know who they are: Charles Bass, David Powell . . .

Then he coughed and nothing else was said.

Prisoner: Jerome Butler, No. 852
Date of execution: April 21, 1990
Last statement:

> I wish everybody a good life. Everything is O.K.

Prisoner: Kenneth Ransom, No. 772
Date of execution: October 28, 1997
Last statement:

> First and foremost I would like to tell the victims' families that I am sorry because I don't feel like I am guilty. I am sorry for the pain all of them have gone through during holidays and birthdays. They are without their loved ones. I have said from the beginning and I will say it again that I am innocent. I did not kill no one. I feel like this is the Lord's will that will be done. I love you all. You know it. Don't cry. Tell my brothers I love them. You all be strong.

Prisoner: Spencer Goodman, No. 999031
Date of execution: January 18, 2000
Last statement:

> To my family, I love them. To Kami, I love you and will always be with you. That's it Warden.

Prisoner: Jackie Wilson
Date of execution: May 4, 2006
Last statement:

> May I speak to my family? Honey, I love you. Be strong and take care of yourselves. Thanks for being there. Take care of yourself. Ms. Irene, thank you for everything you have done. Chaplain Hart, thank you for helping me. Gary, thank you. Maria, Maria, I love you baby. Thank you for being there for me and all these people here will find the one who did this damn crime. I am going home to be with God. Thank you. Thank you, Warden.

Prisoner: Michael Richard
Date of execution: September 25, 2007
Last statement:

> Yes, I would like for my family to take care of each other. I love you Angel. Let's ride. I guess this is it.

Source: Texas Department of Criminal Justice. Retrieved January 6, 2008, from http://www.tdcj.state.tx.us/stat/executedoffenders.htm.

The legal road that a capital case follows is extremely convoluted. The American Bar Association highlighted the many steps that occur from the homicide event to execution. After the homicide, the police conduct an investigation and make an arrest. Then, the courts seek an indictment through the grand jury or the prosecutor directly files the case depending on the jurisdiction. The courts must determine the defendant's competency, hold a trial with separate guilt and penalty phases, and ultimately impose a death sentence. After conviction, the general scenario is as follows:

- Motion for new trial
- Motion denied
- Appeal to state supreme court
- Conviction and sentence upheld
- Motion for rehearing filed
- Motion denied
- Decision affirmed
- Petition United States Supreme Court
- Petition denied
- State postconviction petition filed
- Petition denied
- Appeal to state court of appeals
- Decision affirmed
- Appeal to state supreme court
- Decision affirmed
- Petition Supreme Court for review known as **writ of certiorari**
- Petition granted
- Decision reaffirmed
- Federal postconviction petition filed
- Petition denied in federal district court
- Appeal to United States court of appeals
- Decision affirmed
- Petition Supreme Court for another review
- Petition granted
- Decision affirmed
- Request postconviction loop
- Petition for clemency filed
- Petition denied
- Execution[17]

The bulk of the delay in the administration of capital punishment centers on direct appeals where the condemned offender challenges the decision of the court. Barry Latzer and James Cauthen studied the direct appeals process in 14 states and found the median time from date of death sentence to complete direct appeal was 966 days. Petitioning the United States Supreme Court added 188 days when certiorari was denied and 250 days when it was granted. Virginia and Georgia have the fastest courts of last resort at 295 days

CORRECTIONS HISTORY

Death by Execution: What Went Wrong?

How many attempts at executing a prisoner in this country could be classified as having been botched? Botched means the condemned prisoner experienced prolonged suffering for 20 minutes or more. Records indicate that at least 36 executions have been botched. This number is based on information compiled through news sources, since states do not make this information public according to Michael Radelet, a leading death penalty researcher.

Frank J. Coppola was executed by electrocution in 1982. His death did not come easily. Two jolts of electricity were sent through his body, each lasting approximately 55 seconds. By the end of the second jolt, Frank's head and leg had caught on fire and the chamber smelled liked cooked meat. It took 14 minutes and three separate attempts to electrocute John Evans in 1983. Portions of Evans's torso caught on fire, but his heart kept beating until the final jolt. Officials ushered spectators from the room when Jimmy Lee Gray struggled to survive his execution. Eight minutes after the lethal gas was released, Jimmy was still gasping for air. The executioner was reportedly intoxicated.

It took two jolts to end the life of Alpha Otis Stephens. After the first 2-minute surge of electricity, Stephens was still struggling to breathe. Doctors had to wait 6 minutes for the body to cool before they could examine him and determine that he was still alive. During this interval, Stephens reportedly took 23 breaths. Stephens was considered by one state corrections official as a poor conductor of electricity.

William E. Vandiver took five jolts, and his execution lasted 17 minutes. Randy Woolls and Ricky Ray Rector, both experienced substance users, assisted state officials in locating a usable vein for the intravenous lines that would end their lives. Even with Rector's help, it took five medical personnel working on both sides of his body to establish the intravenous line. Raymond Landry experienced a blowout, according to state officials. The syringe popped out of the vein, spraying the room with the drugs meant for Landry. It took approximately 14 minutes to reestablish the connection. The death of John Wayne Gacy was delayed because the lines feeding the drugs became clogged, stopping the chemicals from entering his body.

Sources: Human Rights Watch. (2006). *So long as they die: Lethal injections in the United States.* Retrieved May 24, 2007, from http://hrw.org/reports/2006/us0406/; Radelet, M. L. (2006). *Some examples of post-Furman botched executions.* Retrieved May 24, 2007, from http://www.deathpenaltyinfo.org/article.php?scid=8&did=478.

and 297 days, respectively. Ohio, Tennessee, and Kentucky are the least efficient courts of last resort with 1,309 to 1,388 days.[18]

A little known fact is that the criminal justice systems automatically appeal their own convictions once an offender is sentenced to death. Of the 37 states with capital statutes, 36 had automatic appeal procedures regardless of the wishes or interests of the defendant. In each jurisdiction, the state's highest appellate court usually conducted the review. If either the conviction or sentence is vacated, the case could be remanded to the trial court for additional proceedings or retrial. As a result of retrial or resentencing, a death sentence could be reimposed. The only exception is South Carolina, where defendants have the right to waive sentence review if they are deemed competent by the courts. The federal system does not have an automatic appeal.[19]

CORRECTIONS IN THE NEWS

DNA Links East End Killer to Four Murders

Credit goes to the Bridgeport Police Department cold case unit. The cold case unit began its review of 15 unsolved murders in 2000. These crimes had occurred in the 1980s and early 1990s. In 2003, two detectives, Heitor Teixeira and Robert Sherback, found crime scene behavior similarities in 10 of the murders. The evidence gathered at the crime scenes and sent to the FBI lab included traces of sperm, a cigarette butt, and skin tissue found under the fingernails of one of the victims. With help from the FBI and information contained in its combined DNA identification system, Emanuel Lovell Webb, age 40, was linked to four of the murders—three of which involved mutilation. The DNA database was not in operation during the time of the killings.

Officers located Webb at the D. Ray James Correctional Facility in Folkston, Ga. At the time, he was being held on a parole violation. In 1994, Webb was charged with the sexual assault and the strangulation murder of Evelyn Charity. In a plea bargain, Webb pleaded guilty to involuntary manslaughter, robbery, and the theft of a motor vehicle and was sentenced to 20 years in prison. He was released on parole in 2001.

Source: Associated Press. (2007). *DNA links Georgia man to Connecticut serial killings*. Retrieved December 28, 2007, from http://www.foxnews.com/story/0,2933,198559,00.html?sPage=fnc.national/crime.

Methods of Execution

The predominant method of execution is lethal injection, which is used in 37 states and the federal system. Nine states use electrocution, four states use lethal gas, three states use hanging, and three states use firing squads. Seventeen states have authorized more than one method; lethal injection is the default and the condemned offender can elect the other method. Several states offer alternative methods of execution in the event that lethal injection is ruled unconstitutional.

Lethal injection involves the intravenous administering of three drugs. First, an anesthetic called sodium thiopental (the trademark name is Sodium Pentothal) puts the condemned offender into a deep sleep within 30 seconds. The anesthetic is about *50 times greater* than that given in normal surgical operations and is itself a lethal dose. Second, a lethal dose of a paralyzing agent called pancuronium bromide (Pavulon) is given, which stops the inmate's breathing by paralyzing the diaphragm and lungs. Third, a toxic agent such as potassium chloride is given at a lethal dose to interrupt the electrical signaling essential to heart functioning and induce cardiac arrest.

Although each of the three drugs used in lethal injection is itself a fatal dose, the method has come under tremendous criticism beginning in 2007. On September 25, 2007, the U.S. Supreme Court agreed to hear a case challenging the use of lethal injection. On April 16, 2008, in *Baze v. Rees*, the Supreme Court held that lethal injection does not constitute cruel and unusual punishment and is therefore constitutional. Shortly after the ruling, on May 6, 2008, Georgia conducted the first execution in the post-*Baze* era and executions have been carried out thereafter in 2008. A listing of executions by state and by method of execution from 1977 to 2005 appears in TABLE 15–3.

Historical Development

As explored in Chapter 2, capital punishment was widespread in colonial America. Death was a routine punishment for upwards of 200 criminal offenses, nearly all of which today would not be considered serious enough to warrant prison, let alone death. The birth of the penitentiary reflected a more tempered American criminal justice system as confinement replaced corporal and capital punishment. The last century of death penalty activity has similarly been marked by wildly contrasting trends.

TABLE 15-3 Executions by State and Method, 1977–2006

State	Number Executed	Lethal Injection	Electrocution	Lethal Gas	Hanging	Firing Squad
U.S. total	1,004	836	152	11	3	2
Federal	3	3	0	0	0	0
Alabama	34	10	24	0	0	0
Arizona	22	20	0	2	0	0
Arkansas	27	26	1	0	0	0
California	12	10	0	2	0	0
Colorado	1	1	0	0	0	0
Connecticut	1	1	0	0	0	0
Delaware	14	13	0	0	1	0
Florida	60	16	44	0	0	0
Georgia	39	16	23	0	0	0
Idaho	1	1	0	0	0	0
Illinois	12	12	0	0	0	0
Indiana	16	13	3	0	0	0
Kentucky	2	1	1	0	0	0
Louisiana	27	7	20	0	0	0
Maryland	5	5	0	0	0	0
Mississippi	7	3	0	4	0	0
Missouri	66	66	0	0	0	0
Montana	2	2	0	0	0	0
Nebraska	3	0	3	0	0	0
Nevada	11	10	0	1	0	0
New Mexico	1	1	0	0	0	0
North Carolina	39	37	0	2	0	0
Ohio	19	19	0	0	0	0
Oklahoma	79	79	0	0	0	0
Oregon	2	2	0	0	0	0
Pennsylvania	3	3	0	0	0	0
South Carolina	35	29	6	0	0	0
Tennessee	1	1	0	0	0	0
Texas	355	355	0	0	0	0
Utah	6	4	0	0	0	2
Virginia	94	67	27	0	0	0
Washington	4	2	0	0	2	0
Wyoming	1	1	0	0	0	0

Source: Snell, T. L. (2007). *Capital punishment, 2006.* Washington, DC: U.S. Department of Justice, Office of Justice Programs, Bureau of Justice Statistics.

As shown in FIGURE 15-1, executions were once a frequent occurrence. During the 1930s, nearly 170 prisoners were executed annually. Approximately 130 executions were performed annually during the 1940s, and around 80 were performed per year during the 1950s. The rapid pace of executions prevented the death row population from becoming too large.

The broad due process reforms of the 1960s forever changed the course of American capital punishment as the general public, for the first time, began to express dissatisfaction with capital punishment. Moreover, the criminal justice system was growing increasingly unnerved by the wide variability in which juries opted for capital punishment and in which executions were conducted (TABLE 15-4).

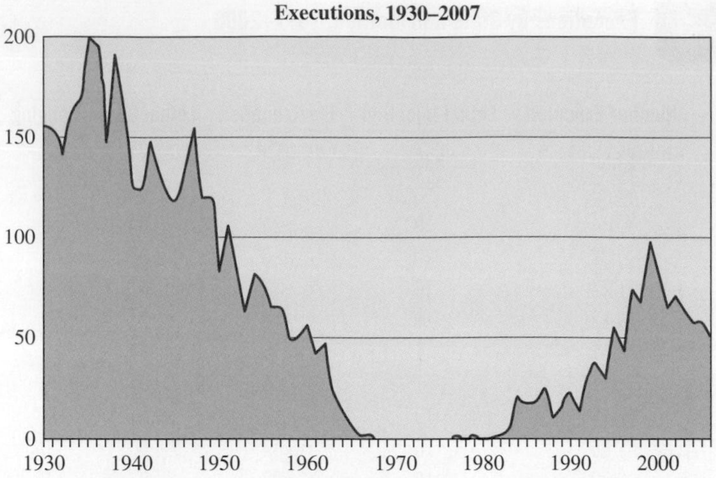

FIGURE 15–1 Executions in the United States. *Source*: Snell, T. L. (2007). *Capital punishment, 2006.* Washington, DC: U.S. Department of Justice, Office of Justice Programs, Bureau of Justice Statistics.

As such, the execution rate plummeted. Only three persons were executed in 1966 and 1967, and from 1968 to 1976 there was a de facto moratorium on the death penalty. From 1972 to 1976, the death penalty was officially held to be unconstitutional. In three cases (***Furman v. Georgia***, *Jackson v. Georgia*, and *Branch v. Texas*) collectively known as the *Furman* decision, the Supreme Court, in a 5–4 decision, held that the manner in which the death penalty was imposed and carried out under the laws of Georgia and Texas was cruel and unusual and overall in violation of the Eighth and Fourteenth Amendments.[20–22] The ruling voided death penalty statutes nationwide and commuted the sentences of more than 600 death row inmates.

The new death statutes with aggravating and mitigating factors to guide sentencing reinstituted the death penalty, but only 11 people were executed between 1977 and 1983. Over the past 20 years, approximately 40 executions have been conducted annually. Consequently, the death row population increased nearly sevenfold between 1980 and 2006 (**FIGURE 15–2**). Since 1977, when Gary Gilmore volunteered to be executed by firing

CORRECTIONS BRIEF

Castrated to Avoid Life in Prison

Bobby James Allen requested and voluntarily agreed to undergo surgical castration in exchange for a shorter sentence. The judge presiding over the case, Judge Michael Overstreet, warned Allen of the physiological consequences of the procedure, but Allen opted for the deal anyway. In return, the judge sentenced Allen to 25 years in prison and 10 years probation. He had been facing life in prison after being convicted on three counts of armed sexual assault for crimes he committed in 1998 and 1999. Florida taxpayers paid for the surgery.

Source: Associated Press. (2007). *Confessed rapist castrated to avoid life sentence.* Retrieved December 31, 2007, from http://www.foxnews.com/story/0,2933,297535,00.html?sPage=fnc.national/crime.

TABLE 15-4 **Executions by Jurisdiction Since 1930**

	Number Executed	
State/Jurisdiction	**Since 1930**	**Since 1977**
U.S. total	4,958	1,099
Texas	702	405
Georgia	406	40
New York	329	0
North Carolina	306	43
California	305	13
Florida	234	64
South Carolina	199	37
Ohio	198	26
Virginia	190	98
Alabama	173	38
Mississippi	162	8
Louisiana	160	27
Pennsylvania	155	3
Oklahoma	146	86
Arkansas	145	27
Missouri	128	66
Kentucky	105	2
Illinois	102	12
Tennessee	97	4
New Jersey	74	0
Maryland	73	5
Arizona	61	23
Indiana	60	19
Washington	51	4
Colorado	48	1
Nevada	41	12
District of Columbia	40	0
West Virginia	40	0
Federal system	36	3
Massachusetts	27	0
Delaware	26	14
Connecticut	22	1
Oregon	21	2
Utah	19	6
Iowa	18	0
Kansas	15	0
Montana	9	3
New Mexico	9	1
Wyoming	8	1
Nebraska	7	3
Vermont	4	0
Idaho	4	1
South Dakota	2	1
New Hampshire	1	0

Note: Military authorities carried out an additional 160 executions between 1930 and 1961.

Source: Snell, T. L. (2008). *Capital punishment, 2007*. Washington, DC: U.S. Department of Justice, Office of Justice Programs, Bureau of Justice Statistics.

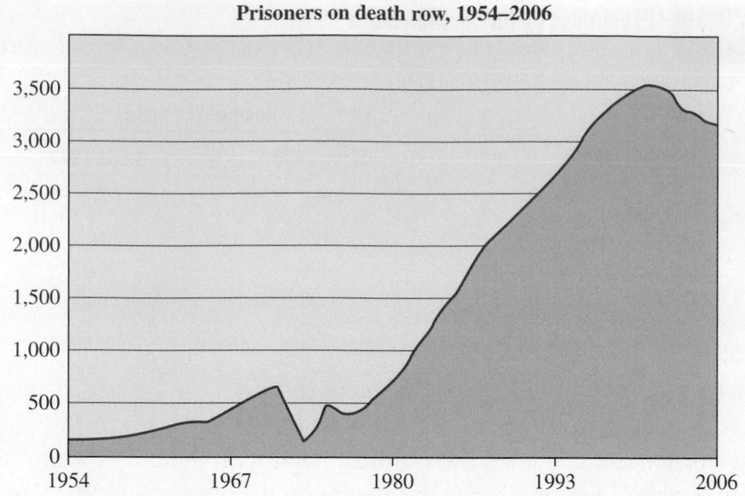

FIGURE 15–2 Death Row Population. *Source*: Snell, T. L. (2007). *Capital punishment, 2006.* Washington, DC: U.S. Department of Justice, Office of Justice Programs, Bureau of Justice Statistics.

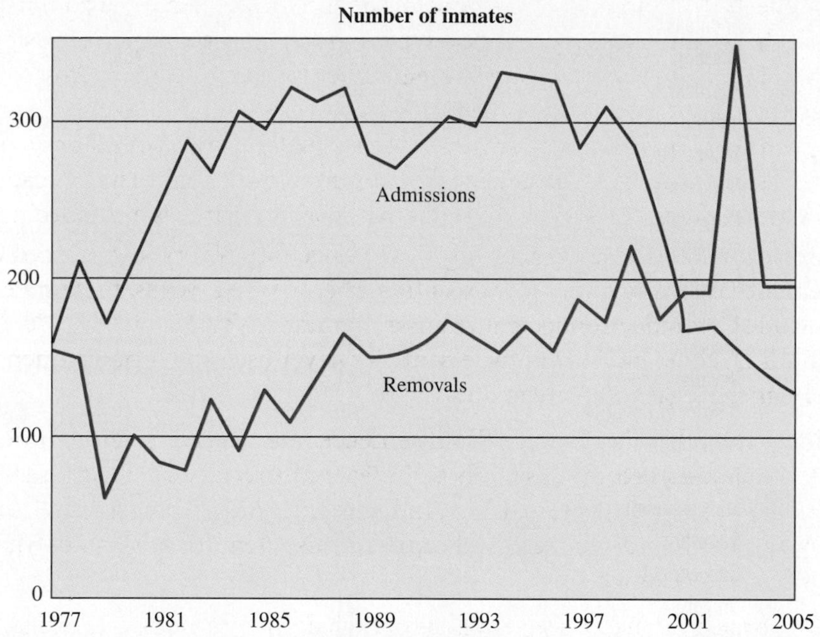

FIGURE 15–3 Removals and Admissions to Death Row. *Source*: Snell, T. L. (2007). *Capital punishment, 2006.* Washington, DC: U.S. Department of Justice, Office of Justice Programs, Bureau of Justice Statistics.

squad in Utah, 1,099 persons have been executed in the United States. In addition, in recent years it is more common for condemned offenders to be removed from rather than admitted to death row (FIGURE 15–3).

Not all persons are eligible for certain criminal punishments because of the mitigating characteristics of specific groups. As described earlier, in 2005, the Supreme Court voided death as a possible punishment for anyone who committed capital crimes under the age of 18. Another group that is *categorically exempt* from capital punishment is criminals who are mentally retarded, defined as those criminals who have an IQ below 70. The major substantive concerns center on whether mentally retarded defendants can appreciate the wrongfulness of their acts, understand the how and why of the death penalty, and can assist in their own defense by competently pursuing appeals. Interestingly, the Supreme Court did an about face on this issue over a 13-year period. In 1989, in a narrow, 5–4 ruling (***Penry v. Lynaugh***), the Court held that executing the mentally regarded was not a violation of the Eighth Amendment.[23] In 2002, in a 6–3 ruling (***Atkins v. Virginia***), the Court held that executing mentally retarded persons *did* constitute cruel and unusual punishment and was a violation of the Eighth Amendment.[24] Although about 3 percent of the general population is mentally retarded, between 12 and 20 percent of death row inmates have historically met the criterion.[25–26]

The overwhelming majority of Americans support capital punishment, and it is one of the few political issues on which Democrats and Republicans agree. Indeed, politicians who steadfastly maintain an anti-death penalty stance risk appearing soft on crime or unable to meet the crime control wishes of the public.[27] James Galliher and John Galliher conducted a study that illustrated the political capital and public opinion of the death penalty. They analyzed the death penalty debate that occurred in New York state from 1977, the time of the first execution after the reaffirmation of the constitutionality of the death penalty, and 1995, which fell during an era when the penalty was reintroduced in New York. They found that the enormous public support for the sanction and faith in its deterrent value was greater than the criminological findings about the death penalty's deterrent effects.[28] In other words, politicians often want to please the public by giving them what they want, and the death penalty is a preferred piece of public policy.

In the 21st century, capital punishment appears at an uncertain crossroads. The federal government and almost 80 percent of the states continue to execute the worst types of criminals. There remains great variation in the speed and efficiency with which correctional systems apply the death penalty. Among jurisdictions that have capital punishment statutes, five general types of states exist in this regard, as explained next.[29]

1. *Inactive states* have a very low death sentence rate, a very low reversal of death sentence rate, and a very low execution rate. In other words, these states, which include Colorado, Connecticut, Kansas, Montana, New Hampshire, New Mexico, South Dakota, and Wyoming, essentially never use capital punishment despite having the legal authority to do so.

2. *Active states* have an average death sentence rate, average reversal of death sentence rate, and average of slightly below average execution rate. States that fit this category include Delaware, Idaho, Indiana, Kentucky, Maryland, Nebraska, New Jersey (which has since removed capital punishment from its statutes), Oregon, Utah, and Washington.

3. *Symbolic states* have an about average or high death sentence rate, average or below average reversal of death sentence rate, and very low execution rate. These states target symbolically reprehensible offenders for execution and include California, Illinois, Nevada, New York, Ohio, Pennsylvania, and Tennessee.

4. *Inefficient states* have a high or very high death sentence rate, high reversal of death sentence rate, and moderate or low execution rate. States that fit this category include Alabama, Arizona, Arkansas, Florida, Georgia, Mississippi, North Carolina, and Oklahoma.

5. *Aggressive states* have a high or very high death sentence rate, limited reversal of death sentence rate, and a high execution rate. These are the states that conduct the majority of executions and include Louisiana, Missouri, South Carolina, Texas, and Virginia.

Among persons sentenced to death, the probability of execution is significantly increasing and the time until execution is declining. Virginia, one of the most active

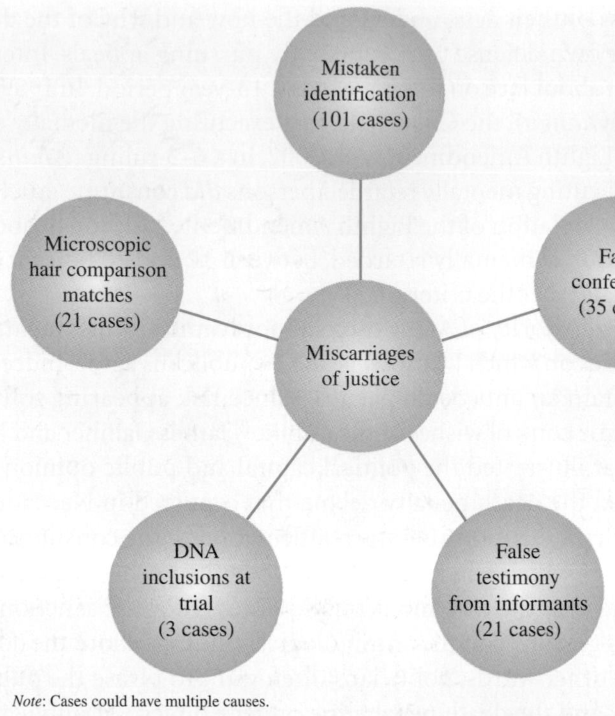

FIGURE 15-4 Causes of Miscarriages of Justice for First 130 Exonerations. *Source*: The Innocence Project. (n.d.). *The causes of wrongful conviction*. Retrieved March 28, 2008, modified from http://www.innocenceproject.org/understand/.

INNOCENCE PROJECT

The Innocence Project works to overturn wrongful convictions through DNA testing and reform of the criminal justice system in the United States. To date, more than 226 people have been exonerated by DNA testing in the United States.

death penalty states, is unquestionably the most severe in terms of likelihood of execution and waiting time until execution. Federal law should only hasten the swiftness of the death penalty with the passage of the Antiterrorism and Effective Death Penalty Act of 1996.[30] Finally, some states that presently do not have the death penalty, such as Iowa, occasionally consider the reinstatement of capital punishment as the only appropriate punishment for persons who commit the most heinous crimes.

On the other hand, the death penalty is also currently facing perhaps its greatest legitimacy crisis in the name of wrongful convictions and miscarriages of justice. At the forefront of this initiative is the Innocence Project. The **Innocence Project** at Cardozo School of Law was created in 1992 by attorneys Barry Scheck and Peter Neufeld. It is a nonprofit legal clinic that handles cases where postconviction DNA testing of evidence can yield conclusive proof of innocence. At this writing, the Innocence Project has exonerated more than 226 persons, 127 of whom had been erroneously sentenced to death.

Several factors contributed to these miscarriages of justice (**FIGURE 15-4**); the most common are mistaken identification, false confessions, erroneous information/testimony from informants, and erroneous microscopic hair matches.[31] Research indicates that prosecutorial misconduct, the discovery of new exculpatory evidence, police misconduct, witness perjury, racial bias, ineffective attorneys, and evidence insufficiency has also contributed to miscarriages of justice in capital cases.[32–35] The exoneration of factually innocent people and the public outrage it engenders is an important policy item and growing area of academic inquiry.[36]

Recently, the Innocence Project mobilized efforts to create **innocence commissions** to monitor, investigate, and address errors in the criminal justice system, much like

CORRECTIONS IN THE NEWS

Prosecutor Agrees to Drop Consideration of the Death Penalty in Decapitation Homicide in Georgia, but Not Florida

In 2008, Gary Michael Hilton confessed to murdering Meredith Emerson and was sentenced to life imprisonment in Georgia. In that case, Hilton was allowed to plead guilty in exchange for a life sentence. Florida authorities are prosecuting Hilton for a similar murder of Cheryl Dunlap, a crime for which he could be sentenced to death if convicted. Both victims were decapitated. Both victims were hikers. Emerson was blitz attacked, kept alive for 3 days, and decapitated after her death. Hilton could also be linked to a double homicide that occurred in North Carolina; this case involved an elderly couple hiking in Pisgah National Forest.

A forestry agent's professional curiosity and a routine check for wants and warrants that came back negative places Hilton near where Emerson's body was found. The information is undeniable evidence that places this man in the area, making Hilton the primary suspect in this murder case. But that's not all. From there, investigators determined that Hilton had used a pay phone at a convenience store in Cumming, Georgia, the day of the murder. Investigators were also able to locate Emerson's wallet and personal identification in a trash bin located in the parking lot of a local grocery store; the same parking lot where Emerson's Labrador was found wandering. Witnesses say they had observed the dog hiking with Meredith in the North Georgia Mountains on New Year's Day. Shortly after New Year's Day, other witnesses place the dog with Hilton. A search of Hilton's minivan uncovered his attempt to wash the interior of the van with a solution of bleach and water. It also appeared as if Hilton had recently vacuumed the inside of the vehicle. In addition, a surveillance video captured Hilton using one of Emerson's credit cards at a bank in Canton, Georgia.

Source: Sheriff: Hiker, Florida woman both decapitated. Retrieved January 10, 2008, from http://www.cnn.com/2008/CRIME/01/10/georgia.hiker/index.html.

the National Transportation Safety Board investigates public transportation disasters. According to Scheck and Neufeld, a federal innocence commission should have the authority to:

1. Investigate any wrongdoing conviction and recommend policy reforms.
2. Order reasonable and necessary investigative services, including forensic testing or autopsies.
3. Subpoena documents, compel testimony, and bring civil actions against any person or entity that obstructs its investigations.

Moreover, Scheck and Neufeld advised that innocence commissions should be protected so that findings and recommendations are not bound to subsequent civil or criminal proceedings and be publicly accountable like other criminal justice entities.[37]

In 2002, North Carolina became the first state to establish an innocence commission with the creation of the North Carolina Actual Innocence Commission. In 2003, the innocence commission for Virginia was founded; it was the first commission to investigate all cases of wrongful conviction. Other states, including California, Connecticut, Illinois, North Carolina, Pennsylvania, and Wisconsin, have established criminal justice reform commissions to evaluate all aspects of criminal justice processing.[38]

Unfortunately, the criminological research on this important issue is often one sided and specious.[39] It has been reported that more than 90 percent of the cases of innocent persons being condemned relied exclusively on the pleadings of the accused or declarations of innocence.[40] By this logic, any criminal defendant who insisted that he or she was innocent should simply be considered innocent. In addition to criminologists, some political leaders, religious leaders, and media figures also contend that innocent persons have been executed or are about to be executed often to fit their preexisting agenda. For example, in 2006, DNA analysis confirmed the guilt of a Virginia man who was executed in 1992. The defendant had maintained his innocence, as did a growing support network. Indeed, no executed convict in the United States has ever been exonerated by scientific testing.[41]

It is clear that the current era of capital punishment appears to be ripe for reforms. For example, Matt DeLisi argues that federal and state governments should assume the responsibility for conducting postconviction DNA analyses to ensure that condemned offenders are indeed guilty of their crimes.[42] It is the state's responsibility to ensure that capital punishment is administered without error, not due process organizations, such as the Innocence Project. Of course, such a policy would forensically affirm the guilt of most condemned offenders and should theoretically increase the speed with which executions are conducted. If DNA technology incontrovertibly confirms one's guilt, why continue endless appeals?

Finally, criminologist Jon Sorensen has convincingly argued that the American death penalty is currently operating at its most efficient and professional level. In the lead article in the newsletter of the Academy of Criminal Justice Sciences, Sorensen assessed that there was not racial bias in the administration of the death penalty and that racial disparities stemmed from legitimate factors, such as actual offending differences by race. Moreover, the danger of executing truly innocent persons has been shown to be virtually zero and there was little chance that miscarriages of justice could occur due to factual innocence. Sorensen concluded that, "the process itself has become more efficient without sacrificing protection for defendants. Capital punishment in active death penalty jurisdictions is at least as efficient as life imprisonment, and perhaps more so."[43, p. 7]

Profile of Condemned Offenders

In March 2008, Jessie Dotson was charged with six counts of first-degree murder and three counts of attempted first-degree murder in Tennessee. The victims include his brother and two child relatives and prosecutors will pursue the death penalty in the case. An aggravating circumstance in Dotson's story is that he had been free for just 2 months after serving a 14-year sentence for a prior conviction for second-degree murder. In that case, Dotson shot a woman in the head after she complained that the crack cocaine she had purchased from Dotson was actually soap shavings. While he was incarcerated, Dotson had more than 30 infractions, including several assaults and at least one stabbing of another inmate.[44]

Unfortunately, lengthy and violent criminal careers among the nation's most serious offenders are commonplace. For instance, in February 2005, Texas authorities executed Dennis Bagwell for convictions for murdering his own mother, his half-sister, and two child relatives (ages 4 and 14)—one of whom was also raped. Records maintained by the Texas Department of Criminal Justice indicated that Bagwell had been on parole for a mere 4 months before committing the quadruple homicide. He was paroled after serving 13 years in prison for a prior conviction for attempted capital murder![45]

Death row inmates tend to have extensive prior involvement in crime. For instance:

- About 66 percent of death row inmates have prior felony convictions before their death sentence.
- Nearly 1 in 10 death row inmates have previously been convicted of homicide *before* being sentenced to death for an additional homicide.
- Approximately 40 percent of death row inmates were already under criminal justice supervision or had pending legal status at the time of their capital crimes.
- Sixteen percent of death row inmates were on parole at the time of their capital crimes.

- Eleven percent of death row inmates were on probation at the time of their capital crimes.
- Nearly 8 percent of death row inmates had charges pending and were on bond at the time of their capital crimes.
- Nearly 4 percent of death row inmates were incarcerated and almost 2 percent were on escape status.[46]

Dorothy Van Soest and her colleagues studied the life histories of 37 death row inmates who had committed heinous crimes. All of these offenders demonstrated an early onset of antisocial behavior during childhood, including alcohol and drug abuse; school behavior problems; reports of conduct problems; and crime. Violence was a predominant theme in their lives across settings, contexts, and ages. Death row inmates who committed heinous crimes experienced sexual abuse, emotional abuse, and neglect and had significantly high rates as the perpetrator and victim of violence.[47]

Condemned offenders exemplify a criminological profile that matches the seriousness of their legal punishment. On average, their lives are startling histories of abuse, victimization, trauma, crime and criminal justice system involvement, substance abuse, and assorted psychiatric and psychopathological problems that are significantly greater than the average prisoner. In their review of the characteristics of death row inmates, Mark Cunningham and Mark Vigen advised that, "It is disturbing that so many inmates on death row are so obviously damaged developmentally, intellectually, educationally, neurologically, and psychologically."[48, p. 207]

There seem to be two general groups of offenders among those ultimately sentenced to death. The first is a career criminal group for whom capital offenses are the culmination of a decades-long pattern of criminal versatility, violence, and recurrent arrest and incarceration. A study of criminals who committed multiple homicides—some of whom were sentenced to death—found that 30 percent were serious, habitual offenders with multiple violent convictions even before being condemned. The second group consists of offenders with minimal criminal records who committed some atrocious act of extreme violence, such as spree killing. In sum, a sustained, intensive, and lifelong involvement in antisocial behavior is typical of persons who reside on death row.[49–50]

Deterrence

Throughout history, death has been used as a punishment for criminal behavior to send a message to potential criminals that violations of the law will not be tolerated. By condemning one offender, it is believed that others will reform their behavior to avoid the same punishment. It is also the case that throughout history, the punishment of death has been used to symbolically destroy the most reprehensible criminals. In short, these are the doctrines of deterrence and retribution, and they are explored next.

Evidence Against

Deterrence is the punishment philosophy that rests on the idea that people are rational thinkers endowed with free will who weigh the costs and benefits of each course of action in their lives and then choose to act. Punishments that are swift, certain, and severe (but proportionate to the crime) should theoretically dissuade potential criminals from choosing to commit crime. For most people, deterrence works pretty well. Most Americans do not engage in felonious behavior for several reasons, one of which is that they are afraid of the prospects of going to prison. In terms of capital punishment, the severity of the sentence should dissuade prospective murderers from killing.

Official policy position of the American Society of Criminology with respect to the death penalty: Be it resolved that because social science research has demonstrated the death penalty to be racist in application and social science research has found no consistent evidence of crime deterrence through execution, the American Society of Criminology publicly condemns this form of punishment, and urges its members to use their professional skills in legislatures and courts to seek a speedy abolition of this form of punishment.

There is no question that most scholarly research has found that the death penalty does not deter murder. Indeed, the American Society of Criminology (ASC) takes an official stance against capital punishment because, according to the ASC, social science research has found no consistent evidence of crime deterrence through execution.[51] William Bailey and Ruth Peterson assessed that the criminological research literature has shown that the death penalty does not deter crime rates, murder rates, and even specific types of capital murder such as the murder of a police officer.[52] Michael Radelet and Ronald Akers surveyed both academic and applied experts for their views on the deterrent effects of capital punishment and found over 84 percent of criminologists and nearly 70 percent of police chiefs and county sheriffs indicated that the death penalty offered no deterrent effect.[53–54]

Early deterrence research employed crude forms of data analysis and were methodologically weak. For instance, the murder rates of contiguous states, one with and one without the death penalty, were compared and offered as evidence against deterrence. Recent research is much more sophisticated but tends to yield the same conclusion even when controlling for an assortment of variables that are known to affect the crime rate. Indeed, Derral Cheatwood even found that capital punishment increased violent crime rates net the effects of other important variables.[55–56]

Several other criminologists have also found that capital punishment can actually produce an increase in homicides. This unexpected antideterrent effect is known as **brutalization**, defined as the increase in violent crime, specifically homicide, in the wake of an execution. Evidence for a brutalization effect has been found using data from South Carolina, Arizona, Oklahoma, and California.[57–60] John Cochran and Mitchell Chamlin, two of the prominent scholars on the brutalization thesis, also found that the effects of the death penalty were contingent on the type of homicide. For instance, California executed Robert Harris in 1992 after a 25-year moratorium in that state. The execution resulted in a decrease in the level of nonstranger felony murders (evidence of deterrence) but an increase in argument-based murders of strangers (evidence of brutalization).[61] However, William Bailey reanalyzed their data and found no evidence for brutalization or deterrence and the death penalty.[62]

Supportive Evidence

Although the bulk of criminological research has found that the death penalty did not deter murder, much of that research was extraordinarily crude in its analysis. Moreover, sociologists conducted the preponderance of death penalty research, and great speculation exists that sociological criminologists were ideologically unwilling to produce evidence of deterrence, were unable to conduct more sophisticated data analysis, or both. Curiously, economists have produced considerable support for the idea that the death penalty deters murder. Isaac Ehrlich conducted the seminal study of death penalty deterrence using highly sophisticated quantitative models that were able to control for a variety of variables that influence crime. Ehrlich found that each execution prevents seven to eight murders from occurring.[63] Ehrlich was vilified for the research finding, and several criminologists hurried to disconfirm his findings. Although some of these reanalyses cast doubt on Ehrlich's work, more studies confirmed that the death penalty actually did deter murder.[64]

Contemporary research continues to suggest an important deterrent effect for the death penalty. For example, Joanna Shepherd recently found that each execution resulted in three fewer murders and that executions affected domestic violence murders and murders of passion—crimes that were previously thought to be beyond the reach of deterrence. She also found that one fewer murder was committed for every 33-month reduction in the wait on death row.[65] A related study found that each execution resulted in 18 fewer murders.[66]

Hashem Dezhbakhsh and Joanna Shepherd recently conducted the most impressive and methodologically sophisticated study of the potential deterrent effects of the death penalty using data from all 50 states and spanning 1960–2000. Dezhbakhsh and Shepherd used the 1972–1976 official moratorium when capital punishment was unconstitutional as a judicial experiment. By comparing the murder rates immediately before and after 1972 and 1976, they could assess the effects of imposing and then lifting the moratorium on the death penalty. They produced several important findings, which include:

- The annual murder rate increased 9.3 percent when the Supreme Court ruled that the death penalty was unconstitutional.
- The murder rate increased 16.3 percent after 2 years and 21 percent after 3 years.
- The annual murder rate dropped 8.3 percent after executions became lawful.
- The murder rate dropped 8.2 percent after 2 years and 4 percent after 3 years.
- The murder rate increased 23 percent between 1972 and 1976.

These results held regardless of the data's aggregation level, the time period used, the specific variable used to measure executions, and of controls for general trends in crime and specific offenses that often lead to murder. They concluded that "we verify that the negative relationship between the death penalty and murder is not a spurious finding."[67, p. 21]

A likely empirical reason for the dispute between the death penalty camps is the timing of the deterrent effect. Theoretically, the deterrent effects of an execution should be immediate and short term, such as within a month. Studies that looked at homicides over a year period were missing the very truncated time period when deterrence should occur. Indeed, criminologists discovered this very point. David Phillips found that homicides decreased 36 percent immediately following a publicized execution and that cases with the greatest publicity resulted in the greatest reductions in killings. No long-term deterrent effect was found.[68]

Steven Stack found that a publicized execution resulted in a drop of 30 homicides in the month of the publicity. Executions that received little to no publicity had no deterrent effect. Importantly, Stack also found that the importance of executions as a means of crime control was exaggerated. For instance, the percent of the population that was in the most homicide-prone age group was 21 times more closely associated with the monthly murder rate than publicized executions.[69]

Finally, Bijou Yang and David Lester conducted a meta-analysis of 30 years of studies on the deterrent effect of the death penalty. Of 95 studies that contained adequate data, 60 of them showed a deterrent effect for capital punishment while only 35 studies showed a brutalization effect. The deterrent effect was most consistently found in methodologically superior time-series or panel studies. Cross-sectional studies, studies of the effect of a single execution, and studies of newspaper and television publicity—all methodologically weaker—tended to not show deterrent effects.[70]

Substantive Problems

Irrespective of the evidence for a deterrent effect for the death penalty, there are major substantive problems to consider. First, executions simply are not conducted soon enough after conviction to adequately explore deterrent effects. Punishment must be swift, certain, and severe to achieve deterrence. Since 1977, the average length of stay on death row until execution was 124 months or more than 10 years. In 2007, offenders waited an average of 135 months before their execution. In other words, among persons who commit capital crimes *today* and are convicted and sentenced to death, we must wait more than a decade until their execution if it is one of the 1 to 2 percent of cases that actually results in execution. With this temporal order, it is impossible to adequately assess the degree to which prospective murderers are deterred by capital punishment.

The second major substantive problem in the administration of the death penalty is the infrequency with which it is actually imposed. Derral Cheatwood studied more than 9,000 homicides from Chicago spanning the years 1879 to 1930 and found that 1.2 percent resulted in a death sentence and less than 1 percent of these cases actually resulted in an execution.[71] In other words, even among inmates sentenced to death, execution is rarely carried out.

Similarly, Steven Levitt assessed that the likelihood of being executed conditional on committing murder was less than one in 200, and that even among those who were condemned, the annual execution rate was 2 percent.[72] Because of the infrequency of executions, others have argued that prison conditions measured by the prisoner death rate are a better method of deterrence. Lawrence Katz and his colleagues found that between 30 and 100 violent crimes and 30 and 100 property crimes were avoided per inmate death in prison.[73] In the end, the evaluation of whether the death penalty deters murder will likely never be answered given the typical way the punishment is administered in the United States.

Retribution

Philosophical and Religious Bases

Retribution is the philosophical rationale that implies the payment of a debt to society and the criminal offender's expiation or atonement for his or her crime. In simple terms, retribution is a form of revenge or retaliation in which the criminal justice system inflicts a proportionate level of suffering to the criminal offender. For capital punishment, the execution is the payback or revenge exacted from the criminal for committing murder. This philosophy was historically described as the *lex talionis,* or law of the claw. The ***lex talionis*** is the law of retaliation such that punishment must be inflicted in the form of an eye for an eye and a tooth for a tooth.

One of the main historical proponents of retribution was the philosopher Immanuel Kant. Kant believed that criminal punishment, even death, recognized the agency, autonomy, and free will of the actor or criminal. Since a criminal chooses to commit homicide, then the state must recognize the criminal's volition and autonomy and respond accordingly. Kant would argue that the deterrent capacity of the death penalty is irrelevant because the sole purpose of an execution is to give the criminal his or her due justice. Kant disposed of arguments calling for the abolishment of capital punishment as sentimentality or humanitarian posturing.[74]

Immanuel Kant was an early proponent of retributive rationales for capital punishment.

Retribution entails reciprocity between the crime and its punishment. It is closely connected with the idea of desert or just deserts. **Just deserts** is the philosophy of justice that assumes that individuals freely choose to violate criminal laws and therefore the state or criminal justice has the legal and moral right and duty to punish them according to the nature of their acts. Many people deeply believe in the idea of just deserts. For example, people who do good things for others are viewed as deserving of rewards or similarly positive treatment. On the other hand, serial killers who are put to death are often described as getting what they deserved.

Capital punishment has been extensively used immemorially in Babylonian society, the kingdoms of Judah and Israel, the Roman Empire, ancient Greece, ancient India, China, under English Common Law, and throughout the majority of American history. The death penalty has an important place among the world's three major religions—Judaism, Christianity, and Islam.[75] Capital punishment was viewed as a righteous, retributive response to criminal offenders who violate the moral order, humanity, or God. But there were mixed feelings about the appropriateness and application of the death penalty, particularly in the Judeo-Christian ethic. Scott Johnson summarized:

> The Bible contained several overt endorsements of capital punishment. Most of these explicit endorsements occur in the Old Testament. The Mosaic Law articulated in the Pentateuch prescribes death as the punishment for several offenses against God and humanity. The New Testament contains no similar overt endorsements. . . . Some New Testament statements appear to support capital punishment; however, these passages do not speak directly to the issue of the death penalty. They mention the death penalty and presume its correctness or these statements demand good citizenship from believers, meaning that believers should accept the death penalty provided it is the policy of a legitimate government.[76, p. 31]

Johnson also identified inconsistencies in the Bible in which murderers were variously executed, condemned but allowed to live, or treated in another manner. In this sense, the arbitrary and capricious application of the death penalty is not new. Curiously, many Americans derive their support or opposition to the death penalty from religious teachings. From one perspective, a retributive death penalty is not only viable policy, but also mandated from scripture. From another perspective, only God can stand in judgment of criminal offenders, thus the death penalty is an affront to God.

Today, the average citizen does not contemplate the arguments of Kant while forming his or her opinion about the death penalty. The overwhelming majority of Americans support the death penalty and arguably the primary basis for their support centers around retribution.[77] The contemporary public philosophy toward retribution is simple and unambiguous. Certain criminal behaviors are considered intrinsically wrong, even evil, and the punishment for these crimes must not only provide just deserts to the offender, but also cleanse the public by removing the person from society. These evil crimes are known as *mala in se* offenses and include murder, rape, abduction or kidnapping, and any sexual-based offense against a child. There is a universal revulsion against these forms of behavior and the persons who commit them. To many Americans, the death penalty is the symbolic vehicle by which evil wrongdoers are legally, lawfully, and morally extinguished from human society. As such, retribution can be viewed as a righteous, philosophically defensible justification for capital punishment.[78]

Harboring retributive views is also part of a larger constellation of ideological values and beliefs. Researchers have found that persons who favor the death penalty tend to hold more conservative political beliefs and invoke a highly moralistic, good-versus-evil worldview in which criminal offenders are considered to be reprehensible monsters who should be punished in the most severe way. For others, retributive death penalty attitudes are correlated with racial prejudice or the attribution of crime to persons of color. Finally, some citizens employ a retributive death penalty stance as a symbolic affirmation of their crime control beliefs.[79]

Modern retribution also is driven by the idea that many citizens are disgusted with the inability of the criminal justice system to adequately control crime. There is widespread public indignation that condemned offenders, many of whom are serious repeat offenders, are seemingly allowed to recurrently commit crime and victimize others. It could be argued that modern retribution is influenced by overemphasis on the due process rights of criminal defendants and a de-emphasis on punishing criminals.[80] Walter Berns summarized the type of retribution that characterizes many Americans' views on the subject: "Anger is the passion that recognizes and cares about justice."[81, p. 152]

Racial Elements

One of the major death penalty controversies centers on the disproportionate number of African Americans who have been executed or await execution on death row. There are comparable numbers of Whites and Blacks on death row despite the huge differences in these racial groups proportion of the population.[82–83] The idea that the death penalty is discriminatory in its application is one of the primary reasons why the American Society of Criminology took an official organizational stance against the death penalty. The American Society of Criminology's decision was motivated by the pioneering research of David Baldus, Charles Pulanski, and George Woodworth, who found that defendants charged with killing White persons were more than four times more likely to be sentenced to death than those charged with killing Blacks.[84] Similarly, many Americans oppose the death penalty because of concerns that it is racially biased in its application.

Irrespective of one's thoughts on potential racial elements of the death penalty, the Supreme Court ruled on this issue in the landmark case ***McClesky v. Kemp*** (1987). In *McClesky*, the Court held that the Baldus study that indicated that Black defendants received the death penalty more often than Whites, especially when the victim was White, was not sufficient to demonstrate that racial considerations enter into capital sentencing determinations. The Court also found that the specific defendant did not show a violation of equal protection under the law (Fourteenth Amendment) because he had not shown that there was purposeful discrimination in his own case. Additionally, the Court found that the Baldus study was "flawed in many respects" and because of these deficiencies "failed to contribute anything of value."[85, p. 481]

Two earlier studies shed further light on the purported racial biases of the death penalty. Michael Radelet examined 637 homicide indictments in 20 Florida counties in 1976 and 1977 and produced the following important findings:

- Crime was mostly intraracial; that is, Whites tended to offend against Whites, and Blacks tended to victimize Blacks.
- When murder was interracial, it tended to be overwhelmingly Black-on-White and involved strangers as offender and victim. Homicides involving strangers were *700 percent* more likely to be Black-on-White than White-on-Black.
- Those accused of murdering Whites faced a higher probability of being indicted for first-degree murder and being sentenced to death.
- Once indicted for first-degree murder, neither the race of the defendant, the victim, nor the interaction between these two variables was significantly related to the probability of being sentenced to death.[86]

Gary Kleck examined race and the death penalty using data spanning 1930 to 1978. Kleck produced five findings that clarified the role of race in the application of the death penalty.

> First, the death penalty has not generally been imposed for murder in a fashion discriminatory toward blacks, except in the South. Elsewhere, black homicide offenders have been less likely to receive a death sentence or be executed than whites. Second, for the 11 percent of executions, which have been imposed for rape, discrimination against black defendants who had raped white victims was substantial. Such discrimination was limited to the South and has disappeared because death sentences are no longer imposed for rape. Third, regarding non-capital sentencing, the evidence is largely contrary to a hypothesis of general or widespread overt discrimination against black defendants, although there is evidence of discrimination for a minority of specific jurisdictions, judges, crime types, etc. Fourth, although black offender-white victim crimes are generally punished more severely than crimes involving other racial combinations, the evidence indicates that this is due to legally relevant factors related to such offenses, not the racial composition itself. Fifth, there appears to be a general pattern of less severe punishment of crimes with black victims than those with white victims, especially in connection with imposition of the death penalty.[87, pp. 798–799]

Recent reanalyses of capital punishment data from Maryland further revealed that earlier showings of racial bias were the result of methodological errors and limitations and that there is not evidence of racial discrimination in the administration of the death penalty.[88]

In the end, the racial bias concern about the death penalty has empirically less to do with race and more to do with the circumstances of capital crimes. The most common scenario that leads to a death sentence is a first-degree murder committed during the course of an armed robbery. This scenario usually involves strangers and satisfies the aggravating circumstances of a felony murder, and armed robbery is the offense that is most disproportionately committed by African American males. These characteristics, not the race of the specific offender and victim, result in capital convictions.

Capital punishment is an extraordinary punishment in that the state can lawfully take the life of condemned offenders. Another unique form of correctional supervision is civil commitment, which involves treating violent offenders as patients rather than punishing them as offenders. This procedure is explored next.

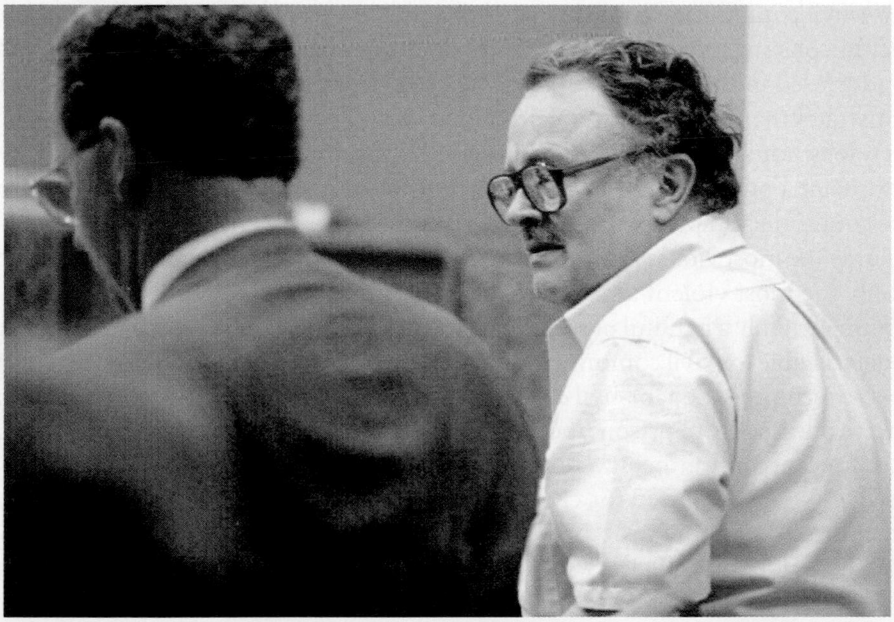

The case of habitual sex offender Leroy Hendricks resulted in the Supreme Court upholding the practice of civil commitment.

Civil Commitment

The case of Leroy Hendricks catapulted the issue of the civil commitment of criminally dangerous persons to the forefront of discussions about the ability of the state to control serious criminals. A pedophile with a lengthy criminal history of sexually assaulting children dating to 1955, Hendricks was released from prison. After his release, Kansas authorities sought his **civil commitment** under its Sexually Violent Predator Act, which permitted the institutionalization of persons likely to engage in predatory acts of criminal violence brought on by mental abnormality or personality disorders. During his civil commitment trial, Hendricks admitted that he experienced continued urges to sexually abuse children despite having received extensive treatment for his pedophilia. Moreover, Hendricks stated that whenever he felt stressed out, the urge to molest became uncontrollable. Kansas authorities determined that Hendricks's pedophilia qualified as a mental abnormality and justified his civil commitment. Consequently, Hendricks was civilly committed.

The Kansas Supreme Court later invalidated the Sexually Violent Predator Act because it did not require that Hendricks suffer from mental illness before imposing the civil commitment. In ***Kansas v. Hendricks*** (1997), the Supreme Court granted certiorari to the case to assess what constitutes mental abnormality and whether substantive due process and double jeopardy provisions were violated. In a narrow 5–4 decision, the Court found:

- The Kansas law did not violate due process because it proved beyond a reasonable doubt that Hendricks had prior sexually violent behavior and a present mental condition that facilitated the likelihood that such violent conduct would recur.
- Civil confinement is permitted as long as the person suffers from an abnormality or personality disorder.
- Release should only occur if the abnormality or personality disorder abates to such a degree that society would be safe from harm by someone who was released.
- Yearly reviews of the civilly committed person are required.[89]

The decision galvanized legal scholars and criminologists who attempted to understand the legality of a civil policy that involuntarily incarcerated violent criminals after they had served sentences imposed by criminal courts.[90] It is important to note that because civil commitment policies are civil and therefore not punitive, the laws are not subject to constitutional concerns such as double jeopardy or ex post facto claims that were addressed in the Hendricks case. The civil commitment ends once the individual demonstrates that he (sexually violent offenders and career criminals are almost always males) does not suffer from a mental disorder or abnormality. Civil commitment is therefore *not* a punishment but an opportunity for the treatment of the mentally sick whose condition and prior conduct pose risks of future violence.

If only the most violent criminals are eligible for capital punishment, it could be said that only the most violent and psychiatrically disturbed offenders are eligible for civil commitment. Only a handful of studies have examined the social and criminal histories of offenders eligible for civil commitment. Jill Levenson studied 229 sex offenders in Florida who were recommended for civil commitment and compared them to 221 sex offenders who were released from prison upon completion of their sentence. She found that those selected for civil commitment were significantly more violent than sex offenders who were released. Offenders selected for civil commitment were more likely to be psychopathic and had higher psychopathy scores, victimized younger persons (children as young as age 10), had more prior victims, had more prior arrests for sexually based offenses, and had more career arrests. In addition, persons selected for civil commitment in Florida had greater likelihood of treatment failure, greater prior use of weapons, greater variety in sexual offenses (e.g., rape, molestation, incest), and greater likelihood to report that they intended to commit future sexually violent offenses.[91]

In a related study, Levenson and John Morin examined which factors predicted selection for civil commitment among Florida sex offenders. Nearly 10 percent of them had prior convictions for murder or attempted murder. Several criminal history factors dramatically increased the likelihood of civil commitment:

- A diagnosis for pedophilia increased the odds of civil commitment by *4,656 percent.*
- A diagnosis for sexual sadism increased the odds of civil commitment by *85,562 percent.*
- A diagnosis for paraphilia not otherwise specified increased the odds of civil commitment by *10,580 percent.*
- Offenders who stated that they intended to commit violent crimes after release were more than *3.7 million percent* more likely to be civilly committed.[92]

In 1990, Washington became the first state to enact civil commitment legislation specifically for sexually violent predators with mental abnormality or personality disorders that made recidivism likely if the person was not in a secure facility. Since 1990, 16 additional states have passed similar laws, including Arizona, California, Florida, Iowa, Illinois, Kansas, Massachusetts, Minnesota, Missouri, New Jersey, North Dakota, Pennsylvania, South Carolina, Texas, Virginia, and Wisconsin. Rebecca Jackson and Henry Richards evaluated the risk profiles of 190 sexually violent predators who were civilly committed in Washington state. They found that nearly 17 percent had a diagnosis for sadism, 57 percent had a diagnosis for pedophilia, and 43 percent had a diagnosis for nonconsent paraphilia. Nearly 85 percent were alcohol or substance abuse dependent. More than 41 percent had antisocial personality disorder, and more than 42 percent had other personality disorder not otherwise specified.[93]

From one perspective, civil commitment is a circumstance where the state can have its cake and eat it, too, because the ability of the state to punish violent criminal offenders extends from the criminal justice system that punishes blameworthiness and *mens rea* to the civil world, immune from constitutional challenges, where the incarcerated are viewed as disordered patients. For this reason, academics have fiercely debated this issue.

Civil commitment is costly. If civilly committed defendants do not experience some convalescence, they will continue to be housed at taxpayer expense. The annual cost to supervise civilly committed sexual predators at the Larned State Hospital in Kansas, where Leroy Hendricks was supervised, is $56,575. In April 2005, Leroy Hendricks, the original civil commitment case, left the state hospital because he completed all five stages of the treatment programs and was in deteriorating health. Hendricks was scheduled to have escorts to monitor his behavior 24 hours a day, 7 days a week, and guard against the likelihood that he could recidivate. The constant surveillance was estimated to cost Kansas taxpayers nearly $280,000 for the first 15 months.[94]

For some, civil commitment raises distressing civil liberty and moral questions. In this view, civil commitment is a clever, legalistic effort to continually punish persons who have already been published criminally. It should be noted that civil commitment is used with great infrequency. Karol Lucken and William Bales studied nearly 800 sex offenders eligible for civil commitment in Florida and found that only 6.5 percent are actually referred to be civilly committed. In addition, *all* referred sex offenders met the requisite legal guidelines to be civilly committed.[95] In this way, civil commitment is a process that the correctional system takes seriously and only those offenders who meet the criteria of sexually violent offenses coupled with mental abnormality/personality disorder receive it. Civil commitment is applied judiciously.

For those who are perhaps rightfully concerned that sexually violent offenders will recidivate, the end may justify the means. Research suggests that the general public is more concerned about protecting the public than alleged civil liberty threats posed by civil commitment. When people feel that sex offenders are not sufficiently punished in the first place by the correctional system, they are significantly more likely to favor civil commitment as a way to correct the punishment imbalance.[96] In the end, civil commitment is a unique approach used by the correctional system to supervise the most disturbed and recidivistic of sex offenders.

WRAP UP

CASE STUDY CONCLUSION

Politics and criminal justice environment play major roles in the death penalty. Conservative, law-and-order states such as Texas execute with relative frequency. Progressive states such as Massachusetts and Minnesota do not have capital punishment. California tends to be more liberal on many social issues, such as crime control, and thus does not proceed with great speed or ambition when it comes to executing condemned offenders. The reason for the considerable length of stay on death row is due almost entirely to a convoluted appeals process that can drag on for years and even decades.

Source: Snell, T. L., (2008). *Capital punishment, 2007*. Washington, DC: U.S. Department of Justice, Office of Justice Programs, Bureau of Justice Statistics.

Chapter Summary

- Capital punishment is the most punitive, sensationalistic, controversial, and infrequently used form of criminal punishment.
- Capital punishment is susceptible to political and public opinion and has been used extensively or sporadically depending on the political era.
- From 1972 to 1976, the death penalty was illegal in the United States because it was applied in a manner that was in violation of the Eighth Amendment's proscription of cruel and unusual punishment.
- Although deterrence is the explicit rationale for capital punishment, the evidence is very mixed about its actual deterrent effects.
- Death sentencing guidelines specify aggravating and mitigating circumstances to determine the appropriateness of capital punishment.
- Retribution is the philosophical rationale that states that the worst criminals deserve death as a means of repayment, retaliation, or deservedness for their crimes.
- Lethal injection, consisting of lethal doses of an anesthetic, a barbiturate to stop respiration, and a toxic agent to induce cardiac arrest, is the most common method of execution.
- Virtually all death sentences are automatically/legislatively reviewed and appealed by the state regardless of the wishes of the condemned defendant.
- Condemned offenders wait more than 10 years on death row primarily due to a convoluted appeals process.
- Despite claims to the contrary, the death penalty is not racially biased in its application and instead reflects legally relevant case variables.
- Civil commitment is the postprison, involuntary confinement of sexually violent offenders with mental abnormalities or personality disorders that increase their likelihood of recidivism.

Key Terms

aggravating circumstances Characteristics that make the crime seem worse in totality and thus deserving of death as the only appropriate punishment.

Atkins v. Virginia Supreme Court case that held that executing mentally retarded persons *did* constitute cruel and unusual punishment and was a violation of the Eighth Amendment, consistent with the evolving standards of decency.

Baze v. Rees Case in which the Supreme Court held that lethal injection does not constitute cruel and unusual punishment and is therefore constitutional.

bifurcated trials Trials in which there are separate deliberations for the guilt and penalty phases of the case.

brutalization The increase in violent crime, specifically homicide, in the wake of an execution.

capital punishment The use of death as a criminal punishment.

civil commitment The institutionalization of persons likely to engage in predatory acts of criminal violence brought on by mental abnormality or personality disorders.

Coker v. Georgia Supreme Court case that invalidated rape as a capital offense.

commute The reduction of a criminal sentence, such as death to life imprisonment.

deterrence The punishment philosophy that rests on the idea that people are rational thinkers endowed with free will who weigh the costs and benefits of each course of action in their lives and then choose to act.

felony murder The commission of a homicide in conjunction with some other serious felony offense, such as kidnapping, rape, armed robbery, child molestation, or additional homicides.

Furman v. Georgia Supreme Court case that held capital punishment to be in violation of the Eighth Amendment.

Gregg v. Georgia Supreme Court case that held that the new death penalty statutes in Florida, Georgia, and Texas were constitutional, and that the death penalty itself was constitutional under the Eighth Amendment.

innocence commission Commission that monitors, investigates, and addresses errors in the criminal justice system.

Innocence Project A nonprofit legal clinic that handles cases in which postconviction DNA testing of evidence can yield conclusive proof of innocence.

just deserts The philosophy of justice that assumes that individuals freely choose to violate criminal laws and therefore the state or criminal justice system has the legal and moral right and duty to punish them according to the nature of their acts.

Kansas v. Hendricks Supreme Court case that upheld civil commitment.

lethal injection The intravenous administering of three drugs to cause death.

lex talionis The law of retaliation such that punishment must be inflicted with an eye for an eye and a tooth for a tooth.

McClesky v. Kemp Supreme Court case that held that although Black defendants received the death penalty more often than Whites, especially when the victim was White, this was not sufficient to demonstrate that racial considerations enter into capital sentencing determinations.

mitigating circumstances Characteristics such as youth, mental retardation, or victimization that render a crime less serious or add context that seems to reduce the overall viciousness of the behavior.

Penry v. Lynaugh Supreme Court case that held that executing the mentally regarded was not a violation of the Eighth Amendment.

proportionality review Judicial review of criminal sentences which helps the state to identify and eliminate sentencing disparities by comparing the sentence in the case with other cases within the state.

retribution The philosophical rationale that implies the payment of a debt to society and the criminal offender's expiation or atonement for his or her crime.

Roper v. Simmons Case in which the Supreme Court ruled that it is unconstitutional to impose the death penalty on offenders younger than 18 at the time of their capital crimes.

writ of certiorari Petition to the Supreme Court for review.

Critical Thinking Questions

1. Are the exonerations achieved by the Innocence Project unconscionable? Do they alone provide an argument for abolishing capital punishment?
2. Is the academic disapproval of capital punishment an elitist response to the public, which overwhelmingly supports it? If so, does this color academic research on the topic?
3. Does the death penalty effectively deter crime? Does it increase it? Can deterrence ever be achieved under the current prolonged methods of actually executing offenders?
4. Would you witness an execution? Which feelings do you think it would elicit?

Notes

1. Sowell, T. (1997). The death penalty is a deterrent. In D. L. Bender (Ed.), *The death penalty: Opposing viewpoints* (pp. 103–107). San Diego, CA: Greenhaven Press.
2. Lyon, A. D., & Cunningham, M. D. (2005). Reason not the need: Does the lack of compelling state interest in maintaining a separate death row make it unlawful? *American Journal of Criminal Law, 33,* 1–30.
3. The quotation from Marquette University political science professor John McAdams appears on the home page of Pro-Death Penalty resource, http://www.prodeathpenalty.com/.
4. Mead, G. H. (1918). The psychology of punitive justice. *American Journal of Sociology, 23,* 577–602.
5. Gelertner, D. (2001). What do murderers deserve? In H. L. Tischler (Ed.), *Debating points: Crime and corrections* (pp. 13–19). Upper Saddle River, NJ: Prentice Hall.
6. DeLisi, M., & Munoz, E. A. (2004). The irrelevant future machinations of human predators: Response to Cunningham, Sorensen, and Reidy. *Criminal Justice Policy Review, 15,* 377–384.
7. Snell, T. L. (2008). *Capital punishment, 2007.* Washington, DC: U. S. Department of Justice, Office of Justice Programs, Bureau of Justice Statistics; Death Penalty Information Center. (2008). *Facts about the death penalty.* Retrieved December 26, 2008, from http://www.deathpenaltyinfo.org/home.
8. Associated Press. (2005). *Connecticut Supreme Court won't block Ross execution.* Retrieved October 20, 2008, from http://www.cnn.com/2005/LAW/05/10/ross.execution/index.html.
9. *Roper v. Simmons,* 543 U. S. 551 (2005).
10. Snell.

11. *Coker v. Georgia,* 433 U. S. 584 (1977).
12. *Gregg v. Georgia,* 428 U. S. 153 (1976).
13. *Jurek v. Texas,* 428 U. S. 262 (1976).
14. *Roberts v. Louisiana,* 428 U. S. 325 (1976).
15. *Proffitt v. Florida,* 428 U. S. 242 (1976).
16. *Woodson v. North Carolina,* 428 U. S. 280 (1976).
17. Rush, G. E. (2000). *The dictionary of criminal justice* (5th ed.). New York: Dushkin/McGraw-Hill, p. 275.
18. Latzer, B., & Gauthen, J. N. G. (2007). *Justice delayed? Time consumption in capital appeals: A multistate study.* Washington, DC: U.S. Department of Justice, Office of Justice Programs, National Institute of Justice.
19. Snell.
20. *Furman v. Georgia,* 408 U. S. 238 (1972).
21. *Branch v. Texas,* 408 U. S. 238 (1972).
22. *Jackson v. Georgia,* 408 U. S. 238 (1972).
23. *Penry v. Lynaugh,* 492 U.S. 302 (1989).
24. *Atkins v. Virginia,* 536 U S. 304 (2002).
25. Acker, J. R., & Lanier, C. S. (1997). Unfit to live, unfit to die: Incompetency for execution under modern death penalty legislation. *Criminal Law Bulletin, 33,* 107–150.
26. Tobolowsky, P. M. (2004). Capital punishment and the mentally retarded offender. *Prison Journal, 84,* 340–360.
27. Mooney, C. Z., & Lee, M. (2000). The influence of values on consensus and contentious morality policy: U. S. death penalty reform, 1956–1982. *Journal of Politics, 62,* 223–239.
28. Galliher, J. M., & Galliher, J. F. (2001). The commonsense theory of deterrence and the ideology of science: The New York State death penalty debate. *Journal of Criminal Law and Criminology, 92,* 307–333.
29. Lofquist, W. S. (2002). Putting them there, keeping them there, and killing them: An analysis of state-level variations in death penalty intensity. *Iowa Law Review, 87,* 1505–1557.
30. Spurr, S. J. (2002). The future of capital punishment: Determinants of the time from death sentence to execution. *International Review of Law and Economics, 22,* 1–23.
31. Innocence Project. (n. d.). *The causes of wrongful conviction.* Retrieved October 20, 2008, from http://www.innocenceproject.org/understand/; also see Scheck, B., Neufeld, P. J., & Dwyer, J. (2000). *Actual innocence: Five days to execution and other dispatches from the wrongly convicted.* New York: Doubleday; Huff, C. R., Rattner, A., & Sagarin, E. (1996). *Convicted but innocent: Wrongful conviction and public policy.* Thousand Oaks, CA: Sage.
32. Harmon, T. R. (2001). Guilty until proven innocent: An analysis of post-Furman capital errors. *Criminal Justice Policy Review, 12,* 113–139.
33. Harmon, T. R. (2001). Predictors of miscarriages of justice in capital cases. *Justice Quarterly, 18,* 949–968.
34. Harmon, T. R. (2004). Race for your life: An analysis of the role of race in erroneous capital convictions. *Criminal Justice Review, 29,* 79–96.
35. Harmon, T. R., & Lofquist, W. S. (2005). Too late for luck: A comparison of post-Furman exonerations and executions of the innocent. *Crime & Delinquency, 51,* 498–520.
36. Leo, R. A. (2005). Rethinking the study of miscarriages of justice: Developing a criminology of wrongful conviction. *Journal of Contemporary Criminal Justice, 20,* 201–223; Forst, B. (2008). *Errors of justice: Nature, sources and remedies.* New York: Cambridge University Press.
37. Scheck, B. C., & Neufeld, P. J. (2002). Toward the formation of "innocence commissions" in America. *Judicature, 86,* 98–105.
38. Gould, J. B. (2008). *The innocence commission: Preventing wrongful convictions and restoring the criminal justice system.* New York: New York University Press.

39. See Bedau, H., & Radelet, M. L. (1987). Miscarriages of justice in potentially capital cases. *Stanford Law Review, 40,* 21–179; Markman, S., & Cassell, P. (1988). Protecting the innocent: A response to the Bedau-Radelet study. *Stanford Law Review, 41,* 121–160. Others contend that both liberals' and conservatives' due process and crime control types are guilty of bias in death penalty research. For instance, see Donohue, J. J., & Wolfers, J. (2005). Uses and abuses of empirical evidence in the death penalty debate. *Stanford Law Review, 58,* 791–846.

40. Leo.

41. Associated Press. (2006). *DNA: Virginia executed the right man.* Retrieved January 12, 2006, from www.cnn.com/2006/LAW/01/12/dna.execution.ap/index.html.

42. DeLisi, M. (2005). *Career criminals in society.* Thousand Oaks, CA: Sage.

43. Sorensen, J. (2004). The administration of capital punishment. *ACJS Today, 29,* 1, 5–7.

44. Aarons, T., & Conley, C. (2008). *Prison stint didn't stop Dotson's violent ways.* Retrieved March 31, 2008, from http://www.commercialappeal.com/news/2008/mar/11/prison-stint-didnt-stop-dotsons-violent-ways/.

45. Texas Department of Criminal Justice. (2008). *Executed offenders.* Retrieved October 20, 2008, from http://www.tdcj.state.tx.us/statistics/deathrow/drowlist/bagwell.jpg.

46. Snell.

47. Van Soest, D., Park, H., Johnson, T. K., & McPhail, B. (2003). Different paths to death row: A comparison of men who committed heinous and less heinous crimes. *Violence and Victims, 18,* 15–33.

48. Cunningham, M. D., & Vigen, M. P. (2002). Death row inmate characteristics, adjustment, and confinement: A critical review of the literature. *Behavioral Sciences and the Law, 20,* 191–210, 207.

49. DeLisi, M., & Scherer, A. M. (2006). Multiple homicide offenders: Offense characteristics, social correlates, and criminal careers. *Criminal Justice and Behavior, 33,* 1–25.

50. DeLisi.

51. American Society of Criminology. (n.d.) *Policy position on the death penalty.* Retrieved October 20, 2008, from http://www.asc41.com/policyPositions.html.

52. Bailey, W. C., & Peterson, R. D. (1997). Murder, capital punishment, and deterrence: A review of the literature. In H. A. Bedau (Ed.), *The death penalty in America: Current controversies* (pp. 135–161). New York: Oxford University Press.

53. Radelet, M. L., & Borg, M. J. (2000). The changing nature of death penalty debates. *Annual Review of Sociology, 26,* 43–61.

54. Radelet, M. L., & Akers, R. L. (1996). Deterrence and the death penalty: The views of the experts. *Journal of Criminal Law and Criminology, 87,* 1–16.

55. Cheatwood, D. (1993). Capital punishment and the deterrence of violent crime in comparable counties. *Criminal Justice Review, 18,* 165–181.

56. Cheatwood, D. (2002). Capital punishment for the crime of homicide in Chicago: 1870–1930. *Journal of Criminal Law and Criminology, 92,* 843–866.

57. King, D. R. (1978). The brutalization effect: Execution publicity and the incidence of homicide in South Carolina. *Social Forces, 57,* 683–696.

58. Bowers, W. J., & Pierce, G. L. (1980). Deterrence or brutalization: What is the effect of executions? *Crime & Delinquency, 26,* 453–484.

59. Cochran, J. K., Chamlin, M. B., & Seth, M. (1994). Deterrence or brutalization? An impact assessment of Oklahoma's return to capital punishment. *Criminology, 32,* 107–134.

60. Thomson, E. (1997). Deterrence versus brutalization: The case of Arizona. *Homicide Studies, 1,* 110–128.

61. Cochran, J. K., & Chamlin, M. B. (2000). Deterrence and brutalization: The dual effects of executions. *Justice Quarterly, 17,* 685–706.

62. Bailey, W. C. (1998). Deterrence, brutalization, and the death penalty: Another examination of Oklahoma's return to capital punishment. *Criminology, 36,* 711–733.

63. Ehrlich, I. (1975). The deterrent effect of capital punishment: A question of life and death. *American Economic Review, 65,* 397–417.

64. The impassioned negative responses to Ehrlich's work lend some support for the idea that some criminologists are simply ideologically unwilling to acknowledge that the death penalty has a deterrent effect. For a sampling of this area of research, see Phillips, D. P. (1980). The deterrent effect of capital punishment: New evidence on an old controversy. *American Journal of Sociology, 86,* 139–148; Phillips, D. P., & Bollen, K. (1985). Same time, last year: Selective data dredging for negative findings. *American Sociological Review, 50,* 101–116; Ehrlich, I. (1977). Capital punishment and deterrence: Some further thoughts and additional evidence. *Journal of Political Economy, 85,* 741–788; Bowers, W. J., & Pierce, G. L. (1975). The illusion of deterrence in Isaac Ehrlich's research on capital punishment. *Yale Law Journal, 85,* 187–208; Passell, P. (1975). The deterrent effect of the death penalty: A statistical test. *Stanford Law Review, 28,* 61–80; Zeisel, H. (1982). Comment on the deterrent effect of capital punishment. *American Journal of Sociology, 88,* 167–169.

65. Shepherd, J. M. (2004). Murders of passion, execution delays, and the deterrence of capital punishment. *Journal of Legal Studies, 33,* 283–322.

66. Dezhbakhsh, H., Rubin, P. H., & Shepherd, J. M. (2003). Does capital punishment have a deterrent effect? New evidence from post-moratorium panel data. *American Law and Economics Review, 5,* 344–376.

67. Dezhbakhsh, H., & Shepherd, J. M. (2006). The deterrent effect of capital punishment: Evidence from a judicial experiment. *Economic Inquiry, 44,* 1–24.

68. Phillips.

69. Stack, S. (1987). Publicized executions and homicide, 1950–1980. *American Sociological Review, 52,* 532–540.

70. Yang, B., & Lester, D. (2008). The deterrent effect of executions: A meta-analysis thirty years after Ehrlich. *Journal of Criminal Justice, 36,* 453–460.

71. Cheatwood, D. (2002). Capital punishment for the crime of homicide in Chicago: 1870–1930. *Journal of Criminal Law and Criminology, 92,* 843–866.

72. Levitt, S. D. (2004). Understanding why crime fell in the 1990s: Four factors that explain the decline and six that do not. *Journal of Economic Perspectives, 18,* 163–190.

73. Katz, L., Levitt, S. D., & Shustorovich, E. (2003). Prison conditions, capital punishment, and deterrence. *American Law and Economics Review, 5,* 318–343.

74. Kant's ethical system appeared in *Foundation for the Metaphysic of Morals* in 1785. An excellent primer on justice and desert, including Kant's work, is Pojman, L. P., & McLeod, O. (1999). *What do we deserve? A reader on justice and desert.* New York: Oxford University Press.

75. Simon, R. J., & Blaskovich, D. A. (2002). *A comparative analysis of capital punishment: Statutes, policies, frequencies, and public attitudes the world over.* Lanham, MD: Lexington Books.

76. Johnson, S. L. (2000). The Bible and the death penalty: Implications for criminal justice education. *Journal of Criminal Justice Education, 11,* 15–34.

77. Ellsworth, P. C., & Gross, S. R. (1994). Hardening of the attitudes: Americans' views on the death penalty. *Journal of Social Issues, 50,* 19–52.

78. Davis, M. (2002). A sound retributive argument for the death penalty. *Criminal Justice Ethics, 21,* 22–26.

79. For studies of the correlates and predictors of retributive beliefs, see Bohm, R. M. (1992). Retribution and capital punishment: Toward a better understanding of death penalty opinion. *Journal of Criminal Justice, 20,* 227–236; Cullen, F. T., Fisher, B., & Applegate, B. K. (2000). Public opinion about punishment and corrections. *Crime & Justice, 27,* 1–79; Finckenauer, J. O. (1988). Public support for the death penalty: Retribution as just deserts or retribution as revenge? *Justice Quarterly, 5,* 81–100; Lotz, R., & Regoli, R. M. (1980). Public support for the death penalty. *Criminal Justice Review, 5,* 55–66; Schadt, A. M., & DeLisi, M. (2007). Is vigilantism on your mind? An exploratory study of nuance and contradiction in student death penalty opinion. *Criminal Justice Studies, 20,* 255–268; Unnever, J. D., & Cullen, F. T. (2005). Executing the innocent and support for capital punishment: Implications for public policy. *Criminology & Public Policy, 4,* 3–38; Barkan, S. E., & Cohn, S. F. (2005). On reducing white support for the death penalty: A pessimistic appraisal. *Criminology & Public Policy, 4,* 39–44.

80. Several criminologists and commentators have written about the moral underpinnings of criminal justice. For a sampling of these works, see Berns, W. (1979). *For capital punishment: Crime and the morality of the death penalty*. Lanham, MD: University Press of America; Murphy, J. G. (2003). *Getting even: Forgiveness and its limits*. New York: Oxford University Press; Rosenbaum, T. (2005). *The myth of moral justice: Why our legal system fails to do what's right*. New York: HarperCollins; Wilson, J. Q. (1993). *The moral sense*. New York: The Free Press.

81. Berns.

82. Longmire, D. R. (2000). Race, ethnicity, and the penalty of death: The American experience. *Corrections Management Quarterly, 4,* 36–43.

83. Schaefer, K. D., Hennessy, J. J., & Ponterotto, J. G. (1999). Race as a variable in imposing and carrying out the death penalty in the U.S. *Journal of Offender Rehabilitation, 30,* 35–45.

84. Baldus, D. C., Pulaski, C., & Woodworth, G. (1983). Comparative review of death sentences: An empirical study of the Georgia experience. *Journal of Criminal Law and Criminology, 74,* 661–753; also see Baldus, D. C., Woodworth, G., & Pulaski, C. A. (1990). *Equal justice and the death penalty: A legal and empirical analysis*. Boston: Northeastern University Press; Baldus, D. C., Woodworth, G., Zuckerman, D., Weiner, N. A., & Broffitt, B. (1998). Racial discrimination and the death penalty in the post-Furman era: An empirical and legal overview, with recent findings from Philadelphia. *Cornell Law Review, 83,* 1638–1770. Earlier, Baldus conducted an analysis of the findings of Thorsten Sellin and Isaac Ehrlich in which he curiously found that Sellin's work was more methodologically sound and credible than Ehrlich's. See Baldus, D. C., & Cole, J. W. L. (1976). A comparison of the work of Thorsten Sellin and Isaac Ehrlich on the deterrent effect of capital punishment. *Yale Law Review, 85,* 170–186.

85. *McClesky v. Kemp,* 481 U. S. 279 (1987).

86. Radelet, M. L. (1981). Racial characteristics and the imposition of the death penalty. *American Sociological Review, 46,* 918–927.

87. Kleck, G. (1981). Racial discrimination in criminal sentencing: A critical evaluation of the evidence with additional evidence on the death penalty. *American Sociological Review, 46,* 783–805.

88. Berk, R., Li, A., & Hickman, L. J. (2005). Statistical difficulties in determining the role of race in capital cases: A re-analysis of data from the state of Maryland. *Journal of Quantitative Criminology, 21,* 365–390.

89. *Kansas v. Hendricks,* 521 U. S. 346 (1997).

90. Entire special issues on sexually violent offenders, their control, and civil commitment occasionally appeared in academic journals, including *Behavioral Sciences and the Law* and *Psychology, Public Policy & Law*. For examples of this research, see Becker, J. V., Stinson, J., Tromp, S., & Messer, G. (2003). Characteristics of individuals petitioned for civil commitment. *International Journal of Offender Therapy & Comparative Criminology, 47,* 185–195; Erickson, P. E. (2002). The legal standard of volitional impairment: An analysis of substantive due process and the United States Supreme Court's decision in *Kansas v. Hendricks*. *Journal of Criminal Justice, 30,* 1–10; Janus, E. S. (2000). Sexual predator commitment laws: Lessons for law and the behavioral sciences. *Behavioral Sciences & the Law, 18,* 5–21; Simon, J. (1998). Managing the monstrous: Sex offenders and the new penology. *Psychology, Public Policy & Law, 4,* 452–467.

91. Levenson, J. L. (2004). Sexual predator civil commitment: A comparison of selected and released offenders. *International Journal of Offender Therapy and Comparative Criminology, 48,* 638–648.

92. Levenson, J. S., & Morin, J. W. (2006). Factors predicting selection of sexually violent predators for civil commitment. *International Journal of Offender Therapy and Comparative Criminology, 50,* 609–629.

93. Jackson, R. L., & Richards, H. J. (2007). Diagnostic and risk profiles among civilly committed sex offenders in Washington state. *International Journal of Offender Therapy and Comparative Criminology, 51,* 313–323.

94. Weslander, E. (2005). *Notorious sex offender is moving to Lawrence*. Retrieved April 2, 2008, from http://www2.ljworld.com/news/2005/apr/01/notorious_sex_offender/.

95. Lucken, K., & Bales, W. (2008). Florida's sexually violent predator program: An examination of risk and civil commitment eligibility. *Crime & Delinquency, 54,* 95–127.

96. Carlsmith, K. M., Monahan, J., & Evans, A. (2007). The function of punishment in the "civil" commitment of sexually violent predators. *Behavioral Sciences and the Law, 25,* 437–448.

GLOSSARY

abeyance Suspended charges until the defendant successfully completes the treatment protocol that was originally ordered.

abscond To violate the conditions of a sentence of escaping or failing to report.

Access to Recovery A program within the Substance Abuse and Mental Health Services Administration that provides people seeking drug and alcohol treatment with vouchers to pay for a range of community services.

active participant model A situation in which the offender takes part in the decision-making process when examining the risks, needs, and community factors that affect his or her involvement in crime and then uses this information to strategically address personal criminogenic needs.

actuarial assessment Tools that are offender classification and assessment instruments based on standardized, objective criteria that are used to distinguish the criminal population to determine the most appropriate treatment and punishment modalities.

actuarial prediction instruments Method that uses behavioral and social indicators on an offender's record to inform decisions about correctional placement.

adjudicated To be found guilty in juvenile court.

adjudicatory hearing Juvenile trial.

administrative control model Inmate behavior approach that points to prison officials, administrators, and governance generally as the most important determinants of inmate behavior.

administrative institutions Federal prison facilities with special missions.

Administrative-Maximum United States Penitentiary Prison in Florence, Colorado, that houses the most dangerous and notorious prisoners in the federal system.

Adult Internal Management System (AIMS) Classification system that relies on two instruments to identify inmates who are likely to pose a risk to the safe and secure operation of the facility.

aftercare Community follow-up component of treatment in third-generation boot camps (aftercare is also used to describe parole in the juvenile justice system). (Chapter 7)

aftercare Juvenile parole. (Chapter 13)

aggravating circumstances Characteristics that make the crime seem worse in totality and thus deserving of death as the only appropriate punishment.

aggravating factors Circumstances that seem to increase the culpability of the offenders.

Alderson First women's federal prison, founded in 1927.

American Correctional Association (ACA) The oldest professional association developed by and devoted to the correctional profession.

American Probation and Parole Association The official professional organization for probation and parole officers.

argot The prisoner language.

Aryan Brotherhood A White prison gang.

Ashurst-Sumners Act Law that authorized federal prosecution of violations of state laws enacted pursuant to the Hawes-Cooper Act, and subsequent amendments to this law in 1940 strengthened federal enforcement authority by making any transport of prison-made goods in interstate commerce a federal criminal offense.

Atkins v. Virginia Supreme Court case that held that executing mentally retarded persons *did* constitute cruel and unusual punishment and was a violation of the Eighth Amendment consistent with the evolving standards of decency.

Auburn system Response to the Pennsylvania system; used congregate inmate organization.

Augustus, John Founder of probation in the United States.

automated probation A form of unsupervised probation that entails no supervision, services, or personal contacts.

automatic appellate review Automatic review of death sentences established by *Gregg v. Georgia.*

automatic parole The immediate granting of parole to low-risk offenders even though they were sentenced to prison by the courts.

bail A form of pretrial release in which a defendant enters a legal agreement or promise that requires his or her appearance in court.

Bail Reform Act of 1966 Legislation that authorized the use of releasing defendants on their own recognizance in noncapital federal cases when appearance in court can be shown to be likely.

Bail Reform Act of 1984 Legislation that reinforced the community ties clause of the Bail Reform Act of 1966 but also provided for the preventive detention of defendants deemed dangerous or likely to abscond.

bail revocation If a defendant does not comply with the conditions of bail, the court can withdraw the defendant's previously granted release.

balancing test Prisoners retain their First Amendment rights while incarcerated unless those rights are inconsistent with their status as prisoner or inconsistent with the legitimate penological goals of the institution.

banishment Penalty in which wrongdoers were excommunicated or excluded from the community entirely.

banked probation A form of unsupervised probation that entails no supervision, services, or personal contacts.

Baze v. Rees Case in which the Supreme Court held that lethal injection does not constitute cruel and unusual punishment and is therefore constitutional.

Bazelon Center for Mental Health Law The nation's leading advocate for children, adolescents, and adults with mental disabilities.

Bazelon, David Federal appeals judge whose rulings pioneered the field of mental health law.

Bearden v. Georgia Supreme Court decision that held that for crimes that are punishable by imprisonment, judges must first consider whether the defendant could pay fines on an installment basis or use another community-based sanction before being detained for nonpayment of fines.

Beccaria, Cesare Philosopher who wrote *On Crimes and Punishments,* which liberalized criminal justice.

bifurcated trials Trials in which there are separate deliberations for the guilt and penalty phases of the case.

Bill of Rights The first 10 amendments to the United States Constitution.

binding over for good behavior An early form of community release that sometimes took the form of a pardon and other times that of a suspended sentence.

Black Guerilla Family (BGF) An African American prison gang.

blended sentencing Method by which juvenile courts combine juvenile and adult punishment that is tailored to the needs of the individual offender.

Blueprints for Violence Prevention program A national violence prevention initiative that identifies programs that meet the most scientifically rigorous standards of program effectiveness.

Board of Pardons v. Allen Supreme Court case that held that any statute that mandates parole creates a presumption that the parole release will be granted.

bond A pledge of money or some other assets offered as bail by an accused person or his or her surety (bail bondsman) to secure temporary release from custody.

bondsperson A social service professional who is contractually responsible for a criminal defendant once the defendant is released from custody.

boot camps/shock incarceration Short-term incarceration programs that incorporate the strict discipline, hard labor, and physical training of military basic training followed by an aftercare program that contains conditions and treatment.

bounty hunter A person hired by bondspersons to enforce the conditions of bail and recover the investment asset of the bondsperson.

Breed v. Jones Court case that ruled that juveniles could not be waived to criminal court following adjudication in juvenile court because it violated the double jeopardy clause of the Fifth Amendment.

brutalization The increase in violent crime, specifically homicide, in the wake of an execution.

Bureau of Prisons (BOP) The federal prison system.

capital punishment The use of death as a criminal punishment.

caseload The roster of probationary clients that a single probation officer supervises.

casework style Parole officer style that refers to counseling, advising, and assisting parolees with their problems.

cash-only bonds Bond in which the defendant must post 100 percent of the bond in cash to be released.

Child Savers Progressive social movement that put juveniles in houses of refuge.

civil commitment The institutionalization of persons likely to engage in predatory acts of criminal violence brought on by mental abnormality or personality disorders.

civil death The loss of legal and civic rights after criminal conviction.

Client Management Classification (CMC) System System designed to identify the level of supervision needed for individual correctional clients, their service needs, and the resources required to meet those needs.

clinical assessment Decision making based on the experience, education, training, and gut feeling of correctional staff.

clinical predictions Correctional assessments based on expert opinion.

close custody *See* maximum security.

close-security prisons Another name for maximum-security state prisons.

Code of Hammurabi Ancient body of laws during the reign of the Babylonian King Hammurabi in 1780 BCE.

coercive mobility The dual processes of mass incarceration and reentry that disrupt the social networks of disadvantaged communities and lead to increased social problems.

Coker v. Georgia Supreme Court case that invalidated rape as a capital offense.

collateral consequences of imprisonment The assorted societal issues that are impacted by the incarceration and return of prisoners.

collective incapacitation Criminals are prevented from committing crime because they are incarcerated.

Commission on Law Enforcement and the Administration of Justice Part of President Johnson's 1965 war on crime, which created youth bureaus to divert juvenile offenders from confinement to community organizations.

committed Status of a juvenile who has received a prison sentence.

Common Law The customary criminal justice and legal traditions or doctrines that the United States inherited from England.

community corrections Sanctions that allow criminal offenders to remain in the community as long as they abide by certain conditions, such as maintaining employment, participating in drug treatment, or undergoing psychological treatment.

community courts Specialized courts that address community problems in addition to prosecuting offenders.

community probation An extension of the community policing approach to crime control where community residents and organizations work with criminal justice officials to address neighborhood disorder and related problems.

community service A form of restitution that involves civic participation toward the improvement of the community.

commute The reduction of a criminal sentence, such as death to life imprisonment.

Comprehensive Strategy for Serious, Violent, and Chronic Juvenile Offenders A research-based framework of strategic responses to help local and state juvenile justice systems respond to delinquency.

concentrated disadvantage Neighborhoods with extreme poverty, racial segregation, and high crime rates.

conditions The terms that the defendant must abide by to remain in compliance with the court.

consensual model A mix of the control and responsibility models characterized by relaxed control of staff routines but fairly rigid control of inmate routines.

consent decree Court order for correctional officials to improve prison conditions.

continuum of sanctions A range of sanctions or legal penalties that balance punishment, treatment, and supervision concerns with the seriousness of the offense and the offender's criminal convictions.

contraband Materials prohibited in correctional facilities, such as weapons, drugs, and cell phones.

control model Inmate behavior model that asserts that highly rigid control of every aspect of inmate life and staff routines is required to ensure safe prison environments.

convicts Offenders sentenced to prison.

Cooper v. Pate Case that resulted in a ruling that inmates were permitted to practice their religion provided that the following three basic conditions were met: (1) the religion must be an established religion (not contrived by the inmate); (2) the inmate's religious practices must conform to the tenets of the religion; and (3) the religious practices cannot pose a security risk or disrupt prison operations.

corporal punishment Sanctions that inflict physical pain on the offender.

corrections The collection of local, state, and federal agencies that supervise and treat criminal defendants.

cosigned recognizance bond A bond on which a family member, close friend, or business associate signs his or her name to guarantee the defendant's appearance in court.

courts A major component of the criminal justice system comprised of prosecutors, defense counsel, and judges that perform a variety of functions, foremost of which is to serve as a check and balance on the police.

Craig v. Boren Supreme Court case that ruled that classifications by gender must serve important governmental objectives and must be substantially related to achievement of those objectives.

criminal history An offender's prior arrests and convictions, which are used for sentencing decisions.

criminal parole violations New criminal offenses committed while an offender is on parole.

criminality The propensity towards antisocial behavior that a defendant embodies.

criminogenic Something that is correlated to crime or contributes to criminal behavior.

Crofton, Sir Walter Disciple of Maconochie who employed similar reforms in Irish prisons.

curfew enforcement Policies that limit the opportunities youths have to engage in delinquency.

cycle of violence Common profile of female offenders in which physical abuse, sexual abuse, and neglect incurred during childhood dramatically increase the risks for delinquency and a host of maladaptive behaviors during adolescence and adulthood.

danger risk The level of danger that the defendant poses toward himself or herself, the specific victim in the current case, or society at large.

day fines Used in Europe, a method of setting variable fine amounts that are punitive and address the economic differences among offenders.

day reporting Sanction that requires defendants to report to an official criminal justice facility, such as a jail, on a daily basis to check in and demonstrate to correctional staff that they are complying with the conditions of their current legal status.

day reporting centers Facilities that provide an assortment of services, such as substance abuse treatment, cognitive restructuring, anger management classes, batterer education classes, parenting skills education, mental health treatment, and others designed to reduce antisocial attitudes and behaviors that lead to crime.

decertification The undoing of a waived case.

decertification process The official process where a prison gang member repudiates his or her membership and provides intelligence to correctional officials.

defendant The person accused of a criminal violation.

deferred judgment *See* deferred prosecution.

deferred prosecution Widely used and cost-effective ways for the courts to control the correctional population by diverting first-time offenders or persons who have never been contacted for violent crimes.

deferred prosecution, judgment, or sentence A sentence whereby the defendant pleads guilty in exchange for a suspended sentence that will be voided and expunged if the defendant complies with certain conditions.

deferred sentences *See* deferred prosecution.

deliberate indifference Standard that affirms that the conditions at a prison are not unconstitutional unless it can be shown that prison administrators show deliberate indifference to the quality of life in prisons and inmates' most basic needs.

delinquency petition Juvenile filing of charges.

delinquent *See* juvenile delinquent.

delinquent offenses Violations of criminal law.

demand waiver Type of waiver into criminal court that occurs when a delinquent chooses criminal prosecution.

departure The judge's act of going outside the sentencing guidelines when imposing a sentence.

deposit bail system System in which the court acts as bondsperson and the defendant posts a percentage of the total bond.

deprivation model Inmate behavior model that proposes that inmate behavior is primarily a function of the oppressive structural features posed by the prison facility itself.

design capacity The number of inmates that planners intended for the facility.

detained Status of a juvenile in jail confinement while awaiting court proceedings.

determinate sentencing Sometimes known as flat or straight sentencing, where a specific term is imposed upon conviction.

deterrence The punishment philosophy that rests on the idea that people are rational thinkers endowed with free will who weigh the costs and benefits of each course of action in their lives and then choose to act.

direct sentence *See* automatic parole.

direct supervision Supervision design where inmates mix in a central common room and are continuously supervised by staff.

discretion The latitude to choose one course of action or another.

discretionary parole Release that occurs when parole boards have the discretionary authority to conditionally release prisoners based on a statutory or administrative determination of eligibility.

disintegrative shaming Type of shaming that stigmatizes both the offender and his or her crimes and serves to ostracize criminals from society.

disposition Juvenile sentence.

diversion Any procedure that prevents official entry into the criminal justice process.

draconian Tough criminal justice policies.

drug courts Specialized criminal courts that link supervision, judicial oversight, and treatment for drug-using criminal offenders.

due process Laws and criminal procedures that are reasonable and applied in a fair and equal manner.

DWI courts Specialized courts that target drunk driving offenders using the drug court model.

earned discharge parole Type of parole in which parolees receive a reduction in their sentence upon completion of prosocial activities, such as completing drug treatment, work, or educational programs.

Eddings v. Oklahoma Court ruling that established that age is a mitigating factor in capital sentencing.

Eighth Amendment Amendment to the Bill of Rights of the United States Constitution that states that "excessive bail shall not be required, nor excessive fines imposed, nor cruel and unusual punishments inflicted."

elect to serve Option to choose prison over a probation sentence.

electronic monitoring (EM) The use of surveillance technology to monitor offenders in the community. *Also see* home detention and house arrest.

Estelle v. Gamble Case in which the Court held that deliberate indifference to a prisoner's serious medical needs constituted cruel and unusual punishment.

Ex parte Hull Case that loosened the hands-off doctrine that characterized American corrections.

Ex parte United States Supreme Court case that held that federal courts had no power to suspend criminal sentences and suggested probation legislation as a remedy.

expiation Based upon the belief that crime arouses the anger of the gods against the entire community, and the only way to reduce the anger is to destroy the offender.

expungement The complete removal of a criminal record from existence.

extralegal variables Factors that influence criminal justice discretion but are not legally relevant, such as demographic characteristics.

faith-based programs Programs that use religious instruction and prayer to reduce problem behaviors.

false-negative Label applied to serious offenders who were predicted to be nonserious offenders.

false-positive Label applied to nonserious offenders who were predicted to be serious offenders.

family courts Specialized courts that handle legal matters pertaining to children and families.

Federal Bureau of Prisons (BOP) The prison component of the federal system.

federal correctional complexes Clusters of BOP facilities located within close proximity to each other.

federal correctional institutions Another name for low-security institutions.

Federal Pretrial Services Act of 1982 Legislation that established pretrial services for defendants in the United States district courts.

federal prison camps Another name for minimum-security institutions.

Federal Prison Industries Federal prison labor program founded in 1934.

federal probation Probation for offenders convicted of federal crimes.

felon disenfranchisement The denial of voting rights of persons with various criminal justice system statuses.

felony murder The commission of a homicide in conjunction with some other serious felony offense, such as kidnapping, rape, armed robbery, child molestation, or additional homicides.

field or home visits Searches of probation clients' place of work or homes to determine their compliance with supervision.

Fifth Amendment Constitutional amendment that states that no person shall be held to answer for a capital, or otherwise infamous crime, unless on a presentment or indictment of a grand jury, except in cases arising in the land or naval forces, or in the militia, when in actual service in time of war or public danger; nor shall any person be subject for the same offense to be twice put in jeopardy of life or limb; nor shall be compelled in any criminal case to be a witness against himself, nor be deprived of life, liberty, or property, without due process of law; nor shall private property be taken for public use, without just compensation.

fines Monetary payments imposed on criminal offenders as a way to repay society for the offenders' violations of the law.

First Amendment Constitutional amendment that states that Congress shall make no law respecting an establishment of religion, or prohibiting the free exercise thereof; or abridging the freedom of speech, or of the press; or the right of the people peaceably to assemble, and to petition the government for a redress of grievances.

first-generation boot camps Boot camps that stressed military discipline, physical training, and hard work.

fixed-fine system *See* tariff system.

flight risk Likelihood that a released offender will abscond or miss a court appearance.

Ford v. Wainwright Case that ruled that the Eighth Amendment prohibits a state from carrying out a sentence of death upon a prisoner who is insane.

Forever Free A voluntary, 4-month intensive residential treatment program for drug-abusing women that includes an aftercare component.

forfeiture The loss of ownership of some property or asset for its illegal use.

formal social control Official, administrative control policies.

Fourteenth Amendment Constitutional amendment that states in Section 1: All persons born or naturalized in the United States, and subject to the jurisdiction thereof, are citizens of the United States and of the state wherein they reside. No state shall make or enforce any law which shall abridge the privileges or immunities of citizens of the United States; nor shall any state deprive any person of life, liberty, or property, without due process of law; nor deny to any person within its jurisdiction the equal protection of the laws.

Fourth Amendment Constitutional amendment that states that the right of the people to be secure in their persons, houses, papers, and effects, against unreasonable searches and seizures, shall not be violated, and no warrants shall issue, but upon probable cause, supported by oath or affirmation, and particularly describing the place to be searched, and the persons or things to be seized.

Furman v. Georgia Supreme Court case that established that capital punishment is cruel and unusual and violates the Eighth Amendment.

Gagnon v. Scarpelli Supreme Court case that held that probationers are entitled to due process for preliminary and final hearings before probation can be revoked.

gendered pathways Gender-specific ways that offending is related to women's social and economic marginality.

gender-responsive strategies Treatments that address the unique needs of female offenders.

general deterrence The large number of potential criminals who might be discouraged from committing crime because of the punishments received by others.

good time Time spent in prison without major disciplinary incidents.

Greenholtz v. Inmates Supreme Court case that held that the decision to grant parole is a subjective, potential outcome—it is not guaranteed.

Gregg v. Georgia Supreme Court case that held that the new death penalty statutes in Florida, Georgia, and Texas were constitutional, and that the death penalty itself was constitutional under the Eighth Amendment.

Griffin v. Wisconsin Supreme Court case that held that parolees can be searched based upon reasonable suspicion of the officer. (Chapter 11)

Griffin v. Wisconsin Supreme Court case that held that warrantless searches of probationer's home by probation officers is reasonable under the Fourth Amendment. (Chapter 8)

guiding principle 1 (gender) Gender-responsive strategy that promotes acknowledging that gender makes a difference.

guiding principle 2 (environment) Gender-responsive strategy that suggests creating an environment based on safety, respect, and dignity.

guiding principle 3 (relationships) Gender-responsive strategy that suggests developing policies, practices, and programs that are relational and promotes healthy connections to children, family, significant others, and the community.

guiding principle 4 (services and supervision) Gender-responsive strategy that promotes addressing substance abuse, trauma, and mental health issues through comprehensive, integrated, and culturally relevant services and appropriate supervision.

guiding principle 5 (socioeconomic status) Gender-responsive strategy that recommends providing women with opportunities to improve their socioeconomic conditions.

guiding principle 6 (community) Gender-responsive strategy that suggests establishing a system of community supervision and reentry with comprehensive, collaborative services.

Gurney Fry, Elizabeth Quaker who was instrumental in spearheading the humane and dignified treatment of female offenders.

habeas corpus The legal doctrine that grants correctional clients access to the courts to challenge the legality of their sentences.

halfway houses/residential treatment Describes the confinement status of a criminal defendant who is partially confined and partially integrated into the community.

hands-off doctrine Little judicial oversight of the practices and operations of prisons and other sanctions, which were largely shut off from the press and academia.

Hawes-Cooper Act Enabled states to implement laws regarding the acceptance or prohibition of prison-made goods coming within its borders.

High risk Security level that applies to costly inmates, including highly aggressive prisoners, sexual predators, gang members, mentally ill inmates, and prisoners with severe medical problems and related special needs.

high-security institutions Federal prisons with highly-secured perimeters featuring walls or reinforced fences, multiple and single occupancy cell housing, the highest staff-to-inmate ratio, and close control of inmate movements.

Hill, Matthew Davenport Founder of probation in England.

Historical, Clinical, and Risk Scales (HCR-20) A pop-ular violence risk assessment tool.

home detention, house arrest, and electronic monitoring Community corrections that permit offenders to serve sentences in their homes while maintaining employment and community ties.

home incarceration programs Programs that allow criminal defendants to remain in the community so that they can continue working, fulfilling family responsibilities, and participating in treatment.

Homeboy Industries Organization that provides free services and work opportunities for former offenders.

hostageship Situation in which a person volunteers to be prosecuted and punished in the place of the actual suspect in the event that the suspect fails to appear for court proceedings.

house arrest A sanction where the offender must not leave his or her home with the exception of court-approved times for work and treatment also see home detention and electronic monitoring. *Also see* home detention and electronic monitoring.

Howard, John English sheriff who caused reforms of English jails and prisons.

Hudson v. Palmer Court case in which the Court ruled that inmates do not have a reasonable expectation of privacy.

importation model Argued that prisoner behavior and the conditions of prisons were mostly a function of the characteristics, values, beliefs, and behaviors that criminals employed on the outside of prison.

in personam Forfeiture in which the criminal defendant whose property is the target of the forfeiture can only occur after criminal conviction.

In re Gault Case that established a juvenile's right to notice of charges, right to counsel, right to question, confront, and cross-examine witnesses, and the right of privilege against self-incrimination.

In re Winshop Court case that established that in delinquency matters, the state must prove its case beyond a reasonable doubt.

in rem Civil forfeiture that targets property; it does not require formal adversarial proceedings and adjudication of guilt.

incapacitation The inability to act; refers to the use of imprisonment to preclude the ability of an offender to victimize members of society.

indigent Poor defendants.

Industrial Prison Era Time that spanned approximately 1900–1935 during which an emphasis was placed on inmate labor and commerce.

informal social control Unofficial sanctions that arise from informal family and friendship networks. (Chapter 2)

informal social control Ways that inmates and correctional staff tacitly coexist to maintain institutional safety. (Chapter 10)

inmate (or prisoner) A defendant who has been sentenced to jail or prison.

inmate code The subculture that governs inmate behavior and social systems that exist in various prison facilities.

Innocence Commission Commission that monitors, investigates, and addresses errors in the criminal justice system.

Innocence Project A nonprofit legal clinic that handles cases in which postconviction DNA testing of evidence can yield conclusive proof of innocence.

institutional corrections Confinement or the physical removal from society as a means of supervision.

integrated/multilevel model Explanation of inmate behavior that uses both inmate and facility variables.

intensive supervised probation (ISP) The most highly restrictive form of punishment that is designed to supervise criminal offenders who embody the most risk factors for continued involvement in crime.

interdependency The extent to which individuals participate in networks where they are dependent on others and others in turn are dependent on them.

intermediate sanctions Any form of correctional supervision that falls between the most lenient types of punishment, such as diversion and unsupervised probation, and the most severe types of punishment, such as prison confinement.

internal management system System used to determine how prisoners should be housed within a particular facility or complex based upon varying levels of aggressiveness and vulnerability that are measured using a questionnaire.

jail A local correctional facility usually operated by a county sheriff's department and used for the short-term confinement of petty offenders, misdemeanants, persons convicted of low-level felonies, and persons awaiting transport to some other criminal justice or social service agency.

Johnson v. Avery Court case in which the Court ruled that access to courts to present legal complaints cannot be denied or obstructed.

Jones v. Cunningham Supreme Court case that held that parolees are considered in custody and can invoke the habeas corpus statute to challenge their sentence.

judicial waiver Transfer of a case to criminal court by a judge based on the severity of the charges and/or the severity of the youth's delinquent record.

just deserts The philosophy of justice that assumes that individuals freely choose to violate criminal laws and therefore the state or criminal justice system has the legal and moral right and duty to punish them according to the nature of their acts.

juvenile conference committee Panel of six to nine volunteers from the community who meet monthly to hear juvenile complaints referred by the family court.

juvenile court Court with original jurisdiction over minors.

juvenile delinquent Minor found guilty of a crime.

Juvenile Justice and Delinquency Prevention Act of 1974 Act that provides federal funding to states and communities for prevention and treatment programs especially diversion programs that deinstitutionalize adolescents convicted of status offenses.

juvenile justice system The set of agencies that process persons under the age of 18 for violations of the law.

juvenile probation The oldest and most widely used way to provide court-ordered services in the juvenile justice system.

Kansas v. Hendricks Supreme Court case that upheld civil commitment.

Kent v. United States Court case that established that essentials of due process must apply to waivers.

La Nuestra Familia A Hispanic prison gang.

labeling theory A school of thought that asserts that defining people as delinquent or criminal leads to social ostracism, solidifies a delinquent self-image, and leads to increased antisocial behavior.

Law of the Twelve Tables A comprehensive and codified legal code to replace the oral, informal, and largely unfair prior tradition.

legal variables Legally relevant factors, such as offense severity, prior criminal record, and number of charges.

legislative waiver Type of waiver into criminal court that occurs because certain offenses are statutorily excluded from prosecution in juvenile court and require adult prosecution.

lethal injection The intravenous administering of three drugs to cause death.

Level of Service Inventory-Revised (LSI-R) The most widely used actuarial tool in corrections.

Lewis v. Casey Court case in which the Court ruled that prisoners who claim that they have been denied access to the courts and that the prisons failed to comply with *Bounds v. Smith* must show that their rights were prejudiced as a result of the denial of these rights in order to recover in a Section 1983 suit.

lex talionis The law of retaliation such that punishment must be inflicted with an eye for an eye and a tooth for a tooth.

Lifestyle Criminality Screening Form (LCSF) Actuarial instrument that measures the criminal lifestyle.

linear supervision Traditional jail design with long rows of individual cells.

low-security institutions Federal prisons with double-fenced perimeters, mostly dormitory or cubicle housing, and strong work and program components. The staff-to-inmate ratio is higher in these institutions compared to minimum-security facilities.

Maconochie, Alexander Administrator of Norfolk Island (Australia) penal colony who devised the mark system and other innovations that influenced American penology.

Magna Carta Codified set of laws from England in 1215 that was the forerunner of the United States Constitution with its dual goals of cautiously empowering the state and granting rights and protections to the public.

mala in se Acts that are intrinsically wrong and violations of natural law.

mala prohibita Offenses are crimes made illegal by legislation, not by natural law.

mandatory parole Type of parole that occurs in jurisdictions using determinate sentencing statutes where inmates are conditionally released from prison after serving a portion of their original sentences minus any good time.

Manhattan Bail Project Project that used community ties rather than ability to pay to determine pretrial release.

mark system System devised by Maconochie in which credits (marks) against a sentence allowed inmates to be released once they earned the required number of marks through good behavior.

Martinez v. California Supreme Court case that held that parole boards have absolute immunity from litigation stemming from third-party accusations of negligence.

Mathews v. Eldridge Supreme Court case that specified due process considerations of probation supervision.

Maximizing Opportunities for Mothers to Succeed (MOMS) A gender-responsive program that promotes the healthy development of children by increasing the capacity of their incarcerated mothers for self-sufficiency, increasing parenting skills with an emphasis on successful parent-child bonding, and reducing recidivism among incarcerated pregnant women and incarcerated mothers of young children.

maximum-security Security level for inmates who engage in misconduct and are subject to the strictest supervision and control with fewer treatment amenities.

maximum-security state prisons Prisons that house the highest risk prisoners in terms of their sentence, institutional adjustment, criminal history, and other factors.

McClesky v. Kemp Supreme Court case that held that although Black defendants received the death penalty more often than Whites, especially when the victim was White, this was not sufficient to demonstrate that racial considerations enter into capital sentencing determinations.

McKeiver v. Pennsylvania Court case that established that jury trials are not constitutionally required in juvenile court hearings.

medium-security Security level for inmates who require more supervision than minimum-security inmates but still have work and programming opportunities.

medium-security institutions Federal prisons with strengthened perimeters, usually double fences with electronic detection systems, mostly cell-type housing, a wide variety of work and treatment programs, higher staff-to-inmate ratios, and overall greater internal controls.

medium-security state prisons Prisons that house medium- or moderate-security inmates in terms of their sentence, institutional adjustment, criminal history, and other factors.

mental health courts Specialty criminal courts that address the special needs of defendants with mental illnesses.

Mentoring Children of Prisoners Program A program within the Department of Health and Human Services that awards competitive grants to eligible organizations supporting mentoring programs for children with incarcerated parents.

meta-analysis Quantitative study of research findings.

Mexican Mafia A Hispanic prison gang.

minimum-security Security level of inmates who require little supervision and are afforded considerable work and living opportunities in confinement.

minimum-security institutions Federal prisons that have dormitory housing, low staff-to-inmate ratios, and little to no perimeter fencing.

minimum-security state prisons Prisons that house the lowest security inmates in terms of their sentence, institutional adjustment, criminal history, and other factors.

Minnesota v. Murphy A 1984 Supreme Court decision that held that probation officers are not obligated to provide Miranda advisement to defendants prior to interviews.

misconduct Inmate violations of prison rules and regulations.

Mistretta v. United States A 1989 Supreme Court decision that upheld the constitutionality of sentencing guidelines.

mitigating circumstances Characteristics such as youth, mental retardation, or victimization that render a crime less serious or add context that seems to reduce the overall viciousness of the behavior.

moral reconation therapy A cognitive-behavioral treatment that attempts to instill moral, prosocial thinking and decision making strategies.

Morrissey v. Brewer Supreme Court case that held that due process rights expressed in the Fourteenth Amendment establish the right of a parolee to a preliminary and final hearing before his or her parole can be revoked.

Mothers and Infants Nurturing Together (MINT) BOP community residential program for women who are pregnant at the time of commitment.

multiple-problem youth Offenders with overlapping problems relating to crime, substance use, and mental illness.

National Pretrial Reporting Program A national initiative sponsored by the Bureau of Justice Statistics, which collects detailed information about the criminal history, pretrial processing, adjudication, and sentencing of felony defendants in state courts in the 75 largest counties in the United States.

natural law The belief that the human world is organized by a positive or good natural order that should be obeyed by all humans.

net widening The growing of the correctional population by supervising increasing number of offenders in the community.

new generation jails Jails with podular design and direct supervision whereby inmates were housed in single-occupancy cells that adjoined a larger communal area.

new penology The management of groups or subpopulations of offenders based on their actuarial risk to society.

New York Mount Pleasant Female Prison First independent women's prison, founded in 1835.

nothing works Philosophy that argues that for all intents and purposes, correctional treatment is ineffective.

offense seriousness The level of legal seriousness and harm in criminal conduct that is used for sentencing decisions.

Office of Juvenile Justice and Delinquency Prevention (OJJDP) Federal agency that funded research to evaluate juvenile justice programs and disseminated research findings on the juvenile justice system.

operational capacity The number of inmates that can be accommodated based on the facility's staff, programs, and services.

pains of imprisonment Deprivations of liberty, autonomy, security, goods and services, and heterosexual relationships.

parens patriae Doctrine that asserts that the state is the ultimate guardian of children.

parole Form of correction in which the convicted person completes a prison sentence in the community rather than in confinement.

parole agency State agency that administers parole.

parole boards Administrative entities that are legally charged with the discretionary authority to conditionally release prisoners based on a statutory or administrative determination of eligibility.

parole conditions Mandated conditions that are intended to serve the treatment and supervision needs of a person on parole.

parole contract A legal document containing the terms and conditions of parole.

parole officer Agent who supervises parolees, monitors them for parole violations, and has the authority to arrest parolees for failing to comply with their sentence.

parole plan The offender's plan after release from prison in terms of proposed employment, living arrangements, and other life circumstances.

parole revocation Situation that occurs when parolees have their parole sentence terminated and are resentenced to prison.

parole violation Violation of the terms of parole.

parolee A person on parole.

Pell v. Procunier Case that established the balancing test.

penitent Feeling or expressing remorse for one's misdeeds or sins.

penitentiaries Early prison that used silence and isolation to force inmates to be penitent.

Penitentiary of New Mexico Prison that experienced the deadliest prison riot in U.S. history, which resulted in 33 inmate murders.

Pennsylvania Board of Probation and Parole v. Scott Supreme Court case that held that the costs of allowing a parolee to avoid the consequences of his or her violation are compounded by the fact that parolees are more likely to commit criminal offenses than average citizens.

Pennsylvania system Quaker-inspired system that created the penitentiary.

penologists Criminologists who study prisons.

Penry v. Lynaugh Supreme Court case that held that executing the mentally regarded was not a violation of the Eighth Amendment.

police Also known as law enforcement, the part of the criminal justice system that responds to citizen complaints, provides basic services such as traffic control, enforces the criminal law, and in doing so, initiates criminal cases.

police diversion Officer discretion to use a variety of tactics, resources, and community agencies to address the criminal behavior of defendants.

police–probation partnerships Collaborative method of juvenile corrections in which juvenile probation officers go on patrol with law enforcement officers to conduct home visits of probationers, explain the terms of the sentence to the probationers, conduct searches of probationers for drugs, weapons, and other contraband, and provide basic services.

postbooking diversion Program in which defendants are connected with appropriate services in lieu of prosecution.

posttrial or postadjudication The stage of the criminal justice system after defendants have pleaded guilty or been found guilty.

prebooking diversion Program in which law enforcement transports offenders to mental health agencies for evaluation and treatment.

precedent A decision by the appellate court (usually the Supreme Court) that serves to guide all future legal decisions that encompass a similar topic.

presentence investigation (PSI) report A report prepared for the court that summarizes the defendant's social and criminal history for the purpose of sentencing.

presumption of innocence Guideline that ensures that defendants are considered innocent until proven guilty.

pretrial service officers Staff who interview criminal defendants and gather information about the offenders' social and criminal histories.

pretrial supervision The correctional supervision of a defendant who has been arrested, booked, and bonded out of jail.

Preventing Parole Crime Program (PPCP) California initiative with programs for parolees geared toward substance abuse education, math and literary skills development, housing assistance, and other services.

prevention The provision of social resources to at-risk groups early in life to enhance their prosocial development while buffering their risk factors for crime.

prison A correctional facility used to confine persons convicted of serious crimes and serving sentences of usually more than 1 year.

prison gangs Organizations that operate within prison systems as criminal organizations consisting of a select group of inmates who have established an organized chain of command and are governed by an established code of conduct that centers on criminal activity and other forms of intimidation.

Prison Industry Enhancement Certification Program (PIECP) Program that allows inmates to work for a private employer in the community and earn the same wage as nonimprisoned workers.

Prison Rape Elimination Act Legislation that required the Bureau of Justice Statistics to conduct a comprehensive statistical review and analysis of the incidence and effects of prison rape and sexual abuse.

Prisoner Management Classification (PMC) System Classification system based on an interview to rate the inmate on 11 objective background factors that assess an inmate's social status and offense history.

Prisoner Reentry Initiative An extension of the Ready4Work program that provides services to 6,250 exprisoners annually.

prisoners Offenders sentenced to prison. *Also see* inmate.

prisonization The socialization process whereby inmates embrace the oppositional and antisocial culture of the prisoner population.

private prisons Private, for-profit businesses hired by the government to supervise lower risk inmates.

private probation Probation supervised by a private business rather than governmental agency.

probation A sanction for criminal offenders who have been sentenced to a period of correctional supervision in the community in lieu of incarceration.

Probation Act Legislation enacted in 1925 that established probation as a sentence in the federal courts and authorized the appointment of probation officers.

probation officer The practitioner who oversees and monitors a probationer's case to determine that the defendant is complying with all conditions of probation.

probation violation Act by a probationer that violates the conditions of his or her probation sentence.

probationers Persons sentenced to probation.

problem-solving courts *See* specialized courts.

Procunier v. Martinez Case whose ruling set the precedent that mail correspondence between inmates and outside parties was speech protected by the First Amendment.

Project Greenlight An intensive reentry program that is delivered during the 8 weeks immediately proceeding an offender's release from custody.

property bonds Houses, real estate, or vehicles that may be cosigned to the court as collateral against pretrial flight.

proportionality review Judicial review of criminal sentences which helps the state to identify and eliminate sentencing disparities by comparing the sentence in the case with other cases within the state.

Proposition 36 (Prop 36) California policy that diverted drug offenders by framing drug use as a public health rather than criminal justice issue.

prosecutorial waiver Type of judicial waiver into criminal court that occurs when the district attorney, county attorney, or prosecutor uses his or her discretion to prosecute a youth as an adult in criminal court.

Provo Experiment An intermediate sanction conducted from 1959 to 1965 in Utah that provided community-based, nonresidential, unstructured, group-oriented treatment unlike the traditional methods of probation.

Psychological Inventory of Criminal Thinking Styles (PICTS) Actuarial device designed to assess the eight criminal thinking styles.

psychopathic personality A personality disorder characterized by severe behavioral and interpersonal traits.

Psychopathy Checklist-Revised (PCL-R) The most widely used measure of psychopathy.

Pugh v. Locke Case that established the totality-of-conditions test.

punitive conditions Burdens placed on probationers convicted of the most serious crimes, such as residency limitations for offenders convicted of sexual offenses.

rabble Term used to describe marginalized groups found in American jails.

rated capacity The number of beds or inmates assigned by a rating official to institutions within a jurisdiction.

Ready4Work A Department of Labor program that uses faith-based and community organizations to help ex-offenders find work and escape cycles of recidivism.

recidivate (recidivism) To reoffend after release from correctional supervision.

recidivism Reoffending after release from criminal justice custody.

recidivism risk Likelihood that a released offender will continue to commit crime.

recognizance bond A written promise to appear in court in which the criminal defendant is released from jail custody without paying or posting cash or property.

reentry The process of preparing and supporting offenders incarcerated in adult prisons and juvenile correctional facilities as they complete their terms and return to society.

Reese v. United States Supreme Court case that established that bounty hunters were proxy pretrial officers who had complete control of returning absconders to the court.

reformatory Response to penitentiary movement, popularized by the reforms of Zebulon Brockway.

rehabilitation Restoration of an offender to a law-abiding lifestyle.

reintegrative shaming Type of shaming that punishes and stigmatizes the criminal act while acknowledging the fundamental decency and goodness of the offender.

relapse prevention groups Treatment programs designed to educate offenders about signs, precursors, and situations that can lead to relapses in drug abuse.

reparative probation A restorative justice concept that focuses on communication and problem solving among offenders, victims, and community residents rather than enforcement and punishment as a way to address crime.

rereleases Parolees recently imprisoned for parole violation or a new offense committed while on parole.

residency restrictions laws Laws that restrict where sex offenders can live. Restrictions range from 1,000 to 2,500 feet from places such as schools, parks, day care centers, bus stops, or other places where children congregate.

residential reentry centers (RRCs) Federal halfway houses that provide assistance to federal inmates nearing release.

residential treatment *See* halfway houses/residential treatment.

residential treatment facilities Contemporary term for halfway house.

responsibility model A more liberal, flexible inmate behavior approach where staff and inmates enjoy relative autonomy intended to facilitate self-governance.

restitution Money paid to the crime victim to recoup some of the harm caused by the offender's wrongful acts.

restoration A theory of justice that emphasizes repairing the harm caused by crime.

restorative justice An alternative justice model that seeks to repair the harm caused by delinquency by bringing together the offender, victim, and societal members to collectively resolve the issues caused by the crime.

retribution The philosophical rationale that implies the payment of a debt to society and the criminal offender's expiation or atonement for his or her crime.

reverse waiver Type of judicial waiver that occurs when a transferred case that qualifies for criminal prosecution is sent back to juvenile court to be processed.

revocation The termination of a probation sentence for noncompliance.

revocation by consent Situation that occurs when a parolee waives right to a formal revocation hearing, acknowledges responsibility for the alleged violation, and accepts a specified revocation penalty determined by the parole commission based on the specifics of the case.

Rhodes v. Chapman Case that resulted in a ruling that double celling at a prison does not constitute cruel and unusual punishment where there is no evidence that the conditions in question inflict unnecessary or wanton pain, or are disproportionate to the severity of crimes warranting imprisonment.

riots Disturbances of prison order involving multiple inmates and usually resulting in property damage and violence.

Roper v. Simmons Case in which the Supreme Court ruled that it is unconstitutional to impose the death penalty on offenders younger than 18 at the time of their capital crimes.

salient factor score An actuarial risk assessment instrument used by federal parole officials to determine parole readiness.

Scared Straight Ineffective program designed to deter juvenile delinquents from a life of crime.

Schall v. Martin Case that established that preventive pretrial detention of juveniles is allowable under certain circumstances, such as the likelihood of recidivism.

school-based probation A variation of juvenile probation in which a juvenile probation officer is housed in a school to provide direct supervision of students on probation.

second-generation boot camps Boot camps that emphasized rehabilitation by adding substance abuse treatment and prosocial skills training.

Section 1983 Part of the United States Code that covers inmate allegations and petitions for money damages or injunctive relief from their sentence.

secured bonds Bonds that require the payment of cash or other assets to the courts in exchange for release from custody.

security threat groups (STGs) An organized inmate gang that engages in predatory, criminal behavior behind bars.

selective incapacitation The use of prison to selectively target high-rate, career criminals.

sentence The penalty imposed by a court on a person convicted of a crime.

sentencing guidelines Federal guidelines designed to (1) incorporate philosophical purposes of punishment, such as deterrence, deserts, and incapacitation; (2) provide certainty and fairness in sentencing by avoiding unwarranted disparity among offenders with similar characteristics while permitting sufficient flexibility to account for relevant aggravating and mitigating circumstances; and (3) reflect knowledge of human behavior as it relates to criminal justice.

Sentencing Reform Act of 1984 Legislation that established determinate sentencing, abolished parole, and reduced the amount of good time inmates could earn.

Serious Violent Offender Reentry Initiative (SVORI) A collaborative federal initiative that addresses reentry outcomes in the areas of criminal justice, employment, education, health, and housing.

sex offender probation A specialized unit within a probation office in which practitioners exclusively supervise offenders convicted of sexually based offenses.

Sex Offender Risk Appraisal Guide (SORAG) An actuarial tool that assesses violence and sexual violence among male offenders.

sex offenders Persons who commit sexually based offenses, such as rape, child molestation, incest, and related offenses.

shaming All processes of expressing disapproval that have the intention or effect of invoking remorse in the person being shamed and/or condemnation by others who become aware of the shaming.

shock incarceration *See* boot camps/shock incarceration.

SHU syndrome Condition characterized by inmate thought disturbances, perceptual changes, thought, concentration, and memory difficulties, extreme anxiety, and other symptoms of mental illness that appear to be produced by the sensory deprivations of solitary confinement in SHU or supermax units.

Silverlake Experiment Experiment conducted between 1964 and 1968 in Los Angeles, which found youths who received community treatment did not pose any added risk to public safety compared to traditional sentences such as probation and detention.

snitches Inmate informants.

sober living houses Drug- and alcohol-free residences for paroled offenders who want to maintain their sobriety.

solitary confinement Isolation in one's cell for the purpose of contemplation, prayer, and penitence to reform prisoners.

special management *See* high risk.

specialized courts Courts that attempt to remedy the problems associated with criminal behavior using social services in conjunction with the justice system and not relying exclusively on punishment.

specific deterrence The individual offender being sentenced and punished.

split sentence Sentence that includes both incarceration and probation.

stake in conformity An offender's commitment to conventional, prosocial behaviors and responsibilities.

standard conditions Universal mandates that apply to all probationers.

Stanford v. Kentucky Court case that established that juveniles age 16 or 17 are eligible for the death penalty.

status offenses Violations of criminal law that only apply to children and adolescents.

structured fines Used in the United States, fines designed to be proportionate to the seriousness of the offense while having similar economic impact on offenders with differing financial resources.

Substance Abuse and Mental Health Services Administration (SAMHSA) A public health agency within the Department of Health and Human Services responsible for improving the accountability, capacity, and effectiveness of the nation's substance abuse prevention, addictions treatment, and mental health services delivery system.

summary probation A sentencing option where the judge accepts a plea or verdict of guilty for a misdemeanant, suspends execution of the sentence, and summarily (without the use of a presentence investigation) imposes a period of unsupervised probation.

summons and release System also known as book and release in which defendants are taken to jail, interviewed by police, booked and processed by sheriff's deputies, and issued a summons or ticket with a court date.

supermaximum-security (supermax) state prisons Special prisons used to house inmates who pose extraordinary risks to institutional safety because of their involvement in prison misconduct and violence.

supervised release In the federal system, a term of supervision that the court imposes to follow a period of imprisonment.

suppression effect Reduction in arrests following a criminal justice intervention.

surety A guarantor who assures criminal justice officials that defendants will appear in court.

surveillance effect The idea that increased correctional surveillance will result in greater noncompliance and technical violations.

surveillance style Parole officer style that involves offender monitoring and enforcement of the conditions of parole.

tariff system Narrow fine amounts set by statute.

Tate v. Short Supreme Court decision that held that for crimes that do not have imprisonment as an authorized penalty, an offender cannot be imprisoned for failure to pay a fine unless the failure to pay is willful.

Taylor v. Taintor Supreme Court case that clarified that bounty hunter behavior must conform to law, but was not bound by Fourth Amendment as is police behavior.

technical parole violations Violations of the specific conditions of the sentence.

technical violations Probation violations that indicate noncompliance rather than new criminal behavior.

Teen court A restorative justice approach where first-time offenders publicly admit guilt before a group of peers, who, in turn, impose a sentence.

therapeutic community A prison programming technique where treatment offenders are removed from the general population and are placed in settings devoted to treatment.

third-generation boot camps Boot camps that have replaced the military components with educational and vocational skills training and often include a follow-up component in the community known as *aftercare*.

Thompson v. Oklahoma Case that established that the execution of persons under 16 is unconstitutional.

Three Penitentiary Act Legislation in 1891 that authorized the building of the first three federal prisons at Leavenworth, Kansas: Atlanta, Georgia: and McNeil Island, Washington.

totality-of-conditions test The standard that is used to evaluate the overall quality of a prison environment.

transfer *See* waiver.

Treatment Alternatives to Street Crime (TASC) A national diversion program devoted to providing substance abuse treatment for offenders.

treatment conditions Conditions that address a problem or issue that, if resolved, will help the offender remain crime free, such as participation in drug treatment.

Trop v. Dulles Established the evolving standards of decency doctrine.

truancy Nonattendance of school.

truth in sentencing The correspondence between the sentence imposed upon those sent to prison and the time actually served prior to prison release.

typologies Categorical classification systems of offenders.

UNICOR Another name for Federal Prison Industries.

United States Board of Parole The federal board of parole, which was founded in 1930.

United States Immigration and Customs Enforcement (ICE) Agency responsible for enforcement of immigration laws.

United States Parole Commission The federal parole board after its name change in 1976.

United States Penitentiaries Another name for high-security institutions.

United States Sentencing Commission (U.S.S.C.) An independent commission in the judicial branch that was established by the Sentencing Reform Act provisions of the Comprehensive Crime Control Act of 1984 to establish sentencing guidelines for the federal courts and install a formal system of determinate sentences.

United States v. Booker A 2005 Supreme Court decision that determined that a jury must determine the facts that result in an upward departure from federal sentencing guidelines.

United States v. Knights Supreme Court case that held that searches of parolees based on reasonable suspicion are permitted because there is enough likelihood that criminal conduct is occurring.

unsupervised probation A sentence that is similar to a deferred sentence reserved for first-time or low-level offenders with little to no probation conditions.

U.S. Probation and Pretrial Services System The community corrections arm of the federal judiciary charged with supervising criminal defendants during the pretrial and postadjudication phases.

victim impact panels Interactive sessions where DWI victims tell their stories of hardship to DWI offenders.

victim impact statements Testimonials from crime victims about how their victimization has affected their life.

Violence Risk Appraisal Guide (VRAG) A popular risk assessment tool for violence risk; related to the Sex Offender Risk Appraisal Guide (SORAG), which measures risk for sexual recidivism.

Violent Crime Control and Law Enforcement Act of 1994 Federal legislation that attempted to rectify the lack of truth-in-sentencing by assuring that offenders served a larger portion of their sentences.

waiver Prosecution of a juvenile in criminal court.

Walsh-Healey Act Legislation passed by Congress in 1936; prohibited the use of inmate labor to fulfill certain federal contracts in excess of $10,000.

weekender Programs in which offenders work in the community but live in a weekender module of the jail on weekends for some specified period of time.

Weems v. United States Case that established that criminal punishments must be graduated, proportionate, or commensurate to the seriousness of the underlying crime.

wergeld The assessed value of a person's life and considered their bail value in medieval England and Germany.

what works Doctrine that uses evidence-based information to inform and design effective correctional treatment programs.

White House Office of Faith-Based and Community Initiatives Executive-branch unit charged with leading a comprehensive effort to enlist, equip, enable, empower, and expand the work of faith-based and other community organizations.

Wilkinson v. Austin Supreme Court case that held that supermax classification does not violate due process (Fourteenth Amendment) rights of prisoners.

Wolff v. McDonnell Case in which the ruling specified the due process guidelines for major prison disciplinary proceedings.

work release Programs that allow inmates to leave prison to work in the community during business hours and then return to prison for nights and weekends.

writ of certiorari Petition to the Supreme Court for review.

writ of mandamus Extraordinary remedies used when the plaintiff has no other way to access the courts for relief and he or she seeks to compel a governmental duty.

INDEX

Note: *Italicized* pages indicate a photo/figure; tables are noted with a *t*.

A

B

E

F

G

H

K

L

N

O

P

S

T

Y

Z

CREDITS

Chapter Opener photos © AbleStock

Part Opener 1 © Thomas Moens/ShutterStock, Inc.

Chapter 1

page 6 © Fred Prouser/Reuters/Landov; **page 8** © Tim Harman/ShutterStock, Inc.; **page 11** © Todd Plitt/Pool/AP Photos; **page 15** © Corbis; **page 23** © Abraham Menashe/Alamy Images; **page 25** © LiquidLibrary; **page 32** © Chee-onn Leong/Dreamstime.com

Chapter 2

page 47 © National Library of Medicine; **page 50 (top and bottom)** Eastern Kentucky University Archives, Richmond, KY; **page 51 (left and right)** Photo courtesy of Ron Arons, Author of *The Jews of Sing Sing*. Wood engraving from Cornelia Cotton Gallery; **page 52** Courtesy of New York State Archives; Criminal Justice, B0095; **page 53** The Library Company of Philadelphia; **page 59** Eastern Kentucky University Archives, Richmond, KY

Chapter 3

page 82 Courtesy of Steve Petteway, Collection of the Supreme Court of the United States; **page 86** © Bill Fritsch/age fotostock; **page 90** © John Hart, *Watertown Daily Times*/AP Photos; **page 91** © David Duprey/AP Photos; **page 94** © Kristen Wyatt/AP Photos

Part Opener 2 © Robin Loznak, *Great Falls Tribune*/AP Photos

Chapter 4

page 116 © Michael Ging/Pool/AP Photos; **page 119** © ThinkStock/age fotostock; **page 122** © AbleStock; **page 128** © Cheryl Guerrero, *The Plain Dealer*/AP Photos; **page 135** © Thinkstock/age fotostock

Chapter 5

page 155 © Bill Fritsch/age fotostock; **page 156** © Jack Star/PhotoLink/Photodisc/Getty Images; **page 157** © Lucy Pemoni/Reuters/Landov; **page 163** © Bill Fritsch/age fotostock; **page 170 (left)** © Kevin P. Coughlin/*Bloomberg News*/Landov; **page 170 (right)** © Mario Anzuoni/Reuters/Landov

Chapter 6

page 191 © Jack Dagley Photography/ShutterStock, Inc.; **page 194** © Lisa F. Young/ShutterStock, Inc.; **page 202** © Corbis; **page 212** © RubberBall Productions/Alamy Images

Chapter 7

page 228 Courtesy of MIEMSS; **page 233** © Photodisc/Getty Images; **page 237** © Dale Sparks/AP Photos; **page 240** © Michael Fuery/ShutterStock, Inc.; **page 245** © Reuters/Bay County Sheriffs Office/HO/Landov; **page 248** © Rodrigo Abd/AP Photos

Chapter 8

page 272 © Reuters/HO/Landov; **page 273 (top)** © Ann Heisenfelt/AP Photos; **page 273 (bottom)** Courtesy of the American Probation and Parole Association; **page 282** © Bonnie Kamin/PhotoEdit, Inc.

Part Opener 3 © Photos.com

Chapter 9

page 297 Homeboy Industries logo and Nothing Stops a Bullet Like A Job are trademarks of Homeboy Industries, Inc., reproduced with permission; **page 298** © David Bjerke/UPN/AP Photos; **page 300** Courtesy of Gerald L. Nino/U.S. Customs and Border Protection; **page 305** © JustASC/ShutterStock, Inc.; **page 318** © Jeff Geissler/AP Photos; **page 321** © California Department of Corrections/AP Photos

Chapter 10

page 337 Courtesy of Ohio State Penitentiary; **page 341** © E.J. Harris, *East Oregonian*/AP Photos; **page 348** © Charlie Riedel/AP Photos; **page 350** © Eric Risberg/AP Photos

Chapter 11

page 372 (left and right) © Connecticut State Police/AP Photos; **page 381** © Ken Hammond/USDA; **page 382** © Bill Fritsch/age fotostock; **page 391** © George Rizer, *Boston Globe*/Landov

Chapter 12

page 407 © Robin Nelson/PhotoEdit, Inc.; **page 411** Courtesy of Mate 3rd Class Joshua Karsten/U.S. Navy; **page 415** Courtesy of www.familywatchdog.us; **page 421** © charles taylor/ShutterStock, Inc.; **page 424** © Eugenijus Marozas/ShutterStock, Inc.

Part Opener 4 © Kiichiro Sato, File/AP Photos

Chapter 13

page 444 © Martin Smith-Rodden/Pool/Reuters; **page 452** © ClassicStock/Alamy Images; **page 454** © Richard Lord/PhotoEdit Inc.; **page 463** © Robin Nelson/PhotoEdit Inc.; **page 465** © 2004 Kayte Deioma/PhotoEdit, Inc.

Chapter 14

page 478 © Reuters/HO/Landov; **page 481** © Steve Pope/AP Photos; **page 485 (top)** Courtesy of the University of Texas Libraries, The University of Texas at Austin; **page 485 (bottom)** © Mike Segar/Reuters/Landov; **page 487** © Jason Maehl/ShutterStock, Inc.; **page 491** © Jack Dagley Photography/ShutterStock, Inc.

Chapter 15

page 511 © HO/AP Photos; **page 524** Courtesy of Innocence Project. www.innocenceproject.org; **page 528** Courtesy of American Society of Criminology; **page 531** © National Library of Medicine; **page 533** © Wichita Eagle/MCT/Landov